Developmental Contexts in Middle Childhood

During middle childhood, the period between ages 5 and 12, children gain the basic tools, skills, and motivations to become productive members of their society. Failure to acquire these basic tools can lead to long-term consequences for children's future education, work, and family life. In this book the editors assemble contributions from fifteen longitudinal studies representing diverse groups in the United States, Canada, New Zealand, and the United Kingdom to learn what developmental patterns and experiences in middle childhood contexts forecast the directions children take when they reach adolescence and adulthood. The editors conclude that, although lasting individual differences are evident by the end of the preschool years, a child's developmental path in middle childhood contributes significantly to the adolescent and adult that he or she becomes. Families, peers, and the broader social and economic environment all make a difference for young people's future education, work, and relationships with others.

Aletha C. Huston is Priscilla Pond Flawn Regents Professor of Child Development at the University of Texas at Austin. She is a developmental psychologist who specializes in understanding the effects of poverty on children and the impact of child care and income support policies on children's development. She is a Principal Investigator in the New Hope Project, a study of the effects on children and families of parents' participation in a work-based program to reduce poverty, and collaborator in the Next Generation Project. She was a member of the MacArthur Network on Successful Pathways Through Middle Childhood and an Investigator for the National Institute of Child Health and Human Development Study of Early Child Care and Youth Development. She is President of the Society for Research in Child Development and Past President of the Division of Developmental Psychology of the American Psychological Association.

Marika N. Ripke is the Director of Hawaii Kids Count and an affiliate faculty member of the Center on the Family at the University of Hawaii at Manoa. Her research specializes on the effects of poverty on children and the impact of out-of-school activities on child and youth development. As director of Hawaii Kids Count, she assesses (and advocates for) the well-being of Hawaii's children and families by monitoring various health, economic, and educational indicators over time. She directs the data collection and analysis of a study examining the quality and availability of education and health supports for Native Hawaiian families and their young children. She holds a governmental position as a voting member of the State of Hawaii's Commission on Fatherhood. Her publications have appeared in the *Handbook of Child Psychology* and in such scholarly journals as *Developmental Psychology*, *Review of Research in Education*, and *New Directions in Youth Development*.

Cambridge Studies in Social and Emotional Development

General Editor: Carolyn Shantz, *Wayne State University*

Advisory Board: Nancy Eisenberg, Robert N. Emde, Willard W. Hartup, Lois W. Hoffman, Franz J. Mönks, Ross D. Parke, Michael Rutter, and Carolyn Zahn-Waxler

Recent books in the series:

Conflict in Child and Adolescent Development
Edited by Carolyn Uhlinger Shantz and Willard W. Hartup

Children in Time and Place
Edited by Glen H. Elder, Jr., John Modell, and Ross D. Parke

Disclosure Processes in Children and Adolescents
Edited by Ken J. Rotenberg

Morality in Everyday Life
Edited by Melanie Killen and Daniel Hart

The Company They Keep
Edited by William M. Bukowski, Andrew F. Newcomb, and Willard W. Hartup

Developmental Science
Edited by Robert B. Cairns, Glen H. Elder, and Jane E. Costello

Social Motivation
Edited by Jaana Juvonen and Kathryn R. Wentzel

Emotional Development
By L. Alan Sroufe

Comparisons in Human Development
Edited by Jonathan Tudge, Michael J. Shanahan, and Jaan Valsiner

Development Course and Marital Dysfunction
Edited by Thomas Bradbury

Mothers at Work
By Lois Hoffman and Lise Youngblade

The Development of Romantic Relationships in Adolescence
Edited by Wyndol Furman, B. Bradford Brown, and Candice Feiring

Emotion, Development, and Self-Organization
Edited by Marc D. Lewis and Isabela Granic

Developmental Psychology and Social Change
Edited by David S. Pillemer and Sheldom H. White

Developmental Contexts in Middle Childhood

Bridges to Adolescence and Adulthood

Edited by

ALETHA C. HUSTON
University of Texas at Austin

MARIKA N. RIPKE
University of Hawaii at Manoa

CAMBRIDGE
UNIVERSITY PRESS

CAMBRIDGE UNIVERSITY PRESS
Cambridge, New York, Melbourne, Madrid, Cape Town, Singapore, São Paulo

Cambridge University Press
40 West 20th Street, New York, NY 10011-4211, USA

www.cambridge.org
Information on this title: www.cambridge.org/9780521845571

First published 2006

Printed in the United States of America

A catalog record for this publication is available from the British Library.

Library of Congress Cataloging in Publication Data

Developmental contexts in middle childhood : bridges to adolescence and adulthood /
edited by Aletha C. Huston, Marika N. Ripke.
    p.   cm. (Cambridge studies in social and emotional development)
Includes bibliographical references and index.
ISBN-10: 0-521-84557-2 hardback
1. Child development – Longitudinal studies.   2. Child psychology – Longitudinal
studies.   3. Children – Longitudinal studies.   4. Preteens – Longitudinal studies.
I. Huston, Aletha C.   II. Ripke, Marika N., 1972–   III. Series.
HQ769.D446   2006
305.231 – dc22   2005025326

ISBN-13   978-0-521-84557-1 hardback
ISBN-10   0-521-84557-2 hardback

Contents

Contributors

Aletha C. Huston is Priscilla Pond Flawn Regents Professor of Child Development for the Human Development and Family Sciences, University of Texas at Austin.

Marika N. Ripke is Director of Hawaii Kids Count and Affiliate Faculty for the Center on the Family, University of Hawaii at Manoa.

Karl L. Alexander is John Dewey Professor of Sociology at Johns Hopkins University.

John E. Bates is Professor of Psychology at Indiana University.

Jay Belsky is Professor of Psychology at Birkbeck College, University of London.

Cathryn Booth-LaForce is Professor of Family and Child Nursing and Research Affiliate at the Center on Human Development and Disability, University of Washington.

Paul Boxer is Assistant Professor of Psychology at the University of New Orleans.

Robert H. Bradley is Professor of Education in the Center for Applied Studies in Education, University of Arkansas at Little Rock.

Jennifer L. Brooks is Senior Associate at Caliber Associates.

John Bynner is Professor of Social Sciences in Education at the Centre for Longitudinal Studies, Bedford Group, Institute of Education, University of London.

Susan B. Campbell is Professor and Chair of the Developmental Program in the Department of Psychology, University of Pittsburgh.

David M. Casey is Community and Policy Research Partnerships Coordinator in the International Collaborative Centre for the Study of Social and Physical Environments and Health, Faculty of Medicine, University of Calgary.

Hrishikesh Chakraborty is Data Analyst for the Research Triangle Institute.

Alison Clarke-Stewart is Professor in the School of Social Ecology, University of California at Irvine.

David J. Cleary is a Graduate Student in the Department of Human Development and Family Studies, Auburn University.

W. Andrew Collins is Professor at the Institute of Child Development, University of Minnesota.

Robin Corley is Senior Research Associate at the Institute for Behavioral Genetics, University of Colorado at Boulder.

Sylvana Côté is Assistant Professor at the School of Psycho-Education, University of Montreal.

Danielle A. Crosby is Postdoctoral Scholar at the Center for Human Potential and Public Policy, University of Chicago.

Pamela E. Davis-Kean is Assistant Research Professor of the Institute for Social Research and the Institute for Research on Women and Gender.

John C. DeFries is Professor at the Institute for Behavioral Genetics, University of Colorado at Boulder.

Kenneth A. Dodge is Director of the Center for Child and Family Policy, Duke University.

Eric F. Dubow is Adjunct Faculty Associate in the Department of Psychology, Bowling Green State University.

Greg J. Duncan is Professor of Education and Social Policy at the Institute for Policy Research, Northwestern University.

Jacquelynne S. Eccles is Wilbert McKeachie Collegiate Professor of Psychology, Women's Studies, and Education at the University of Michigan.

Doris R. Entwisle is Research Professor of Sociology at Johns Hopkins University.

Sylvia R. Epps is a Doctoral Student in Human Development and Family Sciences at the University of Texas at Austin.

Leonard D. Eron is Adjunct Professor of Psychology at the Institute for Social Research, University of Michigan.

Abdeljelil Farhat is Statistician for the Center of Excellence in Early Childhood Development, University of Montreal.

Leon Feinstein is Reader in the Economics of Education at the Institute of Education, University of London.

Jennifer A. Fredricks is Assistant Professor in Human Development at Connecticut College.

Sarah L. Friedman is Project Scientist/Scientific Coordinator for NICHD – National Institute of Child Health and Human Development.

Anna Gassman-Pines is a Doctoral Student in the Department of Psychology, New York University.

Lisa Gennetian is Senior Research Associate for MDRC – Manpower Demonstration Research Corporation.

Alain Girard is Statistician for the Research Unit on Children's Psycho-Social Maladjustment, University of Montreal.

Erin B. Godfrey is a Doctoral Student in the Department of Psychology, New York University.

Robert C. Granger is President of the William T. Grant Foundation.

Lori D. Harach is Assistant Professor in the Department of Human Ecology, University of Alberta.

Penny Hauser-Cram is Professor at the Lynch School of Education, Boston College.

John K. Hewitt is Professor and Director of the Institute for Behavioral Genetics, University of Colorado at Boulder.

Kathy Hirsh-Pasek is Professor of Psychology at Temple University.

Amy Holtzworth-Munroe is Professor in the Department of Psychology, Indiana University.

Renate Houts is Data Analyst for the Research Triangle Institute.

L. Rowell Huesmann is Professor of Communication Studies and Psychology and Senior Research Professor at the Institute for Social Research, University of Michigan.

Sara R. Jaffee is Assistant Professor in the Department of Psychology, University of Pennsylvania.

Christa Japel is Professor in the Department of Specialized Education and Training, University of Quebec at Montreal.

Ariel Kalil is Associate Professor at the Harris School of Public Policy Studies, University of Chicago.

Jean F. Kelly is Research Professor in Family and Child Nursing at the University of Washington.

Bonnie Knoke is Project Data Coordinator for the Research Triangle Institute.

Katherine Magnuson is Assistant Professor of Social Work at the University of Wisconsin, Madison.

Amy D. Marshall is Postdoctoral Fellow for the National Center for Post Traumatic Stress Disorder.

Kathleen McCartney is Professor at the Graduate School of Education, Harvard University.

Sharon M. McGroder is Research Consultant and Senior Scientist at the Lewin Group.

Kristin A. Moore is President and Senior Scholar at Child Trends.

Pamela Morris is Deputy Director for the Policy Area on Family Well-Being and Children's Development, MDRC – Manpower Demonstration Research Corporation.

Fred Morrison is Professor of Psychology at the University of Michigan.

Marion O'Brien is Professor in the Human Development and Family Studies School of Human Environmental Sciences, University of North Carolina at Greensboro.

Linda Steffel Olson is Associate Research Scientist in the Department of Sociology, Johns Hopkins University.

Linda S. Pagani is Professor at the School of Psycho-Education, University of Montreal.

C. Chris Payne is Assistant Professor in the Department of Human Development and Family Studies, University of North Carolina at Greensboro.

Gregory S. Pettit is Human Sciences Professor in Human Development and Family Studies at Auburn University.

Deborah Phillips is Professor of Psychology at Georgetown University.

Robert Pianta is Professor of Clinical and School Psychology at the University of Virginia.

Robert Plomin is Professor and Deputy Director in Social, Genetic, and Developmental Psychiatry at the Research Centre Institute of Psychiatry, King's College London.

Richie Poulton is Director of Dunedin Multidisciplinary Health and Development Research Unit, Department of Preventive and Social Medicine, Dunedin School of Medicine, University of Otago.

Amanda L. Roy is a Doctoral Student in the Department of Psychology, New York University.

Mi Suk Shim is Social Science/Humanities Research Associate IV at the University of Texas at Austin Division of Instructional Innovation and Assessment Measurement and Evaluation Center.

Selcuk R. Sirin is Assistant Professor of Applied Psychology at New York University.

Sandra D. Simpkins is Assistant Professor for the Department of Family and Human Development, Arizona State University.

Susan Spieker is Professor of Family and Child Nursing at the University of Washington.

Jennifer Stadler is Regional Director of the Citizen Schools at Boston.

Laramie D. Taylor is Assistant Professor of Communication at the University of California at Davis.

Richard E. Tremblay is Research Chair in Child Development and Professor for the Departments of Psychology, Psychiatry, and Pediatrics, University of Montreal.

Manfred van Dulmen is Assistant Professor of Psychology at Kent State University.

Deborah Vandell is Professor of Educational Psychology at the University of Wisconsin at Madison.

Sally J. Wadsworth is Senior Research Associate at the Institute for Behavioral Genetics, University of Colorado at Boulder.

Marji Erickson Warfield is Social Scientist for the Heller School for Social Policy and Management, Brandeis University.

Marsha Weinraub is Professor of Psychology at Temple University.

Hirokazu Yoshikawa is Associate Professor of Psychology and Public Policy at New York University.

Martha J. Zaslow is Director of Early Childhood Development Research for Child Trends.

Foreword

Robert C. Granger

In 1994, the MacArthur Foundation invited fourteen scholars to form an interdisciplinary research network. The network's goal was to advance knowledge about middle childhood, the period from roughly age five to twelve. I think it is a fair characterization that, at the outset, none of us in the network saw ourselves as "middle childhood" scholars. Like many researchers interested in child development, we came to the task with backgrounds in early childhood or adolescence. In principle, we all thought middle childhood mattered, but the belief was buttressed more by theory and personal experience (many of us had children in or just leaving the age range) than it was by empirical research.

The MacArthur Network on Successful Pathways Through Middle Childhood functioned for seven years and generated a lot of good work. But it was not until I read the draft chapters for this volume, three years after the Network ended, that I was sure there were definitive data on the question "does middle childhood matter?" Thank goodness, as richly shown in this volume, it does.

Aletha Huston and her former student and current colleague Marika Ripke have done a great service to developmental science by executing the project that became this book. Having been there at the project's outset, but unconflicted by any substantial involvement, I can certify that the effort took clear thinking, countless hours, and all the intellectual and social skills that the chapter authors ascribe to healthy adults.

As with many important efforts, the book is grounded on a few elegant and important questions: Does middle childhood matter over and above the early childhood years and, if so, why and how?

To address these issues, Huston and Ripke identified research teams with data sets that met certain criteria. The teams had to possess longitudinal data covering middle childhood and the period before and/or after (often both); good measures of the contexts that shape development, such as family, school, and peers; strong measures of both good and bad developmental outcomes; and diverse samples of adequate size. This compilation of criteria represents a difficult standard, and I was therefore impressed that Huston and Ripke found fifteen such teams. As readers will understand, this aggregation represents millions of dollars of effort, from far-flung teams, working in some cases for more than forty years. It is extraordinary.

Beyond the power of the underlying data, the strength of the volume is its discipline and its freshness. This book is the antithesis of an edited volume where disparate chapters are loosely tied together. Rather, almost all of these chapters are driven by new analyses and a strong editorial hand that helps the reader. Chapters begin with a few clear questions and some theory, followed by the analysis strategy, the findings, and a discussion of the implications. As with any edited volume, there will be a tendency to read the editors' introduction and their closing synthesis. Readers who use that approach will get a clear exposition of the volume's storyline, but they will miss chapters that deserve individual attention and citation.

Although written for other developmental scientists, the volume's subtext is an issue that is important to policymakers and practitioners. That is, in a world of limited financial resources, how important is the middle childhood period? Should policies steer resources toward that age range? This work will not settle those questions, but the analyses surely leave them on the table. For example, in this volume we learn that families, schools, and peers all influence children in middle childhood in ways that go beyond their influences during early childhood. We also learn that the unique influence of middle childhood is most obvious when, across time, there is change in the environment; when a child's family becomes stronger or weaker; when schools get better or worse; or when peers are more or less competent. This is important. In the lives of most children, stability is the norm, and this can lead to the erroneous conclusion that genetics plus early influences inevitably determine later life. But this is only because the contextual influences tend to remain relatively stable. By capitalizing on the modest natural variation that does exist, coupled with an occasional data set from an intervention trial, the chapters in this volume repeatedly show the potential of the middle childhood years. This is instructive to all who are interested in improving the lives of young people. It suggests the following strategy: maintain the strengths of positive settings while adjusting incentives and resources to improve the contexts when children are doing less well.

Having assured us that middle childhood is uniquely important, the authors do not claim to understand how the developmental contexts influence development or exactly what to do when development goes awry. Time and again chapter authors note that the agenda can now turn from "does middle childhood matter" to "because middle childhood matters, how can we improve it for many children?" That is a worthy shift, made viable by this excellent work. In the language we use at the William T. Grant Foundation, this will require a combination of descriptive and intervention studies that are simultaneously grounded in theory and the daily lives of children. When doing such work, we argue for a shift from the study of the normative development of children to an understanding of how contexts evolve and how they can be improved. In effect, we suggest shifting the unit of analysis from the child to the child and setting in dynamic transaction over time. Understanding development in this framework will help us all do a better job of creating successful pathways into, through, and beyond middle childhood.

Acknowledgments

This volume is an outgrowth of seven years of rich intellectual exchange and collaboration fostered and generously supported by the John D. and Catherine T. MacArthur Foundation Research Network on Successful Pathways Through Middle Childhood (http://childhood.isr.umich.edu). The network organized a series of meetings among the investigators preparing chapters for the book to plan and coordinate analyses around a core set of questions. Earlier versions of many of the chapters were presented as papers at a network-sponsored conference on "Building Pathways to Success: Research, Policy, and Practice on Development in Middle Childhood" in Washington, D.C., in June 2003. The network also provided valuable support for preparing this volume. We thank Professor Jacquelynne Eccles, Network Chair, for her intellectual contributions and support for this project; Dr. Todd Bartko, Executive Director, for his contributions to its implementation; and the other members of the network. They include Phyllis Blumenfeld (University of Michigan), Catherine Cooper (University of California at Santa Cruz), Greg Duncan (Northwestern University), Cynthia Garcia Coll (Brown University), Robert Granger (William T. Grant Foundation), Jennifer Greene (University of Illinois – Urbana-Champaign), Hanne Haavind (University of Oslo), James Johnson (University of North Carolina at Chapel Hill), John Modell (Brown University), Diane Scott-Jones (Boston College), Deborah Stipek (Stanford University), Barrie Thorne (University of California at Berkeley), and Heather Weiss (Harvard University). We are grateful to Catherine Malerba for her excellent editing and to Shannon Moore for her assistance in preparing the manuscript.

1

Middle Childhood

Contexts of Development

Aletha C. Huston and Marika N. Ripke

In 1981, the National Research Council organized the expert Panel to Review the Status of Basic Research on School-Age Children, which produced a seminal volume, *Development During Middle Childhood: The Years From Six to Twelve* (Collins, 1984). The panel concluded that middle childhood is a time of marked change in capacities and typical behaviors that have long-term implications for adolescent and adult patterns. Although several chapters dealt with family, school, peer, and cultural influences on development, most of the research reviewed was designed to understand normative developmental patterns rather than individual differences. The panel noted gaps in available knowledge about what characteristics of middle childhood environments influence developmental change and about the range of environments experienced by children in the different "ecocultural niches" that are defined by such characteristics as ethnic group, socioeconomic characteristics, family structure, and geographic location (Weisner, 1984). Because "Middle childhood behavior and performance have repeatedly been found to predict adolescent and adult status . . . more reliably than do early childhood indicators," the panel recommended additional research on the processes by which middle childhood contributes to later development (Collins, 1984, p. 409).

WHAT DOES MIDDLE CHILDHOOD EXPERIENCE CONTRIBUTE?

In 1994, the MacArthur Foundation formed a Research Network on Successful Pathways Through Middle Childhood, comprising an interdisciplinary group of scholars, with the goal of advancing knowledge about this age group. One of the network's activities involved gathering a group of investigators to analyze longitudinal studies around a common set of questions about middle childhood. The purpose of this book is to assemble what we have learned since 1981 about how children's environments in middle childhood influence development, using contributions from these

15 different longitudinal studies. We hope to advance theory and basic knowledge by presenting cutting-edge research using a range of strong methodological approaches and to inform policy and practice by providing information about how contexts can be used to promote successful development.

Although the preschool years establish the base for future development, experiences in middle childhood can sustain, magnify, or reverse the advantages or disadvantages that children acquire in the preschool years. At the same time, middle childhood is a pathway to adolescence, setting trajectories that are not easily changed later. Therefore, two overriding questions in these chapters are *How do developmental patterns, both stability and change, in middle childhood relate to developments in adolescence and adulthood? What do environmental contexts in middle childhood contribute to long-term developmental patterns?* Several themes guide the analyses and discussion.

Developmental Importance of Middle Childhood

To the extent possible, we attempt to identify the "unique" contribution of middle childhood – that is, what middle childhood adds to the skills and characteristics formed in early childhood, and what effects endure when children reach adolescence and adulthood. Throughout the volume we ask: What are the important contributions of middle childhood development and experiences, above and beyond those in the preschool years, to educational attainment, emotional adjustment, and social functioning in adolescence and adulthood? What aspects of middle childhood development and experience have long-term consequences for adolescent and adult patterns?

Contexts

We emphasize developmental contexts. Earlier longitudinal studies of child development provided detailed evidence about the stability of individual differences, but relatively little information about children's environments, particularly those outside the family. We attempt to determine what characteristics of contexts promote positive or negative developmental trajectories. What environments increase or decrease developmental continuity? We are interested in naturally occurring environments as well as interventions in middle childhood. Because children select and affect their families, schools, peers, and other contexts as well as being affected by them, some of the work explicitly tests reciprocal models of causal relations.

Continuity and Discontinuity

Continuity and stability are the "norm" in child development. Children who are intelligent or aggressive early tend to be intelligent or aggressive later. But we can learn a great deal from *dis*continuities in developmental patterns. What conditions are associated with discontinuous development (e.g., changes in trajectories of achievement or aggression)? What leads to these changes in direction? Do these discontinuities predict later development, or do individuals ultimately return to an earlier trajectory? We are less interested in the stability or instability of a particular trait than in knowing the conditions under which it is changeable or continuous and the long-term implications of continuity and discontinuity.

Successful Development

"Success" is positive behavior, not merely the absence of such problems as delinquency, early pregnancy, and mental illness. Not surprisingly, many of the investigators define successful development as academic performance, motivation and engagement in school, educational and occupational attainment, and adult labor force participation and earnings, but some studies also include a wider range of skills in such areas as athletics, leadership and the arts, and positive self-concepts about one's abilities. Adult success is marked by strong, positive, and nonaggressive *social* relationships with coworkers, friends, partners, and one's own children and by psychological well-being. Although different domains of development (e.g., cognition, emotion, and social relationships) are often investigated separately, we assume that they are interdependent.

Individual and Group Differences

The ecocultural niches resulting from culture, race, and economic advantage or disadvantage not only generate different experiences for children, but also may lead to different impacts of family conditions, schools, and neighborhoods. Some authors in this book ask whether generalization from group to group is appropriate and identify group differences in the relations of contexts to behavior. The samples in these chapters represent Canada, the United Kingdom, and New Zealand as well as the United States, so there are some opportunities to compare across English-speaking countries. We also address whether boys and girls or children with different temperamental predispositions have different opportunities and supports or respond to developmental contexts differently.

TABLE 1.1. *Percentage of U.S. Children in Different Ethnic and Racial Groups,* *1980–2020*

Ethnic Group	1980	2000	2020 (projected)
White non-Hispanic	74	64	55
Black non-Hispanic	15	15	14
Hispanic	9	16	23
Asian	2	4	6
American Indian/Pacific Islander	1	1	1

Source: U.S. Department of Health and Human Services (2004). *Trends in the well-being of America's children and youth.* Table PF1.3, p. 22.

MIDDLE CHILDHOODS ARE PLURAL AND DIVERSE

Demographic Trends

Childhoods in the United States and in many other developed countries are increasingly diverse as immigrants, people of color, and ethnic minorities become a larger proportion of the population and as economic and structural features of families change. The Collins (1984) volume provides a detailed demographic analysis of children in 1980. In this section, we examine changes from 1980 to the early twenty-first century in the contexts surrounding children in the United States, using data compiled by the U.S. Department of Health and Human Services (USHHS) (2004).

Although the number of children in the United States continues to increase, it is becoming a smaller percentage of the total population. The number of 6- to 11-years olds was 20.8 million (9.1% of total population) in 1980 and 24.8 million (8.5% of total population) in 2001; by 2020, a total of 26.9 million (8.0% of total population) is projected.[1]

Ethnic Diversity. Ethnic diversity increased dramatically during the last part of the twentieth century, largely because of increases in immigration from Latin America and Asia. Although the percentage of Black non-Hispanic and American Indian/Alaska Native children remained steady, the proportion of children identified as Hispanic or Asian/Pacific Islander nearly doubled between 1980 and 2001, with proportional declines in the percent of White non-Hispanic children. By 2020, one-third of the population is expected to be Hispanic or Asian (see Table 1.1).

Family Composition. The proportion of children living with only one parent has increased since 1980. From 1970 to 1995, the percentage of children

[1] Calculations from figure in table PF1.1, p. 37 (HHS, 2004).

TABLE 1.2. *Percentage of U.S. Children in Different Family Structures,*
1980–2002

	Number of Parents in Child's Household	1980	1995	2002
All ethnic groups	Two	77	69	69
	One	12	27	28
	None	3	4	4
White non-Hispanic	Two	NA	78	77
	One	NA	19	20
	None	NA	3	3
Black non-Hispanic	Two	42	33	38
	One	46	56	53
	None	12	11	8
Hispanic	Two	75	63	65
	One	22	32	30
	None	3	4	5

Source: U.S. Department of Health and Human Services (2004). *Trends in the well-being of America's children and youth.* Table PF2.2A, p. 51.

living with two married parents declined and then leveled off. Among Black families, there was even a slight increase in the percentage of children living in two-parent married families (Table 1.2). Although the percentage of children living with neither parent remained stable at 4%, the rate of foster care almost doubled from 4.2 per 1,000 children in 1982 to 7.3 in 2002. Black children constituted 37% of the children in foster care in 2002 – a rate much higher than their proportion in the population (USHHS, 2004).

Poverty. During the late twentieth century, the United States continued to have relatively large numbers of children living in poverty, even though more parents, particularly mothers, were employed. From 1980 to 2002, the poverty rate for families of children ages 6–17 declined from 17% to 15.4%, after reaching a high of 19% in 1985 (USHHS, 2004).[2] Black or Hispanic children and those living with one parent were *much* more likely to suffer economic disadvantage than their counterparts in other ethnic groups or two-parent families. Median incomes of Black and Hispanic families were about half those of White families (USHHS, 2004).

After relatively stable rates of poverty and employment for single mothers between 1980 and 1995, dramatic changes occurred between 1995 and 2002. Single mothers entered the labor force, and, even though public

[2] Calculations from figure in table PF1.2, p. 39 (HHS, 2004).

TABLE 1.3. *Poverty, Income, and Employment in Families of Children With Single Mothers*

	1980	1995	2002
Income below poverty (%)[a]	45.5	44.6	36.5
Average annual income ($)	17,502	19,032	22,637
Receiving AFDC (%)	11.3	13.2	5.7
Mother employed (%)[a]	67	69	81
No employed adult in household (%)[a]	33	31	19

[a] Data are for children ages 6–17.

Source: U.S. Department of Health and Human Services (2004). *Trends in the well-being of America's children and youth.* Tables ES1.2A, p. 81; ES 1.1, p. 77; ES 2.2, p. 89; ES 3.1A, p. 98; ES 3.1B, p. 99.

cash assistance declined, their families were less likely to live in poverty. Nonetheless, their incomes remained low. In both 1980 and 2002, the median income of single-mother families was 35% of that for two-parent married families (see Table 1.3).

In summary, some but not all of the trends noted in 1980 have continued into the early twenty-first century in the United States. Perhaps the greatest change is the large increase in Hispanic and Asian ethnic groups, with a corresponding decline in the proportion of White Non-Hispanic children. Although more children live in single-parent families now than in 1980, that trend leveled off in the late 1990s. After a rise in the early 1990s, poverty among school-age children has declined slightly, but children in Black, Hispanic, and single-parent families are still much more likely to live in poverty than are children in other ethnic groups or those in married-couple families. Children at all income levels are more likely to have employed parents today than in 1980, and that is especially true for children in single-mother families.

How Children Spend Their Time

Popular literature is filled with concerns about how modern children spend their time. On the one hand, images of couch potatoes in front of a television set abound as the rate of child obesity rises, and visions of "latchkey" children suffering neglect as their parents pursue careers are rampant. On the other hand, critics worry about overly structured, programmed children who are driven endlessly from soccer to band to French lessons, with little time just to play. The evidence from systematic studies of children's time use in nationally representative samples does not support either of these extremes. In a comparison of time-use diaries for children ages 3–12 in 1981 and 1997 (Hofferth & Sandberg, 1998), there was very little change in the time devoted to television (about 13 to 14 hours per week). Children spent, on average, a little over an hour per week on computers and video games in 1997 (Wright et al., 2001). Participation in sports increased, with 76% of children engaging in some sports activity in 1997, but other extracurricular activities were not reported separately. Older children spent less time with parents than younger children did at both times of measurement (Hofferth & Sandberg, 1998, 2001).

WHY MIDDLE CHILDHOOD?

Although there are no points of sudden demarcation in children's development, periods of transition form important developmental markers. Between the ages of about 5 and 7, children in most societies enter formal education, learn to read, and gain new cognitive abilities that permit them to reflect on and regulate their own behavior. Around ages 10 to 12, biological, intellectual, and social changes occur as children approach or reach puberty, develop new cognitive capabilities, and, in the United States, enter middle or junior high school.

Middle Childhood Is Often Neglected

Middle childhood has been neglected at least since Freud relegated these years to the status of an uninteresting "latency" period. We hear a great deal about early childhood, with some people even arguing that development is fixed in the first three years; and adolescents attract a lot of attention because adults worry about sex, drugs, crime, and "rock-n-roll." Research specializations in infancy and adolescence have burgeoned into separate journals and professional organizations, but no comparable trend has occurred for middle childhood. In fact, the term is often confused with middle school.

Maybe we tend to neglect middle childhood because people think it is freer of major hazards than are very early childhood or adolescence. To the extent that this view is accurate, middle childhood should be valued as a window of opportunity, as a period to "grow by." Because children in this age period have increased cognitive capabilities and self-awareness without the strong pressures of adolescence, it may be a good time to maximize the potential for positive growth and to introduce supports and opportunities that help children along successful pathways to adulthood.

Normative Development in Middle Childhood

Although this book is about contexts, their effects on individual differences can be understood only within the framework of normative development and change. Middle childhood is the period when children gain the fundamental skills needed for adult life, undergo the early stages of puberty, develop self-awareness and self-regulation, and form the foundations for social relationships with age-mates.

Skills for Adult Life

In Erikson's (1950, 1963/2005) theory, the crucial task in middle childhood is developing a sense of industry – mastering the basic tools and skills needed for adult life in one's culture. The corresponding hazard is a sense of inferiority if one's abilities and tools are inadequate or if one despairs of becoming productive in ways that are valued in society. Erikson's theory is explicitly cross-cultural – different societies require different tools and skills.

In developed and developing countries, academic skills are central to economic and occupational attainment in adulthood. In almost every society that provides formal education, children begin school between ages 5 and 7, suggesting some universal recognition that capabilities needed for such schooling emerge during this age period. These capabilities are cognitive, social, and behavioral (e.g., the ability to sit still, follow directions, or perform autonomously). The early school years are critical for children's educational futures. Although first grade achievement does not forecast well, by third grade, a child's level of achievement is a strong predictor of high school and later performance (Collins, 1984).

Social advantage also arises from proficiency in sports, music, drama, visual arts, computers, languages, leadership, and many forms of social exchange. By the end of middle childhood, most American children know how to ride a bicycle and how to swim, and many have played softball and basketball, played a musical instrument, sung in a choir, gone to camp, learned drawing and crafts, created science projects, and spent many hours on a personal computer. A child who reaches adolescence without the rudiments in these skills may face a handicap, not only for acquiring competence in the specific skills, but for being able to participate fully in social activities that include them.

Cognitive Changes. The grand theories of cognitive development have been replaced in recent years by theories that emphasize gradual and nonlinear changes in memory, reasoning, and conceptual structures (e.g., DeLoache, Miller, & Pierroutsakos, 1998; Kuhn, 1998; Schneider & Bjorkland, 1998). Nonetheless, all agree that, between ages 5 and 12, children develop new cognitive skills that allow them to think more flexibly and intentionally than preschoolers usually do. Examples include grasping logical concepts, the ability to use multiple categories simultaneously, metacognition (e.g., being able to analyze thought and memory processes and to plan ahead), explicit rather than implicit understanding, and self-reflection. Cognitive developmentalists no longer talk of isolated maturational processes within the child. Virtually all recent research emphasizes processes of change involving constant interactions of the child with the physical and social environment. For example, Rogoff (1998) describes learning as a collaborative process involving the child's interactions with adults and peers embedded in a system of sociocultural activities.

Physical and Biological Changes. Middle childhood was once considered a period of sexual latency because it was assumed that hormones influencing sexual motivation and behavior are at very low levels. We now know that the hormonal changes associated with puberty begin between ages 7 and 9 (Buchanan, Eccles, & Becker, 1992) and that growth spurts and other body changes associated with the first stages of puberty begin toward the end of this period (e.g., widening of hips, development of testes and breasts), although there are large individual differences in timing. Menarche occurs for the average White girl in the United States at about age 12.6 to 12.8, and there has been little change since 1946 (Demerath et al., 2004). There is some evidence of earlier menarche for Black girls (Herman-Giddens & Slora, 1997).

Self-Direction, Self-Concept, and Identity. Although families and parents continue to play a crucial role, children's increasing independence from parents is associated with an increasing ability to regulate themselves, to take responsibility, and to exercise self-control – abilities that are essential as they enter adolescence (Eccles, Wigfield, & Schiefele, 1998). Children in middle childhood form identities – a sense of who they are and where they fit in the larger scheme of things. They acquire complex understandings of gender, race, ethnic and cultural heritage, and religious affiliation that depend not only on developing cognitive capacities, but also on the social context in which they live (Garcia Coll et al., 1996; Ruble & Martin, 1998; Harter, 1998). During middle childhood, children also form concepts of what they do well and what they do not – whether they are smart, good at sports, and popular, to name a few examples (Eccles et al., 1998).

Social Relationships. Success in adult life is marked not only by getting a college education and a good job but also by establishing healthy and harmonious relationships with one's romantic partners, friends, family, and coworkers. Relationships with parents in the early years form one basis for social competencies. In middle childhood, learning to interact with peers and with adults outside the family and making friends are critical developmental tasks. Social skills and friendships during this period are important foundations for later social adjustment (Hartup, 1984; Rubin, Bukowski, & Parker, 1998). The social skills children acquire during this period are based in part on cognitive changes that allow more sophisticated moral reasoning, the ability to reflect on oneself, and the ability to perceive others' thoughts and feelings (Shantz, 1983). Good relationships with peers and adults are also important for acquiring competencies in and out of school during this period (e.g., Eccles et al., 1998; Entwisle & Alexander, 1999; Ladd & Burgess, 1999).

CONTEXTS OF DEVELOPMENT: SUPPORTS AND OPPORTUNITIES

During middle childhood, children's worlds expand beyond family to schools, peers, activities outside school hours, and adults outside the family. The larger social environment, including public policies affecting parents' employment, income, and resources available to children, in turn, influences these experiences (Bronfenbrenner & Morris, 1998).

Family

Family Environment. At the center of children's expanding worlds, the family remains the core, although there is considerable dispute about the importance of parenting practices *per se* (e.g., Harris, 1998; Collins, Maccoby, Steinberg, Hetherington, & Bornstein, 2000; Vandell, 2000). Family influences are partly genetic, and the environmental effects of families begin in early childhood. Because most families do not change dramatically over time, separate contributions of middle childhood family experiences may be difficult to detect. Nevertheless, our analyses demonstrate that both the cognitive and emotional supports in the family matter for development in middle childhood. Family problems, including conflict and parental depression, affect children's well-being during middle childhood in ways that carry over into adolescence. Children learn about relationships first through their interactions with parents, carrying what they learn in the crucible of the family into their relationships with other children and with adults (Rubin et al., 1998).

Family Management. Children spend less time with their parents as they get older, regardless of whether parents are employed (Hofferth & Sandberg, 2001). As children and parents have less direct interaction, parents' roles as "managers" of their children's environments and activities become more salient (Furstenberg, Cook, Eccles, Elder, & Sameroff, 1999). Parents often take considerable pains to arrange and monitor their children's lives by selecting schools, neighborhoods, peer groups, out-of-school activities, and media (e.g., Scott-Jones & Cho, 2003). Their choices are constrained by the family's resources and by the opportunities provided by public and private entities, so some parents probably settle for less-than-optimal settings, but this very important family management component of parenting is often overlooked in arguments about "effects" of parents.

Peer Relationships: Helpful or Harmful?

Peer relationships are central to development in middle childhood (Rubin et al., 1998). Deviant peers can lead children astray, and prosocial peers can support positive directions. In either case, friendships and social skills are crucial influences on children's well-being and future relationships. A child who is socially inept or who has few friends during the elementary years is at risk of emotional problems and social maladjustment later in life (Hartup & Moore, 1990; Rubin et al., 1998). Because conformity to peers peaks sometime around age 12, children in this period are especially susceptible to both prosocial and antisocial group norms.

Several chapters in this volume demonstrate that peer relations and competence with peers during middle childhood are important forerunners of later social adjustment and of ability to function in the workplace. Children with good peer relationships in middle childhood show better academic performance in adolescence, are more likely to be engaged with school and to like going there, are more successful in the workplace when they reach adulthood, and are more likely to feel secure in romantic relationships.

Schools

Although many children attend preschool, entry into elementary school is a nearly universal experience in most societies. School provides opportunities for learning academic subject matter, but it also confronts children with frequent assessments of their abilities and comparisons with others. They learn to evaluate themselves in ways that reflect the standards of the society around them and to make judgments about whether they are fulfilling their own or others' expectations for competence (Eccles et al., 1998). Children's initial experiences in elementary school (e.g., retention and tracking) may have long-term effects on their future achievement and adult attainment (e.g., Entwisle, Alexander, & Olson, 1997).

Children's attitudes about school and their motivations for being a part of the school agenda emerge in our analyses as central to academic success as well as to psychological well-being. As children get older, their engagement with school and their academic motivation tend to decline, but schools that provide supportive environments – ones that enable children to feel safe and to feel that they belong – counteract that trend to some degree (Eccles et al., 1998). Schools can also increase motivation by encouraging children to be self-directed learners, to evaluate themselves positively, and to gain a sense of their own competence.

Out-of-School Activities

In the United States, school occupies about seven hours a day for 180 days a year. Even with ten hours of sleep, children have seven hours out of school on an average school day, and they have 185 days with no school. Much of that time is filled with "leisure" activities. Most of the research on out-of-school activities deals with adolescents, despite the fact that lessons, sports, clubs, and religious groups are significant parts of life for many children in middle childhood (Mahoney, Larson, & Eccles, 2005).

One consequence of expanding independence is that children have increasing control over the environments in which they spend their time. They build their own "niches" (Scarr & McCartney, 1983). Parents, teachers, and communities are gatekeepers who can find and offer opportunities outside of the classroom as well as prohibit access to disapproved activities, but, even when activities are available, some children will use them more enthusiastically than others.

Children who spend time in activities that are structured by adult leadership, that have group goals and organization, and that promote socially positive values are, on average, better students with more positive social skills than nonparticipants (Mahoney et al., 2005). In these activities, children can learn many skills beyond those taught in school (e.g., sports, music); they can experience mentoring relationships with adults (e.g., coaches) as well as a range of interactions with peers. They can incorporate group value systems (e.g., service activities, religious youth groups) and develop a sense of their own identity as they move gradually to the larger world outside their families.

Conversely, spending extended amounts of time in unstructured activities with little or no adult supervision (e.g., hanging out with peers or watching television) at this age may place children at risk for physical or psychological harm (e.g., Pettit, Bates, Dodge, & Meece, 1999). Television is the most frequent unstructured activity in most children's lives. Children in middle childhood are heavy viewers, averaging two or three hours per day. The impact of television on children depends on its content. Preschool children often watch educational programs, but during the years from 6 to 12, viewing preferences shift from child-oriented programs to adult entertainment fare, which often shows violence, social stereotypes, and explicit sex (Huston & Wright, 1998a, 1998b).

Cultural, Economic, and Policy Contexts

Children and families live in a larger social context defined by the cultural and economic characteristics of their families and communities, which are influenced in part by social policies. As we noted earlier, ethnic group, family structure, and family income create different contexts for children, and each of these is associated with the chances for successful development (Duncan & Brooks-Gunn, 2000; Garcia Coll et al., 1996). Public policies affecting cash assistance and programs for families have direct effects on family income, and policies vary over time and across the nations represented in this book. On occasion, we can use this variation to draw inferences about the effects of family income and parent employment, for example, on children's developmental trajectories.

ORGANIZATION OF THIS BOOK

The chapters in this book are the products of 17 new data analyses conducted by investigators associated with 15 different longitudinal studies. The MacArthur Research Network on Successful Pathways Through Middle Childhood gathered researchers from studies carried out in the United States, Canada, the United Kingdom, and New Zealand to plan and conduct analyses of their data addressing the major questions of interest. The longitudinal studies were selected to meet some of the following criteria, though none met all of them: (a) they include longitudinal data covering middle childhood as well as the period before and/or after (preferably both); (b) they contain measures of context as well as measures of both positive and negative developmental status in middle childhood; (c) they have high-quality measurement, including high reliability, validity, standardized tests, multiple sources of report (i.e., child, parent, teacher), and adequate sample sizes for appropriate analyses to be conducted; (d) they contain diverse samples; and (e) they have unique methodological or design characteristics, such as random-assignment experiments or controls for genetic similarity of family members.[3] The chapters are arranged approximately by the contexts investigated, but some include multiple contexts.

Family and Peers

In the first set of chapters, family influences are studied, but several of the chapters also point to the importance of peer competence and peer relations in middle childhood as a predictor of later intellectual and social functioning. In Chapter 2, Collins and van Dulmen report predictors of competence in relationships with coworkers, friends, and romantic partners at age 23, using information collected from birth to adulthood in the Minnesota Longitudinal Study of Parents and Children. They conclude that peer competence in middle childhood appears to contribute uniquely

---

[3] Most of the chapters are based on papers presented at the Conference on Successful Pathways Through Middle Childhood, sponsored by the MacArthur Network, in June 2003 in Washington, DC.

and distinctively to competence in key domains of early adult functioning, such as work roles and satisfaction in romantic relationships, and that peer competence mediates the impact of early parental relationships on girls' later competence in work and relationships.

In Chapter 3, Pettit and his colleagues also examine romantic relationships for participants in the Child Development Study, who were followed from age 5 to age 19. The results provide evidence of different pathways to partner violence versus feelings of inadequacy in romantic relationships at age 19. Partner violence is associated with such early socialization experiences as harsh parenting and an antisocial peer group that may foster aggression. Feelings of inadequacy are associated more with interpersonally distant social relationships, including intrusive parenting and difficulties in peer relationships. Peer competence and acceptance in middle childhood uniquely contributed to the prediction of late-adolescent relationship insecurity, but not to relationship violence.

In Chapter 4, Huesmann and colleagues follow participants in the Columbia County Longitudinal Study from age 8 to age 48. They find stability of both achievement and aggression over 40 years. Both high family SES and low levels of negative family interaction at age 8 predict low adult aggression and high intellectual achievement. Although higher age-8 IQ predicts adult occupational success for both males and females, the effect is direct for females but is mediated through lower aggression and higher popularity with peers for males.

Drawing from the Colorado Adoption Project, Wadsworth and colleagues examine genetic and environmental influences on reading achievement at ages 7, 12, and 16 in Chapter 5. They conclude that continuity in reading achievement is due to genetics and shared environmental influences, both of which have largely exerted their influence by age 7. *Change* over middle childhood and adolescence is almost entirely due to nonshared environmental influences – that is, to environmental conditions that affect different children in the same family differently. Among the environmental variables analyzed, positive peer relations at age 7 is the only direct predictor of achievement at age 16.

In Chapters 6 and 7, the relations of family dysfunction and parent mental health problems to children's psychological adjustment are investigated. In Chapter 6, using data from the Dunedin Multidisciplinary Health and Development Study in New Zealand, Jaffee and Poulton test models of reciprocal influence between parents' internalizing symptoms and their reports of children's anxiety/depression and antisocial behavior over the age period from 5 through 15 years. They find some evidence that mothers' internalizing symptoms are reciprocally related to children's anxious/depressed behavior and, for girls, to antisocial behavior, but their results suggest unidirectional relations of mothers' internalizing symptoms to increases in boys' antisocial behavior during middle childhood and to decreases in boys' antisocial behavior in early adolescence.

In Chapter 7, Pagani and her associates examine the relations between trajectories of family dysfunction and children's development from ages 2 to 11 in the Canadian National Longitudinal Survey of Children and Youth. They find consistent relations between middle childhood life-course patterns of family dysfunction and trajectories of children's physical aggression, depression, and prosocial behavior.

Family and School

Four chapters investigate the school context, often in conjunction with family characteristics. One emerging theme is the importance of school context as an influence on children's motivation, engagement, sense of safety, and interest in school.

In Chapter 8, Magnuson and colleagues examine a range of contexts in middle childhood, including family and school, as predictors of age 13–14 academic achievement and problem behavior, using the United States National Longitudinal Survey of Youth. Despite considerable continuity in contexts between the preschool years and middle childhood, middle childhood contexts make a small but unique contribution to predicting adolescent achievement. Both a stimulating home learning environment and children's perceptions of teachers' knowledge and school safety are associated with relatively high academic achievement and low behavior problems at ages 13 and 14.

Entwisle and colleagues address issues of educational tracking in Chapter 9, using information from first grade to age 22 in the Beginning School Study in Baltimore. They find that children who are retained during elementary school are likely to be placed in low math tracks in middle school, and that middle school math tracks are strongly related to subsequent educational attainment (e.g., attending college). Tracking effects are not simply a function of achievement level. Tracking occurs between schools as well as within. Children in some middle schools are more likely to attend college than those in other schools, and the differences are accounted for by family socioeconomic status. Both school context and family expectations and resources appear to influence children's educational trajectories.

In Chapter 10, Hauser-Cram and colleagues report on the relations between school contexts and trajectories of learning in the School Transition Study, following children living in very low-income families from school entry through fifth grade. Children in schools with high concentrations of poverty develop literacy skills more slowly than do children with similar skills who attend economically mixed schools. Children in schools with more positive academic climates show less deleterious declines in engaged "self-directed learning," and changes in self-directed learning predict changes in literacy skills. Learning and engagement are iterative. Not only do young children who are more engaged in the academic challenges of school become better readers, but children who become better readers are also more able to engage in a range of academic challenges.

The NICHD Study of Early Child Care and Youth Development provides data for analyses reported in Chapter 11, investigating the relations of observed classroom contexts in first and third grades to children's classroom involvement and social behavior patterns from first through fourth grade. Classrooms in which the overall climate is positive, the teachers are involved and sensitive, and instructional time is used productively have children who are more attentive, engaged, and self-reliant. By contrast, when teachers frequently discipline, correct, or punish students, children are less involved and more disruptive. Although classroom climates and children's classroom behavior are unstable from first to third grade, there is some evidence for cumulative relations of classroom experiences, particularly high discipline, to increases in children's behavior problems. The authors suggest conceptualizing the child and classroom as an interacting system that is affected both by children's personal dispositions *and* by the environment of the classroom.

Out-of-School Time

Four chapters provide in-depth information about children's out-of-school time. Three of them investigate organized activities, consistently finding positive associations of structured activities, particularly sports, with academic achievement and positive social behavior. The fourth is a review of information about children's most frequent leisure activity – television. We included this review because none of the studies had rich data about media use that could be used for new analyses.[4]

In Chapter 12, Morris and Kalil report on participation in sports, clubs, and lessons for 6- to 12-year-old children in low-income families in the Canadian Self-Sufficiency Project. Participation in a combination of all three structured activities (sports, lessons, and clubs) is consistently associated with higher school achievement and prosocial behavior. Similar but less consistent benefits are found for children who participate only in sports. The findings are replicated in analyses that control for unobserved family characteristics, including genetic similarity, by examining differences between siblings.

In Chapter 13, using children from low-income families in the Milwaukee New Hope Project, Ripke and colleagues examine five structured activities (sports, lessons, clubs, religious groups, and community centers) for children from ages 6 to 15. Participation in structured activities is associated

---

[4] The Columbia County Study and a cross-national study (Huesmann, Moise-Titus, Podolski, & Eron, 2003) have generated findings about the relations of viewing violence to adult aggression and other behaviors.

with increased positive social behavior (competence with peers, compliance to adults, and autonomy) over three years and with children's reports of efficacy and satisfaction with their friendships, but also with some increases in externalizing and delinquent behavior. Participation in sports is most consistently related to positive development. Recreation and community center participation is the one activity associated with some negative outcomes – delinquency and low academic performance.

Simpkins and colleagues (Chapter 14) report on children from kindergarten through twelfth grade in the Childhood and Beyond Study, conducted in southern Michigan. They find that parents' beliefs and efforts to get their children involved in out-of-school activities influence both their children's participation and their children's developing expectancies and values. Participation during middle childhood predicts children's perceptions of their abilities and their beliefs about the value of activities, which in turn account for adolescent participation. Being involved in sports during adolescence predicts competent adolescent functioning in multiple domains.

In Chapter 15, Huesmann and Taylor review the literature about mass media influences on aggression, social stereotypes, obesity, and school achievement. They conclude that exposure to television during middle childhood has major impacts on children's behaviors, beliefs, and achievement that last into adolescence and adulthood. Children learn aggressive behaviors and positive attitudes about aggression from viewing television violence and playing violent video games in middle childhood; what they learn influences their behavior as adults. Children learn about gender roles and ethnic stereotypes from television and movies; the content of what they learn depends on what they watch. Although there are correlations of high amounts of television viewing with obesity and with low school achievement, the causal links are not well understood.

Economic and Public Policy Contexts

Families' economic circumstances place them in a broader social context that affects not only family resources and processes, but also the schools, neighborhoods, out-of-school activities, and other opportunities available to their children. In this section, the authors tackle issues of social exclusion and public policies for low-income families to understand how changes in these larger contexts affect later development.

Feinstein and Bynner report analyses of individuals followed from ages 5 to 30 in the 1970 British Cohort Study (Chapter 16). They first examine stability and change between ages 5 and 10, comparing children whose achievement or problem behavior is consistently high or consistently low with children who improved or declined. They find that development in the middle childhood period carries important signals about the risks of adult social exclusion measured at age 30 (e.g., low educational attainment, being in a workless household). Many children whose school achievement improved between ages 5 and 10 escape the risk implied by poor early performance, but those from lower SES families were less likely to show such improvement than were children from more advantaged families.

Three chapters are based on random-assignment experiments testing public policies for low-income families, so they allow causal inferences about effects of contexts on behavior. Both Chapters 17 and 18 are drawn from the National Evaluation of Welfare to Work Child Outcomes Study (NEWWS), in which parents receiving cash assistance were randomly assigned to programs that required efforts to find employment (work first) or participation in education and training (education first). The control group remained in the welfare system that existed at the time. Children were followed from ages 3–5 to ages 8–10. In Chapter 17, McGroder and colleagues find relatively few enduring effects of either policy on children's achievement, behavior, and health, but there were different impacts in different geographic sites. The authors suggest that characteristics of the population served, local economic conditions, welfare benefit levels, and the ethos and practices of the local welfare office are key for understanding impacts on children and families.

In Chapter 18, Yoshikawa and associates examine differential impacts on children's academic achievement for White, African American, and Latino families. Mandatory education-first programs, in particular, had more beneficial effects for Black and Latino children than for their White counterparts. The reasons for the African-American/White differences are not clear, but Latino parents' value for education partially accounts for their children's more positive responses. The authors propose a person–environment fit hypothesis. If the policy fits the parents' values and motivations, the parents respond positively, and their children's achievement in middle childhood improves.

In Chapter 19, Huston and colleagues report a follow-up of children in the Milwaukee New Hope Study, a random-assignment experiment offering wage supplements and subsidies for child care and medical care to low-income working adults. Children were followed from ages 6–11 to ages 11–16. New Hope increased children's school performance, school motivation, and some aspects of social behavior, particularly for boys. The authors propose that improved economic well-being, child care, and structured out-of-school experiences produced by the New Hope program may account for the endurance of positive impacts from middle childhood to adolescence.

Summary and Conclusions

In Chapter 20, the editors bring together the results from this large array of longitudinal data, evaluating the evidence in relation to the two major questions with which we began. First, how do developmental patterns, both stability and change, in middle childhood relate to developments in adolescence and adulthood? We conclude that, although lasting patterns of ability and behavior are formed by the end of the preschool years, a child's developmental path in middle childhood makes a significant contribution to the emerging adolescent and adult that child becomes. Individual differences in behavior stabilize during middle childhood, and patterns formed in middle childhood sometimes last through the perturbations of adolescence to reemerge in adulthood. Developing social competence with peers (e.g., making friends, interacting positively, resolving conflicts nonaggressively) is a particularly important "task" of middle childhood with long-term consequences for later occupational and social success.

Second, what do experiences in the family, peer group, school, out-of-school time, and the larger economic and cultural milieus of middle childhood contribute to long-term developmental patterns? Environmental contexts in middle childhood make modest but significant contributions to long-term developmental patterns above and beyond genetic heritage and early childhood experiences. Magnuson et al. (Chapter 8) estimate that middle childhood contexts account for 1 to 3% of the variability in adolescent achievement and behavior problems once experience in preschool and the child's level of performance or behavior at age 5–6 years old is controlled.

The stability or instability of behavior patterns depends partly on the stability of contexts. Families, some school characteristics, and socioeconomic status are relatively stable over the course of development for most children; these stable contexts tend to maintain or amplify individual differences in performance and behavior as children grow older. The separate contribution of middle childhood is most evident when there are discontinuities of context or developmental trajectories that forecast adolescent and adult accomplishments, behavior, and social relationships. The intellectual and emotional supports provided to children during middle childhood by families, peer interactions, schools, out-of-school activities, and the broader social and economic context make a difference in the pathways they follow through adolescence and into adulthood.

References

Bronfenbrenner, U., & Morris, P. A. (1998). The ecology of developmental processes. In W. Damon (Series Ed.) & R. M. Lerner (Vol. Ed.), *Handbook of child psychology: Vol. 1. Theoretical models of human development* (5th ed., pp. 993–1028). New York: Wiley.

Buchanan, C. M., Eccles, J. S., & Becker, J. B. (1992). Are adolescents the victims of raging hormones? Evidence for activational effects of hormones on moods and behavior at adolescence. *Psychological Bulletin, 111*, 62–107.

Collins, W. A. (1984). *Development during middle childhood: The years from six to twelve.* Washington, DC: National Academies Press.

Collins, W. A., Maccoby, E. E., Steinberg, L., Hetherington, E. M., & Bornstein, M. H. (2000). Contemporary research on parenting: The case for nature and nurture. *American Psychologist, 55,* 218–232.

DeLoache, J. S., Miller, K. F., & Pierroutsakos, S. L. (1998). Reasoning and problem solving. In W. Damon (Series Ed.) & D. Kuhn & R. S. Siegler (Vol. Eds.), *Handbook of child psychology: Vol. 2. Cognition, perception, and language* (5th ed., pp. 801–850). New York: Wiley.

Demerath, E. W., Li, J., Sun, S. S., Chumlea, W. C., Remsberg, K. E., Czerwinski, S. A., et al. (2004). Fifty-year trends in serial body mass index during adolescence in girls: The Fels Longitudinal Study. *American Journal of Clinical Nutrition, 80*(2), 441–446.

Duncan, G. J., & Brooks-Gunn, J. (2000). Family poverty, welfare reform, and child development. *Child Development, 71,* 188–196.

Eccles, J. S., Wigfield, A., & Schiefele, U. (1998). Motivation to succeed. In W. Damon (Series Ed.) & N. Eisenberg (Vol. Ed.), *Handbook of child psychology: Vol. 3. Social, emotional, and personality development* (5th ed., pp. 1017–1096). New York: Wiley.

Entwisle, D. R., & Alexander, K. (1999). Early schooling and social stratification. In R. C. Pianta and M. J. Cox (Eds.), *The transition to kindergarten.* Baltimore: Paul H. Brookes.

Entwisle, D. R., Alexander, K. L., & Olson, L. S. (1997). *Children, schools, and inequality.* Boulder, CO: Westview Press.

Erikson, E. H. (2005). *Childhood and society.* New York: W. W. Norton & Company, Inc.

Furstenberg, F. F., Cook, T. D., Eccles, J. S., Elder, G. H., Jr., & Sameroff, A. (1999). *Managing to make it: Urban families and adolescent success.* Chicago: University of Chicago Press.

Garcia Coll, C., Lamberty, G., Jenkins, R., McAdoo, H. P., Crnic, K., Wasik, B. H., et al. (1996). An integrative model for the study of developmental competencies in minority children. *Child Development, 67,* 1891–1914.

Harris, J. R. (1998). *The nurture assumption: Why children turn out the way they do.* New York: Free Press.

Harter, S. (1998). The development of self-representations. In W. Damon (Series Ed.) & N. Eisenberg (Vol. Ed.), *Handbook of child psychology: Vol. 3. Social, emotional, and personality development* (5th ed., pp. 553–618). New York: Wiley.

Hartup, W. W. (1984). The peer context in middle childhood. In W. A. Collins (Ed.), *Development during middle childhood: The years from six to twelve* (pp. 240–282). Washington, DC: National Academies Press.

Hartup, W. W., & Moore, S. G. (1990). Early peer relations: Developmental significance and prognostic implications. *Early Childhood Research Quarterly, 5*(1), 1–18.

Herman-Giddens, M. E., & Slora, E. J. (1997). Secondary sexual characteristics and menses in young girls seen in office practice: A study from the pediatric research in office settings network. *Pediatrics, 99*(4), 505–512.

Hofferth, S. L., & Sandberg, J. (1998). *Changes in American children's time, 1981–1997.* Ann Arbor, MI: University of Michigan.

Hofferth, S. L., & Sandberg, J. F. (2001). How American children spend their time. *Journal of Marriage & the Family, 63,* 295–308.

Huesmann, L. R., Moise-Titus, J., Podolski, C. P., & Eron, L. D. (2003). Longitudinal relations between childhood exposure to media violence and adult aggression and violence: 1977–1992. *Developmental Psychology, 39*(2), 201–221.

Huston, A. C., & Wright, J. C. (1998a). Mass media and children's development. In I. Sigel & K. A. Renninger (Eds.), *Child psychology in practice* (5th ed., pp. 999–1058). New York: Wiley.

Huston, A. C., & Wright, J. C. (1998b). Television and the informational and educational needs of children. *Annals of the American Academy of Political and Social Science, 557,* 9–22.

Kuhn, D. (1998). Afterword to Volume 2: Cognition, perception, and language. In W. Damon (Series Ed.) & D. Kuhn & R. S. Siegler (Vol. Eds.), *Handbook of child psychology: Vol. 2. Cognition, perception, and language* (5th ed., pp. 979–981). New York: Wiley.

Ladd, G. W., & Burgess, K. B. (1999). Charting the relationship trajectories of aggressive, withdrawn, and aggressive/withdrawn children during early grade school. *Child Development, 70,* 910–929.

Mahoney, J. L., Larson, R. W., & Eccles, J. S. (2005). *Organized activities as contexts of development: Extracurricular activities, after-school and community programs.* Mahwah, NJ: Lawrence Erlbaum.

Markus, H. J., & Nurius, P. S. (1984). Self-understanding and self-regulation in middle childhood. In W. A. Collins (Ed.), *Development during middle childhood: The years from six to twelve* (pp. 147–183). Washington, DC: National Academies Press.

Pettit, G. S., Bates, J. E., Dodge, K. A., & Meece, D. W. (1999). The impact of after-school peer contact on early adolescent externalizing problems is moderated by parental monitoring, perceived neighborhood safety, and prior adjustment. *Child Development, 70,* 768–778.

Rogoff, B. (1998). Cognition as a collaborative process. In W. Damon (Series Ed.) & D. Kuhn & R. S. Siegler (Vol. Eds.), *Handbook of child psychology: Vol. 2. Cognition, perception, and language* (5th ed., pp. 679–746). New York: Wiley.

Rubin, K. H., Bukowski, W., & Parker, J. G. (1998). Peer interactions, relationships, and groups. In W. Damon (Series Ed.) & N. Eisenberg (Vol. Ed.), *Handbook of child psychology: Vol. 3. Social, emotional, and personality development* (5th ed., pp. 619–700). New York: Wiley.

Ruble, D. N., & Martin, C. L. (1998). Gender development. In W. Damon (Series Ed.) & N. Eisenberg (Vol. Ed.), *Handbook of child psychology: Vol. 3. Social, emotional, and personality development* (5th ed., pp. 993–1016). New York: Wiley.

Scarr, S., & McCartney, K. (1983). How people make their own environments: A theory of genotype –> environment effects. *Child Development, 54,* 424–435.

Schneider, W., & Bjorkland, D. F. (1998). Memory. In W. Damon (Series Ed.) & D. Kuhn & R. S. Siegler (Vol. Eds.), *Handbook of child psychology: Vol. 2. Cognition, perception, and language* (5th ed., pp. 467–522). New York: Wiley.

Scott-Jones, D., & Cho, E. Y. (2003, June). *Children of color, children of immigrants in Philadelphia: Challenges of childrearing and challenges of school.* Paper presented at the Building Pathways to Success: Research, Policy, and Practice on Development in Middle Childhood Conference, MacArthur Network on Successful Pathways through Middle Childhood, Washington, DC.

Shantz, C. U. (1983). Social cognition. In J. H. Flavell & E. M. Markman (Eds.), *Cognitive development* (3rd ed., pp. 495–555). New York: Wiley.

U.S. Department of Health & Human Services (2004). *Trends in the well-being of America's children and youth: 2003*. Washington, DC: U.S. Department of Health and Human Services Office of the Assistant Secretary for Planning and Evaluation. http://aspe.hhs.gov.

Vandell, D. L. (2000). Parents, peers, and other socializing influences. *Developmental Psychology, 36,* 699–710.

Weisner, T. S. (1984). Ecocultural niches of middle childhood: A cross cultural perspective. In W. A. Collins (Ed.), *Development during childhood: The years from six to twelve* (pp. 335–369). Washington, DC: National Academy of Science Press.

Wright, J. C., Huston, A. C., Vandewater, E. A., Bickham, D. S., Scantlin, R. M., Kotler, J. A., et al. (2001). American children's use of electronic media in 1997: A national survey. *Journal of Applied Developmental Psychology, 22,* 31–48.

2

The Significance of Middle Childhood Peer Competence for Work and Relationships in Early Adulthood

W. Andrew Collins and Manfred van Dulmen

Middle childhood is a period of rapidly intensifying transitions. Between age 5 and adolescence, transitions occur in physical maturity, cognitive abilities and learning, the diversity and impact of relationships with others, and exposure to new settings, opportunities, and demands. These changes inevitably alter the amount, kind, content, and significance of children's interactions with a rapidly expanding social network (Collins, Madsen, & Susman-Stillman, 2002). This chapter addresses the impact of one feature of that network – increasingly salient relationships with other children – and the significance of these challenges and achievements for work-related attitudes and relationship competence in early adulthood.

   The chapter is divided into four sections. The first outlines several possible reasons for links between the development of competence in relations with peers in middle childhood and competence in work and close relationships in early adulthood. The second describes our approach to testing these linkages in data from a longitudinal study following children from birth to age 23. The third section outlines findings regarding links between middle childhood development and functioning in early adult work roles and social relationships. The chapter ends with a discussion of the impact of middle childhood experiences on functioning in later periods of life and identifies possible implications of the findings for children's lives.

DEVELOPMENT DURING MIDDLE CHILDHOOD: WHY EXPECT LINKS TO LATER LIFE?

Competence has been defined in varied ways, but the common thread is an emphasis on the capacity to draw upon personal and environmental resources to achieve good developmental outcomes. Individuals who are judged as competent in one period of life typically fare well in negotiating the challenges of subsequent periods. Derived from an attachment model of development, this view holds that competence at each age is predicted by competence at each earlier age and lays the foundation for competence in later periods. Development is cumulative, and – although a good foundation in early life is demonstrably important – later experiences also play a role in successful adaptation at subsequent ages (Carlson, Sroufe, & Egeland, 2004; Waters & Sroufe, 1983).

In what ways might middle childhood be expected to contribute distinctively to competence in early adulthood? Though middle childhood and adulthood occur at notably different points in the life span, the two periods nevertheless resemble each other in terms of certain key developmental tasks. In particular, the transitions experienced in middle childhood as children increasingly encounter persons and settings beyond the family and develop more advanced mastery of physical and intellectual skills foreshadow the transitions in social contexts, social roles, and relationships that occur in early adulthood (Arnett, 2000). So extensive are the transitions that Arnett (2000) has proposed that "emerging adulthood" (approximately ages 18–25 years) should be regarded as a distinctive developmental period. Though taking no position on Arnett's proposal and, indeed, preferring the term early adulthood for the period of 18–25 years, this chapter reflects the premise that early adulthood entails a rapidly intensifying range and diversity of transitions and that earlier experiences with similarly intensive transitions, such as those in middle childhood, may contribute to an individual's competence to adapt to them. Thus, it is the parallel characteristics of development during the two periods, rather than the obvious differences between them, that underlie the central hypotheses of the present study.

Two transitions of early adulthood are especially reminiscent of middle childhood transitions. First, the premise that middle childhood contributes uniquely to later development is consistent with Erikson's contention that middle childhood is a period during which "industry," or making things work, becomes a developmental emphasis. Industry goals may be exercised in school or out-of-school settings (e.g., Goodnow, 1988; Goodnow & Collins, 1990), and middle childhood appears to be a prime time for formative experiences of this kind (e.g., Collins et al., 2002).

Second, with respect to romantic relationships, we have proposed that reciprocity and nurturance in caregiving relationships between parents and children establish and maintain foundations for intimacy and autonomy beginning in early life and that these foundations set the stage for children's relationships with peers in middle childhood that are elaborated and expanded upon in later periods (Collins & Sroufe, 1999). Sullivan (1953) has argued that middle childhood friendships "provide opportunities for validation of self-worth and a unique context for exploration and development of personal strengths" that set the stage for positive developmental trajectories in later periods. Effective, satisfying relationships in early adulthood reflect cumulative experiences of effective, satisfying relationships in earlier periods of life (Collins & Sroufe, 1999; Furman & Wehner, 1994).

The conviction that similarities in developmental tasks may underlie significant links between functioning in middle childhood and early adulthood derives partly from the general hypothesis that children bring from each prior developmental period both a way of engaging the world and a set of expectations concerning the self and others. Specific skills and competence gained earlier in life are carried forward and differentially applied in the negotiation of later developmental tasks (Collins, Hickman, Hyson, & Siebenbruner, 2003; Hyson, Hennighausen, & Egeland 2002). Previous analyses of the longitudinal data on which this chapter is based have shown that middle childhood plays a distinctive role in key aspects of functioning in early adulthood. For example, Hyson et al. (2002) reported that initiative in middle childhood predicted to early adult work competence, over and above measures of caregiving quality from early childhood and measures of initiative and academic achievement in adolescence. Similarly, Collins and Madsen (2002) showed that middle childhood peer relations significantly predict *involvement* in romantic relationships in early adulthood, whereas early childhood measures do not contribute additional variance. By contrast, both early childhood and middle childhood variables contribute significantly to the prediction of romantic relationship *quality*. In short, different salient indicators from earlier developmental periods predict success in the negotiation of developmental issues typical of early adulthood.

The goal of this chapter is to illustrate how prospective assessments from the prenatal period to the mid-twenties can be used to test the prediction that experiences in salient contexts and developmental tasks of middle childhood predict over and above relationships in infancy and early childhood and, further, subsume the variance contributed by adolescent relationships (at ages 16 and 19). Although we do not claim that competence and adjustment "crystallize" in this age period for most children – just as we do not claim that later adaptation is determined by early attachment – we do think that middle childhood experiences, including the nature and course of individual adaptation between the ages of 5 and 12, may be especially salient for key aspects of later functioning, especially in arenas beyond the family of origin (e.g., Collins & Sroufe, 1999; Sullivan, 1953; Youniss, 1980).

PREDICTING EARLY ADULT COMPETENCE: EXAMINING THE ROLE OF MIDDLE CHILDHOOD COMPETENCE

This section outlines the strategy for addressing the foregoing possibilities in data about early adult competence in work and relationship from 162 individuals who have been followed from birth to age 23 in the Minnesota Longitudinal Study of Parents and Children.

Participants

The mothers of sample participants had been recruited during the third trimester of pregnancy from the prenatal clinics at the Minneapolis Health Department, so the sample was originally at risk due to poverty (Egeland & Brunnquell, 1979). Mothers were recruited while receiving prenatal care at public health clinics in Minneapolis in 1975. At the time of delivery, the mothers ranged in age from 12 to 34 years ($M = 20.60$, $SD = 3.57$); 58% of the mothers were single. Forty-one percent of the mothers had not completed high school. Fifty-eight percent of the mothers were Caucasian, 16% were mixed race, 14% were African American, and the remaining 3% were Native American or Latino. Based on U.S. Census occupational categories, heads of households were employed as sales, clerical, or service workers, or craftsmen (50%), in professional or administrative positions (18%), or as laborers (13%) when the children were in third grade. An additional 15% were unemployed, and 4% were students.

Prorated IQ scores for these participants ranged from 49 to 142 ($M = 105.30$, $SD = 15.13$, $N = 164$). These scores came from an abbreviated form of the Wechsler Intelligence Scale for Children-Revised (WISC-R) (Wechsler, 1974), which was administered to children at the end of the third grade. IQ scores were derived from Vocabulary, Similarities, and Block Design subtest scores using Sattler's (1982) formula.

The participants were assessed seven times in the child's first year, twice in each of the next three years, yearly through grade 3, and at ages 12, 13, 16, 17 1/2, 19, and 23. Both children and parents participated individually and jointly through age 16. Information thus came from both parents and participants, as well as from teachers and classmates. Since age 19, assessments have involved the children (now adults), both singly and with their close relationship partners and their own children. Thus, information has been provided by the participants, teachers (as long as they were enrolled in formal schooling), and romantic partners.

In a typical year, participants in the study were enrolled in more than 100 classrooms in 100 different schools. Schools employed varying policies and procedures, and each classroom was unique. The several hundred teachers interviewed had different biases and observational abilities. These potential sources of variation are inevitable features of long-term longitudinal research; consequently, data reduction procedures included provisions for handling occasional missing data. Throughout the study, data were combined to minimize subject loss, to use all information available, to cancel out some sources of error, to keep the number of variables in the analyses as small as possible, and to insure high quality data. In some cases, this involved averaging multiple assessments. For example, rank order measures of peer competence were averaged across early grades. This procedure not only counteracts idiosyncrasies of individual teachers, but also maintains an adequate sample size (if data were not available for a subject in a given year, the average from the other two years would be adequate). In the present analyses, although sample size varies slightly among regression analyses, the major Structural Equation Modeling analyses involve all participants for whom age 23 data were available ($n = 162$). A multiple imputation method using the EM algorithm was used in these latter analyses to handle missing data (Schafer, 1997).

Sixty-seven percent of the participants at age 23 were White/Caucasian, 11% African-American, 18% mixed-race, 1% Hispanic, and 3% Native American. Seventeen percent of the participants were currently neither working nor in school, 64% were currently only working, 2% were currently only in school, and 17% were currently both working and in school. Fourteen percent did not earn a degree and 19% earned a GED. Forty-seven percent earned a high school degree and 20% earned a college degree (vocational school, two-year college, or four-year college). Thirty-two percent were currently not in a romantic relationship. Forty-six percent of the participants were dating while 10% were engaged. Twelve percent of the participants were in a married/committed relationship. Thirty-seven percent of the participants were parents.

Measures

Several of the constructs assessed during early and middle childhood and adolescence were relevant to the question of whether middle childhood individual and social variables, relative to predictors from earlier and later periods, forecasted early adults' competent functioning in work roles. From middle childhood, the predictor of greatest relevance was peer competence during first, second, and third grades. To address the possibility that competence with peers in middle childhood reflected the children's earlier history of caregiving relationships in their families, the analyses also included a composite measure of supportive care in early childhood and a measure of security of attachment at 12 months. A further possibility was that experiences with parents and peers during adolescence might provide a pathway by which middle childhood competence would affect early-adult competence. Consequently, the analyses included measures of quality of parent–adolescent interaction at age 13 and quality of friendships at age 16. In addition to these earlier and later experiences in significant relationships, possible variations in findings for females and males also were examined.

Early Adult Outcomes. Assessments at age 23 focused on two general aspects of functioning during early adulthood: competence in work roles and competence in relationships, including both relationships with a romantic partner and participation in a network of associates from whom social support might be derived. To assess *competence in work roles*, participants completed a semi-structured School and Work Experience Interview and a paper-and-pencil Work Experience Questionnaire. The instruments were designed by the staff of the Minnesota Longitudinal Study of Parents and Children. The staff also created three 5-point rating scales for coding these data. The *career reflectivity scale* assessed the extent and complexity of the participant's thinking about a career plan. The *career exploration scale* dealt with the degree to which participants have explored possible career choices. The *career maturity scale* assessed the degree to which participants had thought about and evaluated their job or career goals. Reliabilities, as assessed by intraclass correlation coefficients, ranged from .74 to .84.

Data regarding *competence in relationships in early adulthood* came from extensive interviews which included a series of specific questions about the activities shared with dating partners and feelings about the partner and the relationship (e.g., "Describe a time when you felt especially close to your partner"; "Describe the biggest fight or argument you had with your partner in the past month"). For those in romantic relationships of 4 months or more at age 23 ($N = 93$), we rated responses on 5-point scales of *overall quality of reported relationships*. As expected, relationships receiving the highest ratings were characterized by mutual caring, trust, support, and emotional closeness. Intraclass correlations for these ratings ranged from .85 to .93.

The *quality of observed interactions* between participants and their romantic partners was assessed in our lab at ages 20–21 for those participants who had been in a self-defined romantic relationship for at least 4 months. The participant and partner visited our laboratory. The members of the couple first responded separately to an extensive interview about the relationship, and then the couple participated jointly in two collaborative problem-solving tasks. Using videotapes of these couple interactions, the coding team achieved a very respectable reliability of .95 on ratings of the overall quality. Both members of the couple also provided self-ratings of their *satisfaction with the relationship* during the observational procedure at age 21. The instrument for this self-report was the Relationship Assessment Scale (Hendrick, 1988), a widely used self-report measure of relationship satisfaction in dating and married couples.

Measures of *romantic relationship violence perpetration and victimization* were drawn from the eight items of the "physical aggression" subscale of the Conflict Tactics Scale (Straus, 1979). Continuous scores of perpetration

TABLE 2.1. *Overview Correlations and Descriptive Statistics*

	1	2	3	4	5	6	7	8
1. Early care	1.0							
2. 12 month attachment	.11	1.0						
3. Middle childhood peer competence	.24	.21	1.0					
4. Adolescent friendship quality	.10	.03	.23	1.0				
5. Adolescent family quality	.32	.04	.20	.14	1.0			
6. Young adulthood relationship satisfaction	.05	.28	.21	.32	.20	1.0		
7. Young adulthood work competence	.19	−.06	.25	.03	.14	.13	1.0	
8. Young adulthood relationship violence	−.10	−.07	−.22	−.21	−.10	−.28	−.14	1.0
M	−.03	2.01	47.45	4.58	4.83	5.83	2.94	.49
SD	.71	.67	23.67	1.36	.86	.73	1.32	.74

and victimization were formed by weighing and summing the items for the participants' reports of their own use of physical aggression and for their reports of their partners' use of physical aggression, respectively. Natural log transformations were used to correct for skewness in these two variables. Table 2.1 includes means and standard deviations for all variables included in the analyses described in this chapter, as well as intercorrelations among the variables.

Childhood and Adolescent Predictor Variables. To examine the significance of competence with peers during middle childhood for later competence in key areas of early adult competence, analyses included a measure of peer competence in grades 1–3. In addition, gender was included in analyses whenever sample size permitted to assess whether findings varied for different subgroups of individuals.

The primary predictor from middle childhood was *competence with peers*. The measure of peer competence was a teacher nomination procedure developed by staff of the longitudinal study. Teachers were asked to rank order the students in their classes based on a written description of peer competence with the child most closely resembling the description to be ranked at the top. The description specified the following criteria for peer competence: (a) sociability, that is, fairly frequent social contact with peers; (b) popularity, that is, wide acceptance among other children;

(c) friendship, that is, one or more special companions with whom there seems to be a well-meshed relationship; and (d) social skills and leadership qualities, that is, techniques of social interactions that promote social relations; for example, understanding another child's perspectives and desire, negotiating different play themes if a particular overture to play is not accepted, accepting the other child's ideas as a starting point for interaction, and using clear, comprehensible communications toward peers. Others want to be with this child and do what (s)he is doing; and this child knows how to lead them to interesting and fun activities.

Thus, the measure characterizes the socially competent child in middle childhood and adolescence as a child who effectively engages peers. Use of rankings rather than ratings in part counters rating bias (e.g., tendencies to use high, medium, or low ratings in general) and also allows this information to be gathered without the teacher's knowing whom the target child was (which could introduce a bias that the child must be troubled).

A child's score on each of these measures was the ratio of the inverse of the child's rank divided by the number of students in the class (i.e., if the child was ranked 11th in a class of 30, the child received a score of .66 = (30 − 11 + 1/30). The average rankings in each domain across grades 1, 2, and 3 were used in these analyses. Because a single teacher completed the rank orders (no one else had comparable knowledge of the child), reliability figures are not available for the scales with this sample. In a separate study, however, multiple counselors independently rank-ordered children participating in a 4-week summer camp and reported interrater reliability coefficients ranging from .63 to .81 (Elicker, Englund, & Sroufe, 1992). Teacher rankings show significant stability from year to year (Hiester, Carlson, & Sroufe, 1993).

Control Variables from Early Childhood and Adolescence. Finally, to address the possibility that measures of middle childhood functioning were redundant with measures of functioning in earlier and/or later periods, we controlled for significant relationships in early childhood and adolescence. From early childhood, a composite variable of *early supportive care* was derived to capture the overall quality of maternal support in varied tasks during the child's first four years of life. The composite was the sum of z-scored values from Strange Situation (Ainsworth et al., 1978) assessments of attachment security at 12 and 18 months, child's experience in an observed problem-solving task with the mother at 24 months, and mother's supportive presence as observed in a teaching task at 42 months. The two latter measures were formed as follows.

Mother's support in problem solving at 24 months was assessed in a laboratory problem-solving procedure in which the child is challenged to solve a series of problems of graded difficulty with mother available to help (Matas, Arend, & Sroufe, 1978). Overall quality of mother's problem-solving support was rated on a 5-point Likert-type scale. At the high end of the scale (rating = 5), mother was rated as excellent in problem-solving support: consistent, patiently supportive, and helpful without being overcontrolling. At the low end of the scale (rating = 1), mother was rated as so over-controlling or so lax in providing guidance that the child had a negative problem-solving experience or had no personal experience of problem solving. Two independent coders coded assessments. Pearson product moment reliability was .87. The overall measure of parental support has been shown to be a powerful predictor of later socioemotional functioning (Erickson, Sroufe, & Egeland, 1985; Renken, Egeland, Marvinney, Mangelsdorf, & Sroufe, 1989).

At 42 months, *quality of mother's supportive presence* was assessed in a series of teaching tasks (see Erickson et al., 1985). Mother was asked to assist the child to (a) build block towers of specific proportions, (b) name things with wheels, (c) match colors and shapes on a form board, and (d) trace a preset pattern through an Etch-a-Sketch maze. Mother and child were rated on a series of 7-point Likert-type scales. Two independent coders coded assessments. Average interrater reliability across all rating scales was .78 for 87 participants. These ratings of quality of mother support have been shown to predict socioemotional functioning in both preschool and middle childhood (Erickson et al., 1985; Renken et al., 1989). In the analyses reported here, average ratings from two scales, mother's quality of instruction and mother's ability to provide structure and set limits, were used. Ratings and scores from the three assessments were standardized and averaged to derive the composite *early childhood care* variable. Selection of these and other scales for analysis were all made without reference to outcome data.

Adolescent family functioning was based on observations of mother–child problem-solving interactions at age 13. Adolescents and their mothers were videotaped in a laboratory situation. (Because only 44 men who were the primary male figures for these participants were living with them at age 13, triadic data are not reported here.) The dyads completed four structured interaction tasks: (a) plan an anti-smoking campaign; (b) assemble a series of puzzles while the parent was blindfolded (the child was asked to guide the assembly); (c) discuss the effects of two imaginary/hypothetical happenings; and (d) complete a Q-sort of an ideal person. Coders rated the dyadic interactions on a series of 7-point rating scales (Sroufe, 1991). For these analyses, the measure of parent–child functioning was the sum of scales measuring the degree of balance between individuals in the problem-solving task and the relation between the parent–child relationship system and the external world (i.e., the degree to which the dyad easily became engaged in the tasks and worked as a team to complete the tasks or solve the problem). Two coders rated a subsample of 129 dyadic assessments (kappa = .78).

Adolescent friendship quality was based on interview responses at age 16 regarding a specific friendship. In addition to providing information about the friendship (length, status, how they met), participants were asked what they liked and disliked about the friendship, to explain how their friend treated them, and to describe several positive and negative emotional experiences in the friendship. They also were asked to describe the biggest fight they had ever had with their friend, including the topic, circumstances of the argument, reactions of both individuals, and resolutions. Coders rated audiotapes of these interviews on several 7-point scales. *Ratings of security* assess the extent to which the adolescent feels that the friend is accepting and will be available in times of need. Salient issues considered in this rating include authenticity, mutuality, openness of communication, availability, help, and durability.

Presence of conflict assesses the degree to which the friendship is dominated by conflict and/or tension. This rating considers the frequency, severity, and content of the conflict. Conflict resolution assesses the degree to which the friends are capable of resolving conflicts that arise. This rating considers maturity and equity of resolution strategies, as well as the presence of victimization or exploitation. Disclosure assesses the extent to which the adolescent verbally shares emotional experiences with the friend. The content, ease, and degree of disclosure are all considered in this rating. Closeness captures the degree to which the adolescent feels connected to and values the friend. Each audiotape was coded by at least two trained observers, and the intraclass correlations between two coders' scores ranged from .74 to .84.

Principal components analysis was used to examine the overlap among the scales, which were highly intercorrelated. The number of factors was not specified, and an unrotated solution was requested. One factor emerged (loadings ranged from .61 to .93); therefore, a decision was made to form a composite variable labeled "friendship quality" by summing security, presence of conflict (reverse-coded), conflict resolution, disclosure, and closeness. This scale had high internal reliability ($\alpha = .88$). Possible scores ranged from 5 to 35, with higher scores indicating higher friendship quality.

FROM MIDDLE CHILDHOOD TO EARLY ADULT COMPETENCE IN WORK AND RELATIONSHIPS: FINDINGS

Statistical analyses evaluated the adequacy of structural equation models in which middle childhood peer competence was expected to predict early-adult work and relationship measures, while accounting for associations with quality of early caregiving, adolescent family functioning, and adolescent friendship quality. As follow-up analyses, we tested mediational models, with middle childhood peer competence as a potential mediator of the relation between relationships in early childhood and early-adult outcomes. The potential moderating role of gender was addressed in all analyses. Correlations among all of the predictor and outcome variables appear in Table 2.1.

Competence in Early Adult Work Roles

The 162 participants varied with respect to work outcomes at age 23. Eighty-six percent of participants had earned a high school diploma or GED by age 23, 45% had attended at least some college, and 13% had earned a two- or four-year college degree. In addition, while almost three fourths of participants were engaged full-time in work, school, or a combination of both for the majority of time between ages 21 and 23, just under two thirds were satisfied with their job at the time of the interview, only a little more than half demonstrated a "good" or outstanding work ethic, only just over a third exhibited a "high" or "very high" level of career maturity, and only approximately 1 in 10 was employed in a job that matched his or her career goals. The latter was determined by the degree to which individuals were working currently in the types of jobs or the fields to which they aspired. Females and males were not different in their likelihood of being employed at age 23. However, analysis of variance revealed that males' current jobs ranked significantly higher on occupational status than females' current jobs, $F (1,160) = 4.95$, $p < .001$. By contrast, females scored higher on work ethic than males did, $F (1,158) = 6.47$, $p < .01$. No gender differences appeared on career reflectivity or career maturity.

To answer the question of what variables most consistently predict the competent negotiation of the transition to work in early adulthood, longitudinal path analyses were computed for each of the work outcomes (work reflectivity, work exploration, and career maturity). A model in which middle childhood peer competence directly predicted early adult work competence, while controlling for early childhood caregiving quality and adolescent friendship quality, represented the data well (RMSEA = .065). Middle childhood peer competence ratings significantly predicted early-adult work competence ($\beta = .23$, $t = 2.25$). Neither early care, adolescent family functioning, nor adolescent friendship quality were significant predictors of early-adult status, despite significant associations between middle childhood peer competence and both early care and adolescent friendship quality.

Follow-up regression analyses were conducted to investigate whether peer competence mediated the relation between early supportive care and early adult work competence. Results showed that peer competence partially mediated the relation between early supportive care and early adult work competence, as shown in Figure 2.1. The statistically significant

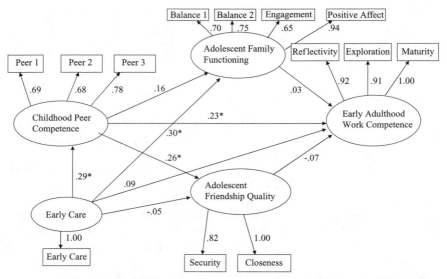

FIGURE 2.1. Results of SEM model predicting early adulthood work competence (N = 161). χ^2 (57) = 95.99; RMSEA = .065

association between early supportive care and early adult work competence ($\beta = .19, p < .05$) became nonsignificant after accounting for the effect of middle childhood peer competence ($\beta = .13, p =$ ns). Further inspection by gender showed that middle childhood peer competence ratings predicted early-adult work competence for girls more strongly than for boys, but there was insufficient statistical power to detect the significance of these differences.

Competence in Early Adult Relationships

In the organizational-developmental model that guides the Minnesota Longitudinal Study of Parents and Children, both parent–child relationships and peer relationships across time should foster the interpersonal competencies needed to negotiate the complex developmental task of forming and maintaining close relationships. The present analyses examined the relations among these variables with respect to romantic relationships and appropriate networks of social support.

Romantic Relationship Competence. The analyses provided information about the adequacy of a model in which middle childhood peer competence predicted the quality of, and satisfaction in, romantic relationships. The model did not provide a good fit to the interrelations of middle childhood

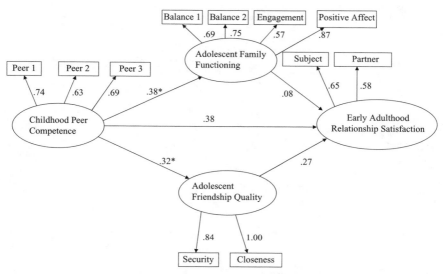

FIGURE 2.2. Structural Equation Modeling analyses predicting early adulthood relationship satisfaction (N = 75). χ^2 (39) = 66.87; RMSEA = .098

competence with peers and early-adult relationship satisfaction (RMSEA = .098), as shown in Figure 2.2. Middle childhood peer competence was positively, but not statistically, associated with reported relationship satisfaction at age 21. Follow-up analyses revealed that middle childhood peer competence partially mediated the relation between attachment at 12 months in the Strange Situation and relationship satisfaction in early adulthood. Middle childhood peer competence reduced the statistically significant association between attachment at 12 months and relationship satisfaction at age 21 ($\beta = .32, p < .05$) to marginal significance ($\beta = .22, p = .05$).

Violence in Relationships. With respect to experiences of violence in relationships, however, the same Structural Equation Model that failed to account for links between middle childhood and positive relationships represented the data linking middle childhood and relationship violence reasonably well (RMSEA = .079). This model appears in Figure 2.3. Sample size was inadequate for testing gender differences in these analyses.

DISCUSSION AND CONCLUSIONS

Peer competence in middle childhood appears to contribute uniquely and distinctively to competence in key domains of early adult functioning,

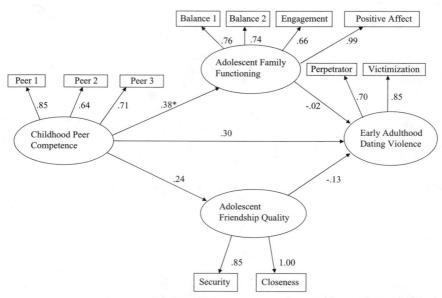

FIGURE 2.3. Structural Equation Modeling analyses predicting early adulthood dating violence (N = 90). χ^2 (39) = 60.65; RMSEA = .079

such as work roles and satisfaction in romantic relationships. This relation is especially apparent for girls. In addition, peer competence mediates the impact of early caregiving relationships on girls' later competence in work and relationships. Although middle childhood functioning with peers did not appear to be an important forerunner of all forms of early-adult relationship competence, the significance of middle childhood experiences with peers for key aspects of later competence is clearly evident in these findings.

These findings provide support for theoretical formulations about the relevance of middle childhood to developmental trajectories in key domains of adult competence and also raise provocative questions about optimal familial, school-based, and other societally influenced experiences common to the middle childhood period. Although these data appeared to show pervasive effects for females rather than males, the present analyses lacked the power to detect significant gender differences. Indeed, descriptive analyses revealed no gender differences on peer competence rankings in grades 1–3, nor were girls and boys different on the degree of relation between peer competence and early measures of IQ. Moreover, although gender differences occurred in the relation between peer competence and school achievement in these early elementary-school years, the relation appeared stronger for boys than for girls.

The suggestion that individual differences in middle childhood peer competence might be related to measures of work-related competence in early adulthood for girls and so weakly related for boys awaits further studies with greater statistical power for examining these contrasts. If such differences were found, they might imply that competence in the gender-segregated peer groups of middle childhood bring females, more than males, into contact with peers who support career concerns and goals. Although contrary to the longstanding stereotype of male gender-role orientations as instrumental and female gender-role orientations as expressive (Parsons, 1955), this interpretation could account for the stronger association for females between individual differences in peer competence and early adult work maturity and planning in a period of increasing tolerance for instrumental orientations in females.

A troubling implication of this interpretation, however, is that a secular trend toward less male investment in achievement, if confirmed, casts doubt on the longstanding assumption that group activities in childhood and adolescence contribute significantly to male socialization. If males' functioning in work and relationships is not significantly shaped by competent functioning in the male peer groups of earlier life, popular and tacit scholarly assumptions about male socialization may need to be revised. Clearly, future research should include additional examination of gender-related variations in the conditions under which competence in extrafamilial settings is significant for functioning in later life periods.

The finding that peer competence in middle childhood predicts early adulthood dating violence more strongly than more proximal predictors from adolescence (viz., family functioning, friendship quality) raises two interesting possibilities regarding interventions to reduce the later likelihood of violent relationships. First, the present results provide new evidence that the almost exclusive focus on early family violence as the primary factor in the likelihood of children's later violent relationships provides an incomplete picture of the development of romantic aggression. Linder and Collins (2005) recently reported that quality of parent–child relationship experiences and friendship quality in adolescence predicted romantic aggression more strongly than early childhood parent–child relationships did. It is unlikely that romantic aggression is the result of experiences in any one relationship context; rather, it emerges from a combination of experiences in different contexts. Second, although prevention efforts to date have focused on adolescent and early adult groups, the indications in the present findings that middle childhood predicts more strongly to early adulthood dating violence than adolescent predictors imply that middle childhood may be an especially promising period for attempting to forestall later violence. A developmental perspective on romantic relationship violence that encompasses potential predictors from multiple age periods may enable researchers to design more effective efforts to prevent partner violence and victimization before it begins (Linder & Collins, 2005).

It is important to note that this evidence of the significance of middle childhood experiences is compatible with, rather than contrary to, the premise that development during each stage of life builds on prior experiences and feeds forward to the distinctive experiences of later periods (Carlson et al., 2004). The present findings underscore that, far from being a period of latency in this dynamic process, as Sigmund Freud's (1954) classic theory implied, middle childhood contributes fundamentally to the ongoing development of Freud's two classic facets of human motivation: to work and to love.

Preparation of this chapter was supported by a grant from the National Institute of Mental Health to Byron Egeland, L. Alan Sroufe, and W. Andrew Collins and by funds from the MacArthur Foundation Network on Successful Pathways Through Middle Childhood.

References

Ainsworth, M., Blehard, M., Waters, E., & Wall, S. (1978). *Patterns of attachment: A psychological study of the Strange Situation*. Hillsdale, NJ: Lawrence Erlbaum Associates.

Arnett, J. J. (2000). Emerging adulthood: A theory of development from the late teens through the twenties. *American Psychologist, 55*, 469–480.

Carlson, E. A., Sroufe, L. A., & Egeland, B. (2004). The construction of experience: A longitudinal study of representation and behavior. *Child Development, 75*, 66–83.

Collins, W. A., Hickman, S., Hyson, D. M., & Siebenbruner, J. (2003, April). Middle childhood roots of early adult competence in work and relationships. In R. Huesmann (Chair), *Middle childhood contextual influences on later outcomes*. Symposium at the biennial conference of the Society for Research in Child Development, Tampa, FL.

Collins, W. A., & Madsen, S. D. (2002, August). Relational histories and trajectories of later romantic experiences. In W. A. Collins & S. Shulman (Organizers), *Trajectories in the development of romantic relationships: Childhood and adolescent precursors of interpersonal transitions*. Symposium at the conference of the International Society for the Study of Behavioral Development, Ottawa, Canada.

Collins, W. A., Madsen, S. D., & Susman-Stillman, A. (2002). Parenting during middle childhood. In M. Bornstein (Ed.), *Handbook of parenting* (2nd ed., Vol. 1) (pp. 103–134). Hillsdale, NJ: Erlbaum.

Collins, W. A., & Sroufe, L. A. (1999). Capacity for intimate relationships: A developmental construction. In W. Furman, B. B. Brown, & C. Feiring (Eds.), *The development of romantic relationships in adolescence* (pp. 125–147). New York: Cambridge University Press.

Egeland, B., & Brunnquell, D. (1979). An at-risk approach to the study of child abuse: Some preliminary findings. *Journal of the American Academy of Child Psychiatry, 18*, 219–225.

Elicker, J., Englund, M., & Sroufe, L. A. (1992). Predicting peer competence and peer relationships in childhood from early parent-child relationships. In R. Parke & G. Ladd (Eds.), *Family-peer relationships: Modes of linkage* (pp. 77–106). Hillsdale, NJ: Erlbaum.

Erickson, M., Sroufe, L. A., & Egeland, B. (1985). The relationships between quality of attachment and behavior problems in preschool in a high-risk sample. In I. Bretherton & E. Waters (Eds.), Growing points of attachment theory and research. *Monographs of the Society for Research in Child Development, 50*(1–2, Serial No. 209), 147–186.

Freud, S. (1954). *Collected works, standard edition.* London: Hogarth Press.

Furman, W., & Wehner, E. (1994). Adolescent romantic relationships. In R. Montemayor, G. R. Adams, & T. P. Gullotta (Eds.), *Personal relationships during adolescence* (pp. 168–195). Thousand Oaks, CA: Sage.

Goodnow, J. J. (1988). Children's household work: Its nature and functions. *Psychological Bulletin, 103,* 5–26.

Goodnow, J. J., & Collins, W. A. (1990). *Development according to parents: The nature, sources, and consequences of parents' ideas.* Hillsdale, NJ: Erlbaum.

Hendrick, S. (1988). A generic measure of relationship satisfaction. *Journal of Marriage and the Family, 50,* 93–98.

Hiester, M., Carlson, E., & Sroufe, L. A. (1993, March). *The evolution of friendship in preschool, middle childhood, and adolescence: Origins in attachment history.* Paper presented at the biennial meeting of the Society for Research in Child Development, New Orleans, LA.

Hyson, D. M., Hennighausen, K. H., & Egeland, B. (2002, April). Competence in emerging adulthood: Developmental antecedents. In A. Masten (Chair), *Developmental tasks in emerging adulthood.* Symposium at the biennial conference of the Society for Research on Adolescence, New Orleans, LA.

Linder, J. R., & Collins, W. A. (2005). Parent and peer predictors of physical aggression and conflict management in romantic relationships in early adulthood. *Journal of Family Psychology, 19,* 252–262.

Matas, L., Arend, R., & Sroufe, L. A. (1978). Continuity of adaptation in the second year: The relationship between quality of attachment and later competence. *Child Development, 49,* 547–556.

Parsons, T. (1955). Family structure and the socialization of the child. In T. Parsons & R. F. Bales (Eds.), *Family, socialization, and interaction process* (pp. 35–131). Glencoe, IL: Free Press.

Renken, B., Egeland, B., Marvinney, D., Mangelsdorf, S., & Sroufe, L. A. (1989). Early childhood antecedents of aggression and passive-withdrawal in early elementary school. *Journal of Personality, 57,* 257–281.

Sattler, J. (1982). *Assessment of children's intelligence and special abilities* (2nd ed.). San Diego, CA: Jerome M. Sattler.

Schafer, J. L. (1997). *Analysis of incomplete data* [*Monographs on Statistics and Applied Probability, No. 72*]. Boca Raton, FL: Chapman & Hall/CRC.

Sroufe, J. (1991). Assessment of parent-adolescent relationships: Implications for adolescent development. *Journal of Family Psychology, 5,* 21–45.

Straus, M. (1979). Measuring intrafamily conflict and violence: The conflict tactics (CT) scales. *Journal of Marriage and the Family, 41,* 75–88.

Sullivan, H. S. (1953). *The interpersonal theory of psychiatry*. New York: Norton.

Waters, E., & Sroufe, L. A. (1983). Social competence as a developmental construct. *Developmental Review, 3*, 79–97.

Wechsler, D. (1974). *Wechsler Intelligence Scale for Children-Revised*. New York: The Psychological Corporation.

Youniss, J. (1980). *Parents and peers in social development: A Sullivan-Piaget perspective*. Chicago: University of Chicago Press.

3

Aggression and Insecurity in Late Adolescent Romantic Relationships

Antecedents and Developmental Pathways

Gregory S. Pettit, John E. Bates, Amy
Holtzworth-Munroe, Amy D. Marshall,
Lori D. Harach, David J. Cleary,
and Kenneth A. Dodge

Experiences in the family and peer group play important roles in the development of interpersonal competencies across the childhood and adolescent years. Toward the end of adolescence, stable and supportive romantic relationships increasingly serve adaptive functions in promoting individual well-being and in fostering a sense of connection and security to others (Collins, Hennighausen, Schmit, & Sroufe, 1997; Conger, Cui, Bryant, & Elder, 2000; Furman, 1999). Romantic relationships marked by conflict and violence pose risks for current and longer-term adjustment and can compromise the health and well-being of the partner to whom the violence is directed (Capaldi & Owen, 2001). Romantic relationships in which one or both partners are wary, jealous, and insecure can stifle growth and fuel disagreements and disharmony (Holtzworth-Munroe, Meehan, Herron, Rehman, & Stuart, 2000).

Relationship insecurity and relationship violence covary to some degree (Holtzworth-Munroe & Stewart, 1994), suggesting that they may be linked in the development of romantic relationship dysfunction. Within the marital violence literature, insecurity has been proposed as a key pathway through which relationship violence develops. Consistent with this perspective, Holtzworth-Munroe et al. (2000), in their examination of types of male batterers, found that one type of batterer could be characterized by insecurity and a tendency to confine violence to an intimate relationship. Holtzworth-Munroe et al. (2000) speculate that insecurity plays an etiological role in the development of partner violence. If this were the case, then insecurity might serve as a mediating link between social experience (e.g., of rejection and intimidation) and subsequent violence.

In this chapter, we test an alternative perspective in which interpersonal insecurities and a proclivity to engage in violence toward one's partner are viewed as correlated but distinguishable features of romantic relationships. Holtzworth-Munroe et al. (2000) note that there are differing developmental pathways leading to partner violence, one of which involves relationship insecurity. But for other individuals, being violent with a romantic partner may have little to do with relationship fears and insecurities (e.g., those for whom violence stems more from a general antisocial orientation). Similarly, many insecure individuals may harbor fears and resentments that do not translate into overt acts of violence toward their partner.

Of central interest in this chapter is whether insecurity and violence have distinct antecedents, and whether these antecedents represent coherent pathways through which the two markers of romantic relationship quality may develop. As markers of relationship quality, each would seem to represent a fairly distinct set of correlates and antecedents. Violence is outer- (and other-) directed and likely follows from aggressogenic experiences with parents and peers (Magdol, Moffitt, Caspi, & Silva, 1998; Swinford, DeMaris, Cernkovich, & Giordano, 2000). Insecurity is less directly dangerous to a partner, and likely reflects internalized views of relationship inadequacy and maladaptive representations of relationships that stem from prior experiences of rejection. In this chapter we use prospective, longitudinal data to trace family and peer experience antecedents of both forms of relationship dysfunction.

Individual differences in the qualities of romantic relationships have been hypothesized to derive from both parent–child relationships, particularly in adolescence, and child–peer relationships in middle childhood and adolescence (Collins et al., 1997). Ineffective and negative family socialization practices, such as lack of warmth and inadequate supervision, have been linked with subsequent couple conflict and partner-directed aggression (Andrews, Foster, Capaldi, & Hops, 2000; Conger et al., 2000). Research on relationship insecurity (including insecure attachment to the relationship partner), on the other hand, has tended to focus more on attachment-based explanations of links between insecurity and parenting quality, as well as links between insecurity and peer relations in general and friendships in particular (Collins et al., 1997). Collectively, these research perspectives suggest that harsh and rejecting experiences with parents and peers may foster the development of antisocial behavioral orientations that subsequently are manifested in partner-directed aggression, whereas lack of close and supportive relationships with parents and peers may contribute to the development of anxious and insecure ways of relating to partners.

Contemporary socialization models stress the role of early and continuing social experiences in the development of interpersonal skills and competencies, with some kinds of relationships (e.g., those with peers) playing especially important roles during some developmental periods (e.g., middle childhood) (Collins & Sroufe, 1999; Furman, 1999; Magdol et al., 1998). In this chapter, we examine children's experiences in the parent–child relationship context and in the peer relationship context. We consider the relations between these experiences across early childhood, middle childhood, and early and middle adolescence, and subsequent aggression toward romantic partners and feelings of insecurity about romantic relationships. Of special interest is whether social experiences in earlier developmental periods account for unique variance in late adolescent relationship outcomes independently of experiences in later developmental periods, or whether the impacts of earlier experiences (especially in early and middle childhood) are rendered nonsignificant after controlling for later experiences. Findings showing the latter pattern would be consistent with an experiential mediation socialization perspective, that is, that social experiences in adolescence follow from, and explain, the link between early social experiences and subsequent interpersonal outcomes.

The developmental period that serves as the key, connecting link in these analyses – because social experience data are available both prior to and subsequent to this period – is that of middle childhood. This allows us to examine continuities in relationship qualities across early childhood, middle childhood, and adolescence, and to consider, in line with the experiential mediation model described above, whether middle childhood experiences with parents and peers (a) predict subsequent relationship insecurity and violence, and (b) mediate the association between earlier family experiences and subsequent relationship insecurity and violence. Assuming significant associations between middle childhood experiences and later outcomes, then we also can test whether (c) the association between middle childhood experiences and late adolescent relationship insecurity and violence is itself mediated by subsequent early-to-middle adolescent family and peer relationship qualities.

Also of interest is whether developmental risk factors operate similarly for males and females and for individuals from higher versus lower socioeconomic status (SES) families. In terms of main effects, it might be expected that males would report higher levels of partner-directed violence, in line with a large body of research showing more externalizing-type problems in males than in females (Coie & Dodge, 1998). However, there is some evidence that, in community samples, partner-directed violence rates are comparable for males and females (e.g., Sorenson, Upchurch, & Shen, 1996). Other studies have shown that female-reported partner-directed violence may even exceed that of male-reported partner-directed violence (e.g., Swinford et al., 2000; but note that only the frequency, and not the severity, of violence was evaluated). With respect to relationship insecurity, it might be expected that females would tend to report higher levels, insofar as insecurity is construed as an internalizing-type problem outcome, on which girls tend to be rated higher. However, because at the present time there is relatively little research directly bearing on insecurity in relationships, there currently is little basis for making sex-difference predictions in overall level of relationship insecurity. Because problem behaviors of all types tend to occur more frequently in economically disadvantaged populations, it was expected that both violence and insecurity scores would be higher among children from lower SES families compared with children from higher SES families.

Of greater interest in the context of sex and SES differences is whether antecedent–outcome relations depend on these background factors. Few differences are expected with respect to child sex because problem-behavior predictors have been found to show comparable patterns for boys and girls (e.g., Deater-Deckard, Dodge, Bates, & Pettit, 1998). On the other hand, SES might be expected to play a somewhat pronounced role in moderating linkages between child and adolescent risk factors and romantic relationship outcomes. Low SES, with its attendant stresses, might serve as a potentiator of certain risks (e.g., exposure to antisocial peers). High SES, and the economic and social advantages that accrue from it (e.g., access to better schools and more extensive involvement in adult-supervised extracurricular activities), might serve as a protective factor in buffering children from the adverse effects of experiential risk (Pettit, Bates, & Dodge, 1997). For example, the relation between harsh parenting and later partner-directed violence, or between harsh parenting and later relationship insecurity, might be stronger for children in lower SES families than for children in higher SES families.

This investigation makes use of data collected as part of the ongoing Child Development Project (Dodge, Bates, & Pettit, 1990; Pettit et al., 1997), a prospective, longitudinal study of a community sample of children and their families initially recruited and assessed when children were age 5, with follow-up assessments conducted annually through age 20. The sample is diverse with respect to gender, ethnicity, and socioeconomic background. Approximately 75% of the original sample of 585 participated in the romantic relationship follow-up phase of the study at age 18. The overarching goal of the Child Development Project is to chart the developmental course of both antisocial and adaptive behavior from childhood through early adulthood, with a focus on the role of social experiences with parents and peers and children's construal of those experiences.

METHOD

Data Collection Overview

In assessments conducted in project year 1 (the summer prior to kindergarten), the family was visited in the home by a team of interviewers. Parents provided detailed accounts of children's developmental history, social experiences, and behavioral characteristics. In grades 1 through 4 (ages 6 through 9, on average) children's peer experiences were assessed via classroom sociometric interviews and through teachers' ratings of the children's social skills and behavior. During each summer following grades 1 through 4, mothers completed a battery of questionnaires, including instruments designed to assess their parenting practices. In the summer prior to grade 6, when most children were 10 years old, mothers were interviewed about aspects of the parent–child relationship. Later that year (during grade 6, when most children were 11 years old) children were interviewed about their friendships and their affiliation with the broader peer group.

During the summer following grade 10, when most participants were 16 years old, a home visit interview and observation session were conducted. Mothers and teens were interviewed separately and asked questions bearing on qualities of the parent–teen relationship and (for the adolescents) the teens' friendships. During a video-recorded, semistructured observational session, mothers and teens engaged in problem-solving and conflict-resolution discussions. In the summer following grade 12 (age 18), the teens were asked in an interview whether they were presently involved in a romantic relationship. For those so reporting, follow-up questions were administered regarding the occurrence of violence in the relationship and feelings of relationship security, jealousy, and confidence.

Whenever possible, we selected measures with previously established psychometric properties and predictive validity. Separate sets of measures were used for each antecedent developmental period. Prekindergarten mother interview data were used to index early parent–child relationship quality. Elementary school data (sociometrics and teacher ratings) and the questionnaires completed by mothers during these years comprise the middle childhood data on peer relationship quality and parenting. Mother interview data at age 12 (grade 6) were used to form indexes of early adolescent parent–child relationships; child interview data at age 13 (grade 7) were used to create indexes of early adolescent peer relationships. Both interview and observational data at age 16 yielded measures of parent–teen and teen–friend relationship quality.

Measures by Developmental Epoch

Early Childhood Parenting. Guided by the literature and our own previous findings, we selected two parenting variables to represent generally positive and negative features of early parenting. Interviewer ratings of parents' reported discipline practices across the first four years and the past year were used to index parents' use of harsh discipline ($\alpha = .81$; interrater $r = .78$). Parents' endorsement of positive, proactive strategies as a means of averting child misbehavior was indexed by interviewer ratings of mothers' responses to hypothetical vignettes ($\alpha = .70$; interrater $r = .54$). Both variables have been found to incrementally predict adjustment outcomes through early adolescence (Pettit et al., 1997).

Middle Childhood Parenting and Peer Experiences. Sociometric nomination data were used to create three indexes of classroom peer experience (described in Criss, Pettit, Bates, Dodge, & Lapp, 2002; Dodge
et al., 2003; Lisonbee & Cleary, 2003). The first is the average social preference score (difference between standardized "liked most" and "liked least"
nominations) across first, second, and third grades. The second index,
reciprocated friendships, was the cross-year average number of reciprocated "5s" on a 5-point peer liking scale. The third index can be referred to
as mutual antipathy and is the cross-year average number of reciprocated
"1s" on the 5-point peer liking scale. Teacher ratings on the Dodge Teacher
Checklist (averaged across grades 1 and 2) provided a measure of children's
social skill with peers. These variables were fairly highly correlated and
were composited (reverse scored as needed) to form a psychometrically
reliable index of middle childhood peer competence ($\alpha = .73$).

The questionnaires completed by mothers in the summers following
grades 1 through 4 included three items (spanking, using a belt or paddle,
or slapping or hitting), rated on a 3-point scale, reflecting use of harsh
physical discipline. A psychometrically reliable cross-year average was
computed ($\alpha = .82$).

Early Adolescent Parenting and Peer Experience. Harsh parenting at age
12 was indexed by mother interview responses to the same three harsh-
discipline items used in the earlier questionnaire assessments ($\alpha = .71$).
Mothers also responded to nine items designed to tap their knowledge and
awareness of their children's whereabouts and companions. These items
were standardized and summed to create an index of parental monitoring
($\alpha = .71$; see Pettit, Bates, Dodge, & Meece, 1999).

At age 13, the children rated the quality of their relationship with their
best friend using a modified version of the Friendship Qualities Scale
(Bukowski, Hoza, & Boivin, 1994). An overall friendship quality score was
created by summing (reverse scoring as necessary) the twenty-seven items
($\alpha = .86$). The children also reported the extent to which they felt they
belonged to a peer group, and then rated, on a 5-point scale, the extent to
which members of the group engaged in five antisocial behaviors (see
Lansford, Criss, Pettit, Dodge, & Bates, 2003). A peer group antisocial
behavior score was computed as the average of the five items ($\alpha = .74$).

Middle Adolescent Parenting and Peer Experience. As part of the home
visit assessment at age 16, teens were interviewed about their parents'
use of control and about the quality of their relationships with their
best friend. An index of teen-reported parental psychological control was
derived from ten items suggested by the work of Barber (1996). These
items (e.g., "My mother is always trying to change how I feel or think

about things") were rated on a 3-point scale and were averaged to produce a maternal psychological control score ($\alpha = .75$). An index of friendship quality was derived from six items suggested by Bukowski et al. (1994) ($\alpha = .87$). Mothers also were interviewed about their relationships with their teens. Items were adapted from Brown, Mounts, Lamborn, & Steinberg (1993) and Dishion, Patterson, Stoolmiller, & Skinner (1991) to create a five-item index of maternal monitoring knowledge (i.e., the extent to which mothers reported that they believed they knew of the adolescent's typical activities, whereabouts, and companions; $\alpha = .67$).

Following the interviews, a forty-five-minute parent–teen interaction session was videotaped. The session consisted of a series of tasks designed to elicit problem solving and conflict resolution strategies, and parent–teen communication about rules, roles, and responsibilities. Using a modified version of the Melby and Conger (2001) coding protocol, extensively trained coders made highly differentiated 9-point ratings of parent and teen behavior. Two multi-item scales are of interest here, representing positive and negative aspects of the parent–teen relationship: positive relationship quality (responsiveness, warmth, and communication clarity; average interrater $r = .70$; $\alpha = .90$) and parental hostility (contempt, anger, and negative affect; average interrater $r = .50$; $\alpha = .77$).

Late Adolescent Romantic Relationships. Interviews were conducted at age 18 and included instruments designed to assess dating behavior, involvement in romantic relationships, and feelings of security in relationships. Of the 447 teen participants interviewed, 235 (101 males, 134 females) were currently in a dating relationship. As part of a pilot study of target–partner agreement, data also were collected from 78 partners (59 males, 19 females). The target participants were interviewed about relationship perceptions and conflict; partners were interviewed only about conflict in the relationship.

Participants in a relationship were compared with those not in a relationship on all antecedent variables. Of fifteen comparisons, only two were significant. Females were more likely to report being in a relationship, compared to males (62% and 46%, respectively, $t(1) = 10.75, p < .001$), and those in a relationship reported higher levels of friendship support at age 16 compared with those not in a relationship ($Ms = 4.49$ and $4.71, t(420) = -4.20, p < .01$).

Three instruments, adapted by Holtzworth-Munroe et al. (2000), were administered to tap beliefs about the self in the context of romantic relationships. These included (a) Preoccupied and Fearful Attachment, from the Bartholomew and Horowitz (1991) Relationship Styles Questionnaire, used to create a measure of relationship insecurity (e.g., "I find it difficult to depend on other people"; eleven items; $\alpha = .88$); (b) the

Fear of Abandonment scale, derived by Holtzworth-Munroe et al. (2000) from the MCMI (Choca & Van Denburg, 1997) (e.g., "I worry a great deal about being left alone and having to take care of myself"; five items; $\alpha = .75$); and (c) the Interpersonal Jealousy Scale (Mathes & Severa, 1981), modified for the current report (e.g., "If my boyfriend/girlfriend were to help someone of the opposite sex with work or homework, I would feel suspicious"; seven items; $\alpha = .84$). These scales were moderately correlated and were summed to create an index of general relationship insecurity ($\alpha = .70$).

The adolescents also completed a modified version of the Revised Conflict Tactics Scale (CTS2; Straus, Hamby, Boney-McCoy, & Sugarman, 1996). This instrument consists of thirty items describing behaviors used by self and partner in conflict situations, ranging from benign, prosocial conflict resolution behaviors, to moderately aggressive behaviors (e.g., grabbing), to violent behaviors (e.g., punching, slapping, kicking), rated in terms of frequency of occurrence over the past year (i.e., from once to twenty or more times). The Holtzworth-Munroe (Holtzworth-Munroe & Stewart, 1994) scoring convention was used, whereby seven physically aggressive behaviors were scored for severity and frequency. Based on scoring guidelines from the original CTS (Straus & Gelles, 1990), each CTS2 violence item was assigned a weight, reflecting likelihood of injury, and multiplied by the frequency of occurrence of the behavior in the past year. This yielded an item severity weighted score ($\alpha = .80$).

A common approach to creating conflict scores using the CTS is to compare partners' reports (which were highly correlated, $r = .85$) and select the higher of the two to index conflict and aggression (Holtworth-Munroe et al., 2000). We first created a score in this manner and correlated it with target participants' reports. The two scores were correlated .91, providing empirical justification for using only the target participants' reports (and thereby increasing the size of the subsample available for analyses).

CONTROL VARIABLES. Separate family socioeconomic status scores, computed using the Hollingshead (1975) four-factor approach, were constructed for the early childhood era, the middle childhood and early adolescent eras (combined), and the middle adolescent eras. For analyses using cross-era predictors a composite SES score was computed (average SES across the three eras; $\alpha = .82$). Participant sex also was used as a control variable.

RESULTS

Descriptive Findings and Intercorrelations Among Study Variables

All variables used in data analysis are listed in Table 3.1. Because the middle childhood peer competence composites summarize a fairly broad set of

TABLE 3.1. *Intercorrelations Among Developmental Antecedents and Romantic Relationship Outcomes*

Variable	2	3	4	5	6	7	8	9	10	11	12	13	14	15	16	17	18	19	20	21
Age-18 Outcomes																				
1. Aggression to partner	.21[b]	-.15[a]	.08	-.11	.16[b]	.16[a]	.14[a]	-.07	.01	.06	-.13[a]	-.08	-.21[b]	-.06	.22[b]	-.05	-.20[b]	.21[b]	.14[a]	-.01
2. Relationship insecurity	—	-.04	.12	-.21[b]	.01	.02	.01	-.16[a]	.15[a]	-.19[b]	-.19[a]	-.09	-.10	.08	.03	-.14	.00	.27[c]	-.14[a]	-.08
Control Variables																				
3. SES		—	-.07	.20[c]	-.32[c]	-.23[c]	.19[c]	-.01	-.09[a]	.28[c]	.18[c]	.25[c]	-.30[c]	-.12[a]	.05	.25[c]	-.17[b]	-.05	.09	-.02
4. Child sex			—	.01	-.10[a]	-.08	.10[a]	-.02	-.05	.19[c]	.11[a]	.14[b]	-.04	-.09	-.01	.06	.05	.08	.06	.29[c]
Early Childhood Predictors																				
5. Proactive parenting				—	-.06	-.08	.03	-.05	-.03	.15[c]	.06	.15[b]	-.07	-.01	.05	.07	.05	-.03	.06	-.03
6. Harsh discipline					—	.52[c]	-.22[c]	-.05	.10[a]	-.25[c]	-.21[c]	-.23[c]	.39[c]	.06	.05	-.16[b]	.17[b]	.10[a]	-.10[a]	-.05
Middle Childhood Predictors																				
7. Harsh discipline						—	-.25[c]	-.04	.13[b]	-.28[c]	-.23[c]	-.27[c]	.51[c]	.08	.07	-.21[c]	.20[c]	.13[b]	-.14[b]	-.02
8. Peer group acceptance							—	.47[c]	-.46[c]	.57[c]	.85[c]	.22[c]	-.17[c]	-.10[a]	-.04	.26[c]	-.14[b]	-.14[b]	-.17[c]	.12[b]
9. Reciprocated friendships								—	-.24[c]	.23[c]	.66[c]	.09	.04	.05	-.07	.15[b]	-.03	-.13[b]	.08	.07
10. Mutual antipathies									—	-.39[c]	-.71[c]	-.15[c]	.09	.07	-.03	-.13[b]	.13[b]	.06	-.14[b]	-.02
11. Social skillfulness										—	.74[c]	.24[c]	-.24[c]	-.16[b]	.01	.24[c]	-.14[b]	-.13[b]	.21[c]	.17[c]
12. Overall peer competence											—	.23[c]	-.16[b]	-.08	-.02	.26[c]	-.14[b]	-.15[b]	.20[c]	.13[b]
Early Adolescent Predictors																				
13. Monitoring												—	-.23[c]	-.30[c]	.02	.22[c]	-.18[c]	-.14[b]	.33[c]	.17[c]
14. Harsh discipline													—	.12[a]	-.05	-.21[c]	.13[a]	.01	-.04	-.05
15. Peer group antisocial behavior														—	.03	-.11[a]	.16[b]	.15[b]	-.17[c]	-.17[c]
16. Friendship Quality															—	.02	-.02	-.01	.01	.01
Mid-Adolescent Predictors																				
17. Parent-teen relationship quality																—	-.35[c]	-.32[c]	.37[c]	.11[a]
18. Parent hostility																	—	.18[c]	-.20[c]	-.02
19. Psychological control																		—	-.22[c]	-.04
20. Monitoring																			—	-.02
21. Friendship quality																				—

Note: Ns = 164 to 238 for correlations involving partner-directed aggression and relationship insecurity; Ns = 345 to 585 for correlations among control and predictor variables.
[a] = significant p < .05.   [b] = significant p < .01.   [c] = significant p < .001.

indicators, both the overall composites and their constituents are shown in the table.

Fifty-five participants reported partner-directed violence (23% of the dating subsample). Females (27%) and participants from lower SES families were somewhat more likely to report violence toward a partner than were males (18%) and children from higher SES families. Relationship insecurity was unrelated to child sex or family SES. Partner-directed violence and relationship insecurity were positively correlated, $r = .21$.

Correlations within and between predictors and outcomes are shown in Table 3.1. Several correlations are noteworthy. Higher family SES generally was associated with more positive parenting and peer group experiences. Child sex also was correlated with several of the antecedent variables; the general pattern suggested higher levels of social skill and better quality friendship relations for girls than for boys. There were modest to moderate levels of cross-era stability in negative parenting, but less stability in positive, proactive parenting. Within-era associations between positive and negative parenting and the quality of peer relations also were found, with correlations in the expected directions.

Partner violence was modestly and significantly correlated with social experience indicators from each era. Children who had experienced harsher (and generally lower-quality) parenting, lack of monitoring, and a relatively higher degree of involvement with antisocial peers reported more partner-directed violence. Relationship insecurity was predicted by social experience indicators from early childhood, middle childhood, and middle adolescence. Children who had experienced less positive and proactive parenting, more problems in peer relationships, and more parental intrusive control reported more relationship insecurity.

Regression Analyses

Predicting Romantic Relationship Violence and Insecurity from Within- and Cross-epoch Antecedent Measures. Regression analyses were computed in four steps. First, within-era social experiences were used to predict age-18 relationship violence and insecurity (in separate analyses). The age-relevant SES score, child sex, and the alternate outcome (i.e., relationship insecurity in the prediction of partner violence; partner violence in the prediction of relationship insecurity) were entered into the first step as controls. The relevant within-era, social experience indicators were entered next. Of interest was whether the social experience scores accounted for variance in the age-18 outcomes, and which individual predictors made significant contributions.

Second, because the literature suggests possible sex-differentiated patterns of antecedents for relationship violence and competence, we considered whether child sex moderated the relation between predictors and age-18 outcomes by constructing interaction terms (the multiplicative product of child sex and each individual predictor) and entering them in the last step of the regression in separate analyses. A similar strategy was followed to evaluate the impact of SES as a moderator of links between social experience predictors and late adolescent romantic relationship outcomes. All predictors and moderators were centered before being multiplied to create product terms.

Third, we evaluated the cumulative impact of antecedent predictors in a single regression analysis for relationship violence and for relationship insecurity (after controlling for child sex and average SES levels). To simplify the analyses and increase power, we selected only those antecedent variables that significantly predicted the age-18 outcomes in the within-era regressions. This approach allowed us to examine whether predictors from earlier developmental periods continued to be significant after controlling for predictors from later periods, or whether both earlier and later predictors incrementally predicted relationship violence and insecurity. As with the within-period analyses, interaction terms between child sex and family SES and each individual predictor were entered in the final step of each regression.

Predicting Partner-Directed Aggression. After controlling for child sex, family SES, and relationship insecurity, the early childhood parenting block accounted for a near-significant ($p = .059$) 2% of the variance in partner-directed aggression. Higher levels of harsh discipline were associated with more partner-directed aggression, standardized $\beta = .16$, $p = .02$. Proactive parenting was not significantly related to partner-directed aggression. These relations were not moderated by SES or child sex.

The middle childhood predictor block consisted of the cross-year harsh parenting composite and the cross-year, cross-informant peer competence composite. After entering the control variables, the predictor set failed to account for a significant R^2 increment. There was, however, a significant ($p < .01$) interaction effect between SES and harsh parenting. Using the approach described by Aiken and West (1991), predictor-outcome slopes were computed at high (1 standard deviation above the mean), medium (average score), and low (1 standard deviation below the mean) levels of the moderator (SES). The relation (slope) between middle childhood harsh punishment and late adolescent partner-directed violence was positive and significant at low levels of SES (slope $= .69$, $p = .01$), but was nonsignificant at medium and high levels of SES (slopes $= .23$ and $-.22$, respectively).

Because of interest in fully exploring the middle childhood predictors of partner-directed violence, we examined each peer relations constituent separately in single regression analyses. None were significant. There were no significant interactions with child sex or family SES.

Early adolescent parent–child relations were indexed by parental monitoring and harsh discipline, and peer relations were indexed by friendship quality and affiliation with antisocial peers. After entering the control variables, the set of social experience variables significantly incremented the prediction of partner-directed violence, $R^2 = .08$, $p = .02$. Higher levels of partner-directed aggression were associated with less parental monitoring, $\beta = -.15$, $p = .09$, and a more antisocial peer group, $\beta = .19$, $p = .03$. The monitoring effect was moderated by child sex and SES (both $p < .05$). Follow-up analyses revealed that monitoring was unrelated to boys' subsequent partner-directed aggression (slope $= .95$, ns), but predicted lower levels of girls' subsequent partner-directed aggression (slope $= -1.54$, $p = .001$). For the SES interaction, slopes were again examined for high, medium, and low levels of the moderator. Low monitoring was significantly associated with later relationship violence for children from low SES families (slope $= -1.00$, $p = .01$). There was no significant relation between monitoring and later romantic relationship violence at medium and high levels of SES (slopes $= -.29$ and $.41$, respectively).

The middle adolescent predictor set contained four indicators of parent–child relations: observed positive relationship quality, parental hostility, mother-reported monitoring, and teen-reported psychological control, and one indicator of peer relations, teen-reported friendship quality. This predictor set accounted for significant variance in partner-directed violence, after controlling for child sex and family SES, $R^2 = .06$, $p = .04$. The only significant or near-significant predictor was observed hostility. Teens whose parents were more hostile in their interactions with them were more likely to aggress toward romantic partners two years later, $\beta = .16$, $p = .05$. A significant interaction between parental hostility and SES also was found. Slopes computed at three levels of SES revealed that parental hostility was more strongly linked with relationship violence at low levels of SES (slope $= .32$, $p = .01$) than at either medium or high levels of SES (slopes $= .08$ and $-.17$, respectively).

In sum, partner-directed aggression at age 18 was anteceded by harsh discipline in early childhood, a more antisocial peer group in early adolescence, and hostile parenting in middle adolescence. There also was a trend for high levels of middle childhood harsh parenting and low levels of early adolescent monitoring to be associated with partner-directed violence. The links between partner-directed violence and middle childhood harsh discipline, early adolescent parental monitoring, and middle adolescent parental hostility were moderated by SES.

The measures of harsh discipline in early childhood, involvement with antisocial peers in early adolescence, and hostile parenting in middle adolescence were entered as a block in a regression analysis, following the control variables. The increment in prediction was, as would be expected, significant, $R^2 = .10$, $p = .001$. Each antecedent was significantly ($p = .05$)

associated with later partner-directed aggression (βs = .16, .21, and .15, respectively), suggesting a cumulative developmental progression in risk of partner violence. There were no interactions with child sex, but interactions between SES and both antisocial peer involvement and hostile parenting were significant ($p < .05$).

Consistent with the findings summarized earlier, the impact of family and peer risk factors were conditional on level of SES. The relation between antisocial peer involvement and partner-directed violence was positive and significant at low levels of SES (slope = .59, $p = .01$) but not at medium or high levels of SES (slopes = .28 and −.04). A similar pattern (replicating the within-period analysis described above) was observed for hostile parenting: Its link with relationship violence was positive and significant at low levels of SES (slope = .27, $p = .05$) but not at medium or high levels of SES (slopes = .05 and −.17).

Predicting Relationship Insecurity. The early childhood parenting block significantly predicted age-18 relationship insecurity after controlling for child sex, family SES, and age-18 partner-directed violence, $R^2 = .04$, $p = .02$. Lower levels of proactive parenting were associated with higher levels of relationship insecurity, standardized $\beta = −.19$, $p = .005$. Harsh discipline was unrelated to relationship insecurity. There were no significant interactions with child sex.

With respect to the middle childhood predictors, after entering the control variables, the social experience block accounted for a significant portion of variance in relationship insecurity, $R^2 = .04$, $p = .02$, with low levels of peer competence predicting higher levels of subsequent relationship insecurity, $\beta = −.20$, $p = .007$. Harsh parenting was not associated with relationship insecurity. Neither child sex nor family SES moderated these relations.

Once again, because of interest in exploring more fully the middle childhood predictors of age-18 outcomes, in this instance relationship violence, we considered each peer relations constituent separately in a single regression analyses. The overall regression step was significant, $R^2 = .05$, $p = .05$, but only one predictor was significant: Teacher-rated social skillfulness was associated with lower levels of subsequent relationship insecurity, $\beta = −.19$, $p = .031$. There were no significant interactions with child sex or family SES. After controlling for child sex and family SES, the early adolescent parenting and peer experience variables did not predict age-18 relationship insecurity, $p > .5$. No significant interactions were found with child sex.

The middle adolescent predictor set significantly predicted relationship insecurity, after entering the control variables, $R^2 = .12$, $p = .001$. Higher levels of psychological control and poorer quality friendships at age 16 predicted higher levels of romantic relationship insecurity at age 18,

βs $= .24$ and $-.21$, respectively, $p = .01$. Interactions with child sex were found for relationship quality and psychological control. Low levels of parent–child positive relationship quality were associated with relationship insecurity for boys (slope $= -.52$, $p = .01$) but not for girls (slope $= .22$, *ns*). High levels of psychological control were associated with more relationship insecurity for girls (slope $= 2.23$, $p = .001$) but not for boys (slope $= -.17$, *ns*).

In summary, relationship insecurity at age 18 was anteceded by low positive, proactive parenting in early childhood, low levels of competence with (and acceptance by) peers in middle childhood, and poorer quality friendships and more intrusive parenting in middle adolescence. A final regression evaluated the independent versus overlapping nature of these predictive relations. As would be expected, the combined predictive set was significantly related to relationship insecurity after controlling for child sex and family SES, $R^2 = .12$, $p = .001$. Significantly predictive relations ($p = .05$) were shown by three antecedent variables: low proactive parenting in early childhood, $\beta = -.21$; low peer competence in middle childhood, $\beta = -.14$; and high intrusive parenting in middle adolescence, $\beta = .20$. There were no significant interactions with child sex or family SES.

These findings support a cumulative, developmental perspective on romantic relationship insecurity. Of special note are the additive impacts of key markers of effective and supportive parenting across distinct developmental periods. Also of note is the finding that poor peer relationships in middle childhood forecasted the development of relationship insecurity independently of either earlier or later parenting or peer experiences.

CONCLUSIONS

These results, summarized in Table 3.2, provide evidence of different pathways to partner violence versus feelings of inadequacy in romantic relationships, with the former associated more with aggressogenic socialization experiences (harsh parenting and an antisocial peer group) and the latter associated more with interpersonally distant social relationships (intrusive parenting and difficulties in peer relationships). Additional analyses, not summarized above, indicate that partner violence is associated with key markers of externalizing problems in adolescence (e.g., previous record of having been arrested) whereas relationship insecurity is associated with socially relevant indicators of internalizing problems (e.g., having been referred for treatment for depression or anxiety). As such, the findings are consistent with research on temperament, personality, and behavior-problem development that suggest that, despite some evidence of co-morbidity in externalizing-type and internalizing-type problems, there is evidence that each is associated with a fairly distinct set of correlates. In the present context, those experiences giving rise to a violent-prone

TABLE 3.2. *Summary of Findings: Unique Within- and Cross-Epoch Predictors of Romantic Relationship Violence and Insecurity*

Early Childhood	Violence	Insecurity
Harsh discipline	Yes*	No
Proactive parenting (low)	No	Yes*
Middle Childhood		
Harsh discipline	Low SES only	No
Peer competence (low)	No	Yes*
Early Adolescence		
Harsh discipline	No	No
Parental monitoring (low)	Girls only; Low SES only	No
Antisocial peers	Yes*	No
Friendship quality (low)	No	No
Middle Adolescence		
Parent–teen relationship quality (low)	No	Boys only
Parental hostility	Low SES only*	No
Parental monitoring (low)	No	No
Parental psychological control	No	Girls only*
Friendship quality (low)	No	Yes

Note: All analyses control for SES, child sex, and the alternate romantic relationship outcome. "Yes" denotes significant within-era associations. Asterisks (*) indicate unique cross-epoch predictors.

orientation in relationships could be distinguished from those experiences contributing to feelings of jealousy and insecurity in such relationships.

Research focusing on antecedents of internalizing-type outcomes has been sparser than that concerned with externalizing outcomes, perhaps reflecting greater societal concern with outer-directed antisocial behavior and its antecedents and consequences. Several theoretical models might be applied to account for the finding that relationship violence is linked with earlier harsh parental treatment, lack of monitoring and supervision, and involvement with antisocial peers, including social learning theory (see Coie & Dodge, 1998), family coercion theory (Patterson, Reid, & Dishion, 1992), and social interactional theory (Thornberry & Krohn, 2001). Each perspective emphasizes the role that exposure to, and reinforcement for, aggressive behavior plays in trajectories of increasingly violent behavior. Such pathways are characterized by disengagement from the family unit, and from other conventional social institutions, and gravitation toward marginalized and antisocial peer groups. This is the classic antisocial profile that has been found to represent one important pathway to partner violence (Holtzworth-Munroe et al., 2000) and is consistent with a substantial body of research on the social-experiential antecedents of romantic relationship violence (Andrews et al., 2000; Capaldi, Dishion, Stoolmiller, & Yoerger, 2001; Lavoie et al., 2002; Swinford et al., 2000).

The antecedents of relationship insecurity show greater similarity with the smattering of findings that bear on family and peer predictors of victimization and low self-regard. These include findings of links between intrusive and manipulative parenting and children's victimization experiences (Ladd & Ladd, 1998), between parents' use of psychological control and adolescents' difficulties in self-expression and autonomous functioning (Barber, 2002), and between low peer acceptance and children's psychological distress (Gazelle & Ladd, 2003). Relationship insecurity with a romantic partner likely also has roots in the parent–child relationship qualities thought to undergird attachment insecurity, such as insensitive and intrusive early and continuing care (Collins et al., 1997).

One would expect some cross-outcome overlap in these antecedent experiences, given typological evidence that some forms of partner-directed violence stem in part from feelings of jealousy and insecurity (i.e., insecurity represents a pathway through which an orientation toward relationship violence may develop; Holtzworth-Munroe et al., 2000). And, in the present study, relationship violence and relationship insecurity empirically overlapped to a modest but significant degree. Thus, it is not surprising that, especially at the bivariate level, the two outcomes shared a number of predictors. However, it is noteworthy that a more differentiated predictive pattern was apparent when multiple variable domains, across multiple developmental periods, were considered (see Table 3.2). It is also worth noting that these predictions held even after controlling for the alternative romantic relationship outcome. It therefore would seem that violence and insecurity, as measured here (and as represented by a single data point from age 18), reflect fairly distinct relational outcomes with fairly distinct sets of experiential precursors.

The two contextual factors of child sex and family SES were evaluated both in terms of their main effects (of which there were several) and their moderating impacts on the main predictors (of which there were a few), mainly restricted to the relationship-violence outcome. The child sex main effects were consistent with past research and indicated that girls are supervised more closely than are boys, and have better quality friendships and peer relationships than do boys. Girls were more likely to be in romantic relationships and somewhat more likely to be violent in those relationships. The latter finding must be understood in relation to research showing that there are few differences between women and men when global and frequency-based measures of violence are used, but that men tend to use more extreme and health-compromising forms of violence with their partners (Sorenson et al., 1996; Swinford et al., 2000). It also is likely that some of the violence toward their partners that women report is a self-defense reaction to violence that their partners have directed toward them.

Sex-differentiated patterns in predictive links between family experience and relationship violence were found for monitoring, and between family experience and relationship insecurity for psychological control and observed relationship quality. Parental early adolescent monitoring was more strongly related to girls' age-18 partner-directed violence, a finding that is consistent with our earlier work on sex differences in links between monitoring and externalizing behavior problems (Pettit, Laird, Bates, Dodge, & Criss, 2001). Lack of monitoring appears to pose a particular risk for girls' development and continuation of aggressive behavior problems. Girls tend to be monitored more closely than boys, and through this heightened vigilance mothers may become aware of their girls' developing behavior problems and modify their monitoring and supervision strategies accordingly. When such monitoring is largely absent, girls may gravitate to antisocial peer groups in which aggressive behavior is both modeled and reinforced.

Parental psychological control was more strongly linked to girls' than boys' relationship insecurity. Girls' emerging sense of confidence and competence in interpersonal relationships may be more susceptible to, and at greater risk of being undermined by, parents' psychologically controlling and manipulative behavior. On the other hand, poor relationship quality – that is, low levels of positive communication observed between mother and teen – was more strongly linked with feelings of insecurity and inadequacy for boys compared to girls. It may be that the closeness and support that teenage boys receive from their mothers plays an especially important role in the boys' developing sense of competence and agency in romantic relationships.

Several main effects also were found for SES, with the general pattern being consistent with what has been previously reported in the literature (e.g., lower quality parenting and poor quality peer relationships in low SES groups compared to high SES groups). For the most part, aggressogenic experiences (i.e., experiences that have been empirically and theoretically linked with the development of aggression) were more strongly related to relationship violence in the context of low (versus high) family SES. Specifically, harsh parenting, lack of parental supervision, and hostile parenting were associated with relationship violence only among those children from low SES families. It may be that living in a high-stress, low-resource home, assuming that low SES homes can be so characterized, amplifies the effects of such experiences, fueling the development of an antisocial orientation that carries over into later relationship contexts and partners. Alternatively, rather than being due to resource and stress differences, the moderating effect of SES may be due to subcultural values concerning romantic relationships that amplify (in the case of lower SES) or buffer against (in the case of higher SES) the effects of adverse experiences with parents and peers.

Another goal of this report was to evaluate the role of earlier versus later social experiences in the prediction of age-18 relationship violence and insecurity. Developmental perspectives on early experience suggest that early family and peer group experience could play an important role in the development of romantic relationship violence and insecurity in late adolescence, especially if there is some degree of continuity in the quality of such experiences over time (Sroufe & Fleeson, 1986). But "psychometric" perspectives would stress the likely greater impact of developmentally more recent experiences in relation to age-18 outcomes (Belsky, Jaffee, Hsieh, & Silva, 2001).

Our data set is not ideally suited for contrasting the relative impact of early versus later experiences because measures of family and peer experience are not uniform across developmental periods. We might argue, however, that sensitivity to developmental context requires a consideration of which measures might best represent key relationship experiences in each period, some of which may be period-specific (e.g., peer competence and acceptance in middle childhood). Our findings suggest that the developmental pathways to the two relationship outcomes are cumulative in nature, with successive "risky" experiences providing additional explanatory power in the prediction of partner-directed violence and self-reported insecurity. Collectively, these findings suggest that both early and continuing social experiences pave the way for the development of distinct styles of romantic relationship difficulty in late adolescence.

We realize that the tests conducted to evaluate the "mediated effects" versus "cumulative (direct) effects" issue were neither conservative nor statistically elegant. It will be important for future work to construct structural models that can be directly compared and the significance of direct and indirect pathways estimated. Minimally, this kind of model testing will yield information on the relative extent to which later experiential factors serve as partial pathways (i.e., by partially accounting for direct paths) through which early experience becomes linked with late adolescent relationship outcomes.

Again, because the same measures of experience were not available for each developmental period, it cannot be said with confidence that particular experiences within a developmental period are more or less important, in terms of their predictive links, than particular experiences in other developmental periods. So, even though peer competence and acceptance in middle childhood emerged as a fairly robust predictor of relationship insecurity, and even though harsh discipline in middle childhood emerged as a more modest predictor (in the context of low SES) of relationship violence, it is reasonable to be cautious in asserting any kind of formative or functional role for these experiences. Still, when one considers that these predictions held even after controlling for relevant family background factors, and for a range of both antecedent and consequent family and peer experiences, the predictiveness of the middle childhood factors begins to look a bit more impressive. Nonetheless, the most consistent story from these data appears to be that it is the cumulation of positive and negative experiences in family and peer contexts across the childhood and adolescent years that lays the groundwork for interpersonal relationship functioning with romantic partners in later life.

The Child Development Project has been supported by research grants from the National Institute of Mental Health and the National Institute of Child Health and Human Development. Correspondence should be addressed to Gregory Pettit, Human Development and Family Studies, Auburn University, AL 36849. E-mail: gpettit@auburn.edu.

References

Aiken, L. S., & West, S. G. (1991). *Multiple regression: Testing and interpreting interactions.* Newbury Park, CA: Sage.

Andrews, J. A., Foster, S. L., Capaldi, D., & Hops, H. (2000). Adolescent and family predictors of physical aggression, communication, and satisfaction in young adult couples: A prospective analysis. *Journal of Consulting and Clinical Psychology, 68,* 195–208.

Barber, B. K. (1996). Parental psychological control: Revisiting a neglected construct. *Child Development, 67,* 3296–3319.

Barber, B. K. (Ed.). (2002). *Intrusive parenting: How psychological control affects children and adolescents.* Washington, DC: American Psychological Association.

Bartholomew, K., & Horowitz, L. M. (1991). Attachment styles among young adults: A test of a four-category model. *Journal of Personality and Social Psychology, 61,* 226–244.

Belsky, J., Jaffee, S., Hsieh, K., & Silva, P. A. (2001). Child-rearing antecedents of intergenerational relations in young adulthood: A prospective study. *Developmental Psychology, 37,* 801–813.

Brown, B. B., Mounts, N., Lamborn, S. D., Steinberg, L. (1993). Parenting practices and peer group affiliation in adolescence. *Child Development, 64,* 467–482.

Bukowski, W. M., Hoza, B., & Boivin, M. (1994). Measuring friendship quality during pre- and early adolescence: The development and psychometric properties of the friendship qualities scale. *Journal of Social and Personal Relationships, 11,* 471–484.

Capaldi, D. M., & Owen, L. D. (2001). Physical aggression in a community sample of at-risk couples: Gender comparisons for high frequency, injury, and fear. *Journal of Family Psychology, 15,* 425–440.

Capaldi, D. M., Dishion, T. J., Stoolmiller, M., & Yoerger, K. (2001). Aggression toward female partners by at-risk young men: The contribution of male adolescent friendships. *Developmental Psychology, 37,* 61–73.

Choca, J., & Van Denburg, E. (1997). *Interpretative guide to the Millon Clinical Multiaxial Inventory* (2nd ed.). Washington, DC: American Psychological Association.

Coie, J. D., & Dodge, K. A. (1998). Aggression and antisocial behavior. In W. Damon (Ed.) & N. Eisenberg (Vol. Ed.), *Handbook of child psychology: Vol. 3. Social, emotional, and personality development* (5th ed., pp. 779–862). New York: Wiley.

Collins, W. A., Hennighausen, K. C., Schmit, D. T., & Sroufe, L. A. (1997). Developmental precursors of romantic relationships: A longitudinal analysis. In S. Shulman & W. A. Collins (Eds.), *Romantic relationships in adolescence: Developmental perspectives: New directions for child development research* (pp. 69–84). San Francisco: Jossey-Bass.

Collins, W. A., & Sroufe, L. A. (1999). Capacity for intimate relationships: A developmental construction. In W. Furman et al. (Eds.), *The development of romantic relationships in adolescence. Cambridge studies in social and emotional development* (pp. 125–147). New York: Cambridge University Press.

Conger, R. D., Cui, M., Bryant, C. M., & Elder, G. H., Jr. (2000). Competence in early adult romantic relationships: A developmental perspective on family influences. *Journal of Personality and Social Psychology, 79*, 224–237.

Criss, M. M., Pettit, G. S., Bates, J. E., Dodge, K. A., & Lapp, A. L. (2002). Family adversity, positive peer relationships, and children's externalizing behavior: A longitudinal perspective on risk and resilience. *Child Development, 73*, 1220–1237.

Deater-Deckard, K., Dodge, K. A., Bates, J. E., & Pettit, G. S. (1998). Multiple risk factors in the development of externalizing behavior problems: Group and individual differences. *Development and Psychopathology, 10*, 469–493.

Dishion, T. J., Patterson, G. R., Stoolmiller, M., & Skinner, M. L. (1991). Family, school, and behavioral antecedents to early adolescent involvement with antisocial peers. *Developmental Psychology, 27*, 172–180.

Dodge, K. A., Bates, J. E., & Pettit, G. S. (1990). Mechanisms in the cycle of violence. *Science, 250*, 1678–1683.

Dodge, K. A., Lansford, J. E., Burks, V. S., Bates, J. E., Pettit, G. S., Fontaine, R., & Price, J. M. (2003). Peer rejection and social information processing factors in the development of aggressive behavior problems in children. *Child Development, 74*, 374–393.

Furman, W. (1999). Friends and lovers: The role of peer relationships in adolescent romantic relationships. In W. A. Collins & B. Laursen (Eds.), *Relationships as developmental contexts. The Minnesota symposia on child psychology: Vol. 30* (pp. 133–154). Mahwah, NJ: Erlbaum.

Gazelle, H., & Ladd, G. W. (2003). Anxious solitude and peer exclusion: A diathesis-stress model of internalizing trajectories in childhood. *Child Development, 74*, 257–278.

Hollingshead, W. (1975). *The Hollingshead four factor index of socioeconomic status.* Unpublished manuscript, Yale University, New Haven, CT.

Holtzworth-Munroe, A., Meehan, J. C., Herron, K., Rehman, U., & Stuart, G. L. (2000). Testing the Holtzworth-Munroe and Stuart (1994) Batterer Typology. *Journal of Consulting and Clinical Psychology, 68*, 1000–1019.

Holtzworth-Munroe, A., & Stewart, G. L. (1994). Typologies of male batterers: Three subtypes and the differences among them. *Psychological Bulletin, 116*, 476–497.

Ladd, G. W., & Ladd, B. K. (1998). Parenting behaviors and parent-child relationships: Correlates of peer victimization in kindergarten? *Developmental Psychology, 34*, 1450–1458.

Lavoie, F., Hebert, M., Tremblay, R., Vitaro, F., Vezina, L., & McDuff, P. (2002). History of family dysfunction and perpetration of dating violence by adolescent boys: A longitudinal study. *Journal of Adolescent Health, 30*, 375–383.

Lansford, J. E., Criss, M. M., Pettit, G. S., Dodge, K. A., & Bates, J. E. (2003). Friendship quality, peer group affiliation, and peer antisocial behavior as moderators of the link between negative parenting and adolescent externalizing behavior. *Journal of Research on Adolescence, 13*, 161–184.

Lisonbee, J., & Cleary, D. J. (2003, April). *Mutual antipathies, reciprocated friendships, and school adjustment in middle childhood: Concurrent and longitudinal relations.* Poster presented at the Society for Research in Child Development, Tampa, FL.

Magdol, L., Moffitt, T. E., Caspi, A., & Silva, P. A. (1998). Developmental antecedents of partner abuse: A prospective-longitudinal study. *Journal of Abnormal Psychology, 107*, 375–389.

Mathes, E. W., & Severa, N. (1981). Jealousy, romantic love, and liking: Theoretical considerations and preliminary scale development. *Psychological Reports, 49*, 23–31.

Melby, J. N., & Conger, R. D. (2001). The Iowa Family Interaction Rating Scales: Instrument summary. In P. Kerig & K. Lindahl (Eds.), *Family observation coding systems: Resources for systemic research* (pp. 33–58). Mahway, NJ: Erlbaurm.

Patterson, G. R., Reid, J. B., & Dishion, T. J. (1992). *Antisocial boys.* Eugene, OR: Castalia.

Pettit, G. S., Bates, J. E., & Dodge, K. A. (1997). Supportive parenting, ecological context, and children's adjustment: A seven-year longitudinal study. *Child Development, 68*, 908–923.

Pettit, G. S., Bates, J. E., Dodge, K. A., & Meece, D. (1999). The impact of after-school peer contact on early adolescent externalizing problems is moderated by parental monitoring, perceived neighborhood safety, and prior adjustment. *Child Development, 70*, 768–778.

Pettit, G. S., Laird, R. D., Bates, J. E., Dodge, K. A., & Criss, M. M. (2001). Antecedents and behavior-problem outcomes of parental monitoring and psychological control in early adolescence. *Child Development, 72*, 583–598.

Sorenson, S. B., Upchurch, D. W., & Shen, H. (1996). Violence and injury in marital arguments: Risk patterns and gender differences. *American Journal of Public Health, 86*, 35–40.

Sroufe, L. A., & Fleeson, J. (1986). Attachment and the construction of relationships. In W. Hartup & Z. Rubin (Eds.), *Relationships and development* (pp. 27–47). Hillsdale, NJ: Erlbaum.

Straus, M. A., & Gelles, R. J. (1990). *Physical violence in American families.* New Brunswick, NJ: Transaction.

Straus, M. A., Hamby, S. L., Boney-McCoy, S., & Sugarman, D. B. (1996). The Revised Conflict Tactics Scales (CTS2): Development and preliminary psychometric data. *Journal of Family Issues, 17*, 283–316.

Swinford, S. P., DeMaris, A., Cernkovich, S. A., & Giordano, P. C. (2000). Harsh physical discipline in childhood and violence in later romantic involvements: The mediating role of problem behaviors. *Journal of Marriage and the Family, 62*, 508–519.

Thornberry, T. P., & Krohn, M. D. (2001). The development of delinquency: An interactional perspective. In S. O. White (Ed.), *Handbook of youth and justice* (pp. 289–305). New York: Plenum.

4

Middle Childhood Family-Contextual and Personal Factors as Predictors of Adult Outcomes

L. Rowell Huesmann, Eric F. Dubow,
Leonard D. Eron, and Paul Boxer

Early models of behavior development tended to de-emphasize the importance of the middle childhood years, labeling this time period a "latency" phase between the theoretically more active periods of early childhood and adolescence (Freud, 1923/1961). As more recent models attest, middle childhood actually is a period critical for the development of important psychosocial functions such as cognitive skill acquisition (e.g., Piaget, 1965), social relationship formation (e.g., McHale, Dariotis, & Kauh, 2003), and self-concept consolidation (e.g., Jacobs, Bleeker, & Constantino, 2003). Contemporary social cognitive theories consider middle childhood a critical time for the development of social scripts, normative beliefs, and world schemas that influence behavior throughout life (Huesmann, 1998; Huesmann & Guerra, 1997). Behaviors established in middle childhood have been shown to display substantial continuity into adulthood (e.g., aggression: Huesmann, Eron, Lefkowtiz, & Walder, 1984; academic achievement: Jimerson, Egeland, Sroufe, & Carlson, 2000). A key concern therefore is identifying which factors exert important influences on children during middle childhood and what adult outcomes are affected by those factors.

In this chapter, we present findings from the Columbia County Longitudinal Study (CCLS), a long-term prospective study that began in 1960 with the entire third grade population of Columbia County, New York. In the most recent wave of data collection, we resampled those individuals at approximately 48 years of age. Our primary concern in this chapter is the degree to which family-contextual and child-personal factors during middle childhood predict three important domains of adult behavioral outcomes: *aggressive behavior*, *intellectual/educational achievement*, and *occupational success*. We also examine the moderating effects of gender on the prediction of adult outcomes.

FAMILY-CONTEXTUAL INFLUENCES DURING MIDDLE CHILDHOOD

Families are embedded in the broader social-economic context of the community. Leventhal and Brooks-Gunn (2000) suggested that communities characterized by socioeconomic disadvantage have relatively few institutional resources to support children's development. Those authors noted that, for example, school achievement should be influenced by the availability and use of libraries, museums, and literacy programs; social competence should be influenced by the availability and use of parks, sports programs, and youth groups, assuming that the program participants and facilitators are appropriate role models. Further, socioeconomic disadvantage is associated with crime and violence in the community that provides children with normative models of antisocial behavior. Tolan, Gorman-Smith, and Henry (2003) found that a composite score representing community-structural characteristics (i.e., concentrated neighborhood poverty, ethnic heterogeneity, economic investment, neighborhood violent crime) played an etiological role in adolescent gang membership and violence.

At the level of interactions within the family, it is well established in social learning models (e.g., Huesmann, 1998) that parents exert substantial influence on their children's behavior. For example, children exposed to more rejecting and aggressive parenting contexts, as well as interparental conflict, display greater aggression (Cummings & Davies, 1994; Eron, Walder, & Lefkowitz, 1971; Huesmann et al., 1984; Lefkowitz, Eron, Walder, & Huesmann, 1977; Patterson, 1982). Presumably, children learn aggressive problem-solving styles as a result of repeated exposure to such models.

INDIVIDUAL/PERSONAL INFLUENCES DURING MIDDLE CHILDHOOD

Negotiating academic demands and peer relationships are among the most important tasks of middle childhood (e.g., Erikson, 1963). Individual/personal attributes such as intellectual ability, social competence (e.g., popularity), and behavior regulation (e.g., aggressiveness) contribute to the child's success at those tasks. These attributes are somewhat stable over time (e.g., Coie & Dodge, 1983; Huesmann et al., 1984). For example, Coie and Dodge (1983) found that 42% of fifth graders identified as "rejected" remained rejected by ninth grade, and 29% of fifth graders identified as "popular" remained so in ninth grade. Using data from the CCLS, Huesmann (2001) reported that 36% of third graders classified as *high* (upper quartile) in aggression remained in this position through adolescence and adulthood, and 37% of third graders classified as *low* (lower quartile) in aggression remained in this position through adolescence and adulthood.

Despite the moderate stability from middle childhood onward in these attributes, the results are consistent with instability as well. Thus, it is important to consider also the extent to which contextual factors uniquely account for later outcomes of these middle childhood attributes (Phelps, Furstenberg, & Colby, 2002; Pulkkinen & Caspi, 2002). For example, Kokko and Pulkkinen (2000) found that individuals who displayed higher levels of aggression during middle childhood were more likely than others to enter a "cycle of maladaptation" involving poorer educational outcomes and greater unemployment. However, such individuals fared better if they experienced supportive family contexts during middle childhood (as indicated by retrospective reports), and if they exhibited higher levels of prosocial behavior during that time period (Pulkkinen, Nygren, & Kokko, 2002).

THE ROLE OF GENDER

Gender is probably the most extensively examined individual/personal variable in any study of development. For many years, we have explored gender differences in aggressive behavior, and how those differences can be explained on the basis of differential socialization of boys and girls (Eron et al., 1971; Huesmann, 2001, Lefkowitz, Eron, Walder, & Huesmann, 1973). We also have noted the recent reduction in this difference and have ascribed it to changes over the years in the socialization of the two sexes (Eron & Huesmann, 1989). Important gender differences also have been identified for educational achievement and occupational attainment (Eccles, 1994). Thus, one goal of the current investigation is to examine whether there are gender differences in the relations of our criterion variables of interest in middle childhood to outcomes in middle adulthood.

In this chapter, based on data from the Columbia County Longitudinal Study, we examine how well we can predict three psychosocial outcomes of interest over a 40-year span from middle childhood (age 8) to middle adulthood (age 48). The three adult outcomes are *aggression* (physical aggression, aggressive personality, spousal abuse, physical punishment), *intellectual/educational achievement* (verbal and arithmetic skill, years of education, self-perceptions of cognitive competence), and *occupational prestige*. Using structural equations and path modeling, we evaluate whether those outcomes are better predicted by their behavioral predecessors (e.g., early aggression to later aggression) or by the middle childhood contextual influences of family SES and family interaction variables. We also consider whether the prediction of adult outcomes varies by gender.

METHOD

Design of the Columbia County Longitudinal Study

The CCLS began in 1960 and has so far culminated in the collection of four waves of data over a 40-year span on children who were living in Columbia County, NY, in 1960. The entire population of third graders ($N =$ 856; 436 boys, 420 girls) in Columbia County, a semirural area of New York State, participated in the first phase of this project in 1960 (Eron et al., 1971). We denote them as generation G2 and their parents as generation G1. The dominant issues in selecting the sample were cost, geographic proximity, availability, representativeness, and low mobility. At that time, 85% of the participants' mothers and 71% of their fathers were also interviewed. Follow-up assessments of G2 were conducted in both 1970 ($n =$ 427) and 1981 ($n = 409$); in 1981 we also were able to obtain data on 76 children of the original subjects (i.e., G3). We do not present findings from the 1970 and 1981 assessments in this chapter; the interested reader is directed to Lefkowitz et al. (1977; 1970 follow-up) or Huesmann et al. (1984; 1981 follow-up) for more information.

In our most recent wave of data collection (Huesmann et al., 2002), between 1999 and 2002, we reinterviewed 284 of the G2 participants in person and another 239 by mail/telephone, for a total of 523 (268 males, 255 females). By also obtaining archival data from the New York State Divisions of Criminal Justice and Motor Vehicles, we obtained follow-up data on 683 of the original G2 participants. We obtained interviews from "second persons" who knew the participants very well (mostly spouses) for 394 participants. We collected some data on 705 of these participants' G3 children, and completed interviews with 551 G3 children (ages 4 years old and older). We attempted to interview up to two children per family – generally the oldest and youngest. We interviewed at least one child for 82% of our reinterviewed participants who had at least one child. The mean age of the interviewed children was 19.97 years ($SD = 5.77$).

Analyses for this chapter are based on data collected about G2, the original participants, during Waves 1 (age 8) and 4 (age 48). We also draw on data provided about the original participants by their parents (G1) in 1960 and by their children (G3) and spouses in 1999–2002.

Description of Sample in Waves 1 and 4

Columbia County, NY, is semirural with a few heavy industries. Of its approximately 63,000 current residents, about 11,000 live in the largest city and county seat, Hudson. The county has had a depressed economy for the last 50 years, although it has begun to benefit from the encroachment of the New York City metropolitan area. At the time the study was started, there were 38 public and private third-grade classrooms in the county, all of which were included in the sample. Over 90% of the original sample of 856 participants were Caucasian; 51% were male and 49% were female. The number of ethnic minorities (i.e., 3% African American, < 1% Asian or Pacific Islanders, < 1% Hispanic) was too small to allow separate analyses. The participants came from a broad range of socioeconomic backgrounds (mean of 4.3 on Warner's scale of fathers' occupational status, i.e., middle class; Warner, Meeker, & Eells, 1960) and displayed a wide range of intelligence (mean IQ of 104, $SD = 14$).

For the 523 participants reinterviewed during 1999–2002, the mean age was 48.85 years old ($SD = .81$); the average education level was between some college and a college degree; the average occupational attainment reflected middle class status (the average occupational prestige code using Stevens & Hoisington's [1987] prestige scores reflected jobs such as sales, bookkeepers, secretaries); and 69% of the original participants were living with their spouses.

Differences Between the Original Sample and the 1999–2002 Resample. In the 40-year follow-up, we collected some data on 80% (683) of our original participants, and interviewed 61% (523) of them extensively. The number of relocated participants who refused to be interviewed (despite substantial financial incentives) was higher than expected ($n = 144$), but the completed reinterview rate of 61% over 40 years still provides us with a substantial sample for analysis. However, we must ask whether attrition introduced bias into the sample. In most longitudinal studies, more aggressive and antisocial participants, and those of lower socioeconomic status, are somewhat less likely to be resampled. We found that the reinterviewed participants had lower levels of age-8 aggression compared to those who were not reinterviewed at Wave 4. Nevertheless, the plots of the distributions reveal that many of the high aggressive participants *were* resampled and there was no substantial reduction of range that might have made it hard to detect relations between aggression and other variables. There was no significant difference in 1960 father's occupational level between reinterviewed participants and dropouts, but reinterviewed participants' parents in 1960 had higher levels of education and value of housing. There was no significant difference between reinterviewed participants and dropouts in an index of negative family interaction processes.

Procedures in Waves 1 and 4

The methods of data collection across the first three waves of the Columbia County Longitudinal Study have been reported elsewhere (e.g., Eron et al., 1971; Lefkowitz et al., 1977; Huesmann et al., 2002; Huesmann et al., 1984).

In Wave 1 in 1960, two main sources of data were used: classroom-based peer nominations and extensive individual parent interviews.

For the 40-year follow-up, interviews were conducted by computer in a field office and by mail/telephone for those participants who could not come to the office.[1] Interviews in the field office were up to four hours in duration for original participants, three hours for their second-persons/spouses, and two hours for their children. Original participants were paid $100, second-persons/spouses were paid $75, and children were paid $50 for their participation.

Measures

Our analyses for the present chapter focus on the effects of family-contextual and individual/personal factors during middle childhood (age 8) on adult outcomes 40 years later.

Family-Contextual Factors During Middle Childhood. We examined two domains of family-contextual factors: *family background (SES)* and *negative family interaction*. For these variables, if two parents were interviewed, their scores were averaged.

FAMILY BACKGROUND (SES) VARIABLES. (a) *Father's occupational level* (Warner et al., 1960) ranges from 1 = laborer to 7 = professional; (b) *Parents' educational level* (Eron et al., 1971) reflects the parents' levels of educational attainment, ranging from 1 = under 7 years to 7 = graduate/professional training; (c) *Value of family housing* (Eron et al., 1971) ranges from 1 = inexpensive rental to 4 = expensive owned.

NEGATIVE FAMILY INTERACTION. Negative family interaction (see Eron et al., 1971) was measured by three indicators: (a) *Parental rejection* is the sum of scores on 10 items about how "unsatisfied" the parent is with the child; for example, "Are you satisfied with your child's manners? Does your child read as well as he/she should?" (yes/no) ($\alpha = .75$). (b) *Parents' endorsement of hitting the child as a form of punishment* was the sum of parents' endorsement of physical punishment in response to two vignettes depicting child transgressions; for example, "If your child was rude to you, would you. . . ." For each of these two vignettes, one physical punishment

---

[1] There were mean differences by interview type for four adult outcome variables. Compared to participants interviewed in person, those interviewed by mail/phone had higher levels of education and occupational status, and lower levels of self-reported severe physical aggression and spouse-reported partner aggression. However, a series of hierarchical regressions showed no evidence that interview type moderated the relations of the middle childhood personal or contextual factors with the adult outcomes. The obtained differences are not surprising given that geographic mobility is highly related to SES. Personal interviews were obtained almost exclusively from participants who still lived in or near Columbia County, New York.

was included: "spank your child until he/she cries?" or "slap your child in the face?" (yes/no). Thirty-five percent of the fathers and 36% of the mothers endorsed at least one of the two physical punishment items. (c) *Parental disharmony* measures the amount and seriousness of disputes between the parents. It is the sum of 10 items of the form; for example, "Do you or your spouse ever leave the house during an argument?" and "Do arguments between you and your spouse ever settle anything?" (yes/no) ($\alpha = .77$).

Individual/Personal Variables During Middle Childhood. We included three individual/personal variables that were assessed when the child was 8 years of age.

CHILD'S PEER-NOMINATED AGGRESSION. Eron et al. (1971) defined aggression as "an act whose goal response is injury to another object" (p. 30). Their 10 aggression items cover physical (e.g., "Who pushes and shoves other children?"), verbal (e.g., "Who says mean things?"), acquisitive (e.g., "Who takes other children's things without asking?"), and indirect (e.g., "Who makes up stories and lies to get other children into trouble?") aggressive acts. The score represents the proportion of times the child was nominated by classmates on any of 10 items. This measure is described in detail elsewhere (Eron et al., 1971; Huesmann et al., 1984), has been widely used, and has an $\alpha = .90$ in cross-national samples (Huesmann & Eron, 1986).

CHILD'S PEER-NOMINATED POPULARITY. This score represents the proportion of times the participant was nominated by his or her classmates on two popularity items; for example, "Who would you like to have as a best friend?" ($\alpha = .87$) (Eron et al., 1971).

CHILD'S IQ. The child's IQ was assessed with the California Short-Form Test of Mental Maturity (Sullivan, Clark, & Tiegs, 1957). Kuder-Richardson reliability coefficients range from .87–.89 across grades; the total score correlates approximately .75 with other IQ measures.

Adult (Age 48) Outcomes. We examined the effects of the family-contextual and individual/personal variables assessed at age 8 on three domains of adult outcomes at age 48: aggression, intellectual/educational achievement, and occupational status.

AGGRESSION. Aggression was evaluated with four measures: (a) *Severe physical aggression* was assessed through participants' self-reports of how often in the last year they engaged in each of four behaviors (e.g., choked, slapped or kicked, punched or beat someone; 1 = never to 4 = a lot) ($\alpha = .66$). (b) *Aggressive personality* was measured by taking the sum of scales 4, 9, and F from the *Minnesota Multiphasic Personality Inventory* (MMPI; Hathaway & McKinley, 1940). In earlier studies by our group (e.g., Huesmann et al., 1984; Huesmann, Lefkowitz, & Eron, 1978), the summed T-scores of these three scales reflected a reliable and valid measure of aggressive behavior. For these scales, participants read 143 statements and indicated whether each was true (1) or false (0) in describing themselves. T-scores were computed for each scale, and a total score for each respondent was computed from the sum of the three T-scores ($\alpha = .78$). (c) *Aggression toward spouse* was measured by nine items from the *Home Violence Questionnaire* (Straus, Giles, & Steinmetz, 1979). Participants who were currently married or had recently lived with a partner or spouse indicated the frequency with which they directed threatening (e.g., with a knife or gun) or physically aggressive (e.g., pushed or shoved, beat up) acts towards their partner in the last 12 months. They made ratings on a 10-point scale ranging from zero to "9 or more." The original participants self-reported on their behavior toward their spouses, and spouses reported on the participant's behaviors toward them ($\alpha = .72$ for self-reports and .90 for other reports). For the present analyses, a composite score was calculated to reflect the average of the participants' and spouses' (if available) reports. (d) *Parent hitting child as a form of punishment* was measured. Original participants indicated the frequency with which they engaged in various forms of punishment while their children (generally the oldest and youngest) were growing up. Five of the punishments reflected *hitting* (e.g., slap in face, spank or beat with a stick or belt) with a 4-point response scale (1 = never, 2 = seldom, 3 = sometimes, 4 = often). Using the same measure, spouses and up to two children over age 19 rated the degree to which the original participant used hitting as a form of punishment. Coefficient alphas across reporters (self, children, spouse) were above .70. A composite score was calculated to reflect the average punishment-hitting score across up to six potential reports.

INTELLECTUAL/EDUCATIONAL ACHIEVEMENT. Intellectual/educational achievement was assessed using three measures: (a) The participant's standard scores were compiled from the *Wide Range Achievement Test-Revised* (Jastak & Jastak, 1978) arithmetic and verbal sections (reading test for personal interviews, spelling test for phone interviews; arithmetic in personal interviews only); (b) *Years of education* ranged from 1 = did not complete high school to 7 = doctoral/law degree; (c) *Perceived cognitive competence* was assessed using two self-report items (Harter, 1985) presented as pairs of opposing descriptions (e.g., "Some adults feel they are intelligent, BUT other adults question whether they are intelligent"; $\alpha = .70$). Participants select which description applies best to them, and then they indicate whether the description is "sort of true" or "really true" for them.

OCCUPATIONAL SUCCESS. Occupational success was estimated using prestige codes following Stevens and Hoisington (1987). Prestige codes are provided for 889 specific occupations within 13 occupational categories (e.g., executive, administrative, and managerial; professional specialty; technicians; sales; protective service; mechanics/repairers; machine operators and inspectors). Higher codes indicate greater prestige. The codes range from 153 (ushers) to 810 (physicians). Two raters coded the participants' occupations. On a subsample of 162 occupations coded by each rater, the correlation between their assigned prestige codes was $r = .81$.

RESULTS

Overview of Analyses

We first examine gender differences in middle childhood family-contextual and personal factors and the age 48 outcome variables. Next, we examine the predictive effects of the middle childhood contextual and personal factors on each of the three domains of age-48 outcomes (aggression, intellectual/educational achievement, occupational success). For each domain, we present: (a) correlations of the age-8 personal factor with the associated measures of the same domain of behaviors at age 48, as an indication of the degree of continuity in the behavior over 40 years; (b) contemporaneous correlations between the age-8 family-contextual factors and the age-8 personal variable; (c) correlations of the middle childhood family-contextual and personal factors with each age-48 measure; and (d) a multiple-group (males and females) structural model using AMOS (Arbuckle, 1997) to examine the effects of middle childhood family-contextual and personal factors in predicting the age-48 outcome construct. In all analyses the log transformation of peer-nominated aggression (age 8) and self-reported severe aggression (age 48) were used because their distributions were highly skewed.

Gender Differences in Middle Childhood Factors and Age-48 Outcomes

There are no gender differences in the middle childhood family background (SES) measures (i.e., father's occupation, parental education, and value of housing). There are gender differences in two of the middle childhood negative family interaction measures: (a) parents reported higher levels of rejection (dissatisfaction) toward boys than toward girls, $t (705) = 4.32, p < .01$; and (b) parents reported more endorsement of hitting as a form of punishment toward their boys than toward their girls, $t (697) = 1.98, p < .05$. At age 8, boys $(M = 16.0, SD = 15.7)$ are rated as more aggressive by their classroom peers than are girls $(M = 9.4, SD = 11.0)$, $t (854) = 7.74, p < .01$, but there are no gender differences in peer-nominated popularity or IQ.

At age 48, we find no gender differences on the measures of aggression toward spouse or aggressive personality. However, males score higher than females on severe physical aggression, $t (481) = 2.80, p < .01$. Females score

TABLE 4.1. *Contemporaneous Correlations of the Age-8 Family-Contextual Factors with the Age-8 Personal Variables*

| | Age-8 Personal Variables | | | | | |
| | Males | | | Females | | |
Age-8 Factors	Log Agg	IQ	Pop	Log Agg	IQ	Pop
Family background (SES)						
Father's occupation		.10+			.13+	
Parent education		.31**	.24**	−.14**	.35**	.22*
Value of housing	−.17**	.36**	.22**	−.13*	.29**	.17**
Negative family interaction						
Rejection	.23**	−.18**	−.14**	.33**	−.14*	−.30**
Punishment (hitting) of child			−.11*	.15**		
Parental disharmony				.17**		−.11+

Note: Log Agg log-transformed peer-nominated aggression; Pop = peer-nominated popularity. Non-significant correlations are not shown.
$^{+}p < .10.$ $^{*}p < .05.$ $^{**}p < .01.$

higher than males on the WRAT-R verbal test, $t (519) = 3.45$, $p < .01$, but males score higher than females on the WRAT-R arithmetic test, $t (279) = 2.10$, $p < .05$. There are no significant gender differences in years of education attained by age 48 or on self-perceptions of cognitive competence. There is no significant gender difference in occupational prestige.

Predicting Age-48 Aggression from the Middle Childhood Factors

There is some continuity of aggression over 40 years despite the very different methods of measuring aggressive behavior at those time points. For males, age-8 peer-nominated aggression is related positively to three indices of age-48 aggression: aggressive personality ($r = .32$, $p < .01$), severe physical aggression ($r = .15$, $p < .05$), and aggression toward spouse ($r = .14$, $p < .01$), and to a composite aggression variable created by summing the subject's z-scores for each aggression measure ($r = .28$, $p < .01$). For females, age-8 peer-nominated aggression is related positively to punishment (hitting) of child ($r = .22$, $p < .01$), aggressive personality ($r = .14$, $p < .05$), and the composite aggression measure ($r = .19$, $p < .01$).

Table 4.1 shows the contemporaneous correlations of the middle childhood family-contextual variables with the middle childhood personal variables. The relations among middle childhood family-contextual variables and aggression are generally modest in magnitude; the strongest indicate that higher levels of parental rejection are related to higher levels of peer-nominated aggression for both genders.

Table 4.2 shows the correlations of the middle childhood aggression and family-contextual variables with the age-48 aggression measures. Several of these are significant but are generally modest in magnitude. Specifically, for males, higher levels of family SES background variables and lower levels of negative family interaction during middle childhood are related to lower levels of adult aggression (most consistently for the composite aggression score and for aggressive personality). For females, fewer correlations are significant, but three of the middle childhood family-contextual variables (lower father's occupation and parental education, and higher parental disharmony) predict how much they use hitting as a form of punishing their children.

Next, we computed a multiple-group structural model (males and females) of the relations of the middle childhood contextual variables and aggression to adult aggression. We constrained the measurement parameters for the family background (the construct is labeled "SES" on the figures) indicators and for the negative family interaction indicators to be equal across gender, but we allowed the measurement parameters to vary across gender for adult aggression because adult aggression appears to comprise different combinations of the age-48 aggression variables for males and females. We allowed the paths among the latent variables to vary by gender. The fit of the multiple-group model is fair (RMSEA = .044, GFI = .93), indicating that the measurement of the constructs and the relations among them – albeit at different levels of magnitude for each gender – approximately describe the obtained pattern of correlations. Figure 4.1 shows that for males, lower middle childhood SES and higher negative family interaction are related directly to higher age-48 aggression, and the effect of negative family interaction on age-48 aggression also is mediated by age-8 aggression. Figure 4.1 also shows that for females, the effect of age-8 aggression on age-48 aggression is not significant: Only lower middle childhood SES significantly predicts higher age-48 aggression for females.[2]

Predicting Age-48 Intellectual/Educational Achievement from the Middle Childhood Factors

As was shown in Table 4.1, for both males and females, higher levels of middle childhood family SES indices are related modestly to age-8 IQ, but only one negative family interaction measure, parental rejection, is related modestly to lower IQ scores. Table 4.3 shows the correlation of middle childhood IQ and family-contextual variations with the age-48 achievement measures. As shown in Table 4.3, for both males and females, higher

---

[2] A model in which the structural paths were constrained to be equal across genders provided a significantly poorer fit to the data as indicated by the chi-square difference test, $\chi^2(6) = 43.895$, $p < .000$.

TABLE 4.2. *Correlations of the Age-8 Family-Contextual Factors with Age-48 Aggression Measures*

	Age-48 Aggression Measures									
	Males					Females				
Age-8 Factors	Agg Per	Log Sev Agg	Agg to Spouse	Pun-Hit of Child	Agg Comp	Agg Per	Log Sev Agg	Agg to Spouse	Pun-Hit of Child	Agg Comp
Age-8 aggression	.32**	.15*	.14*	.15*	.29**	.14*			.24**	.21**
Family background (SES)										
Father's occupation					-.14+				-.17+	
Parent education	-.15*	-.24**			-.21**			-.14+	-.25**	
Value of housing	-.30**	-.14+	-.26**		-.25**				-.15+	-.23**
Negative family interaction										
Rejection						.13+			.15+	
Punishment (hitting) of child	.16*		.21**		.18**	.14*			.13+	.12+
Parental disharmony	.27**		.12+	.16*	.29**				.17*	

Note: Agg per = aggressive personality; Agg comp = composite aggression score. Nonsignificant correlations are not shown.
+$p < .10.$ *$p < .05.$ **$p < .01.$

Males

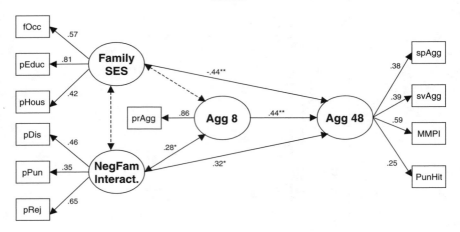

Females

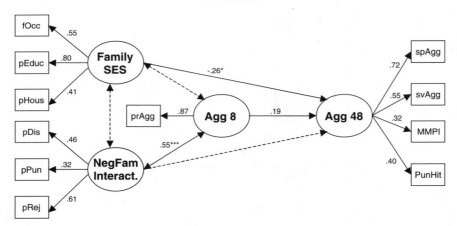

FIGURE 4.1. Structural models showing the effects of age-8 family-contextual factors on aggressive behavior at ages 8 and 48, with path coefficients for 234 males (top) and for 234 females (bottom) (multiple-group chi-square = 182.3, df = 93, RMSEA = .044, GFI = .93). Broken lines represent paths in the model for which the path coefficients are less than one standard error different from zero. FOcc = Father's occupation, 1960; pEduc = Parents' education, 1960; pHous = Value of family housing, 1960; pDis = Parental disharmony, 1960; pPun = Physical punishment of child, 1960; pRej = Parental rejection of child, 1960; prAgg = Peer-nominated aggression (logged), 1960; spAgg = Subject/spouse reports of subjects' aggression to spouse, 2000; svAgg = Subject's severe physical aggression (logged), 2000; MMPI = Sum of F, 4, 9 scales of MMPI, 2000; PunHit = Subject/spouse/child reports of subjects' use of physical punishment, 2000.

$* p < .05, ** p < .01, *** p < .001.$

TABLE 4.3. *Correlations of the Age-8 Family-Contextual Factors with Age-48 Intellectual/Educational Achievement Measures*

	Age-48 Intellectual/Educational Achievement Measures									
	Males					Females				
Age-8 Factors	WRAT Verbal	WRAT Math	Years of Educ	Cog Comp	Ach Comp	WRAT Verbal	WRAT Math	Years of Educ	Cog Comp	Ach Comp
Age-8 IQ	.49**	.56**	.35**	.33**	.52**	.41**	.54**	.38**	.32**	.51**
Family background (SES)										
Father's occupation			.23**		.18*	.18*	.18+	.26**		.23**
Parent education	.28**	.20*	.38**	.21**	.39**	.35**	.33**	.29**	.17*	.37**
Value of housing	.28**	.26**	.18**	.15*	.28**	.21**	.26**	.34**		.28**
Negative family interaction										
Rejection	-.26**	-.16+	-.17*	-.16*	-.27**	-.21**	-.25**	-.22**	-.25**	-.30**
Punishment (hitting) of child				-.13+						
Parental disharmony			-.11+		-.13*					

Note: Cog comp = perceived cognitive competence; Ach comp = composite achievement score. Nonsignificant correlations are not shown.
+*p* < .10. **p* < .05. ***p* < .01.

levels of family SES in middle childhood are associated with higher educational and intellectual achievement at age 48. Of the three family interaction variables, only parental rejection in middle childhood is associated
consistently with low achievement at age 48.

A multiple-group structural model (males and females) of the relations of the middle childhood family-contextual variables and age-8 IQ
to adult intellectual/educational achievement is shown in Figure 4.2. We
constrained the measurement parameters for the family background indicators (labeled in the figures as "SES") and for the negative family interaction indicators to be equal across gender and to be equal to the measurement parameters for these constructs found in the earlier aggression
models. We also constrained the measurement parameters for the age-
48 intellectual/educational achievement construct to be equal across genders. We included bidirectional relations of the middle childhood family-
contextual factors and middle childhood IQ. The fit of the multiple-group
model is adequate (RMSEA = .037, GFI = .94) and the relations among
the variables are similar for males and females.[3] As expected, for both
males and females, higher levels of age-8 IQ are related moderately to
age-48 intellectual/educational achievement. In addition, higher levels of
middle childhood SES and lower levels of negative family interaction are
directly related to higher levels of intellectual/educational achievement
at age 48.

Predicting Age-48 Occupational Prestige from the Middle Childhood Factors

Although there is no corresponding personal factor at age 8 for age-48
occupational prestige, as Table 4.4 shows, the correlations of the age-8
aggression, popularity, and IQ with age-48 occupational prestige are significant for both males and females. As expected childhood aggression
predicts less occupational success while greater popularity and higher
IQs predict more success. Parental rejection of the child at age 8 is also
inversely related to the child's eventual occupational prestige 40 years later
for both genders. However, the family background SES variables relate to
the child's eventual occupational prestige more strongly for males than for
females.

To examine the combined effect of these middle childhood variables
in predicting occupational success later in life, we computed a multiple-
group model (males and females) of the relations of the middle childhood
family-contextual variables and age-8 IQ, popularity, and aggression to
adult occupational prestige. We computed composite family background

---

[3] A model in which the structural paths were not constrained to be equal across genders
provided no better fit to the data; $\chi^2(5) = 4.9$, $p = .432$.

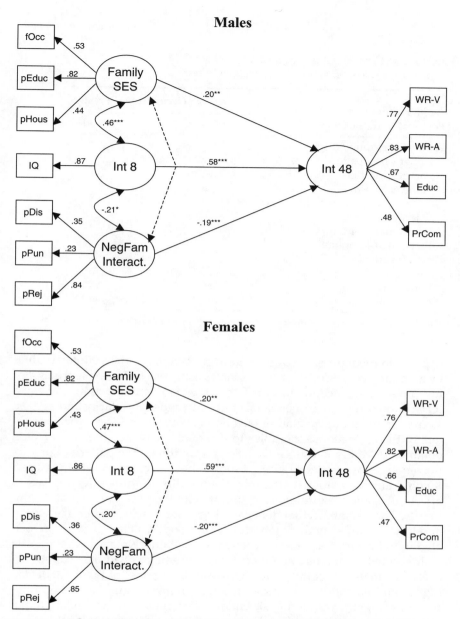

FIGURE 4.2. Structural models showing the effects of age-8 family-contextual factors on intellectual ability at ages 8 and 48, with path coefficients for 234 males (top) and for 234 females (bottom) (multiple-group chi-square = 165.5, df = 101, RMSEA = .037, GFI = .94). Broken lines represent paths in the model for which the path coefficients are less than one standard error different from zero. For variables not duplicating Figure 4.1: IQ = Subject's IQ score on Short Form Test of Mental Maturity, 1960; WR-V = Verbal score on Wide Range Achievement Test (WRAT), 2000; WR-A = Arithmetic score on WRAT, 2000; Educ = Level of educational attainment by 2000; PrCom = Perceived cognitive competence.
$* p < .05, ** p < .01, *** p < .001.$

TABLE 4.4. *Correlations of Age-8 Family-Contextual Factors and Personal Variables with Age-48 Occupational Prestige*

Age-8 Factors and Personal Variables	Age-48 Occupational Prestige	
	Males	*Females*
Family background (SES)		
Father's occupation	.22**	.16+
Parent education	.25**	.14+
Value of housing	.14*	
Negative family interaction		
Rejection	−.20**	−.21**
Punishment (hitting) of child		
Parental disharmony		
Personal variables		
Aggression	−.26**	−.16*
Popularity	.26**	.15*
IQ	.28**	.32**

Note: Nonsignificant correlations are not shown. $^+p < .10$. $^*p < .05$. $^{**}p < .01$.

(labeled in the figures as "SES") and negative family interaction variables by summing the z-scores for the variables comprising those constructs. For this model, we conceptualized SES, negative family interaction, and age-8 IQ as intercorrelated exogenous factors with age-8 popularity and aggression as endogenous mediating factors. We constrained the error parameters of the endogenous variables to be equal across genders. A fair fit is obtained (RMSEA = .058, GFI = .987), and a differential pattern of prediction emerges by gender. Figure 4.3 shows that for males, the effect of age-8 IQ on adult occupational attainment is not direct – rather, IQ appears to affect occupation by influencing middle childhood aggression and popularity. That is, intellectual deficits are associated with higher aggression and lower popularity during middle childhood, which in turn are associated with lower levels of adult occupational status. Note also that middle childhood SES remains a significant direct predictor of adult occupational status for males. In contrast, for females (lower panel of Figure 4.3), *only* higher middle childhood IQ significantly predicts higher age-48 occupational prestige. No other middle childhood variables in the model predict occupational prestige for females at a statistically significant level.[4]

---

[4] A model in which the structural paths were constrained to be equal across genders provided a significantly poorer fit to the data as indicated by the chi-square difference test, $\chi^2(13) = 30.173$, $p < .01$.

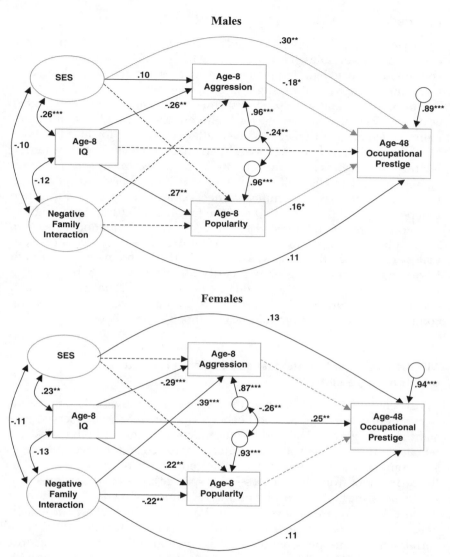

FIGURE 4.3. Structural models showing the mediated effects of age-8 family-contextual factors and IQ through age-8 aggression and popularity on occupational prestige at age 48, with path coefficients for 160 males (top) and for 139 females (bottom) (multiple-group chi-square = 11.928, df = 6, RMSEA = .058, GFI = .987). The broken lines represent paths in the model for which the path coefficients are less than one standard error different from zero.

$* p < .05, ** p < .01, *** p < .001.$

DISCUSSION

Family-contextual factors (i.e., family SES, negative family interactions) and personal variables (i.e., aggression, IQ, popularity) during middle childhood predicted adult outcomes (i.e., aggression, intellectual achievement, and occupational prestige) in important ways. Higher family SES during middle childhood predicted lower adult aggression and higher adult intellectual achievement for both genders and higher adult occupational achievement for males, even after controlling for middle childhood family interaction factors and personal variables. Negative family interaction variables in middle childhood predicted lower levels of adult aggression and intellectual achievement for both males and females as well but did not have a significant effect on adult occupational prestige independently of the child's IQ and the family's SES (despite the significant correlation of childhood rejection with lower occupational success). Although higher age-8 IQ predicted adult occupational success for both males and females, the effect was direct for females and mediated through lower aggression and higher popularity for males. These results add to the growing body of knowledge on the course of individual development, and raise some provocative questions concerning mechanisms affecting continuity and change from middle childhood to adulthood.

Middle Childhood Contextual and Personal Predictors of Adult Aggression

Consistent with prior research on the continuity of individuals' aggression over time (e.g., Farrington, 1990; Loeber & Dishion, 1983), we observed substantial (for a 40-year lag) and significant correlations for both males and females between age-8 peer-nominated aggression and the age-48 aggression composite score. However, notable gender differences were found in the correlations from child aggression to specific kinds of adult aggression. For females, the highest correlation was to "hitting your child" and the next highest was to aggressive personality. For males, the highest correlation was to aggressive personality. For males but not for females, there were correlations to interpersonal physical aggression and aggression "against your spouse." These patterns of longitudinal relations are consistent with the principle that each gender displays aggression consistent with gender roles for the culture.

Striking gender differences were also evident in the extent to which middle childhood factors predicted adult aggression. First, the continuity coefficient for aggression (i.e., age-8 aggression to age-48 aggression), when these other childhood factors were considered was considerably larger for males than for females. Second, the influence of childhood family-contextual factors differed by gender. For males, negative family interactions during middle childhood exerted an effect on aggression 40 years later even after accounting for its effects on aggression during middle childhood. However, for females, the deleterious effects of negative family interactions on aggression occurred only during middle childhood.

Although biological factors obviously play an important role in gender differences in aggression, these results suggest that differential socialization in middle childhood is also important. Boys, more than girls, are socialized to display a certain degree of overt "tough" and masculine aggressive behavior; girls with aggressive tendencies must therefore find more socially acceptable ways to express aggression. Thus, we have observed differences over time in males' tendency to display more public forms of aggression, with females limiting their aggression to more private situations such as child rearing (Eron & Huesmann, 1989). Furthermore, because females' aggression after middle childhood is likely to be more indirect and less public, individual differences in parental responses to overt "bad" behavior reflected by the Negative Family Interaction variables are less likely to be predictive of individual differences in females' subsequent aggressive behavior.

Middle Childhood Contextual and Personal Predictors of Adult Intellectual Achievement

The relations between middle childhood IQ and middle adulthood achievement demonstrated moderate continuity across a variety of specific adult measures. These results consistent with research on the short-term and long-term stability of intellectual and educational achievement (e.g., Chen, Lee, & Stevenson, 1996; Zax, Cowen, Beach, & Rappaport, 1972).

Longitudinal structural models predicting adult intellectual achievement from middle childhood IQ as well as family-contextual variables were more consistent across gender than were models of aggression. Both family SES and negative family interactions in middle childhood exerted significant direct effects on adult achievement, *over and above the best prediction from age-8 IQ*. This is a very important finding. Much of the contemporary literature on achievement outcomes, particularly from childhood into young adulthood, emphasizes the crucial role of family factors such as child rearing variables (e.g., discipline, warmth), parent characteristics (e.g., achievement expectations), and SES in the emergence and maintenance of academic success (Davis-Kean, 2003; Duncan, Brooks-Gunn, & Klebanov, 1994; Mistry, Vandewater, Huston, & McLoyd, 2002). The results of the current investigation underscore the importance of those factors by demonstrating their continuing influence into middle adulthood.

Middle Childhood Contextual and Personal Predictors of Adult Occupational Prestige

Our findings with regard to the prediction of age-48 occupational prestige present a complex picture of the ways in which family-contextual and personal factors differentially influence development by gender. Of the two middle childhood family-contextual predictors, only family SES had a direct long-term relation to age-48 occupational prestige in the structural models, and only for males. Higher childhood SES was associated with greater adulthood occupational prestige for males. Negative family interactions in middle childhood had no substantial effect for either males or females. For females, only age-8 IQ among the personal variables was related independently to adult occupational success. However, for males the effect of age-8 IQ on adult occupational success was mediated almost entirely by IQ's relations to age-8 aggression (inverse) and age-8 popularity (direct). For males, occupational prestige in middle adulthood appears to be more the product of the possible effect that lower IQ has on depressing social competence than on any direct effect of IQ on occupational prestige. From a social capital perspective (Eccles, Templeton, Barber, & Stone, 2003; Parke, 2004), it is possible that higher SES parents provided tangible opportunities for their boys' vocational development (e.g., business opportunities, connections to jobs in the community through their own personal networks). Perhaps more socially skilled boys were better able to take advantage of these opportunities. Given the period during which the Columbia County cohort was growing up (i.e., in the 1950s and 1960s), societal expectations for occupational attainment might have been less critical for girls, so those opportunities might not have been provided for them. For girls to achieve higher occupational attainment later in life, their intellectual abilities might have been more important.

Implications

Our findings provide an initial look at the ways in which middle childhood family-contextual and personal factors continue to exert influence on important domains of functioning into middle adulthood. Our analyses highlight the predictive value of middle childhood variables for explaining aggression, intellectual competence, and occupational prestige over 40 years. However, the results also raise a critical overarching question: What processes or mechanisms account for continuity or discontinuity over time?

Contextual factors are thought to influence the development of attitudes and beliefs that in turn lead to the emergence and continuity/discontinuity of behavior (e.g., Bandura, 1986; Huesmann, 1998; Wigfield & Eccles, 2000). Cognitive processing models posit that behavior is maintained over time through the formation and application of attitudes and beliefs that emerge initially through observational and direct learning experiences to which the child is exposed across multiple contexts; cognitions then crystallize and are strengthened through adolescence and adulthood. For example, males who come to believe that aggression is acceptable (perhaps through cumulative exposure to aggressive models in the home, media, etc.) should be more likely to behave aggressively in the long run, which will interfere with social relations and make success in life more difficult. Females who value educational attainment (perhaps through exposure to higher SES family contexts where cognitively stimulating resources are available) should show higher achievement in childhood and be more likely to experience academic and vocational success. In other words, it may be that females develop their motivation to achieve through their positive experiences with schooling, whereas males might develop similar motivation through positive social interactions. Thus, higher IQ for females leads to reinforcement of an achievement-oriented self-concept through academic successes, whereas social facility for males leads to reinforcement of an achievement-oriented self-concept through social success.

In sum, our analyses have identified middle childhood family-contextual factors that predict adult outcomes. However, we recognize that this is only a first step toward understanding the specific processes by which these factors operate to affect adult development, and how these processes might operate differentially by gender.

This project was supported by funding from the National Institute of Child Health and Human Development (R01 HD 036056-06). We acknowledge the assistance of David Slegers in the preparation of this manuscript. Address all correspondence to L. Rowell Huesmann, Ph.D., Research Center for Group Dynamics, 5035 ISR, University of Michigan, 426 Thompson Street, Ann Arbor, MI 48106. Email: huesmann@umich.edu.

References

Arbuckle, J. L. (1997). *AMOS users' guide version 3.6.* Chicago: SmallWaters Corporation.

Bandura, A. (1986). *Social foundations of thought and action: A social cognitive theory.* Englewood Cliffs, NJ: Prentice-Hall.

Chen, C., Lee, S., & Stevenson, H. W. (1996). Long-term prediction of academic achievement of American, Chinese, and Japanese adolescents. *Journal of Educational Psychology, 88,* 750–759.

Coie, J. D., & Dodge, K. A. (1983). Continuities and changes in children's social status: A five-year longitudinal study. *Merrill-Palmer Quarterly, 29,* 261–282.

Cummings, E. M., & Davies, P. T. (1994). *Children and marital conflict.* New York: Guilford.

Davis-Kean, P. E. (2003, April). *The influence of parent education on child outcomes: The mediating role of parents' beliefs and behaviors.* Paper presented at the biennial meeting of the Society for Research in Child Development, Tampa, FL.

Duncan, G. J., Brooks-Gunn, J., & Klebanov, P. K. (1994). Economic deprivation and early childhood development. *Child Development, 65,* 296–318.

Eccles, J. S. (1994). Understanding women's educational and occupational choices: Applying the Eccles et al. model of achievement-related choices. *Psychology of Women Quarterly, 18,* 585–609.

Eccles, J., Templeton, J., Barber, B., & Stone, M. (2003). Adolescence and emerging adulthood: The critical passage ways to adulthood. In M. H. Bornstein, L. Davidson, C. L. M. Keyes, & K. A. Moore (Eds.), *Well-Being: Positive development across the life course* (pp. 383–406). Mahwah, NJ: Lawrence Erlbaum Associates.

Erikson, E. H. (1963). *Childhood and society* (2nd ed). New York: W. W. Norton & Company.

Eron, L. D., & Huesmann, L. R. (1989). The genesis of gender differences in aggression. In M. A. Luscz & T. Nettlebeck (Eds.), *Psychological development: Perspectives across the life span* (pp. 55–67). Amsterdam: Elsevier.

Eron, L. D., Walder, L. O., & Lefkowitz, M. M. (1971). *Learning of aggression in children.* Boston: Little, Brown.

Farrington, D. P. (1990) Childhood aggression and adult violence: Early precursors and later life outcomes. In D. J. Pepler & K. H. Rubin (Eds.), *The development of childhood aggression.* Hillsdale, NJ: Erlbaum.

Freud, S. (1961). The ego and the id. In J. Strachey (Ed. & Trans.), *The standard edition of the complete psychological works of Sigmund Freud* (Vol. 19, pp. 3–66). London: Hogarth Press. (Original work published 1923.)

Harter, S. (1985). *Manual for the Self-Perception Profile.* Denver, CO: University of Denver.

Hathaway, S. R., & McKinley, J. C. (1940). A multiphasic personality schedule (Minnesota): I. Construction of the schedule. *Journal of Psychology, 10,* 249–254.

Huesmann, L. R. (1998). The role of social information processing and cognitive schema in the acquisition and maintenance of habitual aggressive behavior. In R. G. Geen & E. Donnerstein (Eds.), *Human aggression: Theories, research, and implications for social policy* (pp. 73–109). San Diego, CA: Academic Press.

Huesmann, L. R. (2001). *Gender differences in the continuity of aggression from childhood to adulthood: Evidence from some recent longitudinal studies.* Paper presented at the 2001 G. Stanley Hall Symposium on Gender and Aggression. Williams College, Williams, Massachusetts.

Huesmann, L. R., Dubow, E. F., Eron, L. D., Boxer, P., Slegers, D., & Miller, L. S. (2002, November). *Continuity and discontinuity of aggressive behaviors across three generations.* Paper presented at the meeting of the Society for Life History Research on Psychopathology, New York.

Huesmann, L. R., & Eron, L. D. (1986). *Television and the aggressive child: A cross-national comparison.* Hillsdale, NJ: Erlbaum.

Huesmann, L. R., Eron, L. D., Lefkowitz, M. M., & Walder, L. O. (1984). Stability of aggression over time and generations. *Developmental Psychology, 20,* 1120–1134.

Huesmann, L. R., & Guerra, N. G. (1997). Children's normative beliefs about aggression and aggressive behavior. *Journal of Personality and Social Psychology, 72,* 408–419.

Huesmann, L. R., Lefkowitz, M. M., & Eron, L. D. (1978). The sum of MMPI scales F, 4, and 9 as a measure of aggression. *Journal of Consulting and Clinical Psychology, 46,* 1071–1078.

Jacobs, J. E., Bleeker, M. M., & Constantino, M. (2003). The self-system during childhood and adolescence: Development, influences, and implications. *Journal of Psychotherapy Integration, 13,* 33–65.

Jastak, J. F., & Jastak, S. (1978). *Wide Range Achievement Test-Revised.* Wilmington, DE: Jastak Associates.

Jimerson, S., Egeland, B., Sroufe, L. A., & Carlson, B. (2000). A prospective longitudinal study of high school dropouts examining multiple predictors across development. *Journal of School Psychology, 38,* 525–549.

Kokko, K., & Pulkkinen, L. (2000). Aggression in childhood and long-term unemployment in adulthood: A cycle of maladaptation and some protective factors. *Developmental Psychology, 36,* 463–472.

Lefkowitz, M. M., Eron, L. D., Walder, L. O., & Huesmann, L. R. (1973). Preference for televised contact sports as related to sex differences in aggression. *Developmental Psychology, 9,* 417–420.

Lefkowitz, M. M., Eron, L. D., Walder, L. O., & Huesmann, L. R. (1977). *Growing up to be violent.* New York: Pergamon.

Leventhal, T., & Brooks-Gunn, J. (2000). The neighborhoods they live in: The effects of neighborhood residence upon child and adolescent outcomes. *Psychological Bulletin, 126,* 309–337.

Loeber, R., & Dishion, T. (1983). Early predictors of male delinquency: A review. *Psychological Bulletin, 94,* 68–99.

McHale, S. M., Dariotis, J. K., & Kauh, T. J. (2003). Social development and social relationships in middle childhood. In R. M. Lerner & M. A. Easterbrooks (Eds.). *Handbook of psychology: Vol. 6, Developmental psychology* (pp. 241–265). New York: John Wiley & Sons, Inc.

Mistry, R. S., Vandewater, E. A., Huston, A. C., & McLoyd, V. C. (2002). Economic well-being and children's social adjustment: The role of family process in an ethnically diverse low-income sample. *Child Development, 73,* 935–951.

Parke, R. D. (2004). Development in the family. *Annual Review of Psychology, 55,* 365–399.

Patterson, G. R. (1982). *Coercive family process.* Eugene, OR: Castalia.

Phelps, E., Furstenberg, F. F., & Colby, A. (2002). *Looking at lives: American longitudinal studies of the 20th century.* New York: Russell Sage Foundation.

Piaget, J. (1965). *The child's conception of the world.* Totowa, NJ: Littlefield, Adams.

Pulkkinen, L., & Caspi, A. (Eds.) (2002). *Paths to successful development: Personality in the life course.* Cambridge, UK: Cambridge University Press.

Pulkkinen, L., Nygren, H., & Kokko, K. (2002). Successful development: Childhood antecedents of adaptive psychosocial functioning in adulthood. *Journal of Adult Development, 9,* 251–265.

Stevens, G., & Hoisington, E. (1987). Occupational prestige and the 1980 U.S. labor force. *Social Science Research, 6,* 74–105.

Straus, M. A., Giles, R. J., & Steinmetz, S. K. (1979). *Behind closed doors: Violence in the American family*. New York: Doubleday/Anchor.

Sullivan, E. T., Clark, W. W., & Tiegs, E. W. (1957). *California Short Form Test of Mental Maturity*. Los Angeles: California Test Bureau.

Tolan, P. H., Gorman-Smith, D., & Henry, D. B. (2003). The developmental ecology of urban males' youth violence. *Developmental Psychology, 39*, 274–291.

Warner, W. L., Meeker, M., & Eells, K. (1960). *Social class in America*. New York: Harcourt.

Wigfield, A., & Eccles, J. S. (2000). Expectancy-value theory of motivation. *Contemporary Educational Psychology, 25*, 68–81.

Zax, M., Cowen, E. L., Beach, D. R., & Rappaport, J. (1972). Longitudinal relationships among aptitude, achievement, and adjustment measures of school children. *Journal of Genetic Psychology, 121*, 145–154.

5

Genetic and Environment Influences on Continuity and Change in Reading Achievement in the Colorado Adoption Project

Sally J. Wadsworth, Robin Corley, Robert Plomin, John K. Hewitt, and John C. DeFries

Mastery of reading skills in childhood has far-reaching implications for development. Serving as a foundation for all academic learning, reading performance affects not only educational attainment, but also employment options, interpersonal relationships, and emotional well-being. Although this essential skill continues to develop throughout adolescence and adulthood, measures of reading achievement are highly stable, with correlations ranging from .23 to .96 over intervals of 1 to 8 years (e.g., Bast & Reitsma, 1998; DeFries, 1988; DeFries & Baker, 1983; Shaywitz, Escobar, Shaywitz, Fletcher, & Makuch, 1992; Wadsworth, Corley, Hewitt, & DeFries, 2001; Wagner et al., 1997; Williams & McGee, 1996). Results obtained from both twin and adoption studies have provided compelling evidence for substantial genetic influences on individual differences in reading performance from age 7 to adulthood, with heritability estimates ranging from .18 to .81 (e.g., Alarcn & DeFries, 1995; Cardon, DiLalla, Plomin, DeFries, & Fulker, 1990; Knopik & DeFries, 1999; Stevenson, Graham, Fredman, & McLoughlin, 1987; Wadsworth et al., 2001). Despite the striking evidence for stability and heritability, reading achievement also shows some change as a function of environmental influences. All of these factors – genes and environment, continuity and change – are needed for a complete understanding of the development of reading achievement.

The evidence that individual differences in reading achievement are both stable and heritable throughout development suggests that genetic influences contribute to continuity. Genetic influences that are important at an early age may also be important at later ages. Recent studies which have begun to assess the etiology of continuity and change in reading achievement using data from adoptive and nonadoptive sibling pairs have obtained high genetic correlations (see Appendix for details on calculation of genetic and environmental correlations) between the measures of reading achievement at different ages, indicating that genes substantially affect reading achievement from age 7 through age 16, accounting for as much as 70% of the observed age-to-age stability (e.g., Wadsworth et al., 2001; Wadsworth, Fulker, and DeFries, 1999). Moreover, in a recent analysis of sibling data from the Colorado Adoption Project (CAP), Wadsworth et al. (2001) found that the heritability of reading achievement at age 16 was significantly higher than that at ages 7 and 12, suggesting the possible amplification of genetic influences in late adolescence (DeFries, Plomin, & LaBuda, 1987). In other words, a high genetic correlation from age to age in the face of increasing heritability implies that the same genes affect reading achievement at both ages but that these genes have a greater effect later in development. This is consistent with results of studies of cognitive ability demonstrating higher heritability in late adolescence and adulthood (e.g., McGue, Bouchard, Iacono, & Lykken, 1993; Plomin, Fulker, Corley, & DeFries, 1997).

Although genetic influences on reading achievement and on age-to-age continuity in reading achievement are impressive, these same data demonstrate that environmental factors also make important contributions. At the simplest level, genetic research provides the best available evidence for the importance of the environment. Heritability estimates for reading achievement at a given time point are typically about 40%, which means that more than half of the variance in reading achievement is due to environmental factors. Moreover, behavioral genetic research distinguishes two types of environmental influence. *Shared environment* refers to experiences that are shared by siblings growing up in the same family, thus contributing to their resemblance. *Nonshared environment* refers to all other environmental influences that do not contribute to siblings' similarity, including measurement error. This distinction is important because most environmental theories assume that family background, which should be manifest as shared environment, contributes significantly to reading achievement. However, it is important to note that nonshared environment may also include aspects of the home environment that affect siblings differently. Our sibling adoption research suggests that nonshared environment is much more important than shared environment in the etiology of reading.

The sibling adoption design is the most powerful design for estimating the influence of shared environment because it relies on the resemblance of adoptive siblings, genetically unrelated siblings adopted into the same family. Adoptive sibling correlations, which are usually less than .10, directly estimate shared environmental influence. The remainder of the environmental variance (which accounts for about 50% of the total variance) is attributable to nonshared environment. Thus, in pursuing the environmental causes of individual differences in reading achievement, it is important to look for nonshared environmental factors that do not contribute to sibling resemblance.

With respect to continuity in reading achievement, Wadsworth et al. (2001) found that environmental influences shared by members of sibling pairs accounted for 8%–13% of the observed continuity, and nonshared environmental influences accounted for up to 30%. In contrast, *change* in reading achievement was almost entirely due to nonshared environmental influences.

These longitudinal genetic analyses of reading achievement provide three important clues about the etiology of continuity and change. First, genetic effects on early reading at age 7 are largely the same genetic influences that operate at later ages, even in adolescence at age 16. Second, shared and nonshared environmental influences also contribute to continuity. Third, age-to-age change in reading achievement is not due to genetic factors or to shared environment – change is explained entirely by nonshared environment.

Although there is currently considerable interest in attempting to identify specific genes responsible for genetic influence on reading achievement (Fisher & DeFries, 2002), there has also been a long-standing interest in identifying environmental influences on reading. Numerous studies have investigated the relations between achievement and measures of the home environment and parenting, finding that socioeconomic status (SES), quality of the home environment, and positive parenting were related to changes in achievement (e.g., Jimerson, Egeland, & Teo, 1999; Koutsoulis & Campbell, 2001; Robinson, Lanzi, Weinberg, Ramey, & Ramey, 2002). Although parenting and the home environment have been related to achievement, it is important to note that such measures are confounded with genetic relationships between parents and their offspring (Plomin, 1994). This potential confound remains even when analyzing age-to-age change in achievement.

Unfortunately, most previous attempts to identify environmental influences on reading achievement have not employed genetically sensitive designs that can control for the substantial genetic contribution to reading. The adoption design can assess genetic mediation of associations between ostensible measures of the environment and children's achievement by comparing such associations in nonadoptive families (in which parents share nature as well as nurture with their children) with associations in adoptive families (in which parents share only nurture with their children). In addition, as noted above, shared and nonshared sources of environmental influence can be distinguished.

Associations between environmental factors and achievement may also be mediated by such characteristics of the children as IQ or motivation. In one study (Koutsoulis & Campbell, 2001), children's motivation was an important mediator of parental psychological support as it is associated with achievement. In another, 22% of the observed stability, and one third of the genetic stability between reading achievement at age 7 and that at age 12, was due to influences shared with IQ (Wadsworth & DeFries, 2003).

Candidate mediators must meet two criteria: They must be correlated with the environmental factor and with achievement. One such candidate mediator supported by a body of research is the child's social competence (Robinson et al., 2002). Deficits in social competence may lead to communication difficulties between students and their teachers or peers, which may interfere with learning. Conversely, effective social skills may provide for better teacher–student and peer relationships, thereby enhancing the learning environment. Welsh, Parke, Widaman, & O'Neil (2001) examined the relation between teacher and peer assessments of social competence and children's academic achievement in 163 school-aged children. The investigators tested hypotheses that social competence influenced later academic achievement, that academic achievement influenced later social competence, and that the relationship was one of reciprocal influence. Results suggested that academic achievement influenced social competence to second grade, whereas the two were reciprocally related from second to third grade.

Previous studies have only begun to elucidate the genetic and environmental contexts contributing to continuity and change in reading achievement from middle childhood through adolescence. Therefore, the goals of the present study were to

1. Assess the etiology of continuity and change in reading achievement using multivariate behavioral genetic methods with data from a sample of adoptive and nonadoptive sibling pairs tested at ages 7, 12, and 16 in the Colorado Adoption Project.
2. Explore putative shared and nonshared environmental contexts that may influence reading achievement and its observed continuity and change from middle childhood through adolescence.
3. Investigate children's social competence and IQ as possible mediators of associations between environmental factors and reading achievement.

METHOD

Subjects

The subjects are participants in the Colorado Adoption Project (CAP), an ongoing longitudinal study of genetic and environmental influences on behavioral development. Beginning in 1975, adoptive families were recruited through two adoption agencies in Denver, Colorado. Data from a variety of measures were collected from both adoptive and biological parents, and are currently being obtained from adoptive children and their unrelated siblings. Adoptive children were separated from their biological parents within a few days of birth and placed in adoptive homes within one month. The CAP foundation sample consists of 245 adoptive families

TABLE 5.1. *Sample Sizes by Family Type, Individual Type, and Sex*

Family and Individual Type	Males			Females		
	Age 7	Age 12	Age 16	Age 7	Age 12	Age 16
Adoptive						
Proband	112	108	107	97	90	92
Unrelated sibling	46	43	28	52	54	40
Nonadoptive						
Proband	124	123	119	103	102	104
Related sibling	60	54	45	47	45	29

and 245 nonadoptive control families, which were matched to the adoptive families according to age, education, and occupational status of the father, gender of the adopted child, and number of children in the family. Detailed descriptions of the CAP design and sample, including socioeconomic status (SES) and parental education level, representativeness of the sample, and evidence for little or no selective placement, have been provided by DeFries, Plomin, and Fulker (1994); Petrill, Plomin, DeFries, & Hewitt, (2003); Plomin and DeFries (1985); and Plomin, DeFries, & Fulker (1988). Sample sizes for those subjects with data at a given age are presented by family type (adoptive vs. nonadoptive), individual type (proband vs. sibling) and sex in Table 5.1.

Measures

The primary dependent measure was reading achievement of children. For this we used the Peabody Individual Achievement Test (PIAT; Dunn & Markwardt, 1970), Reading Recognition subtest, administered to the children at 7, 12, and 16 years of age. The Reading Recognition subtest has a median test-retest reliability of .89 across grades K–12. At age 7, the subtest has a correlation of .66 with teacher ratings of reading achievement, and an average correlation of .57 with the various school-administered achievement test scores available for this sample, which are first administered widely at age 9.

Family environmental measures included socioeconomic status (SES), maternal reading, and several measures of parenting and the home environment atmosphere. SES was measured by years of education of the rearing mother, reported when the children were 7 years of age. Mother's education was more highly correlated with measures of children's achievement than father's education or occupational rating of either parent. Maternal reading was assessed using the Reading Recognition subtest of the PIAT, administered to the adoptive and nonadoptive control mothers when the children were 7 years of age.

Two measures assessed parenting and home environment atmosphere. The Family Environmental Scale (Moos & Moos, 1981), cohesion and conflict subscales, were obtained by parental report during early childhood (age 3), middle childhood (age 7), and adolescence (age 12). The Parent Report of Childrearing Behavior (Dibble & Cohen, 1974) "superscales," including positive parenting, inconsistent parenting, and control were obtained when the children were 7 and 12 years of age. The positive parenting superscale consists of items such as degree of child-centeredness, acceptance of the child as a person, acceptance of the child's autonomy, sensitivity to feelings of the child, and consistent enforcement of discipline. The inconsistent parenting superscale consists of items relating to detachment and inconsistent enforcement of discipline. The control superscale consists of items suggesting control through anxiety, guilt, hostility, or withdrawal of relationship. Although a number of other measures were examined as possible environmental predictors of reading achievement, such as television viewing, sibling interaction, and stressful life events, these were not included in the current analyses because their correlations with reading achievement were near zero in this sample.

IQ and social competence were investigated as possible mediators of associations between environmental measures and achievement. IQ was assessed using the Wechsler Intelligence Scale for Children-Revised (WISC-R; Wechsler, 1974), administered at ages 7 and 12, and the Wechsler Adult Intelligence Scale-Revised (WAIS-R; Wechsler, 1981), administered at age 16. Parent and teacher ratings of social competence were assessed by the CAP Social Competence Scale, which is based on the Walker-McConnell Scale of Social Competence and School Adjustment (Walker & McConnell, 1988). A composite of parent and teacher ratings was obtained when the children were 7 years of age, and teacher ratings were used at ages 12 and 15. The total social competence scale is a composite of leadership, popularity, confidence, and problem behavior subscales.

Longitudinal Genetic Analysis of Reading Achievement

The adoptive sibling design is based on a comparison of the correlations of adoptive (unrelated) siblings to those of nonadoptive (related) siblings (e.g., Plomin, DeFries, & Fulker, 1988). Whereas adoptive siblings are genetically unrelated, and share only family environmental influences, related siblings share half of their segregating genes, on average, as well as family environmental influences. Therefore, in the absence of genetic nonadditivity, the phenotypic correlation between related siblings is a function of one half the heritability of the trait, plus shared environmental influences, which are assumed to be no more highly correlated for related siblings than for unrelated siblings. In contrast, the phenotypic correlation between

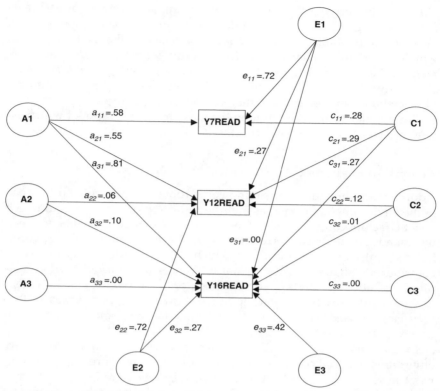

FIGURE 5.1. Cholesky decomposition of the variance in reading at the three ages into genetic (A1, A2, A3), shared environmental (C1, C2, C3), and nonshared environmental (E1, E2, E3) components.

genetically unrelated adoptive siblings results only from shared environmental influences (in the absence of selective placement). Therefore, by analyzing these correlations, the contributions of genetic, shared environmental and nonshared environmental influences can be estimated.

For the genetic analyses, a Cholesky decomposition model (Neale & Cardon, 1992) was used to partition the factor structure underlying the measures of reading achievement at the three ages into its genetic, shared environmental and nonshared environmental components. The Cholesky decomposition model allows for the first latent factor to contribute to the variance of all measures, whereas the second factor contributes to the variance of all measures except the first, etc. As a result, each factor assesses entirely new influences on the corresponding measure, independent of the preceding factor(s). Figure 5.1 depicts the genetic (A1, A2, A3), shared environmental (C1, C2, C3) and nonshared environmental (E1, E2, E3) factor structures underlying the measures of reading achievement at each age, for one sibling only. Using this model, the etiology of the relation between measures of reading achievement at the three ages – that is, the extent to which continuity or change in individual differences in reading achievement at the three ages is due to genetic, shared environmental and nonshared environmental influences – can be assessed. In addition, estimates of heritability, shared and nonshared environmentality, and genetic and environmental correlations among the measures are computed with relative ease (see Appendix for details).

Analysis of Environmental Measures

Adoptive and nonadoptive sibling correlations were calculated for each of the environmental measures in order to (a) explore the extent to which genetic factors contribute to ostensible environmental measures (as seen by nonadoptive sibling correlations that exceed adoptive sibling correlations), (b) assess the extent to which such environmental measures contribute to shared environmental influences (as indexed by the magnitude of adoptive sibling correlations), and (c) investigate the extent to which such environmental measures show sibling differences so that they can be used as nonshared environmental correlates of *changes* in achievement.

Exploratory analyses were conducted to assess the influence of family environment, social competence, and IQ on measures of reading achievement at the three ages. First, simple correlations were computed. Path analyses were then conducted to assess the causal relationships among the measures. Social competence and IQ were further examined as possible mediators of environmental effects on reading achievement. These mediators were subjected, along with reading achievement, to Cholesky decomposition analysis to assess the genetic and environmental contributions to the interrelations among the measures. For all analyses of environmental measures, multigroup models were estimated to determine if the causal relationship differed for boys and girls and for adopted and nonadopted participants.

RESULTS

Genetic Analysis

Sibling correlations for reading achievement are presented in Table 5.2. Whereas unrelated sibling correlations for reading achievement at each age average .05, those for related siblings average .26, suggesting a moderate effect of genetic influences on individual differences in reading achievement, and a small influence of shared environment. Within-person stability

TABLE 5.2. *Sibling Correlations for Reading Achievement*

	Sib1			Sib 2		
	Y7 READ	Y12 READ	Y16 READ	Y7 READ	Y12 READ	Y16 READ
Sibling 1						
Y7 READ	1.00	.65	.56	.07	.14	.16
Y12 READ	.57	1.00	.80	.02	.10	.00
Y16 READ	.54	.58	1.00	−.02	.08	−.02
Sibling 2						
Y7 READ	.27	.20	.36	1.00	.68	.57
Y12 READ	.27	.25	.40	.57	1.00	.82
Y16 READ	.30	.06	.26	.63	.64	1.00

Note: Unrelated sibling correlations above the diagonal; related sibling correlations below the diagonal.

correlations are .62 between the measure of reading achievement at ages 7 and 12, .71 between ages 12 and 16, and .58 between ages 7 and 16, averaged across siblings and adopted and nonadopted children.

Results of fitting the full genetic/environmental Cholesky to reading achievement data from the sibling pairs are presented in Figure 5.1. Consistent with results of previous studies, these results suggest a substantial contribution of genetic influences to the variance in reading achievement at each age, as well as to the covariances among the measures. Of particular interest is the lack of substantial new genetic influence at either age 12 or age 16. Therefore, the genetic influences manifested at ages 12 and 16 appear to be the same as those manifested at age 7 in this sample.

In contrast, shared environmental influences are modest at each age. Moreover, similar to the genetic results, the shared environmental influences on reading achievement at ages 12 and 16 appear to be largely the same as those present at age 7; therefore, the only substantial influences on reading achievement at ages 12 and 16, independent of those at age 7, are environmental influences not shared between siblings, as evidenced by the relatively large magnitude of the path coefficients from E2 to Y12READ and from E3 to Y16READ.

Estimates of genetic, shared environmental and nonshared environmental contributions to the variance in the measures of reading achievement at each age (i.e., heritability and environmentality) are presented on the diagonals of Table 5.3. Because the heritability estimate for reading achievement is somewhat higher at age 16 than at ages 7 and 12, these results suggest that the genetic influences observed at the earlier ages may be amplified in their expression in later adolescence (e.g., DeFries et al., 1987; Wadsworth et al., 2001).

TABLE 5.3. *Genetic, Shared Environmental and Nonshared Environmental Correlations Among Measures of Reading Performance at 7, 12, and 16 Years of Age*

	Genetic		
	Age 7	Age 12	Age 16
Age 7	**.34**	.53	.86
Age 12	1.00	**.31**	.62
Age 16	.99	1.00	**.67**
	Shared Environmental		
	Age 7	Age 12	Age 16
Age 7	**.08**	.14	.14
Age 12	.93	**.10**	.10
Age 16	1.00	.88	**.07**
	Nonshared Environmental		
	Age 7	Age 12	Age 16
Age 7	**.59**	.34	.00
Age 12	.35	**.59**	.27
Age 16	.00	.51	**.25**

Note: Proportions of variance accounted for by genetic or environmental influences (i.e., heritability and environmentality) are given on the diagonal; proportions of phenotypic covariance accounted for are given above the diagonal.

Estimates of the genetic and environmental correlations among the measures of reading achievement at the three ages are presented below the diagonals in Table 5.3. The genetic correlations are all near unity, again suggesting that the same genetic influences are manifested in reading achievement at all three ages. Further, as indicated above the diagonal, shared genetic influences account for 53% of the observed continuity in individual differences in reading achievement between ages 7 and 12, 62% of that between ages 12 and 16, and 86% of that between ages 7 and 16.

Shared environmental correlations are also high, suggesting that the shared environmental influences are largely the same from age 7 through age 16. However, these influences account for only 10% to 14% of the phenotypic continuity from age 7 to age 16. Nonshared environmental correlations are relatively low. Although nonshared environmental influences account for 34% of the observed continuity in individual differences in reading achievement between ages 7 and 12, and 27% of that between ages 12 and 16, they account for none of the continuity between ages 7 and 16. Thus, in contrast to the genetic and shared environmental results, nonshared environmental influences are primarily responsible for changes in reading achievement, as indicated by the magnitude of age-specific non-shared environmental paths.

To test the statistical necessity of individual parameters or groups of parameters, indices of model fit were compared both with and without the parameters in the model. Parameters included in the full model could be constrained to include only one genetic factor ($\Delta \chi_3^2 = .00$, $p = 1.00$), or one shared environmental factor ($\Delta \chi_3^2 = .05$, $p > .99$), without significant reduction in model fit. Alternatively, the nonshared environmental common factors could be dropped, leaving all genetic and shared environmental influences, but only nonshared environmental specifics ($\Delta \chi_3^2 = 5.27$, $p > .10$).

These three models could then be combined, leaving a model with only one genetic common factor, one shared environmental common factor, and nonshared environmental specifics ($\Delta \chi_6^2 = 7.57$, $p > .20$). The shared environmental common factor could then be dropped from the model ($\Delta \chi_3^2 = 1.56$, $p > .50$) so that the most parsimonious model with no significant reduction in fit included one genetic common factor, no shared environmental influences, and nonshared environmental specifics. As expected, the corresponding model omitting all genetic influence and allowing only one shared environmental common factor and nonshared environmental specifics provided a significantly worse fit to the data ($\Delta \chi_3^2 = 274.03$, $p < .001$). Although only one genetic common factor was necessary, indicating that the same genetic influences were manifested at the three ages, the magnitude of genetic influence on individual differences in reading achievement at ages 7, 12, and 16 could not be equated without significant reduction in fit ($\Delta \chi_2^2 = 46.83$, $p < .001$), supporting possible amplification of genetic influence in later adolescence.

Analysis of Environmental Measures

Sibling correlations were calculated for the measures of home environment atmosphere and parenting. The average sibling correlation for these parent-reported parenting measures was .56 – not at all near unity – thus indicating that parents discriminate their parenting toward their two children. The average correlations across measures of cohesion, conflict, positive parenting, inconsistent parenting, and parental control for adoptive (unrelated) and nonadoptive (related) siblings were .53 and .60, respectively, indicating modest genetic influence plus environmental effects that are due to both shared and nonshared factors.

Phenotypic correlations were also computed between the environmental measures included in the exploratory analyses and the measures of reading achievement at the three ages (Table 5.4). The correlations are low, even for contemporaneous correlations (e.g., year 7 parenting and year 7

TABLE 5.4. *Phenotypic Correlations between Putative Measures of the Environment and Reading Achievement at Ages 7, 12, and 16*

	Y7 Reading	Y12 Reading	Y16 Reading
Y3 cohesion	.12	.04	.05
Y3 conflict	−.08	−.06	−.02
Y7 cohesion	.07	.00	.05
Y7 conflict	−.04	−.05	.01
Y12 cohesion	.07	.09	.14
Y12 conflict	.00	−.05	−.02
Y7 positive parenting	.07	.01	.00
Y7 inconsistent parenting	−.03	−.07	−.09
Y7 controlling parenting	−.09	−.12	−.10
Y12 positive parenting	.06	.07	.04
Y12 inconsistent parenting	−.02	−.08	−.07
Y12 controlling parent	−.09	−.12	−.13
Y7 mother's education	.11	.10	.01
Mother's reading	.09	.09	.05

reading), ranging from −.13 to .14. The highest correlation (.14) was between Y12 cohesion and Y16 reading. Thus, environmental influences found to affect reading achievement in the genetic analyses appear to be features of the environment that are not measured in this study, including measurement error.

Exploratory path analysis of the relations among measures of family environment, social competence, and achievement suggest unique contributions of middle childhood to the development of reading performance. However, only social competence at age 7 influenced reading achievement directly ($p < .02$), with measures of parenting and home environment providing only indirect influence, through social competence. Social competence in adolescence had no significant additional influence on achievement when controlling for social competence in middle childhood ($p > .3$).

Analysis of Mediators

Finally, children's IQ and social competence were investigated as possible mediators of environmental effects on reading achievement at age 7. Both IQ and social competence are significantly correlated with reading achievement at age 7 (.37 and .26, respectively). In addition, measures of social competence at age 7 are significantly correlated with measures of the family environment atmosphere (cohesion, $r = .22$) as well as with positive parenting ($r = .32$), inconsistent parenting ($r = −.21$), and parental control

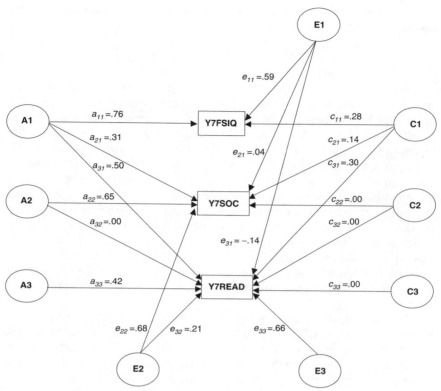

FIGURE 5.2. Results of analysis of mediator variables.

$(r = -.22)$, suggesting that parenting and the family environment may indirectly influence reading achievement, mediated by social competence.

Adoptive and nonadoptive sibling correlations at age 7 are, respectively, .03 and .33 for IQ, and −.08 and .20 for social competence, suggesting genetic influence for both mediators. The phenotypic correlation between IQ and social competence was .27. A trivariate genetic analysis of Full Scale IQ (Y7FSIQ), social competence (Y7SOC), and reading achievement (Y7READ) measured at age 7 suggested that this correlation is almost entirely mediated genetically (Figure 5.2), as indicated by the small negative path from C1 to Y7SOC and the near-zero path from E1 to Y7SOC. In addition, genetic and nonshared environmental influences contributed to the phenotypic correlation between social competence and reading achievement (.26) to similar degrees. Moreover, more than 50% of the phenotypic relationship between these variables is due to genetic influences shared with IQ, that is, $(.31 \times .50)/.26$, and all of the genetic relationship between social competence and reading is due to influences shared with IQ. However, there is substantial independent genetic and nonshared environmental variation in both social competence and reading.

DISCUSSION

Results of our analyses confirm earlier findings of moderate genetic influence on individual differences in reading achievement at each age. The finding of higher heritability for the older age group is consistent with results of studies of cognitive ability demonstrating higher heritability in late adolescence and adulthood (DeFries et al., 1987; McGue et al., 1993; Plomin et al., 1997). Also consistent with previous studies of reading achievement based on data from the CAP (e.g., Wadsworth et al., 2001), there is evidence for substantial and significant genetic influence on the continuity of individual differences in reading achievement from 7 to 16 years of age, some of which may be mediated through cognitive ability, for which substantial and significant genetic continuity has also been demonstrated (e.g., Cherny, Fulker, & Hewitt, 1997; DeFries et al., 1987; Fulker, Cherny, & Cardon, 1993; Fulker & Cherny, 1995). In addition, there is evidence for modest influence of shared and nonshared environment on continuity.

Although these results suggest substantial age-to-age continuity for reading achievement, largely due to genetic influences common to the three ages, there is also evidence for significant *independent* variation at each age, due almost entirely to nonshared environmental influences (i.e., individual experiences that do not contribute to sibling resemblance). Some potential nonshared environmental influences include extrafamilial factors, such as instructional methods, teachers, and peers (Harris, 1998). It is also important to note that measurement error is included in estimates of nonshared environmental influences. A feature of the adoption design is that siblings are tested based on their age, rather than based on the proband's age. As a result, comparable measures for members of a sibling pair are typically collected an average of three years apart, increasing the opportunity for nonshared environmental influences to operate.

Analysis of environmental influences in the current study suggests that both parenting style and social competence appear to have exerted their influence by middle childhood. However, whereas social competence appears to have a direct influence on reading achievement, the effects of parenting are indirect, possibly mediated by social competence; that is, positive parenting may contribute to social competence which, in turn, may influence achievement, possibly due to positive relationships with teachers and peers and/or resistance to negative peer pressure, resulting in a more effective learning environment.

Genetic designs are powerful for identifying shared and nonshared environmental influences while controlling for genetic influences. Multivariate genetic approaches can decompose the covariance between environmental measures and achievement into genetic, shared and nonshared environmental mediation and can be extended to explore age-to-age change and continuity as a function of measured environments. In the present study, such multivariate genetic analyses of environmental measures were not possible because measures of home environment atmosphere and parenting are too weakly related to measured reading achievement. It is, of course, possible that these measures of family "atmosphere" are not as likely to show associations with reading as are other measures of the family environment such as parental attitudes toward education.

Analysis of the relationship between mediators (IQ and social competence) and reading achievement indicated that the phenotypic correlation between social competence and reading achievement is attributable to both genetic and nonshared environmental influences, and that nearly half of the phenotypic relationship between these variables is due to influences shared with IQ. In addition, all of the genetic relationship between social competence and reading is due to genetic influences shared with IQ.

Results of this study highlight the importance of social competence in the development of achievement within the normal range of scores. However, the underlying processes driving this relationship are unspecified. As suggested earlier, social competence may promote better teacher–student and peer relationships which, in turn, enhance the learning environment; social skills deficits may have a negative effect on these relationships and/or decrease resistance to peer pressure, hindering learning. What is clear is that research on the environmental correlates of reading should begin to focus on nonshared environment because of the major influence of nonshared environment on the variance of reading and especially on age-to-age change in reading, independent of genetic and family environmental factors.

A possible limitation of adoption studies is that shared environmental influences may be underestimated due to putative restricted range of family environmental quality (Stoolmiller, 1998, 1999). In the CAP, adoptive and nonadoptive families are matched on demographic variables such as parental education and occupation. Further, means and variances on other measures of family environment are similar for the two groups (Rhea & Corley, 1994). As a result, the internal consistency of the adoption design is not compromised. However, due to the nature of the adoption process, extreme environmental conditions are not represented in the CAP. Thus, CAP families, and therefore results of these analyses, are primarily representative of middle-class Caucasian families, and may not be applicable to children at risk for achievement difficulties.

Another limitation of the current study is the relatively small number of younger siblings with data at the older ages, particularly when divided by family type and sex. As data on more siblings becomes available at the older ages, it will be possible to test hypotheses about environmental influences on adolescent reading achievement more rigorously.

In conclusion, the results of this study suggest that genetic and shared environmental influences operating on academic achievement at ages 7, 12, and 16 are highly stable, launching children on a trajectory by age 7 that will largely be maintained through age 16. However, whereas shared environmental influences are consistently modest at each age, genetic influences appear to be more important in later adolescence, as reading development matures. Perturbations from this trajectory are due to nonshared environmental influences, which do not persist across wide age ranges. This finding suggests that achievement may be facilitated or impeded by strong extrafamilial influences, such as the school environment or peers. However, characteristics of the child, such as social competence and IQ, both of which show moderate genetic influence, may mediate the relationship between measures of the environment and reading achievement. In addition, social competence is influenced, at least in part, by positive parenting.

Future analyses should explore further the etiology of these relationships to isolate other possible common factors. The CAP is ongoing, and additional siblings, as well as a longitudinal sample of twin pairs, are still being tested at age 16 as well as at later ages. Therefore, as more data become available, future CAP analyses will have greater power to test hypotheses about the etiology of the relationship between environmental influences, social competence, IQ, and academic achievement, as well as about continuity and change from middle childhood through late adolescence and into early adulthood.

APPENDIX

Calculation of Heritability, Environmentality, and Genetic and Environmental Correlations

Proportions of variance in reading achievement at each age due to genetic (heritability) and environmental (environmentality) influences are calculated from the standardized path coefficients as the sum of the squared paths from common and specific factors to each measure. For example, from Figure 5.1, the heritability (a^2) of Y7READ is simply the square of the path from A_1 to Y7READ (i.e., a_{11}^2), whereas the heritability of Y12READ is the square of the path from A_1 to Y12READ, plus the square of the path from A_2 to Y12READ (i.e., $a_{21}^2 + a_{22}^2$). Estimates of shared (c^2) and nonshared (e^2) environmental influences are obtained in a corresponding manner.

Estimates of the genetic, shared environmental and nonshared environmental correlations between the measures (i.e., the extent to which the same genes or environmental factors are influencing reading achievement at the different time points, r_A, r_C, and r_E, respectively) are also obtained from the standardized path coefficients. For example, $(a_{21} \times a_{31}) + (a_{22} \times a_{32}) = a_{Y12READ} \times r_A \times a_{Y16READ}$, the phenotypically standardized genetic correlation, where a is the square root of the heritability of the indicated measure, and r_A is the genetic correlation. Thus, the genetic correlation may be estimated from the ratio of the phenotypically standardized genetic correlation to the product of the square roots of the two heritabilities (i.e., $r_A = a_{Y12READ} \times r_A \times a_{Y16READ} / a_{Y12READ} \times a_{Y16READ}$). Further, the ratio of the phenotypically standardized genetic correlation to the phenotypic correlation estimates bivariate heritability, the proportion of the observed covariation due to shared genetic influences, i.e., $[(a_{21} \times a_{31}) + (a_{22} \times a_{32})] / r_P$ (Plomin & DeFries, 1979).

Model Specification

Because of the variability in patterns of missing data in the CAP, raw data were modeled for the genetic analyses using the Mx statistical modeling package (Neale, Boker, Xie, & Maes, 2002), thus allowing the use of all available data and the maximum likelihood estimation of parameters. In the case of data from sibling pairs, this involves the calculation of twice the negative log-likelihood ($-2LL$) for each observation (i.e., each sibling pair), and the summation of these across all pairs. For model comparisons, the difference between $-2LL$ for the two models is distributed asymptotically as a chi-square, with degrees of freedom equal to the difference in the number of free parameters estimated in each model. The full sibling model includes a total of 30 free parameters: 18 estimated path coefficients and 12 estimated means (means for probands and siblings at each of three time points for both adoptive and nonadoptive pairs, which are required when modeling raw data rather than covariance matrices).

The Colorado Adoption Project is supported by grants HD-10333 and HD-18426 from the National Institute of Child Health and Human Development (NICHD), and grant MH-43899 from the National Institute of Mental Health (NIMH). The continued cooperation of the many families participating in the CAP is gratefully acknowledged.

References

Alarcn, M., & DeFries, J. C. (1995). Quantitative trait locus for reading disability: An alternative test [Abstract]. *Behavior Genetics, 25,* 253.
Bast, J., & Reitsma, P. (1998). Analyzing the development of individual differences in terms of Matthew effects of reading: Results from a Dutch longitudinal study. *Developmental Psychology, 34,* 1373–1399.

Cardon, L. R., DiLalla, L. F., Plomin, R., DeFries, J. C., & Fulker, D. W. (1990). Genetic correlations between reading performance and IQ in the Colorado Adoption Project. *Intelligence, 14*, 245–257.

Cherny, S. S., Fulker, D. W., & Hewitt, J. K. (1997). Cognitive development from infancy to middle childhood. In R. Sternberg & E. Grigorenko (Eds.) *Intelligence, heredity, and environment* (pp. 463–482). Cambridge: Cambridge University Press.

DeFries, J. C. (1988). Colorado Reading Project: Longitudinal analyses. *Annals of Dyslexia, 38*, 120–130.

DeFries, J. C., & Baker, L. A. (1983). Parental contributions to longitudinal stability of cognitive measures in the Colorado Family Reading Study. *Child Development, 54*, 388–395.

DeFries, J. C., Plomin, R., & Fulker, D. W. (1994). *Nature and nurture during middle childhood*. Oxford: Blackwell.

DeFries, J. C., Plomin, R., & LaBuda, M. (1987). Genetic stability of cognitive development from childhood to adulthood. *Developmental Psychology, 23*, 4–12.

Dibble, E., & Cohen, D. J. (1974). Companion instruments for measuring children's competence and parental style. *Archives of General Psychiatry, 30*, 805–815.

Dunn, L. M., & Markwardt, F. C. (1970). *Examiner's Manual: Peabody Individual Achievement Test*. Circle Pines, MN: American Guidance Service.

Fisher, S. E., & DeFries, J. C. (2002). Developmental dyslexia: Genetic dissection of a complex cognitive trait. *Nature Reviews: Neuroscience, 3*, 767–782.

Fulker, D. W., & Cherny, S. S. (1995). Genetic and environmental influences on cognition during childhood. *Population Research and Policy Review, 14*, 283– 300.

Fulker, D. W., Cherny, S. S., & Cardon, L. R. (1993). Continuity and change in cognitive development. In R. Plomin & G. E. McClearn (Eds.), *Nature, nurture, and psychology* (pp. 99–120). Washington, DC: American Psychological Association.

Harris, J. R. (1998). *The nurture assumption: Why children turn out the way they do.* New York: The Free Press.

Jimerson, S., Egeland, B., & Teo, A. (1999). A longitudinal study of achievement trajectories: Factors associated with change. *Journal of Educational Psychology, 91*, 116–126.

Knopik, V. S., & DeFries, J. C. (1999). Etiology of covariation between reading and mathematics performance: A twin study. *Twin Research, 2*, 226–234.

Koutsoulis, M. K., & Campbell, J. R. (2001). Family processes affect students' motivation, and science and math achievement in Cypriot high schools. *Structural Equation Modeling, 8*, 108–127.

McGue, M., Bouchard, T. J., Jr., Iacono, W. G., & Lykken, D. T. (1993). Behavioral genetics of cognitive ability: A life-span perspective. In R. Plomin & G. E. McClearn (Eds.) *Nature, nurture, and psychology* (pp. 59–76). Washington, DC: American Psychological Association.

Moos, R. H., & Moos, B. S. (1981). *The Family Environmental Scale manual*. Palo Alto, CA: Consulting Psychologists Press.

Neale, M. C., & Cardon, L. R. (1992). *Methodology for genetic studies of twins and families*. NATO ASI series. Dordrecht, The Netherlands: Kluwer Academic Press.

Neale, M. C., Boker, S. M., Xie, G., & Maes, H. H. (2002). Mx: Statistical modeling. *(6th ed.) [Computer software]*, Richmond, VA: Department of Psychiatry, Virginia Commonwealth University.

Petrill, S. A., Plomin, R., DeFries, J. C., & Hewitt, J. C. (2003). *Nature, nurture, and the transition to early adolescence.* New York: Oxford University Press.

Plomin, R. (1994). *Genetics and experience: The interplay between nature and nurture.* Newbury Park, CA: Sage Publications.

Plomin, R., & DeFries, J. C. (1979). Multivariate behavioral as genetic analysis of twin data on scholastic abilities. *Behavior Genetics, 9,* 505–517.

Plomin, R. & DeFries, J. C. (1985). *Origins of individual differences in infancy: The Colorado Adoption Project.* Orlando, FL: Academic Press.

Plomin, R., DeFries, J. C., & Fulker, D. W. (1988). *Nature and nurture during infancy and early childhood.* Cambridge: Cambridge University Press.

Plomin, R., Fulker, D. W., Corley, R., & DeFries, J. C. (1997). Nature, nurture, and cognitive development from 1 to 16 years: A parent-offspring adoption study. *Psychological Science, 8,* 442–447.

Rhea, S. A., & Corley, R. (1994). Applied Issues. In J. C. DeFries, R. Plomin, & D. W. Fulker (Eds.) *Nature and nurture during middle childhood* (pp. 295–309). Oxford: Blackwell.

Robinson, N. M., Lanzi, R. G., Weinberg, R. A., Ramey, S. L., & Ramey, C. T. (2002). Family factors associated with high academic competence in former head start children at third grade. *Gifted Child Quarterly, 46,* 278–290.

Shaywitz, S. E., Escobar, M. D., Shaywitz, B. A., Fletcher, J. M., & Makuch, R. (1992). Evidence that dyslexia may represent the lower tail of a normal distribution of reading ability. *New England Journal of Medicine, 326,* 144–150.

Stevenson, J., Graham, P., Fredman, G., & McLoughlin, V. (1987). A twin study of genetic influences on reading and spelling ability and disability. *Journal of Child Psychology and Psychiatry, 28,* 229–247.

Stoolmiller, M. (1998). Correcting estimates of shared environmental variance for range restriction in adoption studies using a truncated multivariate normal model. *Behavior Genetics, 28,* 429–441.

Stoolmiller, M. (1999). Implications of the restricted range of family environments for estimates of heritability and nonshared environment in behavior-genetic adoption studies. *Psychological Bulletin, 125,* 392–405.

Wadsworth, S. J., Corley, R., Hewitt, J. K., & DeFries, J. C. (2001). Stability of genetic and environmental influences on reading performance at 7, 12, and 16 years of age in the Colorado Adoption Project. *Behavior Genetics, 31,* 353–359.

Wadsworth, S. J., & DeFries, J. C. (2003). Etiology of the stability of reading performance from 7 to 12 years of age and its possible mediation by IQ. In S. A. Petrill, R. Plomin, J. C. DeFries, & J. K. Hewitt (Eds.) *Nature, nurture, and the transition to early adolescence* (pp. 49–61). New York: Oxford University Press.

Wadsworth, S. J., Fulker, D. W., & DeFries, J. C. (1999). Stability of genetic and environmental influences on reading performance at 7 and 12 years of age in the Colorado Adoption Project. *International Journal of Behavioral Development, 23,* 319–332.

Wagner, R. K., Torgesen, J. K., Rashotte, C. A., Hecht, S. A., Barker, T. A., Burgess, et al. (1997). Changing relations between phonological processing abilities and word-level reading as children develop from beginning to skilled readers: A 5-year longitudinal study. *Developmental Psychology, 33,* 468–479.

Walker, H. M., & McConnell, S. W. (1988). *Walker-McConnell Scale of Social Competence and School Adjustment.* Austin, TX: Pro-Ed.

Welsh, M., Parke, R. D., Widaman, K., & O'Neil, R. (2001). Linkages between children's social and academic competence: A longitudinal analysis. *Journal of School Psychology, 39,* 463–482.

Wechsler, D. (1974). *Examiner's manual: Wechsler Intelligence Scale for Children-Revised.* New York: The Psychological Corporation.

Williams, S., & McGee, R. (1996). Reading in childhood and mental health in early adulthood. In J. H. Beitchman, N.J. Cohen, M. M. Konstantareas, & R. Tannock (Eds.), *Language, learning, and behavior disorders: Developmental, biological, and clinical perspectives* (pp. 530–554). Cambridge: Cambridge University Press.

6

Reciprocal Effects of Mothers' Depression and Children's Problem Behaviors from Middle Childhood to Early Adolescence

Sara R. Jaffee and Richie Poulton

Children whose mothers are depressed are at risk for a range of difficulties in childhood and adolescence, including emotional and behavioral problems, attachment and academic difficulties, and problems in self-regulation, peer relationships, and sleep regulation (see reviews by Cummings & Davies, 1994; Downey & Coyne, 1990; Goodman & Gotlib, 1999; Herring & Kaslow, 2002; Teti, Gelfand, & Pompa, 1990). In this chapter, we focus specifically on the association between mothers' anxious, depressed symptoms and children's emotional problems (e.g., anxious, depressed behavior, also called internalizing problems) and behavioral problems (e.g., aggressive, disruptive, undercontrolled behavior, also called externalizing problems). We refer to emotional and behavioral problems, collectively, as "problem behaviors." The mechanisms by which mothers' depression has been hypothesized to influence children's problem behaviors include genetic transmission of risk for psychopathology, neurodevelopmental insult in the prenatal or perinatal periods, difficulties in parent–child interaction, and social stressors that may impinge on parent and child functioning alike (Goodman & Gotlib, 1999).

These hypotheses about the association between maternal depression and children's outcomes assume that maternal depression plays a causal role in the development of children's problem behaviors. However, relatively little research has considered the possibility that children's problem behaviors may be implicated in the etiology or maintenance of a mothers' depression, even though a sizeable body of literature exists to show how parents' behavior often changes in response to their children (Anderson, Lytton, & Romney, 1986; Bell & Harper, 1977; Bell & Chapman, 1986; Brunk & Henggeler, 1984; Buss, 1981; Grusec & Kuczynski, 1980; Lytton, 1990; Mink & Nihira, 1986; Patterson, Reid, & Dishion, 1992; Yarrow, Waxler, & Scott, 1971). Evidence for a bidirectional association between mothers' depression and children's behavior comes from (a) correlational studies that test for effects of children's behavior on mothers' depression and, to a lesser degree, (b) evaluations of how treatment for maternal depression affects children's behavior or how treatment for children's problem behaviors affects mothers' depression.

EVIDENCE FOR CHILD EFFECTS ON MOTHERS' DEPRESSION AND FOR BIDIRECTIONAL INFLUENCES IN THE ASSOCIATION BETWEEN MOTHERS' DEPRESSION AND CHILDREN'S PROBLEM BEHAVIORS

Feske and colleagues (2001) found that depressed mothers cited child-related stressors such as children's noncompliant or disobedient behavior as important precursors of their depressive episodes. Other studies have shown that parent and child psychological distress are reciprocally related. In a study of 8–16-year-old children and their clinically depressed and nondepressed mothers, Hammen, Burge, and Stansbury (1990) detected a cycle of negative, mutual influence in which poor maternal functioning (as indexed by the severity of the mother's current symptomatology, degree of impairment, and negative communication with her child) was related to child maladjustment, and child maladjustment reciprocally contributed to poor maternal functioning.

In a longitudinal follow-up of this sample, Hammen, Burge, and Adrian (1991) reported that the timing of mothers' and children's episodes of depression was strongly associated. In approximately half of the dyads, the onset of the child's depression followed a worsening of the mother's depression, and in the other half the onset of the child's depression was followed by a worsening of the mother's depression. In a sample of adolescents followed from seventh through ninth grade, Ge, Conger, Lorenz, Shanahan, and Elder (1995) reported that levels of parents' and children's psychological distress (i.e., symptoms of depression, anxiety, and hostility) were reciprocally related, even taking into account the stability of psychological distress over time. Finally, a study by Kim, Conger, Elder, and Lorenz (2003) found evidence for reciprocal relations over time between adolescents' experiences of life stressors and their internalizing and externalizing problems. To the extent that parents' mental health problems represent a potent life stressor (Hammen et al., 1991), the study by Kim and colleagues (2003) provides further support for the hypothesis that the association between parents' and children's psychological distress can be bidirectional.

Two types of experimental intervention studies provide evidence of bidirectional parent–child effects, although the evidence is weak in both cases. Experimental interventions that are designed to decrease children's behavior problems have shown that improvements in children's behavior are associated with decreases in mothers' depressive symptoms, although only in combination with cognitive behavioral therapy for the mothers' depression (Sanders, Markie-Dadds, Tully, & Bor, 2000; Sanders & McFarland, 2000).

One study of treatment for postpartum depression showed greater improvements in mothers' reports of the mother–infant relationship among mothers who received treatment versus those who did not (Cooper & Murray, 1997). Moreover, children whose mothers' depression remitted at a relatively early stage were less likely to show insecure attachment compared to children whose mothers' depression persisted. However, other measures of children's outcomes (e.g., cognitive attainment, observed mother–child interaction, early infant sleeping and feeding problems) were unaffected by treatment of the mothers' depression and improvement in maternal mood (Cooper & Murray, 1997). Although studies of treatment for postpartum depression tend not to follow children beyond early childhood, nonexperimental, longitudinal studies have failed to find significant changes in children's behavior after a mother's depression has remitted (Lee & Gotlib, 1991; Timko, Cronkite, Berg, & Moos, 2002). Taken together, these studies suggest that although a mother's depression may be implicated in the etiology of her children's behavior problems and vice versa, psychological distress of one or both members in the dyad is maintained by additional factors, such that targeting only the mother's depression or the child's problem behavior is insufficient to produce change in the behavior of the other member of the dyad.

AGE- AND GENDER-RELATED CHANGES IN THE ASSOCIATION BETWEEN MOTHERS' DEPRESSION AND CHILDREN'S PROBLEM BEHAVIORS

Timing of Maternal Depression

Although there is evidence to support the hypothesis that mothers' and children's psychological distress may be reciprocally related, the strength of reciprocal effects may change over time as a function of the timing of the mother's depression and the child's age. Depression recurs in the vast majority of individuals who have a first episode, but the importance of psychosocial stressors in provoking recurrent episodes of depression diminishes over time (Post, 1992). To the extent that children's problem behaviors represent a potent psychosocial stressor, it would be expected that (a) their effect would be strongest relatively early in childhood when most mothers will have experienced fewer episodes of depression, and (b) that the effect of a child's problem behaviors would weaken over time as the stability of the mother's depression became a stronger predictor of her future episodes.

Moreover, the effects of mothers' depression on children's behavior might be strongest during periods of transition in childhood. In middle childhood, children are making transitions to school and to a larger peer group and children need a range of social and academic skills in order to be successful in these settings. During such transitions, children may rely more heavily on parents as sources of social and emotional support. Children who are facing such major life transitions in addition to their mothers' depression may be particularly at risk for problem behaviors, especially if children cannot find support from other members of their family or from other individuals. Thus, it might be expected that mothers' depression would have the strongest effect on children's problem behaviors during the transition to middle childhood and, again, during the transition to adolescence when children are faced with a new set of social challenges and biological changes.

Our other work has shown that a mother's depressive symptomatology during the early and middle childhood period is more strongly associated with her child's clinical depression if her child had a first episode of major depressive disorder in childhood or adolescence, rather than in young adulthood (Jaffee et al., 2002). However, because of sample size limitations, and because diagnoses of depression were first made when the individuals were 11 years old, we were unable to determine whether maternal depressive symptomatology was more prevalent in families where individuals first became depressed in middle childhood versus early adolescence.

Gender Effects

Several studies have shown that maternal depression is more strongly associated with daughters' rather than sons' problem behaviors (Davies & Windle, 1997; Fergusson, Horwood, & Lynskey, 1995; Hops, 1992; for an exception, see Ge et al., 1995). Developmental accounts of how mothers' depression influences children's outcomes have hypothesized that boys are more strongly affected by a mothers' depression in childhood than in adolescence. In contrast, girls are hypothesized to be more vulnerable to a mother's depression in adolescence versus childhood. Compared to boys, adolescent girls are thought to use more relationship-focused and fewer instrumental behaviors to cope with the psychosocial stressors associated with a mother's depression. This coping style is itself a risk factor for adolescent depression (Cummings & Davies, 1994; Davies & Windle, 1997; Hops, 1995; Petersen, 1988).

Some support for this hypothesis has been found. Davies and Windle (1997) reported that although family discord characterized the homes of depressed mothers of sons and daughters to equal degrees, family discord accounted for the link between mothers' depression and daughters' (but not sons') internalizing and externalizing problems. Similarly, Fergusson et al. (1995) reported that family discord mediated the association between mothers' and daughters' depression. Hops (1992; 1995) found that the association between mothers' and daughters' depression was stronger for girls in adolescence than for younger girls and that mothers' dysphoric mood predicted daughters' mood over a four year period. Although there was a concurrent association between fathers' and sons' dysphoric mood, there was no association over time. However, Ge and colleagues (1995) failed to support the hypothesis that mothers' psychological distress (e.g., depression, anxiety, hostility) would be a stronger predictor of adolescent daughters' versus sons' psychological distress. These discrepant findings across studies might have been due to differences in how psychological distress was measured.

Another hypothesis is that maternal depression is linked to boys' externalizing problems and to girls' internalizing problems (Cummings & Davies, 1994), although little empirical support for this hypothesis has been provided (Sheeber, Davis, & Hops, 2002). This hypothesis is based on the epidemiology of children's problem behaviors. Boys have higher rates of externalizing problems than girls, and girls have higher rates of internalizing problems than boys. According to this hypothesis, children react to psychosocial stressors by manifesting whichever disorder is sex-typical. An extension of this hypothesis posits that daughters of depressed mothers are more vulnerable than boys to depression because family socialization processes may normalize or encourage girls' depressive behavior (for a review, see Sheeber et al., 2002). However, strong sex differences in internalizing problems do not emerge until adolescence (Cyranowski, Frank, Young, & Shear, 2000; Hankin et al., 1998; Hankin & Abramson, 2001), whereas sex differences in externalizing problems narrow in adolescence (Keenan & Shaw, 1997; Moffitt, Caspi, Rutter, & Silva, 2001; Silverthorn & Frick, 1999). Thus, it might be expected that, in childhood, maternal depression would be associated with boys' but not girls' externalizing problems and with both boys' and girls' internalizing problems. In contrast, in adolescence, mothers' depression would be associated with girls' but not boys' internalizing problems and with both boys' and girls' externalizing problems.

The current study was designed to test whether mothers' symptoms of depression predicted changes in children's problem behaviors, whether children's problem behaviors predicted changes in mothers' symptoms of depression, or whether mothers' and children's mental health problems interacted in a mutually negative, reciprocal fashion. The current study was also designed to test whether the association between mothers' depression and children's problem behaviors was the same or different in middle childhood versus early adolescence and for girls and boys. Based on our reading of the literature, we made the following hypotheses.

Hypothesis 1: Given the evidence of bidirectional effects between parents' and children's psychological distress, we predicted that mothers' depression and children's problem behaviors would be reciprocally related over time.

Hypothesis 2: The effect of children's problem behaviors on mothers' depression would be strongest in early childhood given the finding that psychosocial stressors become less potent predictors of depression over time (Post, 1992).

Hypothesis 3: Given that children are most vulnerable to psychosocial stressors during periods of transition, the effects of a mother's depression on children's problem behaviors would be strongest during the transition to middle childhood and the transition to adolescence.

Hypothesis 4: Because some studies have shown that mothers' depression is specifically linked to girls' outcomes, we predicted that mothers' depression would predict girls' but not boys' problem behaviors.

Hypothesis 5: Given the evidence that children react to psychosocial stressors by manifesting whichever disorder is typical of their sex, we predicted that mothers' depression would be linked to boys' externalizing and internalizing problems in middle childhood and to girls' internalizing problems in middle childhood. We also predicted that mothers' depression would be linked to boys' externalizing problems in adolescence and to girls' internalizing and externalizing problems in adolescence.

METHOD

Participants

Participants are part of the Dunedin Multidisciplinary Health and Development Study, a longitudinal investigation of health and behavior in a complete birth cohort (Silva & Stanton, 1996). The study members were born between April 1, 1972, and March 31, 1973, in Dunedin, New Zealand. Of these, 1037 children (91% of eligible births; 52% male) participated in the first follow-up at age 3 years, forming the base sample for the longitudinal study. Cohort families are primarily white and represent the full range of socioeconomic status in the general population of New Zealand's South Island.

The Dunedin sample has been assessed with a diverse battery of psychological, medical, and sociological measures with high rates of participation at age 3 ($n = 1,037$), 5 ($n = 991$), 7 ($n = 954$), 9 ($n = 955$), 11 ($n = 925$), 13 ($n = 850$), 15 ($n = 976$), 18 ($n = 993$), 21 ($n = 992$), and, most recently, 26 ($n = 980$; 96% of the living cohort members). The research procedure involves bringing four study members per day (including emigrants living overseas) to the research unit within 60 days of their birthdays for a full day of individual data collection. Each research topic is presented, in private, as a standardized module by a different trained examiner in counterbalanced order throughout the day. In addition, data are gathered from sources such as parents, partners, and courts.

TABLE 6.1. *Descriptive Statistics for Mothers' Internalizing Symptoms and Children's Problem Behaviors*

Variable (Child's Age When Variable Was Measured)	Means (Standard Deviation)	Range
Mother's internalizing symptoms (5)	2.30 (2.89)	0–18
Mother's internalizing symptoms (7)	1.93 (2.44)	0–14
Mother's internalizing symptoms (9)	1.88 (2.48)	0–14
Mother's internalizing symptoms (11)	2.84 (3.16)	0–18
Mother's internalizing symptoms (13)	2.88 (3.38)	0–17
Mother's internalizing symptoms (15)	2.81 (3.22)	0–19
Child antisocial behavior (5)	2.43 (2.04)	0–12
Child antisocial behavior (7)	2.07 (1.99)	0–11
Child antisocial behavior (9)	1.95 (1.93)	0–11
Child antisocial behavior (11)	1.71 (1.86)	0–10
Child antisocial behavior (13)	6.89 (7.33)	0–60
Child antisocial behavior (15)	8.43 (8.41)	0–56
Child anxious/depressed behavior (5)	1.95 (1.80)	0–9
Child anxious/depressed behavior (7)	2.23 (1.77)	0–9
Child anxious/depressed behavior (9)	2.35 (1.80)	0–10
Child anxious/depressed behavior (11)	2.05 (1.82)	0–10
Child anxious/depressed behavior (13)	3.44 (3.34)	0–20
Child anxious/depressed behavior (15)	3.97 (3.49)	0–19

Measures

Descriptive statistics for all measures are reported in Table 6.1. Reliabilities for all measures exceeded $a = .70$ (McGee, Williams, Kashani, & Silva, 1983; McGee, Williams, & Silva, 1985, 1986; Quay & Peterson, 1987).

Mothers' Internalizing Symptoms. Mothers' internalizing symptoms were assessed when the study members were 5, 7, 9, 11, 13, and 15 years of age. At ages 5 and 7, mothers' internalizing symptoms were assessed with the Malaise Inventory (Rodgers, Pickles, Power, Collishaw, & Maughan, 1999), which includes 24 items that measure physical and psychological symptoms of depression and anxiety (e.g., "Do you often feel miserable and depressed?" "Are you frightened of going out alone or meeting people?"). Individuals received a score of 1 if they endorsed an item and 0 if they did not. Scores were summed. Although not a measure of clinical symptomatology, the Malaise Inventory has been shown to discriminate those with recent psychiatric morbidity and contact with services (Rodgers et al., 1999). When the study members were ages 9, 11, 13, and 15, mothers' internalizing symptoms were assessed with a 19-item version of the Malaise Inventory that was modified to assess psychological and physical symptoms of depression more fully and that did not assess anxious symptomatology (McGee et al., 1983). This modified measure was scored identically to the Malaise Inventory.

Child Problem Behaviors. When the study members were 5, 7, 9, 11, 13, and 15 years of age, mothers provided reports of children's anxious/depressed and antisocial behaviors (referred to collectively as "problem behaviors"). When study members were 5–11 years of age, mothers used the Rutter Child Behavior Scale (Rutter, Tizard, & Whitmore, 1970) to report children's anxious/depressed behavior (5 items; e.g., "often worried," "often appears miserable") and antisocial behavior (12 items; e.g., "frequently fights," "has stolen things"). Each item was scored on a 3-point scale (0 = "doesn't apply" to 2 = "certainly applies"), and scores were summed.

When the study members were 13 and 15 years of age, their mothers used the Revised Behavior Problem Checklist (Quay & Peterson, 1987) to report children's problem behaviors. Items were scored on a 3-point scale (0 = "doesn't apply" to 2 = "certainly applies"), and scores were summed. Items from the 39-item antisocial scale include "truants from school" and "irritable, hot-tempered." Items from the 11-item anxious/depressed scale include "says nobody loves him/her" and "generally fearful or anxious."

RESULTS

Our hypotheses posed five specific questions about the association between mothers' internalizing symptoms and child problem behaviors, but for the sake of parsimony, our analysis plan is organized around the two types of children's problem behaviors (antisocial and anxious/depressed) and three broad issues that cut across the hypotheses: reciprocal effects (versus parent or child effects), gender, and timing. First, for each child behavioral outcome, we will determine if the association between mothers' internalizing symptoms and the children's problem behavior is the same for boys and girls. Second, we will examine the reciprocal effects model between mothers' internalizing symptoms and their children's problem behavior (by sex if warranted). Finally, we will consider the importance of the timing of mother's depression and children's problem behaviors across middle childhood and early adolescence.

Table 6.2 presents the correlations among mothers' internalizing symptoms measured from age 5 to 15 and children's problem behaviors measured over the same period. Mothers' internalizing symptoms and children's behavior problems were stable over time, as indexed by correlations that were moderate to large in magnitude. For example, correlations across the six waves of data collection ranged from .45 to .71 for measures of mothers' internalizing symptoms, from .36 to .72 for measures of children's antisocial behavior, and from .25 to .66 for measures of children's anxious/depressed behavior. Correlations between mothers' internalizing

TABLE 6.2. *Correlations Between Mothers' Internalizing Symptoms and Children's Problem Behaviors from Age 5 to 15*

		1	2	3	4	5	6	7	8	9	10	11	12	13	14	15	16	17	18
1	M Int 5	1.00																	
2	M-Int 7	.63	1.00																
3	M- Int 9	.58	.63	1.00															
4	M-Int 11	.47	.54	.60	1.00														
5	M-Int 13	.47	.49	.55	.71	1.00													
6	M-Int 15	.45	.49	.52	.63	.65	1.00												
7	ASB 5	.28	.25	.20	.18	.17	.20	1.00											
8	ASB 7	.27	.31	.26	.24	.23	.20	.57	1.00										
9	ASB 9	.21	.23	.24	.21	.21	.18	.51	.68	1.00									
10	ASB 11	.28	.30	.30	.31	.28	.29	.47	.56	.64	1.00								
11	ASB 13	.24	.24	.28	.33	.32	.34	.40	.47	.53	.59	1.00							
12	ASB 15	.23	.19	.22	.24	.26	.31	.36	.38	.45	.53	.72	1.00						
13	Ax/Dep 5	.24	.20	.17	.19	.18	.17	.35	.20	.18	.15	.17	.13	1.00					
14	Ax/Dep 7	.24	.28	.18	.22	.20	.16	.25	.36	.23	.19	.17	.09	.49	1.00				
15	Ax/Dep 9	.19	.23	.24	.23	.20	.17	.26	.28	.38	.24	.20	.12	.50	.55	1.00			
16	Ax/Dep 11	.24	.29	.26	.19	.26	.22	.23	.24	.28	.41	.27	.19	.40	.49	.58	1.00		
17	Ax/Dep 13	.16	.22	.22	.31	.33	.28	.24	.27	.29	.33	.51	.31	.30	.36	.45	.52	1.00	
18	Ax/Dep 15	.16	.22	.19	.28	.26	.26	.20	.19	.24	.26	.35	.37	.25	.28	.34	.44	.66	1.00

Note: M-Int = Mothers' Internalizing Symptoms; ASB = Children's Antisocial Behavior; Ax/Dep = Children's Anxious/Depressed Behavior. All $p <.01$.

symptoms and children's antisocial behavior ranged from .17 to .34 over time and correlations between mothers' internalizing symptoms and children's anxious/depressed behavior ranged from .16 to .33. All correlations were significant at $p < .01$.

Mothers' Internalizing Symptoms and Child Antisocial Behavior

Autoregressive, cross-lagged models were estimated using LISREL 8 (Jöreskog & Sörbom, 1996). One model was estimated for the association between mothers' internalizing symptoms and children's antisocial behavior, and a separate model was estimated for the association between mothers' internalizing symptoms and children's anxious/depressed behavior (see Table 6.3). A covariance matrix was used to estimate the cross-lagged, autoregressive models. Measurement errors for a given measure were correlated in adjoining time periods. Errors between measures were also correlated within each time period (e.g., measurement errors for mothers' internalizing symptoms at age 5 were correlated with measurement errors for children's problem behavior at age 5). Given their skewed distributions, measures of mothers' internalizing symptoms and children's problem behaviors were square root transformed to approximate normality.

The goal of fitting different structural equations is to account for the observed covariance structure using the most parsimonious number of parameters or to compare the fit of different theoretical models (e.g., parent effect versus child effect models). To compare the fit of different models, we used three model-selection statistics. The first was the χ^2 goodness-of-fit statistic. Large values indicate poor model fit to the observed covariance structure. When two models are nested (i.e., identical with the exception of constraints placed on the sub-model), the difference in fit between them can be evaluated with the χ^2 difference, using as its degrees of freedom the df difference from the two models. When the χ^2 difference is not statistically significant, the more parsimonious model is selected, as the test indicates that the constrained model fits equally well with the data. The second model-selection statistic was the Root Mean Square Error of Approximation (RMSEA), which is an index of the model discrepancy, per degree of freedom, from the observed covariance structure (MacCallum, Browne, & Sugawara, 1996). Values less than .05 indicate close fit and values less than .08 indicate fair fit to the data (Browne & Cudeck, 1993). Because the χ^2 tends to be significant when sample sizes are large, the third model-selection statistic was the Bayesian Information Criterion (BIC), where increasingly negative values correspond to increasingly better-fitting models. In comparing two models, differences in BIC larger than 10 represent strong evidence in favor of the model with the smaller value (Raftery, 1995). An advantage of the BIC statistic is that it can be used to compare non-nested models.

TABLE 6.3. *Fit Statistics for Models of the Association Between Mothers' Internalizing Symptoms and Children's Problem Behaviors*

	χ^2	df	p	RMSEA	BIC	χ^2_{diff} (df)
Child antisocial behavior & mothers' internalizing symptoms						
Sex variant model	71.70	64	.24	.019 (0–.038)	−347.48	
Sex invariant model	104.94	84	.06	.027 (0–.042)	−445.23	33.24 (20), p <.05
Males						
Reciprocal model	29.57	32	.59	.00 (0–.036)	−157.98	
Invariant over time	52.40	40	.09	.030 (0–.050)	−182.03	22.83 (8), p <.01
Equal reciprocal effects	41.67	37	.27	.019 (0–.044)	−175.18	12.10 (5), p <.05
Child effects model	48.54	37	.10	.030 (0–.051)	−168.13	18.97 (5), p <.01
Parent effects model	37.42	37	.45	.006 (0–.038)	−179.43	7.85 (5), ns
Invariant parent effects	54.36	41	.08	.031 (0–.051)	−185.93	16.94 (4), p <.01
Females						
Reciprocal model	42.13	32	.11	.030 (0–.053)	−145.14	
Invariant over time	64.42	40	.009	.042 (.021–.060)	−169.67	22.29 (8), p <.01
Equal reciprocal effects	46.70	37	.13	.028 (0–.050)	−169.83	4.57 (5), ns
Child effects model	76.57	37	.001	.056 (.038–.073)	−139.96	34.44 (5), p <.001
Parent effects model	50.92	37	.06	.033 (0–.054)	−165.61	8.79 (5), ns
Child anxious/depressed & mothers' internalizing symptoms						
Sex variant model	63.18	64	.51	.00 (0–.032)	−354.80	
Sex invariant model	72.66	84	.81	.00 (0–.020)	−475.93	9.48 (20), ns
Reciprocal model	36.78	32	.26	.015 (0–.033)	−172.21	
Invariant over time	62.68	40	.01	.029 (.014–.042)	−198.56	25.90 (8), p <.01
Equal reciprocal effects	48.99	37	.09	.022 (0–.037)	−192.65	12.21 (5), p <.05
Child effects model	81.31	37	.001	.042 (.030–.054)	−160.33	44.53 (5), p <.001
Parent effects model	47.77	37	.11	.021 (0–.036)	−193.87	10.99 (5), ns

Note: Best fitting models are in italics.

df = degrees of freedom; RMSEA = Root Mean Square Error of Approximation; BIC = Bayesian Information Criterion.

Is the Association Between Child Antisocial Behavior and Mothers' Internalizing Symptoms Different for Boys Versus Girls? To test whether the association between children's antisocial behavior and mothers' internalizing symptoms differed for boys and girls, a two-group model was estimated. The fit of a model in which all parameters were free to differ for boys versus girls (sex-variant model) was compared to a model in which the path coefficients between the measures of child antisocial behavior and mothers' internalizing symptoms were constrained to be equal for boys and girls (sex-invariant model). The constrained model fit significantly worse than the sex-variant model, indicating that the pattern of effects was different for boys and girls (Table 6.3). Consequently, the analyses were conducted separately by sex. Results are reported first for boys and then for girls.

Boys

RECIPROCAL MODEL. For boys, the fit of the reciprocal model was adequate as indicated by the nonsignificant χ^2, the RMSEA < .05, and the GFI = .99 (Table 6.3; Reciprocal Model). Boys' antisocial behavior and mothers' internalizing symptoms showed strong stability over time, with coefficients ranging from .53 to .99 and from .63 to .95, respectively. Mothers' internalizing symptoms more consistently predicted changes in boys' antisocial behavior than boys' antisocial behavior predicted changes in mothers' internalizing symptoms.

MAGNITUDE OF EFFECTS FROM CHILDHOOD TO ADOLESCENCE. We tested whether the effect of parent and child effects was the same across middle childhood and into early adolescence by constraining the paths from mothers' internalizing symptoms to boys' antisocial behavior to be equal in every period and constraining the paths from boys' antisocial behavior to mothers' internalizing symptoms to be equal in every period. The fit of the constrained model was significantly worse than the fit of the reciprocal model, indicating that the strength of the effect of mothers' internalizing symptoms on boys' antisocial behavior changed over time, as did the effect of boys' antisocial behavior on mothers' internalizing symptoms (Table 6.3; Invariant over Time Model). That is, mothers' internalizing symptoms predicted higher levels of boys' antisocial behavior at ages 7 and 11, but lower levels of boys' antisocial behavior at age 15. The effect of boys' antisocial behavior on mothers' internalizing symptoms was strongest when boys were younger.

We also tested whether parent and child effects were of equal magnitude to each other by constraining the cross-lagged paths to be equal within each period. For example, the path from boys' antisocial behavior at 5 to mothers' internalizing symptoms at 7 was constrained to be equal to the path from mothers' internalizing symptoms at 5 to boys' antisocial behavior at 7. Thus, this is a reciprocal effects model that adds the constraint that mothers' effects on children must be of similar magnitude to children's effects on parents. The constrained model fit significantly worse than the reciprocal model, indicating that the magnitude of parent and child effects differed within each period (Table 6.3; Equal Reciprocal Effects Model).

PARENT EFFECTS AND CHILD EFFECTS MODELS. To test the child effects model, all paths from mothers' internalizing symptoms to boys' antisocial behavior were constrained to zero and the paths from boys' antisocial behavior to mothers' internalizing symptoms were freely estimated. The fit of the child effects model was significantly worse than the fit of the reciprocal model (Table 6.3). To test the parent effects model, all paths from boys' antisocial behavior to mothers' internalizing symptoms were constrained to zero and the paths from mother's internalizing symptoms to boys' antisocial behavior were freely estimated. The fit of the parent effects model was not significantly worse than the fit of the reciprocal effects model (Table 6.3). Thus, for boys, a model in which mothers' internalizing symptoms predicted changes in boys' antisocial behavior fit better than a reciprocal or child effects model. Additionally, we tested whether the effect of mothers' internalizing symptoms on boys' antisocial behavior changed in magnitude over time by comparing the fit of the parent effects model to a model in which the effect of mothers' internalizing symptoms was constrained to be equal in every period. The fit of the constrained model was significantly worse than the fit of the unconstrained parent effects model, indicating that the magnitude of parent effects did differ significantly over time (Table 6.3; Invariant Parent Effects Model). Thus, the best-fitting model shows that mothers' internalizing symptoms predicted increases in boys' antisocial behavior during the transition to middle childhood (from age 5 to 7 years) and from age 9 to 11 years. However, in early adolescence (from age 13 to 15 years), mothers' internalizing symptoms predicted decreases in boys' antisocial behavior.

Girls

RECIPROCAL MODEL. For girls, the fit of the reciprocal model was adequate (Table 6.3). Girls' antisocial behavior and mothers' internalizing symptoms showed moderate to strong stability over time, with coefficients ranging from .45 to .96 and from .56 to 1.0, respectively. Mothers' internalizing symptoms were a more consistent predictor of changes in girls' antisocial behavior than the reverse, but girls' antisocial behavior did predict mothers' internalizing symptoms.

MAGNITUDE OF EFFECTS FROM CHILDHOOD TO ADOLESCENCE. We tested whether parent and child effects were constant across middle childhood and into early adolescence by constraining the paths from mothers' internalizing symptoms to girls' antisocial behavior to be equal in every period and constraining the paths from girls' antisocial behavior to mothers' internalizing symptoms to be equal in every period. The fit of the constrained model was significantly worse than the fit of the reciprocal model, indicating that the effect of mothers' internalizing symptoms on girls' antisocial behavior varied over time, as did the effect of girls' antisocial behavior on mothers' internalizing symptoms (Table 6.3; Invariant over Time Model).

We also tested whether parent and child effects were of equal magnitude by constraining the paths to be equal within each period. For example, the path from girls' antisocial behavior at 5 to mothers' internalizing symptoms at 7 was constrained to be equal to the path from mothers' internalizing symptoms at 5 to girls' antisocial behavior at 7. Thus, this is a reciprocal effects model that adds the constraint that the magnitude of the effect of mothers' internalizing symptoms on girls' antisocial behavior must equal the magnitude of the effect of girls' antisocial behavior on mothers' internalizing symptoms. The constrained model did not fit significantly worse than the reciprocal model, indicating that the magnitude of parent and child effects within each period was similar (Table 6.3; Equal Reciprocal Effects Model).

PARENT AND CHILD EFFECTS. For girls, the fit of the child effects model was significantly worse than the fit of the reciprocal model. The parent effects model did not fit significantly worse than the reciprocal model (Table 6.3). However, the equal reciprocal effects model was chosen as a better-fitting model than the parent effects model (even though these models were not nested) because it was also more parsimonious than the reciprocal model and because it had a smaller χ^2 value, a smaller RMSEA, and a more negative BIC than the parent effects model. The model showed that mothers' internalizing symptoms and girls' antisocial behavior were significantly, reciprocally related across middle childhood but not in early adolescence.

Mothers' Internalizing Symptoms and Children's Anxious/Depressed Behavior

Is the Association Between Children's Anxious/Depressed Behavior and Mothers' Internalizing Symptoms Different for Boys Versus Girls? To test whether the association between children's anxious/depressed behavior and mothers' internalizing symptoms differed for boys and girls, a two-group model was estimated. The fit of a model in which all parameters were free to differ for boys versus girls (sex-variant model) was compared to a model in which the path coefficients between the measures of children's anxious/depressed behaviors and mothers' internalizing symptoms were constrained to be equal (sex-invariant model). The constrained model did not fit significantly worse than the sex-variant model, indicating that the pattern of effects was similar for boys and girls (Table 6.3). Consequently, the analyses were conducted on the whole sample combining boys and girls.

Reciprocal Model. The fit of the reciprocal model was adequate (Table 6.3). Children's anxious/depressed behaviors and mothers' internalizing symptoms were moderately to highly stable over time, with coefficients ranging from .45 to .93 and from .60 to .96, respectively.

Magnitude of Effects from Childhood to Adolescence. We tested whether parent and child effects were constant over time by constraining them to be the same across the six measurement periods. The fit of the constrained model was significantly worse than the fit of the reciprocal model, indicating that the magnitude of parent effects and child effects varied over time. We also tested whether parent and child effects were similar in magnitude by constraining these to be equal within each period. The fit of the constrained model was significantly worse than the fit of the reciprocal model, indicating that in some periods parent effects were stronger than child effects and in other periods the reverse was true.

Parent and Child Effects. The fit of the child effects model was significantly worse than the fit of the reciprocal effects model (Table 6.3). Although the chi-square difference test indicated that the parent effects model provided as good a fit to the data as the reciprocal model, the χ^2 difference narrowly missed significance (critical $\chi^2_{diff} = 11.07$ versus obtained $\chi^2_{diff} = 10.99$), suggesting that the fit of the parent effects model was marginally worse than the fit of the full reciprocal effects model. Moreover, although the BIC statistic indicated that the parent effects model fit better than the reciprocal model, the RMSEA indicated the reverse (Table 6.3). Thus, the reciprocal model was selected over the parent effects model as best fitting although, clearly, both models are plausible representations of the data. The reciprocal model showed that children's anxious/depressed behavior predicted increases in mothers' internalizing symptoms only during the transition to middle childhood (from age 5 to 7 years), whereas mothers' internalizing symptoms predicted increases in children's anxious/depressed behavior during the transition to middle childhood (from age 5 to 7 years), from age 9 to 11 years, and during the transition to early adolescence (from age 11 to 13 years).

DISCUSSION

Support was found for some, but not all, of our hypotheses and tended to be stronger with respect to the association between mothers' internalizing symptoms and children's anxious/depressed behavior than for antisocial behavior. The first hypothesis predicted a bidirectional association between mothers' and children's behavior. We found that mothers' internalizing symptoms were reciprocally related with girls' antisocial behavior and children's anxious/depressed behavior, but not with boys' antisocial behavior. Mothers' internalizing symptoms predicted increases in boys' antisocial behavior during middle childhood (and decreases in boys' antisocial behavior in early adolescence), but boys' antisocial behavior did not predict changes in mothers' internalizing symptoms.

Our second hypothesis was that the effect of children's problem behaviors on mothers' depression would be strongest in early childhood. Support for this hypothesis was found for children's anxious/depressed behavior, but not for children's antisocial behavior. Children's anxious/depressed behavior predicted increases in mothers' internalizing symptoms between the ages of 5 and 7 years, but not thereafter. In contrast, girls' antisocial behavior predicted increases in mothers' internalizing symptoms throughout middle childhood and boys' antisocial behavior did not predict increases in mothers' internalizing symptoms at all. It is possible that only limited support was found for this hypothesis because our measure did not assess mothers' clinical depression, but rather her depressed and anxious symptomatology. Although some of the mothers in the sample would have met criteria for a diagnosis of depression at each time point, most mothers would not have done (McGee et al., 1983).

Our third hypothesis was that the effect of a mother's depression on her children's problem behaviors would be strongest during periods of transition. Limited support was found for this hypothesis. Mothers' internalizing symptoms predicted increases in children's anxious/depressed behavior during the transition to middle childhood (from age 5 to 7) and during the transition to early adolescence (from age 11 to 13), but also from age 9 to 11. However, mothers' internalizing symptoms predicted increases in girls' antisocial behavior throughout middle childhood and predicted increases in boys' antisocial behavior during the transition to middle childhood, but not during the transition to early adolescence.

Finally, our fourth and fifth hypotheses concerned the differential effects of mothers' internalizing symptoms on boys' and girls' problem behaviors. No support was found for these hypotheses. In contrast to our fourth hypothesis, which predicted that mothers' internalizing symptoms would be linked only to girls' problem behaviors, mothers' internalizing symptoms predicted changes in both girls' and boys' anxious/depressed and antisocial behaviors. In contrast to our fifth hypothesis, boys and girls did not respond to mothers' depression by exhibiting only sex-typical problem behaviors. Mothers' depression was linked to anxious/depressed and antisocial behaviors for both girls and boys in middle childhood. Sex differences were detected in the association between mothers' internalizing symptoms and children's antisocial behavior. These revealed a bidirectional association between mothers' and daughters' symptomatology, but a unidirectional association from mothers' to sons' symptomatology. That girls' but not boys' antisocial behavior predicted changes in mothers' internalizing symptoms is, perhaps, counterintuitive. For instance, in middle childhood, boys' antisocial behavior is more prevalent and more extreme than girls' and, consequently, more of a stressor for the mother. It is possible, however, that girls' antisocial behavior, because it is relatively sex-atypical in middle childhood, is a more potent stressor for mothers. Mothers may expect a certain level of noncompliant and aggressive behavior from their sons, but not from their daughters.

Implications for Research and Theory

These findings are largely consistent with a growing body of research that demonstrates a reciprocal association between children's and parents' behavior. Although the bulk of this literature has demonstrated (a) the ways in which children's behavior influences parents' disciplinary style (Anderson et al., 1986; Bell & Harper, 1977; Bell & Chapman, 1986; Buss, 1981; Ge et al., 1996; Grusec & Kuczynski, 1980; Jaffee, Caspi, Moffitt, Polo-Tomas, & Taylor, 2004; Lytton, 1990; O'Connor, Deater-Deckard, Fulker, Rutter, & Plomin, 1998; Patterson et al., 1992; Yarrow et al., 1971), and (b) the cycles by which children's problem behaviors and parents' disciplinary responses escalate over time (Caspi & Moffitt, 1995; Patterson et al., 1992), relatively little work has considered the degree to which parents and children mutually influence one another's psychological well-being. That children's problem behaviors lead to increases in mothers' depression is wholly consistent with a large body of literature on the role of life stressors in risk for depression (e.g., Monroe & Hadjiyannakis, 2002). Children who are hard to manage or who are anxious and depressed are likely to be a source of stress for parents (Crnic & Low, 2002; Feske et al., 2001). Given that children of depressed parents are likely to be genetically vulnerable to a range of problem behaviors (Goodman & Gotlib, 1999), depressed parents may be at greater than average risk of having to cope with such a child.

Moreover, our finding that mothers' depression and children's problem behaviors were reciprocally related is consistent with research showing that life stressors are not always independent events that impinge on the individual at random. Individuals who are already depressed or who are at risk for depression may, as a function of their poor psychological well-being, intentionally or unintentionally create situations that, ultimately, prove stressful (Kim et al., 2003). For instance, mothers who are depressed are more likely to use harsh disciplinary practices with their children compared to mothers who are not depressed (Downey & Coyne, 1990). However, the experience of harsh discipline increases risk for children's problem behaviors. Thus, the use of harsh discipline by depressed mothers may promote children's problem behaviors, which, in turn, become yet another source of stress for mothers.

The Uniqueness of Middle Childhood

Our findings showed that mothers' internalizing symptoms had a stronger effect on children's problem behaviors during the transition to middle childhood and throughout the middle childhood period than they did in early adolescence. It is possible that if we had measures of mothers' internalizing symptoms and children's problem behaviors later in adolescence, we might have detected a stronger association then. Unfortunately, measures of mothers' internalizing symptoms were not collected beyond age 15, so we cannot address this issue in our data. However, our pattern of findings is consistent with the hypothesis that the influence of parents' behavior (or, at least, some aspects thereof) on children's outcomes declines during adolescence as children's worlds broaden beyond the home. As children enter school, they interact with a growing number of individuals, including teachers and peers. However, children's activities are far more directed by parents during the middle childhood period than they are in adolescence (Eccles, 1999) and, consequently, children may rely more heavily on parents to be sources of support during middle childhood than they do later on. Thus, when parents' ability to provide such support is compromised by an episode of depression, younger children (versus adolescents) may be affected because their opportunities to find support elsewhere are relatively limited. Studies that assess mothers' depression and children's problem behaviors throughout middle childhood and the entire period of adolescence will be needed to test this hypothesis.

Limitations

Our findings are qualified by several limitations. First, measures of mothers' internalizing symptoms and children's problem behaviors came from the same source, the mother. Thus, shared informant variance may have accounted, in part, for the association between these measures. It should be noted, however, that this measurement error was explicitly modeled in the path analyses. Moreover, depressed mothers have been shown to be reliable reporters of their children's problem behaviors (Richters, 1992; but see Najman et al., 2001). Nevertheless, it would be desirable to replicate our findings in samples in which mothers' depression and children's problem behavior were assessed by multiple raters.

Second, our sample is from New Zealand. Although rates of psychiatric disorder in New Zealand match those in other developed Western nations (Kessler, McGonagle, Zhao, Nelson, & Hughes, 1994; Newman et al., 1996), our findings must be replicated with other samples from other nations and cohorts. It is encouraging, in this respect, that our findings replicate those from U.S. samples (Ge et al., 1995; Hammen, et al., 1990; Hammen et al., 1991;), although our study covered a different time span in children's lives than did these U.S. studies.

Third, our measure of mothers' depression assessed anxious/depressed symptomatology as opposed to clinical depression. It is possible that the association over time between a mother's clinical depression and her children's outcomes differs from the association we detected in our analyses.

Fourth, one of the challenges associated with the transition to adolescence is the onset of puberty. Given individual differences in the timing of puberty in our sample (Caspi, Lynam, Moffitt, & Silva, 1993; Caspi & Moffitt, 1991), it is possible that our findings with respect to parent and child effects in adolescence would have been different had we been able to distinguish between those who had made the transition to puberty and those who had not. For example, Ge and colleagues (1995) found that the association between fathers' and daughters' psychological distress was stronger during girls' transition to menarche than during other periods. However, data on the transition to puberty are available only for girls in our sample, who reported on age at menarche. Finally, it is possible that mothers' internalizing symptoms and children's problem behaviors are causally related to some other factor, such as poverty, marital conflict, or a shared genetic liability. Future research is necessary to rule out the possibility of such third variable effects.

CONCLUSION

Developmental psychologists have become increasingly aware of the reciprocal nature of parents' and children's relationships. A developmental perspective further considers *when* parents play a particularly important role in influencing children's behavior and *when* children are important influences on parents. Our findings provide preliminary evidence that the association between parents' and children's psychological distress is characterized by reciprocity in the middle childhood period that is less evident at later stages of children's development.

The Dunedin Multidisciplinary Health and Development Study is supported by the Health Research Council of New Zealand. This study was supported by grants MH45070 and MH49414 from the United States National Institute of Mental Health, by grant G0100527 from the United Kingdom Medical Research Council, and by fellowships from the University of Wisconsin. We would like to thank Air New Zealand, HonaLee Harrington, Phil Silva, and the Dunedin Study members and staff.

References

Anderson, K. E., Lytton, H., & Romney, D. M. (1986). Mothers' interactions with normal and conduct-disordered boys: Who affects whom? *Developmental Psychology, 22,* 604–609.
Bell, R. Q., & Chapman, M. (1986). Child effects in studies using experimental or brief longitudinal approaches to socialization. *Developmental Psychology, 22,* 595–603.

Bell, R. Q., & Harper, L. V. (1977). *Child effects on adults*. Hillsdale, NJ: Lawrence Erlbaum Associates.

Browne, M. W., & Cudeck, R. (1993). Alternative ways of assessing model fit. In K. A. Bollen & J. S. Long (Eds.), *Testing structural equation models* (pp. 136–162). Newbury Park, CA: Sage.

Brunk, M. A., & Henggeler, S. Q. (1984). Child influences on adult controls. *Developmental Psychology, 20*, 1074–1081.

Buss, D. M. (1981). Predicting parent-child interactions from children's activity level. *Developmental Psychology, 17*, 59–69.

Caspi, A., Lynam, D., Moffitt, T. E., & Silva, P. (1993). Unraveling girls' delinquency: Biological, dispositional, and contextual contributions to adolescent misbehavior. *Developmental Psychology, 29*(1), 19–30.

Caspi, A., & Moffitt, T. E. (1991). Individual differences are accentuated during periods of social change: The sample case of girls at puberty. *Journal of Personality and Social Psychology, 61*, 157–168.

Caspi, A., & Moffitt, T. E. (1995). The continuity of maladaptive behavior: From description to understanding in the study of antisocial behavior. In D. Cicchetti & D. J. Cohen (Eds.), *Developmental Psychopathology* (1st ed., pp. 472–511). New York: Wiley.

Cooper, P. J., & Murray, L. (1997). The impact of psychological treatments of postpartum depression on maternal mood and infant development. In L. Murray & P. J. Cooper (Eds.), *Postpartum depression and child development* (pp. 201–220). New York: Guilford.

Crnic, K., & Low, C. (2002). Everyday stresses and parenting. In M. H. Bornstein (Ed.), *Handbook of parenting: Vol. 5: Practical issues in parenting* (2nd ed.) Mahwah, NJ: Lawrence Erlbaum Associates.

Cummings, E. M., & Davies, P. T. (1994). Maternal depression and child development. *Journal of Child Psychology and Psychiatry, 35*, 73–112.

Cyranowski, J. M., Frank, E., Young, E., & Shear, K. (2000). Adolescent onset of the gender difference in lifetime rates of major depression. *Archives of General Psychiatry, 57*, 21–27.

Davies, P. T., & Windle, M. (1997). Gender-specific pathways between maternal depressive symptoms, family discord, and adolescent adjustment. *Developmental Psychology, 33*, 657–668.

Downey, G., & Coyne, J. C. (1990). Children of depressed parents: An integrative review. *Psychological Bulletin, 108*, 50–76.

Eccles, J. S. (1999). The development of children ages 6 to 14. *The future of children, 9*, 30–44.

Fergusson, D., Horwood, L. J., & Lynskey, M. (1995). Maternal depressive symptoms and depressive symptoms in adolescents. *Journal of Child Psychology and Psychiatry, 36*, 1161–1178.

Feske, U., Shear, M. K., Anderson, B., Cyranowski, J., Strassburger, M., Matty, M., et al. (2001). Comparison of severe life stress in depressed mothers and nonmothers: Do children matter? *Depression and Anxiety, 13*, 109–117.

Ge, X., Conger, R. D., Cadoret, R. J., Neiderhiser, J. M., Yates, W., Troughton, E., et al. (1996). The developmental interface between nature and nurture: A mutual influence model of child antisocial behavior and parent behavior. *Developmental Psychology, 32*, 574–589.

Ge, X., Conger, R. D., Lorenz, F. O., Shanahan, M., & Elder, G. H. J. (1995). Mutual influences in parent and adolescent psychological distress. *Developmental Psychology, 31*, 406–419.

Goodman, S. H., & Gotlib, I. H. (1999). Risk for psychopathology in the children of depressed mothers: A developmental model for understanding mechanisms of transmission. *Psychological Review, 106*, 458–490.

Grusec, J. E., & Kuczynski, L. (1980). Direction of effects in socialization: A comparison of the parent's versus the child's behavior as determinants of disciplinary techniques. *Developmental Psychology, 16*, 1–9.

Hammen, C., Burge, D., & Adrian, C. (1991). Timing of mother and child depression in a longitudinal study of children at risk. *Journal of Consulting and Clinical Psychology, 59*, 341–345.

Hammen, C., Burge, D., & Stansbury, K. (1990). Relationship of mother and child variables to child outcomes in a high-risk sample: A causal modeling analysis. *Developmental Psychology, 26*, 24–30.

Hankin, B. L., & Abramson, L. Y. (2001). Development of gender differences in depression: An elaborated cognitive vulnerability-transactional stress theory. *Psychological Bulletin, 127*, 773–796.

Hankin, B. L., Abramson, L. Y., Moffitt, T. E., Silva, P. A., McGee, R., & Angell, K. E. (1998). Development of depression from preadolescence to young adulthood: Emerging gender differences in a 10-year longitudinal study. *Journal of Abnormal Psychology, 107*, 128–140.

Herring, M., & Kaslow, N. J. (2002). Depression and attachment in families: A child-focused perspective. *Family Process, 41*, 494–518.

Hops, H. (1992). Parental depression and child behavior problems: Implications for behavioral family intervention. *Behavior Change, 9*, 126–138.

Hops, H. (1995). Age- and gender-specific effects of parental depression: A commentary. *Developmental Psychology, 31*, 428–431.

Jaffee, S. R., Caspi, A., Moffitt, T. E., Polo-Tomas, M., Price, T. S., & Taylor, A. (2004). The limits of child effects: Evidence for genetically-mediated child effects on corporal punishment, but not on physical maltreatment. *Developmental Psychology, 40*, 1047–1058.

Jaffee, S. R., Moffitt, T. E., Caspi, A., Fombonne, E., Poulton, R., & Martin, J. (2002). Differences in early childhood risk factors for juvenile-onset and adult-onset depression. *Archives of General Psychiatry, 59*, 215–222.

Jöreskog, K. G., & Sörbom, D. (1996). *LISREL 8 user's reference guide.* Chicago, IL: Scientific Software International, Inc.

Keenan, K., & Shaw, D. (1997). Developmental and social influences on young girls' early problem behavior. *Psychological Bulletin, 121*, 95–113.

Kessler, R. C., McGonagle, K. A., Zhao, S., Nelson, C. B., Hughes, M., Eshleman, S., et al. (1994). Lifetime and 12-month prevalence of DSM-III-R psychiatric disorders in the United States: Results from the National Comorbidity Study. *Archives of General Psychiatry, 51*, 8–19.

Kim, K. J., Conger, R. D., Elder, G. H. J., & Lorenz, F. O. (2003). Reciprocal influences between stressful life events and adolescent internalizing and externalizing problems. *Child Development, 74*, 127–143.

Lee, C. M., & Gotlib, I. H. (1991). Adjustment of children of depressed mothers: A 10-month follow-up. *Journal of Abnormal Psychology, 100*, 473–477.

Lytton, H. (1990). Child and parent effects in boys' conduct disorder: A reinterpretation. *Developmental Psychology, 26*, 683–697.

MacCallum, R. C., Browne, M. W., & Sugawara, H. M. (1996). Power analysis and determination of sample size for covariance structure modeling. *Psychological Methods, 1*, 130–149.

McGee, R., Williams, S., Kashani, J. H., & Silva, P. A. (1983). Prevalence of self-reported depressive symptoms and associated social factors in mothers in Dunedin. *British Journal of Psychiatry, 143*, 473–479.

McGee, R., Williams, S., & Silva, P. A. (1985). Factor structure and correlates of ratings of inattention, hyperactivity, and antisocial behavior in a large sample of 9-year-old children from the general population. *Journal of Consulting and Clinical Psychology, 53*, 480–490.

McGee, R., Williams, S., & Silva, P. A. (1986). An evaluation of the Malaise Inventory. *Journal of Psychosomatic Research, 30*, 147–152.

Mink, I. T., & Nihira, K. (1986). Family life-styles and child behaviors: A study of direction of effects. *Developmental Psychology, 17*, 610–616.

Moffitt, T. E., Caspi, A., Rutter, M., & Silva, P. A. (2001). *Sex differences in antisocial behaviour: Conduct disorder, delinquency, and violence in the Dunedin Longitudinal Study.* Cambridge: Cambridge University Press.

Monroe, S. M., & Hadjiyannakis, K. (2002). The social environment and depression: Focusing on severe life stress. In I. H. Gotlib & C. L. Hammen (Eds.), *Handbook of depression* (pp. 314–340). New York: Guilford Press.

Najman, J. M., Williams, G. M., Nikles, J., Spence, S., Bor, W., O'Callaghan, M., et al. (2001). Bias influencing maternal reports of child behaviour and emotional state. *Social Psychiatry and Psychiatric Epidemiology, 36*, 186–194.

Newman, D. L., Moffitt, T. E., Caspi, A., Magdol, L., Silva, P., & Stanton, W. R. (1996). Psychiatric disorder in a birth cohort of young adults: Prevalence, comorbidity, clinical significance, and new case incidence from age 11 to 21. *Journal of Consulting and Clinical Psychology, 64*, 552–562.

O'Connor, T. G., Deater-Deckard, K., Fulker, D., Rutter, M., & Plomin, R. (1998). Genotype-environment correlations in late childhood and early adolescence: Antisocial behavioral problems and coercive parenting. *Developmental Psychology, 34*, 970–981.

Patterson, G. R., Reid, J. B., & Dishion, T. J. (1992). *A social learning approach. IV. Antisocial boys.* Eugene, OR: Castalia.

Petersen, A. C. (1988). Adolescent development. *Annual Review of Psychology, 39*, 583–607.

Post, R. M. (1992). Transduction of psychosocial stress into the neurobiology of recurrent affective disorder. *American Journal of Psychiatry, 149*, 999–1010.

Quay, H. C., & Peterson, D. R. (1987). *Manual for the Behavior Problem Checklist.* Miami, FL: Authors.

Raftery, A. E. (1995). Bayesian model selection in social research. *Sociological Methodology, 25*, 111–163.

Richters, J. E. (1992). Depressed mothers as informants about their children: A critical review of the evidence for distortion. *Psychological Bulletin, 112*, 485–499.

Rodgers, B., Pickles, A., Power, C., Collishaw, S., & Maughan, B. (1999). Validity of the malaise inventory in general population samples. *Social Psychiatry and Psychiatric Epidemiology, 34*, 333–341.

Rutter, M., Tizard, J., & Whitmore, K. (1970). *Education, health and behaviour.* London: Longman.

Sanders, M. R., Markie-Dadds, C., Tully, L. A., & Bor, W. (2000). The Triple-P Positive Parenting Program: A comparison of enhanced, standard, and self-directed behavioral family intervention for parents of children with early onset conduct problems. *Journal of Consulting and Clinical Psychology, 68,* 624–640.

Sanders, M. R., & McFarland, M. (2000). Treatment of depressed mothers with disruptive children: A controlled evaluation of cognitive behavioral family intervention. *Behavior Therapy, 31,* 89–112.

Sheeber, L., Davis, B., & Hops, H. (2002). Gender-specific vulnerability to depression in children of depressed mothers. In S. H. Goodman & I. H. Gotlib (Eds.), *Children of depressed parents: Mechanisms of risk and implications for treatment* (pp. 253–274). Washington, DC: American Psychological Association.

Silva, P. A., & Stanton, W. R. (1996). *From child to adult: The Dunedin Multidisciplinary Health and Development Study.* Auckland, New Zealand: Oxford University Press.

Silverthorn, P., & Frick, P. J. (1999). Developmental pathways to antisocial behavior: The delayed-onset pathway in girls. *Development and Psychopathology, 11,* 101–126.

Teti, D. M., Gelfand, D. M., & Pompa, J. (1990). Depressed mothers' behavioral competence with their infants: Demographic and psychosocial correlates. *Development and Psychopathology, 2,* 259–270.

Timko, C., Cronkite, R. C., Berg, E. A., & Moos, R. H. (2002). Children of parents with unipolar depression: A comparison of stably remitted, partially remitted, and nonremitted parents and nondepressed controls. *Child Psychiatry and Human Development, 32,* 165–185.

Yarrow, M. R., Waxler, C. Z., & Scott, P. M. (1971). Child effects on behavior. *Developmental Psychology, 5,* 300–311.

7

Middle Childhood Life Course Trajectories

Links Between Family Dysfunction and Children's Behavioral Development

Linda S. Pagani, Christa Japel, Alain Girard, Abdeljelil Farhat, Sylvana Côté, and Richard E. Tremblay

In their extensive review of the literature on family adversity, Repetti, Taylor, and Seeman (2002) offer their conception of "risky families" as those that offer low warmth and support and are neglectful. Children in such families are likely to show disruptions in emotion processing, social cognition, and regulatory systems involving stress responses, as well as poor health behaviors across the life span. Exposure to conflict and aggression, frequent concomitants of prolonged dysfunctional family relations, encourages deficits in the control and expression of emotion and social competence, disturbances in physiologic and neuroendocrine system regulation, and health threatening addictions. That is, persistent family stress may disrupt the basic homeostatic processes that are central to development by repeatedly activating important bodily systems. Drawing upon the cumulative risk concept of allostatic loading (McEwan, 1998), the biopsychosocial challenge model suggests that children growing in risky environments face a compounded "cascade of risk" for mental and physical health disorders across the life span.

In youngsters, such outcomes manifest themselves most often as behavior problems (Tremblay, Vitaro, Nagin, Pagani, & Séguin, 2003). Some behavior-based research has documented an increased risk of behavioral difficulty in association with parental conflict (Emery, 1999; 2001; Fincham, Grych, & Osborne, 1994; Grych, Fincham, Jouriles, & McDonald, 2001; Wagner, 1997), control (Barber, 1996), coercion, and counter-coercion (Rothbaum & Weisz, 1994; O'Connor, Deater-Deckard, Fulker, Rutter, & Plomin, 1998; Patterson, 2002). Other research, using a broader scope of methods and measures, reliably links family dysfunction with aggression, oppositional-defiant, and conduct-disordered behaviors (Steinberg, Lamborn, Darling, Mounts, & Dornbush, 1994), depression, anxiety, and even suicidal behavior (Chorpita & Barlow, 1998; Kaslow, Deering, & Racusia, 1994).

Albeit less researched, links between family functioning and prosocial behavior are well established (Eisenberg, Fabes, & Murphy, 1996; Eisenberg et al., 1999; Jones, Abbey, & Cumberland, 1998; McGrath, Zook, & Weber-Roehl, 2003). Some behavioral genetics evidence indicates that prosociality may be less affected by biological dysregulation processes than antisocial behavior (Deater-Deckard, Dunn, O'Connor, Davies, & Golding, 2001), suggesting that social learning processes within family contexts that model and encourage helping, support, and acceptance are the predominant influences on prosocial behavior.

Childhood perceptions of parental expectations also seem to have a socializing influence, operating according to some kind of internalization principle (Grusec & Goodnow, 1994). For example, expected parental reactions predict both higher levels of prosocial behavior and lower levels of delinquency and aggression (Wyatt & Carlo, 2002). Children and adolescents develop expectancies regarding their parents' reactions to their social behaviors, which are influenced by a childrearing environment that features functional communication and problem solving.

In this chapter, family dysfunction is composed of indicators of less-than-optimal immediate kin relationships during childhood: poor support, communication, acceptance, and problem solving in the family. Although it would be unreasonable to believe that childhood experiences are the sole determinants of later adjustment, the literature suggests that childhood rearing context influences the features and selection of later experiences through indirect chain reactions (Rutter, Champion, Quinton, Maughan, & Pickles, 1995). In other words, later life chances are not independent of earlier contexts because those experiences shape later self-selection of contexts, goals, and relationships. This is perhaps why, compared to predictors concurrent with adult outcome variables, some childhood factors can exert an influence on life chances as much as 40 years later (Huesmann, Dubow, Eron, & Boxer, 2006). Individuals experiencing socioecological risks as youngsters tend to be less competent in establishing supportive relationships and avoiding peer rejection, and consequently are more likely to experience depression, psychopathologies, and poor social and occupational functioning in adulthood (Bagwell, Newcomb, & Bukowski, 1998; Collins & van Dulmen, 2006; George, 1999; Johnson, Cohen, Kasen, Smailes, & Brook, 2001; Parker & Asher, 1987).

Of course, these studies cannot always adequately address the issue of directionality. The relationship between family functioning and later outcomes could also be explained by gene–environment interactions and competing explanatory variables. The behavioral genetics literature underscores an important effect of inherent predispositions; it also provides evidence for the direct and indirect influence of family dysfunction (Rutter, 2002). There is evidence of environmentally-mediated influences of negative parenting upon children's externalizing behavior in adoptive families' independent of inherent predispositions that the child brought to the adoptive family (O'Connor et al., 1998). Similar results regarding risky family environments were noted in a recent twin study (Asbury, Dunn, Pike, & Plomin, 2003). In a propective study of parenting behavior, Johnson et al. (2001) found associations between maladaptive parental practices and later risk of child psychopathology in late adolescence and early adulthood above and beyond the influence of inherent parent and child mental health characteristics.

An important caveat is that genetic influence can also operate *through* negative family functioning and parenting (Kaslow et al., 1994; Suomi, 1997). That is, family adversity could be an intermediate factor in the expression of genetic risk. This makes discussions about the complexities of gene–environment interactions and directionality between family influences and children's outcomes even more tentative. In the present study, family dysfunction is treated as a shared characteristic, implicating both parents and children and not just the relationship between one parent and a target child. Although this global approach to the home environment does not allow us to estimate the independent effect of heredity, it has the strength of testing the larger ecological context of communication, support, and problem solving experienced by the child. As a result, any competing explanatory variables must also be treated as shared characteristics.

In this study, we examine four possible explanatory variables, the first three of which are structural in nature; the fourth is inherently a parental characteristic. Socioeconomic status is both a correlate and an outcome of risky family environments (Repetti et al., 2002). Family size plays a role as a correlate of family and child functioning (e.g., Baydar, Brooks-Gunn, & Furstenburg, 1993), and family structure has been prospectively associated with individual trajectories of behavioral adjustment during the middle childhood years (Pagani, Boulerice, Tremblay, & Vitaro, 1997). Lastly, maternal depression plays an important role in adding to the directionality of family influences upon children's outcomes through both its undeniable transmission of biological risk and its impact on the family process via maternal negativity, irritability, and unresponsiveness (Jaffee & Poulton, 2006; Nolen-Hoeksema, Wolfson, Mumme, & Guskin, 1995). A recent monozygotic twin differences study, conducted by Asbury et al. (2003), found that nonshared environmental influences (i.e., independent of genetic predisposition) on internalizing, externalizing, and prosocial behavior are *stronger* in higher risk environments featuring low SES, greater family chaos, and greater maternal depression.

In this chapter, we use the life course analytical framework (Elder, 1995; 1996), which comprises four central principles (Benson, 2001; Magnusson & Cairns, 1996): (a) developmental change is a continuous process, (b) biopsychosocial life course trajectories are intimately connected and have reciprocal effects on one another, (c) development is determined by a multitude of social and historical contexts, and (d) the ultimate impacts of prevention and intervention efforts are sensitive to particular stages in the life course. The life course perspective also considers the sequence of socially constructed, normatively ordered phases, events, and transitions (Mayer & Muller, 1986). Our interest for this chapter is middle childhood, the socially constructed phase marked by the beginning and end of the primary school years. During this period of development, children learn the skills they need to become increasingly autonomous and industrious in their academic work; they practice social competence and physical prowess; and their bodies gradually enter prepubertal status. Our unique contribution to the above literature is the application of the life course analytical framework to examine the relation between the trajectories of two middle childhood variables: family dysfunction and behavioral development. Our goal is to examine family dysfunction as a global contextual factor in middle childhood and to consider its relation to the developmental pathways of physical aggression, depression, and prosocial behavior in boys and girls while considering the relations between family dysfunction and other factors in the home environment that could provide competing explanations for children's behavioral development.

Classic models of cumulative risk (Egeland, Carlson, & Sroufe, 1993; Garmezy & Masten, 1994; Masten & Wright, 1997; Rutter, 1987; 1990) concur that potential damage comes from prolonged exposure to challenging or adverse circumstances. Studies of extreme privation point to the predictive value of the duration and dosage of risky rearing conditions in estimating child outcomes (see Rutter, 2002, for a review). Because the middle childhood life course trajectories of family dysfunction emerge from the data themselves, our study can be viewed as a naturalistic experiment of varying rearing conditions. Dose–response variations are used to test the influence of the most risky family environments and how these are linked to behavioral development. We expect that prolonged duration of high doses of family dysfunction will be associated with the most extreme trajectories of psychosocial maladjustment during middle childhood.

METHOD

Participants

This study includes three data cycles of the Canadian National Longitudinal Survey of Children and Youth (NLSCY). The first wave of data collection (Cycle 1) took place in 1994–95 and was followed by subsequent cycles at two-year intervals. Data about family life course and children's adjustment are from the computer-assisted personal interview (CAPI) completed with the person most knowledgeable (PMK) about the child and the family.

	Age	Age	Age	Age	Age	Age	Age	Age
Cycle 1	4	5	6	7	8	9	10	11
Cycle 2	4	5	6	7	8	9	10	11
Cycle 3	4	5	6	7	8	9	10	11

FIGURE 7.1. Three data sets were obtained for children who were ages 4 to 7 at Cycle 1, whereas the accelerated design yielded two data sets for children who were ages 8 and 9 at Cycle 1.

In most cases (89.9% at Cycle 1), the biological mother of the target child was the PMK.

The initial cross-sectional sample consisted of 22,831 Canadian children aged newborn to 11 years. Children who were 4- to 9-years-old at Cycle 1 were selected for our middle childhood sample using an accelerated design. This sampling procedure yielded complete longitudinal data on 5,809 children (2,909 girls and 2,900 boys). As shown in Figure 7.1, three age periods could be obtained for children from ages 4 to 7 at Cycle 1, whereas for 8- and 9-year-old children at Cycle 1, this design yielded two age periods.

Measures

Family Dysfunction (FDF) Trajectories. Information on family character-istics and child behavior was provided by the PMK. Family functioning was assessed with a widely used 12-item scale developed by researchers at Chedoke-McMaster Hospital, McMaster University. Items include (a) "Planning family activities is difficult because we misunderstand each other," (b) "In times of crisis we can turn to each other for support"(reverse scored), (c) "We cannot talk to each other about sadness we feel," and (d) "Individuals (in the family) are accepted for what they are" (reverse scored). For each item, the PMK indicated which response best described his/her family using the indicators "strongly agree," "agree," "disagree," or "strongly disagree." This yielded a total score between 0 and 36, with higher scores indicating greater levels of family dysfunction. Family dys-function trajectories were established with all available data (ages 2 to 11) from the accelerated design of the NLSCY ($N = 8,176$).

Behavioral Trajectories. We assessed children's physical aggression, prosocial behavior, and depression by using items from the Social Behavior Questionnaire (see Tremblay, Pihl, Vitaro, & Dobkin, 1994, for details). PMKs were asked to rate their child's behavior on a response scale from "never or not true," "sometimes or somewhat true," to "often or very true." The *physical aggression scale* consists of three items: (a) "Kicks, bites, or hits other children," (b) "Gets into many fights," and (c) "Reacts with anger and fighting when accidentally hurt by another child" (ages 2 to 4) or "Physically attacks people" (ages 4 to 11). A high score on this scale indicates the presence of direct, physically aggressive behaviors associated with conduct disorder. The *depression scale* comprises three items: (a) "Seems to be unhappy, sad or depressed," (b) "Cries a lot," and (c) "Has trouble enjoying him/herself." A high score on this scale indicates the presence of behaviors generally associated with depression in children. The *prosocial behavior scale* comprises ten items that indicate children's levels of altruism; for example, (a) "Spontaneously helps pick up objects which another child has dropped," (b) "Will invite bystanders to join in a game," or (c) "Comforts a child who is crying or upset."

Explanatory Variables

Once the trajectories were established using the MOC procedure, we used crosstabs to identify any possible explanatory variables to incorporate into the analyses. Four variables were associated with both family dysfunction and child development, so we retained them in the analyses.

Family Transitions. Conjugal changes in family composition from the child's birth to Cycle 3 of the NLSCY were treated as a dummy variable with the reference group (0) not having experienced any family transitions and (1) representing those children whose family had undergone one or more transitions.

Socioeconomic Status (SES). We used a composite score derived from five sources: level of education (PMK and spouse), occupational prestige (PMK and spouse), and household income (Willms & Shields, 1996). The mean score for the three cycles was calculated and converted to a standardized score. It was transformed into a dummy variable with the reference group (0) being those families located one standard deviation above the mean. Families within one standard deviation above and below the mean were given a reference score of (1). Families beyond one standard deviation below the mean were given a reference score of (2).

Maternal Depressive Symptoms. Mothers were administered an abridged version of the Center for Epidemiological Studies-Depression scale. M. Boyle at Chedoke-McMaster Hospital reduced this scale, which assesses depressive symptoms in the past week, from 20 to 12 items for the NLSCY. The mean on the three cycles was transformed into a dummy variable, the reference group representing mothers with no or few depressive symptoms (0) and those whose score on the scale was situated above one standard deviation of the mean (1).

Family Size. The average number of people residing with the family from Cycle 1 to Cycle 3 was recoded into families with three or fewer members (0; the reference group), families with four or five members (1), and families with more than five members (2).

Data Analysis Strategy

We had two objectives: (a) to identify distinctive groups with regard to family functioning and child adjustment during middle childhood and (b) to determine factors that predict membership in the high family dysfunction group. We used semiparametric mixture modeling (Boulerice, 2001; Broidy et al., 2003; Jones, Nagin, & Roeder, 2001; Nagin, 1999) to identify subjects with distinct patterns of family functioning and behavior during middle childhood. This type of trajectory modeling defines the shape of the trajectory (e.g., rising, falling, stable, or hump-shaped) and the estimated proportion of the population belonging to each trajectory group. Selection of the best fitting model is determined using the Bayesian Information Criterion (BIC), as well as other indices of fit such as the examination of residuals and comparison of fitted versus observed values. The BIC procedure also yields, for every subject, the probability of being classified in each of the trajectory groups. Based on this posterior group probability, individuals are assigned to the trajectory group for which they have the highest probability of belonging (see Broidy et al., 2003, for more on this topic).

Family dysfunction and behavioral trajectories were constructed using *all* available participants from the entire population from ages 2 to 9 at data Cycle 1. Longitudinal data were available for the family dysfunction ($n = 8{,}176$), physical aggression ($n = 8{,}208$), and child depression trajectories ($n = 7{,}981$). Because the prosocial items were administered only from age 4 onward, these trajectories are based on a subsample of 4- to 9-year-old children ($n = 5{,}615$) at Cycle 1.

In the second stage of the analyses, we conducted separate multivariate logit regressions for physical aggression, prosocial behavior, and depression. First, we examined the relationship between these behavioral variables and family functioning (Step 1). We then examined the extent to which the explanatory variables predicted belonging to the high family dysfunction trajectory without taking into account the behavioral variables (Step 2). In Step 3, we introduced both the behavioral and the explanatory variables into the regressions. Finally, to control for possible interactions between

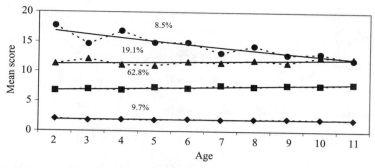

FIGURE 7.2A. Trajectories of family functioning from ages 2 to 11 ($N = 8,178$).

the explanatory variables and behavioral trajectory membership, we took into account possible interactions between behaviors and risk factors (e.g., physical aggression by family transition, physical aggression by maternal depression, etc.).

RESULTS

Life Course Trajectories

Family Dysfunction (FDF) Trajectories. Trajectories of family functioning for the entire sample are shown in Figure 7.2A. The best fitting model yielded four trajectories: the first indicates a persistent, low level of family dysfunction (9.7% of the sample); the second, a medium-low level of family dysfunction (62.8%); the third, a medium-high trajectory (19.1%); and the fourth, a trajectory of high family dysfunction (8.5%). All trajectories seem to be fairly stable through middle childhood with the exception of the high family dysfunction trajectory, which decreases slightly during this period. Separate trajectories for boys and girls are presented in Figures 7.2B and 7.2C, respectively. The shapes of the trajectories and the percentage of

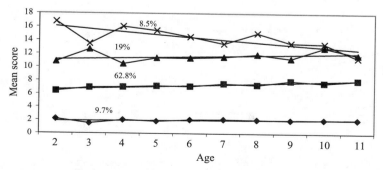

FIGURE 7.2B. Trajectories of family functioning among boys ages 2 to 11 ($N = 4,132$).

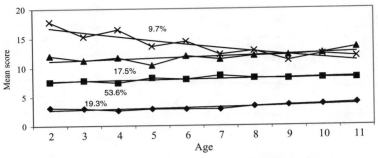

FIGURE 7.2C. Trajectories of family functioning among girls ages 2 to 11 ($N =$ 4, 046).

individuals belonging to a given trajectory are fairly similar for both sexes, with two exceptions. A larger proportion of girls' families are in the low family dysfunction group, compared with boys' families (19.3% vs. 9.7%), and the high family dysfunction trajectory among the girls' families shows a steeper decrease across middle childhood than among the boys' families.

Physical Aggression Trajectories. For both boys and girls, four physical aggression trajectories were extracted from the data. As shown in Figures 7.3A and 7.3B, 31.5% of girls and 21.8% of boys show very low levels of physical aggression in early and middle childhood. A group of girls and boys (15.6% and 20.9%, respectively) show a steep decrease in physical aggression from ages 2 to 4 and remain at a very low level during middle childhood. A bit more than a third of the girls (37.3%) and close to half of the boys (43.5%) follow a gradually declining trajectory with decreasing levels of physical aggression during early and middle childhood. Finally, the data yielded a high physical aggression trajectory that was fairly stable among boys (19.1%) but slightly declining among girls (10.3%) during early and middle childhood.

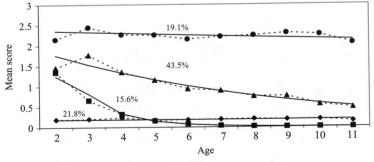

FIGURE 7.3A. Physical aggression trajectories among boys ages 2 to 11.

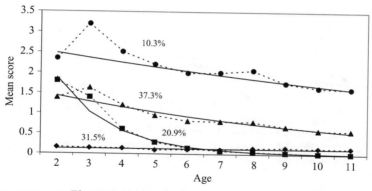

FIGURE 7.3B. Physical aggression trajectories among girls ages 2 to 11.

Depression Trajectories. Figures 7.4A and 7.4B illustrate the depression trajectories for boys and girls from ages 2 to 11. Four distinct trajectories emerged from the data: one low and stable, comprising 14.5% of the girls and 16.2% of the boys; one medium-low, stable trajectory that describes 30.7% of the girls and 29.4% of the boys; one medium-high, slightly increasing trajectory comprising 49.9% of the girls and 44.3% of the boys; and one high, slightly increasing trajectory comprising 4.9% of the girls and 10.1% of the boys. It is noteworthy that the latter two trajectories show an upward trend across middle childhood.

Prosocial Behavior Trajectories. The best-fitting model yielded three trajectories for the prosocial behaviors. Note that in both Figures 7.5A and 7.5B the trajectories are similar for boys and girls. During middle childhood, prosocial behaviors seem to increase among the low prosocial girls (3.2%) and low prosocial boys (8.1%) as well as among the medium prosocial

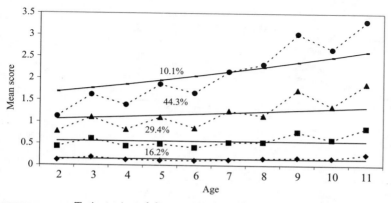

FIGURE 7.4A. Trajectories of depression from ages 2 to 11 for boys.

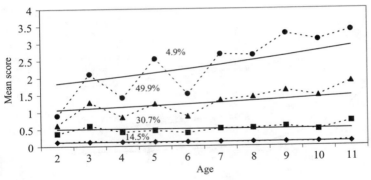

FIGURE 7.4B. Trajectories of depression from ages 2 to 11 for girls.

groups (46.6% of girls and 44.4% of boys). Approximately half of the girls and boys (50.2% and 47.5%, respectively) seem to follow a stable, high prosocial trajectory from ages 4 to 11.

Family Dysfunction and Behavioral Development

Table 7.1 reports the results from the three multivariate logit procedures. In Step 1 we examined the extent to which membership in the highest behavioral trajectories predicted high family dysfunction trajectory membership. Boys from the highest physical aggression trajectory showed 3.4 times greater risk of belonging to a highly dysfunctional family than to a family with the lowest level of family dysfunction. Girls from the highest physical aggression trajectory showed 5.1 times greater risk of belonging to a highly dysfunctional family than to a family with the lowest level of dysfunction. Although physical aggression decreased during middle childhood in the slow-declining trajectory group, both boys and girls in

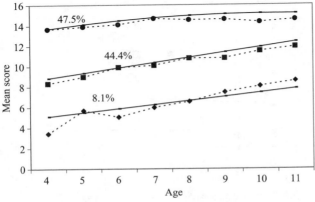

FIGURE 7.5A. Trajectories of prosocial behavior from ages 4 to 11 for boys.

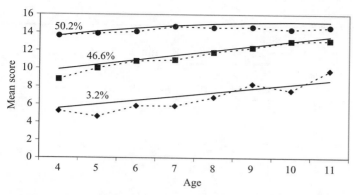

FIGURE 7.5B. Trajectories of prosocial behavior from ages 4 to 11 for girls.

this trajectory also were more likely to belong to a highly dysfunctional family (odds ratios 2.38 and 2.0, respectively; data not presented). However, both boys and girls in the rapidly declining trajectory group did not have a higher risk of belonging to a highly dysfunctional family.

Table 7.1 also shows that, among boys, membership in the highest depression trajectory was associated with 5.9 times greater risk of belonging to a highly dysfunctional family than to a family showing the lowest level of dysfunction. Among girls, membership in the highest depression trajectory increased the risk, by a factor of 20, of belonging to a highly dysfunctional family. Boys and girls in the medium-high, slightly increasing depression trajectory were 4.5 times more likely to belong to a highly dysfunctional family (data not presented). Likewise, belonging to the medium-low, stable depression trajectory increased the risk of high family dysfunction trajectory membership by 1.4 for boys and by 1.7 for girls (data not presented).

Low prosociality was significantly linked to living in the most dysfunctional families in middle childhood. As reported in Table 7.1, girls in the low prosociality trajectory were 4 times more likely to belong to a family with a high dysfunction trajectory; low prosocial boys were 8.2 times more likely to live in a highly dysfunctional family. There was no association between belonging to the medium prosocial group and family dysfunction trajectory membership.

Family Dysfunction and Contextual Factors

Step 2 of the multivariate logit procedure shows the relationship between the explanatory variables and family dysfunction trajectory membership. As reported in Table 7.1, for both boys and girls, having had a family marital transition (compared to not having had a family marital transition) was associated with a greater risk of belonging to

TABLE 7.1. *Predictors of High Family Dysfunction Trajectory Membership (Compared to Those with the Lowest Level of Family Dysfunction) Resulting From the Multivariate Logit Procedure.*

	Physical Aggression		Depression		Prosociality	
	Odds Ratio	90% C.I.	Odds Ratio	90% C.I.	Odds Ratio	90% C.I.
Step 1						
Membership in highest behavioral trajectory*						
Girls	5.1	2.8–9.1	20.0	7.4–52.6	4.0	.08–.81
Boys	3.4	2.3–5.2	5.9	3.1–11.2	8.3	.06–.24
Step 2						
Family transition						
Girls	3.1	2.1–4.7	3.1	2.1–4.7	3.0	1.9–4.9
Boys	2.5	1.6–3.8	2.3	1.5–3.5	2.7	1.5–4.8
Low SES						
Girls	4.8	2.4–9.7	4.2	2.1–8.5	6.6	2.7–16.1
Boys	7.1	3.3–15.6	7.1	3.2–14.9	7.6	2.8–20.8
Maternal depression						
Girls	14.3	8.8–22.2	14.3	8.5–21.3	9.5	5.8–15.6
Boys	14.3	8.8–22.7	14.3	8.8–22.2	13.0	7.5–22.2
Family size						
Girls	.55	.31–.96	.54	.31–.95	.49	.24–.97
Boys	n.s.		n.s.		n.s.	
Step 3						
Membership in highest behavioral trajectory*						
Girls	4.9	2.7–8.9	7.6	2.7–20.8	6.7	.05–.51
Boys	2.0	1.3–3.2	2.4	1.2–4.7	8.3	.06–.26
Family transition						
Girls	3.0	2.0–4.6	3.0	2.0–4.4	3.0	1.9–4.9
Boys	2.5	1.6–3.8	2.2	1.5–3.4	2.8	1.6–5.1
Low SES						
Girls	4.7	2.3–9.6	4.2	2.0–8.5	6.8	2.8–16.7
Boys	7.6	3.5–16.4	6.5	3.0–14.1	7.6	2.8–20.8
Maternal depression						
Girls	13.3	8.3–21.3	11.2	7.1–17.9	10.1	6.1–16.7
Boys	13.3	8.3–21.3	12.2	7.6–19.6	13.9	8.0–23.8
Family size						
Girls	.49	.28–.87	n.s.		.47	.24–.94
Boys	.46	.26–.82	n.s.		n.s.	

* For prosociality, membership in the highest trajectory indicates a high level of prosociality.

the highest family dysfunction trajectory. Being in the lowest income group (compared to the highest income group) was also associated with a higher risk of belonging to the highest family dysfunction trajectory, as was having a mother in the maternal depression group (compared to not being in a maternal depression group).

Interestingly, for girls only, we found a relationship between family size and family dysfunction. Compared to girls in small families (three or fewer members), girls in large families (more than five members) were half as likely to be in the highest family dysfunction trajectory. In other words, girls in larger families were almost twice as likely to be in the lowest family dysfunction trajectory than in the highest family dysfunction trajectory. This was not true for boys.

Family Dysfunction and Behavioral Development and Contextual Factors

Step 3 of the three multivariate logistic regressions shows the odds ratios of belonging to the high family dysfunction trajectory when taking into account both behavioral characteristics of the child and contextual risk factors. As Table 7.1 shows, the predictive power of the explanatory variables is not greatly affected by the introduction of the behavioral trajectories. This suggests that the influence of the behavioral trajectories on the relationship between family functioning and the explanatory variables is not important. Conversely, the relations of children's behavior to family dysfunction were not explained by the contextual risk factors. Children's behavior is strongly associated with family functioning, which is predicted by a number of contextual risk factors. Finally, tests of interactions between the explanatory variables and behavioral trajectory membership showed no significant effect on the relationship between behavior, these risk factors, and family functioning.

DISCUSSION

We generated life course trajectories of family dysfunction and behavioral development for both sexes across middle childhood. These pathways were grounded in the data, making our approach as naturalistic as possible within the limits of a national data set. Across middle childhood, we found a remarkable set of relations of middle childhood life course patterns of family dysfunction with patterns of children's physical aggression, depression, and low prosociality for both boys and girls. When we considered the influence of important co-occurring family context variables, these relations remained robust across all three indicators of psychosocial adjustment.

Although many patterns occurred for both sexes, there were some notable sex differences. Nearly one in five girls' families were in the group with the lowest amount of dysfunction, compared to only one in ten families of boys. There were also sex differences in behavioral development, which is not surprising considering that volumes of research have been written about the problems related to conduct, health, and being less shielded from parental discord that are associated with being male. Adding to this literature is our finding that, among the most highly dysfunctional families, girls' families showed a steeper decline in dysfunctionality across middle childhood than did families of boys. Girls from larger families were comparatively less likely to belong to the most dysfunctional families. Because girls have better average conduct and a more prosocial predisposition than boys (Eisenberg et al., 1999), they may help to stabilize the home environment and needs of larger families (Grusec, Davidov, & Lundell, 2002). Parents of larger families may be very receptive and likely to reward their daughters' inclination to contribute to family functioning (Grusec, 2002).

We found marked gender differences regarding the links between psychosocial adjustment and family dysfunction during middle childhood. Girls from the highest physical aggression and depression trajectory groups were, respectively, five and twenty times more likely to belong to the most dysfunctional families than their peers from the lowest behavioral trajectory groups; whereas, for boys, the same relationship was associated with a three- and six-fold risk. The intensity of the risk relationship suggests a greater vulnerability of girls to family dysfunction, above and beyond the influence afforded by maternal depression as an explanatory variable.

Due to biopsychosocial interactions, we generally think of the prepubertal and pubertal period as being particularly risky for affective maladjustment among girls. Our findings underscore the vulnerability of girls to family stress between ages 6 and 11, far earlier than the current literature would have indicated. Our results also show an unexpected association between stressful family life course and girls' physical aggression during the same period. The relationship between family stress and the intensity of risk associated with problem behavior warrants further research, especially of the kind that can test gene–environment interactions during middle childhood.

From the standpoint of advancing theory in this area, this study adds to the array of strategies used within the life course analytic framework. Three relevant tenets of this perspective were met: (a) Family functioning and behavioral strategies were treated as continuous processes that were documented regularly from early through middle childhood; these two developmental periods are socially constructed and separated by the normative transitions of day or home care, preschool, kindergarten, and primary school. (b) The trajectories generated appeared biopsychosocially interconnected and were assumed to have reciprocal effects on one another. This bidirectionality cannot be avoided, especially because we are looking at shared environmental characteristics. (c) The developmental pathways observed are multidetermined and are most certainly influenced by the sociohistorical context in which the children live.

Our results remained robust even while considering the important influence of competing explanatory variables (family size, family configuration change, and SES). Although these were related to family functioning, they did not explain the association between middle childhood life course pathways of behavior and family dysfunction. Lastly, although our study did not address efforts to optimize human development, our results underscore the importance of being sensitive to family functioning when intervening, either preventively or correctively, during middle childhood. While it is natural for school-age children to move gradually away from the family as a focal source of support, family dysfunction can facilitate premature disengagement on the part of parents and children alike (Emery, 1999).

These results are crucial to our understanding of development beyond middle childhood because life course outcomes derive from continuities and discontinuities in experiences over time (Rutter, 1989; 1994). Prolonged exposure to a risky family context during middle childhood played an important role in explaining the developmental course of aggressive behavior, depression, and low prosociality for boys and girls alike, but especially for girls. Of course, ongoing development can be influenced by relationships with peers, and, toward the end of middle childhood, intimate relationships. Prolonged high doses of family dysfunction during middle childhood might lead to premature disengagement from family involvement, amplifying the perceived importance of peer social relationships. If peers are not deviant, relationships with them can compensate for the support, warmth, and understanding missing from the home front. However, early deviant associations could add to the cascade of risk already in motion.

The design and objectives of this study add a novel dimension to prospective techniques, in that they enabled us to observe natural groupings of individuals over a defined developmental period and test biopsychosocial interconnections among these natural groupings. There are, however, limitations to this technique. Our most important concern is the likelihood that family adversity could represent an intermediate factor in the expression of genetic risk; that is, the environmental dysfunction assessed in this study could have been genetically mediated. As such, the complexities of gene–environment interactions render our results about family influences on children's outcomes tentative. Our second concern is the use of one data source, in this case, the person most knowledgeable about the family (usually the mother). Rutter (2002) warns that we ought to be skeptical about conclusions generated by designs in which common data sources measure both the child outcomes and family risk variables. There is an undeniable possibility that the association is an artifact of caregivers' perceptual biases rather than causal influence. Although the implemented statistical controls could remove some of the bias, we cannot know the degree to which the observed relationships reflect perceptual predispositions. We encourage others with data from multiple sources to replicate and extend our analysis on family adversity, thus advancing the life course conceptual perspective.

References

Asbury, K., Dunn, J. F., Pike, A., & Plomin, R. (2003). Nonshared environmental influences on individual differences in early behavioral development: A monozygotic twin differences study. *Child Development, 74*, 933–943.

Bagwell, C. L., Newcomb, A. F., & Bukowski, W. M. (1998). Preadolescent friendship and peer rejection as predictors of adult adjustment. *Child Development, 69*, 140–153.

Barber, B. K. (1996). Parental psychological control: Revisiting a neglected construct. *Child Development, 67*, 3296–3319.

Baydar, N., Brooks-Gunn, J., & Furstenberg, F. F. (1993). Early warning signs of functional illiteracy: Predictors in childhood and adolescence. *Child Development, 64*, 815–829.

Benson, M. L. (2001). *Crime and the life course.* Los Angeles: Roxbury.

Boulerice, B. (2001). General Nonlinear Mixtures of Curves (*MOC*) [Unpublished statistical software program]. Retrieved from http://lib.stat.cmu.edu/R/CRAN/

Broidy, L. M., Nagin, D. S., Tremblay, R. E., Bates, J. E., Brame, B., Dodge, K. A., et al. (2003). Developmental trajectories of childhood disruptive behaviors and adolescent delinquency: A six site, cross-national study. *Developmental Psychology, 39*, 222–245.

Chorpita, B. F., & Barlow, D. H. (1998). The development of anxiety: The role of control in the early environment. *Psychological Bulletin, 124*, 3–21.

Collins, W. A., van Dulmen, M., & Egeland, B. (2006). The significance of middle childhood peer competence for work and relationships in early adulthood. In A. C. Huston & M. N. Ripke (Eds.), *Developmental contexts in middle childhood: Bridges to adolescence and adulthood* (pp. 23–40). New York: Cambridge University Press.

Deater-Deckard, K., Dunn, J., O'Connor, T. G., Davies, L., & Golding, J. (2001). Using the stepfamily genetic design to examine gene-environment processes in child and family functioning. *Marriage and Family Review, 33*, 131–156.

Egeland, B., Carlson, E., & Sroufe, L. A. (1993). Resilience as process. *Development and Psychopathology, 5*, 517–528.

Eisenberg, N., Fabes, R. A., & Murphy, B. C. (1996). Parents' reactions to children's negative emotions: Relations to children's social competence and comforting behavior. *Child Development, 67*, 2227–2247.

Eisenberg, N., Guthrie, I. K., Murphy, B. C., Shepard, S. A., Cumberland, A., & Gustavo, C. (1999). Consistency and development of prosocial dispositions: A longitudinal study. *Child Development, 70*, 1360–1372.

Elder, G. H. (1995). The life course paradigm: Social change and individual development. In P. Moen, G. H. Elder, & K. Luscher (Eds.), *Examining lives in context: Perspectives on the ecology of human development* (pp. 101–135). Washington, DC: American Psychological Association.

Elder, G. H. (1996). Human lives in changing societies: Life course and developmental insights. In R. B. Cairns, G. H. Elder, Jr., & E. J. Costello (Eds), *Developmental science* (pp. 31–62). New York: Cambridge University Press.

Emery, R. E. (1999). *Marriage, divorce, and children's adjustment* (2nd ed.). New York: Sage.

Emery, R. E. (2001). Interparental conflict and social policy. In J. H. Grych and F. D. Fincham (Eds.), *Interparental conflict and child development: Theory, research, and applications* (pp. 417–439). London: Cambridge University Press.

Fincham, F., Grych, J. H., & Osborne, L. N. (1994). Does marital conflict cause child maladjustment? Directions and challenges for longitudinal research. *Journal of Family Psychology, 8,* 128–140.

Garmezy, N., & Masten, A. S. (1994). Chronic adversities. In M. Rutter, L. Herzov, & E. Taylor (Eds.), *Child and Adolescent Psychiatry* (3rd ed., pp. 191–208). Oxford: Blackwell.

George, L. K. (1999). Life-course perspectives on mental health. In C. S. Aneshensel & J. C. Phelan (Eds.), *Handbook of sociology of mental health.* New York: Kluwer Academic/Plenum Publishers.

Grusec, J. E. (2002). Parenting and the socialization of values. In M. Bornstein (Ed.), *Handbook of parenting* (pp. 143–168). Mahwah, NJ: Erlbaum.

Grusec, J. E., Davidov, M., & Lundell, L. (2002). Prosocial and helping behavior. In P. Smith & C. Hart (Eds.), *Handbook of children's social development* (pp. 457–474). New York: Blackwell.

Grusec, J. E., & Goodnow, J. J. (1994). The impact of parental discipline methods on the child's internalization of values: A reconceptualization of current points of view. *Developmental Psychology, 30,* 4–19.

Grych, J. H., Fincham, F. D., Jouriles, E. N., & McDonald, R. (2001). Interparental conflict and child adjustment: Testing the mediational role of appraisals in the cognitive contextual framework. *Child Development, 71,* 1648–1661.

Huesmann, L. R., Dubow, E. F., Eron, L. D., & Boxer, P. (2006). Middle childhood family contextual factors as predictors of adult outcomes. In A. C. Huston & M. N. Ripke (Eds.), *Developmental contexts in middle childhood: Bridges to adolescence and adulthood* (pp. 62–86). New York: Cambridge University Press.

Jaffee, S. R., & Poulton, R. (2006). Reciprocal effects of mothers' depression and children's problem behaviors from middle childhood to early adolescence. In A. C. Huston & M. N. Ripke (Eds.), *Developmental contexts in middle childhood: Bridges to adolescence and adulthood.* (pp. 107–129) New York: Cambridge University Press.

Johnson, J. G., Cohen, P., Kasen, S., Smailes, E., & Brook, J. S. (2001). Association of maladaptive parental behavior with psychiatric disorder among parents and their offspring. *Archives of General Psychiatry, 58,* 453–460.

Jones, B. L., Nagin, D. S., & Roeder, K. (2001). A SAS procedure based on mixture models for estimating developmental trajectories. *Sociological Methods and Research, 29,* 374–393.

Jones, D. C., Abbey, B. B., & Cumberland, A. (1998). The development of display rule knowledge: Linkages with family expressiveness and social competence. *Child Development, 69,* 1209–1222.

Kaslow, M. H., Deering, C. G., & Racusia, G. R. (1994). Depressed children and their families. *Clinical Psychological Review, 14,* 39–59.

Magnusson, D., & Cairns, R. B. (1996). Developmental science: Toward a unified framework. In R. B. Cairns, G. H. Elder, & E. J. Costello (Eds.), *Developmental science* (pp. 7–30).

Masten, A. S., & Wright, M. O'D. (1997). Cumulative risk and protection models of child maltreatment. In B. B. R. Rossman & M. S. Rosenberg (Eds.), *Multiple victimization of children: Conceptual, developmental, research and treatment issues.* Binghampton, NY: Haworth Press.

Mayer, K. U., & Muller, W. (1986). The state and the structure of the life course. In A. B. Sorenson, F. E. Winert, & L. R. Sherrod (Eds.), *Human development and the life course: Multidisciplinary perspectives* (pp. 217–245). Hillsdale, NJ: Lawrence Erlbaum Associates.

McEwan, B. S. (1998). Protective and damaging effects of stress mediators. *New England Journal of Medicine, 338,* 171–179.

McGrath, M. P., Zook, J. M., & Weber-Roehl, L. (2003). Socializing prosocial behavior in children: The roles of parents and peers. In S. Shohov (Ed.), *Advances in psychological research* (pp. 53–59). Hauppauge, NY: Nova Science Publishers.

Nagin, D. S. (1999). Analyzing developmental trajectories: A semiparametric, group-based approach. *Psychological Methods, 4,* 139–157.

Nolen-Hoeksema, S., Wolfson, A., Mumme, D., & Guskin, K. (1995). Helplessness in children of depressed and nondepressed mothers. *Developmental Psychology, 31,* 377–387.

O'Connor, T. G., Deater-Deckard, K., Fulker, D., Rutter, M., & Plomin, R. (1998). Genotype-environment correlations in late childhood and early adolescence: Antisocial behavior problems and coercive parenting. *Developmental Psychology, 34,* 970–981.

Pagani, L. S., Boulerice, B., Tremblay, R. E., & Vitaro, F. (1997). Behavioural development in children of divorce and remarriage. *Journal of Child Psychology and Psychiatry, 38,* 769–781.

Parker, J. G., & Asher, S. R. (1987). Peer relations and later personal adjustment: Are low-accepted children at risk? *Psychological Bulletin, 102,* 335–389.

Patterson, G. R. (2002). The early development of coercive family process. In J. B. Reid & G. R. Patterson (Eds.), *Antisocial behavior in children and adolescents: A developmental analysis and model for intervention* (pp. 25–44). Washington, DC: American Psychological Association.

Repetti, R. L., Taylor, S. E., & Seeman, T. E. (2002). Risky families: Family social environments and the mental and physical health of offspring. *Psychological Bulletin, 128,* 330–366.

Rothbaum, F., & Weisz, J. R. (1994). Parental caregiving and child externalizing behavior in nonclinical samples: A meta-analysis. *Psychological Bulletin, 116,* 55–74.

Rutter, M. (1987). Psychological resistance and protective mechanisms. *American Journal of Orthopsychiatry, 57,* 317–331.

Rutter M. (1989). Pathways from childhood to adult life. *Journal of Child Psychology and Psychiatry, 30,* 23–51.

Rutter, M. (1990). Psychosocial resilience and protective mechanisms. In J. E. Rolf, A. S. Masten, & D. Cicchetti (Eds.), *Risk and protective factors in the development of psychopathology* (pp. 181–214). Cambridge: Cambridge University Press.

Rutter, M. (1994). Beyond longitudinal data: Causes, consequences, changes, and continuity. *Journal of Consulting & Clinical Psychology. 62*, 928–940.

Rutter, M. (2002). Family influences on behavior and development: Challenges for the future. In J. P. McHale & W. S. Grolnick (Eds.), *Retrospect and prospect in the psychological study of families* (pp. 321–351). New York: Lawrence Erlbaum Associates.

Rutter M., Champion, L., Quinton, D., Maughan, B., & Pickles, A. (1995). Understanding individual differences in environmental risk exposure. In P. Moen, G. H. Elder, & K. Luscher (Eds.), *Examining lives in context: Perspectives on the ecology of human development* (pp. 61–93). Washington, DC: American Psychological Association.

Steinberg, L., Lambron, S. D., Darling, N., Mounts, N. S., & Dornbusch, S. M. (1994). Over-time changes in adjustment and competence among adolescents from authoritative, authoritarian, indulgent, and neglectful families. *Child Development, 65*, 754–770.

Suomi, S. (1997). Early determinants of behavior: Evidence from primate studies. *British Medical Bulletin, 53*, 170–184.

Tremblay, R. E., Pihl, R. O., Vitaro, F., & Dobkin, P. L. (1994). Predicting early onset of male antisocial behavior from preschool behavior: A test of two personality theories. *Archives of General Psychiatry, 51*, 732–739.

Tremblay, R. E., Vitaro, F., Nagin, D., Pagani, L., & Séguin, J. R. (2003). The Montreal longitudinal and experimental study: Rediscovering the power of descriptions. In T. Thornberry and M. D. Krohn (Eds.), *Taking stock of delinquency: An overview of findings from contemporary longitudinal studies* (pp. 205–254). New York: Kluwer Academic/Plenum.

Wagner, B. M. (1997). Family risk factors for child and adolescent suicidal behavior. *Psychological Bulletin, 121*, 246–298.

Willms, D. J., & Shields, M. (1996). *A measure of socioeconomic status for the National Longitudinal Survey of Children and Youth*. Fredericton, NB, Canada: Atlantic Center for Policy Research in Education, University of New Brunswick and Statistics Canada.

Wyatt, J. M., & Carlo, G. (2002). What will my parents think? Relations among adolescents' expected parental reactions, prosocial moral reasoning, and prosocial and antisocial behaviors. *Journal of Adolescent Research, 17*, 646–666.

8

The Contribution of Middle Childhood Contexts to Adolescent Achievement and Behavior

Katherine Magnuson, Greg J. Duncan, and Ariel Kalil

American children spend their elementary school years in diverse conditions. For some children, high family incomes provide large houses, safe neighborhoods, and enriching learning opportunities, while for others, middle childhood is a time of economic deprivation. Some children attend safe schools with highly qualified and caring teachers, while others do not. Some children live with both biological parents during middle childhood; others do not. For some children, relationships with their parents are warm and secure, while for others their relationships are distant and conflicted. For surprisingly many children, these conditions change over the course of middle childhood, and change itself influences children's academic and behavior trajectories.

In this chapter, we assess the extent to which the diverse contexts experienced during middle childhood matter for children's subsequent well-being. Given the established importance of early childhood development and preschool family background conditions, the extent to which contexts during the middle childhood years play a role in shaping the course of academic achievement and problem behavior trajectories is far from clear (Bradley & Corwyn, 2003).

Using data from a national sample of over 2,000 children followed from birth until early adolescence, we assess the extent to which middle childhood contexts add to the explanation of adolescents' academic achievement and problem behavior over and above early childhood environments. We address three specific questions. First, how much variation in adolescents' academic achievement and problem behavior is uniquely explained by the contexts they experience in middle childhood? Second, to the extent that middle childhood contexts matter, which contexts matter most? And third, are the effects of contexts in middle childhood on adolescents' outcomes different for boys and girls and for poor and middle class children? Finally, we provide a brief description of the continuity of contexts between early and middle childhood.

BACKGROUND

During middle childhood, children master such fundamental academic skills as reading and arithmetic and become more self-aware, reflective, and planful (Eccles, 1999). Erikson (1968) characterized this phase of life as a time of "industry," with attention directed at gaining socially-valued competencies and learning how to cooperate with peers and adults. In contrast to the very early years, when the influence of proximal family contexts is paramount, the middle childhood years represent a time of increasing influence of out-of-home environments. Although the family remains an important influence on children's well-being, children participate in school and organized activities and they interact with adults and peers in their community. As a result, they may be influenced by teachers, school environments, and peer groups more during middle than early childhood.

Although children typically enter middle childhood highly optimistic about their abilities, their self-concepts become more differentiated and less positive (albeit, for many, more realistic) by age 10 (Eccles, 1999). Declining self-confidence and motivation in middle childhood, particularly in the academic arena, may lead to a lack of engagement in school and lowered psychological well-being. Indeed, children's personalities, behaviors, and competencies during middle childhood may consolidate and persist into adolescence and adulthood (Collins, Madsen, & Susman-Stillman, 2002). For these reasons, it is clearly important to study the middle childhood years and to identify the factors that promote successful development during this time.

Influences on Development During Middle Childhood

Family and home characteristics, as well as contexts experienced outside the home, have been linked to children's cognitive and social development. Moreover, because children's academic and problem-behavior trajectories differ according to gender and socioeconomic status, the contexts they experience may have differing effects on girls and boys and on children in diverse economic situations (Bongers, Koot, van der Ende, & Verhulst, 2003; Kowaleski-Jones & Duncan, 1999; Pungello, Kuperschmidt, Burchinal, & Patterson, 1996).

Family Income. Correlational and longitudinal research suggests negative effects of low family income on children's cognitive development, and to a lesser extent problem behavior, with stronger negative effects on cognitive development during the preschool years than in later developmental periods (Duncan & Brooks-Gunn, 1997). Findings from a synthesis of the effects of experimental income and work support programs confirm this developmental pattern. The effects of employment and family income supports were more beneficial to preschool-age children's academic achievement as compared with children of other ages (Morris, Duncan, & Clark-Kauffman, 2003).

Family Structure. On average, children raised by single parents have lower levels of social and academic well-being than do children from intact marriages (Cherlin, 1999; McLanahan & Sandefur, 1994). Studies of divorce find that most children have a difficult time during and shortly after the divorce process (Hetherington & Stanley-Hogan, 1999), and that behavior problems are more pronounced than problems in school achievement (McLanahan, 1997). The largest effects of divorce on children are found among children in primary school, and although difficulties may reemerge later in life, recent reviews suggest that the vast majority of children from divorced families do not exhibit severe or enduring problem behaviors (Amato & Keith, 1991).

Divorced families can be distinguished from those in which parents never married or cohabit and from blended and remarried families. Unfortunately, most research has focused only on the effects of divorce on children, or has pooled together all single-parent families (McLanahan, 1997). The few available studies find few differences between children of divorced and never-married parents; both groups are at risk for poorer achievement and behavior as compared to children from intact families (Cooksey, 1997; DeLeire & Kalil, 2002; McLanahan, 1997). In addition, children with stepparents also fare less well than children from intact families. Hill, Yeung, and Duncan (2001) found that time spent in a stepfamily during middle childhood predicts lower educational attainment for girls. Cohabitation and multigenerational coresidence are also prevalent among female-headed families, but their links to child well-being are not well established (Deleire & Kalil, 2002).

Home Environment. The quality of two aspects of the home and family environment – cognitive stimulation and emotional climate – are important influences on children's well-being at all ages. Children and adolescents who have warm and supportive relationships with their parents have better socioemotional adjustment, including lower levels of behavior problems (Bronstein et al., 1996; Patterson, DeBaryshe, & Ramsey, 1989; Wakschlag & Hans, 1999). Parental supportiveness and warmth during interactions with young children have been associated with better cognitive performance and school readiness (Hann, Osofsky, & Culp, 1996; Hubbs-Tait, Culp, Culp, & Miller, 2002; Kelly, Morisset, Barnard, Hammond, & Booth, 1996). However, the importance of parents' emotional supportiveness for academic achievement during middle childhood is less clear (Bradley, Corwyn, Burchinal, McAdoo, & Garcia Coll, 2001;

Bronstein et al., 1996), although several studies have linked positive maternal affect in early childhood to later academic achievement (Estrada, Arsenio, Hess, & Holloway, 1987; Hess, Holloway, Dickson, & Price, 1984).

Parents who are verbally engaging and provide more stimulating toys, activities, and interactions promote children's academic achievement (Espy, Molfeses, & DiLalla, 2001). Using data from the National Longitudinal Survey of Youth, Bradley and colleagues (2001) found that higher levels of learning stimulation were associated with better academic achievement as well as lower levels of behavior problems at all ages, and across several ethnic groups. However, they report that the association between vocabulary and learning stimulation was somewhat larger during early childhood in comparison to middle childhood.

School. As children grow, they spend more time in an array of out-of-home contexts. Key among these is the school environment. Children's sense of "school connectedness," which includes the dimensions of social belonging and relationships with teachers, has been identified as a particularly important influence on middle schoolers' emotional and academic adjustment (Blum, McNeely, & Rinehart, 2002; Roeser, Eccles, & Strobel, 1998). Positive interpersonal relationships in school can fulfill students' needs for belonging and competence, and are in turn hypothesized to promote academic motivation and achievement (Connell & Wellborn, 1991; Eccles & Midgley, 1989; Goodenow, 1992; Roeser et al., 1998). The quality of teacher–student relationships has been found to be an especially important predictor of students' achievement motivation and adjustment during middle childhood (Goodenow, 1992; Wentzel, 1996, 1997, 2002). Resnick and colleagues (1997), for example, found that young adolescents who reported strong emotional attachments to teachers were less likely to use substances or engage in problem behavior. Moreover, positive relationships with teachers were more influential for these behaviors than structural characteristics of the school (e.g., school type, classroom size, attendance, and dropout rates).

Extracurricular Activities. Supervised after-school programs are reported to be the fastest-growing segment of child care services (Pierce, Hamm, & Vandell, 1999). Not only are these arrangements necessary for the supervision and monitoring of school-age children of employed parents, but after-school programs' activities can also provide valuable opportunities for the development of skills and social relationships. Structured, non-school programs can be designed to meet many of the developmental needs of children (Eccles, 1999). Participation in structured activities has been associated with positive changes in adjustment in early adolescence for middle class youth (McHale, Crouter, & Tucker, 2001), although the benefits were not apparent for low-income youth (Posner & Vandell, 1999). Mahoney and Stattin's (2000) analysis of 14-year-olds' leisure time activities concluded that participation in structured activities (e.g., school and community-sponsored athletics, music organizations, and church groups) is correlated with low levels of antisocial behavior. Conversely, unsupervised peer contact after school is associated with increases in problem behavior among children, especially for those in relatively low-income environments (Jarrett, 1997; Pettit, Bates, Dodge, & Meece, 1999; Posner & Vandell, 1994; Vandell & Shumow, 1999).

Neighborhood. The neighborhoods experienced during middle childhood may influence children's development, but most research has considered the effects of neighborhoods on adolescents (Chase-Lansdale, Gordon, Brooks-Gunn, & Klebanov, 1997; Jencks & Mayer, 1990). Physically dangerous neighborhoods may expose children to environmental toxins and to community violence. To protect children from these threats, parents sometimes isolate children in their homes and thus restrict interactions with peers and adults (Jarrett, 1997). Parks, libraries, schools, and other institutions provide more enriching opportunities (and are more available) in higher quality neighborhoods than in less advantaged ones. One recent set of experimental studies showed that increasing neighborhood quality (by randomly assigning families to opportunities to move to low-poverty neighborhoods) improved mental health and decreased problem behaviors for girls but not boys (Orr, Feins, Jacob, & Beecroft, 2003).

Are Middle Childhood Contexts Uniquely Important?

Many of the available studies assess correlations between contexts in middle childhood and concurrent indicators of child well-being, but it is not clear whether the observed child outcomes are the product of concurrent or past contexts. This is a difficult issue to untangle because contexts, as well as behavior, are likely to be stable and thus correlated over time. Developmental theory predicts substantial stability in developmental trajectories, and research on academic achievement and problem behavior has established that early childhood patterns matter for later development (Brame, Nagin, & Tremblay, 2001; Campbell, Shaw, & Gilliom, 2000; Kowaleski-Jones & Duncan, 1999). This stability is not necessarily because behaviors are fixed at an early age and persist, but rather may occur because patterns of interactions between the child and his or her contexts persist until later ages (Caspi, 2000). Typically, studies do not adequately determine whether experiences during middle childhood affect later adjustment over and above developmental trajectories that were established during early childhood. In this chapter, we use a large, nationally representative longitudinal data set to address this issue.

METHOD

Sample

Our data are drawn from the National Longitudinal Survey of Youth (NLSY), a multistage stratified random sample of 12,686 individuals aged 14 to 21 in 1979. Black, Hispanic, and low-income youth were over-represented. Annual (through 1994) and biennial (between 1994 and 2000) interviews with sample members, and very low cumulative attrition in the study, contribute to the high quality of the study's data.

Beginning in 1986, the children born to NLSY female participants were tracked through biennial interview supplements with the mother and direct child assessments. Early cohorts of the child sample were born disproportionately to young mothers. With each additional cohort, the children become more representative, and NLSY children younger than age 14 in 2000 share many demographic characteristics with their broader set of age mates.

Given our desire to track contexts and child achievement from the preschool period through adolescence, our sample consists of all children whose contexts were measured from birth to age 13/14 and whose achievement and behavior was assessed from ages 5/6 to 13/14. Consequently, our sample is composed of children who were ages 5 or 6 in 1986, 1988, 1990, or 1992; their age-13/14 achievement and behavior were assessed in 1994, 1996, 1998, and 2000, respectively. The average age at the final assessment was 13.7 years, with a range from 12.6 to 14.8. Middle childhood contexts were assessed during the intervening biennial interviews, and early childhood contexts were measured annually between birth and age 5/6.

Measures of Child Development

Descriptive statistics for all variables used in analyses are provided in Appendix Table 1. The dependent variables are tests of academic achievement (reading and math) and maternal reports of problem behavior during early adolescence. Academic achievement was assessed with the Peabody Individual Achievement Tests (PIAT) of reading recognition and math. We use the raw PIAT scores, and control for children's age at the time of the final assessment. Children were eligible for the PIAT tests if they were older than 5 years of age, so we control for children's scores on the same tests at the beginning of the middle childhood period.

The reading recognition test measures skills at matching letters, naming names, and reading single words out loud (84 items; $M = 59.4$, $SD = 14$). Overall, the test had an average temporal reliability of .89 (Dunn and Markwardt, 1970). Studies of concurrent validity show moderate correlations with tests of intelligence and reading vocabulary (Davenport, 1976; Wikoff, 1978).

The math subscale is designed so that children are required to apply math concepts to questions rather than to conduct increasingly complicated computations (84 items; $M = 53.8$, $SD = 11$). On average, the test–retest reliability was .74 (Dunn & Markwardt, 1970). Concurrent validity evaluations found that the test correlated moderately with tests of intelligence and math achievement (Davenport, 1976; Wikoff, 1978).

Behavior problems were assessed by mothers' responses to 30 items that asked how true statements were about a child's behavior during the past three months. The internalizing scale is composed of 10 items about such behavior as crying a lot, being fearful and anxious, and being withdrawn ($M = .32$, $SD = .38$). The externalizing scale consists of 20 items about such behavior as cheating or lying, arguing, being disobedient, and acting impulsively ($M = .51$, $SD = .51$).

Middle Childhood Context Measures

Our key independent variables of interest consist of indicators of household income, family structure, urban residence, and the home environment spanning the period from ages 7 to 12, as well as children's perceptions of neighborhood safety, school safety, and their teachers at age 10 or 11. The measure of family income is the percentage of middle childhood years in poverty (family income below the federal poverty threshold), near poverty (1–2 times the poverty threshold), middle income (2–4 times the poverty threshold), and high income (more than 4 times the poverty threshold). The family structure variables are the percentage of middle childhood years children resided in married, divorced, never married, blended, cohabiting, and multigenerational (e.g., grandmother present) households.

The quality of children's home environment was measured by a shortened form of the Home Observation and Measurement of the Environment (HOME) scale, which combines interviewers' ratings of the child's home environment and mothers' responses to questions about the child's home experiences (Caldwell & Bradley, 1984). We use two subscales of the HOME. The cognitive stimulation scale consists of 14 items that measure the quality of learning opportunities, for example, whether the family receives a newspaper and whether the family encourages the child's hobbies. The emotional subscale is comprised of 13 items that measure emotional climate, for example, how often the family gets together with relatives and friends and how often the child was spanked in the prior week.

The reliability for the cognitive stimulation scale when children are 3–5 years old is adequate ($a = .72$), but it drops when children are 6–9 years old ($a = .67$) and over 10 years old ($a = .62$). On the emotional subscale, reliabilities were similar across age groups (a ranged from .58 to .61) (Baker, Keck, Mott, & Quilan, 1993).

When children reached age 10, NLSY interviewers asked them a series of questions about their home, neighborhood, and school experiences. Children's responses to how safe they felt walking and playing in their neighborhood and how safe they felt in their school (1 = very unsafe; 4 = very safe) constituted the measures of neighborhood safety and school safety, respectively. Two items measured children's perceptions of their teachers: "teachers are willing to help with personal problems" and "teachers don't know their subjects well" (1 = very true; 4 = not true at all). We recoded these measures so that a higher score indicates that teachers help with personal problems ("teachers care") and know their subjects. Finally, a single item measured whether children participated in any clubs, teams, or school activities in or out of school (yes = 1; no = 0).

Preschool Control Measures

We control for preschool measures to estimate the unique contribution of middle childhood contexts over and above the early childhood and family background characteristics. The early childhood measures include family income, family structure, home environment, and urban residence. Maternal and interviewer reports of children's temperament, assessed with separate measures of sociability and compliance, are available for children at ages 4 or 5. Compliance was the sum of mothers' responses to 7 items about children's behavioral tendencies; e.g., "the child obeys when told to go to bed" and "turns off the TV when asked" ($a = .59$ for children of all ages, Baker et al., 1993). The sum of three interview ratings of the child's cooperation during the child assessment constituted the sociability scale ($a = .93$, Baker et al., 1993).

An array of child and mother background characteristics were also included: the child's race (Black, Hispanic, or non-Hispanic white) and sex, whether the mother drank alcohol during her pregnancy, her percentile score on the Armed Forces Qualifying Test (AFQT), the age at which she gave birth to the child, whether she ever smoked, her use of marijuana and other drugs during her own early adult or adolescent years, and indicators of whether she got in fights during her own adolescence. Finally, we include missing data dummies for all variables with substantial missing information.

RESULTS

Do Middle Childhood Contexts Matter?

We first consider the extent to which our collection of middle childhood context measures, taken as a whole, accounts for the variation in each of our four early adolescent development measures. A useful point of reference comes from regressions of each of the age-13/14 outcomes on the collection of middle childhood context measures, with no attempt to adjust for preschool contexts, background factors, and achievement and behaviors. The variance explained by middle childhood contexts ranges from 6% and 10% for teen internalizing and externalizing behavior problems to about 20% for math and reading achievement.

These estimates of the variance explained by our set of middle childhood contexts almost certainly overstate the unique role of these contexts because they include the contribution of any early childhood conditions or contexts that are correlated with them. Given the probable continuity of contexts and outcomes across childhood, the possible bias that may result from not controlling for earlier conditions is likely to be substantial.

A more stringent test is of the *unique* contribution of the middle childhood contexts. To accomplish this we first regressed the outcomes on our set of mothers' and children's background characteristics, all of which are measured at or before the entry into middle childhood (age 5/6). Then we add the entire set of middle childhood context measures to the regression, and observe how much additional variation in the outcomes can be explained by the collection of middle childhood contexts.

The results of this analysis are summarized in Figure 8.1. Middle childhood contexts add significantly, but modestly, to explained variance in adolescent achievement and behavior problems. In every case, the additional explained variance amounts to 1–3%. Middle childhood contexts were the strongest unique predictors of children's externalizing behavior, with the R-square increasing from .24 to .27. In the case of internalizing behavior problems, the increase was slightly more modest from .15 to .17. Background factors accounted for much more of the variance in math (32%) and reading (34%) achievement, but again the contributions in explained variance from contexts during middle childhood were small, just 1% in the case of children's reading and 2% for math. With 1–3% incremental explained variance, middle childhood contexts do not appear to be powerful determinants of early adolescent outcomes. Nonetheless, it is possible that some of the middle childhood home and out-of-home contexts are significant predictors of subsequent attainments and behavior.

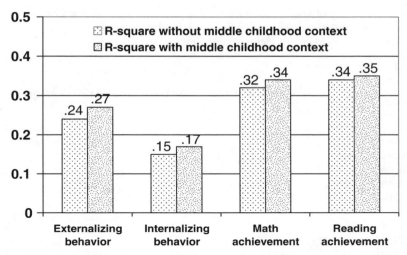

FIGURE 8.1. Explained variance (R-square) with and without middle childhood contexts.

Which Middle Childhood Contexts Matter the Most?

We next examined which contextual measures were most closely associated with behavior problems and achievement in early adolescence. Again, we conducted both simple and more stringent analyses. The simple analyses parallel the regressions presented above – regressions that predict adolescents' outcomes and adjust for other middle childhood contexts but not for preschool measures. Summarized in Table 8.1, results indicate that economic conditions in middle childhood are associated with math and reading achievement, whereas the levels of cognitive stimulation and emotional support in the home strongly predict both achievement and behavior. Most of the out-of-home contextual measures are significant predictors as well.

A stricter test of the unique influence of the middle childhood contextual measures is whether they remain significant after we control for the child's preschool experiences, attainments, and behaviors. Given our ability to control for children's behavior and achievement as they enter middle childhood (age 5/6), as well as a host of preschool family conditions, these regressions provide a rigorous test of whether middle childhood contexts matter. Table 8.2 provides a summary of the results of regressions with a comprehensive set of controls for circumstances at earlier ages.

Among the family environmental measures, only cognitive stimulation in children's home environments predicted all four early adolescent outcomes, promoting higher math and reading achievement and lower levels of behavior problems. In all four regressions, a one standard deviation increase in the home learning environment was associated with about

TABLE 8.1. *Summary of Standardized Regression Coefficients for Middle Childhood Contexts Predicting Early Adolescent Behavior and Achievement Without Controls for Earlier Childhood Behaviors, Achievement, and Contexts*

	Early Adolescent Outcomes			
	Externalizing	Internalizing	Math	Reading
Middle Childhood Family Environments				
% years in poverty	–	–	$-.20^{***}$	$-.15^{***}$
% years divorced	–	–	$.06^{**}$	–
Home cognitive	$-.18^{**}$	$-.15^{***}$	$.28^{***}$	$.30^{***}$
Home emotional	$-.18^{**}$	$-.15^{***}$	$.11^{***}$	–
Middle Childhood Out-of-Home Environments				
Clubs/activities	–	–	$.07^{**}$	–
Neighborhood safety	$-.08^{**}$	$-.07^{**}$	–	$.05^{*}$
School safety	$-.09^{**}$	$-.08^{**}$	$.08^{***}$	$.14^{***}$
Teachers care	–	–	$.05^{**}$	$.06^{**}$
Teachers know subjects	$-.09^{**}$	–	$.12^{***}$	$.12^{***}$

Note: The sample size for all analyses is 2,042. $^{***}p < .01$. $^{**}p < .05$. $^{*}p < .10$. "–" indicates that the standardized coefficient was not statistically significant at $p < .10$.

a tenth of a standard deviation improvement in a given outcome. Positive home emotional climate was also associated with low levels of behavior problems, and again, the magnitude of this effect was near a tenth of a standard deviation. Neither economic conditions nor family structure during middle childhood were significantly related to any of the four outcomes net of preschool conditions.

Out-of-home settings in middle childhood were modestly consistent predictors of adolescent outcomes. Children's perceptions of school safety were associated with lower behavior problems and higher reading achievement. Their perceptions of whether their teachers knew their subjects were also associated with higher achievement and lower externalizing behaviors. Participating in clubs and activities was associated with higher math scores but not other outcomes. Perceptions of neighborhood safety and whether the teachers were helpful with students' personal problems were not related to behavior and academic achievement. Most of these effects were smaller than the estimated effects of children's home environments.

Which Conditions and Contexts in Early Childhood Matter?

Our regressions also provide an assessment of which characteristics and contexts in early childhood matter, net of controls for middle

TABLE 8.2. *Summary of Standardized Regression Coefficients for Middle Childhood Contexts Predicting Early Adolescent Behavior and Achievement with Controls for Early Childhood Achievement, Behavior, and Contexts*

	Early Adolescent Outcomes			
	Externalizing	Internalizing	Math	Reading
Middle Childhood Family Environments				
Poverty/income	–	–	–	–
Family size and structure	–	–	–	–
HOME cognitive	–.08**	–.09**	.11***	.10***
HOME emotional	–.11**	–.09*	–	–
Middle Childhood Out-of-Home Environments				
Clubs/activities	–	–	.04*	–
Neighborhood safety	–	–	–	–
School safety	–.07*	–.06*	–	.09***
Teachers care	–	–	–	–
Teachers know subjects	–.07*	–	.10***	.07**
Preschool Family & Individual Characteristics				
Age 5/6 externalizing behavior	.40***	.20***	–	–
Age 5/6 internalizing behavior	–	.24***	–	–
Age 5/6 math achievement	–	–	.24***	.14***
Age 5/6 reading achievement	–	–	.19***	.34***
Child compliance (age 4/5)	–.16***	–.16***	–	.15***
Child sociability (age 4/5)	–	–	.10**	.10**
HOME emotional (age 5/6)	–.13***	–	–	–
Mom AFQT	–	–	.18***	.12***
Black	–	–	–.10***	–

Note: The sample size for all analyses is 2,042. *** $p < .01$, ** $p < .05$, * $p < .10$; "–" indicates that the standardized coefficient was not statistically significant at $p < .10$.

childhood contexts. Not surprisingly, the measures of the dependent variables at entry into middle childhood (ages 5/6) were the most powerful predictors of early adolescent outcomes. Standardized regression coefficients ranged from .24 for internalizing behavior problems and math achievement, to .34 for reading achievement and .40 for externalizing behavior problems. Reading achievement also predicted later math achievement, and likewise math achievement predicted later reading achievement. Similarly, early externalizing behavior predicted later internalizing behavior, and early internalizing behavior predicted later externalizing behavior, although this association was not especially strong (see Table 8.2). Also noteworthy, children's early reading and math skills were not significant predictors of young adolescents' problem behavior, but early measures of externalizing behavior problems were modestly related to low academic achievement in adolescence (not seen in Table 8.2, standardized coefficients of −.06 for reading and math).

Compliance and sociability at ages 4 or 5 were also predictors of adolescents' outcomes. More compliant children had lower levels of later behavior problems and higher reading achievement. More sociable children had higher subsequent math and reading achievement. A few other early childhood conditions mattered net of the host of other early and middle childhood predictors. More positive home emotional climates were associated with lower levels of adolescent externalizing behavior problems, and mothers' AFQT test scores were positively associated with children's academic achievement. Finally, being Black was associated with lower math achievement in early adolescence.

Do the Patterns Differ by Gender or SES?

We next consider whether the effects of contexts in middle childhood differ according to child gender and early childhood poverty status. To conduct these analyses we ran regressions in which each variable in the estimation model was interacted with child gender and then family poverty (defined as being poor at least half of the time between birth and age 5). The results yielded few significant interactions. In the case of gender, 5 of the 68 tested interactions attained statistical significance at conventional levels. Participating in clubs and activities appeared to have a more positive effect (in particular, math achievement) on girls as compared with boys, and a positive emotional home environment was associated with lower levels of internalizing behavior among girls than among boys.

In the case of early poverty interactions, 7 of the 68 tested interactions were statistically significant at conventional levels, but a sensible pattern did not emerge. Consequently, we conclude that the middle childhood contexts identified as significant for the overall sample (e.g., cognitive stimulation in the home, safe schools) appear to have similar influences on boys and girls and for poor and middle class children.

Continuity of Contexts Across Childhood

Continuity in children's contexts from early to middle childhood presents both conceptual and empirical challenges. If a child's contexts are highly

TABLE 8.3. *Correlations of Key Contexts Over Time*

	Contexts Age 5/6	Contexts Ages 1–5
Contexts 7–12		
Poverty	.43	.66
Near poverty	.30	.36
Medium high income	.31	.35
HOME emotional	.48	–
HOME cognitive stimulation	.56	–
Urban residence	.83	.74
Grandmother in household	.50	.44
Number of children	.77	.63
Never married	.77	.73
Divorced	.67	.52

Note: Correlations are calculated only for observations with non-missing data. All correlations are significant at the $p < .01$ level.

similar in early and middle childhood, it may be impossible to assess the unique contribution of middle childhood contexts to early adolescent well-being. In this section, we assemble various pieces of evidence to show that contexts are far from permanent, and they are certainly variable enough to enable us to assess the unique role of middle childhood contexts.

In Table 8.3 we present simple correlations of the middle childhood context measures with measures of the same contexts at ages 5–6 and ages 1–5. In the cases of time spent in urban areas and family size, these correlations are high indeed, ranging between .63 and .83. In the case of economic conditions, the well-documented fluctuations in families' incomes (Duncan, 1988) produce correlations that average only .40 and range from .30 to .66. Temporal correlations for the two key components of the home environment (cognitive stimulation and emotional climate) are around .50. Any measurement error would attenuate correlations.

Correlations in the range of .40 –.60 are certainly significant in a statistical sense and may be viewed as high in an absolute sense. But, suppose we translate the family poverty (.66) and home cognitive stimulation (.56) correlations into corresponding two-way distribution tables (Table 8.4). The top panel shows that only a little more than one third of children who are poor at least 75% of their early childhood years are poor that much during middle childhood. To be sure, most who escape 75+% poverty still fall into the "often poor" category (i.e., poor 50–75% of the time), but close to one third of those in seeming permanent poverty in early

TABLE 8.4. *(Dis)continuities in Family Economic and Home Cognitive Environments Before and During Middle Childhood*

Family Poverty, Ages 7–12	Family Poverty, Ages 7–12				
	Never or Rarely	Sometimes	Often	Always or Almost Always	Total
Never or rarely poor	68	23	7	2	100%
Sometimes poor	60	23	1	7	100%
Often poor	36	28	20	17	100%
Always or almost always poor	11	21	32	36	100%

HOME Cognitive Environment, Ages 5–6	HOME Cognitive Environment, ages 7–12				
	Lowest	Second	Third	Highest	Total
Lowest quartile	50	31	13	6	100%
Second quartile	28	28	29	16	100%
Third quartile	13	28	33	27	100%
Highest quartile	5	14	28	53	100%

Note: Calculations based on observations with non-missing data. Never or rarely poor = <25% of time; sometimes poor = 25–50% of time; often poor = 50–75% of time; always or almost always poor = >75% of time.

childhood are either never poor or poor less than half of the time in middle childhood.

Similarly, the .56 temporal correlation for home cognitive stimulation translates into considerable change in average conditions between early and middle childhood (bottom panel of Table 8.4). Only half of the children in the lowest quartile of this measure in early childhood were also in the lowest quartile during middle childhood. Likewise, only about one half of the children with early childhood scores in the top quartile were also in the top quartile in middle childhood.

A complementary look at the correlation issue comes from an examination of the precision (standard errors) of the estimates of middle childhood contextual effects with and without controls for early childhood contexts and other conditions. Contexts so highly correlated as to cause troublesome multicolinearity would be reflected in large increases in standard errors when controls for earlier achievement, behavior, and contexts are added to our regression models. In fact, the standard errors hardly increase at all. For example, the standard error of estimates of the impacts of middle childhood home cognitive stimulation stay at .037 for teen externalizing behavior problems, increase from .039 to .042 for internalizing behavior problems, increase from .035 to .036 for math achievement, and decrease slightly from .037 to .036 for reading achievement. Thus, it appears that although early and middle childhood contexts are correlated, they are not so strongly associated as to interfere with estimating the unique contributions of middle childhood contexts to early adolescent outcomes.

SUMMARY AND IMPLICATIONS

Our look at links between middle childhood contexts and teen outcomes leads us to the following conclusions. First, taken as a whole, our measures of middle childhood contexts explain a small, but significant, incremental proportion (1–3%) of the variance in early adolescents' academic and problem behaviors. Despite considerable continuity in contexts between the preschool years and middle childhood, there was not so much continuity that it was difficult to estimate their separate impacts.

Second, elements of both the home and out-of-home environments in middle childhood are associated with positive changes in behavior and achievement. A stimulating home learning environment during middle childhood has the most consistent associations with teen outcomes, predicting lower levels of problem behavior and higher levels of academic achievement. In addition, higher quality home emotional environments predict fewer teen behavior problems.

Looking outside the home, students' perceptions in middle childhood that their "teachers know their subjects" are associated with higher levels of academic achievement and lower levels of subsequent externalizing behavior problems. Similarly, students who reported higher levels of perceived school safety had fewer problem behaviors and higher levels of reading achievement several years later.

Third, with very few exceptions, we found no evidence that effects differed among subgroups of interest. The estimated effects of middle childhood contexts were similar for boys and girls, as well as for children who did and did not experience poverty in early childhood.

Thus, it appears that some middle childhood contexts, but not others, have unique and lasting influences on early adolescents' well-being. Notably absent from this list of important contexts are the economic conditions and family structures of the children's households, both of which were well measured in the survey data. Children in families with higher incomes and two biological parents during middle childhood achieved more and behaved better in adolescence than children in poorer or single-parent families, but these differences disappeared once differences in preschool family conditions and children's own achievement and behavior at the beginning of middle childhood were taken into account.

If we had to select a single context as most important, it appears that a stimulating learning environment – both in the home and school – matters the most. These measures predicted both higher math and reading achievement and lower levels of behavior problems. School safety, which may also contribute to positive learning environments, was also associated with three of the four adolescent outcomes.

Learning opportunities and cognitive stimulation in the preschool years have been identified repeatedly as powerful predictors of school readiness. One result has been public awareness campaigns that encourage parents to read to their children and enrich their children's home learning environments. If confirmed in other studies, the predictive power of cognitive stimulation in home environments during middle childhood emerging from our analysis suggests the possible utility of interventions that successfully promote enriching learning opportunities in children's home environments.

Despite having repeated measurements of a number of contexts across middle childhood, our data fell short of supplying a comprehensive set of contextual conditions. Topping the list of lamented omissions are measures of the peer groups to which the children are exposed, because peers have an increasing influence during this period. Given the element of self-selection in peer groups, it would have been difficult to establish likely casual impacts of peers using our methods. Nevertheless, we suspect that peer influences may account for some of the unexplained variance in our analyses. Also missing are other aspects of the family environment that may be influential such as parents' expectations for their children and their values, and school environment such as the amount and types of instruction.

Finally, the most powerful associations with early adolescent outcomes were found for those experiences, contexts, abilities, and behaviors with which children enter middle childhood. These findings support prior research that has identified strong and enduring associations between early childhood development and adolescent academic achievement and problem behavior (Brame et al., 2001; Campbell et al, 2000; Kowaleski-Jones & Duncan, 1999). Although middle childhood contexts may constitute independent sources of risk and resilience for children, the key to understanding adolescents' achievements and problem behavior is the accumulated experiences and development prior to middle childhood. However, interventions may produce more marked changes in middle childhood contexts than occur naturally, and therefore may be able to bring about larger changes in adolescents' well-being than our analysis indicates.

APPENDIX TABLE 1. *Means and Standard Deviations of Independent Variables*

	Middle Childhood		Age 5/6		Early Childhood	
	M	SD	M	SD	M	SD
Contexts						
% years poverty	.33	.31	.35	.48	.31	.36
% years near poverty	.20	.26	.15	.36	.22	.28
% years middle income	.16	.24	.14	.34	.17	.25
Missing family income	.09	.29	.19	.39	.11	.31
% years divorced	.23	.37	.06	.24	.11	.25
% years never married	.13	.31	.15	.36	.25	.41
% years blended	.09	.22	.20	.40	–	–
% years cohabitation	.02	.12	.04	.19	–	–
% years w/grandmother	.07	.19	.06	.24	.17	.29
HOME cognitive stimulation	.90	.27	.90	.41	–	–
HOME emotional	.97	.31	.77	.36	–	–
Ave # children	2.67	1.08	2.54	1.18	2.21	1.05
Missing HOME cognitive stim.	.04	.19	.10	.31	–	–
Missing HOME emotional	.07	.25	.12	.33	–	–
% years urban residence	.76	.39	.76	.43	.75	.41
Missing urban residence	–	–	.03	.16	.03	.16
Ages 10–11 Contexts						
Neighborhood safety	2.99	1.28	–	–	–	–
School safety	3.07	1.35	–	–	–	–
Teachers care	1.56	.95	–	–	–	–
Teachers know subjects	3.13	1.32	–	–	–	–
Participation in clubs or activities	.50	.50	–	–	–	–
Missing clubs or activities	.17	.37	–	–	–	–
Missing neigh. safety	.09	.29	–	–	–	–
Missing school safety	.10	.30	–	–	–	–
Missing teachers care	.09	.29	–	–	–	–
Missing teachers know	.09	.29	–	–	–	–
Age 5/6: Behavior & Achievement						
Internalizing behavior problems	–	–	.38	.34	–	–
Externalizing behavior problems	–	–	.84	1.24	–	–

(continued)

	Middle Childhood		Age 5/6		Early Childhood	
	M	SD	M	SD	M	SD
Reading (missing data=0)	–	–	14.21	6.52	–	–
Missing reading	–	–	.07	.25	–	–
Math (missing data=0)	–	–	13.28	5.81	–	–
Missing math	–	–	.04	.19	–	–
Maternal Report						
Temperament Age 3/4						
Sociability	–	–	–	66	7.19	5.82
Compliance	–	–	–	–	17.14	1.11
Missing sociability	–	–	–	–	.34	.47
Missing compliance	–	–	–	–	.23	.42
Child & Mother						
Background						
Characteristics						
Mothers education	–	–	12.10	2.14	–	–
Black	–	–	–	–	.33	.47
Hispanic	–	–	–	–	.21	.40
Boy	–	–	–	–	.50	.50
Mom use alcohol during pregnancy	–	–	–	–	.41	.49
Missing alcohol during pregnancy	–	–	–	–	.04	.20
Mother AFQT test score	–	–	–	–	.32	.26
Missing AFQT	–	–	–	–	.03	.18
Mother ever use alcohol	–	–	–	–	.86	.35
Mother fight	–	–	–	–	.29	.74
Mother never smoke	–	–	–	–	.23	.42
Mother marijuana use: occasional	–	–	–	–	.13	.34
Mother marijuana use: moderate or high	–	–	–	–	.11	.31
Mother drug use: occasional	–	–	–	–	.05	.22
Mother drug use: moderate or high	–	–	–	–	.05	.21
Age of mom at birth	–	–	–	–	22.54	2.95
Missing mother fight	–	–	–	–	.05	.21
Missing marijuana use	–	–	–	–	.05	.21
Missing drug use	–	–	–	–	.05	.22

Note: "–" indicates that the measure is not available.

References

Amato, P. R., & Keith, B. (1991). Parental divorce and the well-being of children: A meta-analysis. *Psychological Bulletin, 110,* 26–46.

Baker, P. C., Keck, C. K., Mott, F. L., & Quilan, S. V. (1993). *NLSY Child Handbook, Revised Edition: A guide to the 1986–1990 NLSY child data.* Columbus, OH: Ohio State University, Center for Human Resource Research.

Blum, R. W., McNeely, C. A., & Rinehart, P. M. (2002). *Improving the odds: The untapped power of schools to improve the health of teens.* Minne Center for Adolescent Health and Development, University of Minnesota.

Bongers, I. L., Koot, H. M., van der Ende, J. & Verhulst, F. C. (2003). The normative development of child and adolescent problem behavior. *Journal of Abnormal Psychology, 112,* 179–192.

Bradley, R. H., Corwyn, R. F., Burchinal, M., McAdoo, H. P., & Garcia Coll, C. (2001). The home environments of children in the United States Part II: Relations with behavioral development through age thirteen. *Child Development, 72,* 1868–1886.

Bradley, R., & Corwyn, R. F. (2003). Age and ethnic variations in family process mediators of SES. In M. H. Bornstein & R. H. Bradley (Eds.), *Socioeconomic status, parenting, and child development* (pp. 161–188). Mahwah, NJ: Lawrence Erlbaum.

Brame, B., Nagin, D., & Trembley, R. E. (2001). Developmental trajectories of physical aggression from school entry to late adolescence. *Journal Child Psychology & Psychiatry, 4,* 503–512.

Bronstein, P., Duncan, P., D'Ari, A., Piendiaz, J., Fitzgerald, M., Abrams, C. L., et al. (1996). Family and parenting behaviors predicting middle school adjustment: A longitudinal study. *Family Relations, 45,* 415–426.

Caldwell, B. M., & Bradley, R. H. (1984). *Home observation for measurement of the environment.* Little Rock, AR: University of Arkansas.

Campbell, S. B., Shaw, D. S., & Gilliom, M. (2000). Early externalizing behavior problems: Toddlers and preschoolers at risk for later maladjustment. *Developmental Psychopathology, 12,* 467–488.

Caspi, A. (2000). The child is father of the man: Personality continuities from childhood to adulthood. *Journal of Personality and Social Psychology, 78,* 158–172.

Chase-Lansdale, P. L., Gordon, R. A., Brooks-Gunn, J., & Klebanov, P. K. (1997). Neighborhood and family influences on the intellectual and behavioral competence of preschool and early school-age children. In J. Brooks-Gunn, G. Duncan, & L. Aber (Eds.), *Neighborhood poverty: Vol. 1. Context and consequences for development* (pp. 79–118). New York: Russell Sage Foundation.

Cherlin, A. (1999). Going to extremes: Family structure, children's well-being, and social science. *Demography, 36,* 421–428.

Collins, W. A., Madsen, S., & Susman-Stillman, A. (2002). Parenting during middle childhood. In M. Bornstein, (Ed), *Handbook of parenting: Vol. 1. Children and parenting* (2nd ed., pp. 73–101). Mahwah, NJ: Lawrence Erlbaum Associates.

Connell, J., & Wellborn, J. (1991). Competence, autonomy, and relatedness: A motivational analysis of self-system processes. In M. Gunnar & L. Sroufe (Eds.), *Self processes in development: Minnesota Symposium on Child Development* (Vol. 23, pp. 43–77). Hillsdale, NJ: Lawrence Erlbaum Associates.

Cooksey, E. (1997). Consequences of young mothers' martial histories for children's cognitive development. *Journal of Marriage and the Family, 59,* 245–261.

Davenport, B. M. (1976). A comparison of the Peabody Individual Achievement Test, the Metropolitan Achievement Test, and the Otis-Lennon Mental Ability Test. *Psychology in the Schools, 13,* 291–297.

DeLeire, T., & Kalil, A. (2002). Good things come in 3's: Multigenerational coresidence and adolescent adjustment. *Demography, 39,* 393–413.

Duncan, G., & Brooks-Gunn, J. (Eds). (1997). *Consequences of growing up poor.* New York: Russell Sage.

Duncan, G. (1988). The volatility of family income over the life course. In P. Baltes, D. Featherman, & R. M. Lerner (Eds.), *Life-span development and behavior.* Hillsdale, NJ: Lawrence Erlbaum Associates.

Dunn, L. M., & Markwardt, F. C., Jr. (1970). *Peabody Individual Achievement Test manual.* Circle Pines, MN: American Guidance System.

Eccles, J., & Midgley, C. (1989). Stage-environment fit: Developmentally appropriate classrooms for young adolescents. In C. Ames & R. Ames (Eds.), *Research on motivation in education: Vol. 3. Goals and cognitions* (pp. 13–44). New York: Academic.

Eccles, J. (1999). The development of children ages 6 to 14. The Future of Children, 9(2), 30–44.

Erikson, E. (1968). *Identity, youth, and crisis.* New York: W. W. Norton and Company.

Espy, K. A., Molfeses, V. J., & DiLalla, L. F. (2001). Effects of environmental measures on intelligence in young children: Growth curve modeling of longitudinal data. *Merrill-Palmer Quarterly, 47,* 42–73.

Estrada, P., Arsenio, W. F., Hess, R. D., & Holloway, S. D. (1987). Affective quality of the mother-child relationship: Longitudinal consequences for children's school-relevant cognitive functioning. *Developmental Psychology, 23,* 210–215.

Goodenow, C. (1992). Strengthening the links between educational psychology and the study of social contexts. *Educational Psychologist, 27,* 177–196.

Hann, D. M., Osofsky, J. D., & Culp, A. M. (1996). Relating the adolescent mother-child relationship to preschool outcomes. *Infant Mental Health Journal, 17,* 302–309.

Hess, R. D., Holloway, S. D., Dickson, W. P., & Price, G. G. (1984). Maternal variables as predictors of children's school readiness and later achievement in vocabulary and mathematics in sixth grade. *Child Development, 55,* 1902–1912.

Hetherington, E. M., & Stanley-Hogan, M. (1999). The adjustment of children with divorced parents: A risk and resiliency perspective. Journal of Child Psychology & Psychiatry, *40,* 129–140.

Hill, M. S., Yeung, W. J., & Duncan, G. (2001). Childhood family structure and young adult behaviors. *Journal Population Economics, 14,* 271–299.

Hubbs-Tait, L., Culp, A. M., Culp, R. E., & Miller, C. (2002). Relation of maternal cognitive stimulation, emotional support, and intrusive behavior during Head Start to children's cognitive abilities. *Child Development, 73,* 110–131.

Jarret, R. (1997). African American family and parenting strategies in impoverished neighborhoods. *Qualitative Sociology, 20,* 275–288.

Jencks, C., & Mayer, S. (1990). The social consequences of growing up in a poor neighborhood. In L. Lynn and M. McGeary (Eds.), *Inner-city poverty in the United States* (pp. 111–186). Washington, DC: National Academy Press.

Kelly, J. F., Morisset, C. E., Barnard, K. E., Hammond, M. A., Booth, C. L. (1996). The influence of early mother-child interactions on preschool cognitive/linguistic outcomes in a high-risk-social group. *Infant Mental Health Journal, 17,* 310–321.

Kowaleski-Jones, L., & Duncan, G. J. (1999). The structure of achievement and behavior across middle childhood. *Child Development, 70,* 930–943.

Mahoney, J. L., & Stattin, H. (2000). Leisure time activities and adolescent anti-social behavior: The role of structure and social context. Journal of Adolescence, *23,* 113–127.

McHale, S., Crouter, A., & Tucker, C. (2001). Free-time activities in middle childhood: Links with adjustment in early adolescence. *Child Development, 72,* 1764–1778.

McLanahan, S., & Sandefur, G. (1994). *Growing up with a single parent: What hurts, what helps.* Cambridge, MA: Harvard University Press.

McLanahan, S. (1997). Parent absence or poverty: Which matters more? In G. J. Duncan & J. Brooks-Gunn, (Eds.), *Consequences of growing up poor* (pp. 35–48). New York: Russell Sage Foundation.

Morris, P., Duncan, G. J., & Clark-Kauffman, B. (in press). Child well-being in an era of welfare reform: The sensitivity of transitions in development to policy change. *Developmental Psychology.*

Orr, L., Feins, J. D., Jacob, R., & Beecroft, E. (2003). *Moving to opportunity interim impacts evaluation* (1–178). Washington, DC, U.S. Department of Housing and Urban Development, Office of Policy Development & Research.

Patterson, G. R., DeBaryshe, B. D., & Ramsey, E. (1989). A developmental perspective on antisocial behavior. *American Psychologist, 44,* 329–335.

Pettit, G., Bates, J., Dodge, K., & Meece, D. (1999). The impact of after-school peer contact on early adolescent externalizing problems is moderated by parental monitoring, perceived neighborhood safety, and prior adjustment. *Child Development, 70,* 768–778.

Pierce, K., Hamm, J., & Vandell, D. (1999). Experiences in after-school programs and children's adjustment in first-grade classrooms. *Child Development, 70,* 756–767.

Posner, J., & Vandell, D. (1994). Low-income children's after-school care: Are there beneficial effects of after-school programs? Child Development, *65,* 440–456.

Posner, J., & Vandell, D. (1999). After-school activities and the development of low-income urban children: A longitudinal study. *Developmental Psychology, 35,* 868–879.

Pungello, E. P., Kuperschmidt, J. B., Burchinal, M. R., & Patterson, C. J. (1996). Environmental risk factors and children's achievement: From middle childhood to early adolescence. *Developmental Psychology, 32,* 755–767.

Resnick, M., Bearman, P., Blum, R., Bauman, K., Harris, K., Jones, J., et al. (1997). Protecting adolescents from harm: Findings from the National Longitudinal Study on Adolescent Health. *Journal of the American Medical Association, 278,* 823–832.

Roeser, R., Eccles, J., & Strobel, K. (1998). Linking the study of schooling and mental health: Selected issues and empirical illustrations at the level of the individual. *Educational Psychologist, 33,* 153–176.

Vandell, D. L., & Shumow, L. (1999). After-school child care programs. *Future of Children, 9*(2), 64–80.

Wakschlag, L. S., & Hans, S. L. (1999). Relation of maternal responsiveness during infancy to the development of behavior problems in high-risk youths. *Developmental Psychology, 35,* 569–579.

Wentzel, K. (1996). Social goals and social relationships as motivators of school adjustment. In J. Juvonen & K. Wentzel (Eds.), *Social motivation: Understanding children's adjustment* (pp. 226–247). Cambridge: Cambridge University Press.

Wentzel, K. (1997). Student motivation in middle school: The role of perceived pedagogical caring. *Journal of Educational Psychology, 89,* 411–419.

Wentzel, K. (2002). Are effective teachers like good parents? Teaching styles and student adjustment in early adolescence. *Child Development, 73,* 287–301.

Wikoff, R. L. (1978). Correlational and factor analysis of the Peabody Individual Achievement Test and the WISC-R. (1978). *Journal of Consulting and Clinical Psychology, 46,* 322–325.

9

Educational Tracking Within and Between Schools

From First Grade Through Middle School and Beyond

Doris R. Entwisle, Karl L. Alexander, and
Linda Steffel Olson

To clarify the role of schools in reproducing social stratification, sociologists have focused mainly on high schools, especially curriculum tracking (see e.g., Gamoran & Mare, 1989; Gamoran, 1992). These practices have become less standard over the past two decades (Lucas, 1999), but they are still much in evidence in the United States (Kao & Thompson, 2003). Generally, tracking studies examine curriculum or course-taking differences *within* schools, comparing high- versus low-ability group placements (Gamoran, 1992; Hallinan, 1992; Stevenson, Schiller, & Schneider, 1994). Even so, family SES, which predicts tracks within schools, also predicts tracks *between* schools because the availability and quality of high-level programs vary from school to school, even in the same system (Spade, Columba, & Vanfossen, 1997), and family SES of students predicts this availability (Jones, Vanfossen, & Ensminger, 1995; Spade et al., 1997). Aside from comparisons of public and parochial schools, however, research on effects of between-school tracking is thin.

Ability-group tracking is found in a large majority of U.S. middle schools as well (Braddock, 1990), but research on tracking in middle schools is much less extensive than in high schools, (e.g., Cairns, Cairns, & Neckerman 1989; Eccles, Midgley, & Adler, 1984; Eccles et al., 1993; Feldman & Elliott, 1990; Reynolds, 1992; Simmons & Blyth, 1987). Still, it is in middle school that many students first experience formal tracking, a key organizational change for them (Braddock, Wu, & McPartland 1988; Hoffer, 1992, 1994). Many middle schools place students in English and/or math sections designated by such terms as remedial, regular, and advanced. The limited research on middle school tracks suggests they have effects like those attributed to high school tracks. Students in high tracks tend to learn somewhat more than those in low tracks (Catsambis, 1992; Fuligni, Eccles, & Barber, 1995; Hallinan 1992), but overall heterogeneous grouping does not appear to be an improvement over homogeneous grouping (see Hoffer, 1992, 1994). Whether middle school tracking affects ultimate outcomes is not clear, nor are its precursors; but these questions could be of great consequence for middle school students because taking algebra or advanced math predicts placement in college preparatory courses and college tracks in high school.

A different style of research on tracking, so far rare in the United States is exemplified by Kerckhoff's (1993) work in Great Britain. Beginning in the primary grades, he plotted developmental trajectories over students' entire school careers. He examined tracks between schools *and* within schools at successive levels to see whether placement at one level predicted placement at the next level. His research emphasizes students' social origins at the time they began formal schooling and how those origins are transmitted through tracking systems to life destinations.

Using data from the Beginning School Study (BSS) in Baltimore, this paper takes an explicit life course perspective on school tracking. It examines elementary and middle school (grades 6 to 8) tracks in relation to each other and in relation to life outcomes up to age 22. Middle school may be the crucible period for understanding how curriculum tracking shapes students' ultimate development because students take prerequisites there for college prep programs in high school.

TRANSITIONS

A considerable body of literature deals with the move from grade school to middle or junior high school (see e.g., Eccles et al., 1984; Feldman & Elliott, 1990; Simmons & Blyth, 1987), but little of it focuses on tracking or on the ways in which school organizational structures mesh over that transition (Alexander & Entwisle, 1996; Becker, 1987). Still, school transitions are strategically advantageous for studying tracking because they are points of maximum continuity/discontinuity in the life course. When children enter or leave a school, effects of social context tend to be most apparent (see Dauber, Alexander, & Entwisle, 1996; Simmons & Blyth, 1987). At the beginning of middle school, for example, SES background has more pronounced effects on placements in math than it has on changes in placements during middle school (Dauber et al., 1996). Why? Probably because parent advocacy plays a greater role in initial placements, and higher SES parents are more effective as advocates for their children (see e.g., Lareau, 1987). Academic markers *from the end of elementary school* (fifth grade test scores and marks, retention histories) are also brought into these placement decisions.

An earlier transition, that into first grade, may be even more telling, however (Barr & Dreeben, 1983; Entwisle, Alexander, & Olson, 1997; Entwisle & Hayduk 1978, 1982; Reynolds, 1992), because SES predicts children's cognitive status when they start school (Duncan, Brooks-Gunn, Yeung, & Smith, 1998). Children from homes where socioeconomic resources are scarce start that transition with a smaller vocabulary and/or less numeracy skill than do children from homes with more resources (see Hart and Risley, 1995; U.S. Department of Education, 2003). Children from low SES families thus are at higher risk for retention at the end of first grade and over the rest of elementary school than are children from better-off families (Alexander, Entwisle, & Dauber, 2003; Shepard & Smith, 1989; Reynolds, 1992; Zill, 1996).

In middle childhood, grade retention is a form of tracking but it is seldom explicitly recognized as such. Although the grade retention rate in schools throughout the country is probably 5% or less (see Alexander et al., 2003), rates in schools that enroll mainly disadvantaged children are much higher (see Hauser, 2001). In the early 1990s, about 50% of Baltimore students had been retained by the end of elementary school (Alexander et al., 2003).

Retention tracking *within* elementary schools is only part of the story; tracking *between* elementary schools is also critical. In Baltimore, for example, there is a high inverse correlation (.67) between the average meal subsidy level of students and average first grade California Achievement Tests (CAT) scores in math in elementary schools (Entwisle et al., 1997).[1] Moreover, SES differences between schools tend to increase as children progress up through the grades (see Baltimore City Public Schools, 1988; and Table 4.1 in Entwisle et al., 1997, for more detail). Overall, the gap in reading achievement between the highest and lowest SES schools increased over the elementary school years (see also U.S. Department of Education, 2001, Table 110). SES tracking *between* elementary schools continues in middle schools because they draw from geographically clustered feeder schools. In Baltimore, for example, the correlation is .73 between the meal subsidy rates of the elementary schools and those of the middle schools children are sorted into.

MODELS TO EXPLAIN TRACKING

Track placements within high schools can affect college achievement by several routes: Students in higher groups take more demanding courses than those in lower groups (Gamoran & Berends, 1987); they learn more than students in lower groups (Alexander, Cook, & McDill, 1978); and having been in a higher group has institutional effects (Rosenbaum, 1976) because those in higher groups are judged "better" by virtue of having been in such a group.

In what follows, a series of models examines middle school tracking to understand whether tracks affect achievement and/or have institutional effects, and also how middle school tracks mesh with tracks in the schools

[1] Earlier research found that first grade children's own expectations are amorphous and do not predict their school performance (Alexander & Entwisle, 1988; Finn & Cox, 1992).

children attend before and after middle school. These models clarify track effects within schools *and* between schools in middle childhood, extending from first grade through middle school and beyond to predicting educational outcomes after high school.

The analyses use data from the BSS, a panel of Baltimore youth who have been monitored from first grade into early adulthood (age 22). These models build on prior research by (a) investigating effects of placement in "low tracks" as well as in "high tracks," (b) searching for differences between schools in nominally equivalent tracks, (c) determining whether middle school tracks are predicted by elementary school tracks, and (d) determining whether middle school tracks predict educational status at age 22.

An initial model estimates the cumulative risk of retention over elementary school (grade retention is the only kind of elementary school track examined here). This model is then expanded to determine whether tracking in elementary school predicts middle school placement. The critical question is whether track effects carry over from one level of schooling to the next.

The next model focuses on the equivalence of math tracks in *different* middle schools in the same school system. Do students in advanced tracks learn more math than students in regular or remedial tracks? If so, then do students in advanced sections in some middle schools learn more than students in advanced sections in other middle schools (a between-school issue)? Do determinants of advanced track assignments vary by middle school? For example, is race more important for advanced math placement in some schools than others?

The final model explores whether placements in middle school predict educational outcomes at age 22. Other things equal, do structural characteristics of schools in middle childhood affect educational outcomes in early adulthood? If so, are these effects explained by increased learning or by labeling? This last model is examined also in light of a descriptive analysis of high school tracks. At age 22 does earlier tracking shape the decisions young adults make about how far to go in school and the kinds of postsecondary education to pursue? The full model is illustrated in Figure 9.1.

The analyses focus on mathematics achievement, primarily because middle school algebra is commonly required for college preparatory placements in high school. Math tracking is also more hierarchical and sequenced than is tracking in language arts, the other domain often studied (see Kerckhoff, 1993; Dauber et al., 1996). Criteria for "advanced English," for example, are not easy to define, and no single topic like algebra clearly differentiates among track levels. By contrast, algebra is recognized as the main subject in advanced tracks and is noted in students' records even when advanced tracks are not available in a school. Math achievement

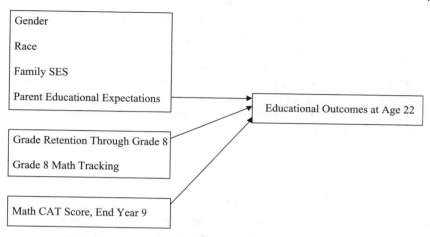

FIGURE 9.1. Model predicting educational outcomes at age 22.

is also of particular interest because it predicts high school completion (Ingels, Curtin, Kaufman, Alt, & Chen, 2002), and math skills taught no later than eighth grade are an important predictor of subsequent wages (Murnane, Willett, & Levy, 1995). Earlier BSS research on the transition to middle school, which examined both verbal and math outcomes (Dauber et al., 1996), concluded that the dynamics of track placements in the two subjects differ in only minor respects.

METHOD

Background and Setting

Data come from the BSS in Baltimore, which has followed a representative, random sample of Baltimore public school children since first grade in 1982 ($N = 790$). Sampling proceeded in two stages. First, a random sample of twenty Baltimore City public elementary schools, stratified by racial mix (six predominantly African American, six predominantly white, eight integrated) and by socioeconomic status (fourteen inner-city or working class and six middle class), was selected. Second, within each school, about a dozen students were randomly sampled from each first-grade classroom. Ninety-seven percent of the randomly selected parents and children consented to participate in the project.

The city public schools at the time enrolled about 77% African Americans (U.S. Census Bureau, 1983), so to sustain racial comparisons the Study oversampled whites. The final sample was 55% African American. Parents' educational levels ranged from less than eighth grade to graduate and professional degrees, averaging 11.9 years ($SD = 2.59$). More white than

African American parents had completed college (14.7% versus 10.3%), but more whites were among those with the least education: Over a third (35.3%) of white parents had completed ten or fewer years of school compared with 17.2% of African American parents. School records show 67% of BSS children qualified for free or reduced price meals, 77% of African Americans and 53% of whites. Overall, about 56% of students resided in two-parent homes at the beginning of first grade, 70% of whites and 44% of African Americans.

Procedures

When children started first grade, their race, gender, and eligibility for subsidized meals were determined from school records. Parents' education, occupations, and expectations for how far children would go in school were ascertained in interviews either prior to or concurrent with the child's enrollment in first grade (see Entwisle et al., 1997). The CAT in math concepts/applications were given fall and spring by the schools each year through the sixth grade, and in the spring of years 7 and 8. In year 9, the BSS staff administered CAT (1979) tests to BSS students. Teachers assigned marks four times a year. Retention decisions at the end of each school year and track placements in middle school came from school records. Educational outcomes by age 22 (years of school completed, kinds of postsecondary schools attended) come from a Young Adult Survey in 1998–99, sixteen years after the students had entered first grade and four to five years after on-time students graduated from high school. The age 22 survey, which was completed by 632 young adults (80% of the original sample), was conducted by telephone when possible (76% of the total), otherwise by face-to-face interviews. The data thus cover the entire span from the first grade transition to early adulthood.

Participants

The multivariate analyses pertain to the 290 individuals who met the following criteria. They were (a) enrolled only in the Baltimore school system through eighth grade, (b) had experienced eighth grade placements in math, (c) had completed the Young Adult Survey at age 22, and (d) had complete information on all variables. This group was 72% African American and 57% female; on average, their mothers had completed 11.7 years of school. At age 6, 71% were on full or partial meal subsidy and 51% lived in two-parent households. This sample has a higher proportion of African Americans (72% versus 55% in the original sample) and somewhat lower SES (71% on meal subsidy) than either the original sample (67%) or the age 22 sample (65%), but compares well on math and reading scores at the beginning of first grade.

The higher level of attrition for white students in the analysis sample reflects the differential choices made by white and African American families to leave the city school system after 1982. Such demographic trends over the 1980s present special difficulties for the analyst, because when students move out of the school system either to private schools or non-city public schools, they are necessarily lost to a complete tracking analysis.

Retention Tracking

A substantial body of literature establishes that retention in elementary school (Brooks-Gunn, Guo, & Furstenberg, 1993; Cairns et al., 1989; Ensminger & Slusarcick, 1992; Garnier, Stein, & Jacobs, 1997) or middle school (Chen & Kaplan, 2003) greatly increases the likelihood of high school dropout. The term "track" is not commonly used in connection with elementary school retention, but retained children – those not promoted at the end of a grade – are effectively placed on a different track from their promoted peers (Entwisle & Alexander, 1993). In repeating a grade, they join new peers, usually go over the same curriculum in the ensuing year, are labeled as "repeaters," and almost always remain "off-time" for the rest of their school careers (see Alexander et al., 2003). Retention placement in elementary school thus has all the earmarks of a track. Retention tracking generally follows SES lines: Parents' income and/or educational level predict whether a child will be retained, and other things equal, males and minority group members more often end up in retention tracks (Alexander, Entwisle, & Kabbani, 2002; Bianchi, 1984; Entwisle & Alexander 1988; Hauser, 2001).

Middle School Tracking

Middle school students in Baltimore are placed in one of three math tracks: remedial, regular, or advanced. In 1988, remedial math courses were available in all thirty Baltimore City middle schools, and twelve middle schools offered advanced math programs. Students selected for advanced sections met standards on achievement tests and marks and were assigned to a middle school with an advanced program that was closest to their neighborhood, except that one "magnet" school offered admission citywide. The programs in the magnet school and one other school were known among parents as top programs. These two schools, which had larger and more sought-after advanced programs than the other ten schools, are designated here as "select schools."

All advanced math students in the twelve middle schools with advanced programs plus all eighth graders who took algebra, even if not in formal advanced programs, are classified as being in advanced sections. In the final sample ($N = 290$), 26% of eighth graders were in advanced sections,

11% were in remedial sections, and the remainder (63%) were in regular sections.

ANALYSIS

Independent variables in the models are race, gender, family SES, parent educational expectations, and cognitive skills (see Table 9.1 for definitions). Family SES is a composite of parents' education, occupation, and the child's eligibility for subsidized meals at school. Parents' educational expectations, measured before or early in first grade, is the parents' estimate of how far their child will go in school. Cognitive skills are standardized test scores in math concepts (CAT, 1979) obtained near the end of the fifth year (1987), the eighth year (1990), and the ninth year (1991), and math marks at the end of elementary school. Tracking variables are (a) grade retention in elementary and/or middle school, and (b) middle school placement in remedial, regular, or advanced math classes.

Determinants of Retention over Elementary School and Middle School Placement

The first goal is to predict retention in elementary school (first column, Table 9.2). Gender, race, family SES, parents' expectations, plus fifth grade test scores and marks serve as independent variables in a logistic regression to explain students' cumulative risk of retention through fifth grade (see Entwisle et al., 1997). Gender is a predictor; boys are twice as likely to be retained as girls. Standardized test scores also predict retention (see Entwisle, Alexander, Pallas, & Cadigan, 1988), but none of the other variables is significant.

The remaining columns in Table 9.2 show the same predictors with one addition, retention by year 5, to address the question: Does track placement in elementary school (retention) predict track placement in middle school? In a multinomial regression (middle panel, Table 9.2), remedial and advanced placements are compared to regular placements in eighth grade math, with advanced students in all middle schools treated as a single advanced group.

Gender does not predict remedial placement (second column, Table 9.2), but African Americans are over six times more likely than whites to be in remedial sections even though they were not more often retained in elementary school. This difference is striking because many other academic predictors of eighth grade placements are controlled. Students in remedial sections have lower CAT scores than students in regular sections (the reference category), but, even with controls for CAT scores, retained students are over eight times as likely to be in remedial sections. This carry-over effect (marginally significant) of early grade retention shows that tracks in elementary school overlap tracks in middle school. Thus, tracking

TABLE 9.1. *Variable Definitions, Means, and Standard Deviations of Measures Used in Analyses (N = 290)*

Variables	Means (SD)	Description of Variable
Demographic & Family Variables		
Proportion female	.57 (.50)	1 = Female 0 = Male
Proportion African American	.72 (.45)	1 = African American 0 = White
Family socioeconomic status	−.12 (.71)	Average of both parent's education and occupational status and participation in federal meal subsidy program (all measures are z-scores) (alpha reliability = .86)
Parent educational expectations	3.07 (1.12)	Parent's expectations for students educational attainment: 1 = not finish high school; 2 = finish high school; 3 = 1–2 yrs college; 4 = 4 yrs college; 5 = > 4 yrs college
Cognitive Skills		
CAT Math Score, end year 5	476 (59.7)	California Achievement Test (Form C)
CAT Math Score, end year 8	548 (72.0)	Math Concepts and Applications
CAT Math Score, end year 9	562 (77.3)	Yrs 5,8,9, scale scores;
CAT Math Score, composite z-score	−.01 (.99)	Composite z-score is year 9 z-score for 270 cases and year 8 z-score for 20 cases
Math Mark, end year 5	2.44 (.83)	Math marks 1 = unsatisfactory; 2 = satisfactory; 3 = good; 4 = excellent
Tracking Variables		
Proportion retained through Grade 5	.40 (.49)	Cumulative retention in grade:
Proportion retained through Grade 8	.47 (.50)	0 = not retained 1 = retained
Grade 8 Math Tracking	%	Math placement in 8th Grade:
Remedial	11.4	1 = Remedial
Regular	62.8	2 = Regular
Advanced	25.9	3 = Advanced
Advanced Non-Select Schools Advanced Select Schools	12.8 13.1	Advanced category is further broken down for some analyses into those in the 2 schools known to have higher level of Advanced program (Select Schools) and those in Advanced programs within other Non-Select Schools

(continued)

TABLE 9.1. (*Continued*)

Variables	Means (SD)	Description of Variable
Age 22 Educational Outcomes		
Level of education attempted by age 22	%	Highest level of education completed or enrolled in by age 22:
Proportion high school dropout	21.7	0 = high school dropout;
Proportion high school graduate	33.1	1 = completed high school;
Prop. in less than 4-yr program	24.8	2 = enrolled in license/certificate/A.A. program;
Proportion enrolled in B.A./B.S.	20.3	3 = enrolled in B.A./B.S. program

actually starts by age 6. For advanced placements (third column, Table 9.2) differences favor whites, but family SES also matters. Achievement scores from fifth grade play a role, but as before, neither marks nor gender is significant with other factors controlled. The odds associated with grade retention again are large, but not significant.

Of the 26% of BSS panel members assigned to advanced math in eighth grade, about half went to the two select schools. The average SES of students in all middle schools offering advanced math in grade 8 was somewhat higher than the SES of students in middle schools without advanced programs (meal subsidy rates of 57% versus 64%). The meal subsidy rate of students in the two select schools, however, was much lower than in the other middle schools offering algebra courses (meal subsidy rates of 37% versus 61%). Parents of students in the non-select schools also had, on average, less than a high school education, compared with parents of students in the two select schools, who averaged about three years of college.

Because of SES differences between schools, the rightmost panel in Table 9.2 (columns 4, 5, and 6) compares two types of eighth grade placements (advanced in non-select schools versus advanced in select schools) to examine differences between middle schools in determinants of advanced placement. The multinomial regression that compares remedial and the two kinds of advanced placements (non-select and select schools) with regular placements tests selection differences between schools. Otherwise, the model is the same as the three-category placement model.

Race differences (Table 9.2, columns 5 and 6) in placement depend upon whether advanced students are in non-select or select schools. Whites are four times more likely to be in advanced sections in the non-select schools, and SES is not significant. By contrast, race is *not* a determinant

TABLE 9.2. *Elementary and Middle School Tracking (Coefficients Are Odds Ratios[1], N = 290)*

	Logistic Regression	Multinomial Logistic Regressions				
	Retention Through Grade 5	Grade 8 Math Track[2]		Grade 8 Math Track[3]		
		Remedial	Advanced	Remedial	Advanced: Non-Select	Advanced: Select
Gender	.50*	.46	1.31	.46	1.40	1.12
Race (African American, White)	1.07	6.65*	.41*	6.60*	.25*	1.29
Family SES Index	.71	.97	1.99*	.98	.98	4.82*
Parent Educational Expectations	.97	1.09	1.69*	1.08	1.65*	1.74+
Math CAT Score, Spring 1987	.09*	.09*	3.11*	.09*	3.51*	3.30*
Math Mark, End Year 5	1.02	.72	1.32	.72	1.32	1.26
Grade Retention through Grade 5		8.43+	.54	8.44+	.71	.23
Pseudo R^2	.43	.45		.44		

[1]The odds ratio coefficients represent the effect of a unit change in the independent variable. Odds ratios for the Family SES Index and Math CAT Score represent the change in relative odds brought about by a one standard deviation increase in the independent variables measured from their means.

[2]Three-category Grade 8 Math Tracking with *Regular Track* as the baseline category.

[3]Four-category Grade 8 Math Tracking. The *Advanced Track* is divided into two categories: Advanced Track in the two *Select Schools* and the Advanced Track in the *Non-Select Schools*. *Regular Track* is the baseline category.

+$p \leq .10$. *$p \leq .05$ (two-sided).

of track assignments in the select schools (1.29), but SES is pivotal: Odds favor higher SES students by nearly 5:1. By far, the strongest predictor of advanced placement in the two select schools is SES.

Between select and non-select schools, some determinants of advanced placement are thus quite different. In non-select schools, being white is an advantage and high SES is not, but in the two select schools the reverse is true. Tracking responds similarly to CAT scores and parents' expectations in the select and non-select schools, however. Clearly, how tracks are defined is key. Among *all* middle schools that offer algebra, whites enjoy an advantage and the impact of family SES is attenuated, but with between-school tracking taken into account (see rightmost panel of Table 9.2), the white advantage is vitiated and SES emerges as most important.

Middle School Achievement

A key question is whether math placements affect achievement. To address this question, Table 9.3 assesses *gains* on standardized tests in math from the beginning of grade 6 through the end of grade 8. Independent variables (gender, race, family SES, parents' educational expectations, retention history) as before predict gains over middle school, but now track placements are added. Two kinds of advanced track placement are evaluated: (a) with advanced placement students pooled over all schools, or (b) with advanced placement students in select and non-select schools separated. To highlight the ways that SES defines tracks, each model is evaluated first with SES omitted, and then with SES included.

To explain gains on standardized tests in math over middle school, coefficients are scaled in test score metric – the coefficients are the gains in test scores. The left half of Table 9.3 summarizes coefficients when advanced sections are pooled over all schools with regular sections as baseline. The equation is estimated without SES (column 1) and then again with SES included (column 2).

Test scores at grade 5 are good predictors of grade 8 test scores. Each test score point in the grade 5 scores accounts for about 60% of a point in the gain over middle school (Table 9.3). Retention through grade 5 reduces gains in middle school about 25 points. As for eighth grade tracking, students in remedial sections gained 30 to 31 fewer points than students in regular sections (the first two columns of Table 9.3). Before SES is taken into account, students in advanced placement gained 32 points more than those in regular sections, but when SES is included, the gain associated with advanced section placement shrinks to 25 points. Students in advanced sections make larger gains than students in remedial or regular sections, so tracking does matter for achievement. Adding SES (column 2), however, makes clear that some of the extra gain by students in advanced sections is explained by SES. Note also that parents' expectations are not significant when SES is

TABLE 9.3. *OLS Regression of Math Test Score Gains over Middle School (Metric Coefficients, N = 321)*

| | Gains in Math CAT Score, End Year 5 to End Year 9 | | | |
	Advanced Tracks Pooled		Separate Advanced Tracks: Select and Non-Select	
Gender	−4.69	−2.85	−3.64	−2.58
Race (African American, White)	−6.61	−4.69	−7.62	−5.91
Parent Educational Expectations	4.88*	2.20	3.87[+]	2.24
Math CAT Score, Spring 1987	.61*	.59*	.62*	.60*
Grade Retention through Grade 5	−26.88*	−25.09*	−25.89*	−24.85*
Grade 8 Math Tracking[1]				
Remedial	−30.18*	−31.46*		
Advanced	31.99*	25.44*		
Grade 8 Math Tracking[2]				
Remedial			−47.23*	−47.68*
Regular			−17.29*	−16.72*
Advanced in Select Schools			30.77*	21.81*
Family SES Index		14.00*		10.36*
R^2	.69	.70	.70	.71

[1]Three-category Grade 8 Math Tracking with *Regular Track* as the baseline category.
[2]Four-category Grade 8 Math Tracking. The Advanced Track is divided into two categories: Advanced Track in the two *Select Schools* and the Advanced Track in the *Non-Select Schools*. Non-Select Schools is the baseline category.
[+]$p = .10$.   *$p \leq .05$ (two-sided).

added. Achievement in advanced sections in select schools is contrasted with achievement in advanced sections in non-select schools, with and without SES in the model, in the analyses shown in columns 3 and 4 of Table 9.3. Here the baseline is advanced placement in a non-select school.

The coefficients for gender, race, and other variables are relatively stable across columns in Table 9.3 except for middle school tracking. Being in an advanced track in a select rather than a non-select school predicts significantly greater achievement gains over eighth grade (31 points; column 3). Advanced students in non-select schools (the baseline category) gained more than students in regular sections (17 points), but in the select schools, students in advanced sections gained almost 48 (31 + 17) points more than those in regular sections (column 3), before SES is added. With SES added (column 4), the coefficient for advanced placement in non-select schools hardly changes (17 points), but the coefficient for advanced placement in select schools shrinks substantially (from 30.8 to 21.8 points). Even allowing for SES, students in advanced sections in select schools still profit by a margin of 39 (17 + 22) points, a benefit over twice that of advanced placement in a non-select school (17 points).

Educational Attainment at Age 22 and Middle School Track Placements

Thus far we have established that middle school tracking predicts increased learning, but those benefits are partially contingent on SES. Now we investigate whether middle school placements predict educational outcomes at age 22. To examine middle school placements in relation to the highest level of schooling attempted, we propose the model in Figure 9.1. This model takes gender, race, parent educational expectations, grade retention, and SES, plus the standardized math score in year 9 and middle school track assignments, as exogenous.

Multinomial regression estimates the predictors of four outcomes: high school dropout (22% of sample), high school graduate (including GED) (33% of sample), ever enrolled in a certification or licensure program or two-year college (25% of sample), and ever enrolled in a four-year college (20% of sample). "Ever enrolled" is the standard because at age 22, postsecondary enrollment is still a "work in progress." Just 27% of those who began postsecondary studies had completed programs, 39% were still enrolled, and 34% had withdrawn without a degree. Clearly, it is premature to screen on degree attainment at this point, but enrollment patterns over a four to five year period preceding age 22 ought to predict eventual prospects. Those who have not started a B.A. program are not very likely to do so.

To highlight the role of SES, again regressions are estimated with and without SES included. Predicting discrete outcomes clarifies nonlinear patterns (see Erikson & Goldthorpe, 2002). The influence of a predictor variable is not necessarily the same at each level of schooling, and this approach looks for such variation in strength or direction of effects. Findings here for dropout, for example, can be compared directly with findings in other studies that pertain only to dropout. This model also separates students who enroll in four-year college programs from those who enroll in other kinds of postsecondary programs, an important distinction for predicting later employment (see Crosby, 2002–03).

The multinomial model (first two columns, Table 9.4) compares students who drop out with students who achieve high school certification, with and without SES included. Females are almost three times as likely as males to drop out, a ratio that needs to be interpreted in light of this sample's distribution. More females than males go on to postsecondary education so the number of females who are just high school graduates is low. As a consequence, comparing female dropouts with females

TABLE 9.4. *Multinomial Logistic Regression Model Predicting Highest Level of Education by Age 22 (Coefficients Are Odds Ratios, N = 290)*

	Highest Educational Level Attempted by Age 22[1]					
	High School Dropout (N = 63)		Proprietary/ Two-Year College (N = 72)		Four-Year College (N = 59)	
Gender	2.94*	2.64*	3.35*	3.76*	2.29+	3.22*
Race (African American, White)	.52	.51	1.66	2.12+	3.86*	9.80*
Parent Educational Expectations	.98	1.08	1.40*	1.31	1.95*	1.56+
Grade Retention through Grade 8	2.69*	2.43+	.86	.87	.53	.40
Grade 8 Math Tracking[2]						
Remedial	.66	.69	.56	.49	.00	.00
Advanced Non-Select Schools	.52	.47	1.05	1.09	1.16	1.57
Advanced in Select Schools	.00	.00	1.93	1.25	7.56*	3.16
Math Cat Score, Spring 91	.39*	.41*	.68	.64	3.86*	2.80*
Family SES Index		.45*		1.75*		4.02*
R^2	.27	.31	.27	.31	.27	.31

[1] Baseline category is *high school graduate* (N = 96). The coefficients represent the effect of a unit change in the independent variable on the odds of being a dropout, attending a *proprietary or two-year college*, or attending a *four-year college* compared with being a *high school graduate*. Odds ratios for the Family SES Index and Math CAT Score represent the change in relative odds brought about by a one standard deviation increase in the independent variables measured from their means.

[2] Four-category Grade 8 Math Tracking. The Advanced Track is divided into two categories: Advanced Track in the two *Select Schools* and the Advanced Track in the *Non-Select Schools*. *Regular Track* is the baseline category.

+$p \leq .10$. *$p \leq .05$ (two-sided).

who are just high school graduates distorts the implications of the analyses for females. Grade retention (odds: 2.69) and low math achievement scores at grade 9 (odds: 0.39) also predict dropout. Remedial placement in middle school, however, does *not* predict dropout when retention is included, suggesting that retention threatens school performance more for reasons of being off-time than for reasons of poor performance (see Roderick, 1993). Family SES (column 2, Table 9.4) predicts dropout (.45) but does not alter the odds of dropout in relation to track placement or grade retention.

The middle panel of Table 9.4 estimates the odds of enrolling in postsecondary education other than a four-year college as compared to stopping with high school certification. Females are more likely (3:1) to enroll in some kind of postsecondary institution that is not a four-year college (middle panel, Table 9.4) as are African Americans (marginal, 2.12) when SES is taken into account. Parent educational expectations are not significant once SES is taken into account, so the parent support effect in the first column transmits some of the advantage and/or disadvantage associated with SES. Track placements are not significant but are orderly and in the expected direction. The predictors of entering sub-baccalaureate training are thus mainly demographic (gender, race, SES) and not related directly to prior school performance or placements.

The rightmost panel of Table 9.4 gives the odds of entering a four-year college. African Americans are favored especially when SES is taken into account (odds increase from 3.86 to 9.80). This finding illustrates the usefulness of discrete attainment benchmarks rather than a continuously scaled outcome like "years of education." Race differences in enrollment are mainly at the top of the education ladder, and are visible only with family SES controlled. Again, the discrete model points up dissimilar effects of exogenous variables at successive levels of enrollment.

Track placement in select middle schools has benefits for four-year college enrollment, but these are explained by the higher status of youth in the select school. With SES controlled, the odds of attending a four-year college among those in a select school fall from 7.56 to a nonsignificant 3.16 (last two columns, Table 9.4). The effect of test scores also shrinks when SES is added (3.86 to 2.80). For the two advanced placement groups combined, the odds (2.46) marginally favor advanced over regular placement, but when SES is added, the odds associated with track placement are not significant (2.10) (data not shown). Test scores and SES thus outweigh track placements in determining attendance at a four-year college.[2]

When we consider the three sets of models together, the main conclusions are (a) retention in elementary school forecasts remedial placement in middle school, (b) students in advanced sections in some middle schools learn more math than students do in advanced sections in other middle schools, and (c) perhaps most important, SES differences between schools can distort evaluations of within-school track effects.

High School Tracking

Middle school tracks may actually play a stronger role than previous analyses show because middle school algebra is a prerequisite for admission to a college preparatory track in high school. To check this conjecture is

---

[2] Following the same logic as the logistic models in Table 9.4, a set of OLS models was estimated to explain years of attainment in response to middle school track placements. Results for this set of models are available from the authors upon request.

TABLE 9.5. *High School Placement in Grade 12 by Middle School Math Track*

| | Middle School Math Tracks (N = 329) | | | |
	Remedial	Regular	Advanced Non-Select	Advanced Select
School Placements				
Magnet high schools in Baltimore City with strong college prep tracks	0	11	12	34
Zoned high schools in Baltimore City	31	119	18	2
Elite private high schools	0	0	0	3
Other high schools outside Baltimore City	1	23	4	2
Dropouts[1]	7	55	7	0
Total	39	208	41	41
High school track placements				
Regular high school track	27 (69%)	95 (46%)	11 (27%)	1 (2%)
Vocational track	4 (10%)	39 (19%)	5 (12%)	0 (0%)
College prep track	1 (3%)	19 (9%)	18 (44%)	40 (98%)
Dropouts[1]	7 (18%)	55 (26%)	7 (17%)	0 (0%)
Total	39 (100.0%)	208 (100.0%)	41 (100.0%)	41 (100.0%)

[1] This tally traces students only into their twelfth year. Close to 50% of students in remedial math tracks did not complete high school.

difficult because BSS data cannot support a full multivariate analysis of high school tracking – by high school many BSS students had either dropped out or moved out of Baltimore City Public Schools. Still, some students do have available high school track assignments, if we include those who attended high schools outside the BCPS system. The upper panel of Table 9.5 tallies high school placements by middle school tracks for BSS students attending high schools both in and outside of Baltimore. The lower panel summarizes high school track placements.

Across all high schools, 3% of those from remedial math tracks and 9% of those from regular math tracks were in a college track in their twelfth year of school. Close to half (44%) of those in advanced tracks in non-select middle schools were in college tracks, but with one exception all the advanced placement students from the two select middle schools (98%) were in college tracks (Table 9.5). A college track in high school is thus virtually guaranteed for those with advanced math placements in the two select middle schools. At the other end, dropping out occurred for 18% of those in remedial tracks,[3] 26% of those in regular tracks, and 17% of those in advanced tracks from non-select schools. No dropouts came from the advanced select schools group.

A college prep program in high school is not the only factor in college admission, of course. Even so, the composition of high school tracks points to a large institutional component in predicting four-year college attendance. In this sample, 65% of those in college tracks in high school actually matriculated as compared to 6% of those in non-college preparatory programs. With regard to the ultimate attainment of Baltimore students, the particular middle schools attended and SES matters while test scores or tracks, as usually construed, matter much less.

DISCUSSION

This chapter reveals a striking parallel between the functioning of U.S. schools in Baltimore and U.K. schools. In the U.K., the 11+ exams (ages 11 or 12) separate students preparing for university from non-university candidates. The middle school math tracks in Baltimore (fifth or sixth grades, ages 11 or 12) have much the same consequence. However, in the U.K. this fork in the road is widely recognized and decided by competitive exams, whereas in Baltimore and elsewhere in the United States (see Kao & Thompson, 2003) a college prep track in high school tends to be seen (mistakenly) as the decisive factor, while the crucible decision is probably algebra in middle school. For students without middle school algebra, the picture is bleak. Moreover, some programs with the same name are much better than others. It is hard to overemphasize the importance of middle school choices made at the beginning of sixth grade. For students like these, *initial* placements change very little over middle school (Dauber et al., 1996). Retention in elementary school (more common for boys and dependent on standardized test scores) greatly reduces the likelihood of college attendance. In short, tracking in middle childhood significantly shapes life chances.

In Baltimore, family SES predicts track placement in middle school and level of education attempted, and we strongly suspect this is true elsewhere. This pattern, coupled with the substantial variation in SES across schools, compels study of between-school tracking as well as within school tracking to evaluate program effects. The common definition of tracking is

---

[3] This figure understates the true extent of dropout because this tally traces students only as they began the twelfth year of school and does not take account of dropouts in years 12, 13, 14, and 15. Close to 50% of students in remedial math tracks in middle school failed to complete high school.

that "students are somehow judged or evaluated and subsequently receive a differential curriculum" (see LeTendre, Hofer, & Shimizu, 2003, p. 44), which implies selection based on objective or academically relevant criteria. This definition fits the process that designates the retention track in Baltimore – students are judged to be ineligible for promotion on the basis of marks and test scores, and then take a different curriculum than their classmates. By contrast, tracking in middle school comes when differences between schools create separate tracks for which some criteria are explicit (test scores) and other criteria are not (SES).

Other Outcomes at Age 22

Research on school tracking mostly overlooks the substantial fraction of youth who do not go on to four-year colleges. Half of the BSS panel stopped with a high school degree or before, and another 30% of the BSS sample went on to some form of postsecondary schooling other than a four-year college. Many good jobs do not require college training, but the consequences of paths non-college-youth take are not clear (Rosenbaum, 2001). The largely buried systems of tracking within and between schools, especially retention, that channel non-college bound students along different pathways need to be more transparent. Retention in elementary school, far more than academic performance, predicts school dropout (Cairns et al., 1989; Ensminger & Slusarcick, 1992; Alexander, Entwisle, & Kabbani, 2001), and the present study shows it also predicts placement in remedial math in middle school, an outcome of retention that, to our knowledge, has not been previously identified. Aside from dropouts, 85% of those in remedial sections did not go on to *any* form of postsecondary education. In predicting age 22 educational attainment, retention, middle school tracks, college prep tracking in high school, and SES are more important than test scores. The imprint of school performance in middle childhood is clearly visible in early adulthood. School tracking channels students, opening doors for some, closing doors for others (e.g., Oakes 1988, 1989/90). Here, as in Kerckhoff's study (1993), tracking starts at the beginning of elementary school, and SES patterns persist across levels of schooling.

The Larger Picture

When Kerckhoff (1993) examined instructional stratification in the U.K., the analog of U.S. retention tracking and the middle school math tracks examined in this paper, he found that (a) school stratification affected attainment, (b) effects of stratification carried over from one level of schooling to the next, and (c) effects at each level accumulated. In Baltimore, we see much the same.

First, school stratification (retention and middle school placements) predicts attainment in math. Second, elementary school tracking predicts middle school tracks, and these tracks forecast high school college prep tracks and later attainment. Whether tracking effects are cumulative (Kerckhoff's third question), cannot be fully addressed with BSS data, but the suggestion is there; retention in elementary school predicts remedial placement in middle school, and students in remedial tracks learn less than those in other tracks. Also, some middle school tracks almost certainly lead to a college track in high school, while others are much less likely to do so. Tracking patterns in Baltimore thus correspond with Kerckhoff's characterization of educational systems as sorting machines.

This meshing of tracks from one school to the next implies that children's academic histories start at age 6 or before and are carried along in more ways than by test scores or marks. The "sorting and selecting" early in middle childhood sets the stage for placements that follow (e.g., Entwisle & Alexander, 1993; Entwisle et al., 1997; Entwisle & Hayduk, 1988; Kerckhoff, 1993; Peterson, DeGracie, & Ayabe, 1987; Stroup & Robins, 1972). First grade track assignments predict test scores and dropout in middle school (Alexander, Entwisle, & Horsey, 1997; Cairns et al., 1989; Ensminger & Slusarcick, 1992). Other things equal, males, minorities, and/or low SES children are more often in "low" tracks in elementary school – low ability groups, retention, and/or special education (Bianchi, 1984; Entwisle & Alexander, 1988).

The idea of an ongoing envelope surrounding the path of attainment is useful for determining at which points the trajectory may be modified (see Alexander et al., 1997; Alexander et al., 2003; Kerckhoff, 1993). The channeling force of trajectories is *not* constant over the entire schooling period: Family resources produce more deflections at educational transition points, for example at the beginning of first grade and when middle school begins or ends rather than from year to year (see Entwisle & Alexander, 1993; Dauber et al., 1996), or as in the present study, when students apply for college. Altering a trajectory must be easiest at the start, however, when children begin school, because initial trajectories respond to preschool and kindergarten experience (see Lazar & Darlington, 1982; Entwisle, Alexander, Cadigan, & Pallas, 1987). Also, parents' expectations boost achievement gains more over first grade than later (Entwisle & Hayduk, 1982; Entwisle et al., 1997, 2004; Duncan et al., 1998). Among the Baltimore middle schools with advanced math programs, two were much more selective by SES, so information not in school records explains how these tracks actually functioned. Between- and within-school tracking effects add up, but between-school tracking can overpower within-school tracking.

We need more research on students' and parents' knowledge about educational tracking. Informed decisions presuppose a familiarity with all the options, knowledge of both the short- and long-term consequences of placements, and open lines of communication between parents and schools. Parents' input into placement decisions is not necessarily "good news," though (Gamoran, 1992). Unless knowledge about school differences in program quality is distributed across all families, parent input may lead to the kind of educational inequality seen here (see, for example, Baker & Stevenson, 1986; Lareau, 1987). Parents may be deeply committed to their children's intellectual development, but they also observe that adult success draws heavily on social capital once school is over. Some parents perceive how the stratification system functions in schools, but many do not. Research in the United States has probably overemphasized the importance of individual choices and underemphasized the importance of institutional arrangements. The institutional structures through which BSS students passed, beginning at age 6, affected their gains on achievements tests, their admission to a college track in high school, whether they would drop out, and/or whether they would matriculate at a four-year college.

Research on the invisible hand of SES tracking is long overdue. The American educational system is often perceived as more "open" than the British. Coleman (Kerckhoff, 1993, p. xv), for example, characterized the U.S. educational system as one with little or no differentiation at any stage, with all children exposed to the same educational environment. To the extent our findings can be generalized, however, the American and British systems seem much the same, especially in terms of strong selection effects in the middle school years.

This research was supported by the W. T. Grant Foundation (95-164195, 98-19298, and 2202010014), the Spencer Foundation (B1517), and the National Science Foundation (SES8510535).

References

Alexander, K. L., Cook, M. A., & McDill, E. L. (1978). Curriculum tracking and educational stratification. *American Sociological Review, 43*(1), 47–66.

Alexander, K. L., & Entwisle, D. R. (1988). Achievement in the first two years of school: Patterns and processes. *Monographs of the Society for Research in Child Development, 53*(2, Serial No. 218).

Alexander, K. L., & Entwisle, D. R. (1996). Educational tracking during the early years: First grade placements and middle school constraints. In A. C. Kerckhoff (Ed.), *Generating social stratification: Toward a new research agenda* (pp. 83–113). New York: Westview Press.

Alexander, K. L., Entwisle, D. R., & Dauber, S. L. (2003). *On the success of failure: A reassessment of the effects of retention in the primary grades* (2nd ed.). New York: Cambridge University Press.

Alexander, K. L., Entwisle, D. R., & Horsey, C. (1997). From first grade forward: Early foundations of high school dropout. *Sociology of Education, 70*(2), 87–107.

Alexander, K. L., Entwisle, D. R., & Kabbani, N. (2001). The dropout process in life course perspective: Early risk factors at home and school. *Teachers College Record, 103*(5), 760–822.

Alexander, K. L., Entwisle, D. R., & Kabbani, N. (2002). Dropout in relation to grade retention: An accounting from the Beginning School Study. In *Can unlike children learn together?* New York: Teachers College Press.

Baker, D. P., & Stevenson, D. L. (1986). Mothers' strategies for children's school achievement: Managing the transition to high school. *Sociology of Education, 59*(3), 156–166.

Baltimore City Public Schools. (1988, February). *School profiles: School year 1987–88.* Baltimore, MD Office of the Superintendent of Public Instruction.

Barr, R., & Dreeben, R. (1983). *How schools work.* Chicago: University of Chicago Press.

Becker, H. (1987). *Addressing the needs of different groups of early adolescents* (Report No. 16). Baltimore, MD: Johns Hopkins University, Center for Research on Elementary and Middle Schools.

Bianchi, S. M. (1984). Children's progress through school: A research note. *Sociology of Education, 57*(3), 184–192.

Braddock, J. (1990). Tracking the middle grades: National patterns of grouping for instruction. *Phi Delta Kappan, 71,* 445–449.

Braddock, J. H. , II, Wu, S. C., & McPartland, J. (1988). *School organization in the middle grades: National variations and effects* (Report No. 24). Baltimore, MD: Johns Hopkins University, Center for Research on Elementary and Middle Schools.

Brooks-Gunn, J., Guo, G., & Furstenberg, F. F. Jr. (1993). Who drops out and who continues beyond high school? A 20-year follow-up of black urban youth. *Journal of Research on Adolescence, 3*(3), 271–294.

Cairns, R. B., Cairns, B. D., & Neckerman, H. J. (1989). Early school dropout: Configurations and determinants. *Child Development, 60*(6), 1437–1452.

California Achievement Test. (1979). *California Achievement Tests: Norms tables, level 18, forms C and D.* Monterey, CA: CTB/McGraw Hill.

Catsambis, S. (1992, March). *The many faces of tracking middle school grades: Between- and within-school differentiation of students and resources.* Paper presented at the Society for Research on Adolescence meeting, Washington, DC.

Chen, Z., & Kaplan, H. B. (2003). School failure in early adolescence and status attainment in middle adulthood: A longitudinal study. *Sociology of Education, 76,* 110–127.

Crosby, O. (2002–03). Associate degree: Two years to a career or a jump start to a bachelor's degree. *Occupational Outlook Quarterly, 46*(4), 2–13.

Dauber, S. L., Alexander, K. L., & Entwisle, D. R. (1996). Tracking and transitions through the middle grades: Channeling educational trajectories. *Sociology of Education, 69*(4), 290–307.

Duncan, G. J., Brooks-Gunn, J., Yeung, W. J., & Smith, J. K. (1998). How much does childhood poverty affect the life chances of children? *American Sociological Review, 63*(3), 406–423.

Eccles, J. S., Midgley, C., & Adler, T. (1984). Grade-related changes in the school environment: Effects on achievement motivation. In J. G. Nicholls (Ed.), *The development of achievement motivation* (pp. 283–331). Greenwich, CT: JAI Press.

Eccles, J. S., Midgley, C., Wigfield, A., Buchanan, C. M., Reuman, D., Flanagan, C., et al. (1993). Development during adolescence: The impact of stage-environment fit on young adolescents' experience in school and families. *American Psychologist, 48,* 90–101.

Ensminger, M. E., & Slusarcick, A. L. (1992). Paths to high school graduation or dropout: A longitudinal study of a first-grade cohort. *Sociology of Education, 65*(2), 95–113.

Entwisle, D. R., & Alexander, K. L. (1988). Factors affecting achievement test scores and marks received by black and white first graders. *The Elementary School Journal, 88*(5), 449–471.

Entwisle, D. R., & Alexander, K. L. (1993). Entry into schools: The beginning school transition and educational stratification in the United States. In *Annual Review of Sociology, Vol. 19* (pp. 401–423). Palo Alto, CA: Annual Reviews, Inc.

Entwisle, D. R., Alexander, K. L., Cadigan, D., & Pallas, A. M. (1987). Kindergarten experience: Cognitive effects or socialization? *American Educational Research Journal, 24*(3), 337–364.

Entwisle, D. R., Alexander, K. L., & Olson, L. S. (1997). *Children, schools, and inequality.* Boulder, CO: Westview Press.

Entwisle, D. R., Alexander, K. L., & Olson, L. S. (2004). Temporary as compared to permanent dropout. *Social Forces, 82*(3), 1181–1205.

Entwisle, D. R., Alexander, K. L., Pallas, A. M., & Cadigan, D. (1988). A social psychological model of the schooling process over first grade. *Social Psychology Quarterly, 51*(3), 173–189.

Entwisle, D. R., & Hayduk, L. A. (1978). *Too great expectations: The academic outlook of young children.* Baltimore, MD: The Johns Hopkins University Press.

Entwisle, D. R., & Hayduk, L. A. (1982). *Early schooling: Cognitive and affective outcomes.* Baltimore, MD: Hopkins Press.

Entwisle, D. R., & Hayduk, L. A. (1988). Lasting effects of elementary school. *Sociology of Education, 61*(3), 147–159.

Erikson, R., & Goldthorpe, J. H. (2002). Intergenerational inequality: A sociological perspective. *Journal of Economic Perspectives, 16*(3), 31–44.

Feldman, S. S., & Elliott, G. R. (1990). *At the threshold: The developing adolescent.* Cambridge, MA: Harvard University Press.

Finn, J. D., & Cox, D. (1992). Participation and withdrawal among fourth-grade pupils. *American Educational Research Journal, 29*(1), 141–162.

Fuligni, A. J., Eccles, J. S., & Barber, B. L. (1995). The long-term effects of seventh-grade ability grouping in mathematics. *Journal of Early Adolescence, 15*(1), 58–89.

Gamoran, A. (1992). Access to excellence: Assignment to honors English classes in the transition to high school. *Educational Evaluation and Policy Analysis, 14*(3), 185–204.

Gamoran, A., & Berends, M. (1987). The effects of stratification in secondary schools: Synthesis of survey and ethnographic research. *Review of Educational Research, 57*(4), 415–435.

Gamoran, A., & Mare, R. D. (1989). Secondary school tracking and educational inequality: Compensation, reinforcement, or neutrality? *American Journal of Sociology, 94*(5), 1146–1183.

Garnier, H. E., Stein, J. A., & Jacobs, J. K. (1997). The process of dropping out of high school: A 19-year perspective. *American Educational Research Journal, 34*(2), 395–419.

Hallinan, M. T. (1992). The organization of students for instruction in the middle school. *Sociology of Education, 65*(2), 114–127.

Hart, B., & Risley, T. R. (1995). *Meaningful differences in the everyday experience of young American children.* Baltimore, MD: Paul H. Brookes Publishing Co.

Hauser, R. M. (2001). Should we end social promotion? Truth and consequences. In G. Orfield & M. Kornhaber (Eds.), *Raising standards or raising barriers? Inequality and high stakes testing in public education* (pp. 151–178). New York: Century Foundation.

Hoffer, T. B. (1992). Middle school ability grouping and student achievement in science and mathematics. *Educational Evaluation and Policy Analysis, 14*(3), 205–227.

Hoffer, T. B. (1994, August). *Cumulative effects of secondary school tracking on student achievement.* Paper presented at the American Sociological Association meeting, Los Angeles, CA.

Ingels, S. J., Curtin, T. R., Kaufman, P., Alt, M. N., & Chen, X. (2002). Coming of age in the 1990s: The eighth grade class of 1988. *Education Statistics Quarterly, 4*(2) 1–12.

Jones, J. D., Vanfossen, B. E., & Ensminger, M. E. (1995). Individual and organizational predictors of high school track placement. *Sociology of Education, 68*(4), 287–300.

Kao, G., & Thompson, J. S. (2003). Racial and ethnic stratification in educational achievement and attainment. In K. Cook & J. Hagen (Eds.), *Annual Review of Sociology, Vol. 29* (pp. 417–442). Palo Alto, CA: Annual Reviews.

Kerckhoff, A. C. (1993). *Diverging pathways: Social structure and career deflections.* New York: Cambridge University Press.

Lareau, A. (1987). Social class differences in family-school relationships: The importance of cultural capital. *Sociology of Education, 60*(2), 73–85.

Lazar, I., & Darlington, R. (1982). Lasting effects of early education: A report from the Consortium for Longitudinal Studies. *Monographs of the Society for Research in Child Development, 47*(2–3), ix–139.

LeTendre, G. K., Hofer, B. K., & Shimizu, H. (2003). What is tracking? Cultural expectations in the United States, Germany, and Japan. *American Education Research Journal, 40*, 43–85.

Lucas, S. R. (1999). *Tracking inequality: Stratification and mobility in American high schools.* New York: Teachers College Press.

Murnane, R. J., Willett, J. B., & Levy, F. (1995). The growing importance of cognitive skills in wage determination. *Review of Economics and Statistics, 77*(2), 251–266.

Oakes, J. (1988). Tracking in mathematics and science education: A structural contribution to unequal schooling. In L. Weis (Ed.), *Class, race, and gender in American education* (pp. 106–125). Albany, NY: State University of New York Press.

Oakes, J. (1989/90). Opportunities, achievement, and choice: Women and minority students in science and mathematics. *Review of Research in Education, 16*(2), 153–222.

Peterson, S. E., DeGracie, J. S., & Ayabe, C. R. (1987). A longitudinal study of the effects of retention/promotion on academic achievement. *American Educational Research Journal, 27*(1), 107–118.

Reynolds, A. J. (1992). Grade retention and school adjustment: An explanatory analysis. *Educational Evaluation and Policy Analysis, 14*(2), 101–121.

Roderick, M. (1993). *The path to dropping out: Evidence for intervention.* Westport, CN: Auburn House.

Rosenbaum, J. E. (2001). *Beyond college for all: Career paths for the forgotten half.* New York: Russell Sage Foundation.

Rosenbaum, J. E. (1976). *Making inequality: The hidden curriculum of high school tracking.* New York: Wiley.

Shepard, L. A., & Smith, M. L. (1989). *Flunking grades: Research and policies on retention.* London: The Falmer Press.

Simmons, R. G., & Blyth, D. A. (1987). *Moving into adolescence: The impact of pubertal change and school context.* Hawthorne, NY: Aldine de Gruyter.

Spade, J. Z., Columba, L., & Vanfossen, B. E. (1997). Tracking in mathematics and science: Courses and course selection procedures. *Sociology of Education, 70,* 108–127.

Stevenson, D. L., Schiller, K. S., & Schneider, B. (1994). Sequences of opportunities for learning. *Sociology of Education, 67*(3), 184–198.

Stroup, A. L., & Robins, L. N. (1972). Elementary school predictors of high school dropout among black males. *Sociology of Education, 45*(2), 212–222.

U.S. Census Bureau. (1983). *Census of population: 1980 Vol 1. Characteristics of the population.* Washington, DC: U.S. Government Printing Office.

U.S. Department of Education. (2001). *Digest of education statistics, 2000* (NCES 2001-034). Washington, DC: U.S. Department of Education, National Center for Education Statistics.

U.S. Department of Education. (2003). *The condition of education 2003* (NCES 2003-067). Washington, DC: U.S. Government Printing Office.

Zill, N. (1996). Family change and student achievement: What we have learned, what it means for schools. In A. Booth & J. F. Dunn (Eds.), *Family-school links: How do they affect educational outcomes?* (pp. 139–174). Mahwah, NJ: Erlbaum.

10

School Environments and the Diverging Pathways of Students Living in Poverty

Penny Hauser-Cram, Marji Erickson Warfield,
Jenny Stadler, and Selcuk R. Sirin

Over the last decade researchers have reported consistently that children differ in their pre-academic skills at the beginning of kindergarten and that those differences are often related to their family's socioeconomic status (SES) and, to a lesser extent, their ethnicity (Lee & Burkam, 2002; Stipek & Ryan, 1997). Our education system should provide the necessary schooling so all children can succeed academically, but there is evidence that the school experiences of children living in poverty differ from those living in middle-income families (e.g., Entwisle & Alexander, 1998; Greenberg, Lengua, Coie, & Pinderhughes, 1999). Yet we know little about the various paths children from low-income families take from the time they enter school through middle childhood. Do children's diverging pathways relate only to their characteristics and skills at school entry or do they also relate to the school environment?

SCHOOL FACTORS RELATED TO ACHIEVEMENT

Schools can be characterized in relation to their structure and climate (Ma, 2001). Structural characteristics usually include school size, location, and the socioeconomic status and ethnicity of students served. School climate is the general character of a school and includes collegiality and community, academic standards, and communication between administrators, teachers, students, and parents. Hoy, Hannum, and Tschannen-Moran (1998) posit that "personality is to individual what climate is to organization" (p. 337). Although the relation of structure and climate to student performance has been established in middle and high schools, it has been examined infrequently in elementary schools (Caldas & Bankston, 1997; Ho & Willms, 1996; Ma, 2001). Even less is known about how these features relate to the differential school outcomes of children living in poverty.

There are several hypothesized mechanisms by which the social demographic composition of the student body and school resources, policies, and climate might have an effect on individual academic performance. First, the influence of peers on the motivation and aspirations of other students, on learning, and on the social behavior of all students may affect student achievement (Kahlenberg, 2001).

Second, the education levels of teachers vary by the proportion of low-income students in a school. Data from the National Center for Education Statistics (1999) indicated that only 37% of teachers had masters degrees in schools where more than 60% of the students were eligible for free or reduced-price lunch. In comparison, more than one half (57%) of teachers had masters degrees in schools where less than 15% of students belonged to low-income families. Lankford, Loeb, and Wyckoff (2002) found that low-income, low-achieving students of color of all ages were more frequently in schools with the least skilled teachers.

Third, tracking and quality of instruction vary by school social demographics. Entwisle, Alexander, and Olson (1997) reported that children in lower-income schools were tracked as "low ability," even though children from low-income areas actually demonstrated a learning pace that was at least equal to that of other children. The quality of instruction was also different for each track of children, with children in low ability tracks receiving instruction at a much lower level (e.g., word-by-word reading as opposed to focusing on clauses). Additionally, children in lower tracks were much more likely to be retained in a grade, which is problematic because it is a significant predictor of dropping out of school (Jimmerson, 1999). Thus, tracking appears to doubly jeopardize low-income students by providing them with poorer quality instruction and increasing the probability of grade retention.

Finally, several measures of school climate have been associated with student achievement. Elementary schools are most effective in producing positive academic outcomes if they maintain a supportive and caring climate coupled with a strong emphasis on academics (Johnson, Livingston, Schwartz, & Slate, 2000). Teachers who emphasize the importance of academics hold high and achievable goals for their students. This emphasis appears to be an important correlate of students' achievement at entry to middle childhood (Goddard, Sweetland, & Hoy, 2000; Hoy & Sabo, 1998).

A school climate that encourages success for all students is also positively related to student achievement. "Collective school efficacy" occurs when all students are expected to achieve high standards and all personnel, including administrative staff, are involved in achieving that goal (Stipek, 2002). Schools with lower-income populations have been shown to have a lower collective efficacy (Stipek, 2002)

Another aspect of climate important in a high-achieving school is the extent of cooperation and collaboration among teachers (Stipek, 2002). In schools where there is collaborative instruction, professional dialogue, and a strong professional community, students are more likely to excel academically (e.g., Baker, Terry, Bridger, & Winsor, 1997). Both a caring, communal focus and high academic standards appear to be the key ingredients for an effective elementary school (Johnson et al., 2000).

One study (Phillips, 1997), however, found that a strong emphasis on academics was more important than a communal, collaborative climate, at least at the middle school level. Phillips reported that schools with demanding curricula and teachers with high expectations had students with higher math scores and higher attendance. Stipek (2002) suggests that this press for learning is created through a number of factors related to climate: strong instructional leadership, clearly articulated standards and consequences for not completing work, parent–teacher communication, teacher collaboration, and frequent assessments.

Although these standards should apply to all schools, the Prospects Study (Abt Associates, 1997) demonstrated that a large gap exists between expectations for children in schools that serve mainly students from low-income versus higher-income families. Students receiving an "A" grade in higher-income schools scored in the 87th percentile on standardized tests, but "A" students in low-income schools scored only in the 36th percentile. Therefore, even students who think they are performing well (based on their grade point average) may be handicapped by the standards of their school environment and the expectations of teachers (Lambert & McCombs, 1998).

SCHOOL PERFORMANCE

Schools emphasize two aspects of academic performance: outcomes and engagement. As evidenced in the Leave No Child Behind Act of 2001 (P.L. 107–110), current education policy places an emphasis on children's acquisition of literacy skills (National Research Council, Committee on the Prevention of Reading Difficulties in Young Children, 1998; National Reading Panel, 2000). For decades there has been speculation that literacy plays a key role in the cognitive skills that students develop and use routinely. Considerable research has shown the importance of acquiring strong literacy skills by the time a child is in middle childhood because such skills enhance access to general knowledge (Stanovich & Cunningham, 1993), and thus are key to future academic success.

Children from lower SES families demonstrate slower gains in literacy during the first school years (e.g., Mullis, Campbell, & Farstrup, 1993). Although this may be due to a variety of family and home characteristics (e.g., parents' low levels of literacy, provision of poor or inadequate nutrition, lack of cognitive resources in the home), school factors may also be important. Esposito (1999) looked specifically at how various measures of school climate affected young students' literacy skills in a sample of low income kindergarten through second grade students (80% African-American, 18% Latino, and 2% Euro-American) living in high-poverty neighborhoods. She found that one aspect of school climate, teacher–student relationships, was positively related to children's reading achievement in first grade, although these relations did not hold for children in kindergarten and second grade. Thus, evidence of the relation between different aspects of school climate and literacy skills for children from low-income families is somewhat inconclusive and perhaps age-specific.

Although literacy has long been a goal in U.S. schools, researchers are finding that children's self-regulation may also be central to their future educational success (National Research Council and Institute of Medicine, 2000). From the perspective of social cognitive theory, children's agency and ability to self-direct is an important facet of learning (Bandura, 1997). Children who exhibit more self-regulated learning take on academic challenges, are curious, follow directions, and are responsive to suggestions from teachers. Children who exhibit greater self-regulation during the early childhood years become more self-directed in their learning at school entry (Bronson, 2000), and are thus more engaged in the academic challenges provided in school.

Marks (2000) compared the patterns of engagement of students in mathematics and social studies classes in elementary, middle, and high schools. She found that school engagement diminishes as grade level increases. At each grade level, however, females, students from higher SES groups, and successful students tend to be more engaged. Alexander, Entwisle, and Horsey (1997), who tracked children from first grade through high school, emphasized the importance of school engagement during the early grades. Children who were less engaged in school in first grade were 2.5 times more likely to drop out of high school than their peers who were more engaged in first grade. Such differences in school engagement may be apparent even in kindergarten. Ladd, Birch, and Buhs (1999) studied the social and academic lives of 200 kindergarten children from a range of economic backgrounds. Although children's cognitive/linguistic maturity and their parent's educational background related to kindergarten achievement, greater school engagement, measured by classroom participation, also predicted higher levels of achievement. The extent to which early school engagement predicts growth in achievement over the following school years, however, is not known.

In this chapter we discuss our study of children living in poverty and the *changes* they demonstrate in two important facets of academic performance: literacy skills and school engagement. We focus on questions of whether children demonstrate predictable pathways of change in these academic areas and whether differences in school structure or climate relate to those pathways.

TABLE 10.1. *Characteristics of Kindergarten Participants and Schools in the School Transition Study*

Characteristic	Mean (SD)	Percent
Child		
Gender (Male)		47.7
Primary language (English)		84.8
Ethnicity		
African-American		40.7
Euro-American		27.2
Latino/a		25.2
Health (excellent)		44.3
Cognitive skills (PPVT)	86.4 (15.0)	
Family		
Maternal income (< $12,000)		79.5
Maternal education (less than high school)		29.1
Maternal marital status (married)		35.0
Life stress (negative life events)	2.0 (1.7)	
School		
Location		
Northeast urban		48.1
Southwest urban		26.7
Northeast rural		25.2
Enrollment	503.2 (244.8)	
Low-income students		61.3
Academic climate	4.0 (1.0)	

METHOD

Participants

Participants included 210 children (48% male) who were part of the School Transition Study (STS),[1] a longitudinal investigation of children living in very low-income families (Table 10.1) who had originally participated in the Comprehensive Child Development Project. Children were assessed in the spring of kindergarten, third grade, and fifth grade.[1] The 210 children were initially distributed among 81 kindergarten classrooms and 59 schools in three locations (urban northeast, rural northeast, and urban southwest). Schools ranged greatly in size but averaged 503 students, and most served a majority of children from low-income families (i.e., eligible for free or

[1] Principal investigators were Deborah Stipek, Heather Weiss, Penny Hauser-Cram, Walter Secada, and Jennifer Greene. This investigation was supported in part by grants from the John D. and Catherine T. MacArthur Foundation Research Network on Successful Pathways through Middle Childhood and the Foundation for Child Development.

reduced-price lunch). Children were mainly from three ethnic groups (40% African-American, 27% Euro-American, 25% Hispanic/Latino, 8% mixed/other). Average yearly income (in 1996–97, when children entered kindergarten) was less than $12,000 for almost 80% of participants' families. Average maternal education was a high school degree or equivalent, although 29% of mothers had completed less than a high school education. Mothers reported that, on average, two negative life events had occurred during the year prior to their child's entry into kindergarten. The most common events were income loss and entry into debt (31.7%) and death of a close friend or immediate family member (29%).

Procedure

Independent examiners assessed children's cognitive skills at 60 months of age; other examiners assessed their skills in literacy during kindergarten, third grade, and fifth grade. Children were assessed in English or Spanish according to their preferred language. Teachers and principals completed questionnaires. Mothers or primary caregivers were interviewed in person.

Constructs and Measures

Child cognitive skills were assessed using the Peabody Picture Vocabulary Test (Dunn & Dunn, 1981) (when children were 60 months), and literacy skills were measured with letter-word identification and word reading subscales of the WJ-R, Woodcock-Johnson (1990), during the spring of kindergarten, third grade, and fifth grade. Children's school engagement was measured during the spring of kindergarten, third grade, and fifth grade, by the self-directed learning subscale of the Teacher Rating Scale of School Adjustment (Ladd et al., 1999), which included four items such as "seeks challenges" and "works independently" rated on a 3-point scale ($\alpha = .87$). Child and family demographic items were based on parent (usually mother) report. Family negative life events were based on the Life Stress Scale of the Parenting Stress Index (Abidin, 1995). Child health was measured by mothers' single item rating of children's health status (excellent to poor).

Measures related to school climate and structure (i.e., school size, location, and proportion of children eligible for free or reduced price lunch) were based on principal report. The school climate measure included items adapted from the School Restructuring Study (Newmann and Associates, 1996) that focused on the schools' academic climate regarding students' learning and included five items rated on a 5-point scale (from strongly disagree to strongly agree). These included questions about academic standards (e.g., "This school is committed to high academic achievement"), school personnel's interest in children ("School personnel take a deep interest in each of their children as individuals"), and teacher communication about children's learning (e.g., "Teachers talk with teachers in the next grade to get an idea of what children should know") ($a = .87$). A set of teacher questionnaires included questions on school climate similar to those completed by the principal. Teachers also reported on their outreach to parents and classroom practices. Such practices included an emphasis on higher-order thinking goals, such as critical thinking, independence and initiative, and creativity ($a = .63$).

Analytic Approach

Data analysis proceeded from descriptive and correlational analyses to analyses using hierarchical linear modeling (HLM) (Raudenbush & Bryk, 2002). HLM is a method appropriate for analyzing longitudinal data. This approach allows the examination of intra-individual patterns of growth (within-person) and inter-individual differences in these patterns (between-persons) by estimating individual and group growth curves. Growth curves were graphed when statistical differences for predictors were found.

Sample attrition was 15.2% between kindergarten and third grade and 18.4% between third and fifth grade. Missing data were treated in two ways. First, when outcome data were missing, the HLM program calculated a growth function based on the data available for the individual and the estimates of parameters for average growth of the full sample. Second, multiple imputation was utilized to substitute estimated values for missing values among the predictor variables (Schafer, 1997). Multiple imputation involves developing a predictive probability distribution for missing values. Each missing value is replaced multiple times with values drawn from the predictive probability distribution to create multiple complete data sets. Four between-person data sets were generated by Schafer's (1997) NORM computer program, and these were used to construct four sufficient statistics matrices (SSM) files. The multiple imputation function of HLM was then used to average the results produced by each SSM file. In another study, four SSM files were found to be adequate to produce reliable results (Hauser-Cram, Warfield, Shonkoff, & Krauss, 2001).

The first step in the HLM analysis involved testing a set of models to determine the best functional form for the unconditional models (within-person models) using the repeated measures data collected at kindergarten, third grade, and fifth grade. Given three time points, we could compare only two models: linear and log. Deviance tests were used to identify the best fitting model. A critical decision when developing the within-person model is how to center the data. Centering the data involves subtracting a constant from the time scale so that the point where time equals zero becomes meaningful. Because we were interested in determining the kindergarten features that would predict change over time, we centered the model at the kindergarten data collection point.

Next, between-person models were constructed to determine significant predictors of status (at kindergarten) and change from kindergarten through fifth grade. Between-person models were developed using the following predictors: child characteristics (gender, ethnicity, health, cognitive skills), family demographics (maternal/caregiver education, income, negative life events), and school characteristics (location, proportion of children in poverty, academic climate). Our overall aim was to determine if school characteristics predicted change in children's growth, controlling for child and family characteristics.[2]

RESULTS

Growth in Literacy Skills

In relation to growth in literacy skills, we found a positive log function provided the best fit to the data. The following model was developed:

$$Y = B_0 + B_1^* [\ln(\text{Grade} + .8)] + E,$$

where Y is the proportion of correct answers on the literacy assessment, B_0 is the intercept (i.e., status parameter) measured at the end of the kindergarten year, B_1 is the slope or rate of change in literacy between kindergarten and fifth grade, ln (Grade + .8) is the natural log of the grade associated with each time point (i.e., kindergarten = 0, third grade = 3, fifth grade = 5) plus .8 of a year to represent the spring data collection (where the model is centered), and E is the residual deviation of each time point from the estimated trajectory. The log function indicated that children's increase in literacy was greatest during the first years of school.

As indicated in Table 10.2, children's literacy skills during kindergarten were positively related to their cognitive skills but not to other characteristics of children, their families, or their schools. After controlling for cognitive skills, positive growth in literacy skills was predicted by a school characteristic: percent of low-income students. Although family income did not predict change in children's literacy skills, children in schools with lower proportions of children in poverty showed the greatest growth in literacy achievement. Figure 10.1 shows an estimated growth trajectory in literacy skills for prototypical children from two schools, one enrolling

[2] Because proportional data were used as the outcome, we also computed a logit transformation at each time point, and ran analyses both with and without the transformation. A similar pattern of results was found.

TABLE 10.2. *Growth Curve Analysis Predicting Trajectories in Literacy Skills*

	B_0 (SE) (Status Kindergarten)	B_1 (SE) (Rate of Change)
Intercepts	.23 (.02)***	.29 (.01)***
Family characteristics		
Income	.001 (.01)	−.001 (.01)
Maternal education	.013 (.01)	−.008 (.01)
Negative life events	−.001 (.01)	.002 (.01)
Child characteristics		
Gender (male)	.010 (.03)	−.201 (.02)
Ethnicity[a]		
African-American	.010 (.04)	−.040 (.02)
Latino/a	.050 (.04)	.024 (.02)
Health	−.013 (.04)	.024 (.02)
Child cognitive skills	.003 (.00)***	−.001 (.00)
School characteristics		
Location[b]		
Northeast rural	−.030 (.04)	.040 (.02)
Southwest urban	.010 (.04)	.030 (.02)
Enrollment		
% low income	−.008 (.09)	−.053 (.02)*
Climate	.040 (.02)	−.020 (.01)

[a] Euro-American children are the reference group.
[b] Northeast urban schools are the reference group. *SE* is standard error.
*$p < .05$. **$p < .01$. ***$p < .001$.

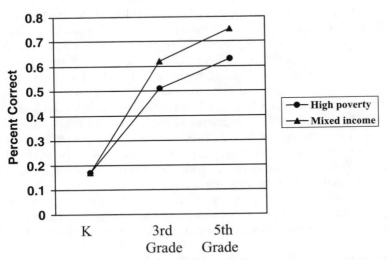

FIGURE 10.1. Changes in literacy skills related to sociodemographics of school population.

TABLE 10.3. *Growth Curve Analysis Predicting Trajectories in School Engagement*

	B_0 (SE) (Status at Kindergarten)	B_1 (SE) (Rate of Change)
Intercepts	9.53 (.19)***	−.165 (.04)***
Family characteristics		
Income	.015 (.10)	−.014 (.03)
Maternal education	.078 (.14)	−.016 (.03)
Negative life events	−.146 (.10)	.042 (.03)
Child characteristics		
Gender (male)	−.819 (.36)*	.052 (.08)
Ethnicity[a]		
African-American	−.138 (.66)	.226 (.12)
Latino/a	−.597 (.52)	.195 (.13)
Health	1.392 (.41)**	−.139 (.10)
Child cognitive skills	.041 (.01)**	−.005 (.00)
School characteristics		
Location[b]		
Northeast rural	.525 (.45)	−.129 (.10)
Southwest urban	.381 (.43)	.027 (.11)
Enrollment		
% low income	1.430 (.88)	−.228 (.19)
Climate	−.260 (.19)	.095 (.04)*

[a] Euro-American children are the reference group.
[b] Northeast urban schools are the reference group. SE is standard error.
*$p < .05$. **$p < .01$. ***$p < .001$.

88% children in poverty, another enrolling 34% children in poverty (these figures represented one standard deviation difference in the distribution). As Figure 10.1 indicates, although children in these two schools display similar skills in kindergarten, their trajectories diverge based on the level of poverty in the school they attend.

Changes in Children's School Engagement

A linear model was determined to be the best fit for the data on school engagement. The model was

$$Y = B_0 + B_1^* \,(\text{Grade} + .8) + E.$$

As indicated in Table 10.3, children's change in school engagement was negative, indicating that teachers rated children as less engaged over time. Females and children in better health as well as those with higher cognitive skills had higher ratings in engagement during kindergarten. Change in school engagement was predicted by one of the three school characteristics

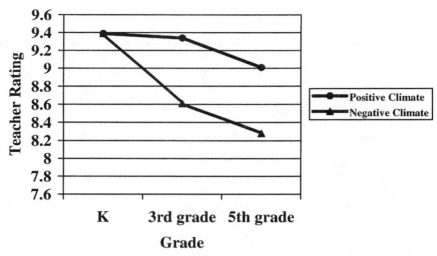

FIGURE 10.2. Changes in school engagement related to school climate.

tested. Children in schools with more positive academic climates showed less decline in school engagement from kindergarten through fifth grade. In Figure 10.2, the change in school engagement of children in schools with a high positive academic climate and those in schools with a less positive academic climate is illustrated. Children enter these two types of schools with similar levels of school engagement but become significantly less engaged in learning over time in schools with less positive academic climates.

The Relation Between Changes in Literacy and in School Engagement

We reasoned that children who become increasingly engaged in school may also become better readers. Therefore, we developed a series of analyses to test the relation between school engagement and literacy at and between the three time points. As shown in Table 10.4, when cognitive performance at school entry was controlled, partial correlations among these outcomes were positive and generally moderate. Although children's school engagement in kindergarten did not relate to their immediate skills in literacy, greater engagement in kindergarten was associated with better literacy skills in both third grade and fifth grade. In order to determine if *changes* in literacy skills were associated with *changes* in school engagement, we tested the following model:

$$Y = B_0 + B_1^* \ [\ln(\text{Grade} + .8) + B_2^* \ \text{SDL} + \text{E},$$

TABLE 10.4. *Partial Correlations Between School Engagement and Literacy*[a]

Literacy	School Engagement		
	Kindergarten	3rd Grade	5th Grade
Kindergarten	.12		
3rd grade	.35***	.39***	
5th grade	.37***	.34**	.20*

[a]Controlling for child cognitive skills at kindergarten entry.
*$p < .05$. **$p < .01$. ***$p < .001$.

where B_2 is each child's school engagement (i.e., self-directed learning) entered as a time varying covariate. Results indicated that changes in school engagement were significantly and positively related to changes in literacy ($B_2 = .29$, $p < .001$). Thus, children with more positive changes in school engagement also exhibited positive changes in literacy.

School Differences Related to Enrollment and Climate

The results indicate that two of the three school factors studied relate to changes in children's school performance. Although school location did not predict change, the social demographics of the school and the school's climate did. We conducted further analyses to learn if schools that differed on each of these two factors differed in other ways as well. Schools in this sample that served a higher proportion of low-income children were significantly larger ($r = .45$, $p < .001$), and kindergarten teachers reported having larger class sizes ($r = .50$, $p < .001$). Teachers in higher poverty schools reported receiving less administrative support than did teachers in schools that served a wider income range (Table 10.5).

Schools with more positive academic climates did not differ from other schools in total enrollment or size of kindergarten classes. As shown in Table 10.5, however, teachers in these schools, in comparison to those in less positive schools, reported establishing more parent outreach, having higher expectations of students, receiving greater administrative support, and having a more collegial faculty and staff. Thus, teachers in schools rated by principals as having a more positive academic climate also viewed their schools as having more positive climates related to both academics and collaborative focus. Further, they worked actively on informing parents about school and classroom activities and welcoming parent involvement. Finally, kindergarten teachers in schools with more positive climates also reported using more effective teaching practices ($r = .24$, $p < .01$), such as balancing instruction in literacy with developing skills in phonics and promoting contextual understanding through whole-language approaches.

TABLE 10.5. *Correlations Between Kindergarten Teachers' Perceptions of Their Practices and the School Climate and Principals' Reports on School Structure and Climate*

	Principal Report	
Teacher Report	Structure: High Poverty[a]	Positive Climate[b]
Teaching practices		
Effective methods	−.05	.24**
Parent outreach	.09	.49***
Climate		
High expectations	.06	.20**
Administrative support	−.18*	.51***
Collegiality	.11	.19*

[a]Proportion of students eligible for free or reduced price lunch.
[b]Rating of academic climate.
$*p < .05.$ $**p < .01.$ $***p < .001.$

DISCUSSION

This investigation focused on children in poverty. Even in a sample with a truncated range of socioeconomic status, children entered school with varying cognitive skills. Consistent with findings from prior studies (e.g., Ladd et al., 1999), children who entered school with higher levels of cognitive performance demonstrated higher skills in literacy and greater engagement in learning during the spring of the kindergarten year. The findings also highlight an advantage for girls in engagement in learning during kindergarten. Similar gender differences in school engagement have been reported in prior studies (Finn & Rock, 1997; Furrer & Skinner, 2003; Marks, 2000). For example, girls have been reported to demonstrate more attentive and cooperative classroom behaviors than do boys (Finn & Rock, 1997).

Brooks-Gunn and Duncan (1997) propose that health is a pathway by which poverty influences other child outcomes including school achievement. Our findings indicate that children in poorer health were less engaged in learning during kindergarten. Allergies and asthma were the most frequently parent-reported specific child health-related problems (affecting approximately 10% and 9.5% of the sample, respectively). Asthma is the most frequent cause of school absence and childhood hospitalization (Newacheck & Halfon, 2000), and children from low-income families with poorly controlled asthma tend to have compromised academic outcomes (Bender, 1995).

The three central findings of this investigation identify the child, family, and school factors that predict *changes* in the academic performance of children living in poverty as they move through the school years in middle childhood:

(1) Children in schools with high concentrations of poverty develop literacy skills more slowly than do children with similar skills and backgrounds in more socioeconomically mixed schools. These patterns remain even when children's cognitive skills at school entry are accounted for.

(2) Children in schools with more positive academic climates show less deleterious declines in being engaged, "self-directed learners" over time.

(3) Changes in self-directed learning are associated with changes in the development of literacy skills, even when cognitive skills at school entry are controlled.

Changes in these outcomes relate to each other, suggesting that an iterative process of learning and engagement occurs for children as they move through middle childhood. Not only do young children who are more engaged in the academic challenges of school become better readers, but children who become better readers are also more able to engage in a range of academic challenges. By fifth grade, teachers expect that children have made a transition from "learning to read" to "reading to learn" (Chall, 1996); children who are strong readers at this point use reading as a means to learn about many topics, including science, history, and social studies. Conversely, children who do not engage in school during the early years fail to develop adequate literacy skills and enter a cycle of continuing disengagement and poor academic performance.

The two outcomes we investigated relate to each other but also are predicted by different aspects of the school environment. Children's growth in literacy skills was predicted by the income characteristics of their schools' population rather than their families' income level. As Entwisle and colleagues (1997) suggest, it is possible that teachers in these schools limit their students' growth by having lower expectations and giving them less rigorous literacy curricula than teachers in middle-income schools. Low expectations of students has been a topic of investigation in many studies, but seldom examined only in low-income samples. In a separate investigation of teacher expectations of the academic competence of kindergarten students in the STS sample, we (Hauser-Cram, Sirin, & Stipek, 2003) found that such expectations were not explained by family socioeconomic status but by teachers' views of educational value differences with parents. Controlling for children's skills, teachers rated children as less academically competent when they perceived value differences with parents.

Although tracking and teacher expectations may in part explain the differences found in literacy skills, other school characteristics may also

affect student outcomes. Higher poverty schools had larger total enroll-
ments and larger class sizes. Teachers in those schools also reported having less administrative support. In a related investigation of this sample,
Stipek (2004) reported that schools with greater proportions of low-income
students had more poorly educated teachers who were more likely to use
ineffective teaching practices.

Allington, Guice, Michelson, Baker, and Li (1996) claimed that another
reason that children in schools serving mainly poor students might develop
literacy skills more slowly is the way in which literary reforms are put
in place. Their study revealed that teachers in these schools often have
difficulty finding time to develop a clear understanding of what a specific
reform entails and sometimes lack broad support for the implementation of
reforms. Since schools serving a high proportion of students in poverty are
more likely to lack administrative support for teachers and have less skilled
teachers with larger classes, literacy reforms may require more time and
support to be successfully implemented. Such implementation difficulties
may partially explain the lower rates of change in literacy found in high
poverty schools.

School climate also is related to children's self-directed learning over
time. Climate (measured as high expectations of students and a strong
emphasis on children's learning) has been linked previously to student
achievement, but seldom considered in relation to children's early school
engagement. This is a serious omission. Our findings indicate that the
path of such engagement begins in kindergarten, with divergent paths for
children in different types of schools quite apparent as children proceed
through middle childhood. Prior studies report that the lack of early school
engagement predicts later school dropout (Alexander et al., 1997) and is
a catalyst for a downward spiral of disengagement in the academic challenges of school (Finn, 1989; Newmann, 1992).

Although children's ability to self-regulate increases with age (Bronson, 2000), the school engagement of children from low-income families
appears to diminish from school entry to middle childhood. Such declines
are not unexpected, given other reported declines in academic motivation
from early through middle childhood (Stipek & Mac Iver, 1989; Wigfield &
Eccles, 2002). These changes may be the result of the increasingly evaluative function of schools, which exacerbates a sense of helplessness in many
low-achieving students (Burhans & Dweck, 1995). Also, as students move
through the middle childhood years, peers become increasingly important
(Adler & Adler, 1998), and students enmeshed in a peer culture that does
not identify with doing well in school may become increasingly disengaged
from academic learning (Fordham & Ogbu, 1986). Our research, however,
indicates that these declines can be somewhat mitigated by school contexts;
students in schools with more positive climates showed less precipitous
declines in school engagement.

Schools with more positive climates had teachers who used more effective teaching practices, made more efforts to reach out to parents, and reported higher expectations for students, greater administrative support, and more staff collegiality. Our investigation suggests that some schools serving a high proportion of children in poverty create climates that promote children's engagement in learning. These schools maintained high standards for academic growth and had students who showed positive self-directed learning.

IMPLICATIONS AND CONCLUSION

Schools serving low-income students are burdened with numerous challenges, including responding to the current emphasis on standards-based reforms while coping with diminishing resources. Given such demands, it may be difficult for school leadership to also focus on ecological features of the school like climate. Yet school climate supports and enhances the quality of teaching and the academic rigor of a school. Creative incentives, such as school–university partnerships and teacher-to-teacher collaborations, may need to be developed for teachers to advance quality teaching in schools serving mainly low-income students. Principals in such schools would benefit from both peer and economic support in taking a leadership role in developing an advantageous school climate. Most important, however, is that at both federal and state levels, economic and social policies prioritize initiatives to effectively decrease the number of children living in poverty in the United States.

Like all investigations, this one has several limitations. First, the study focused on a relatively small sample of students in a relatively large number of schools. Therefore, we were unable to develop multilevel models in which variation within schools could be assessed. On the other hand, the large number of schools allowed assessment of variability across schools. Second, self-directed learning was assessed with teacher reports, which may be prone to bias (e.g., more positive reports in better climate schools). Nevertheless, teachers' perspectives on a student's engagement in learning may be central to the challenges they provide for that student in the classroom.

Our findings suggest that both school structure and school climate relate to children's school performance pathways from kindergarten to middle childhood. Children living in poverty and attending schools that serve a high proportion of students in poverty face double jeopardy. Students in such schools are less likely to make the same advances in literacy as those made by their peers with similar initial skills and backgrounds who attend schools serving more socioeconomically mixed populations of students. School climate also predicts school outcomes. Children from low-income families who attend schools with positive academic environments are more likely to become engaged, self-directed learners. School engagement and the acquisition of literacy skills are intertwined, and we posit that this relation is part of an iterative process by which children enter into *either* advantageous or deleterious pathways as they advance toward middle childhood. Such pathways are forged, at least in part, by the school as it serves as both the context and conduit of student learning.

References

Abt Associates, Inc. (1997). *Prospects: Final report on student outcomes.* Cambridge, MA: Author.

Abidin, R. R. (1995). *Parenting Stress Index* (3rd ed.). Odessa, FL: Psychological Assessment Resources.

Adler, P. A., & Adler, P. (1998). *Peer power.* New Brunswick, NJ: Rutgers University Press.

Alexander, K. L., Entwisle, D. R., & Horsey, C. S. (1997). From first grade forward: Early foundations of high school drop-out. *Sociology of Education, 70,* 87–107.

Allington, R., Guice, S., Michelson, N., Baker, K., & Li, S. (1996). Literature-based curricula in high poverty schools. In M. Graves, P. Van Den Broek, B. Taylor (Eds.), *The first R: Every child's right to read* (pp. 73–96). New York: Teachers College Press.

Baker, J., Terry, T., Bridger, R., & Winsor, A. (1997). Schools as caring communities: A relational approach to school reform. *School Psychology Review, 26,* 586–602.

Bandura, A. (1997). *Self-efficacy: The exercise of control.* New York: Freeman.

Bender, B. G. (1995). Are asthmatic children educationally handicapped? *School Psychology Quarterly, 10,* 274–291.

Bronson, M. B. (2000). *Self-regulation in early education.* New York: Guilford.

Brooks-Gunn, J., & Duncan, G. J. (1997). The effects of poverty on children. *The future of children: Children and poverty, 7*(2), 55–71.

Burhans, K. K., & Dweck, C. S. (1995). Helplessness in early childhood: The role of contingent worth. *Child Development, 66,* 1719–1738.

Caldas, S., & Bankston, C. (1997). Effect of school population socioeconomic status on individual academic achievement. *Journal of Educational Psychology, 90*(5), 269–277.

Chall, J. S. (1996). *Stages of reading development* (2nd ed.). Fort Worth, TX: Harcourt, Brace.

Dunn, L. M., & Dunn, L. M. (1981). *Peabody Picture Vocabulary Test-Revised.* Circle Pines, NM: American Guidance Service.

Entwisle, D. R., & Alexander, K. L. (1998). Facilitating the transition to first grade: The nature of transition and research on factors affecting it. *The Elementary School Journal, 98*(4), 351–361.

Entwisle, D. R., Alexander, K. L., & Olson, L. S. (1997). *Children, schools, and inequality.* Boulder, CO: Westview Press.

Esposito, C. (1999). Learning in urban blight: School climate and its effect on the school population of urban, minority, low-income children. *School Psychology Review, 28*(3), 365–377.

Finn, J. D. (1989). Withdrawing from school. *Review of Educational Research, 59,* 117–142.

Finn, J. D., & Rock, D. A. (1997). Academic stress among students at risk for school failure. *Journal of Applied Psychology, 82*, 221–234.

Fordham, S., & Ogbu, J. U. (1986). Black students' school success: Coping with the "burden of acting White." *Urban Review, 18*, 176–206.

Furrer, C., & Skinner, E. (2003). Sense of relatedness as a factor in children's academic engagement and performance. *Journal of Educational Psychology, 95*, 148–162.

Goddard, R. D., Sweetland, S. R., & Hoy, W. K. (2000). Academic emphasis of urban elementary schools and student achievement in reading and mathematics: A multilevel analysis. *Educational Administration Quarterly, 3*(5), 683–702.

Greenberg, M. T., Lengua, L.J., Coie, J. D., & Pinderhughes, E. E. (1999). Predicting developmental outcomes at school entry using a multiple-risk model: Four American communities. *Developmental Psychology, 35*(2), 403–417.

Hauser-Cram, P., Sirin, S. R., & Stipek, D. (2003). When teachers' and parents' values differ: Teachers' ratings of academic competence in children from low-income families. *Journal of Educational Psychology, 95*(4), 813–820.

Hauser-Cram, Warfield, M. E., Shonkoff, J. P., & Krauss, M. W. (2001). Children with disabilities: A longitudinal study of child development and parent well-being. *Monographs of the Society for Research in Child Development, 66*(3, Serial No. 266).

Ho, E. S., & Willms, J. D. (1996). Effects of parental involvement on eightgrade achievement. *Sociology of Education, 69*, 126–141.

Hoy, W. K., Hannum, J., & Tschannen-Moran, M. (1998). Organizational climate and student achievement: A parsimonious and longitudinal view. *Journal of School Leadership, 8*, 336–359.

Hoy, W. K., & Sabo, D. J. (1998). *Quality middle schools: Open and healthy*. Thousand Oaks, CA: Corwin Press.

Jimmerson, S. R. (1999). On the failure of failure: Examining the association between early grade retention and education and employment outcomes during late adolescence. *Journal of School Psychology, 37*, 243–272.

Johnson, P., Livingston, M., Schwartz, R. A., & Slate, J. R. (2000). What makes a good elementary school? A critical examination. *Journal of Educational Research, 93*(6), 339–345.

Kahlenberg, R. D. (2001). *All together now: Creating middle-class schools through public school choice*. Washington, DC: Brookings Institution Press.

Ladd, G. W., Birch, S. H., & Buhs, E. S. (1999). Children's social and scholastic lives in kindergarten: Relation spheres of influence? *Child Development, 70*(4), 1373–1400.

Lambert, N., & McCombs, B. (Eds.). (1998). *How students learn: Reforming schools through learner-centered education*. Washington, DC: American Psychological Association.

Lankford, H., Loeb, S., & Wyckoff, J. (2002). Teacher sorting and the plight of urban schools: A descriptive analysis. *Education Evaluation and Policy Analysis, 24*(1), 37–62.

Lee, V. E., & Burkam, D. T. (2002). *Inequality at the starting gate: Social background differences as children begin school*. Washington, DC: Economic Policy Institute.

Ma, X. (2001). Stability of school academic performance across subject areas. *Journal of Educational Measurement, 38*(1), 1–18.

Marks, H. M. (2000). Student engagement in instructional activity: Patterns in elementary, middle, and high school years. *American Educational Research Journal,* 37(1), 153–184.

Mullis, I., Campbell, J., & Farstrup, A. (1993). *NAEP 1992 Reading report card for the nation and the states: Data from the national and trial state assessments.* Washington, DC: National Center for Education Statistics.

National Center for Education Statistics (1999). *Teacher quality: A report on the preparation and qualifications of public school teachers (#NCES 1999-080).* Washington, DC: U.S. Department of Education.

National Reading Panel (2000). *Teaching children to read: An evidence-based assessment of the scientific research literature on reading and its implications for reading instruction* (Publication No. 00-4769). Washington, DC: National Institutes of Health .

National Research Council, Committee on the Prevention of Reading Difficulties in Young Children (1998). *Reading difficulties in young children.* Washington, DC: Author.

National Research Council and the Institute of Medicine (2000). *From neurons to neighborhoods.* Washington, DC: National Academy Press.

Newachek, P.W., & Halfon, N. (2000). Prevalence, impact, and trends in childhood disability due to asthma. *Archives of Pediatric and Adolescent Medicine, 154,* 287–293.

Newmann, F. M. (Ed.). (1992). *Student engagement and achievement in American secondary schools.* New York: Teachers College Press.

Newmann, F., & Associates (1996). *Authentic achievement: Restructuring schools for intellectual quality.* San Francisco: Jossey-Bass.

Phillips, M. (1997). What makes schools effective? A comparison of the relationships of communitarian climate and academic achievement and attendance during middle school. *American Educational Research Journal, 34*(4), 633–662.

Raudenbush, S., & Bryk, A. (2002). *Hierarchical linear models: Applications and data analysis methods (2nd ed.).* Newbury Park, CA: Sage.

Schafer, J. L. (1997). *Analysis of incomplete multivariate data.* New York: Chapman & Hall.

Stanovich, K. E., & Cunningham, A. E. (1993). Where does knowledge come from? Specific associations between print exposure and information acquisition. *Journal of Educational Psychology, 85,* 211–229.

Stipek, D. J. (2002). *Motivation to learn: Integrating theory and practice.* Boston: Allyn and Bacon.

Stipek, D. J. (2004). Teaching practices in kindergarten and first grade: Different strokes for different folks. *Early Childhood Research Quarterly, 19,* 548–568.

Stipek, D. J., & Mac Iver, D. (1989). Developmental change in children's assessment of intellectual competence. *Child Development, 60,* 521–538.

Stipek, D. J., & Ryan, R. H. (1997). Economically disadvantaged preschoolers: Ready to learn but further to go. *Developmental Psychology, 33,* 711–723.

Wigfield, A., & Eccles, J. S. (2002). Introduction. In A. Wigfield and J. S. Eccles (Eds.), *Development of achievement motivation* (pp. 1–11). San Diego: Academic Press.

Woodcock, R. W., & Johnson, M. B. (1990). *Woodcock-Johnson Psycho-Educational Battery-Revised.* Allen, TX: DLM Teaching Resources.

11

The Relations of Classroom Contexts in the Early Elementary Years to Children's Classroom and Social Behavior

NICHD Early Child Care Research Network[1]

Beginning formal education represents an almost universal developmental milestone that occurs near the time that children enter middle childhood. Although the major agenda of school is teaching academic skills, schools are social environments with expectations for behavior and social structures to which children need to adapt (Weinstein, 1991). School environments are small communities in which the social interactions are neither totally prescribed nor totally unconstrained. The expected behaviors go well beyond literacy and numerical skills to self-regulation (e.g., involvement in classroom activities, restraining disruptive behavior, attending to the agenda of the classroom, working autonomously), harmonious social interactions with adults (e.g., compliance, clear communications, positive social interactions, absence of defiance or conflict), and positive interactions with peers (e.g., cooperative activity, nonaggressive conflict resolution).

In this chapter, we ask how the social and instructional context of the school classroom contributes to children's social and behavioral competencies during middle childhood. We define context at the level of processes within the classroom that include instructional and emotional support for learning, positive and negative climate, and negative disciplinary interactions between teachers and students. We frame the questions at two levels. First, are there immediate associations between classroom

[1] This study is directed by a Steering Committee and supported by NICHD through a cooperative agreement (U10), which calls for scientific collaboration between the grantees and the NICHD staff. Participating investigators, listed in alphabetical order, are:

Jay Belsky, Cathryn Booth-LaForce, Robert H. Bradley, Susan B. Campbell, Hrishikesh Chakraborty, Alison Clarke-Stewart, Sarah Friedman, Kathy Hirsh-Pasek, Renate Houts, Jean F. Kelly, Bonnie Knocke, Kathleen McCartney, Fred Morrison, Marion O'Brien, C. Chris Payne, Deborah Phillips, Robert Pianta, Susan Spieker, Deborah Vandell, and Marsha Weinraub.

contexts and children's social behavior within the classroom? That is, do children demonstrate different patterns of involvement, peer interaction, or disruptive behavior depending on such features of the classroom as teacher involvement, teacher sensitivity, and instructional style? Second, are any of the "effects" of classroom experiences on children's social skills and behavior problems evident in later years when they are in a different classroom or when they are interacting with their parents? That is, do classroom context effects last over time or generalize from school to home?

We assume from the outset that a child's experiences in a classroom are a product of the classroom features *and* the child's own characteristics; hence, classroom features do not have unidirectional effects. Nevertheless, although individual children elicit different behaviors in the classroom, individual teachers' techniques for teaching and for behavior control affect the extent to which children express and modify positive and problematic social behavior. If children learn and practice social skills, academic motivation, school engagement, or tendencies to misbehave through their repeated experiences in the classroom setting with adults and peers, then some enduring and generalizable changes may emerge.

SCHOOL EXPERIENCES AND SOCIAL BEHAVIOR

Social and behavioral competencies in the early grades, as well as problems in these domains, are important indicators of early school success and harbingers of subsequent outcomes (Entwisle & Alexander, 1999; Ladd & Burgess, 1999; Rimm-Kaufman, Pianta, Cox, & Early, 2000). Teachers often define school readiness in relation to conduct and ability to follow directions (Heaviside & Farris, 1993; Rimm-Kaufman et al., 2000), and large-scale national surveys of children's skills (NCES, 1999) depict wide variation in social and behavioral competencies in the early grades. Children who communicate effectively, follow directions, and cooperate; who are attentive, enthusiastic, and actively involved in classroom activities; and who get along with other children demonstrate a cluster of self-regulatory and social skills that are important for overall school success and for life success as well (Ladd & Burgess, 1999; Meisels, 1999; Rimm-Kaufman et al., 2000). On the other hand, social and behavioral problems including inattention, poor impulse control, difficulties following directions and conforming to classroom rules and routines, disruptive behavior, and aggression toward peers predict continuing problems in adjustment in middle childhood (e.g., Campbell, 1995; Ladd & Burgess, 1999; Schwartz, McFadyen-Ketchum, Dodge, Pettit, & Bates, 1999).

Classroom contexts that provide opportunities for learning and social-emotional supports may facilitate the development of self-regulation and social skills with adults and peers, and chaotic and punitive classrooms with little instructional support may contribute to disruption and withdrawal from the school agenda. Although children's social and behavioral competencies improve over the early school years on average (NCES, 2003), individual differences are somewhat unstable and situation specific, suggesting that classroom environments can influence them (LaParo & Pianta, 2001; NCES, 2003). For example, teachers' sensitive behaviors have been shown to moderate children's on-task behavior in kindergarten (Rimm-Kaufman et al., 2002). Experiences in the early grades may be especially important in forming expectations for appropriate behavior and cultivating the development of such behavior – experiences that may set lasting patterns for future years in school.

Most research on school and classroom characteristics is focused on such structural features as class size and teacher experience; few investigations contain in-depth information about what goes on in the classroom on a day-to-day basis. One exception is an investigation of African American children ages 7–15 showing that classroom features (order and organization, rule clarity, and student involvement in decisions) predicted children's self-regulation, which in turn predicted low levels of aggression, delinquency, and depression. The classroom process measures were obtained, however, from students' reports, so the associations may reflect individual differences among students as well as among classrooms (Brody, Dorsey, Forehand, & Armistad, 2002).

PERSON–ENVIRONMENT FIT

We conceptualize children's adaptation to school classrooms in a broad framework of person–environment fit. Some groups of children are likely to enter school already possessing self-regulatory and social skills that fit well with classroom expectations; others have behavior patterns that are less consistent with the school agenda. In this chapter, we consider possible differences in "fit" based on gender, family income, and ethnic group. On average, girls display less aggression and noncompliance and more adult orientation than boys do (Golombok & Fivish, 1994). Children from low-income families enter school, on average, with fewer language and academic skills, more likelihood of disruptive behavior, and more attention problems (Bradley & Corwyn, 2002). They may experience more discontinuity between behavioral expectations at home and at school than do children from more affluent families. Finally, children from different ethnic groups enter with different average levels of skills and familiarity with the expectations of the classroom (Fisher, Jackson, & Villarruel, 1997). Because teachers are likely to expect more problem behaviors from boys, children from low-income families, and children from some ethnic minority groups, they may perceive such children negatively, contributing to potential problems of "fit" with school expectations.

Although these group differences are well documented, we know little about how children with different initial characteristics respond to different types of classrooms. It is possible that children who enter with fewer skills are more responsive to variations in teacher practices or disciplinary techniques because they have more to learn about school expectations. It is also possible that some children bring behavioral dispositions that make them less responsive to positive or negative classroom contexts or that stimulate teachers and peers to be negative or punitive. In the analyses described below, we ask whether classroom contexts predict behavior differently for boys and girls, children from high- and low-income families, and children from African American and Euro American ethnic groups.

We use a large, national, longitudinal dataset to describe the features of first and third grade classrooms and to examine the relations of these contextual features to children's development of self-regulation and social behavior over time. In the NICHD Study of Early Child Care and Youth Development (NICHD SECCYD) we observed first and third grade classrooms directly for a large sample of children and schools across the country. Because we collected a great deal of information about the children and their families throughout the preschool years, we can control for individual differences in social behavior at school entry and for family characteristics as we examine the relations of classroom contexts to behavior throughout the first four years of school.

We address the following questions: (a) Are there contemporaneous relations between classroom contexts and social behavior while children are enrolled in those classrooms? (b) Do classroom contexts at one grade predict changes in behavior over time, when children are in different classrooms? (c) Do classroom contexts predict behavior across environments; that is, do they predict parent reports of social skills and behavior problems? (d) Do the relations of context to behavior vary by gender, family economic status, or ethnic group?

METHOD

Sample

Families were recruited to the NICHD Study when their children were one month old. Details of the original sampling procedure and characteristics of the sample have been described in a large number of publications (see http://secc.rti.org). The overall design and methods of the study are presented in NICHD ECCRN (2003a).

Of the original 1,364 infants, 841 were observed in both first and third grade classrooms; they compose the sample for this chapter. Ethnicity of the children was as follows: 673 (80.0%) were Non-Hispanic White, 94 (11.2%) African American, 42 (5.0%) Hispanic, and 32 (3.8%) were of other ethnic backgrounds. The average family income-to-needs ratio was less than

2.0 (i.e., less than 200% of the federal poverty threshold) for 212 (25.2%) children. Mothers averaged 14.46 ($SD = 2.42$) years of education. Although the sample reflects a diverse range of family backgrounds in the United States, the NICHD SECCYD excluded children of mothers under 18 years old, mothers who did not speak English, and children who were hospitalized for more than a week at birth or who had a diagnosed disability. Comparison of the sample used in this chapter with those lost to attrition indicated that mothers in our sample had more years of education, children were less likely to be Non-White, and the families' income-to-needs ratios were higher than for those not included.

Classrooms

The study design entailed observing each study child in her or his classroom; therefore, the sample of classrooms was selected because a study child was enrolled in them. Children were observed during the second and fourth years in school, counting kindergarten as the first year. In most instances, they were in first and third grades, respectively. In first grade, the observed classrooms were distributed across 747 different schools, and in third grade there were 780 classrooms. In some instances, two study children were observed in the same classroom, but these observations occurred on different occasions. Most classrooms were located in and around the cities in which the 10 data collection sites were located, although the sample was fairly dispersed by the time the children reached school. Almost all teachers had Bachelor's degrees and were credentialed in elementary education (see NICHD ECCRN, 2002, 2004, in press). Characteristics of these teachers and classrooms are consistent with reports from national samples of elementary school staffing and schools (NCES, 1994).

Classroom Observations

The procedures for classroom observations were similar at first and third grades. Observations took place in the winter and early spring. In first grade, observations were conducted in the morning; in third grade, they took an entire day. At both grades, observers made time-sampled records of context and of children's behavior for a total of 60 minutes (first grade) or 80 minutes (third grade) spread across the observation period. Before and after the time-sampling sessions, observers made global ratings of classroom contexts and children's behavior. These classroom-level global ratings used a scale of 1 to 7. A rating of "1" = "uncharacteristic," "3" = "minimally characteristic," "5" = "very characteristic", and "7" = "extremely characteristic" of the observed classroom. Both the behavior codes and global ratings used the Classroom Observation Systems for First Grade and Third Grade, respectively (NICHD ECCRN, 2002, in press). A detailed manual describes these codes and the coding procedures (see http://secc.rti.org).

Classroom Context. On the basis of factor analyses and theoretical coherence, aggregate measures of classroom context were created. In first grade, there are two composites from the global ratings: *instructional support for student learning* and *emotional support*. Instructional support includes ratings of literacy instruction, evaluative feedback, instructional conversation, and encouragement of child responsibility. Emotional support includes ratings of overcontrol (reflected), positive emotional climate, negative emotional climate (reflected), effective classroom management, teacher sensitivity, intrusiveness (reflected), and detachment (reflected) (see NICHD ECCRN, 2002). In the third grade, many of the specific global rating scales clustered together to form a composite, *positive climate*, which is the sum of teacher detachment (reflected), positive classroom climate, negative classroom climate (reflected), productive use of instructional time, and teacher sensitivity (see NICHD ECCRN, in press).

At both grade levels, a time-sampled indicator was *teacher disciplines*. This scale includes scolding, correction, or punishment of the target child or a group containing the target child. One time-sampled observation category at third grade, *collaborative work*, was chosen as an indicator of the degree to which the classroom context might facilitate positive peer interaction. It was coded when two or more children worked jointly on a classroom-related activity.

Child Behavior. The classroom observations included both time-sampled observations and global ratings of children's behavior. We use three variables from each grade in this chapter. *Positive involvement* is a composite of time-sampled observations of child engagement in classroom activity and positive or neutral interactions with a teacher, as well as a global rating of self-reliance. *Positive peer interaction* is based on time-sampled observations and global ratings of positive and neutral peer interactions. *Disruptive behavior* is time-sampled negative and disruptive behavior.

Observer Reliability. All observers were required to pass a videotaped reliability test before collecting data. Criteria for passing were at least 60% match with a master-coder on specific time-sampled codes and 80% match (within one scale point) on the global rating scales. Average *exact* agreement with the expert codes was .70 for behavioral codes and .63 for the global codes at first grade and .85 for behavioral codes and .79 for global ratings at third grade. Observers also conducted visits in pairs to estimate live reliability. Average live reliability was .71.

Stability of Classroom Observations Over Time. The observations of each target child were conducted on one day, raising the question of how stable or representative the observed classroom contexts and child behaviors were. Because more than one study child was observed in some classrooms (but on different days) ($n = 63$ at first grade; $n = 55$ at third grade), we could examine stability of the classroom context observations across days and children. For the time-sampled codes, the average cross-day correlation was .79 at first grade and .87 at third grade. For the global ratings, the average cross-day correlation was .71 at first grade and .91 at third grade. Thus it appears that the one-day observations reflected features of individual classrooms that remained stable across time and across children.

Stability of Classroom Contexts and Behavior from First to Third Grades. By contrast, there was relatively low stability of the contexts experienced by individual children from first to third grades. The correlations of a child's experience of first grade instructional support for student learning and emotional support with positive climate in third grade were .18, $p < .001$ and .13, $p < .001$, respectively. The correlation of discipline in grades 1 and 3 was $r = .12$, $p < .001$. Similarly, the stability of children's classroom behavior was relatively low. The correlations were child engagement, $r = .20$, $p < .001$; positive peer interaction, $r = .10$, $p < .01$; disruptive behavior, $r = .18$, $p < .001$.

Teacher and Parent Reports of Social Behavior

From first through fourth grades, both teachers and parents completed ratings of children's positive social skills and problem behaviors. Mothers rated children annually over the same time period, except during second grade.

Positive Social Skills. Social skills were measured using the school and home versions of the Social Skills Questionnaire (SSQ) from the Social Skills Rating System (SSRS; Gresham & Elliott, 1990). Subscales are labeled cooperation, assertion, and self-control. The total score is the sum of all 30 items, with higher scores indicating higher levels of perceived social competence. The SSQ was normed on a diverse, national sample of children and shows high levels of internal consistency (median = .90) and test–retest reliability (.75 to .88).

Externalizing and Internalizing Behavior Problems. Behavior problems were assessed with the age-appropriate versions of the Child Behavior Checklist (Achenbach, 1991) or Teacher Report Form (TRF; Achenbach, 1991). Both the parent and teacher versions contain two subscales: *externalizing problems* (e.g., argues a lot) and *internalizing problems* (e.g., too fearful and anxious). The zero-order correlations among the behavior measures (using standardized T-scores) at first and third grades appear in Table 11.1.

TABLE 11.1. *Zero-Order Correlations Among Child Behaviors at First and Third Grades.*

	Positive Involvement	Positive Peer	Disrupts	Social Skills T	Social Skills M	Extern T	Extern M	Intern T	Intern M
Involvement	–	0.011	-0.422	0.227	0.085	-0.143	-0.032	-0.080	-0.028
Positive peer	-0.026	–	0.100	0.082	0.044	-0.038	-0.040	-0.126	-0.073
Disruptive	-0.534	0.236	–	-0.165	-0.102	0.235	0.114	0.000	0.038
Social skills T	0.358	0.077	-0.198	–	0.293	-0.578	-0.236	-0.394	-0.102
Social skills M	0.181	0.112	-0.122	0.232	–	-0.242	-0.475	-0.135	-0.278
Externalize T	-0.307	0.065	0.372	-0.596	-0.219	–	0.322	0.301	0.061
Externalize M	-0.132	-0.086	0.123	-0.298	-0.380	0.390	–	0.072	0.569
Internalize T	-0.171	-0.111	0.136	-0.426	-0.093	0.345	0.100	–	0.153
Internalize M	-0.005	-0.132	-0.041	-0.139	-0.196	0.059	0.555	0.181	–

Note: Correlations above the diagonal are for first grade; those below the diagonal are for third grade. T = teacher report; M = mother report.

At both age levels, there was some consistency between observed behavior and teacher reports, particularly for negative forms of behavior. Similarly, teachers' and mothers' ratings of social skills and externalizing behavior were consistent with one another, but there was less agreement about internalizing, probably because it is less easily observed. Children who displayed positive peer interaction were also more disruptive and slightly lower on internalizing, but not less involved in the classroom. They appear to be children who are sociable and who sometimes disrupt the classroom without reduced engagement in the school agenda.

RESULTS

Do Classroom Contexts Predict Children's Social Behavior in First Grade?

In an earlier paper, we reported the associations of classroom contexts with social behavior during first grade (NICHD ECCRN, 2003b). Children in first grade classrooms with high *instructional* support and high levels of structured activity displayed more positive behavior toward their teachers than did children in classrooms with less instructional support. High levels of *emotional* support were associated with self-reliance and engagement in learning. Although these classroom process indicators predicted behavior in the classroom, they generally did not predict teacher or parent reports of children's positive social skills or behavior problems. The one exception occurred on maternal reports of internalizing problems: mothers reported more internalizing symptoms when their children were in classrooms with low emotional support and high levels of structured activity. All of the analyses included extensive controls for children's preschool levels of behavior, family characteristics, and child care experiences. These findings suggest that classroom contexts in first grade affect children's behavior in the classroom in ways that may set the stage for continuing patterns of social behavior in subsequent classrooms.

Classroom Context and Classroom Behavior in Third Grade

We next examine the relations of both first and third grade classroom features to children's behavior in third grade classrooms. These analyses provide information about the contemporaneous associations of classroom features to behavior within the classroom as well as any lasting effects of first grade experiences.

Three types of behavior in third grade were examined: positive involvement with classroom activities, positive interactions with peers, and disruptive behavior. Each of these was regressed on a set of predictors using ordinary least squares regression procedures. All models included the first grade level of the parallel behavior to control for individual differences in children's initial behavior. In addition, we entered the following set of covariates designed to correct for major selection variables: site; child gender; maternal education; three dummy variables for African American, Hispanic, and "other" ethnic groups (Non-Hispanic Whites are the omitted comparison group); low family income (a dichotomous variable indicating whether family income-to-needs was less than 2.0); teacher ethnic group (1 = African American; 0 = all others); teacher experience; and teacher education. Because the child's initial level of behavior was controlled, we did not include controls for preschool parenting or child care experiences that might have contributed to individual differences at school entry.

With first grade behavior controlled, third grade classroom behaviors were associated with the contemporaneous classroom features, and there was no evidence that first grade classroom features had lasting effects (see Table 11.2). Children in third grade classrooms with positive climates were more involved and less disruptive than were children in less positive climates. Children in classrooms with higher rates of discipline were more likely to be disruptive. Children in classrooms that involved them in collaborative work and/or in classrooms that included more discipline displayed more positive interactions with their peers.

Classroom Features, Social Skills, and Behavior Problems

Both teacher ratings and maternal ratings of children's social skills and behavior problems provide information about whether classroom context effects generalize over time and setting. The measures of social skills and behavior problems were collected from first through fourth grades.

To test the possible lasting effects of classroom features on behavior changes over time, we treated third and fourth grade scores as age-varying dependent variables, using the raw scores. The three first grade classroom features – emotional quality, instructional quality, and discipline – and the three third grade features – positive climate, discipline, and collaborative work – were the major predictors. The first-grade score on the dependent variable was a covariate to control for initial level. The other covariates were grade and those used in the previous hierarchical regression models.

Grade was centered at third grade, so the main effects of the classroom features represent the extent to which each feature predicts behavior in third grade, net of the child's first grade level. That is, the main effects indicate whether the classroom features predict change from first to third grade. The interactions of age with each classroom variable test whether

TABLE 11.2. *Unstandardized Regression Coefficients Predicting Observed Classroom Behavior at Third Grade*

	Positive Involvement		Positive Peer Interaction		Disruptive	
	B	se	B	se	B	se
Emotional quality G1	0.004	0.014	0.003	0.011	0.000	0.003
Instructional quality G1	0.005	0.021	0.022	0.017	−0.002	0.004
Positive climate G3	0.335*	0.025	−0.025	0.020	−0.018*	0.005
Collaborative work 3	0.007	0.017	0.198*	0.013	0.003	0.003
Discipline G1	−0.060	0.056	−0.005	0.044	0.010	0.011
Discipline G3	−0.154*	0.038	0.125*	0.030	0.075*	0.008
Grade 1 behavior	0.209***	0.043	0.008	0.006	0.013**	0.005
Child male	−0.674***	0.142	0.163	0.110	0.133***	0.028
Mother education	0.031	0.034	0.048#	0.026	−0.003	0.007
African American	−0.340	0.253	0.194	0.197	0.106*	0.050
Hispanic	0.039	0.325	0.545*	0.253	0.023	0.064
Other ethnic group	−0.326	0.366	−0.100	0.284	−0.008	0.072
Low income	−0.563**	0.196	−0.411**	0.152	0.011	0.039
Teacher African American	0.812*	0.383	−0.212	0.298	−0.092	0.076
Teacher education	−0.223**	0.071	0.113*	0.056	0.022	0.014
Teacher experience (years)	−0.001	0.007	−0.001	0.005	0.00	0.001
R^2	0.335***		0.272***		0.191***	
ΔR^2 for classroom variables	0.188***		0.208***		0.129***	

Note: All analyses include controls for site.
*$p < .05$. **$p < .01$. ***$p < .001$. #$p < .10$.

the pattern of associations between the predictor and behavior (again net of first grade) are different in fourth grade than in third grade. That is, they indicate the extent to which the classroom features have enduring relations to behavior rated by a new teacher in a new classroom. All covariates were centered at the mean. The results are shown in Table 11.3.

Positive Climate. Children who experienced third grade classrooms with positive climates had slightly higher teacher-rated positive social skills and lower teacher-rated internalizing behavior problems than would have been expected from their first-grade behavior. The interactions of third-grade positive climate with age were not significant, indicating that the

TABLE 11.3. *Regression Coefficients for Classroom Features as Predictors of Social Skills and Problem Behavior*

Factor	SSRS Teacher		SSRS Mother		Externalizing Teacher		Externalizing Mother		Internalizing Teacher		Internalizing Mother	
	B	se	B	se	B	se	B	se	B	se	B	se
Intercept	38.08	1.00	55.25	.89	9.80	.87	7.67	.55	7.98	.64	5.22	.50
Emotional quality G1	-.08	.06	-.05	.05	-.02	.05	.02	.03	-.00	.04	.04	.03
Instructional quality G1	-.02	.09	.10	.08	.05	.08	-.08#	.05	.07	.06	-.10*	.04
Positive climate G3	.18#	.11	.04	.09	-.06	.09	-.05	.06	-.15*	.07	.05	.05
Collaborative work G3	.05	.07	-.01	.06	.04	.06	.03	.04	-.03	.05	-.00	.03
Discipline G1	-.55*	.24	.15	.20	.78***	.21	-.12	.12	.42***	.16	.03	.11
Discipline G3	-.47**	.15	.20	.14	.63***	.13	.08	.08	.08	.10	-.10	.08
Grade	-.05	.35	.48*	.23	-.51#	.28	-.46***	.14	-.44#	.26	-.27*	.12
Emot quality G1 × Grade	-.03	.07	.07	.05	.01	.06	-.02	.03	.00	.05	-.06**	.02
Instruc qual G1 × Grade	.09	.10	.01	.07	.02	.08	.09*	.04	-.03	.08	.13***	.04
Positive clim G3 Grade	.06	.12	.12	.08	-.13	.10	-.04	.05	.07	.09	-.10*	.04
Collaborative G3 × Grade	-.00	.08	-.08	.05	-.02	.07	-.02	.03	-.03	.06	-.01	.03
Discipline G1 × Grade	-.20	.28	.14	.18	-.43#	.22	.06	.11	-.54**	.20	-.02	.09
Discipline G3 × Grade	-.15	.16	-.29*	.12	-.01	.13	.08	.07	.18	.11	.11#	.06
Grade 1 score	.36***	.03	.73***	.03	.39***	.03	.44***	.01	.09***	.02	.32***	.01
Female	2.60***	.51	.98*	.45	-2.96***	.44	-.92**	.28	-.00	.32	.76**	.24
Mother education	.30*	.12	.13	.11	-.15	.10	-.17*	.07	-.17*	.08	-.09	.06
African American	-1.93*	.94	-.91	.82	2.61**	.82	.33	.51	-.44	.60	-.45	.46
Hispanic	-.40	1.14	-1.82	1.01	-.86	1.00	-.92	.63	-.55	.73	-.95	.56
Other	-.98	1.28	-.09	1.14	.88	1.11	-.70	.70	-.08	.81	-.64	.63
Income	3.09***	.70	1.73*	.63	-2.83***	.61	-.51	.39	-1.65***	.45	-.78*	.35
Teacher African Amer.	.26	1.20			-.81	1.00			-.23	.83		
Teacher education	-.45*	.21			.24	.18			.06	.15		
Teacher experience	.06**	.02			-.05**	.02			-.04**	.01		

Note: All analyses include the controls for site.

*p < .05. **p < .01. ***p < .001. #p < .10.

associations of the third grade positive climate with behavior did not decline significantly when children reached fourth grade. Positive climate did not predict teachers' reports of externalizing problems, nor did it predict maternal ratings of any social behavior.

There were no significant relations of first grade instructional or emotional quality to teacher-rated behavior, and there were scattered associations with mother-rated behavior change. Children who experienced high instructional quality showed slightly more decreases in both externalizing and internalizing problems as reported by mothers in third grade, but interactions with age show that these differences had disappeared by fourth grade. Although there was a significant interaction of age with emotional quality, neither the third nor fourth grade coefficients were significantly different from zero.

Discipline. Classroom discipline in both first and third grades was a strong predictor of unfavorable change in teacher-rated behavior. Children who were in first grade classrooms with high rates of discipline had less positive changes in social skills and larger increases in externalizing and internalizing problems as rated by third grade teachers. The relations of discipline to teacher-rated behavior appear to be cumulative in that first and third grade classroom levels made independent contributions to the observed effects for third grade social skills and externalizing problems.

The associations of positive social skills with low levels of discipline in first and third grades lasted into fourth grade. The interactions with age were not significant. Similarly, high levels of first- and third-grade discipline continued to predict high levels of externalizing behavior problems in fourth grade. The interaction of first grade discipline with age was of borderline significance; the interaction of third-grade discipline with age was negligible. By contrast, discipline in the earlier years did not predict fourth-grade internalizing problems.

Discipline had few relations to maternal reports of behavior. For positive social skills and internalizing problems, there were interactions of third grade discipline and age, but neither the third nor fourth grade coefficients were significantly different from zero for either behavior.

Collaborative Work. There were no associations of classroom collaborative work with teacher- or mother-rated social behavior.

Gender, Income, and Ethnic Group Differences

Group Differences. There were average gender differences on a few classroom context dimensions and on most of the measures of social behavior in school. In the classroom observations, boys were in classrooms with slightly more discipline (first grade $r = .14$, $p < .01$; third grade $r = .08$,

$p < .05$), and boys were somewhat less involved and more disruptive in class than were girls (Table 11.2). Both teachers and mothers rated girls higher on positive social skills and lower on externalizing problems than they did boys (see Table 11.3). But mothers rated girls higher than boys on internalizing problems, and there were not gender differences on teacher-rated internalizing (Table 11.3).

Children from low-income families attended classrooms with lower quality and higher levels of discipline than did children from more affluent families. The correlations of *low* income with classroom features were first grade instructional quality $r = -.14, p < .01$; first grade emotional quality $r = -.13, p < .01$; third grade positive climate $r = -.16, p < .01$; first grade discipline $r = .15, p < .01$; and third grade discipline $r = .17, p < .01$.

Children from low-income families displayed somewhat less positive involvement in the classroom and less positive behavior with peers, but they were not more disruptive than those from higher income families (Table 11.2). At third and fourth grades, teachers and mothers rated children from low-income families as having fewer social skills, and more internalizing behavior problems; teachers also rated children from low-income families higher on externalizing behavior problems (see Table 11.3). All of these patterns are net of first grade levels of behavior.

African American children attended classrooms with lower quality and more discipline than did White Non-Hispanic children. The correlations of African American ethnic status with classroom features were first grade instructional quality $r = -.13, p < .01$; first grade emotional quality $r = -.17, p < .01$; third grade positive climate $r = -.22, p < .01$; first grade discipline $r = .20, p < .01$; and third grade discipline $r = .12, p < .01$. There were no significant differences between Hispanic and White Non-Hispanic children's classrooms.

There were few ethnic differences in observed behavior. African Americans were slightly more disruptive than White Non-Hispanic children, and Hispanic children displayed more positive peer interaction than White Non-Hispanic children (Table 11.2). At third and fourth grades, teachers rated African American children more unfavorably on social skills and externalizing problems than they did White Non-Hispanic children, but there were no differences in ratings of internalizing problems. These differences occurred even with controls for teachers' ethnic group. Teachers' ratings of Hispanic children and children from other ethnic groups did not differ from their ratings of White Non-Hispanic children. Mothers' ratings did not differ by ethnic group.

Interactions of Group with Classroom Features. The more interesting question is whether children in different subgroups reacted differently to classroom features. In the regressions on observed classroom behavior, we tested interactions with the third grade classroom features. Child gender interacted with positive classroom climate and with the level of discipline in predicting children's involvement in the classroom as well as disruptive behavior.

We performed separate analyses of boys and girls, which showed that the associations of classroom features with child behavior were slightly stronger for boys than for girls. Specifically, the coefficients for positive climate predicting involvement were boys $\beta = 0.412$, $SE = .038$, $p < .001$; girls $\beta = 0.344$, $SE = .031$, $p < .001$; for positive climate predicting disruptive behavior they were boys $\beta = -0.041$, $SE = .008$, $p < .001$; girls $\beta = -0.011$, $SE = .005$, $p < .05$. The coefficients for discipline predicting involvement were in opposite directions: boys $\beta = -0.051$, $SE = .044$, *ns*; girls $\beta = 0.078$, $SE = .050$, *ns*, but discipline was more strongly related to disruptive behavior for boys than for girls: boys $\beta = 0.059$, $SE = .010$, $p < .001$; girls $\beta = 0.028$, $SE = .008$, $p < .001$.

There were no interactions of ethnic group and classroom features for children's positive involvement or peer interactions, but in the analyses of disruptive behavior, ethnic group interacted significantly with all three classroom variables. In separate analyses of African American (AA) and White Non-Hispanic (W) children, the relations of positive climate and discipline to disruptive behavior were slightly stronger for African American children. The coefficients for positive classroom climate were AA $\beta = -0.043$, $SE = .016$, $p < .001$; W $\beta = -0.016$, $SE = .005$, $p < .001$; the coefficients for discipline were AA $\beta = 0.083$, $SE = .022$, $p < .001$; W $\beta = 0.041$, $SE = .006$, $p < .01$.

There were no interactions of income group with classroom features in the analyses of observed behavior.

In the analyses of the teacher and mother reports of social skills and problem behavior, there were scattered significant interactions with subgroups. Given the many analyses performed, these could well have occurred by chance, so we did not pursue them further.

CONCLUSIONS

The overall goal of this chapter is to identify the immediate and enduring relations of classroom contexts to the development of social behavior. We frame this analysis as a process of interaction between what the child brings to the classroom and what the teacher and school environment provide. As we noted earlier, individual children elicit different behaviors in the classroom, but individual teachers' techniques for teaching and for behavior control affect the extent to which children express and modify positive and problematic social behavior.

At both first and third grades, children's behavior in the classroom is related to the immediate context of that classroom. Classrooms in which the overall climate is positive, the teachers are involved and sensitive, and instructional time is used productively have children who are more attentive, engaged, and self-reliant; who have positive or neutral interactions with teachers; and who are not often disruptive. By contrast, when teachers frequently scold, correct, or punish students, children are less involved and more disruptive. When teachers include collaborative work projects in daily activities, children engage in more positive peer interactions, but they are also more disruptive. Although this finding may seem obvious, it is not trivial. What teachers do in the classroom matters; children's involvement, disruptive behavior, and patterns of peer interaction are not simple manifestations of behavior patterns they bring with them.

However, the patterns of behavior observed in first grade classrooms do not carry over two years later to third grade. The relations of classroom features and children's behavior in a particular classroom appear to be specific to that classroom environment. There are no demonstrated effects of the first grade classroom experience on day-to-day behavior in the third grade classroom.

One reason that first grade classroom characteristics do not predict third grade behavior may be that children experience different classroom contexts from year to year, and their behavior is responsive primarily to the immediate context. Although individual classrooms maintain relatively stable levels of positive or negative climates over the course of the year and for different children, our children experienced little consistency in either positive or negative contexts from first to third grade. When they change classrooms, their behavior adapts to the new classroom environment. If the levels of instructional and emotional quality were consistent from year to year, then one might expect a more cumulative effect.

Children in classrooms with positive climates in third grade did demonstrate slight and lasting increases in positive social skills and reductions in internalizing behavior problems, according to teachers in both third and fourth grades. When teachers provide models of sensitivity, productive time use, and interest in the subject matter, children may not only be more involved during class, but may also learn such social skills as cooperation, assertion, and self-reliance, and may feel less anxious and inhibited.

First grade instructional quality and emotional support did not have lasting relations to social or problem behavior that were independent of third grade experience, but discipline in both first and third grades were strongly related to decreases in social skills and increases in behavior problems from first to third grade. The independent contribution of first grade discipline suggests that the relations of first grade discipline to problem behavior were cumulative. Children who experienced high discipline classrooms in both first and third grades were especially likely to show high levels of behavior problems and relatively low social skills, and these patterns of behavior continued into fourth grade.

The strong associations of discipline with children's behavior raise the question of causal directions. Although our purpose in this chapter is to understand the influence of classroom context, the classroom environment experienced by a particular child is not independent of that child's behavior. Highly disruptive children may elicit discipline rather than discipline causing their behavior. Because classrooms involve ongoing interactions, it seems most reasonable to view the child in context as an interacting system that is affected both by children's personal dispositions *and* by the larger environment of the classroom. Classroom features do not affect all children similarly, but, by the same token, individual differences in behavior are not completely independent of the classroom environment. Most of the classroom context measures were descriptions of events at the small group and classroom level, rather than interactions directed toward the target child individually. Nevertheless, the children's behavior probably affected these classroom characteristics, particularly discipline.

Three features of the results suggest that the classroom contexts experienced by individual children were at least partially independent of children's personal characteristics. The levels of positive climate and discipline within classrooms were quite stable when they were measured for two different children at two different times. By contrast, the levels of positive climate and discipline experienced by the same child in two different classrooms (first and third) were not very stable. If child characteristics were driving the relation between context and behavior, one would expect the reverse – that the levels would vary by child within classroom, but would be similar for a given child across classrooms. Finally, statistical controls for first grade social skills and behavior problems removed some of the effects of initial individual differences among children.

Perhaps the most striking pattern in these findings is the strong relation between teachers' disciplinary actions and children's disruptive and problem behavior – behaviors that continue to be manifested a year later in fourth grade. It appears that these relations are cumulative. Although children with high levels of externalizing behavior display more disruptive behavior in first grade, their experiences with a lot of scolding and punishment may set them on a course of increasingly problematic behavior and disengagement from the classroom. Even though children's initial predisposition to disruptive and negative behavior may elicit such discipline, the snowballing relation of discipline to behavior problems indicates at the very least that punishment and scolding are ineffective ways of altering the trajectories of children who enter school with such predispositions. The findings suggest that a strong instructional and emotionally positive climate is one important way to improve children's social skills and to reduce disruption and behavior problems.

Boys and children from low-income families are more likely than their counterparts to have low engagement in classroom activities, low social skills as perceived by teachers and mother, and high levels of behavior problems. African American children were slightly more disruptive and were rated more negatively by teachers than White Non-Hispanic children. For the most part, the relations of classroom characteristics to children's behavior were similar across subgroups, but there was some tendency for classroom features to predict behavior more strongly for the groups that more often display problems. The relations of contexts, especially discipline, to observed classroom behavior were somewhat higher for boys and African American children than for their counterparts. These differences could result in part from the greater variability in behavior for these groups, but they do suggest that classroom contexts have the potential to counteract or exacerbate children's tendencies toward low involvement and disruptive and problem behavior. There were not, however, consistent differences among groups in the associations of classroom features with teacher- or mother-reported skills and behavior problems.

In conclusion, these direct observations of over 800 children in more than 1400 different classrooms during first and third grades provide evidence that classroom contexts are related to children's immediate behavior, but that behavior is primarily a function of the immediate classroom environment rather than showing strong influences of earlier classroom experiences. We also provide evidence that by third grade, classroom experiences, including positive climates or high levels of punishment and scolding, may contribute to enduring patterns of social skills and problem behavior.

References

Achenbach, T. (1991). *Manual for the Child Behavior Checklist/4–18 and 1991 profile.* Burlington, VT: Author.

Bradley, R. H., & Corwyn, R. F. (2002). Socioeconomic status and child development. *Annual Review of Psychology, 53,* 371–399.

Brody, G. H., Dorsey, S., Forehand, R., & Armistead, L. (2002). Unique and protective contributions of parenting and classroom processes to the adjustment of African American children living in single-parent families. *Child Development, 73,* 274–286.

Campbell, S. B. (1995). Behavior problems in preschool children: A review of recent research. *Journal of Child Psychology and Psychiatry, 36,* 113–149.

Entwisle, D. R., & Alexander, K. (1999). Early schooling and social stratification. In R. C. Pianta and M. J. Cox (Eds.), *The transition to kindergarten.* Baltimore: Paul H. Brookes.

Fisher, C. B., Jackson, J. F., & Villarruel, F. A. (1997). The study of African American and Latin American children and youth. In R. M. Lerner (Ed.), *Theoretical models of human development* (5th ed., pp. 1145–1208). New York: Wiley.

Golombok, S., & Fivush, R. (1994). *Gender development*. New York: Cambridge University Press.

Gresham, F. M., & Elliott, S. N. (1990). *Social skills rating system manual*. Circle Pines, MN: American Guidance Service, Inc.

Heaviside, S., & Farris, E. (1993). *Public school kindergarten teachers' views on children's readiness for school*. (NCES Publication No. 93–410) [On-line]. Retrieved from http://nces.ed.gov/pubs93/93410.pdf

Ladd, G. W., & Burgess, K. B. (1999). Charting the relationship trajectories of aggressive, withdrawn, and aggressive/withdrawn children during early grade school. *Child Development, 70*, 910–929.

La Paro, K., & Pianta, R. C. (2001). Predicting children's competence in the early school years: A meta-analytic review. *Review of Educational Research, 70*, 443–484.

Meisels, S. J. (1999). Assessing readiness. In R. C. Pianta & M. Cox (Eds.), *The transition to kindergarten: Research, policy, training, and practice*. Baltimore: Paul Brookes Publishers.

National Center for Education Statistics. (1994). *School and staffing survey*. Washington, DC: National Center for Education Statistics.

National Center for Education Statistics. (1999). *America's kindergartners*. Washington, DC: National Center for Education Statistics.

National Center for Education Statistics. (2003). *The Condition of Education 2003* (NCES 2003–067). Washington, DC: Institute of Education Sciences, US Dept of Education.

NICHD Early Child Care Research Network. (2002). The relation of global first grade classroom environment to structural classroom features and teacher and student behaviors. *The Elementary School Journal, 102*, 367–387.

NICHD Early Child Care Research Network. (2003a). The NICHD Study of Early Child Care: Contexts of development and developmental outcomes over the first seven years of life. In J. Brooks-Gunn & L. J. Berlin (Eds.), *Early childhood development in the 21st century* (pp. 182–201). New York: Teachers College Press.

NICHD Early Child Care Research Network (2003b). Social functioning in first grade: Association with earlier home and child care predictors and with current classroom practices. *Child Development, 74*, 1639–1662.

NICHD Early Child Care Research Network. (2004). Does class size in first grade relate to changes in child academic and social performance or observed classroom processes? *Developmental Psychology, 40*, 651–654.

NICHD Early Child Care Research Network. (in press). A day in third grade: A large-scale study of classroom quality and teacher and student behavior. *The Elementary School Journal*.

Rimm-Kaufman, S. E., Pianta, R. C., & Cox, M. J. (2000). Teachers' judgments of success in the transition to kindergarten. *Early Childhood Research Quarterly, 15*, 147–166.

Rimm-Kaufman, S. E., Early, D. M., Cox, M. U., Saluja, G., Pianta, R. C., Bradley, R. H., & Payne, C. (2002). Early behavioral attributes and teachers' sensitivity as predictors of competent behavior in the kindergarten classroom. *Applied Developmental Psychology, 23,* 451–470.

Schwartz, D., McFadyen-Ketchum, S. A., Dodge, K. A., Pettit, G. S., & Bates, J. E. (1999). Early behavior problems as a predictor of later peer group victimization: Moderators and mediators in the pathways of social risk. *Journal of Abnormal Child Psychology, 27,* 191–201.

Weinstein, C. S. (1991). The classroom as a social context for learning. *Annual Review of Psychology, 42,* 493–525.

12

Out-of-School Time Use During Middle Childhood in a Low-Income Sample

Do Combinations of Activities Affect Achievement and Behavior?

Pamela Morris and Ariel Kalil

The middle childhood years are characterized by numerous biological, psychological, and social changes (Eccles, 1999). During this period, children master fundamental academic skills such as reading and arithmetic and they also become more self-aware, reflective, and planful. Erikson (1968) characterized this phase of life as a time of "industry," with attention directed at gaining competencies in a variety of tasks and learning how to cooperate with peers and adults. In contrast to children's very early years, when the influence of proximal family contexts is paramount, the middle childhood years represent a time of increasing influences of out-of-home environments. Although the family remains important for children's well-being, children at this age increasingly participate in organized programs and interact with peers in their community or neighborhood; they are also more influenced by teachers, school environments, and peer groups.

Low-income children face several challenges to successful development during this stage of life, and some of these challenges stem from the limitations or outright dangers inherent in their out-of-home environments (Leventhal & Brooks-Gunn, 2000). Physically dangerous neighborhoods (i.e., those in which children experience high levels of victimization) may force children to be isolated in their homes, restricting opportunities for interactions with peers and adults. Less-advantaged neighborhoods also provide fewer enriching opportunities such as parks, libraries, and children's programs.

Just as high quality child care opportunities can boost the development of young children in poverty, researchers have suggested that high quality out-of-school programs can augment the development of children during middle childhood. For low-income children in particular, structured opportunities for learning, sport, or recreation can provide a supervised, safe alternative to time spent unsupervised with peers in potentially dangerous environments. These safe havens can benefit children's cognitive and emotional well-being, as well as their physical safety, and thus can represent an important source of resilience during the potentially risky period of development during middle childhood. Although these opportunities are often thought to be especially critical for adolescents, for whom the prevention of delinquency is critical, few have recognized, or examined, the value of such activities during middle childhood.

This study examines the association of out-of-school time use with the cognitive and emotional well-being of a large sample of low-income children. Our data come from the Canadian Self-Sufficiency Project (SSP), an experimental antipoverty demonstration program in which parents were offered generous earnings supplements if they worked full time and left the welfare system. The intervention had substantial effects on the employment, earnings, and income of single-parent welfare recipients (Michalopoulos et al., 2002). Moreover, SSP produced benefits for elementary school age children's school achievement in both early and later middle childhood (Michalopoulos et al., 2002; Morris & Michalopoulos, 2000; Morris & Michalopoulos, 2003), and, notably for the analysis in this chapter, small increases in structured activity involvement were found for this middle childhood age group as well (Morris & Michalopoulos, 2003).

We use these data to conduct nonexperimental analyses designed to understand the relations of patterns of time use out-of-school with children's cognitive and behavioral adjustment. We employ cluster analysis to understand the patterns of children's participation in activities, then examine whether patterns of participation in activities are related to children's cognitive outcomes and behavioral adjustment. This method adopts the individual child as the unit of analysis rather than the more common variable-based approach of correlating single activity participation with child development outcomes. Using children's patterns of activity involvement more accurately reflects the "bundles" of activities available to and utilized by children and families in the real world.

BACKGROUND

Children's experiences outside the home represent important influences on their development. For example, a large body of literature on child care environments has found evidence of effects of both type and quality of care, with the quality of care being especially important for low-income children's cognitive development (Lamb, 1998; Shonkoff & Philips, 2000). The need for supervised care continues in middle childhood, during after-school, weekend, and vacation hours when parents are away from home. Indeed, supervised after-school programs are reported to be the fastest-growing segment of child care services (Pierce, Hamm, & Vandell, 1999). In 1990, 15% of children ages 5 to 12 with employed mothers were regularly in lessons or activities after school, and an additional 14% were in after-school centers (Vandell & Shumow, 1999). Not only are out-of-school activities often necessary for children's supervision and monitoring, but these activities can also provide valuable opportunities for the development of skills and social relationships. Structured, nonschool programs can be designed to meet many of the developmental needs of children in middle childhood (Eccles, 1999). Conversely, unsupervised peer contact in the out-of-school hours is associated with increases in problem behavior among school-age children, especially for those in low-income environments (Jarett, 1999; Pettit, Bates, Dodge, & Meece, 1999; Posner & Vandell, 1994; Vandell & Shumow, 1999).

Of particular relevance to the present study, the New Hope program, a random assignment antipoverty program similar in nature to SSP, had a significant impact on 9–12-year-old children's participation in organized activities (but did not affect activity participation for children ages 6–8). Most likely this was due to parents' need for such programs in the face of increased employment, but was also potentially related to parents' having more money to pay for costs associated with participation (Huston et al., 2001). The authors of the report suggested that the positive impacts of the program on children's development might be explained by their increased participation in organized activities. In New Hope, there were no program effects on frequency of engaging in unorganized activities (reading, homework, TV viewing, or playing sports without a coach). Similar increases in structured activities were found in SSP as well (Morris & Michalopoulos, 2003).

A larger body of nonexperimental research has examined the components of formal after-school programs as well as structured nonschool related lessons and activities that correlate with children's development. Posner and Vandell (1994), who studied the after-school experiences of low-income third-grade children, found that the time spent on academics and in enrichment lessons, such as art, music, and drama, was positively correlated with children's adjustment at school. In contrast, spending time in unstructured outdoor activities was negatively associated with adjustment. Moreover, children who spent time in academic and enrichment activities were less likely to spend time watching TV or engaging in unstructured outdoor activities. Rosenthal and Vandell (1996) further suggested that children in the third to fifth grades reported more positive experiences in structured programs that offered a larger variety of activities. Mahoney and Stattin's (2000) analysis of 14-year-olds' leisure time activities similarly suggested that participation in highly structured leisure activities (e.g., school and community-sponsored athletics, music organizations, and church groups) is correlated with low levels of antisocial behavior, whereas participation in low-structure activities, such as hanging out at a youth recreation center, is correlated with high levels of antisocial behavior. This particular analysis also suggested that the patterning of activity participation is relevant: The combination of involvement in unstructured activities with no participation in structured activities showed a stronger association with high antisocial behavior for boys, in particular.

In sum, prior research has found that participation in structured activities can benefit the development of children during the middle school years. In general, however, this research has not examined how different patterns of activities are associated with different outcomes for children. Yet, some research suggests the types and combinations of activities may be important, as extensive time spent in unstructured activities appears not to confer the same benefits as time spent in one (or perhaps more) structured activities.

The Present Study

Our analysis plan is as follows: First, we present a detailed examination of activity participation among the children in this sample, employing cluster analytic techniques to identify patterns of activity participation. Next, we link these patterns of activity participation to measures of children's academic and behavioral adjustment, and test whether any observed linkages persist in the face of an array of important control variables. We examine these relations separately for boys and girls. Finally, we examine whether these relations persist in the context of sibling fixed-effect estimates that allow us to control for unobserved family-level characteristics.

METHOD

Sample

Our sample includes 2,127 children (ages 6–12 at the time of assessment) of single-parent welfare recipients in British Columbia and New Brunswick, Canada. These are a subset of the children in the larger evaluation of the Self Sufficiency Project in the specified age range and for whom the relevant measures of interest were collected. Data on children were collected three years after parents entered the study.

SSP was a demonstration program designed to make work a viable alternative to welfare for low-income parents, whose skills and experience would likely relegate them to low-paying jobs. A group of about 6,000 single parents in British Columbia and New Brunswick who had been on welfare for at least a year were selected at random from the welfare rolls between November 1992 and March 1995. Families who agreed to participate in the study were randomly assigned to the program group, which was offered the SSP supplement, or a control group, which was not, but who could continue to receive welfare as usual. SSP's financial supplement, paid to parents who left welfare and worked at least 30 hours per week, was half the difference between their actual earnings and a target level of earnings. Supplement payments were available to program group members for a maximum of three years, and only to sample members who initiated SSP payments by finding full-time work within 12 months of entering the study.

Procedures

A baseline survey administered at the time of random assignment provides background information on the families. A follow-up survey at 36 months after random assignment provides information on children's well-being and participation in structured and unstructured out-of-school activities, as well as their parents' employment, earnings, income, material hardship, and expenditures. The 36-month survey was completed by approximately 77% of the research sample. In addition, at the 36-month assessment point, math tests were given directly to children between the ages of 7 and 12, with response rates of 67% (Morris & Michalopoulos, 2000; Morris & Michalopoulos, 2003).

Measures

Out-of-School Activities. Parents were asked about their children's participation in eight different out-of-school activities in the past year. These activities might have taken place on either weekdays or on weekends. Three *structured activities* were addressed: (a) sports involving teaching or instruction; (b) lessons in music, art, or other non-sport activities; and (c) clubs, groups, or community programs with adult leadership. In addition, *unstructured time* was also addressed: (a) trips to the library, (b) reading for pleasure, (c) doing homework, (d) playing video or computer games, and (e) watching television.[1]

Math Score. A math skills test was administered to children ages 7–12 in grades 2–7. The test, which varied by the child's grade level, consisted of 26 math problems for those in grade 2 and 34 items for those in grades 3 and above. The test included a subset of items from the Canadian Achievement Tests, Second Edition (CAT/2), a mathematics test developed by the Canadian Test Centre that is administered annually in all provinces to approximately 300,000 students from grades 2 up to the end of secondary school and college. The proportion of correct items completed out of the total number of test items was computed for each child.

---

[1] Children's unsupervised "sport" time was also assessed, but because almost all children participated in some physical activity (that included running and riding bikes) this item was excluded from consideration in the analysis.

Academic Achievement. Parents were asked about children's performance in reading, writing, and math. More specifically, parents were asked, "Based on your knowledge of [your child's] school work, including report cards, how did he/she do in the following areas of school in this school year." For each subject, academic functioning was ranked on a 5-point scale ranging from "not very well at all" to "very well." A measure of children's average achievement was computed as the average score across the three academic subjects.

Behavior Problems. Parents reported on children's behavior using a scale developed for use in the National Longitudinal Survey of Children and Youth in Canada (NLSCY). The NLSCY is a unique survey of Canadians from birth to adulthood, and the measure of Behavior Problems has items similar to those in the Behavior Problems Index (a 28-item scale; Peterson & Zill, 1986) used in many U.S. studies of the effects of welfare reform programs (Morris, Huston, Duncan, Crosby, & Bos, 2001). An average score was computed across the items (which were coded on a 3-point scale ranging from "never/not true" to "often/very true"). Items included both internalizing and externalizing aspects of children's behavior. Sample items included "my child is too fearful or anxious," "my child cries a lot," "my child steals at home," and "my child gets into many fights" ($\alpha = .92$ for 27 items).

Prosocial Behavior. Parents reported on children's prosocial behavior using a 5-item scale developed for the NLSCY; items are similar to those in the Positive Behavior Scale used in other welfare demonstration studies (Polit, 1996). Sample items include "my child tries to help someone who is hurt" and "my child comforts a crying child." Scores on the total positive social behavior scale were averages across the five items and ranged from (1) never to (3) often ($\alpha = .80$).

School Behavior Problems. Parents were asked how often in the past school year they were contacted by the school about children's behavior problems in school. This item has been used in a number of recent welfare and work demonstration studies (e.g., Gennetian & Miller, 2002) and ranged from (1) none or one time to (3) four or more times.

Control Variables. A series of baseline child and family background variables that might confound the relation between participation in out-of-school activities and outcomes for children were considered, including *demographic characteristics* (child gender, parent and child age, and parent race/ethnicity), *family composition* (the number of children in the household, the presence of a child age 0 to 5, and the presence of a spouse or partner), *socioeconomic characteristics* (the number of months of welfare receipt in the past year, the number of months of employment in the past year, whether the parent has a high school diploma or GED), the total respondent income (from welfare, earnings, and any program supplements) in the past year, and *study-level variables* (the province in which the family lived and research group status [program or control group assignment]).

RESULTS

Identification of the Clusters

Our first step was to examine out-of-school activity time in greater detail to determine the patterning of activities. Our cluster analysis relies on both hierarchical and iterative methods. As a first step, we employed hierarchical clustering using Ward's minimum-variance clustering method (in SAS, the PROC CLUSTER procedure). Ward's method, like most other clustering methods, is based on an agglomerative hierarchical clustering procedure. In this method, each observation begins in a cluster by itself. The two closest clusters are merged to form a new cluster that replaces the two old clusters. Merging of the two closest clusters is repeated until only one cluster is left. In a cluster analysis, variables with large variances tend to have a greater effect on the resulting clusters than those with small variances. Therefore, in this step of the analysis, we standardize each of the eight time-use variables by its range (see Milligan, 1996, for a discussion of various standardization techniques).

Results from the hierarchical cluster method provide the start values (or "cluster centers") for the iterative approach (in SAS, the FASTCLUS procedure), using a k-means algorithm for determining cluster membership. The goal of the iterative cluster analysis is to minimize the distance within clusters while maximizing the distance between clusters. Theoretically meaningful clusters of children are identified with this technique.

The hierarchical analysis was conducted to determine the cluster solution that would provide theoretically distinct groups of children. The results of the two to six cluster solution resulting from the hierarchical analysis are shown in Figure 12.1. Only the means for the structured activities are presented because nearly all of these solutions produced clusters that were differentiated by their participation in structured, rather than unstructured, activities.

At the two-cluster solution, children were differentiated by their scores on participation in lessons and clubs, with one group of children (Cluster 1–2) with high levels of participation in all three structured activities, and the other (Cluster 2–2) high in only sports activities. At the three-cluster solution, Cluster 1–2 is divided into those children who participate in sports and clubs but not lessons (Cluster 1–3) as distinct from those who participate in all three structured activities (Cluster 2–3). At the four-cluster solution,

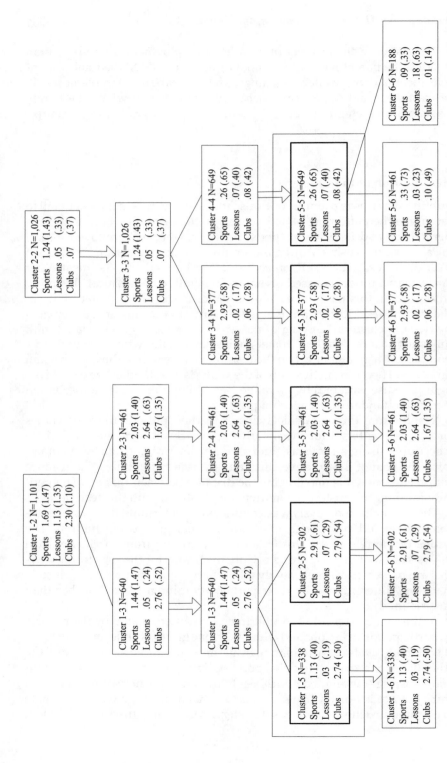

FIGURE 12.1. Results of hierarchical cluster analysis: means of structured activities for each cluster by cluster solution.

the children with high participation in sports (Cluster 2–2) are divided into nonparticipants (those with low values on all three structured activities, Cluster 4–4; and those with high participation in only sports, Cluster 4–5). At the five-cluster solution, the sports and clubs group (Cluster 1–3) is divided into a clubs group with low levels of participation in sports (Cluster 1–5) and a clubs and high sports group (Cluster 2–5). Given prior literature indicating a risk to children who participate in only club/group-like activities (Mahoney & Stattin, 2000), it seemed critical to allow for this differentiation that was highlighted in this fifth cluster solution. The six-cluster solution added little additional explanatory information, dividing the low-participating group into two clusters with very similar levels on the three structured activities. Further inspection of the unstructured activities revealed that this cluster solution parsed this last cluster into children with low scores on the measure of time spent reading (Cluster 6–6, reading mean = .60) as separate from children with high scores on the reading measure (Cluster 5–5, reading mean = 3.15).

The iterative solution used the values generated in the hierarchical analysis as start values for the cluster centers. The final five-cluster solution generated a set of clusters that were differentiated primarily by differences in participation in the three structured activities, but not by participation in the five unstructured activities. The only three activities with sizeable R-square values for predicting the variable from the cluster were clubs (.81), sports with a coach (.81), and lessons (.73). All other R-square values were less than .02. The overall R-square from this analysis was .41.

In Table 12.1, we present the mean levels of participation for all eight activities in each of the five clusters, resulting from the final, iterative cluster analysis. Consistent with the results of the hierarchical analysis, the five groups of children can be defined primarily by their participation in structured activities: (a) high participation in clubs (but low in sports and lessons; $n = 384$), (b) high participation in sports (but low in clubs and lessons; $n = 424$), (c) low participation in all three structured activities (clubs, sports, and lessons; $n = 675$), (d) high participation in sports and clubs (but low in lessons; $n = 293$), and (e) high participation in all three structured activities (clubs, sports, and lessons; $n = 351$).

Background Characteristics of Children in Different Clusters

As indicated earlier, we considered a series of child, family, and background characteristics as potential descriptors of groups of children in each cluster and as covariates in our models. Means on all of these variables are presented in Table 12.2, first for the full sample, and then separately by cluster membership. Pairwise comparisons between clusters were conducted on all background variables, with significance tests adjusted using the

TABLE 12.1. *Means on Activity Participation Variables by Cluster*

	Structured Activities			Unstructured Activities				
	Structured Sports	Lessons	Clubs/Groups	Reading	Library	Homework	TV	Video Games
Cluster 1 – High clubs (N = 384)	0.181	0.229	2.743	2.399	1.493	1.654	0.857	0.198
Cluster 2 – High sports (N = 424)	2.965	0.135	0.079	2.516	1.393	1.491	0.866	0.245
Cluster 3 – Low sports, lessons, and clubs (N = 675)	0.148	0.231	0.028	2.426	1.399	1.479	0.990	0.276
Cluster 4 – High sports and clubs (N = 293)	2.935	0.073	2.835	2.294	1.438	1.713	0.925	0.280
Cluster 5 – High sports, lessons, and clubs (N = 351)	2.401	2.788	1.926	2.891	1.709	1.806	0.724	0.248

Sample size (total = 2,127)

Note: All scales range from 0 to 4 with higher scores indicating higher participation in the activity.

TABLE 12.2. *Covariate Means Overall and by Cluster*

	Full Sample		Cluster 1 High Clubs	Cluster 2 High Sports	Cluster 3 Low Sports, Lessons, & Clubs	Cluster 4 High Sports & Clubs	Cluster 5 High Sports, Lessons, & Clubs	Significant Differences Between Clusters
	Mean	SD	Mean	Mean	Mean	Mean	Mean	
Child is a male	48.9		38.0	56.6	51.3	56.7	40.5	1&5<2,3,4
Child's age	8.8	1.9	8.5	9.1	8.6	9.2	8.9	1&3<2,4
Parent's age	33.8	5.7	33.4	34.4	33.5	34.1	34.0	
Parent's ethnicity is not white	19.6	39.7	18.5	16.7	21.5	19.2	20.8	
Number of kids in the household	2.0	0.9	2.1	2.0	2.1	2.0	1.9	5<1,3
Household's youngest child's age is 0 to 5	18.9		19.5	16.0	20.4	15.0	22.2	
Parent is married or cohabiting	19.1		20.8	16.5	19.1	22.5	17.4	
Total # of months on IA[a], Year 3	8.1	5.1	8.5	7.7	8.4	7.9	8.0	
Total # of months employed, Year 3	4.4	5.1	4.1	4.9	3.8	5.3	4.7	1<4; 3<2,4
Parent has a high school degree or GED	54.3		54.9	56.6	51.1	54.6	56.7	
Total income, Year 3	12,308	7,127	12,071	13,413	11,610	12,660	12,283	2>3
Family lives in New Brunswick province	52.9		64.1	42.9	51.1	67.6	44.2	1&4>2,3,5
In experimental group	50.6		51.8	52.6	50.2	49.5	48.7	
Sample size	2,127		384	424	675	293	351	

[a] IA indicates Income Assistance, Canada's welfare program.

Bonferonni correction for multiple tests. Effects statistically significant at least at the $p < .05$ level are reported.

Boys were more likely to be in the high sports, high sports and clubs, or low participation groups and less likely to be in the high clubs and high participation in all three activities groups; girls show the opposite pattern. Older children were more likely to be in the high sports and high sports and clubs groups than in the three other groups. Children from smaller families were more likely to be in the high participation group than in the low participation or clubs only groups, and those whose parents had a history of more employment were least likely to be in the low participation group and most likely to be in the groups characterized by high sports or high sports and clubs. Children in the low participation group had parents with less income than the high sports group. Finally, more children from New Brunswick were in clusters representing high clubs and high sports and clubs.

These findings provide important information about the individual characteristics, family and economic variables, and social contexts that differentiate among children with different patterns of participation. They also suggest that controlling for these background family and child characteristics may indeed be important in examining the effects of cluster membership on outcomes for children.

Relations of Cluster Membership to Children's Achievement and Behavior

We next conducted a series of OLS regressions to test the association of cluster membership to outcomes for children with and without controls for child and family background characteristics that might underlie relations between particular activity groups and outcomes for children.

We compare achievement and behavior for children with low participation in all three structured activities (Cluster 3) to scores for children who participate in various combinations of structured activities by testing the effects of the four remaining clusters relative to this group. The base model consists of the relations of these four cluster groupings (with Cluster 3 as the omitted category) to the dependent variable; the full model includes the four sets of control variables in addition to the cluster membership variables. Means and standard deviation of the outcome variables are listed to ease interpretation of the parameter estimates.

Results of the achievement analysis are presented in Table 12.3. Effects on the math score were positive and significant for Clusters 4 (high sports and clubs) and 5 (all three structured activities) in comparison to those in no structured activities. Children in Cluster 5 (all activities) and Cluster 2 (high sports) were rated significantly higher in achievement by their parents than those in no structured activities. These effects did not change appreciably with the inclusion of controls for child, parent, and family

TABLE 12.3. *Regression Models Testing the Effect of Cluster Membership on Child Achievement*

	Math Score				Achievement			
	Base Model x = 0.53 s = 0.28		Full Model		Base Model x = 3.66 s = .94		Full Model	
	Parameter Estimate	Standard Error	Parameter Estimate	Standard Error	Parameter Estimate	Standard Error	Parameter Estimate	Standard Error
Cluster 1 – High clubs	-0.015	(0.024)	-0.015	(0.024)	-0.009	0.060	-0.058	(0.060)
Cluster 2 – High sports	0.036	(0.023)	0.022	(0.022)	0.137	0.059*	0.141	(0.058)*
Cluster 4 – High sports and clubs	0.067	(0.025)**	0.064	(0.025)*	0.097	0.066	0.085	(0.066)
Cluster 5 – High sports, lessons, and clubs	0.081	(0.024)**	0.072	(0.024)**	0.274	0.062**	0.216	(0.061)**
Demographics								
Child is a male			0.005	(0.016)			-0.272	(0.040)**
Child's age			0.012	(0.005)*			0.007	(0.011)
Parent's age			-0.001	(0.002)			-0.004	(0.004)
Parent's ethnicity is not white			-0.016	(0.020)			0.081	(0.052)
Family composition								
Number of kids in the household			0.002	(0.010)			-0.072	(0.024)**
Household's youngest child's age is 0 to 5			-0.044	(0.024)			0.0140	(0.057)*

(continued)

TABLE 12.3. (Continued)

	Math Score $x = 0.53$ $s = 0.28$				Achievement $x = 3.66$ $s = .94$			
	Base Model		Full Model		Base Model		Full Model	
	Parameter Estimate	Standard Error	Parameter Estimate	Standard Error	Parameter Estimate	Standard Error	Parameter Estimate	Standard Error
Parent is married or cohabiting			−0.024	(0.022)			−0.035	(0.056)
Socioeconomic Characteristics								
Total # of months on IA,[a] Year 3			−0.002	(0.002)			−0.008	(0.005)
Total # of months employed, Year 3			0.002	(0.002)			0.005	(0.006)
Parent has a high school degree or GED			0.062	(0.016)**			0.204	(0.041)**
Total income, Year 3			0.000	(0.000)			0.000	(0.000)
Province & experimental status								
Family lives in New Brunswick province			−0.038	(0.017)*			0.075	(0.044)
In experimental group			0.022	(0.016)			0.082	(0.041)*
R^2	0.016		0.051		0.012		0.063	
F−statistic	5.220	**	3.990	**	6.210	**	8.070	**
N	1,270		1,270		2,075		2,075	

Note: Cluster 3 (Low sports, lessons, and clubs) was the excluded category in the regressions estimating the effects of cluster membership on child cognitive performance and academic achievement. [a] IA indicates Income Assistance, Canada's welfare program. * $p < .05$, ** $p < .01$.

background variables. These effects suggest that about a fifth to a quarter of a standard deviation change in math scores and parent-reported achievement is associated with membership in Cluster 5.

Results of the analysis for the behavioral outcomes are presented in Table 12.4. Children who participated in all three structured activities manifested fewer behavior problems and more prosocial behavior than did those children who had low participation (Cluster 3). Participation in the high sports group (Cluster 2) is also positively associated with children's prosocial behavior. The effects of participating in Cluster 5 (all activities) are largely sustained with the inclusion of covariates, although the effect for Cluster 2 falls below statistical significance in the full model. There are no effects of cluster membership on parental reports of contact about behavior problems in school.[2] Effects on behavior problems and prosocial behavior are slightly smaller than those for the academic outcomes: 15–20% of a standard deviation difference in child behavior is associated with membership in Cluster 5.

In order to determine whether participation predicted achievement and behavior differently for boys and girls, separate regressions were conducted for males and females, and comparisons were made between the coefficients on the cluster membership variables for each of the child outcomes examined (results not shown). The test statistic used to compare coefficients is the weighted sum of squares of the estimates for the subgroups and has a chi-squared distribution (Cooper & Hedges, 1994; Greenberg, Meyer, & Wiseman, 1993). This analysis is analogous to the more traditional two-way interaction approach, but without assuming homogeneity of variance across groups. In no case were the differences in parameter estimates statistically significantly different for boys and girls, suggesting that these effects pertain to both sexes.

Fixed Effect Analysis

Although a number of child and family characteristics are controlled in the OLS regressions reported above, other unobserved differences among children in the various clusters might have contributed to the associations of clusters with children's behavior. In this section, we report family fixed effects models designed to control for unobserved characteristics by estimating the *difference* in the effects of cluster membership for two (or more) children in the same family and using it to predict the difference between siblings' scores on an outcome. Because the unobserved family effects are

---

[2] Since "contacts about behavior problems in school" is not a true continuous dimension, parallel models were conducted using logistic regression on a dichotomous version of this variable (no contacts vs. any contacts). The conclusions based on this analysis are consistent with those presented in this chapter.

TABLE 12.4. *Regression Models Testing the Effect of Cluster Membership on Child Behavior*

| | Total Problem Behavior Scale $x = 1.41\ s = 0.32$ | | | | Prosocial Behavior Scale $x = 2.60\ s = 0.44$ | | | | School Behavior Scale $x = 1.25\ s = 0.58$ | | | |
| | Base Model | | Full Model | | Base Model | | Full Model | | Base Model | | Full Model | |
	Parameter Estimate	Standard Error	Parameter Estimate	Standard Error	Parameter Estimate	Standard Error	Parameter Estimate	Standard Error	Parameter Estimate	Standard Error	Parameter Estimate	Standard Error
Cluster 1 – High clubs	0.013	(0.021)	0.030	(0.020)	0.030	(0.028)	0.015	(0.028)	−0.068	(0.037)	−0.036	(0.036)
Cluster 2 – High sports	−0.025	(0.020)	−0.027	(0.020)	0.055	(0.027)*	0.045	(0.027)	−0.014	(0.036)	−0.023	(0.035)
Cluster 4 – High sports and clubs	−0.023	(0.022)	−0.028	(0.022)	0.042	(0.031)	0.044	(0.031)	0.003	(0.040)	−0.015	(0.040)
Cluster 5 – High sports, lessons, and clubs	−0.061	(0.021)**	−0.045	(0.021)*	0.120	(0.029)**	0.087	(0.029)**	−0.057	(0.038)	−0.025	(0.037)
Demographics												
Child is a male			0.130	(0.014)**			−0.136	(0.019)**			0.265	(0.025)
Child's age			0.000	(0.004)			0.003	(0.005)			0.008	(0.007)
Parent's age			−0.001	(0.001)			0.000	(0.002)			−0.002	(0.002)
Parent's ethnicity is not white			−0.043	(0.018)*			−0.012	(0.024)			−0.022	(0.032)
Family composition												
Number of kids in the household			−0.002	(0.008)			−0.031	(0.011)**			0.018	(0.014)

	(1)	(2)	(3)	(4)	(5)	(6)
Household's youngest child's age is 0 to 5		0.029 (0.020)		0.024 (0.027)		0.039 (0.035)
Parent is married or cohabiting		0.006 (0.019)		−0.006 (0.026)		0.014 (0.034)
Socioeconomic characteristics						
Total # of months on IA,[a] Year 3		0.000 (0.002)		−0.002 (0.002)		0.005 (0.003)
Total # of months employed, Year 3		−0.001 (0.002)		0.004 (0.003)		0.004 (0.003)
Parent has a high school degree or GED		−0.039 (0.014)**		0.059 (0.019)**		−0.026 (0.025)
Total income, Year 3		0.000 (0.000)		0.000 (0.000)		0.000 (0.000)
Province & experimental status						
Family lives in New Brunswick province		0.008 (0.015)		−0.045 (0.021)**		0.018 (0.027)
In experimental group	0.006	−0.016 (0.014)	0.008	0.015 (0.019)	0.003	−0.005 (0.025)
R^2	0.006	0.056	0.008	0.049	0.003	0.059
F-statistic	3.060*	7.280**	4.390**	6.190**	1.330	7.740**
N	2,090	2,090	2,075	2,075	2,119	2,119

Note: Cluster 3 (Low sports, lessons, and clubs) was the excluded category in the regressions estimating the effects of cluster membership on child behavior. [a] IA indicates Income Assistance, Canada's welfare program. $* p < .05$, $** p < .01$.

assumed to be the same across siblings, they can be "subtracted out" of the difference equation.

Fixed effects models provide unbiased estimates *only* under the assumption that the unobserved effect is static across siblings; that is, the family-level effects are the same for the siblings. If this assumption is violated, then the unobserved family-level effect cannot be "subtracted out" of the equation. Furthermore, fixed effects estimates of activity participation may be identified only if siblings within a family experience different patterns of activity participation.

Sibling fixed effect analyses were conducted on four of the five child outcome measures listed above (the sample for the math score was too small to permit this analysis). Because this analysis relies on the more limited sample of children with siblings, we also conducted parallel OLS models on individual children's scores for this same subsample to provide comparisons between the two different analyses.

Results for these analyses are presented in Table 12.5. The OLS model for the sibling subsample shows positive effects of membership in Cluster 5 for both parent-reported achievement and prosocial behavior (with coefficients of .28 and .15, respectively). Unlike the OLS models with the larger sample, we do not find a positive effect of membership in Cluster 5 for behavior problems – a difference that may be a function of the reduced sample size or the composition of the sibling sample. The coefficients predicting achievement and prosocial behavior remain positive and significant in the fixed effect estimates – with the fixed effect coefficient larger than the OLS estimate for school achievement (.62 standard deviation change in child achievement as a result of membership in Cluster 5), and the fixed effect estimate of comparable size to the OLS for prosocial behavior (.17 standard deviation change in prosocial behavior as a result of membership in Cluster 5).

DISCUSSION

Participation in a combination of all three structured activities considered (sports, lessons, and clubs) is consistently associated with benefits for children. Children in this group scored higher on school achievement and prosocial behavior than those who did not participate in any structured activities. These effects were sustained with controls for parent and child demographic characteristics, family composition, and parents' socioeconomic characteristics, and they were also apparent in analyses that controlled for unobserved characteristics by examining differences between siblings. Similar benefits, but less consistent across outcomes and analyses (OLS versus fixed effects), were found for the clusters representing participation in sports only (for achievement and prosocial behavior) and for participation in sports and clubs (for math test score). The cluster analytic

TABLE 12.5. OLS and Fixed Effect Estimates of the Effects of Cluster Membership on Child Achievement and Behavior

	Achievement		Total Problem Behavior Scale		Prosocial Behavior Scale		School Behavior Problem	
	OLS	Family Fixed Effects	OLS	Family Fixed Effects	OLS	Family Fixed Effects	OLS	Family Fixed Effects
Cluster 1 – High clubs	0.038 (0.092)	0.161 (0.186)	0.001 (0.032)	-0.030 (0.057)	0.064 (0.042)	0.020 (0.061)	-0.043 (0.053)	-0.171 (0.113)
Cluster 2 – High sports	0.035 (0.095)	0.250 (0.158)	-0.011 (0.033)	-0.001 (0.048)	0.119** (0.043)	0.140** (0.051)	0.020 (0.055)	0.036 (0.094)
Cluster 4 – High sports and clubs	0.127 (0.105)	0.661** (0.212)	-0.020 (0.036)	0.041 (0.065)	0.039 (0.047)	0.046 (0.068)	-0.055 (0.060)	-0.009 (0.128)
Cluster 5 – High sports, lessons, and clubs	0.282** (0.107)	0.618** (0.228)	-0.030 (0.037)	-0.024 (0.069)	0.148** (0.049)	0.165* (0.073)	-0.001 (0.062)	-0.146 (0.136)
N (families)		415		418		414		428
N (children)	895	895	903	903	894	894	927	927

Note: The sample used for these analyses includes only those children for whom data is available on multiple children in the family. Cluster 3 (Low sports, lessons, and clubs) was the excluded category in all regressions. Standard errors in parentheses. $* p < .05$, $** p < .01$.

255

approach provided an alternative to the more commonly used variable-oriented approach. In particular, it yielded more insights into the naturally occurring patterns of children's time use in the real world, and the benefits of those patterns for children's behavioral and academic outcomes.

We found no differences between children who participated in clubs only and those with low participation in all three structured activities. These findings are consistent with prior work that finds that the quality and nature of the out-of-school activity is critical in understanding whether participation in those activities will benefit children's development. Although these club-type activities were supervised by an adult, participation in them was not meaningfully related to children's academic achievement and emotional well-being, perhaps because clubs provide less formal instruction or skill building opportunities than, for example, lessons, or perhaps because the nature of the participation is less regular or intensive. Clubs may also have different levels of intensity and quality of adult supervision or opportunities for peer interaction than do other organized activities such as team sports. However, our analysis did not offer a fine-grained look at the quality or nature of clubs, and it is certainly possible that high-quality clubs offer opportunities for skill development or positive social interactions that could confer cognitive and social benefits to children. We would not, therefore, want to conclude that clubs offer no developmental benefits based on the present data.

The natural question arising from this type of cross-sectional analysis is whether we can attribute these observed associations to the causal effect of activity participation, or whether characteristics of children or families account for the observed relations. Parents may play a substantial role in choosing their children's activities, especially given the relatively young age of these children. For example, an especially motivated, involved, or dedicated parent may be more apt to allow, mandate, or encourage participation in team sports or lessons, perhaps because that parent is more willing or able to accept responsibility for transporting the child, to devote time to attending matches, and the like. These parents may also be more motivated to help their children in other ways that are correlated with academic or behavioral adjustment. If this were the case, then the correlation between activity participation and child well-being would not be causal; it would simply reflect parental motivation or involvement.

Differences in family resources, especially in a low-income sample and for a set of activity choices including lessons and team sports, may also play a causal role. Parents with more discretionary income might be more able to enroll their children in lessons or purchase uniforms and the like for a team sport, and that income might benefit children's achievement and behavior as well.

We approach these threats to causal inference at the family level in two ways. Our inclusion of a large set of covariates capturing observed structural and economic characteristics of the family helps to mitigate some of these family-level confounds. In addition, sibling fixed effects models account for stable unmeasured family-level effects, such as preferences for or motivation to participate in different types of activities. By and large, the significant results reported here persist in these analyses. Because of these analyses, we are generally confident that the associations we have obtained here are not merely reflections of unmeasured parental characteristics.

While sibling fixed effect models do a very good job of removing shared family influences on the effects of cluster membership on outcomes, they do little to control for individual child characteristics. For example, children who are more motivated, athletically inclined, or prosocial may be more likely to engage in sports. Or, very socially-inclined children may seek out multiple activities that allow them multiple social interactions. Indeed, research has suggested that selection and causation operate simultaneously in the association between time use and children's adjustment (Posner & Vandell, 1999). Regrettably, our data do not provide a longitudinal assessment of change over time in children's characteristics, nor do they provide a pure test of an experimental change in activity participation (without accompanying changes in parents' employment, welfare receipt, and income), either of which would permit us to examine this causal order.

There are other limitations that deserve note. Our findings are most germane to the effects of activity participation on outcomes for children in single parent, welfare-recipient families. The same benefits of activity participation may or may not occur in more resource-rich families. In addition, although the cluster analytic approach did a good job of differentiating groups of children with different patterns of participation in structured activities, it did not differentiate among children based on their participation in *unstructured* activities. Because of this, our analyses could not test the extent to which unstructured activities might benefit or harm children's development, or even compensate for lack of participation in structured activities. Indeed, although the cluster analysis yielded some interesting results about the relations of activity participation to behavioral and achievement outcomes, it should not be interpreted as the "correct" number of groups in this sample. Finally, the cluster analysis allowed us to test the relations of naturally occurring patterns of activity participation to children's well-being, but the results are consistent with the conclusion that the specific patterning may, in fact, *not* be any more important than the breadth of participation – and this latter effect might have been found using variable-centered analysis.

In sum, our analysis provides evidence that participation in some types of structured, out-of-school activities can benefit children's academic adjustment and emotional well-being. The naturally occurring clusters of activity participation showed that many children participate in multiple kinds of activities, but it appears that not all types of activities confer equal benefits. In general, children showed the greatest benefits when they participated in a combination of sports, clubs, and lessons; there was more limited evidence of benefits from participation in a combination of sports and clubs or sports only. The precise size of these effects varies depending on the analysis and the sample (the OLS estimates find effects from one fifth to one quarter of a standard deviation, while those in the sibling samples and those from the fixed-effect estimates are considerably larger), but all show a benefit that is large enough to be considered noteworthy for children's development.

The common factor among the different groupings of activities associated with positive adjustment is sports participation. Team sports may help children to develop skills that are important to successful development during this stage of life including athletic competencies, emotional and behavioral self-regulation, and the development of ties to peers and other adult mentors. The experiences of success and enjoyment while learning these skills might be expressed in superior academic and behavioral adjustment. Given that successful development in these arenas can help place children on positive trajectories as they move into adolescence, these findings should help to bolster efforts to provide meaningful and enriching opportunities for children during the out-of-school hours.

This chapter was funded in part by a grant from the Social Research and Demonstration Corporation (SRDC), Ottawa, Canada, to the second author. Special thanks go to Reuben Ford at SRDC. We also thank Aletha Huston and Marika Ripke, along with two anonymous reviewers, for helpful comments on earlier drafts of this chapter. The Self Sufficiency Project, upon which this chapter is based, was an evaluation managed by the Social Research and Demonstration Corporation (SRDC) and evaluated by SRDC in collaboration with MDRC. SSP was funded and conceived by Human Resources Development Canada (HRDC).

References

Cooper, H., & Hedges, L. (1994). *The handbook of research synthesis.* New York: Russell Sage Foundation.
Eccles, J. (1999). The development of children ages 6 to 14. *The Future of Children, 9*(2), 30–44.
Erikson, E. (1968). *Identity, youth, and crisis.* New York: W. W. Norton and Company.
Gennetian, L., & Miller, C. (2002). Children and welfare reform: A view from an experimental welfare program in Minnesota. *Child Development, 73*(2), 601–620.
Greenberg, D., Meyer, R. H., & Wiseman, M. (1993). *Prying the lid from the black box: Plotting evaluation strategy for welfare employment and training programs.* Madison, WI: University of Wisconsin, Institute for Research on Poverty.
Huston, A. C., Duncan, G. J., Granger, R., Bos, J., McLoyd, V., Mistry, R., et al. (2001). Work-based anti-poverty programs for parents can enhance the school performance and social behavior of children. *Child Development, 72*, 318–336.
Jarett, R. (1999). Successful parenting in high-risk neighborhoods. *The Future of Children, 9*(2), 45–50.

Lamb, M. (1998). Nonparental child care, context, quality, correlates and consequences. In I. E. Sigel & K. A. Renninger (Eds.) *Handbook of Child Psychology* (4th ed. pp. 73–134). New York: Wiley.

Leventhal, T., & Brooks-Gunn, J. (2000). The neighborhoods they live in: The effects of neighborhood residence on child and adolescent outcomes. *Psychological Bulletin, 126*(2), 309–337.

Mahoney, J. L., & Stattin, H. (2000). Leisure time activities and adolescent antisocial behavior: The role of structure and social context. *Journal of Adolescence, 23*, 113–127.

Michalopoulos, C., Tattrie, D., Miller, C., Robins, P. K., Morris, P., Gyarmati, D., et al. (2002). *Making work pay: Final report on the Self Sufficiency Project for long-term welfare recipients.* Ottawa: Social Research and Demonstration Corporation (SRDC).

Milligan, G. W. (1996). Clustering validation: Results and implications for applied analysis. In P. Arabie, L. J. Hubert, & G. De Soete (Eds.), *Clustering and classification.* River Edge, NJ: World Scientific Publications.

Morris, P., Huston, A., Duncan, G., Crosby, D., & Bos, J. (2001). *How welfare and work policies affect children: A synthesis of research.* New York: MDRC.

Morris, P., & Michalopoulos, C. (2000). *The Self Sufficiency Project at 36 months: Effects on children of a program that increased employment and income.* Ottawa: Social Research and Demonstration Corporation (SRDC).

Morris, P., & Michalopoulos, C. (2003). Findings from the Self Sufficiency Project: Effects on children and adolescents of a program that increased employment and income. *Applied Developmental Psychology, 24*, 201–239.

Peterson, J. L., & Zill, N. (1986). Marital disruption, parent-child relationships, and behavior problems in children. *Journal of Marriage and the Family, 48*, 295–307.

Pettit, G., Bates, J., Dodge, K., & Meece, D. (1999). The impact of after-school peer contact on early adolescent externalizing problems is moderated by parental monitoring, perceived neighborhood safety, and prior adjustment. *Child Development, 70*, 768–778.

Pierce, K., Hamm, J., & Vandell, D. (1999). Experiences in after-school programs and children's adjustment in first-grade classrooms. *Child Development, 70*, 756–767.

Polit, D. F. (1996). *Self-administered teacher questionnaire in the New Chance 42-month survey.* New York: Manpower Demonstration Research Corporation.

Posner, J., & Vandell, D. (1994). Low-income children's after-school care: Are there beneficial effects of after-school programs? *Child Development, 65*, 440–456.

Posner, J., & Vandell, D. (1999). After-school activities and the development of low-income urban children: A longitudinal study. *Developmental Psychology, 35*, 868–879.

Rosenthal, R., & Vandell, D. (1996). Quality of school-aged child-care programs: Regulatable features, observed experiences, child perspectives, and parent perspectives. *Child Development, 67*, 2434–2445.

Shonkoff, J. P., & Philips, D. A. (2000). *From neurons to neighborhoods: The science of early childhood development.* Washington, DC: National Academy Press.

Vandell, D., & Shumow, L. (1999). After-school child care programs. *The Future of Children, 9*(2), 64–80.

13

Low-Income Children's Activity Participation as a Predictor of Psychosocial and Academic Outcomes in Middle Childhood and Adolescence

Marika N. Ripke, Aletha C. Huston, and
David M. Casey

Middle childhood is a time when children become increasingly involved in activities and relationships outside of the home. In middle childhood, children enter formal schooling and, by third to fifth grade, they move out of child care. Parents face new issues of providing adequate supervision, educational experiences, developmental opportunities, and recreation for their children outside of school. These issues are particularly salient for single, employed parents with low incomes.

How children spend their time outside of school can play an important role in their psychosocial and academic development. Researchers studying children's out-of-school time use make distinctions between relaxed leisure (i.e., unstructured) activities and constructive or organized leisure (i.e., structured) activities. Engaging in structured activities is a way to acquire and master skills in both social and academic domains. Structured activities provide children with the opportunity to learn, explore their interests, and interact with their peers in organized settings supervised by adults; children who engage in them are socially skilled and tend to do well in school. Conversely, extended time in unstructured environments with little or no adult supervision (e.g., hanging out with friends in the neighborhood) may put children at risk of physical, emotional, and psychological harm (Agnew & Peterson, 1989; Mahoney & Stattin, 2000; McHale, Crouter, & Tucker, 2001).

A large body of research shows that structured out-of-school activities can serve protective, as well as developmentally enhancing, functions during adolescence, but children in the middle childhood years have received less research attention. Yet, middle childhood is often the time when children begin their involvement in sports, music, and clubs; the skills and interests acquired during this period form a foundation for interests, values, and competence beliefs in adolescence and adulthood (see Simpkins, Fredericks, Davis-Keane, & Eccles, 2006). Structured activities may be especially critical for children in low-income families, because being poor places children at risk for a variety of negative psychosocial and academic outcomes as they move through the middle childhood years (Alexander, Entwisle, & Olson, 2001; Pettit, Laird, Bates, & Dodge, 1997). In this chapter, we examine the relations between low-income children's structured activity participation and their psychosocial and academic development at two times of measurement, three years apart. Hence, we follow some children from middle childhood into the adolescent years.

MIDDLE CHILDHOOD: A WINDOW OF OPPORTUNITY FOR PSYCHOSOCIAL AND ACADEMIC DEVELOPMENT?

Erikson (1968) described middle childhood as a period of "industry" during which children acquire the skills and competencies valued by their culture. Mastering the basic skills needed for adulthood is the crucial developmental task of middle childhood; failure to do so results in "inferiority." Although academic achievement is central to success in modern U.S. culture, competence in such areas as social relationships and athletics is also highly valued. Aber and Jones (1997) identify regulating behavior and emotions, attaining skills in negotiating conflicts, and developing a sense of competence in both social and academic domains as critical tasks in middle childhood.

When children enter school, their social worlds expand and out-of-home environments play an increasing role in their lives. Although family remains important, children increasingly spend time in activities outside of the home (Canadian Council on Social Development, 2001), thus increasing their interactions with other adults (e.g., teachers, coaches) and with peers. By the end of middle childhood, children should have the self-regulatory skills to stay alone without immediate adult supervision.

Psychosocial Development

Children develop feelings of self-esteem, competence, and individuality during middle childhood as they begin comparing themselves with peers. They gain a sense of competence as they acquire the fundamentals of sports, music, social and leadership skills, and languages, to name only a few examples. Children who do not perceive themselves as competent during middle childhood may be at risk for problems down the road such as social isolation, depression, and anger (Cole, 1991; Parkhurst & Asher, 1992).

Along with increased independence comes increasing responsibility for their actions, regulating their behavior, and developing an internalized sense of moral values. Many activities provide opportunities for moral learning and service to others as well as occasions to interact with adults who provide support and guidance. The ability to interact effectively with adults and peers is an important skill to master for life success, particularly because it spans many aspects of one's life. Children in middle childhood are constantly refining their social skills as they exert their independence from the home and family. Well-developed social skills prepare children for successful interpersonal relationships, aid them in making healthy decisions, and sharpen their problem solving skills (Leffert, Benson, & Roehlkepartain, 1997); deficits in interpersonal skills are often associated with later delinquency, substance abuse, school dropout, and poor self-concept (Bukowski & Hoza, 1989).

Relationships with peers are powerful indicators of both current and future adaptive functioning (Coie, Lochman, Terry, & Hyman, 1992; Hymel, Rubin, Rowden, & LeMare, 1990). Friendships promote coping skills and strategies, moral development, and positive self-esteem (Hartup & Stevens, 1999; Piaget, 1965). Understanding social norms, initiating and maintaining social bonds, and defining and sharing leadership roles are all learned through peer relationships (Parker & Gottman, 1989). Developing these social skills during middle childhood may be especially critical as they forecast later social interactions, such as in adolescence and adulthood, when relationships with peers, coworkers, and intimate partners increase.

Out-of-school activities provide a venue for interacting and "networking" with other peers. Vandell and Ramanan (1991) found that children who participated in after-school programs supervised by adults had lower levels of antisocial behaviors, anxiety, and peer conflicts than those who were in the care of single mothers after school. Participation in structured activities also reduces the likelihood of involvement in deviant behavior (Carnegie Corporation, 1992).

Academic Achievement

Some activities not only afford children the opportunity to develop prosocial skills, acquire new competencies and skills, and form relationships with caring and supportive adults, but also strengthen their connection to schools (Eccles & Barber, 1999; Miller, O'Conner, & Wolfson Sirignano, 1995). It is no surprise then that participation in structured activities during middle childhood is associated with school achievement and motivation (Mahoney, Larson, & Eccles, 2005) and, during adolescence, with such long-term outcomes as high school and college GPA, college attendance and graduation, and adult income and earnings (Eccles & Barber, 1999; Barber, Eccles, & Stone, 2001). In several studies, youth participating in out-of-school programs formed attachments to responsible coaches and educators, and these relationships were an important pathway through which core values for school were reinforced (Rehberg, 1969; Rehberg & Schafer, 1968; Tierney, Grossman, & Resch, 1995).

LOW-INCOME FAMILIES

Arranging for supervision outside of school that offers positive developmental opportunities for their children is a particular challenge for low-income parents because: (a) many activities require expensive fees and equipment; (b) few high quality activities are available in their schools, communities, and neighborhoods; and (c) parents often work in jobs with nonstandard and/or irregular work schedules, making it difficult to arrange transportation and consistent attendance for their children. These barriers are especially disconcerting because children from low-income families living in unsafe neighborhoods are at risk for behavior problems and delinquency if they spend a lot of out-of-school time without adult supervision (e.g., hanging out with friends) (Carnegie Corporation, 1992; Pettit, Bates, & Dodge, 1997; Posner & Vandell, 1994, 1999).

Formal after-school arrangements can contribute to social conduct and competence (Posner & Vandell, 1994) and to low levels of internalizing behavior problems (Marshall et al., 1997; Pettit, Laird et al., 1997). The finding that youth who participate in structured activities have less deviant behavior than those who spend after-school time in unsupervised settings with peers is especially true for youth in low-income families and neighborhoods (Carnegie Corporation, 1992; Catalano, Berglund, Ryan, Lonczak, & Hawkins, 1999; Pettit, Bates et al., 1997).

Despite the potential advantages of structured activities, children in low-income families get less experience in them than do more affluent children. U.S. Census data from the Survey of Income and Program Participation (SIPP) shows that only 3% of children ages 6–14 from poor families participated in organized sports, compared to 26% of children from more affluent families (Smith, 2002). Children from economically disadvantaged families are less involved in organized sports, read less, and watch more television (Larson & Verma, 1999; McHale et al., 2001; Medrich, Roizen, Rubin, & Buckley, 1982; Posner & Vandell, 1999; Timmer, Eccles, & O'Brien, 1985). Conversely, children from more affluent families are more likely to be enrolled in lessons, organized sports, and clubs than are children from low-income families (Hofferth, Brayfield, Ciech, & Holcomb, 1991). Low-income parents rely more on community centers and such national youth-serving organizations as the Boys and Girls Club and the YMCA as out-of-school arrangements, while higher-income parents are more likely to avail themselves of school-based out-of-school programs or lessons for their children's out-of-school time (Halpern, 1999; Pettit, Bates et al., 1997).

Welfare and employment programs that increase both parents' employment and their income have shown positive impacts on elementary-school-age children's social behavior and on participation in structured activities (Morris, Huston, Duncan, Crosby, & Bos, 2001). The environments parents select and the arrangements they make for their children when they are not in school (e.g., enrollment in structured activities) may be important pathways by which these positive impacts occur (see Huston et al., 2003).

METHOD

The Study

We examine the relations between children's activity participation and their psychosocial and academic outcomes among children whose parents were part of a larger random assignment experiment in Milwaukee known as the New Hope Project. Participants for New Hope were recruited from July 1994 to December 1995, and were randomly assigned to a program or control group. Program group participants who worked a minimum of 30 hours per week were eligible for income supplements, subsidized health care and child care, and case management; if job searches were unsuccessful, community service jobs were available (see Brock, Doolittle, Fellerath, & Wiseman, 1997). The program led to increases in the amount of parental employment, and to jobs with slightly better wages. Children in program group families had higher levels of reading achievement than those in control families, and program boys displayed more positive social behavior and fewer behavior problems than control group boys. In middle childhood and early adolescence, program group children (especially boys) were more likely to be in formal child care arrangements and to participate in structured out-of-school activities (see Huston et al., 2005).

The Sample

Data for this study come from children who were part of the Child and Family Study (CFS) sample of New Hope, which included all 745 sample members who had one or more children between the ages of 13 months and 10 years 11 months at the time of random assignment. Up to two children in each CFS family were identified as "focal children" to be studied. Parents were predominantly single heads of households (90.4%); 56.8% were African-American, 26.6% were Hispanic, 13.1% were Non-Hispanic White, and 3.5% were Native American.

Data presented in this chapter were collected two and five years after random assignment. Children were between the ages of 6 and 12 at Time 1 of data collection, and 9 and 15 at Time 2 of data collection. There are roughly equal numbers of boys and girls. Sample sizes differ depending on the data source – surveys administered to parents, $N = 405$; children's self-report, $N = 410$; and teacher reports, $N = 189$.

Research Questions

We assess the extent to which participation in five structured activities (sports with a coach, lessons, clubs/youth groups, recreation/community centers, and religious activities) predicts children's academic and psychosocial outcomes. We analyze the association between structured activity participation during middle childhood (i.e., at Times 1 and 2 of data collection) and academic and psychosocial outcomes at Time 2, controlling for children's academic and psychosocial outcomes at Time 1. We examine whether outcomes differ by (a) individual activity, (b) gender, and (c) age. All of the analyses are "nonexperimental"; that is, we examine individual differences in participation controlling for experimental treatment.

Measures

In addition to *structured activity participation*, we assess both positive and negative indicators of children's *psychosocial functioning*. Positive indicators include positive social behavior (social competence, compliance, and autonomy), satisfaction with friendships/peer relations, and feelings of hope/efficacy. Negative indicators include problem behavior (internalizing and externalizing) and delinquency. Indicators of children's *academic achievement* include their standardized math and reading scores, self-concepts of abilities, educational expectations, and teacher-related school performance.

Structured Activity Participation. Mothers reported how frequently their children participated in sports with a team and/or coach, lessons, clubs and youth groups, religious classes and events, and recreation or community centers during the previous year using a 5-point scale ranging from "never" to "about every day." Activities were assessed both two and five years after random assignment, when children were ages 6–12 and 9–15, respectively.

These five activities are classified as "structured activities" because they afford children opportunities for adult supervision, acquiring skills, and socializing with peers. A mean score for structured activity participation was computed for each child. The means for Time 1 and Time 2 activity participation were 2.43 and 2.30, respectively.

Parent and Teacher Report of Positive Behavior. The Positive Behavior Scale (PBS) was originally developed for a study of young children from low-income families whose mothers were participating in an intervention called New Chance (Quint, Bos, & Polit, 1997). It includes 25 items, divided into three subscales: (a) social competence and sensitivity (e.g., gets along well with other children, shows concern for other people's feelings); (b) compliance and self-control (e.g., thinks before he/she acts, usually does what I tell him/her); and (c) autonomy (e.g., tries to do things for him/herself, is self-reliant). Parents and teachers used a 5-point scale, ranging from "never" to "all of the time," to describe the frequency with which the child manifests each behavior ($\alpha = .91$ for parents and .96 for teachers).

Friendship/Peer Relationships. The Loneliness and Social Dissatisfaction Questionnaire (Cassidy and Asher, 1992) is a 16-item measure of children's satisfaction with peer relations and friendships. It uses a 3-point response scale (1 = "no," 2 = "sometimes," 3 = "yes") for 6- to 8-year-olds, and a 5-point response scale (ranging from 1 = "not at all true" to 5 = "always true") for ages 9 and over. Sample items include "Is it easy for you to make new friends?" and "Do you have other kids to talk to?" ($\alpha = .89$).

Hope/Efficacy. The 6-item Children's Hope Scale uses a 6-point scale ranging from "none of the time" to "all of the time." Sample items include "I think I'm doing pretty well" and "Even when others want to quit, I know I can find ways to solve the problem" ($\alpha = .81$) (Snyder et al., 1996). It was administered only at Time 2.

Problem Behavior. Parents and teachers rated children on externalizing and internalizing behaviors using the Problem Behavior Scale of the Social Skills Rating System (Gresham & Elliott, 1990). *Externalizing* problems involve low levels of behavior control, for example, aggression, defiance, and anger ($\alpha = .81$ for parents and .92 for teachers). *Internalizing* problems include social withdrawal, sadness, and anxiety ($\alpha = .61$ for parents and .78 for teachers).

Delinquent Behavior. A 15-item scale was adapted from LeBlanc & Tremblay's (1988) measure assessing self-reported deviant behavior. Youth were asked how often in the last 12 months they had engaged in fighting, stealing, vandalism, and substance use using a 4-point response scale ranging from 1 = "never" to 4 = "5 or more times." For respondents ages 12 and over, two questions were added asking if they had "had sex" and if they had been pregnant or gotten a girl pregnant ($\alpha = .66$) (Gresham & Elliott, 1990). It was administered only at Time 2.

Standardized Achievement Test Scores. To assess reading and math competencies, children completed four individually-administered scales from the Woodcock-Johnson Achievement Battery at Time 2 (Woodcock & Johnson, 1990). Two of these – Letter-Word Identification and Passage Comprehension – are averaged to form the Broad Reading score. The other two – Applied Problems and Calculation – are averaged to form the Broad Math. The total score is the average of all four scales. The mean standard score for the population as a whole is 100; the standard deviation is

15. Reported reliabilities for the broad math and broad reading scales all exceed .90.

Teacher Ratings of Achievement. Teachers responded to the 10-item Academic Subscale of the Social Skills Rating System (Gresham & Elliot, 1990) on a scale of 1 = "lowest 10% of class" to 5 = "highest 10% of class," measuring children's performance in comparison to others in the same classroom on reading skill, math skill, intellectual functioning, motivation, oral communication, classroom behavior, and parental encouragement ($\alpha = .97$).

Children's Educational Expectations. Using a 5-point scale, ranging from "not at all" to "very," children indicated how sure they were that they would complete college.

Children's Self-Concepts of Ability. Items were adapted from Eccles' Self and Task Perception Questionnaire (Eccles & Wigfield, 1995) assessing children's self-concepts of ability in math and English/reading (e.g., "How good at English are you?"). For the English/reading and math items $\alpha = .82$ and .85, respectively.

Data Analysis

We used hierarchical regression analysis to assess the contribution of activity participation in explaining child academic and psychosocial outcomes net of the following covariates: experimental group, child gender, the interaction of experimental group and child gender, child age, parent ethnicity, number of children in household, earnings in the past year, and parent education level; all covariates were measured at baseline.

The dependent variables in all analyses were psychosocial and academic outcomes at Time 2, when children were 9–15 years old. Where possible, the Time 1 score for the dependent variable was included to control for the initial level of that variable. In these cases, the coefficient on the Time 2 dependent variable represents the extent to which participation predicted *change* in behavior over a three-year period. The independent variables were activity participation at Times 1 and 2, entered simultaneously. Participation at Time 1 and Time 2 were significantly correlated ($r = .40, p < .001$). Recall that activity participation at both time points was assessed *the previous year*; therefore, the dependent variables (i.e., psychosocial and academic outcomes) at Time 2 refer to three to four years after Time 1 activity participation, and zero to one year after Time 2 activity participation.

Regressions were conducted separately for overall structured activity participation, and for each individual activity (sports, lessons, clubs/youth groups, religious activities, and community/recreation centers). Finally, the interactions of age and gender with participation (total participation and individual activities) were tested, but the few that were significant could have occurred by chance, so they are not reported.

RESULTS

Sample size and mean activity participation by age, gender, and type of activity are presented in Tables 13.1 and 13.2. Overall, participation tended to increase with age until around 13 or 14, but there was some apparent decline at 15. Although children's involvement in sports and religious activities remained high across ages, the time they spent in lessons and clubs or youth groups peaked around age 11–13. All age groups were more involved in clubs and youth groups at Time 2 than at Time 1, possibly because more of them were available. There were also gender differences, with boys more involved in sports and clubs/youth groups and girls more likely to take lessons. Males and females were about equally involved in religious activities and recreation centers.

All Structured Activities

In general, children who participated in more structured activities displayed more positive psychosocial and academic functioning. The results of the regressions for psychosocial development appear in Table 13.3; participation accounted for 1% to 3% of the variability in the six measures listed. Children who participated more at both Times 1 and 2 had more positive parent-rated social behavior. Participation at Time 1 predicted more satisfaction with friendships, and participation at Time 2 predicted higher levels of hope and efficacy as well as lower teacher-rated internalizing problems. The one "negative" result was that children who participated more at Time 1 also had more teacher-rated externalizing problem behavior and higher self-reports of delinquency.

There were almost no significant associations of participation with academic achievement, but there was some evidence of positive associations with academic motivation (see Table 13.4). Children who participated more at Time 1 had higher self-concepts in English and math, and those who were more involved at Time 2 were more likely to expect to graduate from college.

Type of Activity

At Time 1, children participated most frequently in clubs and youth groups ($M = 3.59$, $SD = 1.44$) followed by religious activities ($M = 2.76$, $SD = 1.36$). At Time 2, children were most often involved in

TABLE 13.1. *Time 1 Mean Activity Participation by Age and Gender**

	Age							Gender	
Activity	6 (n = 78)	7 (n = 81)	8 (n = 80)	9 (n = 79)	10 (n = 74)	11 (n = 77)	12 (n = 65)	Boys (n = 274)	Girls (n = 273)
Sports	1.71	1.92	2.23	2.41	2.26	2.60	2.67	2.34	2.16
Lessons	1.84	2.03	2.12	2.44	2.39	2.55	2.49	2.08	2.44
Clubs/youth groups	1.72	1.80	2.15	2.20	1.86	1.99	1.85	3.85	3.34
Religious	2.24	2.72	2.80	3.11	2.74	2.85	2.85	2.71	2.81
Recreation centers	1.86	2.10	2.49	2.29	2.43	2.61	2.15	1.94	1.94
Total	1.87	2.12	2.36	2.49	2.34	2.52	2.40	2.28	2.32

* Mean activity participation was computed using the following scale: 1 = *Never*, 2 = *Less than once a month*, 3 = *About every month*, 4 = *About every week*, 5 = *About every day*.

269

TABLE 13.2. *Time 2 Mean Activity Participation by Age and Gender**

| Activity | Age | | | | | | | Gender | |
	9 (n = 63)	10 (n = 72)	11 (n = 65)	12 (n = 70)	13 (n = 60)	14 (n = 63)	15 (n = 57)	Boys (n = 241)	Girls (n = 230)
Sports	1.91	2.53	2.68	2.73	2.67	2.58	2.59	2.63	2.43
Lessons	2.09	2.25	2.39	2.36	2.31	2.28	2.14	1.99	2.52
Clubs/youth groups	2.25	2.48	2.80	2.74	2.29	2.41	2.10	2.30	2.60
Religious	2.89	2.94	2.96	2.87	2.66	2.72	2.56	2.75	2.87
Recreation centers	2.25	2.29	2.71	2.64	2.38	2.81	2.22	2.51	2.45
Total	2.26	2.41	2.62	2.50	2.34	2.49	2.19	2.37	2.45

* Mean activity participation was computed using the following scale: 1 = *Never*, 2 = *Less than once a month*, 3 = *About every month*, 4 = *About every week*, 5 = *About every day*.

religious activities ($M = 2.84$, $SD = 1.35$) and sports ($M = 2.56$, $SD = 1.53$).

Sports. Participation in sports was consistently associated with positive outcomes in both psychosocial and academic domains, accounting for 1% to 4% of the variability. As shown in Table 13.3, children who participated in sports at Time 1 showed increases in satisfaction with their friendships and peer relationships three years later and decreases in teacher-rated externalizing behavior. Participation in sports at Time 2 predicted increased positive behavior (parent report), a greater sense of hope and efficacy, reduced externalizing behavior (parent report), and reduced internalizing behavior (teacher report).

In the academic domain (see Table 13.4), sports participation at Time 2 predicted higher scores on reading and math tests, and children who were involved in sports at Time 1 had increases in self-concepts of English and math ability three years later.

Lessons. After sports, participation in lessons had the second highest number of positive associations with child outcomes; lessons were more consistently associated with academic achievement and motivation than with psychosocial functioning. Children who were more involved in lessons at Time 1 had higher hope and efficacy, but also slightly more parent-reported internalizing and externalizing behavior three years later. At the same time, Time 2 participation in lessons was associated with increased positive behavior (parent report) (see Table 13.3).

Academically, participation in lessons at both Times 1 and 2 predicted higher teacher-rated academic skills and self-concepts of ability in English. Children who spent more time in lessons at Time 2 scored higher on standardized reading and math tests, and they had increased self-concepts of math ability.

Clubs and Youth Groups. Children were more frequently involved in clubs and youth groups than in any other activity. Those who participated had slightly better psychosocial functioning, but there was little evidence for a relation to academic skills. Specifically, participation at Time 1 was associated with slightly increased satisfaction with friendships, and at Time 2, more hope/efficacy, slightly increased positive parent-rated social behavior, and less delinquency (see Table 13.3).

Religious Activities. Religious activities also had modest associations with psychosocial well-being and academic achievement. Children who participated in religious activities at Time 1 displayed increased satisfaction with friendships three years later, and those who were most involved at Time 2 had increased positive behavior (parent report) and higher

TABLE 13.3. *Standardized Regression Coefficients for Activity Participation Predicting Psychosocial Outcomes*

Variables	Positive Behavior P/T	Hope/Efficacy	Friendship	Externalize P/T	Internalize P/T	Delinquency
Controls[1]						
E/C group	—	—	—	—	-.19*(P)	—
Child gender	-.23**(T)	-.14*	—	—	—	—
E/C X child gender	—	.18*	—	—	—	—
Child age	—	-.18**	.13*	—	.11†(P)	.21**
Parent education	-.10*(P)	—	.09†	—	—	—
Ethnicity: Black	—	—	—	—	—	—
Ethnicity: Hispanic	—	—	—	—	—	-.19*
Number of children	—	—	—	—	—	—
Earnings past year	—	—	—	—	-.13*(P)	—
Time 1	.42**(P)	n/a	.25**	.56**(P)	.42**(P)	n/a
Outcome	.36**(T)	—	—	.38**(T)	.33**(T)	—
Total activity						
Time 1	.11*(P)	—	.11*	.15*(T)	—	.11*
Time 2	.20**(P)	.15*	—	—	-.14†(T)	—
Adjusted R^2	.23**(P)	.06**	.09**	.14**(T)	.09*(T)	.06**
ΔR^2	.03*(P)	.03**	.01*	.02**(T)	.02*(T)	.01*
Sports						
Time 1	.15*(P)	—	.15**	-.12†(T)	—	—
Time 2	—	.13*	—	-.12*(P)	-16*(T)	—
Adjusted R^2	.21**(P)	.06**	.11**	.29**(P) .14**(T)	.11*(T)	—
ΔR^2	.02*(P)	.02*	.03*	.01*(P) .02*(T)	.03*(T)	—

Lessons						
Time 1	.10* (P)	.09†	–	.13† (T)	.11† (P)	–
Time 2	.20** (P)	.09†	–	–	–	–
Adjusted R^2	.05*	.05*	–	.14** (T)	.18** (P)	–
ΔR^2	.01* (P)	.02*	–	–	.02* (P)	–
Clubs/youth groups						
Time 1	.08† (P)	–	.09†	–	–	–
Time 2	.20** (P)	.12*	–	–	–	−.09†
Adjusted R^2	.05*	.05*	.08**	–	–	.06**
ΔR^2	.01* (P)	.01*	.01*	–	–	.01*
Religious activity						
Time 1	.11* (P)	–	.14*	–	–	–
Time 2	.21** (P)	.13*	–	–	–	–
Adjusted R^2	.06**	.06**	.10**	–	–	–
ΔR^2	.01* (P)	.02*	.01*	–	–	–
Recreation/community center						
Time 1	.10* (P)	–	–	–	–	.10*
Time 2	.22** (P)	–	–	–	–	–
Adjusted R^2	.05*	–	–	–	–	.05*
ΔR^2	.01* (P)	–	–	–	–	.01*

[1] Results shown for control variables are from the regression model with total activity participation (Times 1 and 2) as the independent variables. "n/a" indicates Time 1 outcome not available. P = parent-rated; T = teacher-rated. **$p < .01$. *$p < .05$. †$p < .10$. "–" indicates that standardized coefficients were not statistically significant at $p < .10$.

TABLE 13.4. *Standardized Regression Coefficients for Activity Participation Predicting Academic Outcomes*

Variables	W–J Math	W–J Reading	Academic Skills	Educational Expectations	Self Concept: English	Self Concept: Math
Controls[1]						
E/C group	—	—	—	—	—	-.17†
Child gender	—	-.12†	-.26*	—	—	—
E/C X child gender	—	—	-.22†	-.19*	—	—
Child age	.46**	.34**	—	—	—	-.14*
Parent education	—	—	—	—	—	—
Ethnicity: Black	—	.13	—	—	.17†	—
Ethnicity: Hispanic	—	-.14*	.14*	.18*	—	—
Number of children	—	—	—	—	—	-.13†
Earnings past year	—	—	—	—	—	—
Time 1 outcome	n/a	n/a	.45**	.26***	.13*	.13*
Total activity						
Time 1	—	—	—	—	.14*	.15*
Time 2	.10*	—	—	.09†	—	—
Adjusted R^2	.21**	—	—	.07*	.05*	.11**
ΔR^2	.01*	—	—	.01*	.02*	.03*
Sports						
Time 1	—	—	—	—	.21*	.14*
Time 2	.19***	.14*	—	—	—	—
Adjusted R^2	.24**	.15**	—	—	.08*	.11**
ΔR^2	.04**	.02*	—	—	.04*	.03*

Lessons						
Time 1	–	–	.13†	–	.21*	–
Time 2	.13*	.16**	.16*	–	–	.14*
Adjusted R^2	.22**	.16**	.25**	–	.10**	.11**
ΔR^2	.02*	.03*	.03*	–	.05*	.02*
Club/youth group						
Time 1	–	.09†	–	–	–	–
Time 2	–	–	–	–	–	–
Adjusted R^2	–	.15**	–	–	–	–
ΔR^2	–	.01*	–	–	–	–
Religious activity						
Time 1	.14*	–	–	–	–	–
Time 2	–	.12*	–	–	–	–
Adjusted R^2	.21**	.13**	–	–	–	–
ΔR^2	.01*	.01*	–	–	–	–
Recreation/community center						
Time 1	–	–	–	–	–	–
Time 2	–	–.09†	–.17*	–	–.13†	.12†
Adjusted R^2	–	.14**	.25**	–	.05*	.10*
ΔR^2	–	.01*	.04*	*	.02†	.02†

[1] Results shown for control variables are from the regression model with total activity participation (Times 1 and 2) as the independent variables. "n/a" indicates Time 1 outcome not available. "–" indicates that standardized coefficients were not statistically significant at $p < .10$.
** $p < .01$. * $p < .05$. † $p < .10$.

efficacy (Table 13.3). Participation at one time or the other was associated with better math and reading scores (see Table 13.4).

Recreation and Community Centers. There were very few significant associations of recreation and community center involvement with children's behavior, and those that did appear were almost all negative. High participators at Time 1 reported engaging in more delinquent behavior (see Table 13.3), even though participation at Time 2 was associated with improved parent-rated positive behavior. Children who were frequent participants in recreation and community centers had mixed self-concepts in English and math, but teachers rated them lower on academic skills (compared to their teachers' ratings three years earlier), and they performed less well in reading (see Table 13.4).

Summary of Results

In general, participation in structured activities was related to positive psychosocial and academic outcomes for children, although some activities appear to be more beneficial than others. Of the 15 dependent variables examined (nine psychosocial and six academic), activity participation accounted for a significant amount of variability in 10. Of the five individual activities, sports was most consistently associated with healthy psychosocial functioning and academic achievement; children who had frequent lessons had better academic performance and self-concepts of ability, but had more mixed patterns of psychosocial functioning. Religious activities and clubs were less consistently related to children's behavior, but the associations were all positive. Participation in recreation/community centers was the one activity that did not appear to be beneficial; frequent participants had relatively high delinquency scores and low academic performance.

Some outcomes were more associated with activity participation than others. Parent-rated positive behavior was significantly associated with Time 2 participation for all activities *and* by each individual activity. Delinquency, on the other hand, was positively or negatively related to activity participation, depending on the activity.

DISCUSSION

In this sample of low-income urban families, we expected children's participation in structured activities to contribute to their social competence and academic motivation and achievement. For the most part, the data support this hypothesis. One of the most consistent correlates of participation was positive social behavior, which comprises social competence with peers, compliance to adults, and autonomy. Parents' perceptions of their children's social skills were consistent with the children's own reports of efficacy and satisfaction with their friendships. Reports of lowered internalizing problems also suggest that active children were more comfortable and less inhibited in interacting with peers and adults, and this same level of sociability may also account for the fact that participation predicted increasing externalizing behavior. Development of social skills during middle childhood forecasts successful social interactions and relationships with peers, coworkers, and intimate partners in adolescence and adulthood.

Although positive associations exist between participation and child outcomes for total participation, some activities appear to provide a more consistent climate for developing these skills than do others. Children who spent time in team sports, clubs, youth groups, and religious activities had relatively high levels of psychosocial functioning. These activities provide opportunities for interaction with and supervision by supportive and authoritative adults and for guided interactions with peers. Team sports require and encourage cooperation, and youth groups and religious activities often promote prosocial skills and behaviors.

Participation in sports was associated with academic achievement as well as social skills, a finding that is consistent with earlier research. Several studies document negative relations between sports involvement and delinquent and deviant behavior (e.g., Hastad, Segrave, Pangrazi, & Petersen, 1984; Melnick, Vanfossen, & Sabo, 1988). Additionally, previous research shows positive relations between participation in interscholastic athletics and educational aspirations, expectations, and values for education (e.g., Melnick et al., 1988; Rehberg, 1969; Rehberg & Schafer, 1968). Sports participation may contribute to academic achievement because sports offered through schools often encourage or require minimum grades for participation and because they keep young people connected to their schools.

Children who were involved in lessons were especially likely to perform well academically and to have high self-concepts about their abilities. Lessons in music, dance, or academic subject matter are designed to teach specific skills, often in one-on-one instruction; they may provide less opportunity for interacting with peers, particularly if they are individualized, so it is not surprising that they predict academic skills more consistently than they predict psychosocial functioning.

Recreation and community centers were the one activity associated with negative outcomes – namely, delinquency and low academic performance. These centers may offer less adult supervision and structure than other activities assessed in this study, providing more opportunities for "hanging out" with peers. Although community centers vary greatly, some may attract deviant peers who have antisocial influences on one another. In some ethnographic studies, parents have reported that they did not want their children to attend a local community center because they thought that youth who spent time there were involved with drugs or other antisocial behavior.

Both the age trends in participation and the associations of participation with behavior point to middle childhood as an important juncture for children to become involved with activities and for them to profit from the opportunities offered. For many activities, the rates of participation peak by the time children reach the end of middle childhood (around 11 or 12 years). Most of the relations between participation and behavior were consistent across ages, suggesting that participation can be beneficial across the age range studied.

Causal direction is always an issue in discussing the relations between activity participation and behavior. The longitudinal nature of the data in this study provides information about temporal sequencing that allows some tentative conclusions about causal direction. The activities in which children participated three years prior to the measured behavior predicted not only the behavioral outcomes three years later, but also the *changes* in those behaviors over the three years. Controlling for the Time 1 behavior removes the effects of initial individual differences in behavior. Nonetheless, it is quite possible that children with more positive social behavior and those who change in positive directions seek out activities over the course of development in middle childhood and adolescence. In fact, a reciprocal causal theoretical model seems most sensible for understanding the role of activities in social behavior. Children have a great deal of agency in deciding how much and what kinds of activities they will engage in. Parents and other adults can offer opportunities, and they sometimes require their children to participate (e.g., in religious activities), but children and youth also make decisions about joining and continuing these activities. It seems most likely that such decisions are influenced in part by one's social skills *and* interests, and, in turn, that the experience of participating influences social skills, friendships, and feelings of efficacy and hope for the future.

Future research could be designed to gain a better understanding of the *processes* by which activities contribute to children's lives. It would be useful to know more about what children are actually doing in these various activities, including how much structure is involved, whether the activity has an academic component, the types and content of instruction (i.e., social, academic, or both), and how much adult supervision exists. It would also be useful to assess the peer environments in these activities. Information regarding how long children have been involved in a particular activity would allow investigators to examine how variations in length of participation affect outcomes. Lastly, we know little about what opportunities are available for various age groups or about possible financial barriers to participation.

The population studied in this paper is one that is often considered "at risk" developmentally; thus, they may be particularly open to the beneficial and protective functions of structured activities, particularly those with adult supervision. Policymakers and practitioners who are concerned with how children are spending their out-of-school time might consider assuring that such activities are available, especially in a policy environment that has led many parents to spend long hours in employment that takes them away from home.

Returning to the major theme of this book, we note that participation in activities during middle childhood can set children on a path of future participation, satisfying social interactions with others, and a range of instrumental and intellectual skills. Some of the benefits of programs introduced in adolescence may not be realized unless the groundwork is laid in middle childhood. Middle childhood is the period when children initiate a range of activities; they become increasingly involved over the course of middle childhood; and they can gain confidence, skills, and satisfaction in the process.

References

Aber, J. L., & Jones, S. M. (1997). Indicators of positive development in early childhood: Improving concepts and measures. In R. Hauser, B. Brown, W. Prosser, & M. Stagner (Eds.), *Indicators of children's well-being* (pp. 295–427). New York: Russell Sage.

Agnew, R., & Peterson, D. M. (1989). Leisure and delinquency. *Social Problems, 36*(4), 332–250.

Alexander, K. L., Entwisle, D. R., & Olson, L. S. (2001). Schools, achievement, and inequality: A seasonal perspective. *Educational Evaluation & Policy Analysis, 23,* 171–191.

Barber, B. L., Eccles, J. S., & Stone, M. R. (2001). Whatever happened to the jock, the brain, and the princess? Young adult pathways linked to adolescent activity involvement and social identity. *Journal of Adolescent Research, 16,* 429–455.

Brock, T., Doolittle, F., Fellerath, V., & Wiseman, M. (1997). *Creating New Hope: Implementation of a program to reduce poverty and reform welfare.* New York: Manpower Demonstration Research Corporation.

Bukowski, W. M., & Hoza, B. (1989). Popularity and friendship: Issues in theory, measurement, and outcome. In T. J. Berndt & G. W. Ladd (Eds.), *Peer relationships in child development: Wiley series on personality processes* (pp. 15–45). Oxford, England: John Wiley & Sons.

Canadian Council on Social Development. (2001). *The progress of Canada's children 2001.* Ottawa, ON: Canadian Council on Social Development.

Carnegie Corporation. (1992). *A matter of time: Risk and opportunity in the out-of-school hours.* New York: Carnegie Corporation.

Cassidy, J., & Asher, S. R. (1992). Loneliness and peer relations in young children. *Child Development, 63,* 350–365.

Catalano, R. F., Berglund, M. L., Ryan, J. A. M., Lonczak, H. S., & Hawkins, J. D. (1999). *Positive youth development in the United States: Research findings on evaluations of positive youth development programs.* Report to the U.S. Department of

Health and Human Services, Office of the Assistant, Secretary for Planning and Evaluation and National Institute for Child Health and Human Development. Seattle, WA: Social Development Research Group, University of Washington School of Social Work.

Coie, J. D., Lochman, J. E., Terry, R., & Hyman, C. (1992). Predicting early adolescent disorder from childhood aggression and peer rejection. *Journal of Consulting & Clinical Psychology, 60,* 783–792.

Cole, M. (1991). On putting Humpty Dumpty together again: A discussion of the papers on the socialization of children's cognition and emotion. *Merrill-Palmer Quarterly, 37,* 199–208.

Eccles, J. S., & Barber, B. L. (1999). Student council, volunteering, basketball, or marching band: What kind of extracurricular involvement matters? *Journal of Adolescent Research, 14,* 10–43.

Eccles, J. S., & Wigfield, A. (1995). In the mind of the actor: The structure of adolescents' achievement task values and expectancy-related beliefs. *Personality and Social Psychology Bulletin, 21*(3), 215–225.

Erikson, E. H. (1968). *Identity, youth, and crisis.* New York: Norton.

Gresham, F. M., & Elliott, S. N. (1990). *Social skills rating system manual.* Circle Pines, MN: American Guidance Service, Inc.

Halpern, R. (1999). After-school programs for low-income children: Promise and challenges. *The Future of Children, 9*(2), 81–95.

Hartup, W. W., & Stevens, N. (1999). Friendships and adaptation across the life span. *Current Directions in Psychological Science, 8*(3), 76–79.

Hastad, D. N., Segrave, J. O., Pangrazi, R., & Petersen, G. (1984). Youth sport participation and deviant behavior. *Sociology of Sport Journal, 1,* 366–373.

Hofferth, S. L., Brayfield, A., Ciech, S., & Holcomb, P. (1991). *National child care survey, 1990.* Washington, DC: Urban Institute Press.

Huston, A. C., Miller, C., Richburg-Hayes, L., Duncan, G. J., Eldred, C. A., Weisner, T. S., et al. (2003). *Five-year results of a program to reduce poverty and reform welfare.* New York: Manpower Demonstration Research Corporation.

Huston, A. C., Epps, S. R., Shim, M., Duncan, G. J., McLoyd, V. C., Weisner, .S., et al. (2006). Effects of a family poverty intervention program last from middle childhood to adolescence. In A. C. Huston and M. N. Ripke (Eds.), *Developmental contexts in middle childhood: Bridges to adolescence and adulthood* (pp. 385–408). New York: Cambridge University Press.

Hymel, S., Rubin, K. H., Rowden, L., & LeMare, L. (1990). Children's peer relationships: Longitudinal prediction of internalizing and externalizing problems from middle to late childhood. *Child Development, 61,* 2004–2021.

Larson, R. W., & Verma, S. (1999). How children and adolescent spend time across the world: Work, play, and developmental opportunities. *Psychological Bulletin, 125,* 701–736.

Leblanc, M., & Tremblay, R. (1988). A study of factors associated with the stability of hidden delinquency. *International Journal of Adolescence and Youth, 1,* 269–291.

Leffert, N., Benson, P. L., & Roehlkepartain, J. L. (1997). *Starting out right: Developmental assets for children.* Minneapolis, MN: Search Institute.

Mahoney, J. L., Larson, R. W., & Eccles, J. S. (Eds.). (2005). *Organized activities as contexts of development: Extracurricular activities, after-school and community programs.* Mahwah, NJ: Erlbaum.

Mahoney, J. L., & Stattin, H. (2000). Leisure activities and adolescent antisocial behavior: The role of structure and social context. *Journal of Adolescence, 23,* 113–127.

Marshall, N. L., Coll, C. G., Marx, F., McCartney, K., Keefe, N., & Ruh, J. (1997). After-school time and children's behavioral adjustment. *Merrill-Palmer Quarterly, 43,* 497–514.

McHale, S. M., Crouter, A. C., & Tucker, C. J. (2001). Free-time activities in middle childhood: Links with adjustment in early adolescence. *Child Development, 72,* 1764–1778.

Medrich, E. A., Roizen, J. A., Rubin, V., & Buckley, S. (1982). *The serious business of growing up: A study of children's lives outside school.* Berkeley, CA: University of California Press.

Melnick, M. J., Vanfossen, B. E., & Sabo, D. F. (1988). Developmental effects of athletic participation among high school girls. *Sociology of Sport Journal, 5,* 22–36.

Miller, B. M., O'Connor, S., & Wolfson Sirignano, S. (1995). Out-of-school time: A study of children in three low-income neighborhoods. *Child Welfare, 74,* 1249–1280.

Morris, P. A., Huston, A. C., Duncan, G. J., Crosby, D., & Bos, J. M. (2001). *How welfare and work policies affect children: A synthesis of research.* New York: Manpower Demonstration Research Corporation.

Parker, J. G., & Gottman, J. M. (1989). Social and emotional development in a relational context: Friendship interaction from early childhood to adolescence. In T. J. Berndt & G. W. Ladd (Eds.), *Peer relationships in child development: Wiley series on personality processes* (pp. 95–131). Oxford, England: John Wiley & Sons.

Parkhurst, J. T., & Asher, S. R. (1992). Peer rejection in middle school: Subgroup differences in behavior, loneliness, and interpersonal concerns. *Developmental Psychology, 28,* 231–241.

Pettit, G. S., Bates, J. E., & Dodge, K. A. (1997). Supportive parenting, ecological context, and children's adjustment: A seven-year longitudinal study. *Child Development, 68,* 908–923.

Pettit, G. S., Laird, R. D., Bates, J. E., & Dodge, K. A. (1997). Patterns of after-school care in middle childhood: Risk factors and developmental outcomes. *Merrill-Palmer Quarterly, 43,* 515–538.

Piaget, J. (1965). *The moral judgment of the child.* New York: The Free Press.

Posner, J. K., & Vandell, D. L. (1994). Low-income children's after-school care: Are there beneficial effects of after-school programs? *Child Development, 65,* 440–456.

Posner, J. K., & Vandell, D. L. (1999). After-school activities and the development of low-income urban children: A longitudinal study. *Developmental Psychology, 35,* 868–879.

Quint, J. C., Bos, J. M., & Polit, D. F. (1997). *New chance: Final report on a comprehensive program for young mothers in poverty and their children.* New York: Manpower Demonstration Research Corporation.

Rehberg, R. A. (1969). Behavioral and attitudinal consequences of high school interscholastic sports: a speculative consideration. *Adolescence, 4*(13), 69–88.

Rehberg, R. A., & Schafer, W. E. (1968). Participation in interscholastic athletics and college expectations. *American Journal of Sociology, 73*, 732–740.

Simpkins, S. D., Fredericks, J. A., Davis-Keane, P. E., & Eccles, J. S. (2006). Healthy mind, healthy habits: The influence of activity involvement in middle childhood. In A. C. Huston and M. N. Ripke (Eds.), *Developmental contexts in middle childhood: Bridges to adolescence and adulthood* (pp. 283–302). New York: Cambridge University Press.

Smith, K. (2002). Who's minding the kids? Child care arrangements: Spring 1997. *Current Population Reports, P 70–86*. Washington, DC: U.S. Census Bureau.

Snyder, C. R., Sympson, S. C., Ybasco, F. C., Borders, T. F., Babyak, M. A., & Higgins, R. L. (1996). Development and validation of the state Hope scale. *Journal of Personality and Social Psychology, 70*, 321–335.

Tierney, J. P., Grossman, J. B., & Resch, N. L. (1995). *Making a difference: An impact of Big Brothers-Big Sisters*. Philadelphia, PA: Public-Private Ventures.

Timmer, S. G., Eccles, J., & O'Brien, K. (1985). How children use time. In F. T. Juster & F. P. Stafford (Eds.), *Time, goods, and well-being* (pp. 353–382). Lansing, MI: Survey Research Center Institute for Social Research: The University of Michigan.

Vandell, D. L., & Ramanan, J. (1991). Children of the National Longitudinal Survey of Youth: Choices in after-school care and child development. *Development Psychology, 27*, 637–643.

Woodcock, R. W., & Johnson, M. B. (1990). *Woodcock-Johnson Psycho-Educational Battery-Revised*. Allen, TX: DLM Teaching Resources.

14

Healthy Mind, Healthy Habits

The Influence of Activity Involvement in Middle Childhood

Sandra D. Simpkins, Jennifer A. Fredricks,
Pamela E. Davis-Kean, and Jacquelynne S. Eccles

There is growing evidence that participating in extracurricular and out-of-school activities during adolescence is associated with both short- and long-term indicators of positive development (e.g., Eccles & Barber, 1999; Eccles & Templeton, 2002; Mahoney, 2000). Yet, few researchers have questioned whether these relations are solely the result of activity participation during adolescence or if they are the culmination of a process that began in middle childhood. Middle childhood is marked by many physical, cognitive, social, and contextual changes. It is during this time that children develop multiple cognitive skills, such as reasoning and the ability to reflect on one's accomplishments, experiences, and aspirations. Children's social worlds broaden as they begin to participate in organized out-of-school activities. The changes in children's abilities and skills coupled with the new contexts in which children develop suggest that middle childhood is an important period for the development of skills and beliefs through participation in out-of-school activities. Although entry into adolescence and adulthood brings new abilities and interests, some of the benefits of adolescent participation may not be realized unless the groundwork is laid in middle childhood.

There is little evidence available concerning developmental hypotheses about the reasons or mechanisms for these associations. Longitudinal studies over extended periods of time afford an opportunity to examine positive and negative consequences of participation based on activity characteristics as well as other potential influences such as parental encouragement or child talent. The purpose of this chapter is to extend previous research by examining how participation in academic and nonacademic activities during middle childhood relates to youths' participation in these activities during adolescence, as well as the impact of these choices on positive youth outcomes.

This research is guided by the developmental model presented in Figure 14.1, which is based on the Eccles Expectancy-Value model (see

Sandra D. Simpkins et al.

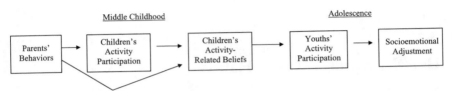

FIGURE 14.1. Theoretical model guiding the current investigation.

Eccles, 1993, for a full description of the model). This model posits that children's motivational beliefs about their ability (self) and about the value of participating in any given activity (task) emerge over middle childhood. Parents' behaviors and children's activity participation during middle childhood can set children on a path of future participation and beneficial outcomes. More specifically, parents affect their children's activity participation through three basic mechanisms: role modeling, direct provision of activity-related experiences (e.g., provision of tools and experiences), and expectancy/value socialization (e.g., by the messages they give regarding their children's competence and potential for different activities). These behaviors are likely to influence the development of children's beliefs about and participation in activities. In turn, children who participate in activities in middle childhood and have formed more favorable self and task beliefs during these ages are more likely to participate in these activities during adolescence, and it is more likely that this adolescent participation will lead to positive outcomes. Given these basic assumptions of the model, we address the following three questions in this chapter:

1. What is the role of parents in promoting math and sport activity participation and activity-related beliefs in middle childhood?
2. What are the associations between children's math and sport activity participation and activity-related beliefs from middle childhood through adolescence?
3. How is youths' activity participation in high school organized sports associated with academic, social, and health promoting behaviors?

METHOD

The Childhood and Beyond Study (CAB) is a longitudinal study of primarily white middle class parents and children who attended 12 public schools in southeastern Michigan. Data collection began in 1987 with approximately 900 children (i.e., 75% of the eligible children) and 65% of their parents when children were in kindergarten, first, and third grade. Nine waves of data were collected: four waves when the children were in elementary school, four when they were in middle and high school, and one approximately at age 20. For example, we have data on the oldest cohort when the participants were in grades 3–6, grades 10–12, and age 20.

Participants

Data from approximately 750 families were used in this report. Information from one child and both parents in each family were included. The majority of the families (97%) had two parents living in the home. Ninety-six percent of mothers, 97% of fathers, and 94% of children were European-American and spoke English. Ninety-eight percent of parents had attained at least a high school degree. Forty percent of mothers and 54% of fathers had also earned a degree from a four-year college. Families' annual household income ranged from $20,000 to over $80,000 (*Mdn* = $60,000–$69,999). This sample was explicitly selected so that family income and neighborhood resources would not be obstacles to parents in providing opportunities for their children's activity involvement.

Data included in this report were collected from children in three different cohorts. At Wave 1, 209 children were in kindergarten (*mean* age of 6.43 years, *SD* = .37), 225 children were in first grade (*mean* age of 7.35 years, *SD* = .36), and 338 children were in third grade (*mean* age of 9.37 years, *SD* = .36). There were relatively equal numbers of boys and girls across the sample (51% female).

We have information on 70 to 80% of the sample at each wave. The missing data rates are comparable to other longitudinal studies. A combination of mailed surveys and telephone interviews (coupled with a variety of tracking strategies, including earlier parent or friend contacts, the State Motor Vehicle Department records, social security numbers, and forwarding address information available from the post office) was used to minimize attrition. All participants were tracked and asked to participate at each wave. The most common source of attrition was moving out of the data collection area. To understand if sample attrition influenced the results, we compared the mean scores for individuals with full data and missing data at each measurement point on demographic and motivational factors (Fredricks & Eccles, 2002). The only significant difference between the two groups was income. Those individuals who dropped out of the study tended to be slightly lower in income. The mean family income of the early attrition group was less than three tenths of a standard deviation lower than the full sample. Because it is unlikely that this small effect constrained variances, we believe the findings were not adversely affected by attrition.

Procedure

The data for this report came from several waves of CAB: Wave 1 (youths were in kindergarten, first grade, and third grade), Wave 3 (second, third, and fifth grades), Wave 4 (third, fourth, and sixth grades), Wave 5 (seventh, eighth, and tenth grades), and Wave 7 (ninth, tenth, and

TABLE 14.1. *Reliability, Means, and Standard Deviations of Youth Reported Activity Participation, Expectancies/Values, and Adolescent Outcomes*

Item	Sports			Math		
	Reliability	M	SD	Reliability	M	SD
Aptitude	N/A	48.96	10.51	N/A	5.13	1.54
Activity participation						
Wave 3	.63	2.92	1.84	N/A	2.54	1.82
Wave 4	.77	3.64	1.69	N/A	2.93	1.68
Wave 5	N/A	3.76	2.12	–	–	–
Math courses – Wave 7	–	–	–	N/A	2.74	1.90
Expectancies/values						
Self-concept – Wave 3	.85	5.56	1.15	.78	5.42	1.02
Interest – Wave 3	.86	6.30	1.33	.81	4.85	1.93
Importance – Wave 3	.84	4.88	1.46	.61	5.36	1.03
Self-concept – Wave 4	.89	5.43	1.61	.85	5.33	1.10
Interest – Wave 4	.89	5.84	1.48	.84	4.70	1.89
Importance – Wave 4	.89	4.53	1.61	.71	5.26	1.02
Adolescent outcomes – Wave 5						
Risky behavior	.90	1.68	0.90			
Depression	.86	1.27	1.61			
Negative friends	.84	2.39	1.10			
Positive friends	.72	3.52	1.11			
School belonging	.73	5.04	1.08			
Self-esteem	.78	3.05	0.57			

Note: Wave 3 = second, third, and fifth grades. Wave 4 = third, fourth, and sixth grades. Wave 5 = seventh, eighth, and tenth grades.

twelfth grades). Children's data were collected at school in the spring of each year. Children's aptitude was measured with the Bruininks-Oseretsky Test of Motor Proficiency for physical abilities at Wave 1 and with teacher's report of children's math skills at Wave 3. During Wave 3, self-administered parent questionnaires were mailed home with a stamped, return envelope. Youths completed questionnaires on their participation, values, self-competencies, and outcomes in their classroom while being supervised by several staff members at Waves 3, 4, 5, and 7. During Waves 3 and 4, the questionnaires were read aloud to the entire class.

Child Measures

Activity Participation. Children described how often they participated in sport and math activities at Wave 3 (i.e., second, third, and fifth grades), one year later at Wave 4 (i.e., third, fourth, and sixth grades), and five years later at Wave 5 (i.e., seventh, eighth, and tenth grades; see Table 14.1 for descriptives). Children reported how often they played organized sport activities with two items at Waves 3 and 4: "How often do you play sports with friends around the neighborhood where someone keeps score" and "How often do you play sports on organized teams where someone keeps score" (0 = *never*, 6 = *a lot*). At Wave 5, youths described about many hours they spent on organized sport activities during the last week (1 = *none*, 8 = *21 or more hours*). At each of the three waves, children also described how often they did other athletic activities for fun. Finally, at Waves 3, 4, and 5, the number of organized sports was assessed through summing the number of activities in which children participated.

In Waves 3 and 4, children reported how often they engaged in math activities after school (0 = *never*, 6 = *a lot*). Adolescents' participation in out-of-school math activities besides time spent on homework wanes. They, however, often make other achievement-related choices in adolescence, such as the math courses they take in high school. Due to this developmental change in youths' math choices, we gauged adolescents' participation in math by summing the number of math courses they took throughout high school. In twelfth grade (i.e., Wave 7 for the oldest cohort), participants reported whether they had taken algebra, algebra II, geometry, precalculus, trigonometry, calculus, and AP calculus/AP analysis courses at any point during high school.

Activity-Related Expectancies/Values. Children described their expectancies and values concerning sports and math at Waves 3 and 4 (Table 14.1). Based on factor analysis and theoretical considerations, scales were created to assess competence (5-item scale; e.g., "How good at math are you?"), interest (3-item scale; e.g., "How much do you like doing math?"), and importance in each of these domains (4-item scale; e.g., "In general, how useful is what you learn in math?"). These scales have excellent face, convergent, and discriminant validity, and strong psychometric properties (Eccles, Wigfield, Harold, & Blumenfeld, 1993).

Adolescent Outcomes. One of the central topics of this chapter is to examine the outcomes associated with *adolescents'* participation in activities. Adolescents were asked a series of questions about a range of outcomes including risk behavior, feelings of depression, self-esteem, school belonging, characteristics of their peer group, and activity participation at Wave 5 (Table 14.1). Adolescent risk behavior described youths' engagement in a variety of behaviors (e.g., skipping school) over the past six months (1 = *never*, 8 = *31 or more times*; 7-item scale). Youths' self-report of depression was drawn from Kovac's (1985) Children's Depression Inventory. Students' self-esteem was measured with Harter's Self-Worth scale (Harter, 1982). The scale measuring school belonging tapped whether students felt that they mattered, belonged, or were left out in school (1 = *never*, 7 = *all of the time*; 5-item scale). Finally, adolescents were asked a series of questions about positive (e.g., think schoolwork is important; 5-item scale) and negative characteristics (e.g., encourage you to disobey your parents; 7-item scale) of their peer group (1 = *none*, 7 = *all*). Indicators of adolescents' outcomes from Wave 5 were included so that we could examine differences in outcomes of youths who are currently involved or uninvolved in activities at Wave 5.

Aptitude. The Bruininks-Oseretsky Test of Motor Proficiency (1978) assessed children's physical aptitude at Wave 1 (see Fredricks & Eccles, 2002, for details). This test has been widely used to assess the proficiency of individuals' motor performance (Hattie & Edwards, 1987). Children's math aptitude was measured with teachers' reports of children's ability and talent in mathematics at Wave 3 (1 = *very little*, 7 = *a lot*).

Parent Measures

Parent Behaviors and Beliefs. During Waves 3 and 4 (i.e., second to sixth grades), parents reported on four different behaviors that were specific to sports and math (see Fredricks, 2000; Simpkins, Davis-Kean, & Eccles, 2005 for details): role modeling (e.g., time spent last week playing sports with friends; 1 = 0 *hours*, 8 = *more than 20 hours per week*), how much they encourage math or sport activities (1 = *strongly discourage*, 7 = *strongly encourage*), provision of activity-related materials (e.g., providing sports equipment in the home; 0 = *no*, 1 = *yes*), and how often they do math or sports activities with their child (1 = *never*, 7 = *almost every day*). In addition, parents reported if they coached their children's sports team (0 = *no*, 1 = *yes*). Mothers' report of coaching a sports team was not included in the analyses because less than 4% of mothers reported coaching. Information was also collected on two parental beliefs concerning sports and math: perceptions of their children's ability and parents' value of their child's participation (perceptions of ability α = .92–.95; perceptions of importance α = .48–.77).

Parent Demographics. Mothers and fathers reported their highest level of educational attainment on a list of precoded responses (1 = *grade school*, 9 = *Ph.D.*). An index was created to characterize the highest level of educational attainment across parents. Parents' incomes were summed to create the average family annual income from a scale listing income brackets in $10,000 increments (minimum = *none*, maximum = *over $80,000*).

RESULTS

Question 1: What Is the Role of Parents in Promoting Math and Sport Activity Participation and Activity-Related Beliefs in Middle Childhood?

In the model presented in Figure 14.1, we hypothesized that parents' behaviors promote children's activity involvement and activity-related beliefs in middle childhood, which, in turn, are associated with adolescent participation. We tested the first part of this model – parent behaviors promote participation and beliefs – by examining the association between parents' behaviors and beliefs and children's math and sport activity participation and beliefs during middle childhood.

In order to understand the associations between parents' behaviors and beliefs and children's activity-related outcomes, we used an approach similar to one utilized by risk/resiliency researchers to create family profiles based on cumulative promotive scores. Risk and resiliency researchers have used cut points on various risk factors to examine the impact of cumulative risk and promotive/protective factors on children's functioning (Rutter, 1988; Sameroff, Bartko, Baldwin, Baldwin, & Seifer, 1998). Because multiple influences can put children at risk, the number of risk/resiliency factors in a child's life may be more important than the specific types of factors. Our qualitative analyses suggest that children engage in particular activities for a variety of reasons (Fredricks et al., 2002). Hence, we have adapted the risk/resiliency approach to examine the relations between parents' beliefs and behaviors and children's activity involvement.

In these analyses, the promotive scores included parents' (a) ratings of children's sport or math competence, (b) value of sports or math, (c) level of encouragement of sports or math, (d) time involvement with their child in sport or math activities, (e) purchases of sport or math materials, and (f) own time involvement in sports or math. Sport promotive scores also included a seventh item: father coaches a team. To create an index of family-level promotive behaviors, mothers' and fathers' behaviors were averaged. Then, parents were given a 1 or 0 for each variable depending on whether they were above or below the top 25% cutoff (i.e., above the cutoff = 1, below the cutoff = 0). All promotive behaviors were summed to create an index of family-level promotive climate. A higher score signified that parents engaged in more behaviors that promote children's sport or math participation and beliefs.

Parents' sport promotive scores ranged from 0 to 7, with a *mean* of 1.76. For subsequent analyses, families with four or more promotive scores were combined into a single group so that there was adequate sample size in each group. Parents' math promotive scores ranged from 0 to 6, with a *mean* of 1.94. Because of the low frequencies of families with 4, 5, or 6 math promotive scores, we combined these family types into one group.

Analysis of covariance (ANCOVA) was used to examine the relations between the number of promotive scores at Wave 3 (second, third, and fifth grades) and each of the standardized scores of children's ability self-concept, interest, importance, and participation at Wave 3 and one year later at Wave 4 (third, fourth, and sixth grades). Separate ANCOVAs were computed for each of the four outcomes at Waves 3 and 4. In the cross-sectional analyses, family income, parent education, child gender, child grade, and aptitude were included as covariates. In the longitudinal analyses, the controls from the cross-sectional analyses and the outcome measured at Wave 3 were included as covariates.

The number of sport and math promotive scores positively predicted children's sport and math ability self-concept, interest, importance, and participation at both waves. Figure 14.2 shows the adjusted means of children's self-concept, interest, importance, and participation by the number of promotive scores. In general, these results show a linear relation between the number of promotive scores and children's beliefs and participation, indicating that promotive scores have a cumulative positive relation to children's motivation and participation. Children's concurrent (i.e., Wave 3) math and sport beliefs and participation were significantly predicted by parents' promotive scores even after controlling for family- and child-level differences. Parents' sport promotive scores also significantly predicted children's sport outcomes one year later (i.e., Wave 4). With the exception of math importance, children's math outcomes at Wave 4 were not predicted by parents' promotive scores once we controlled for children's outcomes measured at Wave 3. That is, parents' promotion of sports predicted increasing involvement and beliefs about sports over the subsequent year, but their promotion of math did not lead to significant increases beyond those observed at Wave 3. The longitudinal predictions of parents' promotive scores were reduced by the stability of these indicators across time.

Question 2: What Are the Associations Between Children's Math and Sport Activity Participation and Activity-Related Beliefs from Middle Childhood Through Adolescence?

The Eccles Expectancy-Value model asserts that children's activity participation and activity-related beliefs reciprocally influence one another across development. In line with this model, we expected that children's activity participation would predict their beliefs, which, in turn, would predict adolescent participation. These two sections of the model presented in Figure 14.1 were tested separately. First, we examined the relations between children's activity participation and beliefs within middle childhood.

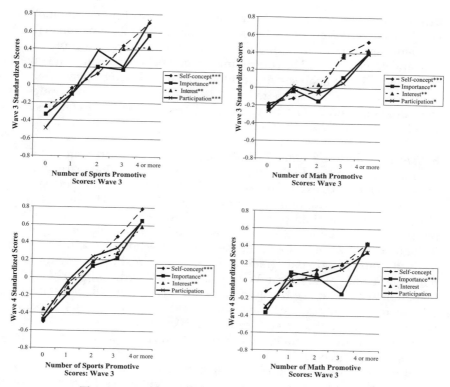

FIGURE 14.2. The standardized adjusted means of children's sport and math expectancies, values, and time use at Wave 3 (second, third, and fifth grades) and Wave 4 (third, fourth, and sixth grades) by the number of parental promotive scores at Wave 3. The significance of the parental promotive scores' main effect in the ANCOVA analyses is designated with *$p < .05$, **$p < .01$, ***$p < .001$.

Second, we tested the associations between children's beliefs in middle childhood and their participation in adolescence.

Participation Predicting Beliefs in Middle Childhood. We hypothesized that children's participation in math and sport activities should positively predict their beliefs concerning math and sports. These associations were tested with cross-sectional (i.e., all indicators were measured in Wave 3 when children were in second, third, and fifth grades) and longitudinal regression analyses (i.e., Wave 3 predictors and Wave 4 outcomes). As in previous analyses, parent education, parent income, grade level, gender, and aptitude were used as controls in both analyses. The controls in the longitudinal analyses also included the outcome measured at Wave 3.

Overall, participation in sport and math activities predicted children's expectancies and values in these domains. Children's beliefs concerning their competence and interest in and the importance of sports and math at Wave 3 were positively predicted by their concurrent participation in these domains (Table 14.2). In addition, participation at Wave 3 also predicted beliefs at Wave 4 even when controlling for their beliefs measured at Wave 3 (Table 14.3). These analyses suggest that the time children spend in math and sport activities is associated with higher expectancies and values in these domains, and that participation predicts increasing expectancies and values over the course of a year.

Beliefs in Middle Childhood Predicting Adolescent Participation. The findings discussed in the previous section suggested that participation predicted children's expectancies and values in middle childhood, specifically in third, fourth, and sixth grades (i.e., Wave 4). The next step in our model was examining our hypothesis that these expectancies and values in middle childhood would be associated with activity participation in high school. As mentioned in the Method section, participants were in third, fourth, and sixth grade at Wave 4 and in seventh, eighth, and tenth grade four years later in Wave 5. In order to predict high school participation at Wave 5, we had to restrict our analyses to the oldest cohort who were in sixth grade in Wave 4 and tenth grade at Wave 5. Separate regressions included competence, importance, and interest to avoid issues of multicolinearity; aptitude, gender, parent education, and parent income were included as controls.

Children's self-perceptions of competence, importance, and interest in sports in sixth grade were positively associated with adolescents' sport participation in tenth grade, after controlling for child and family differences (see Table 14.4). Children's competence and value beliefs were positively related to all three measures of sport participation (i.e., time on organized sport activities, number of organized sport activities, and time on sports for fun). Thus, children are more likely to participate in sports when they perceive that they have ability in sports, value the activity, and enjoy participating in middle childhood.

Adolescents' participation in out-of-school math activities besides time spent on homework is minimal. During adolescence, however, youths can often choose whether they take math courses throughout high school. Due to this developmental change in youths' math choices, we tested the relations between middle childhood beliefs and the number of math courses they took in high school. In addition, youths' math courses and experiences are very different through the years spanning middle childhood through high school. As a result, youths' expectancies and values change across this period (Jacobs, Lanza, Osgood, Eccles, & Wigfield, 2002). We used two sets of analyses to examine the associations between children's beliefs concerning math in middle childhood and the number of math courses they took in high school. First, children's middle childhood beliefs were

TABLE 14.2. *Regression Results Predicting Sport and Math Expectancies and Values at Wave 3 from Activities at Wave 3 (second, third, and fifth grades)*

	Sports			Math		
Model Summary	Competence β	Importance β	Interest β	Competence β	Importance β	Interest β
Predictors						
Time in activities	.36***	.33***	.33***	.15***	.12**	.23***
Aptitude	.10*	.00	.00	.12**	.07t	.14***
Gender	−.28***	−.15***	−.15***	.19***	.05	.08*
Cohort status	−.15***	−.12**	.02	−.06	−.03	−.07
Parent education	.01	.09t	.13*	.00	−.11*	−.09*
Parent income	.01	−.20*	−.23*	.06	.04	.05
Model F^a	44.79***	20.89***	20.54***	8.37***	3.16**	5.60***
Adjusted R^2	.30	.16	.16	.07	.02	.08

[a] $df = 7{,}711$ for sport models; $df = 6{,}569$ for math models.
t$p < .10$. *$p < .05$. **$p < .01$. ***$p < .001$.

TABLE 14.3. *Regression Results Predicting Sport and Math Expectancies and Values at Wave 4 (third, fourth, and sixth grades) from Activities at Wave 3 (second, third, and fifth grades)*

	Sports			Math		
	Competence	Importance	Interest	Competence	Importance	Interest
Model Summary	β	β	β	β	β	β
Predictors						
Time in activities	.19***	.22***	.20***	.04	.09*	.13***
Prior belief	.50***	.39***	.36***	.39***	.35***	.39***
Aptitude	.09*	.05	.10*	.21***	.01	.09*
Gender	−.14***	−.17***	−.15***	.16***	.06	.03
Cohort status	−.10**	−.12**	−.12**	−.05	−.01	−.11**
Parent education	.03	.06	.01	.01	−.01	.03
Parent income	.02	−.15*	−.04	.05	.04	−.05
Model F^a	84.21***	51.05***	39.30***	30.03***	13.05***	24.28***
Adjusted R^2	.49	.37	.31	.28	.14	.24

[a] $df = 8,685$ for sport models; $df = 7,525$ for math models.
*$p < .05$. **$p < .01$. ***$p < .001$.

TABLE 14.4. *Regression Results Predicting Youths' Sport Activities at Wave 5 (tenth grade) from Their Expectancies and Values at Wave 4 (sixth grade)*

Model Summary	Time in Organized Sports			Number of Organized Sports			Time in Sports for Fun		
	β	β	β	β	β	β	β	β	β
Predictors									
Sport competence -6th	.33***	–	–	.32***	–	–	.28***	–	–
Sport importance -6th	–	.29***	–	–	.27***	–	–	.21***	–
Sport interest -6th	–	–	.26***	–	–	.25***	–	–	.23***
Aptitude	.06	.10	.09	.15*	.18**	.17**	.03	.07	.05
Gender	.06	.03	.00	.11*	.08	.07	−.09*	−.13**	−.13**
Parent education	.15*	.13*	.14*	.12	.10	.11	−.03	−.04	−.03
Parent income	−.04	.04	.01	−.02	.06	.03	.08	.14	.12
Model F[a]	11.28***	10.16***	8.58***	12.93***	11.15***	10.77***	10.43***	8.07***	8.77***
Adjusted R²	.11	.10	.09	.15	.13	.12	.11	.08	.09

[a] $df = 7,150$.
*$p < .05$. **$p < .01$. ***$p < .001$.

295

TABLE 14.5. *Regression Results Predicting the Number of Math Courses Taken in High School from Youths' Math Expectancies and Values in Tenth Grade*

Model Summary	β	β	β
Predictors			
Math competence -10th	.55***	–	–
Math importance -10th	–	.23**	–
Math interest -10th	–	–	.32***
Aptitude	.04	.09	.08
Gender	−.13	−.05	−.05
Parent education	.15	.22*	.20*
Parent income	.06	.01	.02
Model F[a]	14.97***	4.00**	5.72***
Adjusted R²	.35	.10	.15

[a]$df = 5, 131$.
*$p < .05$. **$p < .01$. ***$p < .001$.

used to predict their beliefs in adolescence. Second, analyses described the relations between adolescents' beliefs and the number of math courses. Children's math expectancies and values in sixth grade were associated with their expectancies and values in tenth grade (competence $\beta = .43$, $p < .001$; importance $\beta = .20$, $p < .01$; interest $\beta = .32$, $p < .001$). Those expectancies and values in tenth grade were positively associated with the number of math courses youths took during high school (Table 14.5). As in the sport domain, youths who have an interest in math, believe they are good at math, and value math are more likely to take math courses in high school.

Question 3: What Outcomes Are Associated with Youths' Activity Participation in High School Organized Sports?

In the previous sections, we have shown that parents' behaviors and beliefs promote youths' participation in activities during middle childhood. Furthermore, these beliefs predict adolescent involvement in those activities. In this section, we examine the last path of the model presented in Figure 14.1 for sport participation by testing whether participation in organized activities during adolescence acted as a resource that improved adolescents' chances of obtaining optimal levels on later outcomes and/or kept adolescents free from risky outcomes. Because few youths participate in organized math activities (e.g., math clubs) in adolescence, these analyses focus on the correlates of youths' participation in organized sport activities.

In these analyses, we defined thresholds as points at which participation in organized sport activities dramatically increased youths' chances of success and decreased their likelihood of risk. One reason for creating thresholds is that it provides simple but rich measures of the potential benefits of activity involvement that are interpretable by practitioners and policymakers. Specifically, we were interested in whether adolescents who participated at high levels (i.e., 10 or more hours per week) had more optimal developmental outcomes than adolescents who were not involved in athletics. The decision to compare the two groups [high participation ($n = 81$ students) versus no participation ($n = 73$ students)] was based on our hypothesis that the intensity of activity involvement mattered and that high rates of sport involvement would act as a resource that improved adolescents' developmental outcomes.

We compared adolescents in the two groups on negative behaviors including frequency of risk behaviors, association with a negative peer group, and level of depression; and positive behaviors including association with a positive peer group, levels of school belonging, and self-esteem. For each developmental outcome, we created a risk and productive group by examining the distribution of each variable to find the cutoff point where differences between individuals scoring above and below this point were as large as possible on related variables. We patterned our analyses on work by Gambone, Klem, and Connell (2002) and did not include covariates in any of these analyses. First, we examined whether participation in high levels of organized sports helped to lessen the probability of ending up in a risk category in tenth grade. Adolescents with high levels of sport participation were 40% less likely to end up in a negative peer group and 40% less likely to be in the depressed category than youths who did not participate in sports (Figure 14.3). Next, we tested whether organized sport participation increased the probability of ending up in the productive group. Youths who participated at high rates accrued benefits from their participation (Figure 14.3) including a 26% increase in the probability of being in a positive peer group, a 25% increase in the probability of being in the high self-esteem group, and a 53% increase in the probability of ending up in the high school belonging category.

DISCUSSION

Our findings extend the work on out-of-school activities by focusing on the developmental period of middle childhood through adolescence. Although most individuals begin participating in activities during middle childhood, researchers have concentrated on adolescence. As a result, we know very little about why children get involved in activities during middle childhood and the consequences of participation. Researchers have theorized that middle childhood is an important time for youths to develop and form values and beliefs about competence in various domains

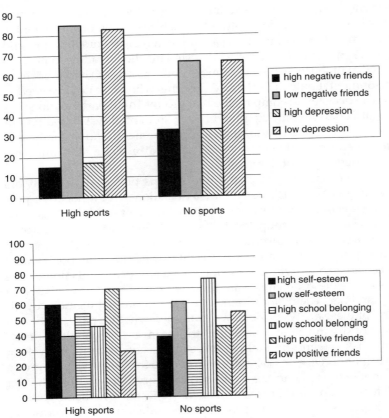

FIGURE 14.3. Percentage of youths who had high or low risky behaviors (i.e., number of negative friends, depression) and high or low productive outcomes (i.e., positive friends, self-esteem, school belonging) for youths participating in a high amount of sports, and youths not participating in sports.

(Erikson, 1982). Our results suggest that (a) parents' efforts to get their children involved in out-of-school activities influence both their children's participation and their children's developing expectancies and values; (b) children's activity participation and their self and task beliefs (ability perceptions and activity value) are linked, such that middle childhood participation predicts beliefs, which, in turn, account for adolescent participation; and (c) sport participation during adolescence predicts better adolescent functioning in multiple domains. These results extend prior research by Eccles and her colleagues on the association between expectancy and values and participation measures by examining the developmental progression of middle childhood activity participation to adolescent outcomes

(Barber, Eccles, & Stone, 2001; Eccles-Parsons, Adler, & Kaczala, 1982; Fredricks & Eccles, 2002).

Our results suggest that parents' beliefs and behaviors can play a substantial role in promoting or discouraging youths' participation in a variety of out-of-school activities, particularly during middle childhood. In fact, a number of supportive behaviors and beliefs predicted children's activities, self-beliefs, and task values. Similar to risk and resiliency research (Sameroff et al., 1998), the number of parental behaviors and beliefs rather than a specific set of practices predicts participation. This more ecologically valid approach for capturing the variety in parents' behaviors and the home environment across children illustrates that various family influences can have a similar effect on children's participation. Parents are one of the first key influences on children's participation in activities, which can have long-term consequences for future participation, academic course selection, and psychosocial outcomes (e.g., risk behavior, self-esteem).

Many researchers have documented the link of competence and expectancy beliefs to activity choice, persistence, and performance in academic domains (Bandura, 1997; Eccles, Wigfield, & Schiefele, 1998; Marsh & Yeung, 1997). The current results replicate and expand on this work by examining the links between activity participation in middle childhood and adolescence through children's expectancies and values. Our findings support the Eccles Expectancy-Value model predicting that youths' participation in activities and their beliefs concerning those domains influence one another. Success and participation in activities led to both increases and decreases in youths' activity value and self-concept of abilities. At the same time, youths who believe they are skilled in a particular domain and/or value the domain are more likely to continue to pursue this endeavor after school than their peers. In other words, youths continue to participate, in part, based on their beliefs concerning that activity. Although children's beliefs become more refined during adolescence as they gain experience, they begin to form their expectancies and values during middle childhood, suggesting that middle childhood experiences in activities are important formative influences. Because middle childhood is the time when the fundamentals of many skills are acquired, these same patterns may hold for other skill-based activities, such as playing a musical instrument or reading.

Across many of our findings, the results were stronger for sports than math. There are several differences between math and sports that may account for these findings. First, there is likely to be more variability in sports than math indicators in our middle-class sample. Athletic activities are more voluntary, and the importance of sports may differ more widely than math across families. Children's performance in math, on the other hand, may be viewed as essential for children's future educational and occupational success. Thus, for example, children may feel math is important regardless of their participation in math out-of-school activities because children may already know it is important for their education. Second, sports are more highly visible activities with greater status and prestige than math activities. Athletic activities provide more opportunities for social interactions with peers, public recognition, and engagement in activities that differ from those which are targeted during the school hours. Finally, there are more opportunities for children to engage in sports through both informal avenues (e.g., pick-up games in the neighborhood) and organized activities (e.g., YMCA, school/community teams) than math activities. It is likely that the distinctive characteristics of the math and sport domains and the differences in participation accounted for the stronger findings in sports.

Engaging in sports is a process that, for many youths, begins in middle childhood and continues through adolescence. Adolescents who spend a lot of time in organized sport activities appear to reap a variety of psychological, social, and behavioral benefits. They are less likely to engage in risky and negative behaviors and more likely to show optimal developmental outcomes. Unlike previous research, this study did not find that sport participation was associated with higher levels of risk behavior, particularly alcohol use (Eccles & Barber, 1999). These results highlight the potential of activities to help adolescents navigate their high school years, and add support to recommendations for more opportunities for youths to be involved in productive and structured activities. Participation in middle childhood, however, is a key step on the pathway to subsequent adolescent and young adulthood outcomes. Unfortunately, out-of-school and extracurricular activities are often viewed as nonessential and are often among the first items to be removed from school budgets during times of economic troubles. Educators and policy makers should reevaluate these assumptions because of the potential developmental benefits of participation for many youths.

This research was supported by Grant HD17553 from the National Institute for Child Health and Human Development to Jacquelynne Eccles, Allan Wigfield, Phyllis Blumenfeld, and Rena Harold; Grant 0089972 from the National Science Foundation to Jacquelynne Eccles and Pamela Davis-Kean; and grants from the W. T. Grant Foundation and the MacArthur Network on Successful Pathways through Middle Childhood to Jacquelynne Eccles. We would like to thank the principals, teachers, students, and parents of the cooperating school districts for their participation in this project. We would also like to thank the following people for their work on the project: Amy Arbreton, Phyllis Blumenfeld, Carol Freedman-Doan, Rena Harold, Janis Jacobs, Toby Jayaratne, Mina Vida, Allan Wigfield, and Kwang Suk Yoon.

References

Bandura, A. (1997). *Self-efficacy: The exercise of control.* New York: W. H. Freeman & Co.

Barber, B. L., Eccles, J. S., & Stone, M. R. (2001). Whatever happened to the jock, the brain, and the princess? Young adult pathways linked to adolescent activity involvement and social identity. *Journal of Adolescent Research, 16,* 429–455.

Eccles, J. S. (1993). School and family effects of the ontogeny of children's interests, self-perception, and activity choice. In J. Jacobs (Ed.), *Nebraska Symposium on Motivation, 1992: Developmental perspectives on motivation* (pp. 145–208). Lincoln, NE: University of Nebraska Press.

Eccles, J., & Barber, B. (1999). Student council, volunteering, basketball, or marching band: What kind of extracurricular involvement matters? *Journal of Adolescent Research, 14,* 10–43.

Eccles, J. S., & Templeton, J. (2002). Extracurricular and other after-school activities for youth. In. W. G. Secada (Ed.), *Review of research in education: Vol. 26* (pp. 113–180). Washington, DC: American Educational Research Association.

Eccles, J. S., Wigfield, A., Harold, R. D., & Blumenfeld, P. (1993). Ontogeny of children's self-perceptions and subjective task values across activity domains during the early elementary school years. *Child Development, 64,* 830–847.

Eccles, J. S., Wigfield, A., & Schiefele, U. (1998). Motivation. In N. Eisenberg (Ed.), *Handbook of child psychology: Vol. 3* (5th ed., pp. 1017–1095). New York: Wiley.

Eccles-Parsons, J., Adler, T., Kaczala, C. M. (1982). Socialization of achievement attitudes and beliefs: Parental influences. *Child Development, 53,* 310–321.

Erickson, E. H. (1982). *The life cycle completed: A review.* New York: Norton.

Fredricks, J. A. (2000). *Girl-friendly family contexts: Socialization into math and sports.* Unpublished doctoral dissertation, University of Michigan, Ann Arbor.

Fredricks, J. A., Alfeld-Liro, C. J., Hruda, L. Z., Eccles, J. S., Patrick, H., & Ryan, A. M. (2002). A qualitative exploration of adolescents' commitment to athletics and the arts. *Journal of Adolescent Research, 17,* 68–97.

Fredricks, J. A., & Eccles, J. S. (2002). Children's competence and value beliefs from childhood through adolescence: Growth trajectories in two males-sex-types domains. *Developmental Psychology, 38,* 519–533.

Gambone, M. A., Klem, A. M., & Connell, J. P. (2002). *Finding out what matters for youth: Testing key links in a community action framework for youth development.* Unpublished manuscript, Philadelphia: Youth Development Strategies, Inc., and Institute for Research and Reform in Education.

Harter, S. (1982). The perceived competence scale for children. *Child Development, 53,* 87–97.

Hattie, J., & Edwards, H. (1987). A review of the Bruininks-Oseretsky Test of Motor Proficiency. *British Journal of Educational Psychology, 57,* 104–113.

Kovacs, M. (1985). The children's depression inventory. *Psychopharmacology Bulletin, 21,* 995–998.

Jacobs, J. E., Lanza, S., Osgood, D. W., Eccles, J. S., & Wigfield, A. (2002). Changes in children's self-competence and values: Gender and domain differences across grades one through twelve. *Child Development, 73,* 509–527.

Mahoney, J. L. (2000). School extracurricular activity participation as a moderator in the development of antisocial patterns. *Child Development, 71,* 502–516.

Marsh, H. W., & Yeung, A. S. (1997). Relations to academic self-concept and achievement. *American Educational Research Journal, 34,* 691–720.

Rutter, M. (Ed.). (1988). *Studies of psychosocial risk: The power of longitudinal data.* New York: Cambridge University Press.

Sameroff, A. J., Bartko, W. T., Baldwin, A., Baldwin, C., & Seifer, R. (1998). Family and social influences on the development of child competence. In M.Lewis (Ed), *Families, risk, and competence* (pp. 161–185). Mahwah, NJ: Lawrence Erlbaum Associates.

Simpkins, S. D., Davis-Kean, P. E., & Eccles, J. S. (2005). Parental socialization and children's engagement in math, science, and computer activities. *Applied Developmental Science, 9,* 14–30.

15

Media Effects in Middle Childhood

L. Rowell Huesmann and Laramie D. Taylor

The telecommunications revolution of the twentieth century has created a new environment for our children. Radio, television, movies, videos, video games, and computer networks have assumed central roles in socializing our children while parents may have lost influence. For better or worse, the mass media have an enormous impact on our children's values, beliefs, and behaviors. No examination of middle childhood environments can be complete without understanding the influences of the mass media.

Of course, it is beyond the scope of this chapter to review all of the effects that the mass media have on youth in middle childhood. Excellent recent reviews of media effects on children are available (Anderson et al., 2003; Comstock & Paik, 1991; Huston & Wright, 1997; Palmer & Young, 2003; Singer & Singer, 2001). Instead, in this chapter, we will first elaborate the theory that has developed to explain the different ways in which media exert both short- and long-term influences on children's behaviors and cognitions. We will also review some of the characteristics of media presentations and some of the individual differences in children that have been shown to moderate these effects. Finally, we will review the empirical evidence on the effects of the exposure to the mass media in childhood on four dimensions of behavior and beliefs: (a) violent and aggressive behavior, (b) body image and obesity, (c) stereotype formation, and (d) learning and academic achievement.

THEORETICAL RATIONALES FOR MEDIA EFFECTS

Media exposure can affect young people in middle childhood through *time displacement effects, short-term content effects,* and *long-term content effects.* Time displacement refers to the role of the mass media in displacing other activities. Short-term content effects are due to (a) priming processes, (b) excitation processes, and (c) the immediate imitation of specific behaviors (Bushman & Huesmann, 2001; Huesmann, 1988, 1998). Long-term content effects seem to be due to (a) lasting observational learning of cognitions and behaviors, (b) activation and desensitization of emotional processes, and (c) didactic learning processes. Of course, these are general psychological processes that explain how children are influenced by what they see and experience whether it is at home, in the neighborhood, or in the media.

Short-Term Effects

Priming. Priming is the process through which spreading activation in the brain's neural network from the locus representing an external observed stimulus excites another brain node representing a cognition, emotion, or behavior (Berkowitz, 1993). The external stimulus can be inherently linked to a cognition (e.g., the sight of a gun is inherently linked to the concept of aggression) (Berkowitz & LePage, 1967), or the external stimulus can be something inherently neutral like a particular ethnic group (e.g., African-American) that has become linked in the past to certain beliefs or behaviors (e.g., welfare) (Valentino, Traugott, & Hutchings, 2002). The primed concepts make behaviors linked to them more likely. Although this effect is short-lived, the primed script, schema, or belief may have been acquired long ago.

Arousal. If mass media presentations arouse the observer, a range of behaviors may become more likely for two reasons: excitation transfer (Bryant & Zillmann, 1979) and general arousal (Berkowitz, 1993; Geen & O'Neal, 1969). Immediately following an exciting media presentation, *excitation transfer* could cause more aggressive responses to provocation, greater sexual arousal in response to sexual stimulation, and greater anxiety in response to anxiety provoking stimuli (e.g., tests). Alternatively, the increased general arousal stimulated by the media presentation may result in a decline in performance on complex tasks, diminished inhibition of inappropriate responses, and the display of dominant learned responses in social problem solving (e.g., direct instrumental aggression).

Imitation. The third short-term process, imitation of specific behaviors, can be viewed as a special case of the more general long-term process of observational learning (Bandura, 1986; Huesmann, 1998). Imitation is a powerful innate learning mechanism in humans that influences behavior from infancy through old age (Huesmann, 2005). Children mimic the social behaviors they see and reproduce these behaviors at later times (Bandura, 1977; Bandura, Ross, & Ross, 1963). Observing expressions on others' faces also leads people to automatically imitate those observed expressions and to experience the emotion that the other was experiencing (Zajonc, Murphy, & Ingelhart, 1989). As children grow into middle childhood, the imitated behaviors and emotions are combined into scripts for sequences of behavior, and by middle childhood, whole social scripts have been acquired through repeated observations.

Long-Term Effects

By middle childhood, according to these social cognitive models (Anderson & Huesmann, 2003; Huesmann, 1998), the scripts, world schemas, and normative beliefs that children acquire through observing others become more firmly encoded, more resistant to change (Huesmann & Guerra, 1997), and capable of exerting very long-term influences. To the extent that these acquired scripts are used and achieve desired goals, they become even more firmly encoded. One of the powerful characteristics of video games is that the act of playing the game involves not only observation of behaviors but also reinforcement of the behaviors that "win" the game.

Long-term effects of the mass media are also increased by the way the mass media and video games affect emotions. Through classical conditioning, fear, anger, or general arousal can become linked with specific stimuli after only a few exposures (Cantor, 1994, 2002; Harrison & Cantor, 1999). These emotions influence behavior in social settings away from the media source through stimulus generalization. Children may then react with inappropriate anger or fear in a novel situation similar to one observed in the media.

Repeated exposures to emotionally activating media or video games also can lead to habituation of certain natural emotional reactions through a process of "desensitization." Behaviors observed by the child viewer that might seem unusual at first start to seem more normative after being viewed many times. Emotions experienced automatically in response to a particular scene decline in intensity after many exposures. For example, most humans have a negative emotional response to observing blood, gore, and violence, as evidenced by increased heart rates, perspiration, and self-reports of discomfort (Cline, Croft, & Courier, 1973; Moise-Titus, 1999). However, with repeated exposure to violence, this negative emotional response habituates, and the child becomes "desensitized." The child can then think about and plan proactive aggressive acts without experiencing negative affect, making proactive aggression more likely.

Interestingly, desensitization of emotional responding does not require effortful cognition. It happens without children being aware of what is happening. Nevertheless, properly presented didactic material and persuasive arguments that engender "central, effortful" processing generally produce more enduring well-integrated cognitions that are resistant to change (Chaiken, Lieberman, & Eagly, 1989). Consequently, carefully scripted presentation about social relations such as those found on *Sesame Street, Mr. Rogers' Neighborhood,* or *Fat Albert and the Cosby Kids* may have enduring socialization effects on middle childhood youth (e.g., Hearold, 1986).

Cognitive changes in middle childhood make children more active processors of media information; they apply the schemas they have acquired and become more interested in the abstract, conceptual meanings of the material presented (Huston, 1983; Huston & Wright, 1989). They become more receptive during this period to the counter-stereotypic (or stereotypic) messages and nuanced perceptions provided by both shows directed at children (e.g., Freestyle, The Wonder Years) and adult programming (e.g., The Cosby Show, The Simpsons, Seinfeld, Friends). Counter-stereotypic messages received from the media during middle childhood (e.g., about alternative life styles) are probably particularly likely to be processed effortfully, resulting in more lasting effects.

MODERATORS OF MEDIA EFFECTS

The effects of media content on children are moderated by (a) characteristics of the presentation, including both form and content; (b) characteristics of the child and how these interact with characteristics of the presentation; and (c) characteristics of the physical and human context in which they are exposed to media. Presentations that do not attract a minimum level of attention will have little influence. Although effects can occur through peripheral processing without cognitive resources being devoted to processing the material in a presentation, they cannot occur without a minimal level of attention (Bandura, 1994).

During "viewing," on average, children look at the television set for less than 40% of the time, though attention increases across middle childhood (Anderson, 1986). Consequently, form and content factors that attract and maintain attention to a presentation are important in determining the magnitude of effects. Factors that facilitate attention for young children include action, special effects, and comprehensible speech; attention is lower when there is lack of movement, extended still shots, eye contact with the viewer, and male voices (Anderson & Burns, 1991; Comstock & Paik, 1991; Huston & Wright, 1989). The latter are all factors that might normally be part of didactic messages directed at an adult audience.

There are clear exceptions to these general patterns (e.g., Mr. Rogers' Neighborhood), and as children develop these formal features become less important. Children in middle childhood attend to the combination of attention-grabbing formal features – movement, music, change of scenes – with content that demands the application cognitive resources to assemble elements into a narrative (Comstock & Paik, 1991). The formal features are still important because children in middle childhood recognize that these formal features signal content of interest (Huston & Wright, 1997).

Once the child attends, individual characteristics interact with the content presented to affect the response. For example, children are more likely to imitate behaviors that are rewarded than those that are not (Bandura et al., 1963). For youth in middle childhood, who already have a conception of the world around them, material that "contrasts" too much with their existing conception will have less effect than material that they can assimilate into their world schemas (Lord, Ross, & Lepper, 1979).

This principle helps to explain why children who already tend to behave in certain ways are more likely increase that behavior in response to media content (Bushman & Huesmann, 2001). Material that is perceived as telling about the world like it really is has more effect than material perceived as pure fantasy (Huesmann & Eron, 1986). The behavior and beliefs of characters with whom the child identifies have more effect than the behaviors and beliefs of other characters (Huesmann, Moise-Titus, Podloski, & Eron, 2003; Leyens & Picus, 1973).

Elements of the setting in which the medium is encountered affect its power. Video games that are played as part of a peer network and that are viewed as accepted and normative have more influence than video games played in isolation (Williams, 2004). Parents who regulate and discuss the movies and TV shows that children view change the impact of those shows (Nathanson, 1999). In summary, the impacts of video games, movies, television, and other media on youth in middle childhood vary substantially depending on their presentation, individual child characteristics, and the social context of exposure.

INFLUENCES ON AGGRESSION AND ANTISOCIAL BEHAVIOR

The methods used to study the relation between media violence and aggression fall into three major classes: (a) experiments in which the researcher manipulates exposure to media violence; (b) correlational studies, or one-time observational studies, in which exposure to violence and concurrent aggressive behavior are measured with surveys or observations; and (c) longitudinal observational studies in which exposure and behavior are measured on the same sample repeatedly over long periods of time. It is critical to integrate the findings of all three methods in reaching any conclusion.

Experiments

Generally, experiments have demonstrated that exposing middle childhood youth to violent behavior on film and TV increases the likelihood that they will behave aggressively immediately afterwards (see reviews by Bushman & Huesmann, 2001; Geen and Thomas, 1986; Paik & Comstock, 1994). In the typical paradigm, randomly selected children are shown either a violent or nonviolent short film and are then observed as they play with each other or with objects such as Bo-Bo dolls. Children who see the violent film clip behave more aggressively immediately afterwards than those viewing nonviolence toward persons (Bjorkqvist, 1985; Josephson, 1987) and toward inanimate objects (Bandura, 1977). For example, Josephson (1987) randomly assigned 7- to 9-year-old boys to watch either a violent or a nonviolent film before they played a game of floor hockey in school. In some conditions, the referees carried a walkie-talkie, a specific cue that had appeared in the violent film, which was expected to remind the boys of the movie they had seen earlier. Among boys who scored above average on a measure of aggressiveness prior to the study, the combination of seeing a violent film and seeing the movie-associated cue stimulated significantly more assaultive behavior than any other combination of film and cue. The effect size was moderate ($r = .25$).

In experiments like this, causal effects have been demonstrated for children from preschool age to adolescence, for boys and girls, for Black children and white children, and for children who are normally aggressive and those who are normally nonaggressive. The average size of the immediate effect produced is about equivalent to a .40 correlation (Paik & Comstock, 1994). In these well-controlled laboratory studies there can be no doubt that it is the children's observation of the violence that is *causing* the changes in behavior. The question then becomes whether these causal effects observed in the laboratory generalize to children's everyday lives. That is, does media violence cause aggression not just in the short run, but in the long run as well?

Cross-Sectional and Longitudinal Studies

Empirical cross-sectional and longitudinal studies of children and youth behaving and watching media in their natural environments provide strong support that there are long-term effects on children's aggressive behavior. Although cross-sectional and longitudinal nonexperimental studies cannot establish causation, when coupled with the results from experiments, their results provide strong support for extending the causal conclusion demonstrated by the experiments.

The great majority of competently done one-time survey studies have shown that children who watch more media violence day in and day out behave more aggressively day in and day out (Paik & Comstock, 1994). The correlations obtained usually are between .15 and .30. Such correlations are not large by the standards of variance explained, but they are moderate by the standards of children's personality measurement, and they can have real social significance (Rosenthal, 1986). In fact, as Rosenthal has pointed out, a correlation of .30 translates into a change in the odds of aggression from 50/50 to 65/35 – not a trivial change. Moreover, the relation is highly replicable even across countries (Huesmann & Eron, 1986; Huesmann, Lagerspetz, & Eron, 1984).

Complementing these one-time survey studies are the longitudinal, nonexperimental studies that have shown correlations between childhood viewing of media violence and later adolescent or adult aggressive behavior (Eron, Huesmann, Lefkowitz, & Walder, 1972; Huesmann et al., 2003; Johnson, Cohen, Smailes, Kasen, & Brook, 2002; Slater, Henry, Swaim, & Anderson, 2003; for reviews see Huesmann & Miller, 1994; Huesmann, Moise, & Podolski, 1997). Analysis of longitudinal data has also shown that early habitual exposure to media violence *in middle childhood* predicts aggressiveness beyond what would be predicted from early aggressiveness.

For example, in their 1972 analysis of males from age 8 to age 19, Eron et al. (1972) showed that the correlation between a preference for viewing violent TV programs at age 8 and aggressive behavior 10 years later was .31. This correlation remained significant even when initial aggressiveness and many other demographic and personal variables (e.g., IQ) were statistically controlled. On the other hand, behaving aggressively in middle childhood did not predict higher subsequent viewing of violence, making it less likely that the correlation was due to aggressive children turning to more violence (Eron et al., 1972).

In a comprehensive three-wave study of children who were interviewed as they moved through middle childhood (ages 6–8 or 8–10), Huesmann and Eron (1986; Huesmann, Eron, & Lagerspetz, 1984) found higher rates of aggression for both boys and girls who watched more television violence even with controls for initial aggressiveness and many other background factors. Children who identified with the portrayed aggressor and those who perceived the violence as realistic were especially likely to show these observational learning effects.

A 15-year follow-up of these children (Huesmann et al., 2003) demonstrated that those who habitually watched more TV violence in their middle childhood years grew up to be more aggressive young adults. For example, male children who were in the upper quartile on violence viewing in middle childhood were more likely to have been convicted of a crime; to have "pushed, grabbed, or shoved their spouse" in the past year; and to have "shoved a person" when made angry in the past year compared to all other males in the study. Among females, high-violence viewers were more likely to have "thrown something at their spouse" in the past year; to have "punched, beaten, or choked" another adult when angry in the past year; and to report committing a crime in the past year. These effects were not attributable to any of a large set of child and parent characteristics including demographic factors, intelligence, and parenting practices. Although there was some tendency for children who were more aggressive in middle childhood to watch more violence in adulthood, the much larger effect was from watching violence in middle childhood to later aggressive behavior.

Another recent longitudinal study found similar bidirectional longitudinal effects for children moving from middle childhood into adolescence. Slater and colleagues (2003) obtained self-reports of violence viewing and aggressive thoughts, beliefs, and behaviors at four times between the middle of the sixth grade and the middle of the eighth grade. Growth curve analyses reveal significant effects of both contemporaneous and prior violence viewing on aggression, but use of violent media viewing was predicted only by contemporaneous aggression, not by prior aggression. At least one other longitudinal study has found a simple relation between the amount of general television viewing in late middle childhood or adolescence and subsequent aggression, but the mechanisms explaining these results remain obscure because content of the programs watched was not assessed (Johnson et al., 2002).

These longitudinal studies, when combined with current thinking about child development, suggest that middle childhood is a critical period for exposure to media violence to have lasting effects. The 7- to 11-year-old child has developed to the point where social cognitions related to aggression begin to be stable (Huesmann & Guerra, 1997). He or she is capable of processing the implied messages inherent in many of the violent shows about the acceptability of violence, and therefore of acquiring lasting scripts and schemas that promote violence. The aggressive behavior that results may make viewing violence on television even more likely because of the children's desire to justify their own behavior and the decreased popularity that aggression is likely to engender (Huesmann & Eron, 1986). This can produce a long-term downward spiral in behavior and viewing (Slater et al., 2003) continuing into adolescence and young adulthood. Although we do not have longitudinal studies that examine the lasting effects of exposure in earlier periods of a child's development, the existing longitudinal studies show that exposure between ages 6 and 11 has lasting effects consistent with this perspective. In contrast, there are few studies that show lasting effects for exposure to media violence for teenagers and young adults.

OBESITY AND BODY IMAGE

Television viewing is often implicated in the dramatic rise in obesity among Americans generally, and among children specifically because viewers are physically inactive and because advertising encourages consumption of calorie-dense foods. Research findings seem to support a relation between viewing and obesity in middle childhood, but there is controversy about the conclusions to be drawn. Similarly, anorexia and other eating disorders have become more prevalent among American female youth, and some have argued that the proliferation of ultrathin females in the media has contributed to this epidemic.

Theoretical Connections Between Television, Obesity, and Body Image Disorders

Obesity and eating disorders, like violence and aggression, are complex phenomena and are not caused by any single factor. Numerous biological and social factors promote or inhibit weight gain (for a review, see Yanovski & Yanovski, 1999). Any influence of television must be considered within a more complex framework; television is neither a necessary nor a sufficient cause of obesity or body image problems. It may be a contributing factor, though research is by no means unequivocal on the question.

Displacement of Activities and Obesity. The most commonly hypothesized mechanism by which television is believed to influence obesity is through time displacement. When children watch television, they are not engaged in physical activity; that sedentary behavior could increase the likelihood of obesity. If this is the case, more television viewing should be correlated with less physical activity, obesity, and poor physical fitness. Media influence is of particular concern because children in middle childhood spend more hours viewing television per day (three to four hours on average) than either adolescents or young adults (Comstock & Paik, 1991). Some scholars argue that television viewing is unlikely to displace physical activity because displacement occurs primarily between similar activities. Thus, passive entertainment like television viewing is most likely to displace other passive entertainment, such as reading, playing video games, or talking on the phone rather than highly active activities (see Neuman, 1995).

Learning and Obesity. The same processes that link media violence to real-life aggression may connect media content to obesity. Television, particularly for child audiences, is rife with commercial messages promoting unhealthy, sugar- and fat-laden foods (Kotz & Story, 1994; Taras & Gage, 1995). Children viewing messages presenting such foods as attractive, appealing, and even healthy may adopt positive attitudes and beliefs about such foods that would lead to greater consumption. Middle childhood is a critical period for shaping health-related attitudes and beliefs because attempts to establish patterns of healthful eating and exercise during this period are more durable than those undertaken later in life (Epstein, McCurley, Wing, & Valoski, 1990) and because obesity or being overweight in middle childhood is a strong predictor of adulthood obesity (Sorenson & Sonne-Holm, 1988).

Learning and Body Image. Television may influence children's body image. Television characters, especially women, tend to be thinner and more fit than typical Americans, and thinner characters are treated better than heavier characters (Fouts & Burggraf, 1999; Silverstein, Perdue, Peterson, & Kelly, 1986). Middle childhood viewers may learn that it is desirable to have a thin, fit body, and that any other body type is undesirable. Such beliefs and attitudes may translate into two very different behavior patterns among those whose bodies do not conform to the ideal. Some may diet or develop eating disorders; for others, reactance may intervene, leading to more (and less healthful) eating. Some individuals may simply respond to the stress of dissonance by eating; obesity researchers have observed that eating is a common response to distress, depression, and loneliness (Banis et al., 1988).

Television Viewing and Obesity: Empirical Data

Although the results of studies exploring the connections between television viewing and obesity are somewhat equivocal, they do suggest a relation between viewing television and being overweight or obese. A number of national studies employing representative sampling techniques have found that children who spend relatively more time watching television are more likely to be overweight or obese than their peers who watch less (Andersen, Crespo, Bartlett, Cheskin, & Pratt, 1998; Dietz & Gortmaker, 1985). This finding has been replicated with smaller, more homogenous yet widely diverse samples (Armstrong, Sallis, Alcaraz, Kolody, & McKenzie, 1998; Gable & Lutz, 2000). Some similar studies have found no relationship between television viewing and obesity (DuRant, Baranowski, Johnson, & Thompson, 1994; Robinson et al., 1993). Among these correlational studies, there is no readily apparent, systematic difference between studies that find significant relationships and those that do not.

Longitudinal studies exploring connections between television viewing during middle childhood and adolescent obesity are rare, and also yield mixed results. Some find a clear relation, with heavy television viewing during middle childhood predicting obesity even after controlling for numerous environmental factors (Gortmaker et al., 1996). Others find no relation (Robinson et al., 1993). No longitudinal analyses of the relation between early viewing and adult obesity are available. The question therefore remains, does viewing television cause obesity, or is it simply correlated with it for other reasons?

A single controlled field experiment suggests that television viewing causes obesity (Robinson, 1999). One group of third- and fourth-grade students in California was exposed to a school curriculum designed to decrease television viewing, while a matched group received no such curriculum. Compared to control students, those who received the intervention watched less television at the end of the study, as indicated by both self- and parental-report, and they also had decreases in Body Mass Index (BMI), skinfold, and other indicators of obesity, even when ethnicity and socioeconomic status were statistically controlled.

Television Viewing, Obesity, and Displacement of Physical Activity. Most research fails to support the time displacement hypothesis, that passive television viewing displaces more active activities, as an explanation for the correlation of viewing with obesity. Although some studies do confirm a correlation between television viewing and physical activity (DuRant et al., 1994; Robinson et al., 1993), such relations are weak and generally occur in studies that do not link television viewing to obesity. Most studies on obesity in middle childhood find no relation between physical activity or physical fitness and television viewing (Andersen et al., 1998; Armstrong et al., 1998; Gable & Lutz, 2000; Robinson, 1999).

Television Viewing, Obesity, Diet, and Nutrition. The alternative hypothesis, that television viewing may influence obesity in middle childhood by influencing children's diets, receives more support. In fact, children who view more television have been found to eat more sugar and junk food (Gable & Lutz, 2000), to have less accurate nutritional knowledge, and to make worse dietary choices (Ross, Campbell, Huston-Stein, & Wright, 1981; Signorielli & Lears, 1992b; Signorielli & Staples, 1997). Children who watch more television gain faulty knowledge about nutrition from commercials for processed foods. This influences their food choices, which in turn may lead to obesity. This process is more likely to occur for children who learned less about nutrition from other sources.

Television Viewing and Body Image: Empirical Data

During middle childhood, some children are clearly influenced by the images of bodies they see on television, but this influence depends on both the nature of the message and how children respond to it. In one study, when fourth- and sixth-grade girls were shown idealized images of women's bodies accompanied by messages that emphasized comparisons between viewers and the images, the girls believed themselves to be less attractive; when the messages emphasized viewers' attractiveness or ability to become attractive, girls perceived themselves as more attractive (Martin and Gentry, 1997). Another study found that early elementary-aged girls who find moderate-weight characters more appealing had fewer symptoms of eating disorders (Harrison, 2000).

Children's unfavorable comparisons of their own bodies with those they see on television could produce stress that leads to excessive dieting or excessive eating. Studies of adults have documented altered eating patterns immediately following exposure to media content that is emotionally provocative (Sheppard-Sawyer, McNally, & Fischer, 2000) or which depicts idealized body images (Harrison, Taylor, & Marske, 2004). Importantly, the way in which individuals respond to thin-ideal or emotionally provocative images is not uniform. In one study, normally restrained eaters increased their consumption of popcorn when watching an upsetting film (compared to a neutral film), although normally less restrained eaters decreased their consumption during the upsetting film (Sheppard-Sawyer et al., 2000). In response to idealized body images, some individuals increase their consumption of available snack foods, some decrease their consumption, and others seem unaffected, depending largely on sex and the size and nature of their self-discrepancies (Harrison et al., 2004).

Given the numerous factors that contribute to body composition, the increasing frequency of childhood obesity, the health risks associated with obesity, and data strongly suggesting a link between television viewing and increased risk of obesity, further research is clearly warranted. Although displacement effects have essentially been ruled out as explanations for the TV-obesity link, other explanations have been inadequately explored. Future research should consider the impact of television viewing on nutrition knowledge, body image, and eating. Further, researchers in this area would be well advised to adopt longitudinal methods, which could provide more clear answers to the role of these factors in a developmental context. Middle childhood is apparently a key time when eating behaviors are shaped; it is imperative that television's role in shaping them be clearly understood.

INFLUENCES OF MASS MEDIA ON STEREOTYPING IN MIDDLE CHILDHOOD

By observing how the world works on television, children develop systematic schemas about the workings of the world around them. Such schemas, when applied to a group of people identified by some salient characteristic, constitute stereotypes. It seems obvious that certain relatively unproblematic stereotypes are learned from television, particularly for groups with which children are unlikely to have extensive experience; such stereotypes may include beliefs that police officers wear uniforms and are helpful, that fire fighters are brave and friendly, or that doctors are intelligent and wear white coats. Other schemas or stereotypes are more problematic.

Television Viewing, Stereotyping, and Gender Roles

Middle childhood is a period of gender role dynamism. Although most children in this stage are well-versed in common gender stereotypes, over the course of middle childhood, changing cognitive abilities allow children to deal with exceptions to gender stereotypes and accommodate more individual information (Stoddart & Turiel, 1985). Theoretically, the schemas developed in childhood will be maintained or amplified throughout the lifespan unless they are meaningfully and persistently countered.

Television frequently depicts fairly rigid and traditional gender roles: Men are leaders and work in male-dominated professions; women are followers, nurturers, frequently employed in support positions or not employed outside the home (Campbell, Breed, Hoffman & Perlman, 2002; Signorielli, 1989; for reviews see Durkin, 1985; Signorielli, 1990). Children who view this content are likely to learn it, just as children who view violent television content are likely to learn aggression-supportive beliefs and attitudes. Because middle childhood is a time when schemas become increasingly nuanced and complex, children may also be receptive to alternative information.

Gender constancy – the certainty that gender is consistent across all situations – is an important developmental milestone usually achieved by age 6 or 7. Some argue that achieving gender constancy allows children to transgress gender stereotypes because they know that gender does not change with behavior (Huston, 1983). If this is the case, then children in middle childhood should be more susceptible than younger children to counter-stereotypical portrayals. Others argue the opposite: that children seek out ways to act consistently with their new certainty about gender (Ruble & Frey, 1991), making them particularly susceptible to gender stereotypes portrayed on television.

Television Viewing and Gender Stereotyping: Empirical Data

A meta-analysis of television viewing and stereotype endorsement concluded that television content contains many sex stereotypes and that there is a relation between viewing sex-stereotyped television and accepting sex stereotypes (Herrett-Skjellum and Allen, 1996). Children who are heavy viewers of television in middle childhood (25 hours or more per week) score significantly higher on measures of gender stereotypes than light viewers (10 hours or less per week), particularly stereotypes about males and appropriate male behaviors (Frueh & McGhee, 1975; McGhee & Frueh, 1980).

Television viewing is correlated with sex-stereotypic attitudes toward household chores. Children who watch more television see chores as more sex-typed than those who watch less, although viewing has no impact on what chores children do (Signorielli and Lears, 1992a). The latter finding does not challenge the influence of television on gender stereotypes, because parents may determine what chores children perform. Elementary school girls who watch relatively more television were more likely to associate negative attributes with female targets than girls who watch less television (Zuckerman, Singer, & Singer, 1980).

Experimental evidence also shows that sex stereotyping can be acquired from television viewing and that viewing can activate and reinforce stereotypes that have already been learned. For example, third graders watched television commercials that depicted women in traditional, stereotypical roles (e.g., serving men or preparing food for children) or women engaged in nontraditional roles (e.g., working as a doctor or farming). After viewing, both boys and girls who saw women in nontraditional roles scored higher on a scale evaluating women's competence and the appropriateness of women filling diverse roles than did children who viewed women in traditional, stereotyped roles (Pingree, 1978).

Even exposure to a single commercial has been shown to increase or decrease stereotyping. Ruble, Balaban, and Cooper (1981) showed 4- and 5-year-old children, who scored either high or low on a measure of gender constancy, a television commercial in which same-sex peers or opposite sex peers played with a gender-neutral toy. After viewing, children who were high in gender constancy spent much less time playing with the featured toy if they had seen the opposite-sex commercial as compared to the same-sex commercial or no commercial at all.

Counter-stereotypical or egalitarian portrayals on television can influence children as well. Perhaps the most notable demonstration is *Freestyle*, a television program developed specifically to challenge sex role stereotypes, particularly those relating to careers, held by children in fourth through sixth grades. This program, which was broadcast nationally and discussed as part of many school curricula, led children to be more accepting of diverse roles for women, especially when they discussed the programs in the classroom (Johnston & Ettema, 1982).

Overall, the research seems to support the notion that children learn schemas about what it means to be male or female from television, and that what they learn depends on what they see. Although a small group of correlational studies have found no such relation (Meyer, 1980; Perloff, 1977), there is ample correlational and experimental evidence that viewing television that is characterized by gender role stereotypes influences children's beliefs about appropriate gender roles, their reactions to characters who behave in ways which are consistent or inconsistent with those roles, and their own aspirations for the future. Although most television content tends to reinforce traditional stereotypes about women and men and their roles in society, counter-stereotypical content that offers attractive models can produce more progressive beliefs and attitudes among child viewers.

Television, Stereotyping, and Race

The same processes that underlie the influence of gender and sex-role stereotypical television content apply to racial and ethnic stereotypes. Although very little research has been conducted which explicitly examines whether viewing television influences the nature of children's schemas about members of other ethnic or racial groups, there is abundant reason to predict that such influence may occur.

Children who have relatively little direct experience with members of other racial and ethnic groups in particular likely form schemas based on media depictions. Content analyses have shown that African Americans are disproportionately depicted as criminals in the news (Dixon & Linz, 2000), as aggressive or irrelevant in advertisements (Coltraine & Messineo, 2000), and as overweight in situation comedies (Tirodkar & Jain, 2003). At the same time, families of color are nearly as prevalent on television as they are in the population of the United States, and those families are diverse in their structure, makeup, and socioeconomic status (Dates & Stroman, 2001). Because there are no systematic content analyses of racial depictions in recent children's television programs clearly more research is needed to identify what information about issues pertaining to race and ethnicity are embedded in such programs.

There is some evidence that children learn racial stereotypes during middle childhood from what they see on television. For example, in one survey, children in third through fifth grades who watched more violent programs tended to endorse stereotypes of Blacks as less competent, and those who watched more programs with predominantly Black casts were more likely to endorse stereotypes of Blacks as superior athletes (Zuckerman et al., 1980). Viewing comedies, dramas, and sports programs was unrelated to racial stereotyping and prejudice.

Children, especially minority children, also learn from portrayals of members of their own racial or ethnic groups on television. Minority children who view more television would be expected to learn from the depictions of race and ethnicity they see. Although depictions of African Americans on television is clearly problematic, there are some indications that viewing more television featuring Black casts predicts relatively higher self-esteem among Black children, but viewing other types of television does not (McDermott & Greenberg, 1984; Stroman, 1986).

Children can and do acquire stereotypes from television during middle childhood. Evidence is strongest for stereotypes about gender but probably holds for stereotypes about race as well. What children learn, however, is strongly dependent on content; counter-stereotypical content can produce counter-stereotypical beliefs and attitudes. Middle childhood is probably a particularly key time for acquiring stereotypes for much the same reason that it is a key time for acquiring aggressive and prosocial behaviors from the mass media. It is during middle childhood that social schemas, scripts, and normative or moral beliefs crystallize, become relatively stable and resistant to change, and begin to predict subsequent behavior. The mass media have powerful influences on such social cognitions at any time, but these influences are most likely to be lasting when they occur in middle childhood.

INFLUENCE OF THE MEDIA ON LEARNING AND ACADEMIC PERFORMANCE

Television is often blamed for lowering children's academic achievement. According to displacement theory, television viewing replaces more intellectually valuable activities, such as reading and homework. However, most evidence shows that, although television and video games may displace some leisure reading in middle childhood, they are more likely to displace movie viewing and radio listening, leaving reading and homework time fairly intact (Neuman, 1988). Television content may teach children to place less value on academic achievement and greater emphasis on other endeavors that are rewarded in the world of television. Television viewing may also directly impair children's ability to focus or engage in mental work (Harris, 1994).

Television and School Achievement: Empirical Data

Though few studies have been undertaken to examine their effects, available evidence shows that educational television programs developed for middle childhood audiences are successful in improving their viewers' problem solving abilities (Hall, Esty, & Fisch, 1990) and science knowledge (Clifford, Gunter, & McAleer, 1995; Goodman, Rylander, & Ross, 1993, as cited in Huston & Wright, 1997). Children can and do learn when they watch educational television which is designed for them.

   Most research on television and learning largely ignores the question of content, however, instead addressing the broad question of whether overall television viewing is linked to diminished academic performance. Some studies fail to find a correlation (Anderson & Maguire, 1978), but much of this research suggests a negative correlation between time spent viewing television during middle childhood and school grades (Ridley-Johnson, Cooper, & Chance, 1983), IQ (Gortmaker, Salter, Walker, & Dietz, 1990), or other measures of intellectual achievement (Neuman, 1988). For example, a study of over 200,000 sixth graders in California revealed a linear decline in achievement test scores as time spent watching TV increased (Comstock & Paik, 1991). The decrement related to TV viewing was greatest for children from higher SES families.

Viewed on a larger scale, the relation between television viewing and academic performance is more complex. Using very large data sets, two studies found that, at low levels of viewing, viewing time is positively correlated with academic achievement. Negative relations were observed only for children who spend a great deal of time watching television (more than 25 hours each week), though "optimal" viewing amounts are much less (closer to 10 hours each week) (Neuman, 1995; Razel, 2001).

The question of whether excessive television viewing actually *causes* diminished academic performance has received less attention (for a review, see Huston & Wright, 1997). One longitudinal analysis of a national, representative sample found that television viewing during middle childhood did not predict IQ or performance on measures of reading and math ability in early adolescence after longitudinal controls were applied (Gortmaker, Salter, Walker, & Dietz, 1990). Displacement of academic activities has not been supported as a cause for the relationship between television viewing and academic achievement; in field studies comparing children in communities with and without television, Schramm, Lyle, and Parker (1961) observed only trivial differences in time spent reading or doing homework. Instead, such factors as parents' TV or reading habits predict both television viewing and academic performance (e.g., Neuman, 1995).

Although inadequate research on television's impact on academic performance is available for children in middle childhood, available research suggests that heavy entertainment television viewing during middle childhood is generally associated with diminished academic and intellectual performance. Television *can* be informative and educational, but very little of it is.

CONCLUSIONS

Exposure to television has a major impact on children's behaviors, beliefs, and achievement during middle childhood. Moreover, the impact of the mass media during middle childhood lasts into adolescence and adulthood. Children learn aggressive behaviors and positive attitudes about aggression from viewing television violence and playing violent video games in middle childhood; what they learn influences their behavior as adults. Children learn about gender roles from television and movies (and probably video games) and acquire more or less egalitarian gender role beliefs depending on what they watch. Children acquire gender and ethnic stereotypes from the mass media, and these stereotypes affect their judgments and behaviors. On the positive side, middle childhood is also the period when mass media counter-stereotypical portrayals can effectively influence children, and prosocial portrayals can effectively stimulate lasting prosocial tendencies.

In other domains of development, the nature of media influence is more ambiguous or less well understood. There is an association between watching large amounts of television and being overweight or obese, but we do not know precisely why. There are links between academic performance and television viewing, but the relation is complex. Despite these gaps in our knowledge, the existing research demonstrates that mass media are among the most influential elements in a child's environment during middle childhood, and they cannot be ignored.

References

Andersen, R. E., Crespo, C. J., Bartlett, S. J., Cheskin, L. J., & Pratt, M. (1998). Relationship of physical activity and television watching with body weight and level of fatness among children. *JAMA, 279*(12), 938–942.

Anderson, C. A., Berkowitz, L., Donnerstein, E., Huesmann, L. R., Johnson, J., Linz, D., et al. (2003). The influence of media violence on youth. *Psychological Science in the Public Interest, 4*(3), 81–110.

Anderson, C. A., & Huesmann, L. R. (2003). Human aggression: A social-cognitive view (pp. 296–323). In M. A. Hogg & J. Cooper (Eds.), *Handbook of social psychology.* Thousand Oaks, CA: Sage Publications.

Anderson, C. C., & Maguire, T. O. (1978). The effect of TV viewing on the educational performance of elementary school children. *Alberta Journal of Educational Research, 24*(3), 156–163.

Anderson, D. R. (1986). Television viewing at home: Age trends in visual attention and time with TV. *Child Development, 57*(4), 1024–1033.

Anderson, D. R., & Burns, J. (1991). Paying attention to television. In J. Bryant & D. Zillmann (Eds.), *Responding to the screen: Reception and reaction processes* (pp. 3–25). Hillsdale, NJ: Lawrence Erlbaum Associates.

Armstrong, C. A., Sallis, J. F., Alcaraz, J. E., Kolody, B., & McKenzie, T. L. (1998). Children's television viewing, body fat, and physical fitness. *American Journal of Health Promotion, 12*(6), 363–368.

Bandura, A. (1977). *Social learning theory.* New York: Prentice-Hall.

Bandura, A. (1986). *Social foundations of thought and action: A social cognitive theory.* Upper Saddle River, NJ: Prentice-Hall, Inc.

Bandura, A. (1994). Social cognitive theory of mass media. In J. Bryant & D. Zillmann (Eds.), *Media effects: Advances in theory and research* (pp. 61–90). Hillsdale, NJ: Lawrence Erlbaum Associates.

Bandura, A., Ross, D., & Ross, S. A. (1963). Imitation of film-mediated aggressive models. *Journal of Abnormal and Social Psychology, 66*, 3–11.

Banis, H. T., Varni, J. W., Wallander, J. L., Korsch, B. M., Jay, S. M., Adler, R., et al. (1988). Psychological and social adjustment of obese children and their families. *Child: Care, Health, and Development, 14*, 157–173.

Berkowitz, L. (1993). *Aggression: Its causes, consequences, and control.* Boston: McGraw Hill.

Berkowitz, L., & LePage, A. (1967). Weapons as aggression-eliciting stimuli. *Journal of Personality and Social Psychology, 7*(2), 202–207.

Bjorkqvist, K. (1985). *Violent films, anxiety, and aggression.* Helsinki: Finnish Society of Sciences and Letters.

Bryant, J., & Zillmann, D. (1979). Effect of intensification of annoyance through unrelated residual excitation on substantially delayed hostile behavior. *Journal of Experimental Social Psychology, 15*(5), 470–480.

Bushman, B. J., & Huesmann, L. R. (2001). Effects of televised violence on aggression. In D. Singer & J. Singer (Eds.), *Handbook of children and the media* (pp. 223–254). Thousand Oaks, CA: Sage Publications.

Campbell, L., Breed, L., Hoffman, L., & Perlman, C. A. (2002). Variations in the gender-stereotyped content of children's television cartoons across genres. *Journal of Applied Social Psychology, 32*(8), 1653–1662.

Cantor, J. (1994). Confronting children's fright responses to mass media. In D. Zillmann & J. Bryant (Eds.), *Media, children, and the family: Social scientific, psychodynamic, and clinical perspectives* (pp. 139–150). Hillsdale, NJ: Lawrence Erlbaum Associates.

Cantor, J. (2002). Fright reactions to mass media. In J. Bryant & D. Zillmann (Eds.), *Media effects: Advances in theory and research* (2nd ed., pp. 287–306). Mahwah, NJ: Lawrence Erlbaum Associates.

Chaiken, S., Lieberman, A., & Eagly, A. H. (1989). Heuristic and systematic processing within and beyond the persuasion context. In J. Uleman & J. Bargh (Eds.), *Unintended thought* (pp. 212–252). New York: Guilford Press.

Clifford, B. R., Gunter, B., & McAleer, J. (1995). *Television and children: Program evaluation, comprehension, and impact.* Hillsdale, NJ: Lawrence Erlbaum Associates.

Cline, V. B., Croft, R. G., & Courrier, S. (1973). Desensitization of children to television violence. *Journal of Personality & Social Psychology, 27*(3), 360–365.

Coltraine, S., & Messineo, M. (2000). The perpetuation of subtle prejudice: Race and gender imagery in 1990s television advertising. *Sex Roles, 42*(5/6), 363–389.

Comstock, G., & Paik, H. (1991). *Television and the American child.* San Diego, CA: Academic Press.

Dates, J. L., & Stroman, C. A. (2001). Portrayals of families of color on television. In J. Bryant (Ed.), *Television and the American family,* (pp. 207–228). Mahwah, NJ: Lawrence Erlbaum Associates.

Davidson, E. S., Yasuna, A., & Tower, A. (1979). The effects of television cartoons on sex-role stereotyping in young girls. *Child Development, 50,* 597–600.

Dietz, W. H., & Gortmaker, S. L. (1985). Do we fatten our children at the television set? Obesity and television viewing in children and adolescents. *Pediatrics, 75,* 807–812.

Dixon, T. L., & Linz, D. (2000). Overrepresentation and underrepresentation of African Americans and Latinos as lawbreakers on television news. *Journal of Communication, 50*(2), 131–154.

DuRant, R. H., Baranowski, T., Johnson, M., & Thompson, W. O. (1994). The relationship among television watching, physical activity, and body composition of young children. *Pediatrics, 94,* 449–455.

Durkin, K. (1985). Television and sex-role acquisition 1: Content. *British Journal of Social Psychology, 24,* 101–113.

Epstein, L. H., McCurley, J., Wing, R. R., & Valoski, A. (1990). Five-year follow-up of family-based treatments for childhood obesity. *Journal of Consulting and Clinical Psychology, 58,* 661–664.

Eron, L. D., Huesmann, L. R., Lefkowitz, M. M., & Walder, L. O. (1972). Does television violence cause aggression? *American Psychologist, 27*(4), 253–263.

Fagot, B. I., & Leinbach, M. D. (1989). The young child's gender schema: Environmental input, internal organization. *Child Development, 60,* 663–672.

Fouts, G., & Burggraf, K. (1999). Television situation comedies: Female body images and verbal reinforcements. *Sex roles, 40*(5), 473–481.

Frueh, T., & McGhee, P. E. (1975). Traditional sex role development and amount of time spent watching television. *Developmental Psychology, 11,* 109.

Gable, S., & Lutz, S. (2000). Household, parent, and child contributions to childhood obesity. *Family Relations, 49*(3), 293–300.

Geen, R. G., & O'Neal, E. C. (1969). Activation of cue-elicited aggression by general arousal. *Journal of Personality & Social Psychology, 11*(3), 289–292.

Geen, R. G., & Thomas, S. L. (1986). The immediate effects of media violence on behavior. *Journal of Social Issues, 42*(3), 7–27.

Gortmaker, S. L., Must, A., Sobol, A. M., Peterson, K., Colditz, G. A., & Dietz, W. H. (1996). Television viewing as a cause of increasing obesity among children in the United States, 1986–1990. *Archives of Pediatrics & Adolescent Medicine. 150*(4), 356–362.

Gortmaker, S. L., Salter, C. A., Walker, D. K., & Dietz, W. H. (1990). The impact of television viewing on mental aptitude and achievement: A longitudinal study. *Public Opinion Quarterly, 54*(4), 594–604.

Hall, E. R., Esty, E. T., & Fisch, S. M. (1990). Television and children's problem-solving behavior: A synopsis of an evaluation of the effects of Square One TV. *Journal of Mathematical Behavior, 9*(2), 161–174.

Harris, R. J. (1994). *A cognitive psychology of mass communication.* Hillsdale, NJ: Lawrence Erlbaum Associates.

Harrison, K. (2000). Television viewing, fat stereotyping, body shape standards, and eating disorder symptomatology in grade school children. *Communication Research, 27*(5), 617–640.

Harrison, K., & Cantor, J. (1999). Tales from the screen: Enduring fright reactions to scary media. *Media Psychology, 1*(2), 97–116.

Harrison, K., Taylor, L. D., & Marske, A. L. (2004, May). *Never say diet (in front of the guys): Women's and men's eating behavior following exposure to ideal-body images and text.* Paper presented at the annual meeting of the International Communication Association, New Orleans, LA.

Hearold, S. (1986). A synthesis of 1043 effects of television on social behaviour. In G. Comstock (Ed.), *Public communications and behaviour: Vol. I.* New York: Academic Press.

Herrett-Skjellum, J., & Allen, M. (1996). Television programming and sex stereotyping: A meta-analysis. In B. R. Burleson (Ed), *Communication yearbook 19* (pp. 157–185). Thousand Oaks, CA: Sage Publications.

Huesmann, L. R. (1988). An information processing model for the development of aggression. *Aggressive Behavior, 14*(1), 13–24.

Huesmann, L. R. (1998). The role of social information processing and cognitive schema in the acquisition and maintenance of habitual aggressive behavior. In R. G. Geen & E. Donnerstein (Eds.), *Human aggression: Theories, research, and implications for social policy* (73–109). San Diego, CA: Academic Press.

Huesmann, L. R. (2005). Imitation and the effects of observing media violence on behavior. In S. Hurley & N. Chater (Eds.), *Perspectives on imitation: From mirror neurons to memes*. Cambridge, MA: MIT Press.

Huesmann, L. R., & Eron, L. D. (Eds.). (1986). *Television and the aggressive child: A cross national perspective*. Hillsdale, NJ: Lawrence Erlbaum Associates.

Huesmann, L. R., & Guerra, N. (1997). Children's normative beliefs about aggression and aggressive behavior. *Journal of Personality and Social Psychology, 72*(2), 408–419.

Huesmann, L. R., Lagerspetz, K., & Eron, L. D. (1984). Intervening variables in the TV violence-aggression relation: Evidence from two countries. *Developmental Psychology, 20*(5), 746–775.

Huesmann, L. R., & Miller, L. S. (1994). Long-term effects of repeated exposure to media violence in childhood. In L. R. Huesmann (Ed.), *Aggressive behavior: Current perspectives* (pp. 153–186). New York: Plenum Press.

Huesmann, L. R., Moise-Titus, J., & Podolski, C. (1997). The effects of media violence on the development of antisocial behavior. In D. Stoff, J. Breiling, & J. Maser (Eds.), *Handbook of antisocial behavior* (pp. 181–193). New York: John Wiley.

Huesmann, L. R., Moise-Titus, J., Podolski, C., & Eron, L. (2003). Longitudinal relations between children's exposure to TV violence and their aggressive and violent behavior in young adulthood: 1977–1992. *Developmental Psychology, 39*(2), 201–221.

Huston, A. C. (1983). Sex-typing. In E. M Hetherington (Ed.), *Handbook of child psychology: Vol 4. Socialization, personality, and social development* (4th ed.) (pp. 387–467). New York: Wiley.

Huston, A. C., & Wright, J. C. (1997). Mass media and children's development. In W. Damon (Series Ed.), I. Sigel, & A. Renniger (Vol. Eds.), *Handbook of child psychology: Vol 4. Child psychology in practice* (5th ed., pp. 999–1058). New York: Wiley.

Huston, A. C., & Wright, J. C. (1989). The forms of television and the child viewer. In G. A. Comstock (Ed.), *Public communication and behavior: Vol. 2* (pp. 103–158). New York: Academic Press.

Johnson, J. G., Cohen, P., Smailes, E. M., Kasen, S., & Brook, J. S. (2002). Television viewing and aggressive behavior during adolescence and adulthood. *Science, 295*, 2468–2471.

Johnston, J., & Ettema, J. S. (1982). *Positive images: Breaking stereotypes with children's television*. Beverly Hills, CA: Sage.

Josephson, W. L. (1987). Television violence and children's aggression: Testing the priming, social script, and disinhibition predictions. *Journal of Personality & Social Psychology, 53*(5), 882–890.

Kotz, K., & Story, M. (1994). Food advertisements during children's Saturday morning television programming: Are they consistent with dietary recommendations? *Journal of the American Dietetic Association, 94*(11), 1296–1300.

Leyens, J. P., & Picus, S. (1973). Identification with the winner of a fight and name mediation: Their differential effects upon subsequent aggressive behaviour. *British Journal of Social & Clinical Psychology, 12*(4), 374–377.

Lord, C. G., Ross, L., & Lepper, M. R. (1979). Biased assimilation and attitude polarization: The effects of prior theories on subsequently considered evidence. *Journal of Personality & Social Psychology, 37*(11), 2098–2109.

Martin, M. C., & Gentry, J. W. (1997). Stuck in the model trap: The effects of beautiful models in ads on female pre-adolescents and adolescents. *The Journal of Advertising, 26*(2), 19–33.

McDermott, S., & Greenberg, B S. (1984). Black children's esteem: Parents, peers, and television. In R. N. Bostrom (Ed.), *Communication yearbook 8* (pp. 164–177). Beverly Hills, CA: Sage.

McGhee, P. E., & Frueh, T. (1980). Television viewing and the learning of sex-role stereotypes. *Sex Roles, 6*(2), 179–188.

Meyer, B. (1980). The development of girls' sex-role attitudes. *Child Development, 51,* 508–514.

Moise-Titus, J. (1999). *The role of negative emotions in the media violence-aggression relation.* Unpublished dissertation, University of Michigan, Ann Arbor.

Nathanson, A. (1999). Identifying and explaining the relationship between parental mediation and children's aggression. *Communication Research, 26*(2), 124– 143.

Neuman, S. B. (1988). The displacement effect: Assessing the relation between television viewing and reading performance. *Reading Research Quarterly, 23*(4), 414–440.

Neuman, S. B. (1995). *Literacy in the television age: The myth of the TV effect* (2nd ed.). Norwood, NJ: Ablex.

Paik, H., & Comstock, G. (1994). The effects of television violence on antisocial behavior: A meta-analysis. *Communication Research, 21*(4), 516–546.

Palmer, E. L., & Young, B. M. (Eds.). (2003). *The faces of televisual media: Teaching, violence, selling to children* (2nd ed.). Mahwah, NJ: Lawrence Erlbaum Associates.

Perloff, R. M. (1977). Some antecedents of children's sex-role stereotypes. *Psychological Reports, 40,* 947–955.

Pingree, S. (1978). The effects of nonsexist television commercials and perceptions of reality on children's attitudes about women. *Psychology of Women Quarterly, 2*(3), 262–277.

Razel, M. (2001). The complex model of television viewing and educational achievement. *The Journal of Educational Research, 94*(6), 371–379.

Ridley-Johnson, R., Cooper, H., & Chance, J. (1983). The relation of children's television viewing to school achievement and I. Q. *Journal of Educational Research, 76*(5), 294–297.

Robinson, T. N. (1999). Reducing children's television viewing to prevent obesity: A randomized controlled trial. *JAMA, 282*(16), 1561–1567.

Robinson, T. N., Hammer, L. D., Killen, J. D., Kraemer, H. C., Wilson, D. M., Hayward, C., & Taylor, C. B. (1993). Does television viewing increase obesity and reduce physical activity? Cross-sectional and longitudinal analyses among adolescent girls. *Pediatrics, 91,* 273–280.

Rosenthal, R. (1986). Media violence, antisocial behavior, and the social consequences of small effects. *Journal of Social Issues, 42*(3), 141–154.

Ross, R. P., Campbell, T., Huston-Stein, A., & Wright, J. C. (1981). Nutritional misinformation of children: A developmental and experimental analysis of the effects of televised food commercials. *Journal of Applied Developmental Psychology, 1*(4), 329–347.

Ruble, D. N., Balaban, T., & Cooper, J. (1981). Gender constancy and the effects of sex-typed televised toy commercials. *Child Development, 52,* 667–673.

Ruble, D. N., & Frey, K. S. (1991). Changing patterns of comparative behavior as skills are acquired: A functional model of self-evaluation. In J. Suls & T. Wils (Eds.), *Social comparison: Contemporary theory and research* (pp. 79–116). Hillsdale, NJ: Lawrence Erlbaum Associates.

Schramm, W., Lyle, J., & Parker, E. (1961). *Television in the lives of our children.* Stanford, CA: Stanford University Press.

Sheppard-Sawyer, C. L., McNally, R. J., & Fischer, J. H. (2000). Film-induced sadness as a trigger for disinhibited eating. *International Journal of Eating Disorders, 28*(2), 215–220.

Signorielli, N. (1989). Television and conceptions about sex roles: Maintaining conventionality and the status quo. *Sex Roles, 21*(5/6), 341–360.

Signorielli, N. (1990). Children, television, and gender roles: Messages and impact. *Journal of Adolescent Health Care, 11*(1), 50–58.

Signorielli, N., & Lears, M. (1992a). Children, television, and conceptions about chores: Attitudes and behaviors. *Sex Roles, 27*(3/4), 157–170.

Signorielli, N., & Lears, M. (1992b). Television and children's conceptions of nutrition: Unhealthy messages. *Health Communication, 4,* 245–257.

Signorielli, N., & Staples, J. (1997). Television and children's conceptions of nutrition. *Health Communication, 9*(4), 289–301.

Silverstein, L., Perdue, L., Peterson, B., & Kelly, I. (1986). The role of mass media in promoting a thin standard of bodily attractiveness for women. *Sex Roles, 14,* 519–532.

Singer, D. G., & Singer, J. L. (Eds.). (2001). *Handbook of children and the media.* Thousand Oaks, CA: Sage Publications.

Slater, M. D., Henry, K. L., Swaim, R. C., & Anderson, L. L. (2003). Violent media content and aggressiveness in adolescents: A downward spiral model. *Communication Research, 30*(6), 713–736.

Sorensen, T. I., & Sonne-Holm, S. (1988). Risk in childhood of development of severe adult obesity: Retrospective, population-based case-cohort study. *American Journal of Epidemiology, 127*(1), 104–113.

Stoddart, T., & Turiel, E. (1985). Children's concepts of cross-gender activities. *Child Development, 56,* 1241–1252.

Stroman, C. A. (1986). Television viewing and self-concept among Black children. *Journal of Broadcasting and Electronic Media, 30*(1), 87–93.

Taras, H. L., & Gage, M. (1995). Advertised foods on children's television. *Archives of Pediatric and Adolescent Medicine, 149,* 649–652.

Tirodkar, M. A., & Jain, A. (2003). Food messages on African American television shows. *American Journal of Public Health, 93*(3), 439–441.

Valentino, N. A., Traugott, M., & Hutchings, V. (2002). Group cues and ideological constraint: A replication of political advertising effects studies in the lab and in the field. *Political Communication, 19*(1), 29–48.

Williams, D. (2004). Trouble in River City: The social life of video games. *Dissertation Abstracts*. AAT3122072, PROQUEST.UMI.COM.

Yanovski, J. A., & Yanovski, S. Z. (1999). Recent advances in basic obesity research. *JAMA*, 282(16), 1504–1506.

Zajonc, R. B., Murphy, S. T., & Inglehart, M. (1989). Feeling and facial efference: Implications of the vascular theory of emotion. *Psychological Review*, 96, 395–416.

Zuckerman, D. M., Singer, D. G., & Singer, J. L. (1980). Children's television viewing, racial and sex-role attitudes. *Journal of Applied Social Psychology*, 10(4), 281–294.

16

Continuity and Discontinuity in Middle Childhood

Implications for Adult Outcomes in the
UK 1970 Birth Cohort

Leon Feinstein and John Bynner

There is a large body of evidence pointing to the importance of the early years of life, in laying the foundations for later childhood development and adult outcomes. The early years – by which we mean the period from birth to age 5 – encompass infancy and the preschool period before kindergarten and formal schooling begin. It is a period of far greater change in apparent abilities, propensities, and physical constitution and brain development than at any other time (Caviness, Philipek, & Kennedy, 1993). The basic elements of cognitive and behavioral functioning are set down during this period as are the more intangible elements of development bound up with "risk" and "protection" (Rutter, 1990; Brooks-Gunn, Duncan, & Maritato, 1997; Bynner, 2001; Schoon et al., 2002). These include family circumstances and the behavior and values of parents as well as the individual attributes of children concerned with disposition and temperament through which personality is formed. Such characteristics lie at the heart of children's resilience or vulnerability to adversity on which much subsequent success will depend.

For these reasons, much attention has been given to interventions in the early years that halt or reverse the negative processes that will impede performance on entry into school. Such initiatives as Early Head Start in the United States and Sure Start in Great Britain (Glass, 1999) reflect the well-established belief in policy circles that the earlier intervention begins, the greater the returns to government investment, reinforcing the personal and external resources that children bring with them into the school age period (Schweinhart, Barnes, & Weikart, 1993).

Although the significance of preschool experience is undeniable, what follows it in middle childhood has been given less attention, perhaps because the institutionalized aspects of early schooling are often seen as offering less scope for individually based interaction. What Kagan (1998) describes as "the lure of infant determinism" tends to mask the continuing importance of the interactions between children and their social and physical environments that extends throughout childhood and beyond (Schaffer, 2002). It is through these interactions that the initial foundations of educational achievement are realized, or fail to be realized, and when the gap between disadvantaged children's family lives and the educational process may begin to emerge. This is also the period when children's social interactions with peers and teachers begin to replace those within the family in shaping development. School entry also offers opportunities for inhibiting, and in some cases reversing, negative processes set in motion earlier. Thus, a supportive school environment and committed teachers have been identified as key factors in the "escape from disadvantage" (Pilling, 1990; Werner, 1989).

The early years matter tremendously, but the critical policy question remains: In what form and in what quantity should resources be allocated across childhood and in the life course more generally? Withdrawal of support may appear to be justified if the intervention has achieved a lasting resilience or capability in the child that enables him or her to overcome subsequent environmental threats, but such an achievement would be a large claim for even the most ardent proponents of early interventions. It is clear therefore that some kind of persistence of intervention is essential from a theoretical as well as an empirical standpoint (as discussed for example in Ramey & Ramey, 2000). In this chapter we use the unique longitudinal research sources supplied by the 1970 British Cohort Study to examine the key features of child development during middle childhood (Ferri, Bynner, & Wadsworth, 2003).

THE LIFE COURSE PERSPECTIVE

Developmental psychologists differ between those who (a) emphasize "stages of development," which imply a degree of homogeneity in progress in the cognitive behavioral and affective domains, and (b) those who emphasize "specificity," that is, interactions but not necessarily strong correlations between the timing and sequencing of developmental processes across the different domains (Hartup, 2002). The life span and life course developmental conceptions embrace the two perspectives by stressing the impact of changing contexts on the timing and sequencing of developmental transitions in different domains, including those brought about through social and economic change (Elder, 1998; Lerner, 1996).

In this last scenario, which forms the basis of our own research approach, patterns of adaptation established earlier dispose the individual towards later success or failure through a series of dynamic interactions between individually and environmentally based characteristics. Thus, risk and protective factors, though increasing the probability of particular negative or positive outcomes, also display a degree of fluidity. Given the right circumstances, negative or positive developmental processes are, to an extent, reversible. As Clarke and Clarke (1998) put it, "probabilities are not certainties and deflections of the life path, for good or ill, are always possible, although always within the powerful limits imposed by genetic, constitutional and social trajectories" (p. 102). Such a conception also shifts the focus away from a relatively passive role for the individual towards that of an active agent, both actively seeking, as well as reacting to, the proximal and distal features of the environment (Bronfenbrenner, 1979). In this sense, revealed differences in cognitive, behavioral, and temperamental attributes (the whole personality) underlie the differentiation in response and adaptation patterns (Caspi, Elder, & Herbener, 1990).

A life course conception sets the parameters of the analysis reported here and the variables needed to operationalize the life span developmental theory, which it espouses. To understand the long-term effect of developmental processes in middle childhood, we need to be able to chart the trajectories across middle childhood in the domains of cognitive functioning and behavior, taking account of development and its long term outcomes up to adulthood. Using British longitudinal data collected from birth to adulthood, the focus of the analysis reported here is on continuities and discontinuities in the developmental processes involved in cognitive performance and maladjusted behavior patterns. We also take into account socioeconomic status and gender.

Our life span developmental orientation extends to anticipating differential effects of childhood developmental processes in the different domains of adult life. Thus, although the predictive capability of cognitive performance at different stages is well established with respect to economic outcomes (see Card, 1999), much less is known about the social or "wider" benefits (although see Hammond, 2002, for a review of the literature on health effects; Feinstein, 2002, for effects on crime; and Davis-Keen & Magnuson, in press, for a review of intergenerational effects).

Behavioral adjustment in childhood has similarly been shown to have long-term consequences in the economic and social spheres of later life. Conduct disorder predicts problems in entry to the labor market, seen as a crucial threshold in adolescent development (Caspi, Moffitt, Entner Wright, & Silva, 1998; Sanford et al., 1993), as well as trouble with the law of various kinds (Farrington, 2000; Moffit & Harrington, 1996; Robins & Rutter, 1990). Behavioral problems are often signs of underlying emotional or environmental problems that may themselves have repercussions for subsequent development and impact on adult outcomes. This may be because of the effect antisocial ("externalizing") behavior has on the attributions of others, such as teachers. The consequence can be exclusion from school, trouble with the police, and other forms of conflict with authority, possibly with long-term effects. Other kinds of behavior problems remain more "internalized" with later manifestations more likely in the form of maladjusted personality and psychiatric difficulties than challenges to social cohesion.

In this chapter, we address three major questions regarding the continuity and change in cognitive and behavioral development from early childhood to adulthood: (a) What are the relations between early cognitive and behavior scores and adult outcomes? (b) How stable are cognitive performance and behavior problems during middle childhood? (c) What are the implications of change during middle childhood for adult outcomes?

METHOD

Participants

The British Cohort Study 1970 (BCS70) data set is particularly suited to our research purposes. This longitudinal study comprises data collected from all 17,500 individuals born in the United Kingdom the week of April 5–11, 1970. Data have been collected in follow-up surveys at ages 5, 10, 16, 26, and most recently 30, with the scope of data collection reflecting the stage of life reached.

Childhood measures of cognitive functioning are included, together with the mother-reported Rutter inventory (Rutter, 1967), broadly categorized in terms of externalizing and internalizing behaviors. Measures of the family's socioeconomic status are assessed from parents' occupation at the time of the child's birth. In the United Kingdom, this measure is often used in isolation from family income and education, though strongly correlated with those factors (Feinstein, 2003).

To enable identification of developmental continuities and discontinuities, we restrict attention to those early childhood (age 5) measures that are repeated in middle childhood (age 10). Clearly, the precise meaning of these variables and, consequently, their validity for our analytic purposes are problematic. Variables were selected on the grounds of broad functional equivalence across time. Adult life data include current statuses and event histories in the domains of education, training and employment, family, housing, income, health and health-related behavior, citizenship, and values.

Measures of Cognitive Development

The age-10 math test was created by the Department of Child Health, Bristol University, which supervised the surveys in 1975 and 1980 (see Butler, Haslum, Barker, & Morris, 1982). The age-10 reading test is the Edinburgh Reading Test. Both show good properties of discrimination. The tests of math and reading ability would not be meaningful at age 5 and were not given. Instead, children's general cognitive ability was tested using human figure drawing tests (Koppitz, 1968; Harris, 1963), the English Picture Vocabulary Test (Brimer & Dunn, 1968), and another specially designed copying test (see Feinstein, 2003, for a validity test).

In order to make an assessment of change between ages 5 and 10 we consider the position of the child in the distribution of scores. At each age we combine the cognitive ability test scores using principal components, maximizing the variation in the resulting index, and then take the position of the child in the distribution as the developmental indicator. The correlation of scores at ages 5 and 10 was 0.53, indicating considerable stability. The rank provides a ground for a meaningful comparison between periods.

Childhood Behavioral Measures

A shortened form of the Rutter inventory was given to the sample children's mothers when the children were ages 5 and 10. This measure of antisocial behavior, originally developed for completion by teachers, has been used as an index of conduct disorder.[1] It predicts ratings based on a standard psychiatric assessment, and children with high scores are at risk of later maladjustment and delinquency (Caspi et al., 1998; Feinstein, 2000).

We differentiated between externalizing and internalizing items on *a priori* theoretical grounds and tested a two-factor model using confirmatory factor analysis (Stata, V8). Eleven of the nineteen items loaded well on the first factor (externalizing) and five items loaded well on the second factor (internalizing). The scores of the high loading items were summed and the mean score taken to create our behavioral measures, externalizing ($\alpha = 0.78$ at age 5 and 0.82 at age 10) and internalizing ($\alpha = 0.57$ at age 5 and 0.65 at age 10). The correlations of age-5 with age-10 scores were $r = 0.45$ for externalizing and $r = 0.37$ for internalizing.

In order to facilitate comparison between results for cognitive and behavioral development we reflected the behavioral scores so that a high score indicated normatively positive outcomes; that is, a low level of externalizing or internalizing problems. The correlations between cognitive and behavior measures ranged from 0.05 to 0.20.

Adult Outcomes

Our theoretical framework predicts differential effects of development in various domains in adult life. The set of outcomes at age 30 are expressed as negative statuses typically identified in the United Kingdom with "social exclusion" (UK Government Social Exclusion Unit, 1998). *Low income* is

---

[1] The test has also been found to have high retest reliability ($r = 0.89$) over a two-month interval and when based on teachers' reports has a retest reliability by a different set of teachers after two months of 0.72 (see Rutter, 1967). Use with mothers raises the possibility that mothers' own mental state might influence the rating, thus biasing the test profile for the children. However, there is good evidence that mothers' ratings on scales of this kind are more accurate than teachers' and children's ratings (e.g., Goodman, 1997, 2001).

identified by hourly wages below 80% of the gender-specific median for those in work at age 30 ($M = 0.17$, $N = 4915$). It is an indicator of low productivity and skills, not of household poverty, as it excludes those out of the labor market and neglects the partner's earnings. *Low qualifications* is defined as failure to attain "Level 2" qualifications ($M = 0.35$, $N = 6725$). This is a particularly important target in UK education, representing a fairly low level of successful exam passes in the tests commonly taken at age 16 (DfES, 2002). *Household worklessness* is membership in a household with children in which no adult is employed ($M = 0.05$, $N = 6733$). It is a major cause of family poverty in both the United Kingdom and the United States (Gregg & Wadsworth, 1996). *Criminality* is assessed by self-report that the sample member has been found guilty by a court more than once since age 16 ($M = 0.09$, $N = 3214$). Because of low female crime rates in the data, we can consider only male offenders. *Teen motherhood* is based on the self-report of the age of the participants' eldest child ($M = 0.05$, $N = 3478$). We cannot assess teen fatherhood as there are too few reported instances in the data. *Smoking* is assessed from a self-report measure of smoking ($M = 0.29$, $N = 6710$). Finally, participants are given a positive score for *depression* if they indicate seven or more positive responses in the Malaise score (Rutter et al., 1970), a 24-item scale comprising symptoms of depression ($M = 0.13$, $N = 6722$).

RESULTS

The Relationship Between Early Scores and Adult Outcomes

Analytic Method. The first issue is the amount of predictive information carried by the age-5 rank positions. For each outcome, we report the odds ratio for those in the top quartile relative to those in the lowest quartile. The odds ratios are derived from logistic regression, appropriate given that the outcome variables are binary. Odds ratios less than 1 indicate the protective capability associated with a top quartile score.

Control Variables and Causality. In order to focus on these descriptive questions we do not include a large set of control variables, although the richness of the data would allow us to do so. Our concern is to allow the middle childhood developmental changes the full chance to predict adult outcomes. Instead of attempting to condition out confounding bias and approximate simple causal solutions, we focus on the less ambitious, but nonetheless important, descriptive question: What are the average adult outcomes of those with different types of continuity and discontinuity in middle childhood?

We do include controls indicating the child's family's socioeconomic status (SES) assessed at the time of the children's birth because of the policy significance of social class. We wish to know whether the benefit of persistently high scores holds even when we condition on SES. We do not assess the differences in effects for high SES and low SES (the interaction), but by controlling for SES we do enable a test of the inference that middle childhood development matters for children of all social class groups. We also include one other control variable, the individual deviation from the quartile-specific mean of age-5 development. For example, children who seem to "escape" early disadvantage may simply be closer to the cutoff between the bottom and second quartiles than those whose low score was persistent. Failure to take this into account would mean that the effect of apparent change between 5 and 10 was rather due to the difference at 5. We therefore condition on the position relative to children of the same quartile at age 5.

In Table 16.1, we report the odds ratios for those in the top quartile of each outcome relative to those in the lowest quartile (behavior scores are reflected so that high scores indicate an absence of problems). For example, the first figure given is 0.33. This is the odds ratio for males, for the low wages outcome, associated with being in the top quartile of cognitive development relative to being in the bottom quartile.

For most adult outcomes, across both genders, the cognitive quartile is the strongest predictor. Among males, externalizing behavior is equally or more predictive of criminality, smoking, and depression. The age-5 cognitive score has particularly large implications for men's membership in a workless household with children. Nonetheless, the results for women are also substantive and statistically significant, $p = 0.001$. Internalizing behavior at age 5 is not a significant predictor of most outcomes, but it does predict depression for both sexes and low education for females. The fact that the score predicts depression 25 years later is evidence that it contains substantive and valid information.

Generally, these results indicate the significance of development to age 5. The position in the distribution at age 5, particularly for cognitive development and externalizing behavior, is a strongly significant predictor of adult outcomes with quite sizable substantive differences in outcomes at age 30 for those at different ends of these distributions at age 5.

Continuity and Discontinuity in Middle Childhood

The degree of stability in each indicator between the ages of 5 and 10 is indicated by transition matrices, which show the empirical probability that a child ranks in a particular quartile at age 10 based on his or her quartile position in the same score at age 5. We group children based on their middle childhood transitions, identifying four groups: Group 1 is the *persistently low scorers*, those children who were in the bottom quartile at ages 5 and 10; Group 2 is the *escapers*, those who were in the bottom quartile at age 5

TABLE 16.1. *Odds Ratios Effects on Adult Outcomes for Top Quartile Age-5 Development Relative to Bottom Quartile Development, in the Three Domains*

		Males		Females	
		Odds Ratio	P-value	Odds Ratio	P-value
Low wages	Cognitive	0.33	0.000	0.29	0.000
	Non-externalizing	0.59	0.001	0.60	0.000
	Non-internalizing	0.89	0.454	0.81	0.143
Low education	Cognitive	0.17	0.000	0.20	0.000
	Non-externalizing	0.40	0.000	0.54	0.000
	Non-internalizing	1.01	0.914	0.75	0.006
Worklessness	Cognitive	0.11	0.000	0.35	0.000
	Non-externalizing	0.37	0.007	0.62	0.004
	Non-internalizing	0.91	0.801	0.85	0.395
Criminality	Cognitive	0.30	0.000		
	Non-externalizing	0.30	0.000		
	Non-internalizing	1.15	0.463		
Teen mother	Cognitive			0.32	0.000
	Non-externalizing			0.55	0.004
	Non-internalizing			1.03	0.898
Smoker	Cognitive	0.61	0.000	0.53	0.000
	Non-externalizing	0.38	0.000	0.55	0.000
	Non-internalizing	1.01	0.921	1.07	0.566
Depressed	Cognitive	0.67	0.013	0.42	0.000
	Non-externalizing	0.55	0.000	0.63	0.000
	Non-internalizing	0.72	0.049	0.68	0.003

Note: Externalizing and internalizing behavior scores are reflected so that high scores indicate the absence of problems. Statistics given are odds ratios and respective P-values taken from 42 logistic regressions (3 developmental indicators *7 outcomes *2 genders). In each regression, for the given gender, the probability of the outcome is regressed on three dummy variables indicating membership of the second, third, or fourth (top) quartiles in the developmental indicator. Results are only reported for the top quartile.

TABLE 16.2. *Continuity and Discontinuity by SES*

	Persistent High Scorers		Persistent Low Scorers	
	High SES	**Low SES**	**High SES**	**Low SES**
Cognitive				
Boys	63	25	38	64
Girls	67	30	30	70
All	65	27	34	67
Non-externalizing				
Boys	47	32	48	52
Girls	44	26	41	57
All	46	32	44	54
Non-internalizing				
Boys	40	31	51	44
Girls	42	34	44	48
All	41	32	47	46

Note: Externalizing and internalizing behavior scores are reflected so that high scores indicate the absence of problems. The persistently high scorer rate is defined as the proportion of those who were in the top quartile at age 5 who remained there at age 10. The persistent low score rate is equivalently defined. In each case, the rates for high and low SES groups are based on the quartile positions defined over all children and not just children of similar SES. Gender-specific rates, on the other hand, *are* based on the positions in the gender-specific distributions. The proportion of fallers can be calculated as 100 minus the high persistence rate. The proportion of escapers can be calculated as 100 minus the low persistence rate.

but not at age 10; Group 3 is the *fallers*, those who were in the top quartile at age 5 but not at age 10; and Group 4 is the *persistently high scorers*, those who were in the top quartile at ages 5 and 10.

We define the *persistent high score rate* as the proportion of children who were in the top quartile at ages 5 and 10, and the *persistent low score rate* as the proportion of children who were in the bottom quartile at ages 5 and at 10. These probabilities are reported by SES for each developmental indicator. SES is a very raw proxy for all kinds of different family processes, available resources, motivations, genetic inheritances, and other determinants of success. No hypotheses are made here about the precise cause of this SES difference; the aim is merely to describe it.

In Table 16.2 we report the equivalent statistics for the three types of development, showing the persistence of high or low scores. This difference by SES is greater for cognitive development than for behavior. The chance of persistently high levels of cognitive attainment at age 10 is 65% for a high SES child and only 27% for a low SES child. The probability of persistent internalizing problems is similar for high and low SES children. The persistence of the most nonproblematic levels of internalizing behavior is more strongly moderated by SES.

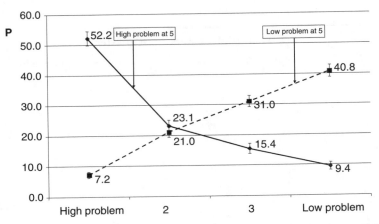

FIGURE 16.1. Externalizing behavior transitions, quartile position at age 10 by quartile position at age 5. Ninety-five percent confidence intervals shown. Behavior indicators reflected.

For all three indices of development, persistence of low scores is more common for high SES boys than similar girls. For example, a high SES boy with an age-5 cognitive score in the bottom quartile has a 38% chance of remaining in the bottom quartile at age 10. The equivalent rate for high SES girls is only 30%. However, for low SES children this gender pattern is reversed: persistent low scores are *more* common for low SES girls than boys; this holds for all three indices of development. For example, a low SES boy with a bottom-quartile age-5 cognitive score has a high 64% chance of remaining in the bottom quartile at age 10. The equivalent rate for high SES girls is even higher at 70%.

Figure 16.1 shows the age-10 externalizing behavior of children who were in the top and bottom quartiles of behavior at age 5. Of the children who were in the bottom quartile at age 5, with the most behavior problems (the downward sloping line), 52% were still in the bottom quartile at age 10; 23% were in the second quartile; and 25% gained above-median scores at age 10, indicating some mobility in performance after age 5. There were similar levels of mobility for children in the top quartile at age 5, with the fewest behavior problems (the upward sloping line); 28% moved below the median at age 10 and 72% still scored above the median.

Figure 16.2 reports the age-10 externalizing behavior outcomes of children who were most externalizing at age 5 (i.e., in the bottom quartile) for two different socioeconomic groups. For high SES children in the bottom quartile at age 5, the probability of remaining in the bottom quartile is 44% compared to 54% for low SES children in the bottom quartile at age 5 ($p = 0.008$).

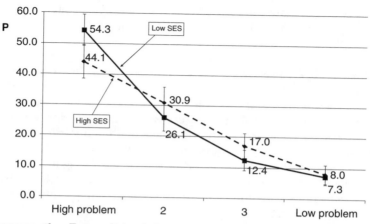

FIGURE 16.2. Externalizing behavior transitions, quartile position at age 10 by SES for externalizing children at age 5. Ninety-five percent confidence intervals shown. Behavior indicators reflected.

The Implications of Change

Next, we consider the relations of the type of continuity/discontinuity experienced in middle childhood to adult outcomes. It is to be expected that high/low development at age 5 offers protection/risk for negative outcomes in adulthood. For those who start out performing well at age 5 but who lose their developmental advantage by age 10, two results are possible. They may have benefits due to their early success, but the risk following their relative decline may either (a) be overridden by the protective advantages of early functioning so that they suffer no significant effects of the decline, or (b) outweigh the early benefit, leaving them with outcomes equivalent to those who started out with roughly median scores.

The first possibility would suggest that early scores dominate and that change (even large change) during middle childhood has no additional effect on adult outcomes. The second possibility would indicate that middle childhood trajectories make important contributions to life course development. The test of which of these cases holds is, therefore, a test of our key hypothesis that middle childhood is an important developmental phase, the successful negotiation of which provides protection against social exclusion in adult life.

We ran the regressions (one each per age-30 outcome, per developmental index, and per gender) in which the major predictor was a set of four dummy variables identifying the four groups established above. All regressions included the control variables discussed earlier. The default category was the set of all children who were in quartiles 2 or 3 at age 5. It is to be expected that membership in Group 1 is particularly bad and in Group 4, particularly good. The main interest is in outcomes for those in Groups 2 and 3. Do escapers catch up with median age-5 children? Do fallers drop back to the median?

Cognitive Development: Persisters. Those with persistent low cognitive development (Group 1) of both genders underperform those in the middle two quartiles at age 5 for all seven outcomes, with the single exception of depression for boys (see Table 16.3). Across both genders, those with persistently high scores (Group 4) outperform the median quartile groups for all seven outcomes. The differences are substantial. For example, the odds ratios for low cognitive persisters for the outcome of being in a workless household with children at age 30 are 2.49 for boys and 2.67 for girls. The largest effects, not surprisingly, are on the educational qualifications variable (3.64 for boys, 3.22 for girls).

Cognitive Development: Escapers. Generally, the odds of negative outcomes for escapers, compared to children in the middle quartiles at age 5, are greater than 1 (see Table 16.3). That is, age-5 score is important and carries risk even for escapers, but the difference is not always statistically significant. For boys, escapers manage odds not greater (at 10% significance) than those in the second and third quartiles of cognitive performance at age 5 for the probabilities of being in a workless household, smoking, and experiencing depression, but they are significantly more likely to have low wages and low education and to engage in criminal behavior. For girls, the difference is not significant for the probabilities of low wages, low education, smoking, and depression but they are significantly more likely to be in a workless household and in teen parenthood. Although escaping the bottom quartile of cognitive development between ages 5 and 10 brings important advantages, some of the risk is carried over.

Hypotheses about the group whose low cognitive performance at age 5 improved by age 10 (Group 2: escapers) were also tested by comparing these children to Group 1 (persistently low scorers). For 8 of the 12 outcomes escapers do significantly better than those with persistently low scores. Both male and females in Group 2 had lower odds than Group 1 of having low wages, low education, or being in a workless household. Differences were also significant for smoking for boys and depression for girls.

There are four cases for Groups 1 and 2 that did not differ at $p < 0.10$. Smoking for girls and depression for boys are trivial cases in the sense that odds for all four groups in these cases are similar. More interesting are criminality for boys and teenage parenthood for girls. For both of these outcomes, odds are much higher for escapers than for those in quartiles 2 or 3 at age 5. Moreover, for these two outcomes, escaping the bottom quartile for cognitive performance is not only worse than not having been

TABLE 16.3. *Results from Logistic Regressions of Adult Outcomes on Middle Childhood Transition Groups*

| | | Odds Ratio | | | | | | SE | | | | | |
| | | Cognitive Development | | Externalizing | | Internalizing | | Cognitive Development | | Externalizing | | Internalizing | |
Outcome	Group	Male	Female	Male	Female	Male	Female	Male	Female	Male	Female	Male	Female
Low wages	1	2.54	2.26	1.26	1.66	0.99	1.04	0.40	0.35	0.24	0.27	0.22	0.19
	2	1.37	1.24	1.01	1.18	1.39	1.01	0.25	0.21	0.21	0.20	0.27	0.19
	3	0.86	0.92	0.82	1.01	1.11	0.94	0.16	0.15	0.13	0.15	0.17	0.14
	4	0.59	0.30	0.66	0.89	0.88	1.06	0.13	0.07	0.13	0.16	0.17	0.18
	n	2544	2401	2392	2278	2391	2276						
Low education	1	3.64	3.22	1.84	1.40	0.95	1.22	0.46	0.38	0.24	0.17	0.14	0.16
	2	1.42	1.21	1.61	0.95	0.91	0.79	0.17	0.14	0.22	0.12	0.13	0.11
	3	0.80	0.87	0.91	0.73	1.16	0.86	0.10	0.10	0.09	0.08	0.12	0.09
	4	0.20	0.16	0.60	0.68	0.74	0.91	0.04	0.03	0.08	0.09	0.09	0.11
	n	3242	3483	3025	3286	3023	3282						
Workless household	1	2.49	2.67	1.12	1.90	1.27	0.92	0.75	0.46	0.46	0.36	0.59	0.22
	2	1.23	1.45	1.59	1.06	0.91	1.11	0.51	0.30	0.61	0.24	0.45	0.25
	3	0.39	1.22	0.41	1.24	1.08	1.08	0.24	0.26	0.20	0.23	0.37	0.19
	4	0.17	0.53	0.64	0.73	0.46	0.79	0.18	0.16	0.32	0.19	0.28	0.19
	n	3246	3487	3028	3290	3026	3286						

(continued)

TABLE 16.3. (*Continued*)

Outcome	Group	Odds Ratio Cognitive Development Male	Female	Externalizing Male	Female	Internalizing Male	Female	SE Cognitive Development Male	Female	Externalizing Male	Female	Internalizing Male	Female
Male offender	1	1.80		2.29		0.69		0.32		0.43		0.20	
	2	2.22		1.63		0.93		0.39		0.34		0.22	
	3	0.97		0.71		1.05		0.21		0.14		0.18	
	4	0.52		0.70		1.04		0.15		0.17		0.22	
	n	3214		2997		2995							
Teen mother	1		2.09		1.66		0.68		0.43		0.37		0.21
	2		1.60		0.95		0.70		0.37		0.26		0.22
	3		0.93		0.92		0.92		0.25		0.21		0.20
	4		0.54		0.74		0.90		0.20		0.23		0.24
	n		3478		3281		3277						
Smoker	1	1.63	1.26	2.12	1.71	0.84	0.82	0.19	0.15	0.28	0.21	0.13	0.12
	2	1.21	1.18	1.37	1.14	1.05	0.85	0.15	0.15	0.19	0.15	0.15	0.12
	3	1.04	0.89	0.73	0.82	1.07	1.02	0.12	0.11	0.08	0.09	0.11	0.11
	4	0.81	0.59	0.74	0.82	0.88	0.92	0.10	0.08	0.09	0.11	0.11	0.12
	n	3232	3478	3015	3282	3013	3278						
Depressed	1	1.23	2.09	2.08	2.01	1.36	1.64	0.21	0.28	0.35	0.29	0.27	0.26
	2	1.04	1.14	0.91	1.13	0.98	1.15	0.19	0.18	0.20	0.19	0.20	0.20
	3	0.98	0.84	0.88	1.01	0.84	1.15	0.17	0.14	0.15	0.14	0.13	0.15
	4	0.71	0.62	0.95	1.05	0.68	0.89	0.14	0.11	0.18	0.17	0.14	0.15
	n	3239	3483	3022	3286	3020	3282						

Note: Group 1 is the persistent low scorers; Group 2, the escapers; Group 3, the fallers; and Group 4, the persistent high scorers. Externalizing and internalizing behavior scores are reflected so that high scores indicate the absence of problems.

there at age 5 but also brings no, or relatively low, advantages compared to not escaping.

Overall, we conclude that change in cognitive performance between ages 5 and 10 is important. For most positive outcomes, relative change brings advantages and relative decline disadvantages. For some outcomes escaping the bottom quartile can completely knock out the effect of the risk of having been there at age 5. For others some residual risk remains but it is substantially reduced. The interesting exceptions are for criminality for boys and teen parenthood for girls; it appears that there is considerable persistence of the effects of poor scores at age 5 that is not significantly reduced by improvement between ages 5 and 10.

Cognitive Development: Fallers. The long-term outcomes of those who dropped out of the top quartile in cognitive performance between ages 5 and 10 (Group 3: fallers) were compared to those in the middle quartiles at age 5. The only outcome for which fallers maintain any significant advantage (at $p < 0.10$) is, for boys, a reduced probability of low educational qualifications. The odds for being in a workless household are low at 0.39 but not quite significant. For no other outcomes (and none for girls) are the benefits of a high age-5 score sustained. For all the outcomes, with the exception of boys' risk of being in a workless household, the odds for fallers are also significantly worse than for high persisters. Thus, losing the age-5 high cognitive score clearly erodes the benefit of having had it.

Externalizing: Persistence. Persistently high externalizers (Group 1) have higher risks of negative adult outcomes than the default group (the middle quartiles at age 5) for all outcomes and both genders, and the disadvantages associated with persistently high externalizing are substantial. For example, odds ratios for smoking are 2.12 for boys and 1.71 for girls (see Table 16.3).

Those with persistently low levels of problem behavior (Group 4) generally outperform the median quartile groups for all seven outcomes and both genders. However, these differences are not always statistically significant. In fact, there is not a significant benefit for this group for worklessness, criminality, and depression for men or for low wages, worklessness, teen parenthood, and depression for women. This appears to indicate nonlinearity in the effect of externalizing behavior, in that it differs from that found at the other end of the distribution. It may be that there are long-term implications of high levels of externalizing behavior problems above some cutoff point, but that below this cutoff there are not substantial differences between those with even quite large differences in score. Moreover, externalizing scores are generally positively skewed, so it is likely that non-externalizers are not as different from the third quartile as the high externalizing group are from the second quartile.

Externalizing: Escapers. Females who escaped age-5 high externalizing behavior (Group 2) are not more likely to suffer any of the seven outcomes than those who were not in the bottom quartile at age 5. Furthermore, their odds ratios are significantly lower than persistent high externalizers (Group 1) for all seven outcomes. Girls who exit high levels of externalizing behavior between ages 5 and 10 overcome all the associated risks for these outcomes (see Table 16.3).

For boys, the story is more mixed. Effects of high externalizing behavior at age 5 persist for low education, criminality, and smoking. For the low education outcome, age-5 male high externalizers have significantly higher odds ratios than median score children, and escapers have no apparent advantage over those who remain in Group 1. For criminality and smoking, however, the negative repercussions are less than for those who did not escape the age 5 behavioral problems. Thus, there are long-term problems for boys with high externalizing behavior at age 5 that persist even if the problems themselves are reduced in middle childhood. Nonetheless, there are clear advantages associated with a decline in externalizing behavior in middle childhood.

Externalizing: Fallers. It seems that there are some benefits of low externalizing behavior at age 5 but that there is no extra risk associated with losing the advantage between ages 5 and 10 (Group 3: fallers). Again, it is likely that this reflects the nonlinearities in levels of externalizing behavior and that the important implications of change are for those with high levels of behavior problems rather than for those at the other end of the distribution.

Internalizing: Persistence. The only substantive effects of persistence of high- or low-quartile internalizing behavior are on the probability of depression at age 30. Persistence of high levels of internalizing behavior (Group 1) is associated with an odds ratio for depression at age 30 of 1.36 for boys (not quite significant at 5% in a one-tailed test) and 1.64 for girls ($p = 0.001$). Effects at the other end of the distribution are weaker and there are not significant effects of persistent low levels of internalizing (Group 4) for girls. This may reflect the cutoff issue discussed above in relation to externalizing behavior, although with an apparent gender difference. High internalizing behavior is a powerful signal for adult depression for women. Low internalizing behavior, on the other hand, is a more powerful predictor for males. Low male internalizing behavior, moreover, is also associated with reduced risk of low educational success for men (see Table 16.3).

Internalizing: Change. Although discontinuity in the childhood measures of internalizing behavior provide signals about mental health twenty years later, they do not provide many indications about other outcomes. For depression, there are important effects of middle childhood change in internalizing behavior in that escapers (Group 2), those who get out of the problematic group between the age of 5 and 10, have odds ratios for depression of 0.98 for boys and 1.15 for girls when compared to children in the middle quartiles at age 5. Neither of these is significantly different from 1. Their odds are significantly less than those for females who remain high on internalizing (Group 1). We conclude, therefore, that escape from problematic levels of internalizing behavior between ages 5 and 10 brings benefits, particularly for girls. Female fallers (Group 3), those whose relative internalizing scores increased from ages 5 to 10, also have relatively high depression probabilities in adulthood that are significantly higher than those for girls who remained in the lowest quartile of internalizing problems (Group 4) ($p = 0.091$). The age-5 level of internalizing is not, therefore, a sufficient indicator of adult female depression risk; age-10 internalizing is an important moderator of the age-5 effect.

CONCLUSIONS AND DISCUSSION

We found that development in the middle childhood period carries important signals about the risks of adult social exclusion. Many children with improvement between ages 5 and 10 escaped the risk implied by poor early performance. One implication of this is that school tracking mechanisms must reflect the importance of these large transitions and that early tracking should remain flexible and able to address changes during middle childhood. More importantly, school resources must continue to be targeted on this developmental period, particularly on identifying the developmental discontinuities observed in these data and responding to them with personalized educational interventions.

We also found interesting gender and social class differences and different patterns of relations across particular outcomes. These results suggest that the relative effectiveness of programs at different points in childhood may differ according to the adult outcomes that one wishes to affect and the context and domain to be targeted. For example, a high level of externalizing behavior at age 5 is a serious problem predicting low educational attainment regardless of developmental progress between ages 5 and 10 for boys, but not for girls. However, there were benefits from escaping an early low-quartile cognitive score during middle childhood for both boys and girls.

Schools do not appear to have been as successful in addressing behavior problems as in confronting low, early cognitive attainment, perhaps because they did not attempt to do so, and/or they were less well equipped to address behavioral problems and issues than academic ones. This suggests a possible high-return area for future research in the mechanisms that lead to early, high externalizing and policy development to strengthen protective processes. Schools and teachers need help in addressing externalizing behavior problems and developing strategies that will put high externalizers on a different developmental path.

For two outcomes, male criminality and teen motherhood, the negative implications of poor cognitive scores at age 5 were not reduced by improvement in scores between ages 5 and 10, a particularly strong argument for appropriately targeted investment in early years' contexts. However, with regard to male criminality, there are clear advantages associated with a decline in externalizing behavior in middle childhood. A focus solely on preschool contexts or solely on cognitive development ignores the importance of both school-age development and behavioral adjustment. The policy implication is that educational investments need to consider behavioral and psychological development and not just cognitive development.

This makes the case for strong school, home, and community links to help ensure that the proximal influences to which the child is subjected, inside and outside the school, all work in positive directions within a holistic framework of support. It is not just in the preschool period that such support is needed, but throughout children's school careers. The benefit of this focus may be experienced in terms of outcomes beyond educational attainment, with subsequent advantages for the individuals concerned as well as the broader society. The life span developmental perspective leads to the conclusion that government departments must operate holistically through cooperation and development in imaginative interagency programs that cut across the traditional divisions.

Although we found substantial risks associated with high levels of externalizing behavior, we found no significant reverse benefits of persistently low levels of externalizing behavior. This nonlinearity is important, suggesting that a persistently low level of externalizing behavior may indicate a degree of passivity or compliance. There are likely to be other nonlinearities in the developmental variables used here, as well as crucial interactions between them.

There are clear and strong relations of context to these discontinuities. Social class differences in patterns of middle childhood development are large. If they are to be successful, middle childhood interventions may have to reproduce or substitute for the protective resources that accompany high SES features such as resource rich and low-stress households (Yeung, Linver, & Brooks-Gunn, 2002), high parental interest in education (Feinstein & Symons, 1999), motivated and able peers (Robertson & Symons, 2003), and beneficial school and out-of-school contexts (Eccles & Gootman, 2002).

Low SES children who were in the top quartile of the cognitive development score at age 5 had only a 27% chance of remaining in the top quartile at 10, compared to 65% for the high SES group. One explanation for the finding is nonrandom measurement error and regression towards the mean for the low SES children. However, Feinstein (2003) shows that, even within SES groups, early scores predict adult outcomes. For a given SES background, children with high quartile scores had significantly better outcomes than those with low quartile scores. It is very unlikely, therefore, that these results follow from random measurement error. We have no reason to believe that when high SES children score well it is because their test scores are reliable, but that when low SES children score well it is due to measurement problems. Most evidence suggests that the bias in testing runs against the success of low SES children, not in favor of it.

For all three indices of development, persistently low scores were more common for high SES boys than for similar girls. Among high SES children, girls were better than boys at escaping early developmental problems by age 10. For low SES children, on the other hand, poor early performance was more likely to persist for girls than for boys. There may be different attitudes to development for boys and girls among different social class groups. Underperforming high SES girls may be more likely than low SES girls to receive extra family resources to compensate. The relative attainment of girls may be more valued by high SES families than by low SES families. Alternatively, the difference in responses may be by schools rather than families. The difference in persistence of high or low scores by SES is more substantial for cognitive development than for behavior, perhaps indicating that behavioral problems are relatively harder to measure. Alternatively, behavioral development may be relatively harder to explain by distal contextual factors.

The measures we have relied on for development in middle childhood were devised in the 1970s and could be improved upon today. Direct measures of behavioral adjustment, through teacher reports and observational ratings, would strengthen the validity of assessments produced by the mothers in this study. However, in other studies where such multiple measurement has been employed, the mothers' ratings have proved consistent with these possibly more objective approaches, strengthening confidence that they are genuinely tapping child attributes largely uncontaminated by the mother's own feelings about herself (Goodman, 1997, 2001). Similarly, the cognitive tests used show high consistency in the way they correlate with later educational achievements. We therefore have confidence that our findings are robust and would stand up well to further replication employing different measurement methods.

Taken together, the results reported here imply that change in cognitive development and behavior between ages 5 and 10 carry important signals for long-term development and adult outcomes. Escaping the bottom quartile of academic development between ages 5 and 10 brings important advantages, and those who do escape have outcomes similar to those who were not in the bottom quartile at age 5 for most outcomes. Discontinuities between ages 5 and 10 substantially alter the children's life chances based on their developmental position assessed at age 5.

Age-5 development, however, is also a strong indicator of adult outcomes, pointing to the continuous nature of developmental processes, and the risk and protection that are their counterparts (Rutter, 1990). The age-5 measures signify the outcomes of development up to that point. What happens subsequently in the child's life builds on these foundations, constituting additional risk or protection depending on the kinds of external influences the child encounters. It is in these early years that the vicious circles that can bedevil many children's developmental progress are set in train. Garmezy (1993) identifies three types of protective influence against such accumulative maladjustment in childhood – child-based, family-based, and community-based. His prescriptions for the form interventions should take – developing personality, autonomy, self-esteem, and positive social orientation in the child; building cohesion in the family; and strengthening support in the community – resonate with our findings and are as relevant for those in middle childhood as they are for preschoolers.

Interventions that supply the protective factors need to be continuous throughout childhood. Programs that achieve enduring success are necessarily expensive, as they have to be persistent. This implies that some degree of targeting may be required, given the constraints on public resources. The findings presented here suggest that targeting based on the age-5 situation can be improved on by information arising between ages 5 and 10 because important changes occur in this period that have long-term implications for children. Practitioners, policy-makers, and academics should not be persuaded into thinking that the preschool years are so crucial that important changes and interventions can occur only before school entry.

References

Brimer, M. A., and Dunn, L. M. (1968). *English Picture and Vocabulary Test*. Newnham, U.K: Educational Evaluation Enterprises.
Bronfenbrenner, U. (1979). *The ecology of human development*. Cambridge, MA: Cambridge University Press.
Brooks-Gunn, J., Duncan, G. J., & Maritato, N. (1997). Poor families, poor outcomes: The well-being of children and youth. In G. J. Duncan & J. Brooks-Gunn (Eds.), *Consequences of growing up poor* (pp. 1–17). New York: Russell Sage.
Butler, N. R., Haslum, M. N., Barker, W., & Morris, A. C. (1982). *Child health and education study. First report to the Department of Education and Science on the 10-Year follow-up*. Bristol: Department of Child Health, University of Bristol.
Bynner, J. (2001). Childhood risks and protective factors in social exclusion. *Children and Society, 15*, 285–301.
Card, D. (1999). The causal effect of education on earnings. In O. Ashenfelter & D. Card (Eds.), *Handbook of labor economics: Vol. 3*. North Holland: Elsevier.

Caspi, A., Elder, G. H., & Herbener, E. S. (1990). Childhood personality and the prediction of life's course patterns. In L. Robins & M. Rutter (Eds.), *Straight and devious pathways from childhood to adulthood* (pp. 13–35). Cambridge: Cambridge University Press.

Caspi, A., Moffitt, T. E., Entner Wright, B. R., & Silva, P. A. (1998). Early failure in the labour market: Childhood and adolescent predictors of unemployment in the transition to adulthood. *American Sociological Review, 63,* 424–451.

Caviness, V. S., Philipek, P. A., & Kennedy, D. N. (1993). Longitudinal research and biology of human brain development and behavior. In D. Magnusson & P. Casear (Eds), *Longitudinal research on individual development: Present status and future perspectives* (pp. 60–74). Cambridge, MA: Cambridge University Press.

Clarke, A. M., & Clarke, A. D. B. (1998). *Early experience: Myth and evidence.* London: Open Books.

Davis-Kean, P. E., & Magnuson, K. (2005). The influence of parent education and family income on child achievement: The indirect role of parental expectations and the home environment. *Journal of Family Psychology, 19,* 294–304.

DfES (2002). *Education and skills – Delivering the results: A strategy to 2006.* London: Department for Education and Skills.

Eccles, J. S., & Gootman, J. (Eds.). (2002). *Communities and youth: Investing in our future.* Washington, DC: National Academy Press.

Elder, G. H. (1998). The life course and human development. In R. M. Lerner (Ed.), *Handbook of child psychology: Vol. 1. Theoretical models of human development.* New York: Wiley.

Farrington, D. P. (2000). Explaining and preventing crime: The globalization of knowledge: The American Society of Criminology 1999 Presidential Address. *Criminology, 38,* 1–24.

Feinstein, L. (2000). The relative economic importance of academic, psychological and behavioral attributes developed in childhood. *Centre for Economic Performance Discussion Paper,* No. 443.

Feinstein, L. (2002). *Quantitative estimates of the social benefits of learning: 1: Crime* (Wider Benefits of Learning Research Report 5). London: Institute of Education.

Feinstein, L. (2003). Inequality in the early cognitive development of British children in the 1970 cohort. *Economica, 70,* 73–98.

Feinstein, L., & Symons, J. (1999). Attainment in secondary school. *Oxford Economic Papers, 51,* 300–321.

Ferri, E., Bynner, J., & Wadsworth, M. E. (2003). *Changing Britain: Changing lives.* London: Bedford Way Papers, Institute of Education.

Garmezy, N. (1993). Developmental psychopathology: Some historical and current perspectives. In D. Magnusson & P. Casaer (Eds.), *Longitudinal research in individual development: Present status and future perspectives* (pp. 95–126). Cambridge: Cambridge University Press.

Glass, N. (1999). Sure Start: The development of and early intervention programme for young children in the United Kingdom. *Children and Society, 13,* 257–264.

Goodman, R. (1997). The Strengths and Difficulties Questionnaire: A research note. *Journal of Child Psychology and Psychiatry, 38,* 581–586.

Goodman, R. (2001). Psychometric properties of the Strengths and Difficulties Questionnaire (SDQ). *Journal of the American Academy of Child and Adolescent Psychiatry, 40*, 1337–1345.

Gregg, P., & Wadsworth, M. (1996). More work in fewer households. In J. Hills (Ed.), *New inequalities: The changing distribution of income and wealth in the U.K.* Cambridge: Cambridge University Press.

Hammond, C. (2002). *Learning to be healthy* (The Wider Benefits of Learning Papers: No. 3). London: Institute of Education.

Harris, D. B. (1963). *Children's drawings as measures of intellectual maturity.* New York: Harcourt, Brace, and World.

Hartup, W. W. (2002). Growing points in developmental science: A summing up. In W. W. Hartup & R. K. Silbereisen (Eds.), *Growing points in developmental science* (pp. 329–344). New York: Psychology Press.

Kagan, J. (1998). *Three seductive ideas.* Cambridge, MA: Cambridge University Press.

Koppitz, E. M. (1968). *Psychological evaluation of children's human figure drawings.* New York: Grure and Stratton.

Lerner, R. (1996). Relative plasticity, integration, temporality and diversity in human development. *Developmental Psychology, 32*, 781–786.

Moffitt, T. E., & Harrington H. L. (1996). Delinquency: The natural history of antisocial behaviour. In P. A. Silva & W. R. Stanton (Eds.), *Child to Adult* (pp. 163–185). Oxford: Oxford University Press.

Pilling, D. (1990). *Escape from disadvantage.* London: The Falmer Press.

Ramey, C., & Ramey, S. (2000). Persistent effects of early childhood education on high risk children and their mothers. *Applied Developmental Science, 4*, 2–14.

Robertson, D., & Symons, J. (2003). Do peer groups matter? Peer group versus schooling effects on academic attainment. *Economica, 70*, 31–53.

Robins, L., & Rutter, M. (1990). *Straight and devious pathways from childhood to adulthood.* Cambridge: Cambridge University Press.

Rutter, M. (1967). A children's behavior questionnaire for completion by teachers: Preliminary findings. *Journal of Child Psychology and Psychiatry, 8*, 1–11.

Rutter, M. (1990). Psychosocial resilience and protective mechanisms. In J. Rolf, A. S. Masten, D. Cicchetti, K. H. Nuechterlein, & S. Weintraub (Eds.), *Risk and protective factors in the development of psychopathology.* Cambridge: Cambridge University Press.

Rutter, M., Tizard, J., & Whitmore, K. (1970). *Education, health and behavior.* London: Longmans.

Sanford, M., Offord, D., McLeod, K., Boyle, M., Byrne, C., & Hall, B. (1993). Pathways into the workforce: Antecedents of school and workforce status. *Journal of the American Academy of Child and Adolescent Psychiatry, 33*, 1036–1046.

Schaffer, H. R. (2002). The early experience assumption: Past, present and future, in W. W. Hartup, & R. K. Silbereisen (Eds.), *Growing points in developmental science.* New York: Psychology Press.

Schoon, I., Bynner, J., Joshi, H., Parsons, S., Wiggins, R. D., & Sacker, A. (2002). The influence, timing and duration of risk experiences for the passage of childhood to midadulthood. *Child Development, 73*, 1486–1504.

Schweinhart, L. J., Barnes, H. V., & Weikart, D. P. (1993). Significant benefits: The High/Scope Perry Preschool Study through age 27. *Monographs of the High/Scope Educational Research Foundation, 10*.

UK Government Social Exclusion Unit. (1998). *Bringing Britain together: A national strategy for neighbourhood renewal*. London: The Stationery Office.

Werner, E. E. (1989). Vulnerability and resiliency: A longitudinal perspective. In M. Bambring, F. Lsel, & H. Skowronick (Eds.), *Children at risk: Assessment, longitudinal research and intervention*. Berlin: Walter de Gruyter.

Yeung, W. J., Linver, M. R., & Brooks-Gunn, J. (2002). How money matters for young children's development: Investment and family process. *Child Development, 73,* 1861–1879.

17

Mandatory Welfare-to-Work Programs and Preschool-Age Children

Do Impacts Persist into Middle Childhood?

Sharon M. McGroder, Martha J. Zaslow,
Kristin A. Moore, and Jennifer L. Brooks

During the 1990s, states experimented with various mandatory welfare-to-work strategies, culminating in the passage of the federal Personal Responsibility and Work Opportunity Reconciliation Act in 1996. This law replaced the Family Support Act of 1988, which marked the first time in national policy that welfare recipients with children as young as 3 years old (or younger, at state option) were required to participate in work preparation activities through the Job Opportunities and Basic Skills Training (or JOBS) Program. As such, policy makers sought information on the impact of these mandatory programs not only on the economic well-being of families but also on the development and well-being of their children particularly, preschool-age children. Consequently, in designing the JOBS Evaluation (later renamed the National Evaluation of Welfare-to-Work Strategies, or NEWWS), federal officials requested a "Child Outcomes Study" to examine short- and longer-term impacts of the JOBS Program on children of enrollees, with a focus on children who were 3 to 5 years old at study entry. The Child Outcomes Study (COS) was designed to assess the impacts of an experimental manipulation of a policy requirement (or mandate) and is a direct test of how changes in this policy context affect children as they move into middle childhood. After providing some background on the JOBS program, this chapter presents a theoretical rationale for why and how a program aimed at the economic well-being of adults may influence children, summarizes findings from the COS, and proposes a revised theoretical framework for investigating effects of welfare policies on children and families.

BACKGROUND

The Family Support Act of 1988 created the JOBS Program, which required states to develop and operate mandatory welfare-to-work programs for welfare recipients. Programs could adopt a "labor force attachment" (LFA) strategy, which emphasized short-term job search assistance and encouraged people to find employment quickly, or a "human capital development" (HCD) strategy, which emphasized skill-building activities prior to seeking employment. The JOBS Program had four main components:

1. Services to enhance the employability of welfare recipients, such as adult basic education (including high school or GED preparation classes, remedial education, and English as a Second Language classes), vocational training, and job search.
2. Required participation in these work preparation activities and financial sanctions for noncompliance with this mandate.
3. Messages about the importance of such activities for self-sufficiency.
4. Case management, to direct and monitor clients' progress through these activities.

The NEWWS examined the impacts of 11 JOBS programs on welfare recipients and their families up to five years after being randomly assigned to either a mandatory JOBS program or to a control group (see Hamilton, 2002, and Hamilton, Brock, Farrell, Friedlander, & Harknett, 1997, for greater detail on study design and a summary of NEWWS findings).[1] Because the Family Support Act marked the first time in national policy that welfare-receiving mothers with preschool-age children (ages 3 to 5) were required to participate in welfare-to-work activities and secure employment, policy makers were particularly interested in impacts on this age group of children.

THEORETICAL FRAMEWORK

An ecological perspective (Bronfenbrenner, 1979) suggests that children can be affected by interventions directed at their parents ("mesosystems") and by the broader contexts in which these programs are implemented ("exosystems"). The "person–process–context" orientation of an ecological perspective directs intervention researchers to examine what works, for whom, under what circumstances, and through what processes. In designing the COS, Zaslow, Moore, and their colleagues applied an ecological perspective to explore how children might be affected by a mandatory welfare-to-work program aimed at their mothers (Zaslow, Moore, Morrison, & Coiro, 1995). Their conceptual framework identified aspects of adult functioning and family life that JOBS might affect that, in turn, had the potential to serve as pathways of influence on child outcomes. These

---

[1] With the passage of PRWORA in 1996, two of the three sites chose to release some (in Grand Rapids) or all (in Atlanta) control group members. As a result, in these two sites, impacts measured as of the end of this follow-up period are probably understated relative to what may have occurred if treatment differences had been maintained in those sites.

included "targeted" outcomes that the JOBS program was designed to change (e.g., educational attainment, employment, and welfare receipt), as well as "derivatives" of these outcomes (e.g., health insurance and child care use) and "nontargeted" outcomes (e.g., maternal psychological well-being). Figure 17.1 presents this conceptual framework.

With respect to targeted outcomes, HCD programs directed mothers toward activities that would enhance their basic educational skills. By attending classes and doing homework, mothers may serve as positive role models, emphasizing the value of learning and study. Improvements in mothers' own reading and math skills may enable them to better support their children's educational progress. Unlike maternal education, the effects of maternal employment on children are less clear. The effects on children could range from negative to neutral to positive, depending on factors such as the mother's preferred work status, job quality, and whether the employment yielded increased economic resources for the family. The NEWWS COS was seen as an important opportunity to explore whether and how children in low-income families were affected by maternal employment that did not occur fully at the mother's own volition.

With respect to nontargeted outcomes, JOBS had the potential to change maternal psychological well-being (e.g., sense of efficacy, sense of stress, and depressive symptoms), parenting behavior (e.g., warmth in the mother–child relationship, harshness in discipline, and cognitive stimulation to the child), and the contexts of parenting (e.g., father involvement in the family, neighborhood safety, and social support available to the mother). But whereas JOBS programs were anticipated to affect targeted outcomes in expected ways (with HCD programs increasing educational attainment, and both HCD and LFA programs increasing employment), there was limited basis for predicting the direction of impacts on nontargeted outcomes. For example, JOBS might increase maternal psychological well-being if employment improved a sense of respect, daily contact with other adults, and feelings of control over one's life, but it might compromise psychological well-being if employment created substantial stress and concerns about child care or involved physically exhausting job demands. Similarly, parenting behavior might improve (for example, if mothers' own level of cognitive stimulation increased through stimulating experiences at work) or deteriorate (if a transition to employment resulted in economic insecurity or high levels of stress).

Because the direction of effects was unclear for some of pathways by which JOBS might influence children, JOBS could have positive, neutral, or negative effects on children. It was important to consider not only whether and in what way JOBS affected the "pathway" variables, but also to consider how multiple pathway variables might accumulate and interact. Countervailing effects might occur. For example, programs might increase maternal educational attainment and employment but simultaneously increase stress in balancing employment and family responsibilities,

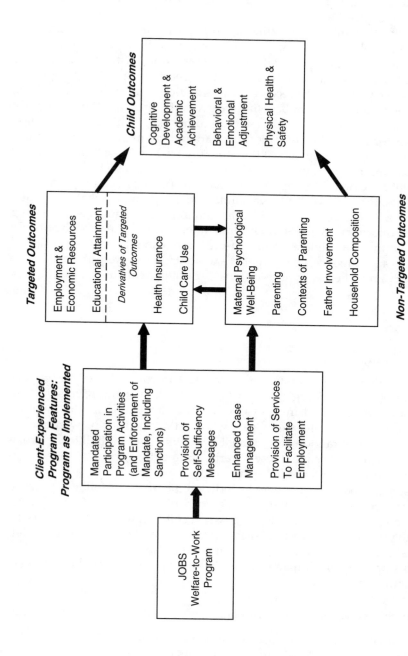

FIGURE 17.1. Conceptual framework.

with the net effect on children depending on which of these pathways had the stronger effect.

Finally, JOBS might have differing impacts on children in families with differing levels of initial barriers to employment based on their histories of welfare receipt, maternal education, recent work history, or number of young children. Because JOBS targeted long-term recipients, "long-term" welfare recipients might receive more attention from JOBS caseworkers; thus, their families might benefit more from the program than long-term recipients *not* enrolled in JOBS. On the other hand, those with stronger work histories and greater educational attainment might be better able to respond to the requirements of the program, leading these "less disadvantaged" families to benefit more than "less disadvantaged" families who were *not* provided the supports and mandates of the JOBS program.

In sum, the NEWWS COS was undertaken early on in what eventually became a "wave" of experimental evaluations of the impacts of varying welfare reform approaches on children. It was critical to establish not only whether and how children were affected, but also which of the potential pathways of influence, both targeted and nontargeted, were affected by the program, and whether impacts differed in families with differing initial risk levels.

METHOD

Study Design

Three NEWWS sites operating both an HCD and an LFA welfare-to-work program (Atlanta, Georgia; Grand Rapids, Michigan; and Riverside, California) were included in the COS. In each site, single mothers with a youngest or only child[2] age 3 to 5 who had applied for or were receiving welfare as of random assignment ("baseline") were eligible. Approximately 5,900 families met these criteria, and nearly 3,700 (62%) were randomly selected to be enrolled in the study.

Just over 3,000 families were included in the two-year follow-up (when children were between about 5 and 7 years old), and 2,332 families were included in the five-year follow-up (when children were between about 8 and 10 years old). For 1,472 of these 2,332 families, teacher reports of children's school performance and behavior were also available.[3] This chapter focuses on program impacts at the five-year point, when children were well into middle childhood.

[2] Except for the Grand Rapids sample, in which about one third of focal children had younger siblings at study entry.

[3] Data from the NEWWS, including the Child Outcomes Study, are available free as public use files from the following HHS website: http://aspe.hhs.gov/hsp/NEWWS/. Restricted access files, which contain additional data, are available for a nominal fee and must be used on site at the National Center for Health Statistics.

Measures

Administrative data on welfare receipt, employment, and earnings, as well as survey information on maternal participation in education and training programs, maternal educational attainment, characteristics of the most recent job (type of job, hours per week, benefits), use of employment-related child care, and abbreviated information on the well-being of each child in the family was available from the larger NEWWS data collection procedures. Information on outcomes for young children was obtained from surveys given to mothers two years after random assignment, and to mothers, children, and teachers five years after random assignment. Standardized assessments were also conducted to tap young children's academic school readiness (at the two-year follow-up) and achievement in math and reading (at the five-year follow-up). Measures of maternal and family well-being were obtained from mothers' reports and through interviewer ratings at both the two-year and five-year follow-up.

Developmental studies increasingly examine both positive and problem outcomes in an effort to more fully understand the complexity of development (see discussions in Moore, Evans, Brooks-Gunn, & Roth, 2001; Moore & Halle, 2001). The COS included measures of both positive and problem outcomes across key domains of development (behavioral, cognitive/academic, and health) at both the two- and five-year follow-ups. Specifically, at the five-year point, child outcomes and measures included math and reading scores as assessed by the Woodcock-Johnson Tests of Achievement-Revised (Woodcock & Mather, 1989, 1990); academic progress and class placement (mother and teacher reports); engagement in school (child and teacher reports; Connell, 1990); positive and problem behavior and social skills from the Social Skills Rating System (mother, child, and teacher reports; Gresham & Elliot, 1990); and maternal reports of the child's attendance, tardiness, general health, and health conditions. (For details and psychometric information, see Hamilton et al., 2001, for five-year child outcome measures; and McGroder, Zaslow, Moore, & LeMenestrel, 2000, for two-year child outcome measures.)

Analytic Method and Standards of Evidence

OLS regression analyses, predicting each outcome measure from the program–control group dummy variable and a set of covariates, were conducted separately within site. (Random assignment occurred within site; thus, to retain the experimental design, impact analyses must be conducted at the site level.) Program–control group adjusted means that differed at $p < .10$ are reported as program impacts. Program–control group adjusted means that differed at $.10 < p < .20$ are discussed (as trends) only if they are consistent with an emerging pattern of findings and/or if the effect size

TABLE 17.1. *Effects Sizes of Impacts on Children's Social Skills and Problem Behavior at Ages 8 to 10[1]*

	Atlanta		Grand Rapids		Riverside	
	LFA	HCD	LFA	HCD	LFA	HCD[2]
Mother report						
Externalizing	−0.20**	−0.13	−0.02	−0.02	−0.10	−0.15
Self-control	0.00	−0.07	0.01	−0.03	0.14	0.29**
Responsibility	−0.06	0.14	0.03	0.01	−0.07	0.24*
Teacher report						
Externalizing	−0.29**	−0.25**	−0.08	0.28*	0.28**	−0.16
Internalizing	−0.33**	−0.25**	−0.13	0.27*	0.27**	−0.15
Hyperactivity	−0.24*	−0.25**	0.03	0.32**	0.29**	−0.01
Self-control	0.15	0.23*	−0.03	−0.14	0.05	0.05
Positive assertion	0.25*	0.21	−0.13	−0.15	0.02	−0.01
Cooperation	0.18	0.17	−0.22*	−0.21	−0.19	−0.03
Interpersonal skills	0.26**	0.30**	−0.07	−0.18	−0.04	−0.03
Child report						
Self-control	0.02	−0.06	−0.15	−0.25**	−0.06	0.08
Positive assertion	−0.01	−0.05	−0.21*	−0.29**	−0.03	0.12
Cooperation	−0.17	−0.06	−0.14	−0.23**	−0.01	0.07

[1] Only variables on which any statistically significant impacts were found are shown in this table. For details on impact estimates (and effect sizes) for *all* child outcomes examined at the five-year point, see Hamilton et al., 2002.

[2] Only mothers deemed to be in need of basic skills were enrolled in Riverside's HCD program. Thus, effect sizes in this column pertain only to this disadvantaged subgroup, unlike effect sizes for other impacts reported in this table.

*$p < .05$. **$p < .01$. ***$p < .001$.

is as large or larger than the statistically significant effect size of a different program on the same outcome.

RESULTS

Impacts on Children in Middle Childhood

Tables 17.1 through 17.3 highlight the impacts of the six JOBS programs on children's social skills and behavior, academic functioning, health, and safety at the five-year point, when children were between about 8 and 10 years old.

Impacts on Children's Social Skills and Behavior. In general, there were few impacts of these JOBS programs on children's social skills and behavior at ages 8 to 10 (Table 17.1), and the impacts that occurred varied across sites. There were more impacts on teacher-reported than on mother-reported behavior. Each of the programs in Atlanta decreased problem behavior and simultaneously increased positive behavior, whereas both programs in Grand Rapids decreased positive behaviors, and Grand Rapids' HCD program increased problem behaviors. Riverside's programs had isolated impacts on children's social skills and behavior. With few exceptions, the magnitude of these impacts on measures of social skills and behavior ranged from .20 to .30 of a standard deviation.

Table 17.1 shows that Atlanta's LFA and HCD programs reduced mothers' and teachers' reports of externalizing behaviors and reduced teachers' reports of internalizing and hyperactive behaviors. Atlanta's LFA program also increased the child's positive assertion (e.g., asking for help) as reported by the teacher, and Atlanta's HCD program increased teacher reports of the child's self-control. By contrast, Grand Rapids' HCD program and Riverside's LFA program increased teachers' reports of children's externalizing, internalizing, and hyperactive behaviors. Grand Rapids' HCD program reduced the child's self-report of positive assertion, cooperation, and self-control. Grand Rapids' LFA program also reduced children's self-reported positive assertion and teacher reports of cooperation. There was a single favorable impact of Riverside's HCD program on behavior, increasing mothers' reports of the child's self-control. None of the six JOBS programs affected mothers' reports of the child's positive assertion, cooperation, internalizing behavior, or hyperactivity; teacher reports of positive approaches to learning; or child self-reports of empathy.

Impacts on Children's Engagement, Achievement, Placement, Problems, and Progress in School. There were fewer impacts on academic functioning, and their patterns were less clear, than was the case for social skills and behavior (Table 17.2). None of the programs affected math or reading achievement test scores, performing below grade-level in reading, performing below grade-level in math, or being placed in a remedial math class. Nonetheless, over half of the academic measures were affected by one or more programs. Both programs in Atlanta increased the proportion of children performing above grade-level in reading. Atlanta's HCD program also increased teachers' reports of the child's engagement in school and reduced teachers' reports of disciplinary problems. Despite the otherwise favorable impacts in Atlanta, the HCD program increased the proportion of teachers reporting that the child had been absent, and the LFA program increased the proportion of teachers reporting that the child had been tardy.

In contrast to generally favorable impacts in Atlanta, Grand Rapids' LFA and HCD programs each reduced child self-reports of school engagement. Grand Rapids' HCD program also increased the proportion of children reported by teachers as having disciplinary problems requiring parental notification. The only favorable impact of Grand Rapids' LFA program was

TABLE 17.2. *Effects Sizes of Impacts on Children's Academic Functioning at Ages 8 to 10*[1]

	Atlanta		Grand Rapids		Riverside	
	LFA	HCD	LFA	HCD	LFA	HCD[2]
Mother Report						
% repeated a grade	0.00	−0.07	0.15	0.13	−0.23**	−0.16
% suspended or expelled	0.10	0.05	−0.13	−0.05	−0.17*	0.08
Teacher Report						
% in remedial reading group	0.00	−0.03	−0.12	0.03	0.23*	−0.02
% above grade level in reading	0.27*	0.25*	−0.11	0.05	−0.17	−0.06
School engagement	0.11	0.21*	−0.04	−0.14	−0.13	0.06
Number of days absent	0.23	0.43**	0.07	−0.09	0.09	0.48**
Number of days tardy	0.44*	0.13	−0.13	0.00	0.09	0.01
% with disciplinary action weekly	−0.17	−0.12	0.06	0.15	0.24*	0.08
% with disciplinary action requiring parental notification	−0.22	0.34***	0.02	0.36**	0.15	0.05
Child report						
School engagement	−0.07	−0.05	−0.30**	−0.21*	−0.02	0.09
Achievement tests						
% "above average" on math test	0.08	0.10	0.20*	0.10	0.16	0.02

[1] Only variables on which any statistically significant impacts were found are shown in this table. For details on impact estimates (and effect sizes) for *all* child outcomes examined at the five-year point, see Hamilton et al., 2002.

[2] Only mothers deemed to be in need of basic skills were enrolled in Riverside's HCD program. Thus, effect sizes in this column pertain only to this disadvantaged subgroup, unlike effect sizes for other impacts reported in this table.

*$p < .05$. **$p < .01$. ***$p < .001$.

its increase in the proportion of children scoring "above average" on the math achievement test.

Riverside's LFA program increased the proportion of teachers reporting weekly disciplinary problems and increased the likelihood that the child was in a remedial reading group, but it also decreased the proportion of children who had repeated a grade or had been suspended or expelled in the previous two years.

Impacts on Children's Health-Related Outcomes. There were few impacts on measures of children's health (Table 17.3). Two programs (Grand Rapids' LFA program and Riverside's HCD program) had unfavorable impacts, reducing the proportion of children rated by their mothers as

TABLE 17.3. *Effects Sizes of Impacts on Children's Health and Physical Conditions at Ages 8 to 10*[1]

	Atlanta		Grand Rapids		Riverside	
	LFA	HCD	LFA	HCD	LFA	HCD[2]
Mother report						
% in "very good" or "excellent" health	−0.12	−0.07	−0.26**	−0.12	−0.07	−0.24*
% with physical, emotional, mental condition impeding mothers' school/work	0.34**	0.18	−0.07	−0.08	−0.10	0.01
% with physical, emotional, mental condition requiring medical attention, equipment, medication	0.30**	0.34***	0.02	0.01	−0.02	−0.02

[1] Only variables on which any statistically significant impacts were found are shown in this table. For details on impact estimates (and effect sizes) for *all* child outcomes examined at the five-year point, see Hamilton et al., 2002.
[2] Only mothers deemed to be in need of basic skills were enrolled in Riverside's HCD program. Thus, effect sizes in this column pertain only to this disadvantaged subgroup, unlike effect sizes for other impacts reported in this table.
*$p < .05$. **$p < .01$. ***$p < .001$.

being in "very good" or "excellent" health. Both Atlanta's LFA and HCD programs increased the proportion of children whose mothers reported that they had "a physical, emotional, or mental condition that required frequent medical attention or the use of medication or special equipment." Atlanta's LFA program also increased the proportion of children whose mothers reported that they had "a physical, emotional, or mental condition that impedes on (the mothers') ability to go to work or school." Atlanta's impacts can be considered unfavorable (if the programs increased the prevalence of these health conditions) or favorable (if the programs increased the detection of preexisting health conditions). None of the programs affected average scores on mothers' ratings of the children's overall health or the proportion of children reported by mothers to have experienced an accident or injury requiring emergency medical treatment in the past two years.

How Do Impacts at Five Years Compare to Those at Two Years?

There were relatively few impacts on children, on average, two years after their mothers enrolled in JOBS (see McGroder et al., 2000), and there were both similarities and differences at the two time points. Impacts on the proportion of children rated by their mothers as being in "very good" or "excellent" health at both the two- and five-year follow-ups were unfavorable, although these impacts were concentrated in Riverside at the two-year point and occurred in both Riverside and Grand Rapids at the five-year point. Another point of continuity was evident in the overall balance of favorable and unfavorable impacts in specific sites. The majority of impacts in Atlanta at both time periods were favorable, regardless of whether mothers were enrolled in the LFA or the HCD program. However, earlier impacts occurred largely on measures of academic school readiness, whereas the majority of longer-term effects occurred for children's social skills and behavior. There was also continuity in Grand Rapids' LFA program, which increased maternal reports of externalizing problems at the two-year point and decreased teacher reports of cooperation and child self-reports of positive assertion three years later.

Some earlier impacts were not sustained. For example, Grand Rapids' HCD program increased the proportion of children scoring in the top 25th percentile on academic school readiness at the two-year point but did not affect math or reading achievement three years later. Indeed, Grand Rapids' HCD program had few favorable impacts on *any* outcome (and, in fact, resulted in a fair number of unfavorable impacts on behavior) at the five-year point. One could argue that more numerous unfavorable impacts would have emerged in this program if not for the earlier "boost" from improved academic school readiness, although this proposition has not been tested empirically.

There appear to have been some "sleeper effects," wherein impacts emerged at the five-year point with no indication that children were affected, or affected in that domain, at the two-year point. Neither of Atlanta's programs affected children's health outcomes at the two-year point, but each increased the proportion of children reported by mothers to have health conditions at the five-year point. Grand Rapids' HCD program did not affect children's behavioral outcomes at the two-year point, but it uniformly worsened them three years later. Grand Rapids' LFA program did not affect children's academic school readiness at the two-year point, but it increased the percent of children scoring above average on the math achievement test three years later. Finally, neither of Riverside's programs affected behavioral or academic outcomes when children were 5 to 7 years old, but Riverside's LFA program tended to worsen young children's behavior, and both improve and worsen different aspects of academic functioning, three years later.

Did Impacts Differ in Subgroups?

The Role of "Family Risk" in Moderating Impacts. In general, impacts at the five-year point did not differ according to baseline levels of family risk,[4] with two exceptions. First, Riverside's LFA program showed a pattern of lower academic performance, lessened school engagement, and increased problem behaviors for children of the "least disadvantaged" mothers. Second, there was a concentration of unfavorable impacts on children of the least disadvantaged mothers in the Atlanta LFA program, including reduced academic progress and placement, and a decline in positive behaviors. These findings are consistent with the patterns found at the two-year point, when impacts tended to be favorable for children in higher-risk families (in four programs) and unfavorable for children in lower-risk families (in three programs) (McGroder et al., 2000).

The Role of Child Gender in Moderating Impacts. Although gender differences in program impacts were not initially predicted, subsequent research showing that New Hope (a voluntary, work-based antipoverty program) affected boys and girls differently (see Huston et al., 2001) led us to examine differences in impacts by child gender. Although these programs had few effects on boys or girls at either time period, in some cases, nonsignificant patterns for the sample as a whole were masking program impacts for one but not the other gender.

PROGRAMS AND OUTCOMES ON WHICH GIRLS FARED BETTER. Each of the six programs either benefited girls more than boys, or had less detrimental impacts on girls than boys, on at least one outcome. The four programs affecting health outcomes (both programs in Atlanta, Grand Rapids' HCD program, and Riverside's LFA program) largely reflect impacts on boys. These gender differences in health impacts were not evident at the two-year point. Of note, each of Atlanta's programs increased the proportion of mothers reporting that their sons had "a physical, emotional, or mental condition that requires frequent medical attention, frequent use of medication, or the use of any special equipment, such as a wheelchair or a breathing mask." Again, this may be a problem, if Atlanta's programs somehow increased the actual prevalence of these health conditions among boys, or it may indicate that Atlanta's programs increased the diagnosis of boys' preexisting health conditions (perhaps by their families' being better connected to services).

Atlanta's LFA program improved math only among girls: It decreased the proportion of girls scoring below-average on the math achievement test, decreased the proportion of girls reported by teachers as being in

---

[4] Mothers who lacked a high-school diploma at study entry, had not worked in the year prior to study entry, and had been receiving welfare for at least two years before the study were defined as the "most disadvantaged." Mothers with one or two of these barriers were considered "moderately disadvantaged," and mothers with none of these barriers were considered "least disadvantaged."

a remedial math group, and increased the proportion of girls rated by teachers as performing above grade level in math. Atlanta's LFA program improved both girls' and boys' academic school readiness at the two-year point, suggesting sustained impacts on cognitive/academic outcomes for girls but not boys in this program.

The favorable five-year impacts of Atlanta's HCD program on social skills occurred mostly for girls. Specifically, the increase in the child's self-control and interpersonal skills and the reduction in hyperactivity and disciplinary problems (as reported by teachers) in the sample as a whole held especially for girls. Despite no aggregate impact of Atlanta's HCD program on mothers' reports of externalizing problems or on teachers' reports of positive assertion at the five-year point, there were favorable impacts on these measures for girls. These findings stand in contrast to those from the two-year follow-up, when neither of Atlanta's programs affected boys' and girls' behavior differently. In Grand Rapids, the HCD program increased teacher reports of boys' externalizing behaviors; increased discipline problems requiring notification of boys' parents; and left boys' hyperactivity (as rated by mothers) unaffected, even though it reduced girls' hyperactive behaviors. These findings stand in contrast to those from the two-year follow-up in which, when found, impacts on boys were favorable, though small.

Finally, despite no evidence of five-year impacts for the sample of children as a whole, Riverside's LFA program increased the proportion of mothers with sons (from 3.5 to 8.9%) who each reported in the five-year survey that her son had not lived with her at some point since the last interview because she couldn't care for him. By contrast, 6.5 percent of program mothers, and 5.6 percent of control group mothers, reported such a separation from their daughters ($p = $ ns).

PROGRAMS AND OUTCOMES ON WHICH BOYS FARED BETTER. The two Riverside programs benefited boys more than girls, or had less detrimental impacts on boys than girls, on multiple outcomes at the five-year point. First, Riverside's LFA program lowered scores on social skills and behavior especially among girls. Specifically, the increase in teacher reports of externalizing, internalizing, and hyperactive behaviors found for the sample as a whole held especially for girls. Second, this program increased for girls (but not for boys) the likelihood that the teacher reported a disciplinary problem. These findings are consistent with behavioral impacts at the two-year point, in which Riverside's LFA program decreased the prevalence of "high" behavior problem scores and reduced slightly the mean frequency of internalizing behavior problems for boys but not girls. Finally, and perhaps most striking, Riverside's HCD program improved boys' math and reading achievement while simultaneously *lowering* the math and reading achievement of girls. These latter impacts completely offset each other, leading to no statistically significant impacts on achievement for the sample as a whole. These gender differences in impacts of Riverside's HCD program on measures of cognitive functioning were not evident at the two-year point.

Pathways Through Which Children Were Affected

Despite the absence of strong impacts on children in either the short run or longer term, the evidence suggests that mandatory welfare-to-work programs aimed at adults can have "spillover" effects on children. Understanding the mechanisms that carry program impacts to children can inform policy makers about how to buffer against potentially negative impacts and bolster positive impacts on young children. So how did these impacts on young children come about? Unfortunately, the answers are not straightforward. There does not appear to be a single pathway through which children were affected by each of these six JOBS programs.[5]

Maternal education may have been an important pathway. At the two-year point, all of the HCD programs and Atlanta's LFA program increased the proportion of mothers receiving either a high school diploma or GED or obtaining a trade degree since study entry. These same programs had predominantly favorable impacts on children, especially those in higher-risk families, at the two-year point. One program (Grand Rapids' employment-focused program) reduced degree receipt at the two-year point, and this program also worsened children's behavior problems. Five years after study entry, two programs continued to have positive impacts on both maternal education and child outcomes, and Grand Rapids' employment-focused program continued to have negative impacts on maternal education and to worsen child outcomes. In the other three programs, maternal education was not affected at the five-year point, even though children were, suggesting either earlier educational changes had lasting effects, or other factors contributed to these effects on children.

Program impacts on mothers' psychological well-being and parenting may underlie effects on children in some cases. At the two-year point the program-induced increase in maternal depressive symptomatology and reduction in warm parenting completely mediated the unfavorable impact of Grand Rapids' employment-focused program on children's externalizing behaviors. Also, improvements in parenting (as well as greater employment) partially mediated the favorable impact of Atlanta's LFA program on children's academic school readiness, and improvements in parenting completely mediated the favorable impact of Atlanta's LFA program on

---

[5] Failure of adult and child impacts to map at the aggregate level does not rule out the possibility that these adult impacts operate as pathways for certain subgroups of families.

children's externalizing behavior (see McGroder et al., 2000, for greater detail).

Income was theorized as another possible pathway, but none of the six JOBS programs altered income, on average. A few programs changed the proportion of families in poverty at the two-year point, which may help to explain impacts on children in middle childhood.[6] Both programs in Grand Rapids increased the proportion of families living below poverty at the two-year point and worsened child outcomes at both the two- and five-year points. The Riverside HCD program decreased poverty, and the Atlanta LFA program decreased "deep" poverty, at the two-year point, and the pattern of impacts for children in these programs was largely favorable three years later.

DISCUSSION

Do impacts on preschool-age children of mandatory welfare-to-work programs persist into middle childhood? The COS provides an experimental test of how changes in family context, brought about by mandatory welfare-to-work programs, affect children.

Persistence of Impacts into Middle Childhood

The strongest evidence of persistence, within program and within developmental domain, can be seen in Grand Rapids, whose LFA program worsened children's behavior at both the early elementary and middle childhood time points. Atlanta's programs had persistently favorable impacts, though they occurred in different developmental domains early and later.

Evidence that impacts were not persistent includes both "sleeper effects" and "fadeout effects." Two programs increased behavior problems in middle childhood despite not having affected behavior in early childhood, and two programs affected academic functioning in middle childhood despite not having affected academic school readiness in early childhood. At the same time, one program improved academic school readiness in early childhood but did not affect math or reading achievement three years later.

Toward a Broader Theoretical Framework

What have we learned in the last 15 years, from the COS and from subsequent evaluations, about whether and how children are affected by their mothers' enrollment in a mandatory welfare-to-work program? As proposed by Zaslow, Moore, and colleagues, children can be affected by

---

[6] Impacts on poverty were not examined at the five-year point, so it is not known whether longer-term changes in material well-being may have played a role in longer-term impacts on children.

welfare-to-work programs; effects can be positive, negative, or neutral; impacts can occur on children's cognitive, behavior, and health outcomes; impacts can differ in different subgroups; and the pathways through which children are affected include both those targeted by welfare policies (e.g., education, employment, income) and those not targeted (e.g., maternal psychological well-being, parenting) (Zaslow et al., 1995).

The overall pattern of findings shows that, while impacts on young children can occur, they most often do not. It may be that the programs did not have sufficiently large or enduring effects on the pathways affecting children, such as stable maternal employment, adequate family income, and supportive environments in children's daily lives (home, child care, school). Also, effects on children's environments may have canceled one another. For example, Atlanta's employment-focused program increased time stress reported by mothers at the two-year point (which predicted greater problem behaviors in children), but it also increased employment and improved mothers' parenting (which predicted fewer problem behaviors). The net effect for children was a slight reduction in behavior problems.

Material Versus Maternal Influence: Are Income Increases Necessary to Improve Children's Outcomes?

Emerging evidence indicates that young children benefit from welfare-to-work programs only when both parental employment and family income are improved. Three recent syntheses of findings from experimental evaluations of welfare-to-work and antipoverty programs found that total income can be affected by programs containing strong financial incentives for work, and that these programs often lead to improved school achievement and behavior for children in middle childhood (Morris, Huston, Duncan, Crosby, &6009"> works, for whom, under what circumstances, and through what processes. In Bos, 2001; Sherman, 2001; Zaslow et al., 2002). Although the JOBS programs evaluated in the COS did not affect average levels of household income, four programs affected families' poverty status in ways consistent with the direction of subsequent impacts on children. This set of findings suggests that examinations of family economic resources need to take into account not only absolute levels of family income but also more subtle variations in relation to the poverty line.

In sum, there is no single answer to the question of why children were affected. Impacts on children reflect the net effect of changes in multiple aspects of family life, some of which, like education and employment, were targeted by the programs, and others, like income and parenting, were not. The pathways though which one program affected children may be different from the pathways through which a different program affected children. Despite the in-depth information collected on children's environments, the evaluation may have failed to measure other conduits through which young children were affected by their mothers' enrollment in a JOBS program.

The Importance of Site

Contrary to hypotheses, the study found few differences in impacts on children according to program approach (human capital vs. labor-force attachment). Instead, impacts varied by site, suggesting that characteristics of the research site – including characteristics of the population served, local economic conditions, welfare benefit levels, and the ethos and practices of the local welfare office – are key for understanding impacts on children and families.

Both population characteristics and welfare administrative practices differed across sites. The relatively large caseload per case worker in Grand Rapids may have made it more difficult to give personal attention to clients, whereas the smaller caseloads in Atlanta, along with this site's "customer-oriented" approach to case management, may have facilitated greater personal attention to clients. Atlanta and Grand Rapids also served different types of clients. We have already noted a pattern of unfavorable impacts on children in lower-risk families – a pattern that has been found in other welfare evaluations (see review in Zaslow et al., 2002). Study families in Grand Rapids appear to have been less disadvantaged at study entry, on average, than families in Atlanta. Compared to their counterparts in Atlanta at study entry, mothers in the Grand Rapids site were less likely to have three or more children, less likely to be living in public or subsidized housing, more likely to have ever been married, more likely to have "higher" literacy, and were more likely to have had earnings in the past 12 months. The Grand Rapids sample was also composed of White, Black, and some Hispanic mothers, whereas the Atlanta sample was predominantly Black. (See Yoshikawa et al., 2006, for an examination of the impacts of JOBS on children according to race and ethnic group.) Though the mechanisms are not yet clear, site demographics and/or the context in which the LFA programs were implemented in Atlanta and Grand Rapids seem to have shaped impacts on children.

The Potential Importance of Child Gender

In most cases, impacts found held equally for boys and girls, although there were some indications that boys and girls responded differently to their mothers' enrollment in a mandatory welfare-to-work program. These gender differences, like impact findings in general, varied across programs and sites. There were more instances of girls being favorably affected than boys, which contrasts with findings from New Hope, in which boys experienced more favorable program impacts than girls (Huston et al., 2001). Of note were the offsetting impacts of Riverside's HCD program on achievement test scores, improving boys' scores but lowering girls' scores (relative to the control group). The inconsistency of these gender differences across sites and across studies suggests that gender differences in the impacts of welfare-to-work and antipoverty programs on children may be highly localized and idiosyncratic.

Policy Implications

The Family Support Act and the JOBS Program introduced key features that are still major elements in today's welfare policies and programs – most notably, the social contract that requires welfare recipients to prepare for and secure employment as a condition of receiving public assistance or face financial repercussions. Consequently, findings from the COS shed light on what might be expected with respect to the shorter- and longer-term impacts of today's mandatory welfare-to-work programs on children as they move from preschool age into middle childhood.

Although the study found few impacts on preschool-age children of single mothers assigned to one of these JOBS programs, the pattern of longer-term impacts on children's behavior may prove to be important, because research has shown that a history of antisocial behavior in childhood is the strongest risk factor for chronic delinquency among adolescents (Farrington, 1987). This may be particularly germane for Grand Rapids' HCD program, which not only reduced positive behaviors but also increased antisocial behaviors (especially among boys) when these children were between 8 and 10 years old. Other chapters in this volume indicate that the patterns formed in middle childhood may serve as a harbinger of things to come in adolescence and early adulthood (e.g., Huston et al., 2001).

Findings of this study also call attention to the potential importance of the context in which a policy is implemented (e.g., caseload, program ethos, population served) for shaping program impacts. Gaining a better understanding of the circumstances under which welfare-to-work programs affect children of various ages can help inform the development, targeting, and implementation of welfare programs and policy.

It is important to keep in mind that, even when they were favorably affected by these programs, children in this study still remained at risk for problem outcomes – especially with regard to academic achievement and school progress – as they moved into middle childhood. In short, the results from the COS might have implications not only for the design of welfare policy and programs, but also for federal, state, and local programs and policies aimed at the education, development, and well-being of low-income children more generally.

This chapter was adapted from a research brief titled "Impacts of a Mandatory Welfare-to-Work Program on Children at School Entry and Beyond: Findings from the NEWWS Child Outcomes Study," by Sharon M. McGroder, Martha J. Zaslow, Kristin A. Moore, & Jennifer L. Brooks and funded by the Office of the Assistant Secretary for Planning and Evaluation (ASPE) in the U.S. Department of Health and Human Services. We would like to thank ASPE for granting us permission to reprint parts of this research brief.

The NEWWS and COS were funded by the Administration for Children and Families and the Office of the Assistant Secretary for Planning and Evaluation in the U.S. Department of Health and Human Services, with additional funding from the U.S. Department of Education, the Foundation for Child Development, and the William T. Grant Foundation. The NEWWS was conducted by MDRC, and the COS was conduced by Child Trends, under subcontract to MDRC. The views expressed in this chapter are those of the authors alone and should not be construed to represent the official views of the U.S. Department of Health and Human Services or the U.S. Department of Education.

We gratefully acknowledge the contributions of Child Trends research and support staff over the years, without whom the COS – and, thus, this chapter – would not have been possible.

References

Bronfenbrenner, U. (1979). *The ecology of human development: Experiments by nature and design*. Cambridge, MA: Harvard University Press.
Connell, J. (1990). *The Research Assessment Package for Schools, Student Self-Report*. (Unpublished report) Rochester, NY: University of Rochester
Farrington, D. P. (1987). Early precursors of frequent offending. In J. Q. Wilson & G. C. Loury (Eds.), *From children to citizens: Families, school, and delinquency prevention*. New York: Springer-Verlag.
Gresham, F. M., & Elliot, S. N. (1990). *Social Skills Rating System manual*. Circle Pines, MN: American Guidance Service.
Hamilton, G. (2002). *Moving people from welfare to work: Lessons from the National Evaluation of Welfare-to-Work Strategies*. Washington, DC: U.S. Department of Health and Human Services, Administration for Children and Families and Office of the Assistant Secretary for Planning and Evaluation, and U.S. Department of Education.
Hamilton, G., Brock, T., Farrell, M., Friedlander, D., & Harknett, K. (1997). *Evaluating two welfare-to-work program approaches: Two year findings on the Labor Force Attachment and Human Capital Development Programs in three sites*. Washington, DC: U.S. Department of Health and Human Services, Administration for Children and Families and Office of the Assistant Secretary for Planning and Evaluation.

Hamilton, G., Freedman, S., Gennetian, L., Michalopoulos, C., Walter, J., Adams-Ciardullo, D., et al. (2001). *National Evaluation of Welfare-to-Work Strategies: How effective are different welfare-to-work approaches? Five-year adult and child impacts for eleven programs. Executive Summary.* Washington, DC: U.S. Department of Health and Human Services, Administration for Children and Families and Office of the Assistant Secretary for Planning and Evaluation, and U.S. Department of Education.

Huston, A. C., Duncan, G. J., Granger, R., Bos, J., McLoyd, V., Mistry, R., et al. (2001). Work-based antipoverty programs for parents can enhance the school performance and social behavior of children. *Child Development, 72,* 318–336.

McGroder, S. M., Zaslow, M. J., Moore, K. A., & LeMenestrel, S. M. (2000). *The National Evaluation of Welfare-to-Work Strategies: Impacts on young children and their families two years after enrollment: Findings from the Child Outcomes Study.* Washington, DC: U.S. Department of Health and Human Services, Administration for Children and Families and Office of the Assistant Secretary for Planning and Evaluation, and U.S. Department of Education.

Moore, K. A., Evans, V. J., Brooks-Gunn, J., & Roth, J. (2001). What are good child outcomes? In A. Thornton (Ed.), *The well-being of children and families: Research and data needs.* Ann Arbor, MI: University of Michigan Press.

Moore, K. A., & Halle, T. G. (2001). Preventing problems vs. promoting the positive: What do we want for our children? In S. Hofferth & T. Owens (Eds.), *Children at the millennium: Where have we come from, where are we going?* Greenwich, CT: JAI Press.

Morris, P. A., Huston, A. C., Duncan, G. J., Crosby, D. A., & Bos, J. M. (2001). *How welfare-to-work policies affect children: A synthesis of research.* New York: MDRC.

Sherman, A. (2001). *How children fare in welfare experiments appears to hinge on income.* Washington, DC: Children's Defense Fund.

Woodcock, R. W., & Mather, N. (1989, 1990). WJ-R tests of achievement: examiner's manual. In R. W. Woodcock M. B. Johnson, *Woodcock-Johnson Psycho-Educational Battery-Revised.* Allen, TX: DLM Teaching Resources.

Yoshikawa, H., Morris, P., Gennetian, L., Roy, A. L., Gassman-Pines, A., & Godfrey, E. B. (2006). Effects of welfare and employment policies on middle childhood school performance: Do they vary by race/ethnicity, and if so, why? In A. C. Huston & M. N. Ripke (Eds.), *Developmental contexts in middle childhood: Bridges to adulthood* (pp. 370–384). New York: Cambridge University Press.

Zaslow, M. J., Moore, K. A., Brooks, J. L., Morris, P., Tout, K., Redd, Z., & Emig, C. (2002). Experimental studies of welfare reform and children. *Future of Children, 12*(1), 79–95.

Zaslow, M. J., Moore, K. A., Morrison, D., & Coiro, M. J. (1995). The Family Support Act and children: Potential pathways of influence. *Children and Youth Services Review, 17,* 231–249.

18

Effects of Welfare and Employment Policies on Middle-Childhood School Performance

Do They Vary by Race/Ethnicity and, If So, Why?

Hirokazu Yoshikawa, Pamela Morris, Lisa Gennetian,
Amanda L. Roy, Anna Gassman-Pines, and
Erin B. Godfrey

In recent years, research examining the effects of welfare and antipoverty policies on children and adolescents has surged (Chase-Lansdale et al., 2003; Gennetian et al., 2002; Morris, Huston, Duncan, Crosby, & Bos, 2001; Huston et al., 2001; Yoshikawa, Rosman, & Hsueh, 2001; Yoshikawa, Magnuson, Bos, & Hsueh, 2003). Much of this interest has stemmed from the implementation of large-scale, nonexperimental and experimental studies assessing the effects of particular welfare-to-work approaches on school performance. These studies, in turn, were motivated by policy developments, starting in the 1980s, that first resulted in the Family Support Act of 1988; then over the course of the 1990s a series of welfare policy waiver programs in many states, and culminated in the passage of the Personal Responsibility and Work Opportunity Reconciliation Act of 1996 (Weaver, 2000). That legislation transformed the welfare system in the United States from an entitlement program to one contingent on work effort and subject to a cumulative lifetime limit of 60 months. As of this writing, that act is still in the process of reauthorization in the U.S. Congress.

Little research has examined whether race/ethnicity might moderate the effects of welfare policies in middle childhood. This question is of interest for several reasons. First, race and ethnicity continue to be major sources of social stratification in the United States. Racial and ethnic gaps in children's school achievement and earlier school readiness are persistent, despite some declines in recent years (Lee & Burkham, 2002; Jencks & Phillips, 1998). These gaps emerge first in early childhood, but widen substantially across middle childhood. Second, predictors of racial and ethnic gaps in middle-childhood school achievement include some factors that are targeted by welfare and antipoverty policy, such as earnings, income, and employment. Third, the soaring percentages of immigrant groups in the United States include substantial populations in poverty (Hernandez, 1999). At the very least, from the standpoint of equity, researchers and policy makers should be interested in whether recent approaches to policy reform may be having differential impacts on children from different racial, ethnic, and immigrant backgrounds.

This chapter considers whether effects of antipoverty policy on children's school performance differ by ethnicity, and if so, why. We explore several hypotheses: those that derive from human capital theory, theories about family structure and family process, and person-environment fit theory. A major finding is that, in addition to the role of human capital, we find evidence to support the hypothesis that person-environment fit matters. That is, the fit between policy contexts and personal values and goals, such as motivation to pursue one's own education, appears to play a role in explaining differences by race and ethnicity in effects of welfare and employment policies on children.

WHY MIGHT EFFECTS OF WELFARE POLICIES IN MIDDLE CHILDHOOD DIFFER BY RACE OR ETHNICITY?

Why might children of different racial or ethnic groups be affected differently by welfare policies? To answer this question, we must ask another question that takes into account the fact that welfare policies are essentially parent-directed interventions: Why might parents of different racial or ethnic groups respond differently to policy requirements, incentives, and messages? This section considers three possible explanations, stemming from three theories of contextual influences on middle-childhood adjustment – human capital theory, theories of family structure, and person–environment fit theory.

Human Capital

Human capital theory was developed to explain how economic resources in one generation translate into higher earnings in the next (Becker, 1964, 1991; Schultz, 1961). Specifically, resources are passed on to children in the form of expenditures on children's health, skills, learning and education, and credentials (Becker & Tomes, 1986; Haveman & Wolfe, 1995; Kalil & DeLeire, 2004). Developmental studies conducted in middle childhood have bolstered human capital theory. National data sets show that a substantial proportion of the association between income, on the one hand, and middle-childhood cognitive outcomes and school performance, on the other, is explained by differences in the amount of observed cognitive stimulation in the home (books, toys, other learning materials and activities) (Bradley & Corwin, in press; Duncan & Brooks-Gunn, 1997; Duncan, Brooks-Gunn, Yeung, & Smith, 1998; Yeung, Linver, & Brooks-Gunn, 2002). No evaluation of welfare policies has examined whether differences in human capital explain differences across race or ethnicity in effects of the policies.

Extending this line of thought to potential racial/ethnic differences in effects of these policies on children, we note the following. First, parents from three major racial/ethnic groups in the United States – White, African American, and Latino – have shown persistent differences in levels of human capital, and these appear linked to differences in their children's educational attainment (Burkham & Lee, 2002; Jencks & Phillips, 1998; Kao, 1999). Specifically, differences in indicators of human capital, such as income, earnings, and education, partially account for observed Black–White and Latino–White differences in academic achievement (usually in middle childhood or adolescence). Similarly, differences in cognitive stimulation, the form of parenting that is most closely linked to economic resources in the home, appear to account for the effect of race and ethnicity as well. Most of these studies have examined Black–White differences in standardized test scores; some have examined Latino–White differences as well. Should effects of antipoverty policies on children differ by race or ethnicity, such a pattern of effects could be explained by differences in effects of the policies on parent human capital.

Family Structure

Effects of welfare policy on family structure, such as marriage, cohabitation or contact with noncustodial parents, may differ across African American, Latino, and White families. Rates of two- versus single-parent families differ across these groups (McLanahan & Sandefur, 1994). In qualitative studies, low-income parents report often stringent conditions for feeling ready to marry; many of the requirements include progress on human capital indicators, such as finding a steady, well-paying job, or achieving educational goals (Gassman-Pines, Yoshikawa, & Nay, in press; Gibson & Edin, 2002). Several studies show that values supporting the importance of marriage and pressures to marry in low-income Mexican American families are stronger than in low-income White or African American families (e.g., Oropesa, 1996). Some ethnographies show that post-immigration families of particular Latino ethnicities undergo changes in the gender roles of mother and father, with mothers' employment becoming more acceptable in the United States. However, when this occurs, expectations regarding mothers' childrearing and housekeeping roles often do not change (Levitt, 2001; Pessar, 1995).

Values and Person–Environment Fit

Finally, person–environment fit theory suggests that characteristics of the individual – for example, developmental stage or values – may, in part, determine how that individual selects or responds to different environmental demands (Eccles et al., 1993; Moos, 1987). Congruence between environmental demands and personal goals, values, and attitudes, for example, could produce higher levels of adjustment and well-being. Such theories have never been applied to policy environments; they could help explain ethnic differences in effects of welfare policies on child development.

Values and goals relevant to work and education are highly salient developmental concerns for parents in young adulthood, who often have young children. Such values and goals might interact with welfare program approaches to influence parents' responses to policy-driven mandates and their children's development. Imagine, for example, a single parent on welfare, without her GED, who has high levels of motivation to pursue her own education. She might fare better in a welfare policy environment that encourages education and job training rather than immediate job search. In a policy environment that encourages immediate work, a parent who prefers working over staying at home with her children might fare better than one who believes that work may interfere with good parenting. Responses to mandates, such as involvement in adult education activities or employment, might then influence children through intervening family processes, such as higher expectations for one's own and children's future education, cognitive stimulation, parent well-being, or monitoring.

Parent Well-Being

Finally, parent well-being or distress, manifested in such indicators as parental depressive symptoms, may help explain ethnic differences in effects of welfare policies on children. Involvement with welfare and employment policy offices and bureaucracies, as well as receipt of welfare itself, can enhance feelings of stigma. High levels of perceived welfare stigma predicted higher levels of subsequent employment, in one recent study (Yoshikawa et al., 2003). Research indicates that the brunt of welfare stigma in public opinion about welfare falls on African Americans, with somewhat lesser but still stigmatized associations with Latinos and Whites. Martin Gilens's research has shown persuasively that the American public's particular hatred of cash welfare assistance (greater in animosity than towards any other public program) was entirely explained by stereotypes about African Americans as lazy or otherwise undeserving (Gilens, 1999). Although welfare stigma may affect all families on welfare to some degree, its effects on well-being may be particularly strong for African Americans.

TYPES OF WELFARE AND EMPLOYMENT POLICIES

In 1996, the U.S. cash assistance system was overhauled, in the most drastic change to policies affecting poor families since the introduction of Aid to Dependent Children in the 1930s. A much stronger emphasis on work was introduced, chiefly through requirements to participate in work activities for welfare recipients, abolishment of welfare as an entitlement program, and the institution of a cumulative lifetime limit of 60 months for the receipt of federal welfare benefits (P.L. 104–193).

Assessing the impact of the 1996 law on child outcomes has been difficult because the law was introduced at the same time in all areas of the United States; there was no "natural experiment," with affected and unaffected areas (Blank, 2002; Smolensky & Gootman, 2003). In addition, a variety of other historical policy and economic changes were in process at the time, and these might have contributed to any observed changes in child development. Most prominent among these were the historically strong economy of the mid- to late-1990s and the expansion of the Earned Income Tax Credit, which, for low-wage workers, rewarded work with increased income. Evidence on the effect of recent welfare policy can be obtained from more indirect sources. Chief among these are a set of experimental demonstrations of welfare and antipoverty policies conducted by the Manpower Demonstration Research Corporation (MDRC) and some other policy institutes, and a few large nonexperimental, longitudinal studies, such as the Three-City Study (Chase-Lansdale et al., 2003).

In this chapter, we focus on experimental data, specifically a set of 16 experimental evaluations of welfare and antipoverty policy, all conducted between the early 1990s and 2000s. This set of evaluations has been described in detail elsewhere (Gennetian et al., 2002; Hamilton et al., 2001; Morris et al., 2001). The evaluations were conducted in a variety of state and local settings, in the United States and Canada. For the most part, the populations they targeted were single parents on welfare; in some cases, particular programs targeted a broader population of low-income parents. The studies all focused on increasing work effort, but in different ways that we will outline below. In each of the studies, eligible families (typically, those recertifying their welfare benefits, or newly applying for them) were randomly assigned to either a new set of rules governing welfare and other benefit receipt (experimental condition) or the then-existing Aid to Families with Dependent Children (AFDC) rules (control group).

The experiments took different approaches to changing welfare rules and regulations. They reflect some of the kinds of policy variation in current Temporary Assistance for Needy Families (TANF) programs, but not all. In one set of programs, which we refer to as *earnings supplement programs*, parents' increased work efforts were rewarded with wage supplements. These occurred in three experiments: (a) the Self-Sufficiency Project, targeting welfare recipients in two provinces in Canada; (b) the Minnesota Family Investment Program, conducted within the welfare system in several counties in that state, which included two experimental conditions in addition to a control condition; and (c) the New Hope Project, conducted outside the welfare system in Milwaukee. The Minnesota program provided not an outright earnings supplement in the form of a check, like the other two programs, but a generous "earnings disregard." An earnings disregard is an alteration in the ratio by which additional earnings are counted against one's welfare benefits. The more generous the earnings disregard, the less that increased earnings reduced welfare benefits, with the result being higher overall income.

In another set of programs, work was mandated, but there were no efforts to supplement income, as in the earnings supplement programs. We call these *mandated employment programs*. That is, if the recipient did not engage in some work-related activity, her welfare benefits were reduced (often referred to as "sanctioning"). Among these programs, there were two subtypes: those in which caseworkers emphasized education and job training (human capital development programs) prior to work, and those in which caseworkers emphasized immediate job experience (labor force attachment programs). This contrast was made possible in the National Evaluation of Welfare-to-Work Strategies, or NEWWS. In three NEWWS cities – Atlanta, Grand Rapids, and Riverside County, California – each of those two conditions were implemented, in addition to a control condition. In the NEWWS programs, no earnings supplement was implemented (that is, for welfare recipients making transitions to work or increasing their work effort, every additional dollar gained in earnings represented a dollar lost in welfare benefits).

Finally, two programs, in Connecticut and Florida, incorporated *time limits*. The Connecticut Jobs First program, implemented in two cities in that state, incorporated a relatively generous earnings supplement, in the form of an earnings disregard, but coupled it with the shortest time limit yet introduced in any of the states: 21 months. The Florida program, implemented in one county in that state, was essentially a work-first program with some additional support services. The Florida Family Transition Program imposed a time limit of 24 out of the last 60 months for most families, for receipt of welfare, and 36 out of 72 months for the least job-ready.

The sample of data from the 16 experiments was restricted in several ways to accommodate our particular analysis questions. First, we required a minimum of 150 families in each racial ethnic group per study. Second, data had to be available on the child outcome measures of interest in middle childhood (between the ages of 6 and 12 at follow-up). In general, we consider those programs in which follow-up assessments of child school performance were conducted between two and four years after random assignment. In addition, in the six NEWWS programs, we consider longer-term (five year) follow-up effects. Analyses examining five-year impacts from some of the other programs are forthcoming but were not completed at the time of this writing.

We cite results from several studies conducted using these experimental data. We focus on several research questions:

1. Do welfare and employment policies' *short-term effects* on middle-childhood school performance differ by race/ethnicity (African American, Latino, or White)? Here we use the most complete set

of experimental programs, investigating differences by type of program approach.

2. Do welfare and employment policies' *long-term effects* on middle-childhood school performance differ by race/ethnicity (African American, Latino, or White)? Here we focus on the mandatory employment programs in the NEWWS evaluation, in which a five-year follow-up was conducted.

3. Do these welfare and employment policies' long-term effects on *school dropout rates* differ by race/ethnicity (African American, Latino, or White)? Here we focus again on the five-year follow-up of the NEWWS programs.

In cases where we do find racial/ethnic differences, we examine whether the differences were due to factors reviewed above, associated with human capital theory, family structure, or person–environment fit theory.

We tested our hypotheses by estimating OLS regression models in which treatment status (e.g., whether in the experimental or control group) varies with parents' race/ethnic group. We accomplished this by constructing a set of interaction terms of race/ethnicity categories (African American, Latino, and White) with the experimental dummy in each program. We also include dummy variables for these racial/ethnic group categories and type of test, plus baseline controls and a measure of the time between baseline and the given achievement assessment. Huber-White methods were employed in all analyses to adjust standard errors for nonindependence of multiple reports per child and multiple children per family.

Do Welfare and Employment Policies' Short-Term Effects on Middle-Childhood School Achievement Differ by Race/Ethnicity?

To answer our first research question, we pooled data from all of our studies (including all nine welfare and antipoverty program experiments). Comprising approximately 30,000 observations of children ages 2 to 15 at the time of random assignment, the majority of whom lived in single-parent families, our data include information about children's academic achievement between two and three years after random assignment as well as detailed histories of parents' employment, welfare use, and income. Academic achievement was measured through teacher report (two programs Connecticut Jobs First and New Hope), standardized math test (one program – the Self-Sufficiency Project), and parent report (other programs). We ran separate regressions for three child age groups, based on age at the beginning of the study (early childhood, ages 2–5; middle childhood, ages 6–9; and early adolescence, ages 10–15). Follow-up periods were two or three years, for the most part, and four years in one program.

We find that while there is some variation in effects across racial ethnic groups, these differences in effects never reach statistical significance at conventional levels. More specifically, we find that effects for the children who were youngest (ages 2–5) at study entry are generally positive for all three racial/ethnic groups, with effects most pronounced for Black and White children (average effect sizes across programs were +.10 for Black children, +.04 for Latino children, and +.06 for White children). Consistent with prior work, positive effects (albeit not always statistically significant) are more consistently found in the programs with generous earnings supplements. Effects for the middle-childhood (ages 6–9) children are neutral across program types and for both generous supplement policies and other program types (average effect sizes across programs were −.02 for Black children, −.01 for Latino children, and +.01 for White children). Finally, effects for the oldest children (ages 10–15 at random assignment) are generally negative and statistically significant Black and Latino adolescents (average effect sizes across programs were −.16 for Black adolescents, −.20 for Latino adolescents, and −.08 for White adolescents). Although the effects are somewhat stronger for Black and Latino adolescents, no significant differences in the size of effects were found among these three groups. In addition, these negative effects were found for both program models. In sum, the pattern of effects mirrors those we have found in prior work on this sample (Gennetian et al., 2002; Morris, Duncan, & Clark-Kauffman, 2004) and does not differ significantly by racial/ethnic group.

Do Welfare and Employment Policies' Long-Term Effects on Middle-Childhood School Performance Differ by Race/Ethnicity?

Here we focus on two programs from the NEWWS evaluation in which five-year follow-ups were conducted. Children were ages 3 to 5 at the time parents entered the study, and between ages 8 and 10 at the follow-up. Hence, this analysis provides information about the effects of the changes in family context brought about by the NEWWS program in early childhood on development in middle childhood. Recall that the NEWWS programs tested the mandating of employment-related activities and did not include earnings supplements. In each of these programs, a three-way random assignment experiment was conducted. The two experimental conditions included an "education-first" approach and a "work-first" approach. In the education-first (or human capital development) approach, caseworkers emphasized engagement in adult basic education, GED classes, English as a Second Language classes, or college prior to or in addition to work. In the work-first (or labor force attachment) approach, caseworkers emphasized short-term job club and job search activities, followed by entry into work.

In both the education-first and work-first approaches, noninvolvement in activities brought about sanctions (reductions in welfare benefits). A control condition represented the third condition; recipients in this condition were subject to the then-current AFDC rules and regulations, which did not require involvement in education or work activities. In one program, in Riverside County, California, our sample consisted of Latino families (primarily Mexican) and White families. In the other, located in Grand Rapids, Michigan, our sample consisted of African American and White families. Our outcome measures were the Woodcock-Johnson (III-R) reading and math tests.

We found some evidence of racial/ethnic differences in experimental impacts on standardized math and reading achievement at age 5. For both math and reading, and in both education-first and work-first comparisons to the control group, Latino families in Riverside experienced more positive impacts on achievement than White families. Similarly, for both math and reading achievement, and in both education-first and work-first comparisons to the control group, African American families in Grand Rapids experienced more positive impacts on achievement than White families. The differences in impacts by race/ethnicity were of a magnitude larger than .20 effect size in six of the eight comparisons. In the case of math achievement in Grand Rapids Education First and Riverside Education First, these differences in impacts were especially large and significant (in Grand Rapids Education First, effect sizes were +.28 and −.28 for African American and White children, respectively; in Riverside Education First, effect sizes were +.24 and −.24 for Latino and White children, respectively; Yoshikawa, Gassman-Pines, Morris, Gennetian, & Godfrey, 2004).

What may explain these differences? We examined this question for the two experiment-by-ethnicity interactions for which we found statistically significant interactions (math scores in Grand Rapids and Riverside). We tested four possible mediators: parents' value for their own education; working parents' human capital (months of education) and cognitive stimulation to the child; family structure (marriage, cohabitation); and maternal depressive symptoms, as assessed by the CES-D measure. All of these were measured at the previous two-year follow-up, except for value of education, which was available only at baseline. For each of these, we tested whether the regression coefficient representing the experiment-by-ethnicity interaction was reduced after including experiment-by-mediator interactions.

In Grand Rapids, none of the possible mediators accounted for the more positive effect of the experimental programs on the math skills of African American children (as compared to White children). In Riverside, months of education partly accounted for the more positive effect of the experimental program on Latino children's math skills in comparison with White children. Latino parents in the education-first condition engaged in higher levels of adult education activities than their Latino or White counterparts in the control conditions, and their White counterparts in the education-first condition. A significant indirect effect was found of the experiment-by-race interaction on math scores, through months of education, which met statistical conditions for mediation (Mackinnon, Lockwood, Hoffman, West, & Sheets, 2002; Shrout & Bolger, 2002).

Do the Welfare and Employment Policies' Long-Term Effects on Dropout Rates Differ by Race/Ethnicity (African American, Latino, or White)?

To answer our third and final question, we used the same two programs – Grand Rapids and Riverside – that were described in the prior section, and the same methods. However, our developmental outcome for these analyses was school dropout, and we focused on the adolescent sample in NEWWS (that is, those who were ages 10 to 14 at random assignment, and ages 15 to 19 at the five-year follow-up), covering the late middle-childhood to adolescent years. A single, mother-reported item measured high school dropout.

The effects of both education-first programs on dropout varied by race/ethnicity. In Grand Rapids, African American adolescents in the education-first group were more likely to have dropped out (20%) than were those in the control group (10%) – a contrast with the positive program effects on their younger siblings. In White families, a slight decrease in dropping out in the experimental group was observed (23% in the control group; 18% in the education-first group). In Riverside, in contrast, a decrease in dropout (17% in the control group, 7% in the education-first group) was observed among Latino families, while an increase (10% in the control group, 20% in the education-first group) was observed among White families (Roy & Yoshikawa, 2004).

Again we tested the potential mediating effects of parents' value for their own education, human capital and cognitive stimulation, family structure, and maternal well-being. In Riverside, the value of the parents' own education accounted for part of the ethnic difference in dropout rates. The experiment reduced dropout only for adolescents whose parents placed a high value on education, and increased dropout for those whose parents placed low value on their own education. This finding supports the person–environment fit hypothesis. In this sample, Latinos placed a higher value on their own education than did the White parents. Prior research has also suggested that immigrant parents place higher value on education than do U.S.-born parents (Kao & Tienda, 1995). Recall that our Latino sample is largely Mexican. The education-first program appears to have provided a better fit with these Latina mothers' goals to pursue their own education; this seems to have translated into lower dropout rates for their children.

Although data on immigration status was unfortunately not collected in the NEWWS evaluation, census data indicate that the majority of Mexican parents in Riverside County living in poverty are immigrant parents. And the majority of these parents were likely to be legal immigrants, as they were in the welfare system. As for Grand Rapids, and the African American and White sample there, the story is less clear. None of the mediators tested reduced the size of the experiment-by-ethnicity interaction on dropout.

THE ROLE OF HUMAN CAPITAL AND PERSON–ENVIRONMENT FIT IN EXPLAINING EFFECTS OF WELFARE POLICY ON CHILDREN FROM DIFFERENT ETHNIC GROUPS

Our research contributes to the overlooked question of whether and why the effects of welfare and antipoverty policies on children might vary by ethnicity. Our goal was to examine whether welfare and employment policies, tested in nine experimental demonstrations, affected middle-childhood school performance differently for children of different races or ethnic groups. Overall, we found few short-term (two- and three-year) differences. As prior research has found (Gennetian et al., 2002; Morris et al., 2004), the effects of welfare policies on children's school performance are generally small and positive for those experiencing them in early child-hood (outcomes in middle childhood), and small and negative for those experiencing them as adolescents. Morris et al. (2004) have found, in pooled analyses across a larger number of programs than we examine here, that the positive effects coincide with the transition to schooling, and that the negative effects coincide roughly with the transition to junior high school. Our current analyses suggest that there are no racial/ethnic differences in this developmental pattern.

However, we did find some striking long-term (five-year) differences in the effects of mandatory work-first and education-first programs on middle-childhood standardized achievement and later school dropout rates. These were generally consistent across the two age groups (those who experienced the policies in early childhood, and those who experienced them in middle childhood and early adolescence). We found that effects of mandatory education-first programs, in particular, had more beneficial effects on Black than White children in Grand Rapids, Michigan, and more beneficial effects on Latino than White children in Riverside County, California.

Why might mandatory education-first programs have had different effects on Black, Latino, and White children? We investigated several hypotheses, including differences in human capital, values placed on parents' own education and work, family structure, maternal well-being, parent monitoring, and cognitive stimulation. None of these hypotheses were supported for the observed differences among Black and White children in the Grand Rapids site. That is, none of the variables representing these factors reduced the size of the experiment-by-ethnicity interaction effect.

The story was different for the Latino/White comparison. We found that the interaction between the value of education and the education-first program explained the Latino/White difference in effects on dropout in Riverside. This indicates that person–environment fit, specifically the fit between parents' motivation to pursue education and mandates that parents engage in education-related activities, may influence children's educational outcomes in early adolescence. To our knowledge, this is the first demonstration of how the match between parental goals and policy approach can influence child development. In addition, the Latino/White difference in effects of the Riverside education-first program on middle-childhood math achievement was mediated by months of adult education activities. We also found that Latino parents in Riverside reported significantly higher levels of valuing education than their White counterparts. Prior research has shown that immigrant parents place higher value on education than U.S.-born parents; we show that this makes a difference for how they respond to policy messages.

These results indicate that tailoring welfare and employment policy implementation to welfare recipients' life goals may have benefits for their children. However, we caution that these results were obtained at one place (Riverside County) at one point in time (the mid-1990s). These results bear additional efforts at replication. Unfortunately, the NEWWS evaluation was the only one of the experiments considered here that gathered data on parents' valuing of their own education.

We also note that the beneficial effects of employment policies on children, which we observed in NEWWS among Blacks and Latinos, were stronger for education-first programs than work-first programs. Current TANF policies in the states de-emphasize adult education activities. The near exclusive focus on "work first," which was made the law of the land in 1996, may be worth reconsidering. Our data show that, for some parents, "education first" may, in the long run, benefit their children's school performance.

Work on the studies reported here was supported by National Science Foundation Grant BCS0004076 to Yoshikawa, Morris, and Gennetian and a William T. Grant Foundation Scholars Award to Yoshikawa. We thank JoAnn Hsueh and Sandra Nay for research assistance and Aletha Huston, Marika Ripke, Gordon Berlin, Greg Duncan, Virginia Knox, Katherine Magnuson, and Jason Snipes for helpful comments on the work presented here.

References

Becker, G. S. (1964). *Human capital: A theoretical and empirical analysis with special reference to education.* Cambridge, MA: National Bureau of Economic Research.

Becker, G. S. (1991). *A treatise on the family: Enlarged edition.* Cambridge, MA: Harvard University Press.

Becker, G. S., & Tomes, N. (1986). An equilibrium theory of the distribution of income and intergenerational mobility. *Journal of Political Economy, 87,* 1153–1189.

Blank, R. (2002). Evaluating welfare reform in the United States. *Journal of Economic Literature, 40,* 1105–1166.

Bradley, R. H., & Corwyn, R. F. (in press). "Family process" investments that matter for child well-being: Time spent in monitoring, enriching activities, socioemotional support, providing for safety, and carefully organizing encounters with the social and physical environment. In A. Kalil & T. DeLeire (Eds.), *Parental investment in children: Resources and behaviors that promote success.* Mahwah, NJ: Lawrence Erlbaum.

Chase-Lansdale, P. L., Moffitt, R. A., Lohman, B. J., Cherlin, A. J., Coley, R. L., Pittman, L. D., et al. (2003). Mother transitions from welfare to work and the well-being of preschoolers and adolescents. *Science, 299,* 1548–1552.

Duncan, G. J., & Brooks-Gunn, J. (1997). Income effects across the life span: Integration and interpretation. In G. J. Duncan & J. Brooks-Gunn (Eds.), *Consequences of growing up poor* (pp. 596–610). New York: Russell Sage Foundation.

Duncan, G. J., Brooks-Gunn, J., Yeung, J., & Smith, J. (1998). How much does childhood poverty affect the life chances of children? *American Sociological Review, 63,* 406–423.

Eccles, J. S., Midgely, C., Wigfield, A., Buchanan, C. M., Reuman, D., Flanagan, C., et al. (1993). Development during adolescence: The impact of stage-environment fit on young adolescents' experiences in schools and families. *American Psychologist, 48,* 90–101.

Gassman-Pines, A., Yoshikawa, H., & Nay, S. (in press). Can money buy you love? The relationship of employment dynamics and anti-poverty policy to entry into marriage among single mothers. In H. Yoshikawa, T. S. Weisner, & E. Lowe (Eds.), *'If you are working, you should not be poor': Low-wage employment, family life, and child development.* New York: Russell Sage Foundation.

Gennetian, L. A., Duncan, G. J., Knox, V., Vargas, W., Clark-Kauffman, E., & London, A. S. (2002). *How welfare and work policies for parents affect adolescents: A synthesis of research.* New York: Manpower Demonstration Research Corporation.

Gibson, C., & Edin, K. (2002). *High hopes but even higher expectations: The retreat from marriage among low-income couples.* Paper presented at the Population Association of America annual meeting, Atlanta, GA.

Gilens, M. (1999). *Why Americans hate welfare: Race, media, and the politics of antipoverty policy.* Chicago: University of Chicago Press.

Hamilton, G., Freedman, S., Gennetian, L., Michalopoulos, C., Walter, J., Adams-Ciardullo, D., et al. (2001). *National Evaluation of Welfare-to-Work Strategies: Five-year impacts on adults and children in eleven programs.* Washington, DC: Administration for Children and Families and Office of the Assistant Secretary for Planning and Evaluation.

Haveman, R., & Wolfe, B. (1995). The determinants of children's attainments: A review of methods and findings. *Journal of Economic Literature, 33,* 1829–1878.

Hernandez, D. J. (1999). (Ed.). *Children of immigrants: Health, adjustment, and public assistance.* Washington, DC: National Academy Press.

Huston, A. C., Duncan, G. J., Granger, R., Bos, J., McLoyd, V., Mistry, R., et al. (2001). Work-based anti-poverty programs for parents can enhance the school performance and social behavior of children. *Child Development, 72*, 318–336.

Jencks, C., & Phillips, M. (1998). (Eds.). *The Black-White test score gap.* Washington, DC: Brookings Institution Press.

Kalil, A., & DeLeire, T. (2004). (Eds.). *Parental investment in children: Resources and behaviors that promote success.* Mahwah, NJ: Lawrence Erlbaum.

Kao, G. (1999). Psychological well-being and educational achievement among immigrant youth. In D. J. Hernandez (Ed.), *Children of immigrants: Health, adjustment, and public assistance* (pp. 410–477). Washington, DC: National Academy Press.

Kao, G., & Tienda, M. (1995). Optimism and achievement: The educational achievement of immigrant youth. *Social Science Quarterly, 76*, 1–19.

Lee, V. E., & Burkham, D. T. (2002). *Inequality at the starting gate: Social background differences in achievement as children begin school.* Washington, DC: Economic Policy Institute.

Levitt, P. (2001). *The transnational villagers.* Berkeley, CA: University of California Press.

Mackinnon, D., Lockwood, C. M., Hoffman, J. M., West, S. G., & Sheets, V. (2002). A comparison of methods to test mediation and other intervening variable effects. *Psychological Methods, 7*, 83–104.

McLanahan, S., & Sandefur, G. (1994). *Growing up with a single parent: What hurts, what helps.* Cambridge, MA: Harvard University Press.

Moos, R. H. (1987). Person-environment congruence in work, school, and health care settings. *Journal of Vocational Behavior, 31*, 231–247.

Morris, P., Duncan, G., & Clark-Kauffman, E. (2004). *Child well-being in an era of welfare reform: The sensitivity of transitions in development to policy change.* Manuscript submitted for publication.

Morris, P. A., Huston, A. C., Duncan, G., Crosby, D., & Bos, J. (2001). *How welfare and antipoverty policies affect children: A synthesis of research.* New York: MDRC.

Oropesa, R. S. (1996). Normative beliefs about marriage and cohabitation: A comparison of non-Latino Whites, Mexican Americans, and Puerto Ricans. *Journal of Marriage and the Family, 58*, 49–62.

P. L. 104–193 (1996). *The Personal Responsibility and Work Opportunity Reconciliation Act.*

Pessar, P. (1995). *A visa for a dream: Dominicans in the United States.* Boston: Pearson, Allyn, and Bacon.

Roy, A. L., & Yoshikawa, H. (2004). *Racial/ethnic differences in the effects of welfare policy on high-school dropout: The role of person-environment fit.* Manuscript submitted for publication.

Schultz, T. W. (1961). Investment in human capital. *American Economic Review, 51*, 1–17.

Shrout, P. E., & Bolger, N. (2002). Mediation in experimental and non-experimental studies: New procedures and recommendations. *Psychological Methods, 7*, 422–445.

Smolensky, E., & Gootman, J. (2003). (Eds.). *Working families and growing kids: Caring for children and adolescents.* Washington, DC: National Academy Press.

Weaver, R. K. (2000). *Ending welfare as we know it.* Washington, DC: Brookings Institution Press.

Yeung, W. J., Linver, M. R., & Brooks-Gunn, J. (2002). How money matters for young children's development: Parental investment and family processes. *Child Development, 73,* 1861–1879.

Yoshikawa, H., Gassman-Pines, A., Morris, P. A., Gennetian, L. A., & Godfrey, E. B. (2004). *Do five-year effects of welfare policy on standardized achievement differ by race/ethnicity?* Manuscript submitted for publication.

Yoshikawa, H., Magnuson, K. A., Bos, J. M., & Hsueh, J. (2003). Effects of welfare and anti-poverty policies on adult economic and middle-childhood outcomes differ for the "hardest to employ." *Child Development, 74,* 1500–1521.

Yoshikawa, H., Rosman, E. A., & Hsueh, J. (2001). Variation in teenage mothers' experiences of child care and other components of welfare reform: Selection processes and developmental consequences. *Child Development, 72,* 299–317.

19

Effects of a Family Poverty Intervention Program Last from Middle Childhood to Adolescence

Aletha C. Huston, Sylvia R. Epps, Mi Suk Shim,
Greg J. Duncan, Danielle A. Crosby,
and Marika N. Ripke

Experiences within the family and in settings outside the family during middle childhood may set patterns of achievement, motivation, and behavior that endure as children make the transition into adolescence. Although many studies demonstrate associations of such experiences with later behavior, two questions often remain. First, to what extent did experiences prior to middle childhood contribute to the patterns observed during middle childhood? For example, if parenting warmth during middle childhood predicts children's prosocial behavior, is that association merely an extension of the effects of earlier parenting warmth? The second question concerns inferences about causal direction when contexts and behavior are correlated. Do contexts affect children's development, or do characteristics of children lead them to select particular contexts, or both? For example, the extensive literature showing that children who participate in extracurricular activities have better school performance and behavior (e.g., Mahoney, Larson, & Eccles, 2005) is based primarily on correlational data and leaves unanswered questions about the causal nature of these relationships.

In this chapter, we use a random assignment experiment evaluating New Hope, a program designed to increase parental employment and reduce family poverty, to examine the impacts of changes in contexts initiated during middle childhood on children's behavior in early to middle adolescence. The experimental design of the study solves the problems of identifying unique effects of contexts in middle childhood and of making causal inferences about the direction of effects on behavior. The major questions are: (a) Do changes in contexts experienced during middle childhood have lasting effects on children's development? and (b) What specific contextual changes account for later development?

New Hope offered working poor adults a set of benefits that were designed to increase family income and to provide work supports in the form of subsidized child care and health insurance. Several features of family context were likely to be affected by New Hope, including parents'

385

employment, family income and resources, parents' psychological well-being, parenting behavior, and children's activities during out-of-school time. Prior research suggests that some of these features are likely to affect children of different ages in different ways.

FAMILY CONTEXT

Employment

Many low-income workers have nontraditional schedules that require evening and weekend work, and their hours are often irregular. Although nontraditional schedules may be stressful for families of preschool children, they pose even more difficulties for families of older children because school schedules often do not mesh with parents' work schedules. An extensive analysis by Presser (2003) demonstrates that school-age children's achievement and behavior is especially likely to suffer when parents work on weekday evenings, often leaving children without an adult to supervise meals, homework, bedtime, and time with peers.

Middle childhood is the time when children begin to form concepts of work and career as well as to pursue interests related to future career possibilities; hence, parental experiences with the rewards and stresses of employment may be particularly likely to shape children's attitudes about work and expectations for their own futures. Proponents of welfare reform propose that employed parents provide good role models; children who see parents going to a job regularly and bringing home a paycheck will accept employment as the "norm" of adult life. Our earlier analyses show that parents' work lives can serve as models for their children (Ripke, Huston, & Mistry, 2001), but both positive and negative messages can be conveyed. When parents' jobs are routine and repetitious or have very low wages, their children may infer that work is boring and unrewarding (see Parcel & Menaghan, 1994, 1997; Moore & Driskoll, 1997). There is some evidence that parents in the New Hope program group had slightly better quality jobs than those in the control group; by the time of the five-year follow-up, their jobs were more stable, and they earned higher hourly wages, so their children may have gotten more positive messages about work (Huston et al., 2003).

Although there is some debate about possible harmful effects of maternal employment on infants (Smolensky & Gootman, 2003), most of the literature on low-income families suggests that children's cognitive and social development is more positive in families with employed mothers than in those with unemployed mothers (Zaslow, Rabinovich, & Suwalsky, 1991; Zaslow & Emig, 1997). It appears, however, that much if not all of this difference is a result of selection-employed mothers having more education, skills, and adaptive personal and psychological attributes that enable them to find and retain employment and that also contribute to their children's development (Zaslow, McGroder, Cave, & Mariner, 1999). If employment increases material resources, its effects on children are likely to be positive (e.g., Harvey, 1999). In short, the available literature suggests that parental employment in low-income families can have both positive and negative effects on children's experiences and behavior.

Income

A large body of literature shows positive associations of family income with achievement and school-related motives (e.g., Bradley & Corwyn, 2002). There is some evidence that poverty during the preschool years is more consistently associated with low cognitive and academic skills than is poverty in middle childhood and adolescence (Bradley & Corwyn, 2002; Duncan & Brooks-Gunn, 1997; Magnuson, Duncan, & Kalil, 2006). For example, analyses of a nationally representative sample demonstrated that parental income in the early years predicted years of completed schooling and non-marital childbearing; the effects were particularly strong for individuals who experienced poverty in the early years (Duncan, Yeung, Brooks-Gunn, & Smith, 1998). In a sample of children born to adolescent mothers, poverty in early childhood was a stronger predictor of dropping out of high school than poverty later in childhood or in adolescence (Brooks-Gunn, Guo, & Furstenberg, 1993). These studies raise questions about whether interventions like New Hope that are intended to raise family income are beneficial for children if the changes in income begin after the preschool years.

On the other hand, there is strong evidence that income loss has effects on older children's psychological and emotional well-being (Conger et al., 1994; Elder, 1974; Elder, Liker, & Cross, 1984; McLoyd, Jayaratne, Ceballo, & Borquez, 1994). In samples of very low-income single mothers, 10–14-year-old children had slightly better psychological well being (lower anxiety) when their mothers entered employment and poor well-being when their mothers left employment, perhaps in part because of changes in family income (Chase-Lansdale et al., 2003).

Experimental studies suggest more positive effects of increased income for children in middle childhood than for adolescents. In the 1960s and 1970s, a set of experiments was designed to test the effects of a "negative income tax" that provided a guaranteed minimum income to families. These income guarantees led to slightly better school achievement for elementary school aged children, but not for high school students (Salkind & Haskins, 1982). In the 1990s, another group of experimental tests of programs designed to increase parent employment and reduce welfare use were conducted. Programs that provided earnings supplements for participating parents raised family income and had positive effects on school achievement and social behavior for children who were ages 3 through 10 when their parents entered the program. Programs that increased parental employment without improving family income had few positive or negative effects on children in this age range (Morris, Huston, Duncan, Crosby, & Bos, 2001).

By contrast, children who were early adolescents when their families entered the same programs showed some negative effects on such achievement indicators as completing school, regardless of whether the programs produced income gains (Gennetian, Duncan, Knox, Vargas, & Clark-Kauffman, 2002). Further analysis of the pooled data from several studies shows the most positive effects of income gains for children who were in preschool at random assignment (and in the early school years at follow-up) and the most negative effects for children who were in or near adolescence (ages 10–15) at random assignment (and were adolescents at follow-up) (Morris, Duncan, & Clark-Kauffman, in press).

The reasons for the differences by age group are not entirely clear. Parents' employment and income can affect the quality of resources available in the home and away from home. The quality of the home environment is particularly important for children's cognitive development during the preschool years, although there is evidence that it also has some effects in middle childhood (see Magnuson et al., 2006). Income and related resources also affect the child care choices available to parents, and there may be more variability in child care quality for preschool children from different income levels than there is in school quality, for example.

Parent Well-Being and Parenting Practices

Although children's lives move beyond the family in middle childhood, parents and family life continue to play a central role. In fact, parents are important mediators of the effects of economic stress on the well-being of their children well into adolescence. Parents' employment experiences and economic strains can affect the quality of the home environment and of parent–child relationships, which in turn affect children's behavior and psychological distress (McLoyd, 1998; Parcel & Menaghan, 1994). Changes in parents' employment and family income are likely to affect children through their impacts on everyday experiences at home and away from home (Huston et al., 2003). There is a great deal of evidence that income affects parents' well-being, which in turn contributes to positive parenting (e.g., McLoyd, 1998).

Child Care and Out-of-School Activities

The quality and type of child care are particularly important influences on children's opportunities to acquire academic skills before they enter school, but quality after-school programs and out-of-school activities can also contribute to both skill and motivation for children in middle childhood. The New Hope program provided child care subsidies that allowed parents to use paid child care for all children under age 13; as a result, New Hope parents used more center-based care and less home-based care for both preschool and school-age children than did control parents (Huston et al., 2001).

Middle childhood is a period of increasing independence from parents; children gradually learn to regulate their own behavior, to take responsibility, and to exercise self-control abilities that are essential as they enter adolescence. Between about third and fifth grade, many children phase out of formal child care programs, and they spend less and less time under the direct supervision of their parents (Belle, 1999). During this normative transition, the scaffolding provided by the larger social environment may be especially important in guiding successful development of autonomy and self-regulation. As parents begin spending more time away from home, leaving children with little supervision and perhaps with responsibility for other children in their households, other resources in the neighborhood and the community may assume an important role in supporting the development of self-regulation skills.

Formal child care and organized youth development activities offer opportunities to build skills and interact with peers in contexts with at least some adult supervision. Youth who participate in activities that are structured or supervised by adults have better school performance and less deviant behavior than do those who spend after-school time in unsupervised activities with peers. This difference is especially apparent for youth in low-income families and unsafe neighborhoods (Catalano, Berglund, Ryan, Lonczak, & Hawkins, 1999; Mahoney et al., 2005; Pettit, Bates, & Dodge, 1997).

In summary, the New Hope intervention provides an opportunity to examine the effects of environmental contexts in middle childhood. The random assignment experimental design assures that the context effects are independent of events in early childhood and that causal inferences can be made. On the other hand, the New Hope program was a package of benefits that affected several different aspects of the child's environment. The design does not permit us to determine with certainty which components or combinations of components were most important, but we can make some inferences by examining how the treatment affected these various contexts.

For this chapter, we examine impacts for children who were school age (6–10 years old) when their parents entered the New Hope study. The New Hope program was available to families in the program group for three years (i.e., until these children were 9–13 years old). At the follow-up approximately five years after random assignment (and two years after the program ended), the children were in early to middle adolescence (11–16 years old).[1] When children were assessed two years and five years after families entered the study, the positive impacts of New Hope on some

---

[1] The larger study included children from ages 1 to 10 years old at random assignment. Results appear in Huston et al. (2003).

indicators were greater for boys than for girls (Huston et al., 2001, 2003), therefore we examine boys and girls separately in some analyses. We explored two principal research questions: (a) Did exposure to the New Hope program in middle childhood affect school achievement, school motivation, and behavior in adolescence? and (b) What changes in context produced by New Hope may have accounted for changes in children's behavior?

METHOD

New Hope Project

The New Hope Project was an experimental antipoverty demonstration program in Milwaukee, Wisconsin that offered the following benefits to participants when they were employed 30 or more hours per week: (a) a wage supplement that ensured that net income increased as they earned more; (b) a child care subsidy for any child under age 13, which could be used for any state-licensed or county-certified child care provider, including preschool programs for young children and extended day programs for school-age children; and (c) subsidized health insurance. The child care subsidies were at least commensurate with those available to some families through the Aid to Families with Dependent Children (AFDC) program, but the income eligibility threshold was higher and they were much more convenient and free of bureaucratic hassles than is often the case in the welfare system (Adams & Roizen, 2002). Benefits decreased gradually as income increased, and were phased out completely if monthly income exceeded $2500. The program provided case management services to assist participants in job searches and other needs. If participants could not find unsubsidized employment, they were offered access to a community service job at minimum wage that counted toward the hours needed for New Hope benefits. A detailed description of the program's implementation appears in Brock, Doolittle, Fellerath, and Wiseman (1997).

Sample

Eligibility for New Hope was limited to two ZIP code-defined neighborhoods in Milwaukee's poorest areas. Applicants for the program had to meet three criteria: be older than 18; have an income at or below 150% of the poverty line; and be willing to work 30 or more hours a week. The 1,357 adult applicants were randomly assigned to either program ($N = 679$) or control ($N = 678$) status. Members of both groups could be eligible for any federal or state public assistance programs; individuals in the experimental program also had access to New Hope benefits.

Adults with at least one child between the ages of 1 year, 0 months and 10 years, 11 months at baseline were identified for a supplemental Child and Family Study (program group $N = 366$; control group $N = 379$). Up to two children in each CFS family were selected as "focal children" to be studied.[2] Surveys were administered to parents and children two and five years after random assignment. The analyses presented in this chapter focus on the 243 families (with 390 focal children ages 6–10 at baseline) who responded to the five-year follow-up survey. A mail survey was sent to teachers of children whose parent gave permission. Teacher-reported outcomes are based on the reports for 245 children.

At baseline, the majority of New Hope families were headed by a single female parent (89%). Most of these women were not employed (55.6%) and were receiving public assistance (81.1%). Their average age was 29; about 55% were African American, and about 30% were Hispanic.

Measures

School Achievement. School achievement information was obtained from three independent sources: individual standardized tests, parent reports, and teacher reports. Children completed four individually-administered scales from the Woodcock-Johnson Achievement Battery-Revised (Woodcock & Johnson, 1990). Two of these (Letter-Word Identification and Passage Comprehension) measure reading skills; their average is the Broad Reading score. The other two scales (Applied Problems and Calculation) measure mathematics skills; they compose the Broad Math score. The total score is the average of all four scales. The standard score for each scale is obtained by comparing the child's score with norms for his/her chronological age group. The mean standard score for the population as a whole is 100; the standard deviation is 15.

Parent ratings of overall level of achievement and performance in reading, mathematics, and written work were collected on 5-point scales. Parents reported negative school progress (whether the child had been in special education, repeated a grade, received poor grades, or dropped out of school). Teachers completed the Academic Subscale of the Social Skills Rating System (SSRS) (Gresham & Elliot, 1990), rating children's performance in reading, math, intellectual functioning, motivation, oral communication, classroom behavior, and parental encouragement, and a mock report card on which they rated the child's achievement in different subject matter areas.

Motivation, Attitudes, and Beliefs. Children's educational expectations were obtained from questions about how sure they were that they would

---

[2] If there were more than two eligible children, the focal children were randomly selected with the restriction that opposite-sex siblings were given preference over same-sex siblings.

finish high school, go to college, and finish college (Cook et al., 1996). Occupational expectation was the occupational prestige score (see Nakeo & Treas, 1990) of the job the child thought she or he would do as an adult. School engagement was assessed with five items (e.g., you feel close to others at your school) adapted from the Adolescent Heath Survey. Two questions asked whether children expected to own more things and to make more money than their parents. Efficacy was measured on the Children's Hope Scale (e.g., "Even when others want to quit, I know I can find ways to solve the problem") (Snyder, Hoza, & Pelham, 1997).

Future goals were grouped into two scales – one referring to individual goals (e.g., obtaining a good job) and the other to community involvement (e.g., improving their community) (adapted from Flanagan, Bowes, Jonsson, Csapo, & Sheblanova, 1998). Work attitudes (e.g., you expect work to be a central part of your life) were assessed with five items taken from the Monitoring the Future Survey. Financial stress was measured with questions about how much the child worried about his or her family lacking enough money for food, rent, and other necessities. Delinquency was measured as self-reported deviant behavior on 15 items measuring fighting, stealing, vandalism, and drugs (adapted from LeBlanc & Tremblay, 1988).

Social Behavior and Peer Relationships. Both parents and teachers rated children's positive and problem behavior. The Positive Behavior Scale includes items about compliance/self-control (e.g., "thinks before he/she acts"), social competence and sensitivity (e.g., "gets along well with other children"), and autonomy (e.g., "is self-reliant") (Quint, Bos, & Polit, 1997). The Problem Behavior Scale from the Social Skills Rating System (SSRS) (Gresham & Elliot, 1990) has two subscales: externalizing (aggression and lack of behavior control) and internalizing problems (social withdrawal and excessive fearfulness). Children completed the Loneliness and Social Dissatisfaction Questionnaire (Asher & Wheeler, 1985; Cassidy & Asher, 1992) to measure perceptions of peer relations and friendships. The Intent Attributions and Feelings of Distress Measure (Crick & Dodge, 1996) presents hypothetical vignettes to assess whether children attribute hostile or benign intent to a person who does something provocative (e.g., bumping into you). Hostile attributions are associated with aggressive behavior; hence, it is used as an indirect indicator of children's aggressive tendencies.

Family Well-Being and Parenting. The material hardship index asked whether the family had been without utilities, medical care, housing, or other necessities (Mayer & Jencks, 1989). Financial health included nine items assessing participants' degree of financial stability and ownership of such assets as a car, a savings account, or cable TV. Satisfaction with standard of living was one question on which the participant rated her/his satisfaction on a 5-point scale from 1 = "unhappy" to 5 = "happy." Depressive symptoms were measured on the CES-D (Center for Epidemiological

Studies – Depression scale; Radloff, 1977). On national norms a score of 16 is the cutoff, suggesting serious depression. General stress was a single item asking how much of the time the parent had felt stressed in the past month. Financial worry was assessed with five questions asking how much the respondent worried about paying bills and lacking money for important needs. Hope was measured with the State Hope Scale (Snyder et al., 1996), which includes belief in one's capacity to initiate and sustain actions and belief in one's capacity to achieve goals.

Measures of parenting included parent reports, child reports, and interviewer ratings. Effective child management was a composite of parents' reports of control, frequency of discipline, parenting stress, and confidence in preventing harm. Warmth was based on parents' reports of warmth (three items; Morris & Michalopoulos, 2000) and interviewers' ratings of parental warmth. Parent monitoring was measured by questions asking whether parents knew what their children were doing and who their friends were. Youth reported on positive youth–parent relations, negative relations (McLoyd et al., 1994), psychological autonomy granting (Steinberg, Lamborn, Dornbusch, & Darling, 1992), and parent monitoring (Kerr & Stattin, 2000).

Child Care and Activities. Parents were asked about the number of months during the prior year that the focal child had been in any center-based care (including child care centers, before/after-school programs), home-based care, providing care for siblings, and unsupervised. Parents rated children's participation in out-of-school activities during the school year and the summer using a 5-point scale ranging from "never" to "almost every day." Five "structured" activities were assessed: lessons, organized sports, clubs and youth groups, religious classes and events, and recreation or community centers. Participation in service and volunteer activities and in paid work and time watching TV were also measured.

RESULTS

The first major question is whether New Hope affected achievement, motivation, and social behavior as children moved from middle childhood to adolescence. Program impacts must be considered in the context of overall age differences and age changes. Older children in the control group had lower test scores and lower parent-reported achievement than did younger children, suggesting strongly that the "normative" pattern for these children was a decline in academic performance as they got older. Moreover, indicators of negative school progress (i.e., grade retention, remedial education, and poor grades) increased with age. There were no overall age differences in teacher ratings, but the instrument administered to teachers asked them to evaluate students in comparison to others in their class, so age differences may have been obscured. On the whole, these findings are consistent with the literature that shows a pattern of increasing school failure and a downward trajectory of achievement for children in low-income families as they progress (or fail to progress) through school.

Within this context of declining achievement, it is noteworthy that adolescents in New Hope families had higher levels of achievement in reading (but not in math) according to both parent and teacher reports than control group children did. Moreover, teachers rated boys in the program group higher than control group boys on the academic subscale of the SSRS. Program group boys were less likely than control group boys to have "negative school progress"; that is, they were less likely to have been retained, placed in special education, or received poor grades. Although the impacts on other indicators of achievement were not significant, the coefficients are all positive. In effect, New Hope partially counteracted the tendency for children's school performance to decline with age, especially for boys (see Table 19.1).

The picture is complicated by the fact that, although the coefficients were positive, there were not significant program effects on Woodcock-Johnson reading test scores, nor on any measure of math achievement. Children were getting better grades in reading and were less likely to be retained or be placed in remedial classes, but their tested skills were not clearly superior. New Hope may have affected school-relevant behaviors such as compliance to adults, self-regulation, attentiveness, ability to work independently, and responsibility that combine with academic skills to affect grades and teacher perceptions. Success in school depends partially on basic academic skills, but it also depends on school-appropriate behavior: for example, doing assignments on time without direct supervision, doing homework, cooperating with the agenda of the school, going through transitions without disruption, and complying with teachers and school rules. These skills are also important for success outside of school and in many facets of adult life.

Motivation

New Hope had positive effects on some measures of school-related motivation, particularly for boys (shown in Table 19.1). Children in New Hope families were more certain that they would complete college, more engaged in school, and more optimistic about attaining their life goals. Compared to control group children, they had higher expectations for educational attainment, higher levels of school engagement, more feelings of hope or efficacy in achieving their goals, and higher aspirations to contribute to their communities in the future. Although these patterns were significant for the whole group, they were especially pronounced for boys. Again, it appears that something about the New Hope program counteracted the tendency for school-related motivation to decline with age.

TABLE 19.1. *Program Impacts on Achievement, Motivation, and Social Behavior Five Years After Random Assignment*

	Boys				Girls				Both Sexes			
Outcome	Control Group	Program Minus Control Difference	SE	Effect Size[a]	Control Group	Program Minus Control Difference	SE	Effect Size[a]	Control Group	Program Minus Control Difference	SE	Effect Size[a]
Woodcock-Johnson Test of Achievement[b]												
Total standard score	88.83	2.65	2.70	0.18	89.86	0.76	1.94	0.05	89.43	1.55	1.53	0.10
Broad reading score	90.51	4.23	3.55	0.26	94.05	−0.54	2.55	−0.03	92.41	1.65	2.00	0.10
Broad math score	87.15	1.07	2.32	0.06	85.65	2.07	1.82	0.13	86.43	1.44	1.41	0.09
Teacher Ratings of Achievement												
SSRS academic subscale	2.66	0.57	0.23**	0.57	3.18	−0.06	0.19	−0.06	2.96	0.21	0.15	0.19
Mock report card – total	2.35	0.38	0.28	0.39	2.75	0.25	0.23	0.26	2.59	0.27	0.16*	0.28
Mock report card – reading	2.43	0.49	0.24**	0.45	2.69	0.31	0.23	0.28	2.61	0.33	0.16**	0.30
Mock report card – math	2.37	0.18	0.25	0.16	2.69	0.04	0.23	0.04	2.55	0.12	0.16	0.09

(continued)

TABLE 19.1. (*Continued*)

Outcome	Control Group	Program Minus Control Difference	SE	Effect Size[a]	Control Group	Program Minus Control Difference	SE	Effect Size[a]	Control Group	Program Minus Control Difference	SE	Effect Size[a]
Parent Ratings of Achievement												
Overall achievement	3.09	0.20	0.18	0.19	3.76	0.14	0.16	0.13	3.45	0.14	0.11	0.12
Reading	3.12	0.22	0.14	0.22	3.68	0.16	0.14	0.16	3.40	0.20	0.10**	0.19
Math	3.17	0.07	0.18	0.06	3.53	0.19	0.16	0.18	3.37	0.10	0.11	0.09
School Progress												
Negative school progress	0.37	−0.09	0.04**	−0.34	0.19	−0.03	0.04	−0.10	0.27	−0.05	0.03*	−0.18
Motivation												
Expects to complete college	3.72	0.47	0.17**	0.43	4.23	−0.04	0.18	−0.04	3.95	0.29	0.13**	0.26
Occupational expectation	63.08	1.01	3.38	0.05	67.67	0.16	3.51	0.01	65.63	0.25	2.43	0.01
School engagement	3.68	0.37	0.17**	0.39	3.82	0.07	0.14	0.08	3.76	0.21	0.10**	0.22
Expects to own more than parents	4.04	−0.09	0.15	−0.09	3.81	0.23	0.13*	0.24	3.92	0.08	0.10	0.09
Expects to earn more than parents	4.33	−0.15	0.13	−0.16	3.91	0.30	0.15**	0.31	4.11	0.08	0.10	0.09
Future beliefs – individual	4.07	−0.03	0.08	−0.05	3.97	0.06	0.07	0.11	4.01	0.02	0.05	0.04

396

Future beliefs – community	4.44	0.12	0.10	0.25	4.50	0.07	0.06	0.14	4.47	0.11	0.05**	0.23
Attitude about employment	4.31	−0.08	0.10	−0.12	4.14	0.08	0.10	0.12	4.23	−0.01	0.07	0.01
Hope	4.50	0.29	0.15*	0.32	4.62	−0.04	0.13	−0.04	4.53	0.18	0.10*	0.20
Positive Behavior												
Parent report	3.69	0.07	0.08	0.13	3.81	0.16	0.07**	0.30	3.75	0.12	0.06**	0.23
Teacher report	3.26	0.27	0.17	0.39	3.63	−0.07	0.12	−0.11	3.46	0.11	0.09	0.14
Problem Behavior												
Externalizing – parent	2.52	−0.13	0.11	−0.18	2.36	0.01	0.11	0.01	2.46	−0.10	0.08	−0.13
Externalizing – teacher	2.11	−0.04	0.18	−0.04	1.97	0.20	0.16	0.23	2.06	0.03	0.11	0.04
Internalizing – parent	2.52	−0.18	0.10*	−0.28	2.47	−0.06	0.11	−0.09	2.49	−0.11	0.07	−0.17
Internalizing – teacher	2.47	−0.18	0.15	−0.26	2.26	0.14	0.11	0.21	2.37	−0.03	0.09	−0.04
Social Relationships												
Peer relationships – kid	4.00	0.25	0.11**	0.36	4.19	0.01	0.11	0.01	4.11	0.10	0.07	0.14
Hostile intent total – kid	3.72	−0.67	0.32**	−0.33	3.05	−0.10	0.29	−0.05	3.31	−0.26	0.21	−0.13

a The effect size is the difference between program and control group outcomes as a proportion of the standard deviation of the outcomes for both groups combined.

This standard deviation is always obtained from the entire research sample, even if the table shows impacts for subgroups.

b Woodcock-Johnson scores are age-standardized with a mean of 100 and a standard deviation of 15.

* p < .10, ** p < .05, *** p < .01.

Because the New Hope program emphasized work, and many social policy makers believed that parent employment would serve as a model for children, we included several measures designed to assess children's attitudes and aspirations about work. There were no program effects on children's expectations about the type of occupation they would have or on their attitudes about the value of work. Girls in New Hope families were more likely to think they would own and earn more than their parents did, perhaps indicating some optimism about their adult lives; but, by and large, New Hope had little impact on children's perceptions of work or expectations about their own future employment.

Social Behavior and Health

In comparison to the control group, parents in the New Hope group rated their adolescents higher on positive social behaviors – social competence, compliance, and autonomy – and they rated boys lower on internalizing behavior problems. Boys reported more satisfaction with their peer relationships (less loneliness), and they were less likely to attribute hostile intent to others, indicating lower probability of aggressive behavior to peers (Table 19.1). Together these findings indicate that New Hope helped to increase social skills and reduce aggressive tendencies, particularly for boys.

Overall, these analyses provide evidence of some positive effects of New Hope on adolescents' school performance, motivation, and behavior. As we noted earlier, the program had several components that might have contributed to these differences, so we turn now to examine program impacts on children's contexts, both in the home and outside the family, in an effort to identify possible pathways by which effects might have occurred. Because some program impacts were stronger for boys than girls, we examine these contexts separately by gender.

Family Well-Being and Parenting

Although New Hope brought about increases in parent employment in the first few years of the program, these effects were reduced to nonsignificance by the time of the five-year follow-up. Overall, however, the rate of employment in both program and control groups was high, so most of the children in the sample had parents who were employed most of the time. Similarly, New Hope led to slight improvements in family income; but, even though they were earning more, many families in both the program and control groups experienced little improvement in total income, in part because of major reductions in public assistance during the period from 1995 to 2000 (see Huston et al., 2003). Similarly, New Hope did not have significant effects on the amount of material hardship, financial health, or worry about finances.

By contrast, New Hope did lead to small improvements in some measures of parents' psychological well-being and parenting in this sample. New Hope parents reported lower levels of depressive symptoms ($\beta = -2.97$, $SE = 1.38$, $p < .01$) and lower levels of general stress ($\beta = -.21$, $SE = .12$, $p < .05$) than did control parents. On the CES-D, which measures depressive symptoms, a score of 16 or higher is considered an indication that significant depression may be occurring and that further diagnosis may be indicated. Of the program group, 43.1% scored at or above 16 compared to 50.1% of the control group. There were no differences, however, on measures of parents' hope for the future or financial well-being.

New Hope parents also reported more effective child management ($\beta = .15$, $SE = .07$, $p < .05$) – that is, they reported that their children were more likely to obey them; they had less occasion to punish their children; they felt less parenting stress; and they had more confidence that they could protect their adolescents from harm. Although these patterns of reduced depressive symptoms and improved child management held for both boys and girls, they were especially pronounced for boys. On the other hand, for girls, New Hope parents reported more warmth ($\beta = .35$, $SE = .19$, $p < .05$), but somewhat less monitoring ($\beta = -.15$, $SE = .09$, $p < .10$), than did control group parents. There were no program effects on children's reports of positive or negative parent–child relationships.

Contexts Outside of the Family

Even though these children were ages 11 through 16, parents still reported "child care" arrangements – that is, formal and informal arrangements for supervision. Children in New Hope families were less likely than those in control families to be either unsupervised or supervised by an adult in a home setting, and boys in New Hope were more likely than control group boys to spend time in a formal setting (e.g., an after-school program or summer program) (see Table 19.2). New Hope adolescents also spent more time than did control adolescents in structured out-of-school activities (e.g., sports, clubs, religious activities, and community centers). For boys, New Hope was especially likely to increase participation in sports; for girls, the impact was especially strong for religious activities (e.g., attending services, social activities, and other events in a religious institution) (see Table 19.2).

DISCUSSION

The first major question addressed in this chapter is whether children whose families had access to the New Hope intervention when the children were in middle childhood would show lasting effects when they reached adolescence. Our findings show this to be true. New Hope had positive

TABLE 19.2. *Program Impacts on School Year Activities and Child Care*

Outcome	Boys				Girls				Both Sexes			
	Control Group	Coefficient	SE	Effect Size[a]	Control Group	Coefficient	SE	Effect Size[a]	Control Group	Coefficient	SE	Effect Size[a]
Child Care												
Months in formal care	1.54	1.25	0.61	0.27**	2.30	−0.09	0.72	−0.02	1.88	0.67	0.49	0.14
Months in home-based care	5.20	−0.48	0.80	−0.09	6.03	−1.23	0.92	−0.23	5.79	−1.17	0.66	−0.23*
Months in unsupervised care	4.33	−1.17	0.77	−0.25	4.49	−1.03	0.83	−0.22	4.37	−1.02	0.58	−0.22*
Months caring for other children	1.65	−0.42	0.58	−0.15	1.68	−0.34	0.51	−0.12	1.65	−0.36	0.39	−0.13
Parent Report of School Year Activities												
Structured activities (5)	2.35	0.26	0.16	0.28*	2.54	0.14	0.16	0.14	2.45	0.19	0.11	0.20*
Lessons	2.06	−0.18	0.19	−0.14	2.62	−0.10	0.21	−0.08	2.35	−0.15	0.15	−0.12
Sports	2.41	0.60	0.27	0.41**	2.48	0.09	0.24	0.06	2.47	0.30	0.18	0.21
Clubs	2.21	0.35	0.25	0.24	2.49	0.18	0.22	0.12	2.34	0.28	0.17	0.19
Religious	2.60	0.29	0.22	0.21	2.62	0.48	0.21	0.36**	2.60	0.41	0.15	0.30***
Community centers	2.43	0.26	0.28	0.17	2.51	0.03	0.25	0.02	2.47	0.14	0.19	0.09

[a] The effect size is the difference between programs and control group outcomes as a proportion of the standard deviation of the outcomes for both groups combined. This standard deviation is always obtained from the entire research sample, even if the table shows impacts for subgroups.

* p < .10, ** p < .05, *** p < .01.

impacts on several indicators of school performance, academic motivation, and social skills for adolescents. Other studies show that both academic achievement and school motivation both tend to decline with age, with a particularly strong dip when children make the transition to adolescence. Many children, including those from low-income families, are generally on a downward trajectory as they move out of middle childhood into adolescence. The reasons proposed in the literature include increasing demands in school in conjunction with a school environment that does not fit the developmental needs of emerging adolescents (Eccles et al., 1993), physical and emotional changes associated with puberty, and increasing exposure to opportunities for deviant behavior along with reduced levels of adult supervision.

The experiences induced by the New Hope intervention helped to counteract these downward trajectories so that adolescents sustained better reading competency and better school performance with less likelihood of school failure. It is noteworthy that New Hope adolescents were less likely to be retained or to be placed in special education, both of which are strongly associated with low educational attainment in later adolescence and adulthood (Entwisle, Alexander, & Olson, 2005). New Hope adolescents also manifested more positive social behavior in several contexts – parents rated them higher on such positive behaviors as social skills, compliance, and autonomy. New Hope boys reported better peer relationships and fewer tendencies to respond aggressively to peers; and, according to their parents, they had fewer internalizing behavior problems.

These findings provide a more complete understanding of the age differences found in two recent meta-analyses of welfare and employment programs. Although one indicated positive effects two to four years later for children who were in preschool or middle childhood at baseline, the other reported some negative impacts on school progress and deviant behavior for children who were adolescents when their parents entered the programs (Morris et al., 2001; Gennetian et al., 2002). This pattern was clarified in a subsequent analysis of the same studies, showing the strongest positive effects on achievement for children who were in preschool at baseline, and the strongest negative effects for those who were ages 10–11 at baseline (Morris et al., in press).

Our study, which follows children from middle childhood into adolescence, contradicts the latter finding. Why did New Hope produce impacts on achievement for older children when most of the other studies included in the Morris et al. (in press) synthesis did not? The New Hope program provided a richer array of benefits than most of the other programs, including community service jobs that enabled parents to gain access to wage supplements and strong support for child care. The evaluation also included more sources of information (i.e., child, parent, and teacher) and more domains of development. Most of the significant impacts of New Hope on achievement occurred for reading, literacy, and academic motivation, none of which was measured separately from total achievement in most other studies. New Hope had impacts on children's own reports of friendship and aggressive attributions; most other studies did not obtain measures of psychosocial well-being from children themselves. Whatever the reason, these findings show that a successful intervention initiated when children are ages 6–11 can produce effects that endure well into adolescence.

Our second purpose was to identify the contexts that contributed to children's behavior. One reason for lasting change in children's behavior could be stability of the contexts affected by New Hope. We examined two major pathways – changes in parental well-being and parenting, and changes in children's experiences outside the family. There was evidence for New Hope impacts on both, but effects on environments outside the family were particularly strong and consistent. New Hope parents did, however, report better psychological well-being and more feelings of efficacy in managing their adolescents than did control group parents. Interestingly, these impacts were more apparent five years after random assignment than they were two years after random assignment, when the children in this sample were in middle childhood and early adolescence (ages 8–12; Huston et al., 2001). Hence, it is possible that changes in parenting and parent well-being were a result of improvements in children's behavior that were brought about by the program. There is some evidence, in fact, that improvements in boys' social behavior, measured two years after random assignment, partially accounted for parents' more effective child management three years later (Epps, 2004). The effects on parenting for girls were more mixed, with parents showing more warmth and less monitoring, a combination that could reflect both affection and lack of supervision.

These findings are of particular interest in relation to normative developmental change. As children enter adolescence, children and parents spend less time together, and parents feel greater concern about their children getting into trouble. If the New Hope intervention partly counteracted this trend, whether by direct effects on children or on parents, it is likely that both adults and children benefit from a slightly more harmonious family environment.

New Hope had consistent effects on the environments in which children and adolescents spent time outside the family and school. At both follow-up points, the youth in New Hope families were more likely to be in formal after-school and summer arrangements (though not in summer school) and to take part in structured extracurricular activities, particularly sports for boys and religious activities for girls. The opportunities for learning, peer contacts, and adult supervision and interaction in these settings may have been particularly important as scaffolding for the development of autonomy and self-regulation as children moved through middle childhood into adolescence. Few children participate in formal after-school programs beyond the elementary school years, so it may be difficult for parents to find programs or to persuade their children to attend them.

Middle childhood may be an important period for children to begin sports, lessons, and other activities. Although many scholars and youth workers consider such activities central to adolescents' development, middle childhood is the time when involvement is often initiated. Participation rates are higher in late middle childhood than in late adolescence (see Simpkins, Fredricks, Davis-Kean, & Eccles, 2006), and children who are not engaged in sports, clubs, and lessons by the time they reach middle school are probably less apt to enter these activities for many reasons. Conversely, children who become involved tend to stay involved as they move into adolescence (Ripke, Huston, & Casey, 2006; Simpkins et al., 2006). When extracurricular activities occur in conjunction with school (e.g., sports teams), they are likely to increase children's sense of engagement with the school, perhaps explaining in part why impacts on school engagement were stronger for boys. Girls in New Hope were likely to participate in religious activities, including services, social events, and other activities in their religious institutions. Parents and young people appear to use religious institutions successfully as sources of support, supervision, and involvement for their young people.

Gennetian et al. (2002) proposed that negative effects of parents' participation in employment programs for adolescents might have resulted from young people assuming household and child care responsibilities while their mothers were working. The negative program impacts across studies occurred only for adolescents who had younger siblings, supporting this interpretation. If that were the case, then one might expect that children who became adolescents after the program began would gradually assume such responsibilities. At both follow-up occasions, we asked children and parents whether and when the children cared for siblings. There was no evidence of New Hope children assuming more household responsibility than controls. At the five-year follow-up, there was a nonsignificant tendency for youth in the program group to spend less time caring for siblings than did those in the control group; there were no differences between girls and boys. One reason may be that younger children in their families were more likely to be in center-based child care and less likely to be cared for at home (Huston et al., 2003). It appears that the program supports helped to establish a pattern of using more formal and structured settings that provided supervision and developmental opportunities and reduced the likelihood that adolescent children would assume maternal responsibilities at home. (There is little information about whether such responsibilities contribute positively or negatively to adolescent development, but it seems likely that there is a point at which the burden can become excessive and stressful.)

In summary, we began with two major questions: (a) Are there lasting effects on children's development as a result of a change of context produced by New Hope during middle childhood? and (b) What contextual changes account for these effects? The answer to the first question is "yes." The New Hope intervention produced effects on school performance, motivation, and social skills that endured as children moved from middle childhood to the adolescent years. The second question is more complex. Most of the families studied were headed by a single mother who was fairly consistently employed, so we cannot evaluate the role of maternal employment in predicting children's development.

The experimental impacts on family and parent well-being and on children's activities outside the home suggest that formal child care and structured activity experiences played an important role in improving children's skills and motivation, but there is also evidence of some positive impacts on parent well-being and parenting. Moreover, parental decisions and encouragement are important influences on children's participation in outside activities, and New Hope increased parents' approval of such activities. Parents allocate the financial resources, transportation, and time for children's outside activities, so participation in these experiences is at least partly a function of parental influences. We can conclude that the mix of supports provided by the New Hope program did have lasting effects on the contexts experienced by children as well as on their school performance, motivation, and social skills during the transition from middle childhood to adolescence.

References

Adams, G., & Roizen, J. A. (2002). More than a work support? Issues around integrating child development goals into the child care subsidy system. *Early Childhood Research Quarterly, 17,* 418–440.

Asher, S. R., & Wheeler, V. A. (1985). Children's loneliness: A comparison of rejected and neglected peer status. *Journal of Consulting and Clinical Psychology, 53,* 500–505.

Belle, D. (1999). *The after-school lives of children.* Mahwah, NJ: Lawrence Erlbaum Associates.

Bradley, R. H., & Corwyn, R. F. (2002). Socioeconomic status and child development. *Annual Review of Psychology, 53,* 371–399.

Brock, T., Doolittle, F., Fellerath, V., & Wiseman, M. (1997). *Creating New Hope: Context, implementation, and service utilization in a work-based anti-poverty program.* New York: Manpower Demonstration Research Corporation.

Brooks-Gunn, J., Guo, G., & Furstenberg, F. F., Jr. (1993). Who drops out of and who continues beyond high school? A 20-year follow-up of black urban youth. *Journal of Research on Adolescence, 3,* 271–294.

Cassidy, J., & Asher, S. R. (1992). Loneliness and peer relations in young children. *Child Development, 63,* 350–365.

Catalano, R. F., Berglund, M. L., Ryan, J. A. M., Lonczak, H. S., & Hawkins, J. D. (1999). *Positive youth development in the United States: Research findings on evaluations of positive youth development programs.* Seattle, WA: Social Development Research Group, University of Washington School of Social Work.

Chase-Lansdale, P. L., Moffit, R. A., Lohman, B. J., Cherlin, A. J., Coley, R. L., & Pittman, L. D. (2003). Mothers' transitions from welfare to work and the well-being of preschoolers and adolescents. *Science, 299,* 1548–1552.

Conger, R. D., Ge, X., Elder, G. H., Jr., Lorenz, F. O., Simons, R. L., & Xiaojia, G. (1994). Economic stress, coercive family process, and developmental problems of adolescents. *Child Development, 65,* 541–561.

Cook, T. D., Church, M. B., Ajanaku, S., Jr., Shadish, W. R., Jeong-Ran, K., & Cohen, R. (1996). The development of occupational aspirations and expectations among inner-city boys. *Child Development, 67,* 3368–3385.

Crick, N. R., & Dodge, K. A. (1996). Social information-processing mechanisms on reactive and proactive aggression. *Child Development 67,* 993–1002.

Duncan, G. J., & Brooks-Gunn, J. (1997). Income effects across the life span: Integration and interpretation. In G. J. Duncan & J. Brooks-Gunn (Eds.), *Consequences of growing up poor* (pp. 596–610). New York: Russell Sage.

Duncan, G. J., Yeung, W.-J., Brooks-Gunn, J., & Smith, J. R. (1998). How much does childhood poverty affect the life chances of children? *American Sociological Review, 63,* 406–423.

Eccles, J. S., Midgley, C. W., Buchanan, C. M., Reuman, D., Flanagan, C., & MacIver, D. (1993). Development during adolescence: The impact of stage-environment fit on young adolescents' experiences in schools and families. *American Psychologist, 48,* 90–101.

Elder, G. H., Jr. (1974). *Children of the Great Depression.* Chicago: University of Chicago Press.

Elder, G., Liker, J., & Cross, C. (1984). Parent-child behavior in the Great Depression: Life course and intergenerational influences. In P. Baltes & O. Brim (Eds.), *Life span development and behavior* (pp. 109–158). Orlando, FL: Academic Press.

Entwisle, D. R., Alexander, K. L., & Olson L. S. (2006). Educational tracking within and between schools: From first grade through middle school and beyond. In A. C. Huston & M. N. Ripke (Eds.), *Developmental contexts in middle childhood: Bridges to adolescence and adulthood* (pp. 173–197). New York: Cambridge University Press.

Epps, S. R., (2004). *Effects of a poverty intervention policy demonstration on authoritative parenting and child social competence: A test of the direction of effects.* Unpublished master's thesis, University of Texas, Austin.

Flanagan, C., Bowes, J., Jonsson, B., Csapo, B., & Sheblanova, E. (1998). Ties that bind: Correlates of adolescents' civic commitments in seven countries. In C. Flanagan & L. Sherrod (Issue Eds.) & P. Katz (General Ed.), Political Development: Youth Growing Up in a Global Community. *Journal of Social Issues, 54 (3),* 457–475.

Gennetian, L. A., Duncan, G., Knox, V., Vargas, W. G., & Clark-Kauffman, E. (2002). *How welfare and work policies for parents affect adolescents: A synthesis of research.* New York: Manpower Demonstration Research Corporation.

Gresham, F. M., & Elliott, S. N. (1990). *Social skills rating system manual.* Circle Pines, MN: American Guidance Service, Inc.

Harvey, E. (1999). Short-term and long-term effects of early parental employment on children of the National Longitudinal Survey of Youth. *Developmental Psychology, 35,* 445–459.

Huston, A. C., Duncan, G. J., Granger, R. C., Bos, J. M., McLoyd, V. C., & Mistry, R. S. (2001). Work-based anti-poverty programs for parents can enhance the school performance and social behavior of children. *Child Development, 72,* 318–336.

Huston, A. C., Miller, C., Richburg-Hayes, L., Duncan, G. J., Eldred, C. A., & Weisner, T. S. (2003). *New Hope for families and children: Five-year results of a program to reduce poverty and reform welfare.* New York: Manpower Demonstration Research Corporation.

Huston, A. C., Mistry, R. S., Bos, J. M., Shim, M. S., Branca, S., Dowsett, C., & Cummings, J. (2003). *Parental employment, family income dynamics, and child well-being: The relations of earnings, earnings supplements, and welfare receipt to children's behavior.* Austin, TX: Report Submitted to the U.S. Department of Health and Human Services, Office of the Assistant Secretary for Planning and Evaluation.

Kerr, M., & Stattin, H. (2000). What parents know, how they know it, and several forms of adolescent adjustment: Further support for a reinterpretation of monitoring. *Developmental Psychology, 36,* 366–380.

LeBlanc, M., & Tremblay, R. (1988). A study of factors associated with the stability of hidden delinquency. *International Journal of Adolescence and Youth, 1,* 269–291.

Magnuson, K., Duncan, G., & Kalil, A. (2006). The contribution of middle childhood contexts to adolescent achievement and behavior. In A. C. Huston & M. N. Ripke (Eds.), *Developmental contexts in middle childhood: Bridges to adolescence and adulthood* (pp. 150–172). New York: Cambridge University Press.

Mahoney, J. L., Larson, R. W., & Eccles, J. S. (Eds.). (2005). *Organized activities as contexts of development: Extracurricular activities, after-school and community programs.* Mahwah, NJ: Lawrence Erlbaum Associates.

Mayer, S., & Jencks, C. (1989). Poverty and the distribution of material hardship. *Journal of Human Resources, 24,* 88–114.

McLoyd, V. C., Jayaratne, T. E., Ceballo, R., & Borquez, J. (1994). Unemployment and work interruption among African American single mothers: Effects on parenting and adolescent socioemotional functioning. *Child Development, 65,* 562–589.

McLoyd, V. C. (1998). Socioeconomic disadvantage and child development. *American Psychologist, 53,* 185–204.

Moore, K. A., & Driscoll, A. K. (1997). Low-wage maternal employment and outcomes for children: A study. *The Future of Children, 7,* 122–127.

Morris, P. A., Duncan, G. J., & Clark-Kauffman, E. (in press). Child well-being in an era of welfare reform: The sensitivity of transitions in development to policy change. *Developmental Psychology*

Morris, P. A., Huston, A. C., Duncan, G. J., Crosby, D., & Bos, J. M. (2001). *How welfare and work policies affect children: A synthesis of research.* New York: Manpower Demonstration Research Corporation.

Morris, P. A. & Michalopoulos, C. (2002). *The Self-sufficiency Project at Thirty-six Months: Effects on Children of a Program That Increased Employment and Income.* New York: Manpower Demonstration Research Corporation.

Nakeo, K., & Treas, J. (1990). Computing 1989 occupational prestige scores. *General Social Survey Methodological Report No 70*. Chicago: NORC.

Parcel, T. L., & Menaghan, E. G. (1994). *Parents' jobs and children's lives*. New York: Aldine de Gruyter.

Parcel, T. L., & Menaghan, E. G. (1997). Effects of low-wage employment on family well-being. *The Future of Children, 7*, 116–121.

Pettit, G. S., Bates, J. E., & Dodge, K. A. (1997). Supportive parenting, ecological context, and children's adjustment: A seven-year longitudinal study. *Child Development, 68*, 908–924.

Presser, H. B. (2003). *Working in a 24/7 economy: Challenges to American families*. New York: Russell Sage Foundation.

Quint, J. C., Bos, J. M., & Polit, D. F. (1997). *New chance: Final report on a comprehensive program for young mothers in poverty and their children*. New York: Manpower Demonstration Research Corporation.

Radloff, L. (1977). The CES-D Scale: A self-report depression scale for research in the general population. *Applied Psychological Measurement, 1*, 385–401.

Ripke, M. N., Huston, A. C., & Casey, D. M. (2006) Low-income children's activity participation as a predictor of psychosocial and academic outcomes in middle childhood and adolescence. In A. C. Huston & M. N. Ripke (Eds.), *Developmental contexts in middle childhood: Bridges to adolescence and adulthood* (pp. 260–282). New York: Cambridge University Press.

Ripke, M., Huston, A. C., & Mistry, R. S. (2001). *Parents' job characteristics and children's occupational aspirations and expectations in low-income families*. Paper presented at the Biennial Meeting of the Society for Research in Child Development, Minneapolis, MN.

Salkind, N. J. & Haskins, R. (1982). Negative income tax: The impact on children from low-income families. *Journal of Family Issues, 3*, 165–180.

Simpkins, S. D., Fredricks, J. A., Davis-Kean, P. E. & Eccles, J. S. (2006). Healthy mind, healthy habits: The influence of activity involvement in middle childhood. In A. C. Huston & M. N. Ripke (Eds.), *Developmental contexts in middle childhood: Bridges to adolescence and adulthood* (pp. 283–302). New York: Cambridge University Press.

Smolensky, E., & Gootman, J. A. (Eds.). (2003). *Working families and growing kids: Caring for children and adolescents*. Washington, DC: National Academies Press.

Snyder, C. R., Hoza, B., Pelham, W. E. (1997). The development and validation of the Children's Hope Scale. *Journal of Pediatric Psychology, 22*, 399–421.

Snyder, C. R., Sympson, S. C., Ybasco, F. C., Borders, T. F., Babyak, M. A., & Higgins, R. L. (1996). Development and validation of the state Hope Scale. *Journal of Personality and Social Psychology, 70*, 321–335.

Steinberg, L., Lamborn, S. D., Dornbusch, S. M., & Darling, N. (1992). Impact of parenting practices on adolescent achievement: Authoritative parenting, school involvement, and encouragement to succeed. *Child Development 63*, 1266–1281.

Woodcock, R. W., & Johnson, M. B. (1990). *Woodcock-Johnson Psycho-Educational Battery-Revised*. Allen, TX: DLM Teaching Resources.

Zaslow, M. J., & Emig, C. A. (1997). When low-income mothers go to work: Implications for children. *The Future of Children, 7*, 110–115.

Zaslow, M. J., McGroder, S. M., Cave, G., & Mariner, C. L. (1999). Maternal employment and measures of children's health and development among families with some history of welfare receipt. In R. Hodson & T. L. Parcel (Eds.), *Research in the sociology of work: Vol. 7. Work and family* (pp. 233–259). Stamford, CT: JAI Press.

Zaslow, M. J., Rabinovich, B. A., & Suwalsky, J. T. D. (1991). From maternal employment to child outcomes: Preexisting group differences and moderating variables. In J. V. Lerner & N. L. Galambos (Eds.), *Employed mothers and their children* (pp. 237–282). New York: Garland Publishing, Inc.

20

Experiences in Middle Childhood and Children's Development

A Summary and Integration of Research

Aletha C. Huston and Marika N. Ripke

Over two decades ago, when a major review of development in middle childhood was published (Collins, 1984), the authors concluded that middle childhood characteristics predict adolescent and adult development better than preschool indicators do. Although many people would not find this conclusion surprising, it contradicted two widespread notions: that a child's future is shaped in early childhood and that little of interest happens in middle childhood compared with "coming of age" in adolescence. The authors called for new research investigating the processes by which the phenomena of middle childhood account for later development, and more inquiry into the effects of middle childhood experiences and environments, particularly economic and cultural backgrounds, using more sophisticated methods to investigate complex developmental questions.

More than 20 years later, we are positioned to address middle childhood processes and environments with several context-rich longitudinal studies, many of which specifically examine economic and cultural variations. Advances in research methods and data analytic techniques allow a variety of new approaches to our central questions.

We address two related questions:

- *How do developmental patterns in middle childhood – both continuous and discontinuous – relate to directions taken in adolescence and adulthood?*
- *What do experiences in the family, peer group, school, out-of-school time, and the larger economic and cultural milieus of middle childhood contribute to long-term developmental patterns?*

We reach the following conclusions. Although lasting individual differences in ability and behavior are evident by the end of the preschool years, a child's developmental path in middle childhood makes a significant contribution to the adolescent and adult that he or she becomes. Individual differences in behavior stabilize during middle childhood, and patterns formed in middle childhood sometimes endure through the perturbations of adolescence to reemerge in adulthood. Developing social competence with peers (e.g., making friends, interacting positively, resolving conflicts nonaggressively) is a particularly important developmental "task" of middle childhood with consequences for later occupational and social success. The separate contribution of middle childhood is most evident when there are discontinuities of development that forecast adolescent and adult accomplishments, behavior, and social relationships.

Environmental contexts in middle childhood make modest, but significant contributions to long-term developmental patterns above and beyond genetic heritage and early childhood experiences. Magnuson et al. (Chapter 8) estimate that middle childhood contexts account for 1% to 3% of the variability in adolescent achievement and behavior problems once experience in the preschool years and the child's level of performance or behavior at ages 5 to 6 is controlled. The intellectual and emotional supports provided to children during middle childhood by families, peer interactions, schools, out-of-school activities, and the broader social and economic context make a difference in the pathways they follow through adolescence and into adulthood.

The stability or instability of behavior depends partly on the stability of contexts. Family functioning, some school characteristics, and socioeconomic status do not change markedly over the course of development for most children. These stable contexts probably maintain or amplify individual differences in performance and behavior as children grow older, but their independent effects may not be evident unless children in them can be compared with those experiencing discontinuity.

STABILITY AND CHANGE DURING MIDDLE CHILDHOOD AS FORERUNNERS OF LATER PATTERNS

It is well established that measured individual differences in ability and behavior stabilize during middle childhood. For example, IQ after age 6 predicts adult IQ better than preschool IQ does; school achievement in third grade predicts adolescent achievement better than individual differences in first grade do (Collins, 1984). But this pattern alone does not mean that changes or events in middle childhood are singularly important because increasing stability could result from genetic expression (e.g., see Chapter 5), or it could result from the increasing similarity between the measures used for a given construct as the age gap between the measures declines (Collins, 1984).

Isolating the Unique Contribution of Middle Childhood

The investigators in this volume use several methods to isolate the "effects" of middle childhood developmental patterns and middle childhood contexts from those of the preschool years on the one hand and subsequent experiences in adolescence on the other. These methods include genetically-informed designs, controls for preschool development, controls for adolescent contexts, "fixed effects" analyses of individual patterns or trajectories of change over time, and random assignment experiments. Some investigators study discontinuities in middle childhood, asking whether naturally occurring changes or alterations brought about by an experimental treatment contribute to later patterns. Finally, several authors investigate individual differences in emerging capacities – particularly peer competence and relationships – that have antecedents but no direct parallels in the preschool years. In Table 20.1, we summarize the pertinent design features of these investigations. No single study includes all possible controls, but as a group, they are a strong set that permits firm conclusions.

Individual Differences Are Stable

Investigations reported in this book support the large body of literature showing that lasting individual differences in children's intellectual functioning and antisocial behavior are already in place by age 5. For example, in the British Cohort Study, high externalizing behavior at age 5 predicted males' criminal behavior at age 30, regardless of whether externalizing had declined by age 10; females had high rates of adult criminal behavior only if high externalizing persisted from age 5 to age 10 (Chapter 16). This pattern echoes the Dunedin study findings that early antisocial behavior is a harbinger of lifelong antisocial tendencies (Moffit, Caspi, Rutter, & Silva, 2001). Aggression was stable from age 8 to 48 for males in the Columbia County Study, but there were no preschool measures in this study, so it is not possible to separate preschool and middle childhood antecedents (Chapter 4).

Stable behavior patterns may result in part from stable contexts. Parents' affection, use of harsh discipline, intellectual stimulation, and values for education are consistent over time (Chapters 6–8), as are the socioeconomic and cultural niches in which families live (e.g., Chapter 8). Therefore, one cannot infer that an ability or behavioral pattern is a fixed, internal characteristic of the child simply because it is stable; some of that consistency may result from continuity in important parts of the child's environment.

Middle Childhood Development Matters

Although stable differences in intellectual skills and social behavior are evident by age 5, developmental changes in ability or behavior during middle childhood contribute to individual variations in adolescence and adulthood. The evidence for this statement comes from investigations showing that discontinuities in developmental patterns predict later functioning and from studies comparing the predictive power of behavior in preschool, middle childhood, and adolescence. One recurring theme is the long-term importance of gaining competence with peers during middle childhood.

TABLE 20.1. *Summary of Study Samples*

Chapter	Sample Characteristics	Age or School Grade Measured				
		Preschool (0–4)	School Entry (5)	Middle (6–12)	Adolescent (13–17)	Adult (18–48)
2	Minnesota, mixed ethnic and income	0–4	5	6–12	to 16 13–16	23
3	U.S., mixed ethnic and income		5	6–12	13–17	18–20
4	New York, white			8		48
5	Colorado, white, primarily middle class			7, 12	16	
6	New Zealand, white		5	7, 9, 11	13, 15	
7	Canada, representative	4	5	6–9		
8	U.S., representative		5–6	6–12	13–14	22
9	Maryland, mixed ethnic and income			1st–5th	5th–8th	22
10	U.S., mixed ethnic, low income		5 (K)	6–10 1st–4th		
11	U.S., mixed ethnic, income	4	5	6–12		
12	Canada, mixed ethnic, low income			6–12		
13	Wisconsin, mixed ethnic, low income			6–12	13–15	
14	Michigan, white, middle income		K	1st–6th	7th–12th	
15	Literature review					
16	British 1970 cohort, representative		5	10		30
17	U.S., mixed ethnic, low income	3–5		8–10	13–17	
18	U.S., mixed ethnic, low income	3–5		6–12	13–15	
19	Wisconsin, mixed ethnic, low income			6–12		

Discontinuities in Middle Childhood Have Enduring Effects. In the report from the British Cohort Study, the authors compare adult patterns for children whose achievement or behavior levels were stable from ages 5 to 10 with children whose levels changed during that period. Although age-5 status was an important predictor of adult attainment and maladaptive behavior patterns, many adult outcomes were different for children whose scores were stably high or low between ages 5 and 10 compared to those who improved or declined in that age period. For example, children who "escaped" being low achievers – that is, they performed better by age 10 than they had at age 5 – had higher levels of adult educational attainment and wages than children whose low academic performance did not improve during middle childhood (Chapter 16).

The authors of the Colorado Adoption Study chapter concluded that continuity in reading achievement across ages 7 to 16 is based at least partly on genetic endowments and shared environments, but *dis*continuities are a function of children's "nonshared" environments. That is, experiences and environments that differ for siblings in the same family during the period between age 7 and age 16 account for changes over time (Chapter 5).

Changes in trajectories during middle childhood that were produced by an experimental program also lasted into adolescence in the New Hope study. When families received a package of benefits designed to support working poor adults, their children demonstrated improved school achievement that endured well after parents had left the program (Chapter 19).

Peer Competence Matters. The quality of peer relationships changes in middle childhood; it is the time when children learn to judge and select friends, accord group status to others, and form the capacity to maintain and extend friendships and intimate relationships (Rubin, Bukowski, & Parker, 1998). Emerging peer competence during middle childhood is a central predictor of later attainment and social relationships in several of the chapters in this book. In the Colorado Adoption Study (Chapter 5), social competence in middle childhood was the only measured environmental feature that predicted reading ability in adolescence, even with controls for genetic influences. In the Columbia County Study, children who were popular with peers along with having low levels of aggressive behavior at age 8 had higher occupational statuses at age 48. Popular and nonaggressive children had higher IQs and cognitive ability at age 8, but their social competence appeared to mediate the effects of cognitive skills on later occupational success (Chapter 4).

Why should peer competence contribute to educational or occupational achievement? Children with good peer relationships and low levels of problem behavior may also be more engaged and motivated to participate in the agenda of the school (e.g., Ladd, Buhs, & Troop, 2002). Moreover, success in many occupations depends partly on good social skills. A person who can "network" and get along with contemporaries as well as authority figures has a strong advantage in attaining a job, retaining a job, and advancing in many occupations. In the Minnesota study, children with high levels of peer competence in middle childhood, compared to less competent children, interacted more effectively on the job and formed more harmonious relationships with their coworkers in young adulthood (Chapter 2).

Work is not the only avenue of adult accomplishment. Middle childhood relationships with peers forecast harmonious and satisfying relationships with friends, spouse or partner, and family; all are important indicators of healthy adult lives. In the Minnesota study, individuals with high peer competence in middle childhood were more satisfied with their close relationships and were less likely to be involved in violent dating relationships as adults, even with controls for adolescent family functioning and friendship quality (Chapter 2). In the Child Development Study children with high levels of peer competence in middle childhood were less apt to experience insecurity in late adolescent romantic relationships, supporting the Minnesota study findings; but middle childhood peer competence did not make an independent contribution (beyond that of early childhood and adolescence) to the likelihood that people would have violent partner relationships as young adults (Chapter 3).

Peer competence has its roots in positive parenting during the preschool years, supporting previous findings that early family interactions form one important base for the emergence of social skills in middle childhood, which, in turn, contribute to secure and nonviolent adult relationships (Chapter 2). In the Colorado Adoption Project, the indirect effects of parenting and maternal education on adolescent reading achievement were mediated by peer competence at age 7 (Chapter 5).

Middle Childhood Sometimes Forecasts Adulthood Better than Adolescence Does. In a few instances, middle childhood patterns establish a basis for adult characteristics that survive the perturbations of adolescence. For example, in the Minnesota Longitudinal Study, peer competence in middle childhood predicted high levels of work competence, satisfying partner relationships, and low levels of dating violence in young adulthood *better* than did family functioning and friendship quality measured during adolescence (Chapter 2).

In summary, evidence from several methods and populations supports the proposition that developments during middle childhood have lasting effects on both achievement and social relationships. Changes in developmental patterns of academic skills and social behavior during middle childhood have long-term consequences for adolescent and adult attainment. Children who acquire competence in interactions with peers have improved chances for adult attainment and harmonious interpersonal relationships.

WHAT DO MIDDLE CHILDHOOD CONTEXTS CONTRIBUTE TO DEVELOPMENTAL PATTERNS?

Although many developmental theories and a great deal of research have given prime place to environmental influences, earlier longitudinal studies are peculiarly bereft of context information in middle childhood, particularly about environments outside of the family. Only recently have longitudinal studies gathered detailed information about children's experiences in their families, schools, out-of-school settings, and broader socioeconomic and cultural milieus.

In evaluating the evidence for the unique contribution of middle childhood contexts, we apply stringent standards, asking such questions as: Does middle childhood experience predict behavior independently of prior preschool context and/or later adolescent contexts? Does middle childhood experience predict *change* in behavior? Does the context predict independently of associated child, family, and socioeconomic characteristics, and other confounding variables?

Overall, environmental contexts in middle childhood make modest but significant contributions to long-term developmental patterns above and beyond genetic heritage and early childhood experiences. Table 20.2 shows the contexts and Table 20.3 shows the domains of development studied in each of the 18 data chapters. The reader should note that peers can be considered a context of development, but we do not include a separate discussion here because almost all of the information in these studies concerns the child's peer competence, already described above. There is little information about the characteristics of the peer groups or friends with whom the child associates, although it is likely that some of the effects of schools and out-of-school time reflect the peers who inhabit those settings. This gap may be addressed as studies of peer relationships that are currently underway follow children beyond middle childhood.

Family

The developmental literature is replete with correlations between parenting and child behavior (e.g., Bornstein, 2002), but controversies about the causal effects of parenting practices surface periodically (e.g., Collins, Maccoby, Steinberg, Hetherington, & Bornstein, 2000; Harris, 1998; Vandell, 2000). Many similarities between parents and children are partly genetically based; for example, punitive parenting and aggressive behavior could reflect a shared genetic predisposition to aggression. Associations of parenting with child behavior could also result from effects of

TABLE 20.2. *Middle Childhood Contexts Measured*

Chapter	Family	School	Out of School	Socioeconomic
2	Maternal relations, Attachment			
3	Parenting (harsh, intrusive)			
4	Negative family interaction			
5	Genetic similarity, Shared environment			
6	Mother internalizing			
7	Family dysfunction, Mother depression, Family composition & size			
8	Home learning environment, Emotional environment, Family structure	Perceived safety, Teachers know subjects		SES, Poverty
9	Parent educational expectations	Retention, tracking, type of school		
10		School climate, % poor children in school		
11		Classroom context observed		
12	Family composition		Participation in activities	
13			Participation in activities	
14	Family management (encouragement of participation)		Participation in activities	
15			Media – mostly TV	
16				SES
17	Supportive parenting practices			NEWWS interventions (parent education, income, employment)

(continued)

TABLE 20.2. (*Continued*)

Chapter	Family	School	Out of School	Socioeconomic
18	Parent value on education			NEWWS & other welfare interventions
19	Parenting warmth and control		Child care, Participation in out of school activities	New Hope intervention (income, employment, child care assistance)

children's behavior on parenting practices; for example, aggressive children may elicit punishment. To the extent that parenting practices do affect children's development, most theories predict that these influences are strongest in the preschool years, and major dimensions of parenting are likely to be stable over time. For all of these reasons, it is difficult to isolate contributions of parenting to middle childhood development if they do exist. The studies reported here use a range of methods to control for genetic influences, child effects, and preschool influences.

Achievement, School Motivation, Educational and Occupational Attainment. Several chapters provide evidence that intellectual stimulation in the home, parents' value for education, and positive family interaction during middle childhood contribute to achievement, motivation, and engagement in school, and to adult educational and occupational attainment. None finds evidence for effects of family structure. In the National Longitudinal Survey of Youth (Chapter 8), middle childhood intellectual stimulation in the home predicted adolescent achievement after controlling for preschool home stimulation and preschool achievement. In the Baltimore study (Chapter 9), parents' educational expectations and values predicted math *gains* in middle school as well as college attendance. Children in the Columbia County Study who experienced negative family interaction (e.g., harsh parenting) in middle childhood had lower academic skills 40 years later, even with controls for IQ, but their occupational attainment did not differ from those with more positive family experiences (Chapter 4). However, in the Colorado adoption study, there was no independent contribution of parenting or home environment beyond the preschool years to reading achievement (Chapter 5).

Parents' educational values and parenting practices also mediate or moderate their children's reactions to outside contexts. In two chapters analyzing the effects of policies designed to promote education and work for low-income, single mothers, children's responses were associated

TABLE 20.3. *Developmental Domains Studied*

Chapter	Achievement/Cognitive/Motivation	Social Behavior/Relationships	Psychological Adjustment	Occupational Success
2		Peer competence (pre–16) Competence in relationships (22)		Competence in work roles (22)
3		Externalizing (5–16) Partner violence, Relationship insecurity (19)	Internalizing problems (5–16)	
4	IQ (8) Educational attainment (48)	Aggressive behavior (8, 48) Popularity (8)		Occupational prestige (48)
5	Reading achievement (7, 12, 16)	Social competence (7, 12, 16) Antisocial problems (7–15)		
6		Aggression (4–9) Prosocial (4–9)	Anxious/depressed (7–15) Depression (4–9)	
7				
8	Reading and math achievement (5–14)	Externalizing problems (5–14)	Internalizing problems (5–14)	
9	Math achievement (5th–12th) Educational attainment (22)			
10	Literacy (K–5th), School engagement (K–5th)			

11	Classroom involvement (1st–3rd)	Externalizing problems (1st–4th)	Internalizing problems (1st–4th)	
12	School achievement (6–12)	Prosocial behavior (6–12)		
13	Achievement, Expectancy of success (9–15)	Positive social behavior, Externalizing (6–15)	Efficacy, Satisfaction with friendships, Internalizing problems (6–15)	
14	Perceived ability and values for math and sports (3rd–6th); School belonging (7th–12th)	Risk behavior, Positive or negative peers (7th–12th)	Depression, Self esteem (7th–12th)	
15	Achievement in school	Aggression	Gender and ethnic identity	
16	Low education (30)	Criminality, Teen birth (30)	Depression (30)	Low wage, Workless household (30)
17	School achievement, School engagement, Retention (8–10)	Behavior problems (8–10)		
18	School achievement (5–18)			
19	Achievement, School engagement, Attitudes about work, Educational expectations (11–15)	Externalizing problems, Aggressive attributions (11–15)	Efficacy, Satisfaction with friendships, Internalizing problems (11–15)	

Note: Numbers in parentheses indicate age or grade level at assessments.

419

with their parents' values and parenting practices. When participation in these policies led to increases in supportive parenting practices, children's achievement and school engagement improved (Chapter 17). When mothers valued education, their required participation in education led to improved achievement for their children (Chapter 18).

Social and Emotional Development. A vast literature on family influences shows that harmonious relationships in families, parents' psychological well-being (vs. depression and distress), and supportive parenting practices (particularly parenting without harsh discipline) are associated with children's prosocial behavior, emotional well-being, and low levels of aggression. In particular, harsh, punitive parenting is consistently correlated with aggression and antisocial behavior. Virtually all of the longitudinal studies in this book show these general patterns, but their findings are mixed regarding the specific influences of parenting *during middle childhood*.

The two studies with detailed observational information about parenting and developmental outcomes from the preschool years through adolescence provide little evidence that parenting during middle childhood had unique effects on later social relationships or behavior problems, largely because many of the effects of supportive or harsh parenting were apparent by the time children reached age 5 or 6. In the Minnesota Longitudinal Study, parenting during middle childhood did not add to early childhood parenting in predicting dating violence or the quality of early adult relationships (Chapter 2). Similarly, in the Child Development Study, parenting in middle childhood did not make a unique contribution, with one exception: harsh punishment in middle childhood predicted partner violence at age 19 for children in low SES families (Chapter 3).

Several other studies using different methods provide tentative evidence that parents' depression or well-being and functional or dysfunctional patterns of family interaction during middle childhood do contribute to variations in children's aggression, antisocial behavior, and anxiety/depression. In a large Canadian sample, children with consistently high levels of aggression and depression and low levels of prosocial behavior were likely to live in stably dysfunctional families, even with controls for SES, family structure, and maternal depression. Children with high levels of aggression in preschool followed different developmental trajectories. Those who remained high or declined slowly were likely to live in dysfunctional families, but those whose aggression declined steeply had families that were similar to families of low aggression children, suggesting that dysfunctional families may sustain the behavior of an initially aggressive child and that families with more adequate levels of functioning may be able to reduce a difficult child's aggression (Chapter 7).

The Dunedin study design specifically examined reciprocal effects of parenting and child behavior over time, showing separate influences of parents' internalizing symptoms and children's problem behavior on one another. In most of the analyses, reciprocal effects of mothers' internalizing symptoms and children's problem behavior were demonstrated. One exception was that mothers' internalizing symptoms predicted increases in boys' antisocial behavior during middle childhood, but decreases by age 15 (Chapter 6). Child effects are suggested in the Canadian NLSCY; boys were more apt to live in dysfunctional families than were girls. Perhaps boys' greater probability of aggression and disobedience contributed to family dysfunction (Chapter 7).

The one major caveat in both of these studies is the fact that mothers reported both parenting and child behavior problems. Maternal reports of children's social behavior are strongly related to mothers' own levels of depression and psychological dysfunction. Hence, they really show relations between mothers' well-being and their *perceptions* of children's behavior.

In the Columbia County study, the measures of aggression and parenting came from independent sources. For men, but not women, negative parenting practices in middle childhood were associated with age-48 aggression, with controls for age-8 aggression (Chapter 4). The experimental design of the NEWWS study provides strong evidence for causal effects of parenting. Changes in maternal depression and warm parenting in response to the experimental programs accounted for changes in children's externalizing behavior at ages 8 to 10, but we do not know if these effects persisted into adolescence (Chapter 17).

Conclusions. Family functioning, parent well-being, and parenting practices are generally continuous from early to middle childhood, so many stable associations of parenting and child behavior are in place by the end of the preschool years. Nonetheless, families do continue to matter in middle childhood. Stimulation and value for education appear to be especially important for intellectual and educational attainment. Parenting practices and the emotional climate of the home are in some cases related to patterns of social and emotional functioning. These conclusions are based on longitudinal evidence comparing developmental patterns of family processes with patterns of child development, controlling for preschool family and child characteristics, and on investigations using experimental manipulations. The latter hint at the possibility that *changes* in family process during middle childhood may have effects on children, but longer follow-ups would be necessary to substantiate this conclusion.

Family Management

Most theory and research on parenting concentrate on the intellectual and emotional quality of parent–child interactions and on disciplinary practices, but these approaches may define parents' roles too narrowly, particularly as children get older. Parents are managers who make important decisions about the people and places their children experience. Because children spend less and less time with their parents as they get older, this parental management role may become more important with age (Fursten-berg, Cook, Eccles, Elder, & Sameroff, 1999). Parents make decisions about schools, out-of-school experiences, neighborhoods, and peers. For example, parental encouragement is a strong predictor of children's participation in out-of-school activities (Chapter 14). Parents serve as gatekeepers and provide scaffolding as children assume more responsibility for themselves and more ability to regulate their own lives. As we examine the influence of contexts beyond parenting, it is well to keep in mind the fact that some of their effects are indirect results of parents' actions or decisions.

School

School is a central and almost universal experience for children in middle childhood, so it is surprising that many longitudinal studies lack detailed information about school environments. Four studies in this book include some information about school contexts, but many questions remain. First, are school contexts stable over time? School differences in structure (e.g., classroom size), policies (e.g., retention and tracking), and populations (e.g., percent of children from low-income families) are fairly consistent over time. Schools also have different "climates" that are probably fairly stable, at least when school leadership is continuous (Chapter 10). The one study examining observed classroom processes, however, shows that individual children experience little consistency from first to third grade in the levels of positive classroom climate or disciplinary practices in their classrooms (Chapter 11).

In general, children's engagement with school and academic motivation decline the longer they are in school, and, for children from minority and low-income families, achievement tends to decline as well (Eccles, Wig-field, & Schiefele, 1998; Chapter 10). The School Transition Study shows, however, that a positive school climate, which includes high academic standards, teacher concern with individual children, outreach to families, and staff communication, helps to counteract this overall trend, maintaining children's engagement and involvement in learning. Children who remain engaged continue to learn more as they reach the upper grades (Chapter 10). In the NLSY study, children who perceived their schools as safe and their teachers as competent (which might be evidence of school involvement) in middle childhood performed better academically and had fewer behavior problems in adolescence, even after controlling for family characteristics and preschool academic performance (Chapter 8).

At a more microscopic level, children are more engaged in learning activities when they are in classrooms with high levels of instructional quality (e.g., literacy instruction, evaluative feedback, instructional conversation, and encouragement of child responsibility) and emotional support (e.g., sensitivity to child needs, effective classroom management, nonintrusive-ness, and teacher involvement). Classrooms that encourage group work have children who display more frequent positive peer interactions. In classrooms with high levels of punishment, scolding, and negative forms of discipline, on the other hand, children are more disruptive (Chapter 11). These analyses show few lasting effects of classroom experiences, how-ever, at least in the first few grades of elementary school, probably because there is little continuity of classroom features. The one exception is that a cycle of teacher discipline, disruptive behavior, poor social skills, and externalizing problems is cumulative over time from first through fourth grades (Chapter 11).

School practices that involve tracking and retention, either within or between schools, appear to have long-term effects on children's achieve-ment and educational attainment. In the Baltimore study, children who had been retained in grade during elementary school not only had low math achievement at the end of grade 5, but also, even with achievement controlled, were more likely to be in remedial classes in middle school. They gained less in middle school and had higher odds of dropping out of high school (Chapter 9).

Longitudinal data on the relations of school contexts in middle child-hood to later development are sparse. The two studies in this volume with direct observations in schools and classrooms do not yet have information about children's behavior after middle childhood. The data we do have provide some evidence that differences among schools associated with SES, school policies (e.g., retention and tracking), and supportive school climate make lasting contributions to learning, achievement, engagement in school, and ultimate educational attainment. Classroom practices (e.g., instructional quality, emotional quality, and discipline) have strong imme-diate relations to engagement in learning and disruptive behavior, but limited lasting effects on social skills or problem behavior, partly because children's classrooms in different grades are highly variable.

Out-of-School Activities

Children who spend time in organized activities that have group goals and organization, adult leadership, and socially positive values are, on aver-age, better students with more positive social skills than nonparticipants (Mahoney, Larson, & Eccles, 2005). Young people can learn many skills in these activities beyond those taught in school, and they can experience mentoring relationships with adults (e.g., coaches) as well as interactions with peers. They can experiment with different interests, using activities to develop their sense of identity (Eccles & Barber, 1999).

Much of the existing research on extracurricular activities is concen-trated on adolescents, but middle childhood is the time when most chil-dren initiate activities and acquire the basic skills needed to advance in them. Children from all SES levels play softball and soccer, take music lessons, join scouts, and engage in many other structured activities, beginning in middle childhood. Participation peaks in early adolescence and then declines. Those who begin activities in middle childhood are likely to continue with them in the teen years (Chapters 13 and 14). Continuity of participation may result from initial individual differences in interests, but it may also reflect the fact that children who gain skills early are more competent than are newcomers in adolescence. For many activities, including sports or playing a musical instrument, the skill requirements for entry accelerate in high school, so starting early confers a clear advantage. For the most part, the studies in this volume show that children who participate in sports, lessons, clubs, and structured out-of-school activities do better in school and have better social skills than do nonparticipants.

Of all the activities sampled, sports participation has the most consistent associations with achievement and positive social adjustment. These patterns occur across samples from different levels of family income and different ethnic and nationality groups. It is likely, of course, that family and individual characteristics affect both participation and children's achievement or social behavior, making it difficult to draw inferences about the extent to which activities influence children's development independently of these confounds, but the studies in this volume use some strong controls. Morris and Kalil compare siblings in order to control for family characteristics (Chapter 12); Ripke and colleagues examine changes in behavior over time, controlling for children's initial characteristics (Chapter 13); Simpkins and associates incorporate parent encouragement in a longitudinal model (Chapter 14); and Magnuson and colleagues use an extensive set of controls for preschool and middle childhood behavior and contexts (Chapter 8). All except Chapter 8 (which has a one-item measure of activities) find positive associations of involvement in structured activities with academic and social development.

Even these controls do not completely account for children's own agency and their families' support as motivations for beginning and maintaining participation. Unlike school, out-of-school activities are voluntary. Although parent encouragement is important, most parents probably do not insist that a child start or remain in an activity the child does not like. Regardless of the reasons for getting into an activity, it can affect development. Once a child is involved, he or she can expand nascent interests, form friendships, and test different identities in a setting with supportive adults and peers. Similarly, children's preferences probably affect their television viewing patterns, but those who watch a great deal of violent television are subject to increases in aggressive and antisocial behavior, regardless of why they watch (Chapter 15; Huston & Wright, 1998). Although exposure to educational TV in the preschool years predicts adolescent achievement (Anderson, Huston, Schmitt, Linebarger, & Wright, 2001), there is less clear evidence for the unique effects of middle childhood media use on school performance, social stereotypes, or obesity.

These data shed little light on the *processes* by which sports, lessons, and clubs may enhance social or academic skills. Many activities bring young people into contact with adults who act as models, mentors, and supervisors in settings that protect them from some of the hazards of dangerous neighborhoods. Playing on a team or working on a project can support positive peer interactions and enable young people to develop and perfect a range of social, intellectual, and athletic skills. Nevertheless, the quality of adult leadership and the characteristics of peers in a particular activity category probably vary enormously. In-depth information about the characteristics of the activity and the nature of children's experiences would be quite useful in advancing our understanding of how such activities can contribute to positive development.

Socioeconomic Status

Socioeconomic status (SES) is typically defined by a combination of parents' education, occupational status, and income, even though these indicators are not perfectly correlated. Using this broad definition, SES is a proxy for material, human, and social capital within and beyond the family, and it predicts patterns of family life, school characteristics, and the nature of opportunities available outside of school (Bradley & Corwyn, 2002).

Children from lower SES families are disadvantaged in early childhood, and their relative disadvantage increases during middle childhood. In the British Cohort study, for example, low SES children who were in the top quartile on cognitive development at age 5 had only a 27% chance of remaining in the top quartile at age 10, compared to 65% of the high SES group. Low SES children in the bottom quartile at age 5 were much less likely than higher SES children to "escape" into higher levels of performance by age 10. These patterns of increasing or decreasing performance in middle childhood predicted adult achievement and well-being (Chapter 16).

Living in a lower SES family in middle childhood raises the odds of low achievement and dysfunctional behavior in adulthood, but we have only a partial understanding of the processes by which socioeconomic status influences development. Even with controls for family or school experiences, children from lower SES families are at higher risk for adolescent and adult aggression (Chapters 3 and 4), poorer educational outcomes (Chapters 4 and 9), and lower occupational attainment (Chapters 4 and 16). Children from lower SES families are more likely to live in families with high levels of psychological dysfunction throughout the early and middle years (Chapters 4 and 7).

The human and social capital associated with high SES may become increasingly important as children are sorted into different school tracks, schools, and opportunity structures. In middle school, higher SES children are more likely than children from lower SES families to be in an advanced track in math and to attend select schools, even with controls for fifth-grade math performance (Chapter 9). Children from low SES families who attend schools with many other poor children have lower achievement gains than they do when their schools are more economically diverse (Chapter 10). At the classroom level, children from low-income families, compared to more affluent children, attend first- and third-grade classrooms with lower instructional quality, less emotionally supportive teachers, and higher rates of punishment and scolding. In turn, they are less engaged in learning, and their teachers perceive them as having lower social skills and more behavior problems than more affluent children (Chapter 11).

Children from lower SES families are less likely to be involved in organized sports, lessons, and clubs than are children from more affluent families, and they watch more television and read less (Chapter 15). It is noteworthy that SES was the only family characteristic predicting adult occupational status for males in the Columbia County study, suggesting that the advantages provided in a high SES family contribute to the opportunities for their children to maintain the social status in which they were raised (Chapter 4).

Income and Other Resources. Although family income is one component of socioeconomic status, it is more volatile over time than education and occupational status (Duncan, 1984), and it can be affected more readily by public policies. Most available research shows that income variations at the low end are most important in predicting children's behavior; increases beyond about the national median income are not associated with improvement in children's development (Bradley & Corwyn, 2002). Hence, in several studies, families living in or near the poverty level are compared with all others. Earlier findings that poverty in the preschool years is more influential than later poverty were supported in one study in this volume; poverty during middle childhood had no effects beyond those that occurred in the preschool years (Chapter 8).

Experimental tests of policies designed to increase employment, income, and other resources suggest that *changes* in income during middle childhood may have positive effects on development. Some of these policies raised overall income, and others did not. A synthesis of several studies demonstrated that when policies improve income and other resources (e.g., child care) in early and middle childhood, there are lasting positive effects on school achievement and social behavior. When they increase parents' employment without raising income, there are few effects on children (Morris, Huston, Duncan, Crosby, & Bos, 2001).

The interventions in the NEWWS study reported in this volume did little to raise family income, and the effects on children's achievement and behavior were scattered or specific to particular groups (Chapters 17 and 18). New Hope, on the other hand, raised income modestly and increased center-based child care and out-of-school activities. Children who were in middle childhood when their families experienced these changes showed lasting improvements in achievement and social behavior well into the adolescent years (Chapter 19).

Parent Education. Parent education is associated with a host of advantages for children, but teasing out the reasons for these correlations is difficult. NEWWS, one of the policy experiments analyzed in two of our chapters, included an experimental treatment designed to increase (very modestly) the educational levels of low-income single mothers. There is some evidence that experimentally-induced improvements in maternal education led to improved academic performance in middle childhood for their children, at least for African American and Hispanic families (Chapters 17 and 18).

Race, Ethnic Group, Nationality

In the United States, it is almost impossible to disentangle race and ethnic minority status from poverty and other sources of social disadvantage. In the few samples containing a range of both ethnic groups and income (see Table 20.1), we find evidence that African American children experience less positive school contexts than do other ethnic groups. The first- and third-grade classrooms attended by African American children, compared to those attended by Non-Hispanic White children, had lower instructional quality and more punitive discipline; in turn, the African American children exhibited slightly more disruptive behavior and were perceived by teachers as having fewer social skills and more behavior problems. Hispanic children's classrooms and behavior did not differ substantially from those of Non-Hispanic Whites (Chapter 11).

African Americans in Baltimore were much more likely to be tracked into remedial math in middle school, even with controls for fifth grade math score, but African Americans who graduated from high school were also more likely than Whites to enroll in a four-year college (Chapter 9). In the NLSY, African American students gained less than Whites from preschool to adolescence on math, but not on reading (Chapter 8).

One of our studies of low-income single mother families shows that African American and Latino children benefited more than White children did from policies requiring their mothers to participate in education and employment activities (Chapter 18). One reason may be that ethnic minorities are more disadvantaged than Whites with similar incomes; therefore, changes that improve their employment or incomes have more positive effects. Other analyses of these studies have shown that the policies tested were most likely to benefit the most disadvantaged families (Chapter 17).

Conclusions

The environments that children experience in middle childhood make a difference in the short run and for the pathways they follow into adolescence and adulthood. Although the influences of family characteristics are evident by the end of the preschool years, what happens within the family and the choices that parents make about their children's exposure to other contexts can make a difference during middle childhood. As young people become increasingly independent of parents, environmental contexts outside the family assume increasing importance. These, in turn, are affected by the position of the child and family in the larger social structure defined by family income and socioeconomic status.

WHAT PROGRESS HAVE WE MADE SINCE 1984?

Understanding Environmental Contexts

In his concluding chapter to the 1984 volume on middle childhood, Collins (1984) laid out some conceptual and methodological areas for future research. The studies in this volume represent major advances in addressing one of those issues – the nature and role of the environment. The investigations were selected because they contained information about the environmental contexts in which children grow, permitting analyses that advance our knowledge about important experiences for middle childhood development. As a set, these investigations go beyond the prevailing tendencies to concentrate almost entirely on the internal interactions of families by including school, peers, out-of-school activities, and sociocultural contexts as well as parents' values and practices.

Diversity

In 1984, data about children from diverse ethnic and income groups were sparse. Many of the chapters in this volume include children and families from different ecocultural niches that are defined by socioeconomic status, family income, and ethnic group. This newer research reflects the increasing ethnic diversity of the United States, and samples in the United Kingdom and Canada similarly encompass the populations of those nations. In a few cases, investigators go beyond showing differences between groups to ask whether the relations of context to behavior are similar within groups (e.g., Chapter 18).

Advances in Data Quality

The last 20 years have seen a shift in the nature of longitudinal data on children from studies planned and carried out by a small number of investigators using convenience samples to large-scale investigations of nationally-representative samples. The National Longitudinal Study of Youth began its Child Development component in 1986 and continues to follow the children of a representative sample of women. The Panel Study of Income Dynamics, which includes a representative sample of adults, added Child Development Supplements in 1997 and 2002. The federal government is sponsoring and collecting data on two cohorts of children, one beginning at birth and one at kindergarten, in the Early Childhood Longitudinal Study. Plans are currently underway to launch a very large National Children's Study to measure health and development. In the United Kingdom, two representative birth cohorts, 1958 and 1970, have been assessed from childhood into adulthood, and the Canadian National Longitudinal Survey of Children and Youth is a representative sample of that country.

These large datasets offer many advantages. They are efficient, cost-effective, and publicly available to large numbers of researchers. Investigators do not need to spend years of their lives collecting data and waiting for children to grow up; they can proceed directly to analyses. The representative samples allow generalization to known populations; the large number of cases provides good statistical power; different studies often use the same or similar measures, making comparisons across studies possible; and, in many cases, there are sufficient numbers of cases to analyze subgroups separately (e.g., different ethnic groups, families in poverty, or boys and girls).

The same datasets also have the limitations inherent in secondary analysis. Someone else decided what to measure. An investigator with a particular question is often frustrated because important variables are either assessed superficially or are completely absent. Studies designed for multiple purposes tend to include a broad range of indicators that are measured briefly in an effort to serve many research needs; hence, they do not cover most topics in depth.

Investigator-initiated studies have complementary strengths and weaknesses. Several of the studies in this volume were designed to study particular topics; for example, early social and emotional development (Chapter 2), aggression (Chapters 3 and 4), achievement motivation (Chapter 14), or schools (Chapter 9). They contain rich, theoretically driven measures that compensate for their smaller and less representative samples. Many of them mix qualitative and quantitative measurement, offering opportunities for a nuanced understanding of the topics under investigation.

The Study of Early Child Care and Youth Development is a third model that falls somewhere in between. The National Institute of Child Health and

Human Development initiated it as a cooperative agreement to study the effects of child care on children born in 1991. The sample is being studied from birth through adolescence. The conceptualization and methods were designed by a consortium of investigators to study specific questions, so the measures are more extensive and theoretically-guided than those in many larger studies. Its sample is larger and more diverse than those in most investigator-initiated studies, but smaller than many national studies, and it is not nationally representative.

Advances in Statistical Methods

New statistical methods along with increases in computing capacity have revolutionized data analysis. Investigators in this volume use structural equation and hierarchical linear modeling techniques that allow tests of complex mediating pathways, reciprocal causality, and longitudinal trajectories, none of which could be addressed very satisfactorily with earlier methods. Methods specifically designed to model change over time have mushroomed, providing a wonderful resource for longitudinal research as well as a continuing challenge to developmentalists who are trying to keep their methodological expertise current.

Comparing longitudinal studies in the early twenty-first century to most of those available in the early 1980s, there are dramatic changes not only in the types of data used and the statistical techniques used, but also in the range of disciplines guiding the work. Many are collaborations among investigators with different disciplinary approaches and different areas of analytic expertise.

DIRECTIONS FOR THE FUTURE

Integration of Developmental Functions and Individual Differences

Many years ago, Cronbach (1957) described the "two disciplines of psychology" – "experimentalists" who study commonalities among people by examining group means and the influence of experimental manipulations on groups, and "correlationalists" who study individual differences with an emphasis on the relative ordering of individuals. He argued that psychology would benefit from more integration across the two "disciplines," but nearly 50 years later, the same division pervades developmental science. A large body of research is devoted to understanding developmental function – the near-universals or average patterns of developmental change – and an equally large body of literature is concentrated on issues of stability and change of individual differences. The two are not inherently in conflict; the ultimate goal of both is to understand the processes accounting for development.

Since 1984, scholars studying developmental functions during middle childhood have generated sophisticated theory and a rich knowledge base about normative developmental patterns of cognition, metacognition, self-perceptions, identity, self-regulation, and emotion, to name only some of the major topics (e.g., Damon, 1998). The earlier volume on middle childhood called for more examination of these important developmental functions and for more attention to children's perceptions and perspectives (Collins, 1984). But, the issues of concern in this book led us to concentrate on studies of individual differences, particularly those that shed light on the contributions of environmental contexts. In some cases, the investigations reflect new knowledge about normative development by including indicators of social cognition or self-perception, for example, but much more could be done. In particular, as noted in 1984, there are few good indicators of children's self-regulation, autonomy, and identity, all of which are important features of middle childhood development. With a few notable exceptions, measures of aggression, anxiety, and internalizing problems represent the perceptions of the adults who know the child – parents and teachers – rather than direct observations or reports by the child him- or herself. We have relatively little information about how children think about their schools, families, and other experiences. We know little about how closely their perceptions correspond to those of adults or observers. Future research could benefit by a closer coordination of advancing knowledge about basic developmental processes with large-scale investigations of individual differences.

Understanding Process

Although there is more emphasis on understanding process, the accumulated body of data falls short of the ideal in several respects that could be addressed in future research. We need more information about the processes by which contexts outside the family operate, including children's day-to-day experiences in them. What are the important elements in school classrooms that contribute to long-term learning and social development? How do various out-of-school experiences operate? How does SES get translated into day-to-day events?

Ethnic Diversity

Research on children from low-income families and on African American children has increased over the past 20 years, but most studies lag behind the major demographic changes in the United States. By the year 2020, almost 30% of the children in the United States will be from Hispanic or Asian ethnic groups (Chapter 1). Recent waves of immigration have brought children and families from many countries and cultures to the

United States, and increases in mixed ethnic marriages have resulted in more multiethnic children. We need more theory and more investigation focused on the forces affecting children in groups with diverse and multiple national, cultural, and social backgrounds if we are to understand the basic processes affecting successful development.

Physical Development and Health

Future research would also benefit by integrating physical and biological changes as well as physical health with the study of children's environmental contexts. The classic longitudinal studies conducted at Berkeley (Honzik, McFarlane, & Allen, 1948) and the Fels Research Institute (Sontag, Baker, & Nelson, 1958) included physical growth and pubertal development as part of the assessment batteries, but their data on environmental contexts were limited. In recent years, public health and medical researchers have conducted much of the longitudinal research focused on health, but these studies are generally not well suited to understand the processes by which multiple environmental contexts influence normal development. One exception is the NICHD Study of Early Child Care and Youth Development, which is collecting high quality measures of physical growth and pubertal development as well as information about children's physical activity and social environments. New data from this study and others can be informative about the conditions affecting growth and such health problems as obesity and asthma.

Peers

A major theme in this volume is the emergence of peers and peer groups as important influences on children's navigation through middle childhood. Children bring social skills and expectations from their families to their interactions with other children, but they must also learn how to negotiate conflicts, to understand others' perspectives, to relate to friends, and to lead as well as follow in situations where adults do not make the rules. We have learned a great deal over the last few decades about processes of peer interaction, formation of friendships, and peer group influences. Longitudinal investigations can benefit from collecting detailed information about the nature of interactions with individuals and groups of peers over time.

Conclusion

This book was motivated by questions about middle childhood. Does the path taken in middle childhood matter, beyond the direction already set in the early years? How do the various environments surrounding a child influence that path? By implication, is middle childhood a propitious time for intervention? If interventions affect children in middle childhood, do those effects last? We conclude that the directions taken in middle childhood do matter for the future, even though stable individual differences among children are clearly evident by age 5. Just as the growth of a young tree is permanently modified by pruning or grafting, the growth of a child depends in part on the directions that the family, school, peer group, and other environments encourage or discourage during the years from ages 6 to 12.

The fact that middle childhood is not fraught with some of the conflicts of adolescence may make it an advantageous time for interventions, particularly because adults have more control over children's environments than they do in the teen years. Because institutions outside the family assume greater importance during this period, it offers a window of opportunity to modify or reverse the effects of perverse family or socioeconomic environments through the influences of schools and out-of-school experiences. As Hanne Haavind, a MacArthur network member stated, "middle childhood is a time to grow by." And, as Erik Erikson sagely observed, it is the time when children gain the basic tools, skills, and motivations to become productive and valued members of their society; if they fail, there are long-term consequences for their future education, work, and family life.

References

Anderson, D. R., Huston, A. C., Schmitt, K. L., Linebarger, D. L., & Wright, J. C. (2001). Early childhood television viewing and adolescent behavior. *Monographs of the Society for Research in Child Development, 66.*

Bornstein, M. H. (2002). *Handbook of parenting* (2nd ed.). Mahwah, NJ: Lawrence Erlbaum.

Bradley, R. H., & Corwyn, R. F. (2002). Socioeconomic status and child development. *Annual Review of Psychology, 53,* 371–399.

Collins, W. A. (1984). *Development during middle childhood: The years from six to twelve.* Washington, DC: National Academies Press.

Collins, W. A., Maccoby, E. E., Steinberg, L., Hetherington, E. M., & Bornstein, M. H. (2000). Contemporary research on parenting: The case for nature and nurture. *American Psychologist, 55,* 218–232.

Cronbach, L. J. (1957). The two disciplines of psychology. *American Psychologist, 12,* 671–684.

Damon, W. (Ed.). (1998). *Handbook of child psychology* (5th ed., Vols. 1–4). New York: Wiley.

Duncan, G. J. (1984). *Years of poverty, years of plenty.* Ann Arbor, MI: Survey Research Center, University of Michigan.

Eccles, J. S., Wigfield, A., & Schiefele, U. (1998). Motivation to succeed. In W. Damon (Series Ed.) & N. Eisenberg (Vol. Ed.), *Handbook of child psychology: Vol. 3. Social, emotional, and personality development* (5th ed., pp. 1017–1096). New York: Wiley.

Eccles, J., & Barber, B. L. (1999). Student council, volunteering, basketball, or marching band: What kind of extracurricular participation matters? *Journal of Adolescent Research, 14*(1), 10–43.

Eccles, J., & Barber, B. L. (1999). Student council, volunteering, basketball, or marching band: What kind of extracurricular participation matters? *Journal of Adolescent Research, 14*(1), 10–43.

Furstenberg, F. F., Cook, T. D., Eccles, J. S., Elder, G. H., Jr., & Sameroff, A. (1999). *Managing to make it: Urban families and adolescent success.* Chicago: University of Chicago Press.

Harris, J. R. (1998). *The nurture assumption: Why children turn out the way they do.* New York: Free Press.

Honzik, M. P., McFarlane, J. W., & Allen, L. (1948). The stability of mental test performances between two and eighteen years. *Journal of Experimental Education, 17,* 309–324.

Huston, A. C., & Wright, J. C. (1998). Mass media and children's development. In W. Damon (Series Ed.), I. Sigel & K. A. Renninger (Vol. Eds.), *Handbook of child psychology: Vol. 4. Child psychology in practice* (5th ed., pp. 999–1058). New York: Wiley.

Ladd, G. W., Buhs, E. S., & Troop, W. (2002). Children's interpersonal skills and relationships in school settings: Adaptive significance and implications for school-based prevention and intervention programs. In P. K. Smith & C. H. Hart, (Eds.), *Blackwell handbook of childhood social development* (pp. 394–415) Malden, MA: Blackwell.

Mahoney, J. L., Larson, R. W., & Eccles, J. S. (2005). *Organized activities as contexts of development: Extracurricular activities, after-school and community programs.* Mahwah, NJ: Lawrence Erlbaum.

Moffitt, T. E., Caspi, A., Rutter, M., & Silva, P. A. (2001). *Sex differences in antisocial behavior: Conduct disorder, delinquency, and violence in the Dunedin Longitudinal Study.* Cambridge, UK: Cambridge University Press.

Morris, P. A., Huston, A. C., Duncan, G. J., Crosby, D., & Bos, J. M. (2001). *How welfare and work policies affect children: A synthesis of research.* New York: Manpower Demonstration Research Corporation.

Rubin, K. H., Bukowski, W., & Parker, J. G. (1998). Peer interactions, relationships, and groups. In W. Damon (Series Ed.) & N. Eisenberg (Vol. Ed.), *Handbook of child psychology: Vol. 3. Social, emotional, and personality development* (5th ed., pp. 619–700). New York: Wiley.

Sontag, L. W., Baker, C. T., & Nelson, V. L. (1958). Mental growth and personality: A longitudinal study. *Monographs of the Society for Research in Child Development, 23* (Serial No. 68).

Vandell, D. L. (2000). Parents, peers, and other socializing influences. *Developmental Psychology, 36,* 699–710.

Author Index

435

Author Index

445

Shimizu, H., 191
Shonkoff, J. P., 204, 238
Shrout, P. E., 379
Shumow, L., 154, 239
Siebenbruner, J., 25
Signorielli, N., 313, 315
Silva, P. A., 42, 58, 111, 112, 113, 125, 329, 411
Silverstein, L., 312
Simmons, R. G., 174
Simons, R. L., 387
Simpkins, S. D., 17, 260, 288, 403, 424
Singer, D. G., 303, 316
Singer, J. L., 303, 316
Sirin, S. R., 198, 211, 217
Skinner, E., 210
Skinner, M. L., 47
Slate, J. R., 199
Slater, M. D., 309, 310
Slora, E. J., 9
Slusarcick, A. L., 179, 192
Smailes, E., 131, 309
Smith, J, 174, 371, 387
Smith, K., 263
Smith, M. L., 175
Smolensky, E., 374, 386
Snyder, C. R., 266, 392, 393
Sobol, A. M., 312
Sonne-Holm, S., 311
Sontag, L. W., 432
Srbom, D., 116
Sorensen, T. I., 311
Sorenson, S. B., 37, 43, 56
Spade, J. Z., 173
Sroufe, L. A., 24–25, 30, 31, 41, 42, 58, 62, 133
Stadler, J., 198, 217
Stanley- Hogan, M., 152
Stanovich, K. E., 200
Stansbury, K., 108
Stanton, W. R., 112
Staples, J., 313
Stattin, H., 154, 239, 245, 260, 393
Stein, J. A., 179
Steinberg, L., 10, 47, 130, 393, 415
Steinmetz, S. K., 63–69
Stevens, G., 64–69
Stevens, N., 262
Stevenson, D. L., 64–81, 173, 193
Stevenson, H. W.
Stevenson, J., 87
Stewart, G. L., 41
Stipek, D., 198, 200, 211–212
Stoddart, T., 315

Stone, M., 67–68
Stone, M. R., 262, 299
Stoolmiller, M., 47, 56, 101
Story, M., 311
Straus, M. A., 28, 48, 63–69
Strobel, K., 153
Stroman, C. A., 317
Stroup, A. L., 192
Stuart, G. L, 41
Sugarman, D. B., 48
Sugawara, H. M., 116
Sullivan, E. T., 24, 25
Suomi, S., 132
Susman-Stillman, A., 23, 151
Suwalsky, J. T. D., 386
Swaim, R. C., 309
Sweetland, S. R., 199
Swinford, S. P., 42, 43, 56
Symons, J., 344
Sympson, S. C., 393

Taras, H. L., 311
Taylor, A., 123
Taylor, L. D., 17, 303, 314
Taylor, S. E., 130
Templeton, J., 283
Templeton, J., 66–82
Teo, A., 89
Terry, R., 262
Terry, T., 200
Teti, D. M., 107
Thomas, S. L., 307
Thompson, J. S., 173, 190
Thompson, W. O., 312
Thornberry, T. P., 55
Tiegs, E. W., 63–68
Tienda, M., 379
Tierney, J. P., 262
Timko, C., 109
Timmer, S. G., 263
Tirodkar, M. A., 317
Tizard, J., 114
Tolan, P. H., 63
Tomes, N., 371
Traugott, M., 304
Treas, J., 392
Tremblay, R., 130, 132, 135, 154, 266, 392
Tschannen-Moran, M., 198
Tucker, C., 154, 260
Tully, L. A., 109
Turiel, E., 315

Subject Index